Dictionary
Italian – English
English – Italian

Dizionario
Italiano – Inglese
Inglese – Italiano

Berlitz Publishing
Union, NJ · Munich · Singapore

Edited by the Berlitz Editorial Staff

Cover photo by ID Image Direkt CD-ROM GmbH, Germany

© 2004 Berlitz Publishing/APA Publications GmbH & Co. Verlag KG
Singapore Branch, Singapore

Berlitz Publishing
95 Progress Street
Union, NJ 07083
USA

Printed in Singapore
ISBN 981-246-374-7

Contents

Indice

	Page		Pagina
Preface	4	Prefazione	5
Introduction	8	Introduzione	190
Guide to Pronunciation	10	Guida della pronuncia	192
ITALIAN-ENGLISH DICTIONARY	13	DIZIONARIO ITALIANO-INGLESE	13
Menu Reader	151	Lessico gastronomico	323
Mini-Grammar	167	Mini-grammatica	336
Italian Abbreviations	180	Abbreviazioni inglesi	345
Numerals	182	Numeri	348
Time	183	L'ora	349
Some Basic Phrases	184	Alcune espressioni utili	184
Measures and Temperature	350	Misure e temperatura	350
ENGLISH-ITALIAN DICTIONARY	195	DIZIONARIO INGLESE-ITALIANO	195

Preface

In selecting the vocabulary and phrases for this dictionary, the editors have had the traveller's needs foremost in mind. This book will prove a useful companion to casual tourists and business travellers alike who appreciate the reassurance a small and practical dictionary can provide. It offers them—as well as beginners and students—all the basic vocabulary they will encounter and have to use, giving the key words and expressions to allow them to cope in everyday situations.

Like our successful phrase books and travel guides, these dictionaries —created with the help of a computer data bank—are designed to slip into your pocket or purse, and thus have a role as handy companions at all times.

Besides just about everything you normally find in dictionaries, there are these Berlitz bonuses:

- simplified pronunciation after each foreign-word entry, making it easy to read and enunciate words whose spelling may look forbidding

- a unique, practical glossary to simplify reading a foreign restaurant menu and to take the mystery out of complicated dishes and indecipherable names on bills of fare

- useful information on how to tell the time and how to count, on conjugating irregular verbs, commonly seen abbreviations and converting to the metric system, in addition to basic phrases.

While no dictionary of this size can pretend to completeness, we are confident this dictionary will help you get most out of your trip abroad.

Berlitz Publishing

Prefazione

Selezionando i lemmi e le accezioni di questo dizionario, i nostri redattori hanno tenuto conto innanzitutto delle necessità di chi viaggia. Questo libro si rivelerà prezioso per i milioni di turisti, viaggiatori, uomini d'affari che apprezzano il contributo che può dare un dizionario pratico e di formato ridotto. Di grande utilità sarà anche per i principianti e gli studenti, perchè contiene tutti i vocaboli di base che sentiranno e dovranno usare, oltre a parole-chiave ed espressioni che permettono di affrontare situazioni correnti.

Come i nostri manuali di conversazione e le nostre guide turistiche, già molto apprezzate, questi dizionari — realizzati grazie a una banca dati — hanno la dimensione giusta per scivolare in una tasca o in una borsetta, diventando così i compagni indispensabili di ogni momento.

Oltre a tutto quanto si trova normalmente in un dizionario, i nostri volumetti contengono:

- una trascrizione fonetica accanto a ogni lemma, al fine di facilitarne la lettura; ciò si rivela particolarmente utile per quelle parole che sembrano impronunciabili
- un pratico lessico gastronomico, inteso a semplificare la lettura del menù in un ristorante straniero e a svelare i misteri di pietanze complicate e di nomi indecifrabili sui conti
- preziose informazioni sul modo di esprimere il tempo, di contare, sui verbi irregolari, sulle abbreviazioni e le conversioni nel sistema metrico, oltre alle espressioni più correnti.

Nessun dizionario di questo formato può pretendere di essere completo, ma il suo scopo è di permettere a chi lo usa di affrontare con fiducia un viaggio all'estero.

Berlitz Publishing

Italian-English

Italiano-Inglese

Introduction

The dictionary has been designed to take account of your practical needs. Unnecessary linguistic information has been avoided. The entries are listed in alphabetical order, regardless of whether the entry word is printed in a single word or in two or more separate words. As the only exception to this rule, a few idiomatic expressions are listed alphabetically as main entries, by order of the most significant word in the expression. When an entry is followed by sub-entries such as expressions and locutions, these, too, have been listed in alphabetical order.

Each main-entry word is followed by a phonetic transcription (see Guide to pronunciation). Following the transcription is the part of speech of the entry word, whenever applicable. When an entry word may be used as more than one part of speech, the translations are grouped together after the respective part of speech.

Irregular plurals of nouns are given in brackets after the part of speech. Italian feminine headwords are shown as follows:

> **abbonato** … *m*, **-a** *f* subscriber
> **campione** … *m*, **-essa** *f* champion
> **compratore** … *m*, **-trice** *f* buyer, purchaser

The feminine forms of these headwords are: **abbonata**, **campionessa**, **compratrice**.

Whenever an entry word is repeated in irregular plurals or in sub-entries, a tilde (~) is used to represent the full entry word.

An asterisk (*) in front of a verb indicates that the verb is irregular. For details, refer to the lists or irregular verbs.

Abbreviations

adj	adjective	*num*	numeral
adv	adverb	*p*	past tense
Am	American	*pl*	plural
art	article	*plAm*	plural (American)
conj	conjunction	*pp*	past participle
f	feminine	*pr*	present tense
fpl	feminine plural	*pref*	prefix
m	masculine	*prep*	preposition
mpl	masculine plural	*pron*	pronoun
n	noun	*v*	verb
nAm	noun (American)	*vAm*	verb (American)

Guide to Pronunciation

Each main entry in this part of the dictionary is followed by a phonetic transcription which shows you how to pronounce the words. This transcription should be read as if it were English. It is based on Standard British pronunciation, though we have tried to take account of General American pronunciation also. Below, only those letters and symbols are explained which we consider likely to be ambiguous or not immediately understood.

The syllables are separated by hyphens, and stressed syllables are printed in *italics*.

Of course, the sounds of any two languages are never exactly the same, but if you follow carefully our indications, you should be able to pronounce the foreign words in such a way that you'll be understood. To make your task easier, our transcriptions occasionally simplify slightly the sound system of the language while still reflecting the essential sound differences.

Consonants

g	always hard, as in **g**o
l^y	like **ll**i in mi**lli**on
ñ	as in Spanish se**ñ**or, or like **ni** in o**ni**on
r	slightly rolled in the front of the mouth
s	always hard, as in **s**o
y	always as in **y**et, not as in eas**y**

Vowels and Diphthongs

aa	long **a**, as in c**a**r
ah	a short version of **aa**; between **a** in c**a**t and **u** in c**u**t
ai	like **air**, without any **r**-sound
eh	like **e** in g**e**t
igh	as in s**igh**
o	always as in h**o**t (British pronunciation)
ou	as in l**ou**d

1) A bar over a vowel symbol (e.g. $\overline{oo}$) shows that this sound is long.
2) Raised letters (e.g. **ah**^{ay}, **eh**^{oo}) should be pronounced only fleetingly.
3) Italian vowels (i.e. not diphthongs) are pure. Therefore, you should

try to read a transcription like **oa** without moving tongue or lips while pronouncing the sound.

4) A few Italian words borrowed from French contain nasal vowels, which we transcribe with a vowel symbol plus **ng** (e.g. **ong**). This **ng** should *not* be pronounced, and serves solely to indicate nasal quality of the preceding vowel. A nasal vowel is pronounced simultaneously through the mouth and the nose.

A

a (ah) *prep* at; to; on

abbagliante (ahb-bah-*l*ʸ*ahn*-tay) *adj* glaring; **abbaglianti** full beam

abbagliare (ahb-bah-*l*ʸ*aa*-ray) *v* blind

abbaiare (ahb-bah-*yaa*-ray) *v* bark

abbandonare (ahb-bahn-doa-*naa*-ray) *v* abandon

abbassare (ahb-bahss-*saa*-ray) *v* lower

abbastanza (ahb-bah-*stahn*-tsah) *adv* enough; fairly, rather, pretty, quite

abbattere (ahb-*baht*-tay-ray) *v* knock down, fell; dishearten

abbattuto (ahb-bah-*tōō*-toa) *adj* low, down

abbazia (ahb-ba-*tsee*-ah) *f* abbey

abbiamo (ahb-bee-*ah*-moa) *v* (pr be)

abbigliamento (ahb-bee-*l*ʸ*ah-mayn*-toa) *m* clothing; **~ sportivo** sportswear

abbonamento (ahb-boa-nah-*mayn*-toa) *m* subscription; season ticket

abbonarsi (ahb-boa-*nahr*-see) *v* subscribe

abbonato (ahb-boa-*naa*-toa) *m*, **-a** *f* subscriber

abbondante (ahb-boan-*dahn*-tay) *adj* plentiful, abundant

abbondanza (ahb-boan-*dahn*-tsah) *f* plenty, abundance

abbottonare (ahb-boat-toa-*naa*-ray) *v* button

abbozzare (ahb-boat-*tsaa*-ray) *v* sketch

abbracciare (ahb-braht-*chaa*-ray) *v* embrace, hug

abbraccio (ahb-*braht*-choa) *m* embrace, hug

abbreviazione (ahb-bray-vyah-*tsyōā*-nay) *f* abbreviation

abbronzante (ahb-broan-*dzahn*-tay) *m* sun-tan lotion

abbronzato (ahb-broan-*dzaa*-toa) *adj* tanned

abbronzatura (ahb-broan-dzah-*tōō*-rah) *f* suntan

abbronzarsi (ahb-broan-*dzahr*-see) *v* get a tan

abete (ah-*bāy*-tay) *m* fir tree

abile (*aa*-bee-lay) *adj* able; skilled, skilful

abilità (ah-bee-lee-*tah*) *f* capacity, ability; art, skill

abisso (ah-*beess*-soa) *m* abyss

abitabile (ah-bee-*taa*-bee-lay) *adj* inhabitable, habitable

abitante (ah-bee-*tahn*-tay) *m* inhabitant

abitare (ah-bee-*taa*-ray) *v* live; inhabit; reside

abitazione (ah-bee-tah-*tsyōā*-nay) *f* house; home

abito (*aa*-bee-toa) *m* frock; suit; dress; **abiti** clothes *pl*; **~ da sera** evening dress

abituale (ah-bee-*twaa*-lay) *adj* common, customary

abitualmente (ah-bee-twahl-*mayn*-tay) *adv* usually

abituare (ah-bee-*twaa*-ray) *v* accustom; **abituarsi a** get used to

abitudine (ah-bee-*tōō*-dee-nay) *f* habit; custom; routine

abolire (ah-boa-*lee*-ray) *v* abolish

aborto (ah-*bor*-toa) *m* miscarriage; abortion

abusivo (ah-*bo*-zee-voa) *adj* unauthorized, illegal

abuso (ah-*bōō*-zoa) *m* misuse, abuse

accademia (ahk-kah-*dai*-myah) *f* academy; **~ di belle arti** art school

*accadere (ahk-kah-*dāy*-ray) *v* occur, happen

accamparsi (ahk-kahm-*pahr*-see) *v*

camp

accanto (ahk-*kahn*-toa) *adv* next-door; **~ a** beside

accappatoio (ahk-kahp-pah-*tōa*-yoa) *m* bathrobe

accarezzare (ak-kah-re-*dzah*-ray) *v* caress; stroke

accelerare (aht-chay-lay-*raa*-ray) *v* accelerate

accelerato (aht-chay-lay-*raa*-toa) *m* stopping train

acceleratore (aht-chay-lay-rah-*tōa*-ray) *m* accelerator

***accendere** (aht-*chehn*-day-ray) *v* *light; turn on, switch on

accendino (aht-chayn-*dee*-noa) *m* cigarette lighter, lighter

accennare (aht-chayn-*naa*-ray) *v* mention; **~ a** allude to

accensione (aht-chayn-*syōa*-nay) *f* ignition; contact

accento (aht-*chehn*-toa) *m* accent; stress

accerchiare (aht-chayr-*kyaa*-ray) *v* circle, encircle

accertare (aht-chayr-*taa*-ray) *v* verify; **accertarsi** make sure

acceso (aht-chay-zoa) *adj* bright; burning; on; running

accessibile (aht-chayss-*see*-bee-lay) *adj* accessible

accesso (aht-*chehss*-soa) *m* access; approach, entrance

accessori (aht-chayss-*sōa*-ree) *mpl* accessories *pl*

accessorio (aht-chayss-*sōa*-ryoa) *adj* additional

accettare (aht-chayt-*taa*-ray) *v* accept

accettazione (aht-chayt-taa-tsyōa-nay) *f* reception; **~ bagagli** check-in

acchiappare (ahk-kyahp-*paa*-ray) *v* *catch

acciaio (aht-*chaa*-yoa) *m* steel; **~ inossidabile** stainless steel

accidentato (aht-chee-dayn-*taa*-toa) *adj* bumpy; rough

acciuga (aht-*chōo*-gah) *f* anchovy

acclamare (ahk-klah-*maa*-ray) *v* cheer

***accludere** (ahk-*klōo*-day-ray) *v* enclose

accoglienza (ahk-koa-*l'ehn*-tsah) *f* reception, welcome

***accogliere** (ahk-*kaw*-l'ay-ray) *v* welcome; accept

accompagnare (ahk-koam-pah-*ñaa*-ray) *v* accompany; *take

acconciatura (ahk-koan-chah-*tōo*-rah) *f* hairdo

acconsentire (ahk-koan-sayn-*tee*-ray) *v* consent

accontentare (ahk-koan-tayn-*tah*-ray) *v* satisfy; **accontentarsi di** content oneself with; be happy with

acconto (ahk-*koan*-toa) *m* down payment

accorciare (ahk-koar-*tʃaa*-ray) *v* shorten; trim

accordare (ahk-koar-*daa*-ray) *v* grant, extend; **accordarsi** *v* agree

accordo (ahk-*kor*-doa) *m* agreement, settlement; approval; deal; **d'accordo!** okay!

***accorgersi di** (ahk-*kor*-jayr-see) notice

***accorrere** (ahk-*koar*-ray-ray) *v* rush

accreditare (ahk-kray-dee-*taa*-ray) *v* credit

***accrescere** (ahk-*kraysh-shay*-ray) *v* increase

accudire a (ahk-koo-*dee*-ray) attend to

accumulatore (ahk-koo-moo-lah-*tōa*-ray) *m* battery

accurato (ahk-koo-*raa*-toa) *adj* careful, accurate; thorough

accusa (ahk-*kōo*-zah) *f* charge; accusation

accusare (ahk-koo-*zaa*-ray) *v* accuse;

charge

accusato (ahk-koo-*zaa*-toa) *m* accused

acerbo (*ah*-chayr-boa) *adj* unripe

acero (*ah*-chay-roa) *m* maple

aceto (ah-*chāy*-toa) *m* vinegar

acido (ah-*chee*-doa) *m* acid

acne (*ahk*-nay) *f* acne

acqua (*ahk*-kwah) *f* water; ~ **corrente** running water; ~ **di mare** sea water; ~ **dolce** fresh water; ~ **ghiacciata** iced water; ~ **minerale** mineral water; ~ **ossigenata** *m* peroxide; ~ **potabile** drinking water

acquaforte (ahk-kwah-*for*-tay) *f* etching

acquario (ahk-*kwah*-ree-oa) *m* aquarium

acquazzone (ahk-kwaht-*tsōa*-nay) *m* shower, downpour

acquerello (ahk-kway-*rehl*-loa) *m* watercolo(u)r

acquisizione (ahk-kwee-zee-*tsyōa*-nay) *f* acquisition

acquistare (ahk-kwee-*staa*-ray) *v* *buy

acquisto (ahk-*kwee*-stoa) *m* purchase

acuto (ah-*kōō*-toa) *adj* acute

adattare (ah-daht-*taa*-ray) *v* adapt; adjust, suit

adattatore (ah-*daht*-tah-*tōā*-ray) *m* adaptor

adatto (ah-*daht*-toa) *adj* proper, suitable, fit; appropriate

addestramento (ahd-day-strah-*mayn*-toa) *m* training

addestrare (ahd-day-*straa*-ray) *v* train, drill

addetto (ahd-*day*-toa) *m*, **-a** *f* person responsible; authorized personnel

addio (ahd-*dee*-oa) *m* goodbye, farewell

addirittura (ahd-*dee*-ree-*too*-rah) even; absolutely

***addirsi** (ahd-*deer*-see) *v* *become,

suit; qualify

additare (ahd-dee-*taa*-ray) *v* point

addizionare (ahd-dee-tsyoa-*naa*-ray) *v* add, count

addizione (ahd-dee-*tsyōā*-nay) *f* addition

addomesticare (ahd-doa-may-stee-*kaa*-ray) *v* tame; **addomesticato** tame

addormentarsi (ahd-doar-mayn-*taar*-see) *v* *fall asleep

addormentato (ahd-doar-mayn-*taa*-toa) *adj* asleep

adeguato (ah-day-*gwaa*-toa) *adj* adequate; suitable

adempiere (ah-*dehm*-pyay-ray) *v* accomplish

adempimento (ah-daym-pee-*mayn*-toa) *m* achievement

adesso (ah-*dehss*-soa) *adv* now

adiacente (ah-dyah-*chehn*-tay) *adj* neighbo(u)ring

adolescente (ah-doa-laysh-*shehn*-tay) *m* teenager

adoperare (ah-doa-pay-*raa*-ray) *v* use

adorabile (ah-doa-*raa*-bee-lay) *adj* adorable

adottare (ah-doat-*taa*-ray) *v* adopt

adulto (ah-*dool*-toa) *adj* grown-up, adult; *m* grown-up, adult

aerare (ah*ay*-*raa*-ray) *v* ventilate

aerazione (ah*ay*-rah-*tsyōā*-nay) *f* ventilation

aereo (ah-*ai*-ray-oa) *m* plane, aircraft; ~ **a reazione** turbojet; **compagnia aerea** airline; **posta aerea** airmail

aerodromo (ah*ay*-*ro*-dro-moa) *m* airfield

aeroplano (ah*ay*-roa-*plaa*-noa) *m* aeroplane; airplane *Am*

aeroporto (ah*ay*-roa-*por*-toa) *m* airport

affabile (ahf-*faa*-bee-lay) *adj* friendly

affacciarsi (ahf-faht-*chahr*-see) *v*

appear

affamato (ahf-fah-*maa*-toa) *adj* hungry

affare (ahf-*faa*-ray) *m* matter, affair, business; bargain; deal; **affari** business; ***fare affari con** *deal with; **per affari** on business

affascinante (ahf-fahsh-shee-*nahn*-tay) *adj* glamorous, enchanting, charming

affascinare (ahf-fahsh-shee-*naa*-ray) *v* fascinate

affaticato (ahf-fah-tee-*kaa*-toa) *adj* weary, tired

affatto (ahf-*faht*-toa) *adv* at all

affermare (ahf-fayr-*maa*-ray) *v* state

affermativo (ahf-fayr-mah-*tee*-voa) *adj* affirmative

afferrare (ahf-fayr-*raa*-ray) *v* grasp, *catch, seize; *take

affettato (ahf-fayt-*taa*-toa) *adj* affected; *m* sliced ham; sliced salami

affetto (ahf-*feht*-toa) *m* affection

affettuoso (ahf-fayt-*twōa*-soa) *adj* affectionate

affezionato a (ahf-fay-tsyoa-*naa*-toa ah) attached to

affidare (ahf-fee-*daa*-ray) *v* commit

affilare (ahf-fee-*laa*-ray) *v* sharpen

affilato (ahf-fee-*laa*-toa) *adj* sharp

affinché (ahf-feeng-*kay*) *conj* so that

affisso (ahf-*feess*-soa) *m* placard

affittacamere (ahf-feet-tah-*kaa*-may-ray) *m* landlord; *f* landlady

affittare (ahf-feet-*taa*-ray) *v* *let; rent

affitto (ahf-*feet*-toa) *m* rent; ***dare in ~** lease; ***prendere in ~** lease

*affliggersi (ahf-fleed-*jayr*-see) *v* grieve

afflitto (ahf-*fleet*-toa) *adj* sad

affogare (ahf-foa-*gaa*-ray) *v* drown

affollato (ahf-foal-*laa*-toa) *adj* crowded

affondare (ahf-foan-*daa*-ray) *v* *sink

affrancare (ahf-frahng-*kaa*-ray) *v* stamp

affrancatura (ahf-frahng-kah-*tōō*-rah) *f* postage

affrettarsi (ahf-frayt-*tahr*-see) *v* rush, hasten, hurry

affrontare (ahf-froan-*taa*-ray) *v* tackle, face

affumicato (ahf-foo-mee-*kah*-toa) *adj* smoked

Africa (*aa*-free-kah) *f* Africa; **~ del Sud** South Africa

africano (ah-free-*kaa*-noa) *adj* African; *m*, **-a** *f* African

agenda (ah-*jehn*-dah) *f* diary

agente (ah-*jehn*-tay) *m* policeman; agent; **~ di viaggio** travel agent; **~ immobiliare** house agent

agenzia (ah-jayn-*tsee*-ah) *f* agency; **~ viaggi** travel agency; tourist office

aggeggio (ahd-*jayd*-joa) *m* gadget

aggettivo (ahd-jayt-*tee*-voa) *m* adjective

aggiornare (ahd-joar-*nah*-ray) *v* update; postpone

aggiudicare (ahd-joo-dee-*kaa*-ray) *v* award

*aggiungere (ahd-*joon*-jay-ray) *v* add

aggiunta (ahd-*joon*-tah) *f* addition; **in ~ a** beyond

aggiustare (ahd-joo-*stah*-ray) *v* repair, fix; settle

aggredire (ahg-gray-*dee*-ray) *v* assault

aggressivo (ahg-grayss-*see*-voa) *adj* aggressive

agiato (ah-*jaa*-toa) *adj* well-to-do

agile (*ah*-jee-lay) *adj* agile

agio (*aa*-joa) *m* comfort, ease

agire (ah-*jee*-ray) *v* act; operate

agitare (ah-jee-*taa*-ray) *v* *shake; **agitarsi** *get worried

agitazione (ah-jee-tah-*tsyōa*-nay) *f* excitement, unrest

aglio (*aa*-l^{y}oa) *m* garlic

agnello (ah-*ñehl*-loa) *m* lamb

ago (*aa*-goa) *m* needle

agosto (ah-*goa*-stoa) August

agricolo (ah-*gree*-koa-loa) *adj* agrarian

agricoltura (ah-gree-koal-*too*-rah) *f* agriculture

agriturismo (ah-gree-too-*ree*-zmoa) *m* farm holidays *pl*

agro (*aa*-groa) *adj* sour

aguzzo (ah-*goot*-tsoa) *adj* keen

aiola (igh-*aw*-lah) *f* flowerbed

airone (igh-*roa*-nay) *m* heron

aiutante (ah-yoo-*tahn*-tay) *m* helper

aiutare (ah-yoo-*taa*-ray) *v* aid, help

aiuto (ah-*yoo*-toa) *m* assistance; help; relief

ala (*aa*-lah) *f* wing

alba (*ahl*-bah) *f* dawn

albergo (ahl-*behr*-goa) *m* hotel

albero (*ahl*-bay-roa) *m* tree; mast

albicocca (ahl-bee-*kok*-kah) *f* apricot

album (*ahl*-boom) *m* album; scrapbook

alce (*ahl*-chay) *m* moose

alcol (*ahl*-koa-oal) *m* alcohol

alcolico (ahl-*kaw*-lee-koa) *adj* alcoholic

alcuno (ahl-*koo*-noa) *adj* any; **alcuni** *adj* some; *pron* some

alfabeto (ahl-fah-*bai*-toa) *m* alphabet

alga (*ahl*-aah) *f* seaweed

algebra (*ahl*-jay-brah) *f* algebra

Algeria (ahl-jay-*ree*-ah) *f* Algeria

algerino (ahl-jay-*ree*-noa) *adj* Algerian; *m*, **-a** *f* Algerian

aliante (ah-*lyahn*-tay) *m* glider

alimentari (ah-lee-mayn-*taa*-ree) *mpl* groceries *pl*, foodstuffs *pl*

alimento (ah-lee-*mayn*-toa) *m* food; **alimenti** alimony

allacciare (ahl-laht-*chaa*-ray) *v* fasten

allargare (ahl-lahr-*gaa*-ray) *v* widen; extend; expand

allarmante (ahl-lahr-*mahn*-tay) *adj* scary

allarmare (ahl-lahr-*maa*-ray) *v* alarm

allarme (ahl-*lahr*-may) *m* alarm; ~ **antincendio** fire alarm

allattare (ahl-laht-*taa*-ray) *v* nurse

alleanza (ahl-lay-*ahn*-tsah) *f* alliance

alleato (ahl-lay-*aa*-toa) *m*, **-a** *f* associate; **Alleati** Allies *pl*

allegare (ahl-lay-*gaa*-ray) *v* enclose

allegato (ahl-lay-*gaa*-toa) *m* annex, enclosure

allegria (ahl-lay-*gree*-ah) *f* cheerfulness

allegro (ahl-*lay*-groa) *adj* cheerful; jolly

allenamento (*ahl-lay-nah-mayn-to*) *m* training

allenatore (ahl-lay-nah-*toa*-ray) *m*, **-trice** *f* coach

allergia (ahl-layr-*jee*-ah) *f* allergy

allergico a (ahl-*layr*-jee-koa) allergic to

allevare (ahl-lay-*vaa*-ray) *v* raise; rear; *breed

allibratore (ahl-lee-brah-*toa*-ray) *m* bookmaker

allievo (ahl-*lyai*-voa) *m*, **-a** *f* scholar

allodola (ahl-*law*-doa-lah) *f* lark

alloggiare (ahl-load-*jaa*-ray) *v* accommodate, lodge

alloggio (ahl-*lod*-joa) *m* accommodation, lodgings *pl*; apartment *Am*; ~ **e colazione** bed and breakfast

allontanare (ahl-loan-tah-*naa*-ray) *v* remove; **allontanarsi** depart; deviate

allora (ahl-*loa*-rah) *adv* then; **da ~** since

allungare (ahl-loong-*gaa*-ray) *v* lengthen; dilute

almeno (ahl-*may*-noa) *adv* at least

Alpi (ahl-*pee*) *fpl* Alps

alpinismo (ahl-pee-*nee*-zmoa) *m*

mountaineering

alquanto (ahl-*kwahn*-toa) *adv* fairly, rather, pretty, quite; somewhat

alt! (ahlt) stop!

altalena (ahl-tah-*lay*-nah) *f* swing; seesaw

altare (ahl-*taa*-ray) *m* altar

alternativa (ahl-tayr-nah-*tee*-vah) *f* alternative

alternato (ahl-tayr-*naa*-toa) *adj* alternate

altezza (ahl-*tayt*-tsah) *f* height

altezzoso (ahl-tayt-*tsoa*-soa) *adj* haughty

altitudine (ahl-tee-*too*-dee-nay) *f* altitude

alto (*ahl*-toa) *adj* high; tall; loud; **verso l'alto** up

altoparlante (ahl-toa-pahr-*lahn*-tay) *m* loudspeaker

altopiano (ahl-toa-*pyaa*-noa) *m* (pl altipiani) plateau, uplands *pl*

altrettanto (ahl-trayt-*tahn*-toa) *adv* as much

altrimenti (ahl-tree-*mayn*-tee) *adv* otherwise, else; *conj* otherwise

altro (*ahl*-troa) *adj* other; different; **l'un l'altro** each other; **l'uno o l'altro** either; **tra l'altro** among other things; **un ~** another

d'altronde (dahl-*troan*-day) besides

altrove (ahl-*troa*-vay) *adv* elsewhere

altura (ahl-*too*-rah) *f* rise

alunno (*ah-loon*-noa) *m*, **-a** *f* pupil, student

alveare (ahl-vay-*aa*-ray) *m* beehive

alzare (ahl-*tsaa*-ray) *v* lift; **alzarsi** *get up, *rise; *come up; *stand up

amaca (ah-*maa*-kah) *f* hammock

amante (ah-*mahn*-tay) *m/f* lover

amare (ah-*maa*-ray) *v* love; *be fond of

amaro (ah-*maa*-roa) *adj* bitter

amato (ah-*maa*-toa) *adj* beloved

ambasciata (ahm-bahsh-*shaa*-tah) *f* embassy

ambasciatore (ahm-bahsh-shah-*toa*-ray) *m*, **-trice** *f* ambassador

ambientarsi (*ahm-byayn-tahr-see*) *v* settle down; become acclimatized

ambiente (ahm-*byayn*-tay) *m* milieu, environment

ambiguo (ahm-*bee*-gwoa) *adj* ambiguous

ambizioso (ahm-bee-*tsyoa*-soa) *adj* ambitious

ambra (*ahm*-brah) *f* amber

ambulanza (ahm-boo-*lahn*-tsah) *f* ambulance

ambulatorio (*ahm-boo-lah-toa-rioa*) *m* surgery, consulting room

America (ah-*may*-ree-kah) *f* America; **~ Latina** Latin America

americano (ah-may-ree-*kaa*-noa) *adj* American; *m* American

ametista (ah-may-*tee*-stah) *f* amethyst

amianto (ah-*myahn*-toa) *m* asbestos

amichevole (ah-mee-*kay*-voa-lay) *adj* friendly

amicizia (ah-mee-*chee*-tsyah) *f* friendship

amico (ah-*mee*-koa) *m*, **-a** *f* friend

ammaccare (ahm-mahk-*kaa*-ray) *v* bruise

ammaccatura (ahm-mahk-kah-*too*-rah) *f* dent

ammaestrare (ahm-mah*straa*-ray) *v* train

ammainare (ahm-migh-*naa*-ray) *v* *strike

ammalarsi (*ahm-mah-laar-see*) *v* *fall ill

ammalato (ahm-mah-*laa*-toa) *adj* ill, sick

ammazzare (ahm-maht-*tsaa*-ray) *v* kill

*ammettere (ahm-*mayt*-tay-ray) *v* admit; acknowledge

amministrare (ahm-mee-nee-*straa*-

ray) v *run

amministrativo (ahm-mee-nee-strah-tee-voa) adj administrative

amministratore (ahm-mee-nee-strah-tōa-ray) administrator; manager

amministrazione (ahm-mee-nee-strah-tsyōa-nay) f administration; direction

ammiraglio (ahm-mee-rah-lʸoa) m admiral

ammirare (ahm-mee-raa-ray) v admire

ammirazione (ahm-mee-rah-tsyōa-nay) f admiration

ammissione (ahm-meess-syōa-nay) f admittance, admission

ammobiliare (ahm-moa-bee-lʸaa-ray) v furnish

ammoniaca (ahm-moa-nee-ah-kah) f ammonia

ammonire (ahm-moa-nee-ray) v caution

ammontare a (ahm-moan-taa-ray) amount to

ammorbidire (ahm-moar-bee-dee-ray) v soften

ammortizzatore (ahm-moar-teed-dzah-tōa-ray) m shock absorber

ammucchiare (ahm-mook-kyaa-ray) v pile

ammuffito (ahm-moof-fee-toa) adj mouldy

ammutinamento (ahm-moo-tee-nah-mayn-toa) m mutiny

amnistia (ahm-nee-stee-ah) f amnesty

amo (aa-moa) m fishing hook

amore (ah-mōa-ray) m love; darling

ampio (ahm-pyoa) adj extensive, broad

ampliamento (ahm-plyah-mayn-toa) m extension

ampliare (ahm-plyaa-ray) v enlarge

amuleto (ah-moo-lāy-toa) m charm

anabbaglianti (ah-nah-bah-lʸahn-tee)

mpl dipped headlights

anagrafe (ah-nah-grah-fay) f registry office

analcolico (ah-nahl-kōa-lee-koa) adj non-alcoholic; n non-alkoholic drink

analfabeta (ah-nahl-fah-bai-tah) m illiterate

analisi (ah-naa-lee-zee) f analysis

analista (ah-nah-lee-stah) m/f analyst

analizzare (ah-nah-leed-dzaa-ray) v analyse; *break down

analogo (ah-naa-loa-goa) adj similar

ananas (ah-nah-nahss) m pineapple

anarchia (ah-nahr-kee-ah) f anarchy

anatomia (ah-nah-toa-mee-ah) f anatomy

anatra (aa-naa-trah) f duck

anca (ahn-kah) f hip

anche (ahng-kay) adv too, also; even

ancora¹ (ahng-kōa-rah) adv yet, still; again; some more; ~ **una volta** once more

ancora² (ahng-koa-rah) f anchor

***andare** (ahn-daa-ray) v *go; ~ **a prendere** *get, fetch; ~ **carponi** crawl; ~ **in macchina** *ride; ***andarsene** *go away, depart

andata (ahn-daa-tah) f going

andatura (ahn-dah-tōo-rah) f walk; pace

andirivieni (ahn-dee-ree-vyai-nee) m bustle

anello (ah-nehl-loa) m ring; link; ~ **di fidanzamento** engagement ring

anemia (ah-nay-mee-ah) f anaemia

anestesia (ah-nay-stay-see-ah) f anaesthesia

anestetico (ah-nay-stai-tee-koa) m anaesthetic

angelo (ahn-jay-loa) m angel

angolo (ahng-goa-loa) m corner; angle

angora (ahng-go-rah) f mohair

anguilla (ahng-gweel-lah) f eel

anguria (ahng-*goo*-ryah) *f*
watermelon

angusto (ahng-goo-stoa) *adj* narrow

anima (*aa*-nee-mah) *f* soul

animale (ah-nee-*maa*-lay) *m* animal;
beast; ~ **da preda** beast of prey; ~
domestico pet

animato (ah-nee-*maa*-toa) *adj* busy

animo (*aa*-nee-moa) *m* heart;
intention; courage

annaffiare (ah-nahf-*fyah*-ray) *v* water

annegare (ah-nay-*gaa*-ray) *v* drown

***annettere** (ahn-*neht*-tay-ray) *v* annex;
attach

anniversario (ahn-nee-vayr-*saa*-ryoa)
m anniversary; jubilee

anno (*ahn*-noa) *m* year; **all'anno** per
annum; ~ **bisestile** leap year; ~
nuovo New Year

annodare (ahn-noa-*daa*-ray) *v* knot,
tie

annoiare (ahn-noa-*yaa*-ray) *v* bore;
annoiarsi *get bored; *be bored

annotare (ahn-noa-*taa*-ray) *v* *write
down, note

annuale (ahn-*nwaa*-lay) *adj* yearly,
annual

annuario (ahn-*nwaa*-ryoa) *m* annual

annuire (ahn-*nwee*-ray) *v* nod

annullamento (ahn-nool-lah-*mayn*-
toa) *m* cancellation

annullare (ahn-nool-*laa*-ray) *v* cancel

annunciare (ahn-noon-t∫*yaa*-ray) *v*
announce

annunciatore (ahn-noon-t∫ah-ray) *m*,
-trice *f* speaker; announcer

annuncio (ahn-*noon*-t∫yoa) *m*
announcement

anonimo (ah-*naw*-nee-moa) *adj*
anonymous

ansia (*ahn*-syah) *f* worry

ansietà (ahn-syay-*tah*) *f* anxiety,
concern

ansimare (ahn-see-*maa*-ray) *v* pant

ansioso (ahn-*syoa*-soa) *adj* anxious,
eager

anteguerra (ahn-tay-*gwehr*-rah): **d'~**
pre-war

antenato (ahn-tay-*naa*-toa) *m*
ancestor

antenna (ahn-*tayn*-nah) *f* aerial

anteriore (ahn-tay-*ryoa*-ray) *adj* prior,
previous

antibiotico (ahn-tee-*byaw*-tee-koa) *m*
antibiotic

antichità (ahn-tee-kee-*tah*) *fpl*
antiquities *pl*; **Antichità** *f* antiquity

anticipare (ahn-tee-chee-*paa*-ray) *v*
anticipate

anticipatamente (ahn-tee-chee-pah-
tah-*mayn*-tay) *adv* in advance

anticipo (ahn-*tee*-chee-poa) *m*
advance; **in ~** in advance

antico (ahn-*tee*-koa) *adj* ancient;
antique; former

anticoncezionale (ahn-tee-koan-
chay-tsyoa-*naa*-lay) *m* contraceptive

antifurto (ahn-tee-*foor*-toa) *m* burglar
alarm; anti-theft device

antigelo (ahn-tee-*jay*-loa) *m*
antifreeze

antipasto (ahn-tee-*pah*-stoa) *m* hors
d'œuvre, starter

antipatia (ahn-tee-pah-*tee*-ah) *f*
antipathy, dislike

antipatico (ahn-tee-*paa*-tee-koa) *adj*
unpleasant, nasty

antiquario (ahn-tee-*kwaa*-ryoa) *m*
antique dealer

antiquato (ahn-tee-*kwaa*-toa) *adj*
ancient, old-fashioned; quaint

antologia (ahn-toa-loa-*jee*-ah) *f*
anthology

anzi (*ahn*-tsee) *adv* rather, on the
contrary

anziano (ahn-*tsyaa*-noa) *adj* aged,
elderly

ape (*aa*-pay) *f* bee

aperitivo (ah-pay-ree-*tee*-voa) *m* aperitif, drink

aperto (ah-*pehr*-toa) *adj* open; **all'aperto** outdoors

apertura (ah-payr-*too*-rah) *f* opening

apice (*aa*-pee-chay) *m* zenith

appagamento (ahp-pah-gah-*mayn*-toa) *m* satisfaction

apparato (ahp-pah-*raa*-toa) *m* appliance; pomp

apparecchio (ahp-pah-*rayk*-kyoa) *m* appliance, apparatus, machine

apparente (ahp-pah-*rehn*-tay) *adj* apparent

apparentemente (ahp-pah-rayn-tay-*mayn*-tay) *adv* apparently

apparenza (ahp-pah-*rehn*-tsah) *f* appearance; semblance

*apparire (ahp-pah-*ree*-ray) *v* appear

appartamento (ahp-pahr-tah-*mayn*-toa) *m* flat; suite; apartment *Am*; **blocco di appartamenti** apartment house *Am*

*appartenere (ahp-pahr-tay-*nay*-ray) *v* belong

appassionato (ahp-pahss-syoa-*naa*-toa) *adj* passionate; keen

appello (ahp-*pehl*-loa) *m* appeal; call

appena (ahp-*pai*-nah) *adv* hardly, barely; just; **non ~** as soon as

*appendere (ahp-*pehn*-day-ray) *v* *hang

appendice (ahp-payn-*dee*-chay) *f* appendix

appendicite (ahp-payn-dee-*chee*-tay) *f* appendicitis

appetito (ahp-pay-*tee*-toa) *m* appetite

appetitoso (ahp-pay-tee-*toa*-soa) *adj* appetizing

appezzamento (ahp-payt-tsah-*mayn*-toa) *m* plot

appiccicare (ahp-peet-chee-*kaa*-ray) *v* *stick

appiccicaticcio (ahp-peet-chee-kah-*teet*-choa) *adj* sticky

applaudire (ahp-plou-*dee*-ray) *v* clap

applauso (ahp-*plou*-zoa) *m* applause

applicare (ahp-plee-*kaa*-ray) *v* apply; **applicarsi** apply

applicazione (ahp-plee-kah-*tsyoa*-nay) *f* application

appoggiare (ahp-poad-*jaa*-ray) *v* support; **appoggiarsi** *lean

apposta (ahp-*po*-stah) *adv* on purpose

*apprendere (ahp-*prehn*-day-ray) *v* learn; *hear

apprendista (ahp-reayn-*dee*-stah) *m/f* apprentice

apprezzamento (ahp-prayt-tsah-*mayn*-toa) *m* appreciation

apprezzare (ahp-prayt-*tsaa*-ray) *v* appreciate

approfittare (ahp-proa-feet-*taa*-ray) *v* profit, benefit

appropriato (ahp-proa-*pryaa*-toa) *adj* appropriate, proper

approssimativo (ahp-proass-see-mah-*tee*-voa) *adj* approximate

approvare (ahp-proa-*vaa*-ray) *v* approve; approve of

approvazione (ahp-proa-vah-*tsyoa*-nay) *f* approval

appuntamento (ahp-poon-tah-*mayn*-toa) *m* appointment, date

appuntare (ahp-poon-*taa*-ray) *v* pin

appuntito (ahp-poon-*tee*-toa) *adj* pointed

appunto (ahp-*poon*-toa) *m* note; **blocco per appunti** pad, writing pad

apribottiglie (ah-pree-boat-*tee*-lʸay) *m* bottle opener

aprile (ah-*pree*-lay) April

*aprire (ah-*pree*-ray) *v* open; unlock; turn on

apriscatole (ah-pree-*skaa*-toa-lay) *m* tin opener, can opener

aquila (*ah*-kwee-lah) *f* eagle

Arabia Saudita (ah-*raa*-byah sou-*dee*-

tah) Saudi Arabia

arabo (ah-rah-boa) adj Arab; m, **-a** f Arab

arachide (ah-raa-kee-day) f peanut

aragosta (ah-rah-goa-stah) f lobster

arancia (ah-rahn-chah) f orange

aranciata (ah-rahn-chaa-tah) f orangeade

arancione (ah-rahn-chōa-nay) adj orange

arare (ah-raa-ray) v plough

aratro (ah-raa-troa) m plough

arbitrario (ahr-bee-traa-ryoa) adj arbitrary

arbitro (ahr-bee-troa) m umpire; referee

arbusto (ahr-boo-stoa) m shrub

arcata (ahr-kaa-tah) f arch; arcade

arcato (ahr-kaa-toa) adj arched

archeologia (ahr-kay-oa-loa-jee-ah) f archaeology

archeologo (ahr-kay-o-loa-goa) m, **-a** f archaeologist

architetto (ahr-kee-tayt-toa) m architect

architettura (ahr-kee-tayt-tōō-rah) f architecture

archivio (ahr-kee-vyoa) m archives pl

arcivescovo (ahr-chee-vay-skoa-voa) m archbishop

arco (ahr-koa) m bow; arch

arcobaleno (ahr-koa-bah-lāy-noa) m rainbow

*ardere (ahr-day-ray) v *burn; glow

ardesia (ahr-dāy-syah) f slate

area (aa-ray-ah) f area

arena (ah-rāy-nah) f bullring

argenteria (ahr-jayn-tay-ree-ah) f silverware

Argentina (ahr-jayn-tee-nah) f Argentina

argentino (ahr-jayn-tee-noa) adj Argentinian; m, **-a** f Argentinian

argento (ahr-jehn-toa) m silver;

d'argento silver

argilla (ahr-jeel-lah) f clay

argine (ahr-jee-nay) m dike, dam; river bank, embankment

argomentare (ahr-goa-mayn-taa-ray) v argue

argomento (ahr-goa-mayn-toa) m argument; theme

aria (aa-ryah) f air; tune; **ad ~ condizionata** air-conditioned; **~ condizionata** air conditioning; ***aver l'aria** look

arido (aa-ree-doa) adj arid

arieggiare (ah-ryayd-jaa-ray) v air

aringa (ah-reeng-gah) f herring

arioso (ah-ryōa-soa) adj airy

aritmetica (ah-reet-mai-tee-kah) f arithmetic

arma (ahr-mah) f (pl armi), arm, weapon

armadio (ahr-maa-dyoa) m cupboard

armare (ahr-maa-ray) v arm

armatore (ahr-mah-tōa-ray) m shipowner

armonia (ahr-moa-nee-ah) f harmony

arnese (ahr-nāy-say) m tool, utensil

arpa (ahr-pah) f harp

arrabbiarsi (ahr-rahb-byaar-see) v get angry

arrabbiato (ahr-rahb-byaa-toa) adj angry, cross

arrampicare (ahr-rahm-pee-kaa-ray) v climb

arrangiarsi (ahr-rahn-jahr-see) v manage; **~ su** agree on

arredamento (ahr-ray-daa-mayn-toa) m furniture; interior design

*arrendersi (ahr-rehn-dayr-see) v surrender

arrestare (ahr-ray-staa-ray) v arrest

arresto (ahr-reh-stoa) m arrest

arretrato (ahr-ray-traa-toa) adj overdue

arricciare (ahr-reet-chaa-ray) v curl

arrischiare (ahr-ree-*skyaa*-ray) *v* venture

arrivare (ahr-ree-*vaa*-ray) *v* arrive

arrivederci! (ahr-ree-vay-*dayr*-chee) goodbye!

arrivo (ahr-*ree*-voa) *m* arrival; **in ~** due

arrogante (ahr-roa-*gahn*-tay) *adj* snooty

arrossire (ahr-roass-*see*-ray) *v* blush

arrostire (ahr-roa-*stee*-ray) *v* roast

arrotondato (ahr-roa-toan-*daa*-toa) *adj* rounded

arrugginito (ahr-rood-jee-*nee*-toa) *adj* rusty

arte (*ahr*-tay) *f* art; **arti e mestieri** arts and crafts; **belle arti** fine arts; **opera d'arte** work of art

arteria (ahr-*tai*-ryah) *f* artery; thoroughfare

articolazione (ahr-tee-koa-lah-*tsyoa*-nay) *f* joint

articolo (ahr-*tee*-koa-loa) *m* article; item; **articoli da toeletta** toiletry

artificiale (ahr-tee-fee-*chaa*-lay) *adj* artificial

artigianato (ahr-tee-jah-*naa*-toa) *m* handicraft

artigiano (ahr-tee-jah-noa) *m* craftsman; **-a** *f* craftswoman

artiglio (ahr-*tee*-l³oa) *m* claw

artista (ahr-*tee*-stah) *m/f* artist

artistico (ahr-*tee*-stee-koa) *adj* artistic

arto (ahr-*toa*) *m* limb

ascella (ah-*shayl*-lah) *f* armpit

*ascendere (ahsh-*shayn*-day-ray) *v* ascend

ascensione (ahsh-shayn-*syoa*-nay) *f* ascent

ascensore (ahsh-shayn-*soa*-ray) *m* lift; elevator *Am*

ascesa (ahsh-*shay*-sah) *f* rise; climb; ascent

ascesso (ahsh-*shehss*-soa) *m* abscess

ascia (*ahsh*-shah) *f* axe

asciugacapelli (ahsh-shoo-gah-kah-*payl*-lee) *m* hairdryer

asciugamano (ahsh-shoo-gah-*maa*-noa) *m* towel, bath towel

asciugare (ahsh-shoo-*gaa*-ray) *v* dry; wipe

asciutto (ahsh-*shoot*-toa) *adj* dry

ascoltare (ah-skoal-*taa*-ray) *v* listen

ascoltatore (ah-skoal-tah-*toa*-ray) *m*, **-trice** *f* listener

asfalto (ah-*sfahl*-toa) *m* asphalt

Asia (*aa*-zyah) *f* Asia

asiatico (ah-*zyaa*-tee-koa) *adj* Asian

asilo (ah-*zee*-loa) *m* kindergarten; nursery; **~ politico** asylum

asino (*aa*-see-noa) *m* donkey

asma (*ah*-zmah) *f* asthma

asola (*aa*-zoa-lah) *f* buttonhole

asparago (ah-*spaa*-rah-goa) *m* asparagus

aspettare (ah-spayt-*taa*-ray) *v* wait, await; expect; **aspettarsi** expect

aspettativa (ah-spayt-tah-*tee*-vah) *f* expectation

aspetto (ah-*speht*-toa) *m* look; appearance; aspect; **di bell'aspetto** good-looking

aspirapolvere (ah-spee-rah-*poal*-vay-ray) *m* vacuum cleaner; **passare l'aspirapolvere su** hoover; vacuum *vAm*

aspirare (ah-spee-*raa*-ray) *v* inhale; aspire; **~ a** aim at

aspirazione (ahss-pee-rah-*tsyoa*-nay) *f* suction; aspiration

aspirina (ah-spee-*ree*-nah) *f* aspirin

aspro (*ah*-sproa) *adj* harsh

assaggiare (ahss-sahd-*jaa*-ray) *v* taste

assai (ahss-*sigh*) *adv* very, quite

*assalire (ahss-sah-*lee*-ray) *v* attack

assassinare (ahss-sahss-see-*naa*-ray) *v* murder

assassinio (ahss-sahss-*see*-ñoa) *m* assassination, murder

assassino (ahss-sahss-*see*-noa) *m*, **-a** *f*
murderer

asse (*ahss*-say) *m* axle; *f* plank, board

assedio (ahss-*sāy*-dyoa) *m* siege

assegnare (ahss-say-*ñaa*-ray) *v* allot; ~
a assign to

assegno (ahss-*sāy*-ñoa) *m* allowance;
cheque; check *Am*; ~ **turistico**
travel(l)er's cheque; **libretto degli
assegni** chequebook; checkbook
Am

assemblea (ahss-saym-*blai*-ah) *f*
assembly, meeting

assennato (ahss-sayn-*naa*-toa) *adj*
sober

assente (ahss-*sehn*-tay) *adj* absent

assenza (ahss-*sehn*-tsah) *f* absence

asserire (ahss-say-*ree*-ray) *v* claim

assetato (ahss-say-*taa*-toa) *adj* thirsty

assicurare (ahss-see-koo-*raa*-ray) *v*
assure; insure; **assicurarsi** ensure,
make sure

assicurazione (ahss-see-koo-rah-
tsyōa-nay) *f* insurance; ~ **sulla vita**
life insurance; ~ **viaggi** travel
insurance

assieme (ahss-*syai*-may) *m* set

assistente (ahss-see-*stehn*-tay) *m/f*
assistant

assistenza (ahss-see-*stehn*-tsah) *f*
assistance

*****assistere** (ahss-*see*-stay-ray) *v* assist,
aid; ~ **a** attend, assist at

associare (ahss-soa-*chaa*-ray) *v*
associate; **associarsi a** *v* join

associato (ahss-soa-*chaa*-toa) *adj*
affiliated

associazione (ahss-soa-chah-*tsyōa*-
nay) *f* association; society, club

assolutamente (ahss-soa-loo-tah-
mayn-tay) *adv* absolutely

assoluto (ahss-soa-*lōō*-toa) *adj* sheer;
total

assoluzione (ahss-soa-loo-*tsyōa*-nay)
f acquittal

assomigliare a (ahss-soa-mee-*l'aa*-
ray) resemble

assonnato (ahss-soan-*naa*-toa) *adj*
sleepy

assorbente (ahs-soar-*bayn*-tay) *f*
sanitary towel, sanitary napkin *Am*; ~
interno tampon

assortimento (ahss-soar-tee-*mayn*-
toa) *m* assortment

assortito (ahss-soar-*tee*-toa) *adj*
assorted

*****assumere** (ahss-*sōō*-may-ray) *v*
assume; engage

assurdo (ahss-*soor*-doa) *adj* absurd

asta (*ah*-stah) *f* auction

astemio (ah-*stai*-myoa) *m*, **-a** *f*
teetotaller

*****astenersi da** (ah-stay-*nayr*-see)
abstain from

astratto (ah-*straht*-toa) *adj* abstract

astronomia (ah-stroa-noa-*mee*-ah) *f*
astronomy

astuccio (ah-*stoot*-choa) *m* case

astuto (ah-*stōō*-toa) *adj* sly

astuzia (ah-*stōō*-tsyah) *f* ruse

ateo (*aa*-tay-oa) *m* atheist

Atlantico (aht-*lahn*-tee-koa) *m*
Atlantic

atleta (aht-*lai*-tah) *m* athlete

atletica (aht-*lai*-tee-kah) *f* athletics *pl*

atmosfera (aht-moa-*sfai*-rah) *f*
atmosphere

atomico (ah-*taw*-mee-koa) *adj* atomic

atomizzatore (ah-toa-meed-dzah-*tōa*-
ray) *m* atomizer

atomo (*aa*-toa-moa) *m* atom

atrio (*aa*-tryoa) *m* lobby

atroce (ah-*trōa*-chay) *adj* horrible

attaccapanni (aht-tahk-kah-*pahn*-
nee) *m* clothes hanger

attaccare (aht-tahk-*kaa*-ray) *v* attach;
assault

attacco (aht-*tahk*-koa) *m* attack; fit; ~

cardiaco heart attack

atteggiamento (aht-tayd-jah-*mayn*-toa) *m* position

attempato (aht-taym-*paa*-toa) *adj* aged

***attendere** (aht-*tehn*-day-ray) *v* await, wait; ~ a attend to

attento (aht-*tehn*-toa) *adj* attentive; careful; ***stare** ~ look out

attenzione (aht-tayn-*tsyoa*-nay) *f* attention; consideration, notice; ***fare** ~ mind, *pay attention, look out, beware; **prestare** ~ a attend to

atterrare (aht-tayr-*raa*-ray) *v* knock down; land

attesa (aht-*tay*-sah) *f* waiting

attestato (aht-tay-*staa*-toa) *m* certificate

attillato (aht-teel-*laa*-toa) *adj* tight

attimo (*aht*-tee-moa) *m* moment

attinenza (aht-tee-*nehn*-tsah) *f* relation

attitudine (aht-tee-*too*-dee-nay) *f* talent; attitude

attività (aht-tee-vee-*tah*) *f* activity; work

attivo (aht-*tee*-voa) *adj* active

atto (*aht*-toa) *m* deed, act; certificate

attore (aht-*toa*-ray) *m* actor

attorno (aht-*toar*-noa) *adv* about; ~ a round

attraccare (aht-trahk-*kaa*-ray) *v* dock

attraente (aht-trah-*ehn*-tay) *adj* attractive

***attrarre** (aht-*trahr*-ray) *v* attract

attrattiva (aht-trah-*tee*-vah) *f* attraction

attraversare (aht-trah-vayr-*saa*-ray) *v* cross; pass through

attraverso (aht-trah-*vehr*-soa) *prep* across; through

attrazione (aht-trah-*tsyoa*-nay) *f* attraction

attrezzatura (aht-trayt-tsah-*too*-rah) *f* gear

attrezzo (aht-*trayt*-tsoa) *m* tool; **attrezzi da pesca** fishing tackle, fishing gear; **cassetta degli attrezzi** tool kit

attribuire a (aht-tree-*bwee*-ray) assign to

attrice (aht-*tree*-chay) *f* actress

attrito (aht-*tree*-toa) *m* friction

attuale (aht-*twaa*-lay) *adj* present; topical

attualmente (aht-twahl-*mayn*-tay) *adv* at present

attuare (aht-*twaa*-ray) *v* realize

audace (ou-*daa*-chay) *adj* brave

audacia (ou-*daa*-chah) *f* courage; nerve

auditorium (ou-dee-*toa*-ryoa) *m* auditorium

augurare (ou-goo-*raa*-ray) *v* wish

augurio (ou-*goo*-ryoa) *m* wish; **tanti auguri!** all the best!

aula (*ou*-lah) *f* classroom

aumentare (ou-mayn-*taa*-ray) *v* increase; raise

aumento (ou-*mayn*-toa) *m* rise, increase; raise *Am*

aurora (ou-*raw*-rah) *f* daybreak, dawn; sunrise

Australia (ou-*straa*-lʸah) *f* Australia

australiano (ou-strah-lʸ*aa*-noa) *adj* Australian; *m*, **-a** *f* Australian

Austria (*ou*-stryah) *f* Austria

austriaco (ou-*stree*-ah-koa) *adj* Austrian; *m*, **-a** *f* Austrian

autentico (ou-*tehn*-tee-koa) *adj* original, authentic; true

autista (ou-*tee*-stah) *m/f* driver, chauffeur

auto (*ou*-toa) *f* car

autobus (*ou*-toa-booss) *m* (pl ~) bus; coach

autocarro (ou-toa-*kahr*-roa) *m* lorry; truck *Am*

autogrill (ou-toa-*greel*) *m* motorway café

autolavaggio (ou-toa-lah-*vahd*-joa) *m* car-wash

automatico (ou-toa-*maa*-tee-koa) *adj* automatic

automazione (ou-toa-mah-*tsyōa*-nay) *f* automation

automobile (ou-toa-*maw*-bee-lay) *f* automobile, motorcar, car; ~ **club** automobile club

automobilismo (ou-toa-moa-bee-*lee*-zmoa) *m* motoring

automobilista (ou-toa-moa-bee-*lee*-stah) *m* motorist

autonoleggio (ou-toa-noa-*layd*-joa) *m* car hire; car rental *Am*

autonomo (ou-*taw*-noa-moa) *adj* autonomous, independent; self-employed

autore (ou-*tōa*-ray) *m*, **-trice** *f* author

autorità (ou-toa-ree-*tah*) *f* authority

autoritario (ou-toa-ree-*taa*-ryoa) *adj* authoritarian

autorizzare (ou-toa-reed-*dzaa*-ray) *v* license

autorizzazione (ou-toa-reed-dzah-*tsyōa*-nay) *f* authorization, permission

autoscuola (ou-toa-*skwaw*-lah) *f* driving school

autostop (ou-toa-*stōap*) *m* hitchhiking; ***fare l'autostop** hitchhike

autostoppista (ou-toa-stoap-*pee*-stah) *m* hitchhiker

autostrada (ou-toa-*straa*-dah) *f* motorway; highway *Am*

autunno (ou-*toon*-noa) *m* autumn; fall *Am*

avanti (ah-*vahn*-tee) *adv* onwards, forward; ahead; ~ **dritto** straight on

avant'ieri (ah-vahn-*tyai*-ree) *adv* the day before yesterday

avanzamento (ah-vahn-tsah-*mayn*-toa) *m* advance

avanzare (ah-vahn-*tsaa*-ray) *v* advance; *get on

avanzo (ah-*vahn*-tsoa) *m* remainder

avaria (ah-vah-*ree*-ah) *f* breakdown

avaro (ah-*vaa*-roa) *adj* miser

avena (ah-*vāy*-nah) *f* oats *pl*

*avere (ah-*vāy*-ray) *v* *have

avido (*aa*-vee-doa) *adj* greedy

avorio (ah-*vaw*-ryoa) *m* ivory

avvelenare (ahv-vay-lay-*naa*-ray) *v* poison

avvenimento (ahv-vay-nee-*mayn*-toa) *m* event

avvenire (ahv-vay-*nee*-ray) *m* future

*avvenire (ahv-vay-*nee*-ray) *v* happen

avventato (ahv-vayn-*taa*-toa) *adj* rash

avventore (ahv-vayn-*tōa*-ray) *m* customer

avventura (ahv-vayn-*tōō*-rah) *f* adventure

avverbio (ahv-*vehr*-byoa) *m* adverb

avversario (ahv-vayr-*saa*-ryoa) *m* opponent

avversione (ahv-vayr-*syōa*-nay) *f* aversion, dislike

avversità (ahv-vayr-see-*tah*) *f* misfortune

avverso (ahv-*vehr*-soa) *adj* averse

avvertimento (ahv-vayr-tee-*mayn*-toa) *m* warning

avvertire (ahv-vayr-*tee*-ray) *v* warn; notice

avviamento (ahv-vyah-*mayn*-toa) *m* start-up; **motorino d'~** starter

avviarsi (ahv-*vyahr*-see) *v* set out

avvicinare (ahv-vee-chee-*naa*-ray) *v* approach; **avvicinarsi** get closer; come closer

avvisare (ahv-vee-*zaa*-ray) *v* warn; notify

avviso (ahv-*vee*-zoa) *m* notice, announcement

avvitare (ahv-vee-*taa*-ray) *v* screw

avvocato (ahv-voa-*kaa*-toa) *m* lawyer; barrister, solicitor, attorney

*avvolgere (ahv-*vol*-jay-ray) *v* *wind; wrap; envelop

avvolgibile (ahv-voal-*jee*-bee-lay) *m* blind

avvoltoio (ahv-voal-$\overline{toa}$-yoa) *m* vulture

azienda (ah-*dzyehn*-dah) *f* concern, business

azione (ah-*tsyōa*-nay) *f* deed, action; share

azoto (ah-*dzaw*-toa) *m* nitrogen

azzardo (ahd-*dzahr*-doa) *m* chance

azzurro (ahd-*dzoor*-roa) *adj* sky-blue

B

babbo (*bahb*-boa) *m* dad

babordo (bah-*boar*-doa) *m* port

bacca (*bahk*-kah) *f* berry

baccano (bahk-*kaa*-noa) *m* noise

bacheca (bah-*kai*-kah) *f* showcase

baciare (bah-*chaa*-ray) *v* kiss

bacino (bah-*chee*-noa) *m* basin; dock; pelvis

bacio (*baa*-choa) *m* kiss

badare a (bah-*daa*-ray) tend, look after; mind

baffi (*bahf*-fee) *mpl* moustache

bagagliaio (bah-gah-*l'aa*-yoa) *m* luggage van; boot; trunk *Am*

bagaglio (bah-*gaa*-l'oa) *m* luggage, baggage; **~ a mano** hand luggage; hand baggage *Am*

bagliore (bah-*l'ōa*-ray) *m* glare

bagnare (bah-*ñah*-re) *v* wet; **bagnarsi** get wet

bagnato (bah-*ñaa*-toa) *adj* wet; moist

bagnino (bah-*ñee*-noa) *m*, **-a** *f* lifeguard

bagno (*baa*-ñoa) *m* bath; bathroom; **costume da ~** bathing-suit; swimming trunks; ***fare il ~** bathe

baia (*baa*-yah) *f* bay

balbettare (bahl-bayt-*taa*-ray) *v* falter

balcone (bahl-*kōa*-nay) *m* balcony

balena (bah-*lāy*-nah) *f* whale

baleno (bah-*lāy*-noa) *m* flash

ballare (bahl-*laa*-ray) *v* dance

balletto (bahl-*layt*-toa) *m* ballet

ballo (*bahl*-loa) *m* dance; ball

balneare (bal-*nay*-ah-ray) *adj* bathing

balsamo (bal-*sah*-moa) *m* conditioner

balzare (bahl-*dzaa*-ray) *v* *leap

bambina (bahm-*bee*-nah) *f* little girl

bambinaia (bahm-bee-*naa*-yah) *f* nurse; babysitter

bambino (bahm-*bee*-noa) *m* child; kid

bambola (*bahm*-boa-lah) *f* doll

bambù (bahm-*boo*) *m* bamboo

banana (bah-*naa*-nah) *f* banana

banca (*bahng*-kah) *f* bank

bancario (bahng-*kah*-ryoa) *adj* banking; *m*, **-a** *f* bank employee

bancarella (bahng-kah-*rehl*-lah) *f* stall

banchetto (bahng-*kayt*-toa) *m* banquet

banchina (bahng-*kee*-nah) *f* platform

banco (*bahng*-koa) *m* bench; counter; stand; reef; **~ di scuola** desk

Bancomat® (bahng-koa-*maht*) *m* cash-point; cash card

banconota (bahng-koa-*naw*-tah) *f* banknote

banda (*bahn*-dah) *f* gang; band

bandiera (bahn-*dyai*-rah) *f* flag

bandito (bahn-*dee*-toa) *m* bandit

bar (bahr) *m* bar; saloon, café, pub

baracca (bah-*rahk*-kah) *f* hut; hovel

baratro (*baa*-rah-troa) *m* chasm

barattare (bah-raht-*taa*-ray) *v* swap

barattolo (bah-*raht*-toa-loa) *m* tin, canister; jar

barba (*bahr*-bah) *f* beard; **farsi la ~** shave

barbabietola (bahr-bah-*byai*-toa-lah) *f* beetroot, beet

barbiere (bahr-*byai*-ray) *m* barber

barbone (bahr-*bōa*-nay) *m*, **-a** *f* tramp

barca (*bahr*-kah) *f* boat; **~ a remi** rowing boat; **~ a vela** sailing boat

barchetta (bahr-*kayt*-tah) *f* dinghy

barcollante (bahr-koal-*lahn*-tay) *adj* unsteady

barile (bah-*ree*-lay) *m* cask, barrel

barista (bah-*ree*-stah) *m/f* bartender, barman; *f* barmaid

baritono (bah-*ree*-toa-noa) *m* baritone

barocco (bah-*rok*-koa) *adj* baroque

barometro (bah-*raw*-may-troa) *m* barometer

barra (*bahr*-rah) *f* rod

barriera (bahr-*ryai*-rah) *f* barrier

barzelletta (bahr-*dzayl*-*layt*-tah) *f* joke

basare (bah-*zaa*-ray) *v* base

base (*baa*-zay) *f* base; basis

basette (bah-*zayt*-tay) *fpl* sideburns *pl*, whiskers *pl*

basilica (bah-*zee*-lee-kah) *f* basilica

basso (*bahss*-soa) *adj* low; short; *m* bass

bassopiano (bahss-soa-*pyaa*-noa) *m* lowlands *pl*

bastante (bah-*stahn*-tay) *adj* sufficient

bastardo (bah-*stahr*-doa) *m* bastard

bastare (bah-*staa*-ray) *v* suffice, *do; **basta!** enough!

bastone (bah-*stōa*-nay) *m* stick; cane;

~ da passeggio walking stick; **bastoni da sci** ski sticks; ski poles *Am*

battaglia (baht-*taa*-l^yah) *f* battle

battello (baht-*tehl*-loa) *m* boat

battere (*baht*-tay-ray) *v* *beat; **~ le mani** clap

batteria (baht-tay-*ree*-ah) *f* battery

batterio (baht-*tai*-ryoa) *m* bacterium

battesimo (baht-*tāy*-zee-moa) *m* christening, baptism

battezzare (baht-tayd-*dzaa*-ray) *v* christen, baptize

battito (*baht*-tee-toa) *m* pulse; beating

bavaglino (bah-vah-*l^yee*-noa) *m* bib

baule (bah-*ōō*-lay) *m* chest; trunk

becco (*bayk*-koa) *m* beak; nozzle

beffare (bayf-*faa*-ray) *v* fool

beige (baizh) *adj* beige

belga (*behl*-gah) *adj* (pl belgi) Belgian; *m/f* Belgian

Belgio (*behl*-joa) *m* Belgium

bellezza (bayl-*layt*-tsah) *f* beauty

bellino (bayl-*lee*-noa) *adj* nice

bello (*behl*-loa) *adj* beautiful; pretty; good-looking; handsome

benché (behng-*kay*) *conj* although

benda (*bayn*-dah) *f* band

bendare (bayn-*daa*-ray) *v* dress

bene (*bai*-nay) *adv* well; **va bene!** all right!

*benedire (bay-nay-*dee*-ray) *v* bless

benedizione (bay-nay-dee-*tsyōa*-nay) *f* blessing

beneficio (bay-nay-*fee*-choa) *m* benefit

benessere (bay-*nehss*-say-ray) *m* welfare

benevolenza (bay-nay-voa-*lehn*-tsah) *f* goodwill

benvenuto (behn-vay-*nōō*-toa) *adj* welcome

benzina (bayn-*dzee*-nah) *f* fuel, petrol; gasoline *Am*, gas *Am*; **~ senza**

piombo unleaded petrol

*bere (*bāy*-ray) *v* *drink

berretto (bayr-*rayt*-toa) *m* cap; beret

bersaglio (bayr-*saa*-l^yoa) *m* mark; target

bestemmia (bay-*staym*-myah) *f* curse

bestemmiare (bay-staym-*myaa*-ray) *v* curse, *swear

bestia (*beh*-styah) *f* beast

bestiame (bay-*styaa*-may) *m* cattle *pl*

bevanda (bay-*vahn*-dah) *f* beverage; **bevande alcooliche** spirits, liquor

biancheria (byahng-kay-*ree*-ah) *f* linen; lingerie; ~ **da letto** bedding; ~ **intima** underwear

bianco (*byahng*-koa) *adj* white

biasimare (byah-zee-*maa*-ray) *v* blame

biasimo (*byaa*-zee-moa) *m* blame

bibbia (*beeb*-byah) *f* bible

biberon (*bee*-bay-*roan*) *m* baby's bottle

bibita (*bee*-bee-tah) *f* drink; ~ **analcoolica** soft drink

biblioteca (bee-blyoa-*tai*-kah) *f* library

bicchiere (beek-*kyai*-ray) *m* glass; tumbler

bicicletta (bee-chee-*klayt*-tah) *f* cycle, bicycle

bidone (bee-doa-nay) *m* dustbin; swindle

biforcarsi (bee-foar-*kahr*-see) *v* fork

biglietteria (bee-l^yayt-tay-*ree*-ah) *f* box office; ~ **automatica** ticket machine

biglietto (bee-l^y*ayt*-toa) *m* note; ticket; ~ **da visita** visiting-card; ~ **gratuito** free ticket

bigodino (bee-goa-*dee*-noa) *m* curler

bilancia (bee-*lahn*-chah) *f* weighing machine, scales *pl*

bilancio (bee-*lahn*-choa) *m* budget; balance

bile (*bee*-lay) *f* gall, bile

biliardo (bee-l^y*ahr*-doa) *m* billiards *pl*

bilingue (bee-*leeng*-gway) *adj* bilingual

bimbo (*beem*-boa) *m*, **-a** *f* toddler

binario (bee-*naa*-ryoa) *m* track; platform

binocolo (bee-*naw*-koa-loa) *m* binoculars *pl*; field glasses

biologia (byoa-loa-*jee*-ah) *f* biology

bionda (*byoan*-dah) *f* blonde

biondo (*byoan*-doa) *adj* fair

birbante (beer-*bahn*-tay) *m/f* rascal

birichinata (bee-ree-kee-*naa*-tah) *f* mischief

birra (*beer*-rah) *f* beer, ale

birreria (beer-ray-*ree*-ah) *f* brewery

biscotto (bee-*skot*-toa) *m* biscuit, cookie *Am*

bisogno (bee-*zōā*-ñoa) *m* want; need; misery; *aver ~ di need

bistecca (bee-*stayk*-kah) *f* steak

bivio (*bee*-vyoa) *m* road fork, fork

bizzarro (beed-*dzahr*-roa) *adj* odd, strange, queer, quaint

blocco (*bloak*-koa) *n* block; pad; blockade

bloccare (bloak-*kaa*-ray) *v* block

blu (bloo) *adj* blue

boa (*baw*-ah) *f* buoy

bocca (*boak*-kah) *f* mouth

boccale (boak-*kaa*-lay) *m* mug

bocchino (boak-*kee*-noa) *m* cigarette holder

bocciare (boat-*chaa*-ray) *v* fail

bocciolo (boat-*chaw*-loa) *m* bud

boccone (boak-*kōā*-nay) *m* bite

boia (*boi*-ah) *m* (pl ~) executioner

Bolivia (boa-*lee*-vyah) *f* Bolivia

boliviano (boa-lee-*vyaa*-noa) *adj* Bolivian; *m*, **-a** *f* Bolivian

bolla (*boal*-lah) *f* bubble; blister

bolletta (boal-*layt*-tah) *f* bill; note

bollire (boal-*lee*-ray) *v* boil

bollitore (boal-lee-$\overline{too}$-ray) *m* kettle

bollo (boal-loa) *m* stamp; **marca da ~** revenue stamp

bomba (*boam*-bah) *f* bomb

bombardare (boam-bahr-*daa*-ray) *v* bomb

bonifico (boa-*nee*-fee-koa) *m* money transfer

bordello (boar-*dehl*-loa) *m* brothel

bordo (*boar*-doa) *m* edge; border, verge; **a ~** aboard; **~ del marciapiede** curb

borghese (boar-$g\overline{ay}$-say) *adj* middle-class, bourgeois; *m/f* civilian

borsa¹ (*boar*-sah) *f* bag; **~ del ghiaccio** ice bag; **~ dell'acqua calda** hot-water bottle; **~ per la spesa** shopping bag

borsa² (*boar*-sah) *f* grant; **~ di studio** scholarship

borsa³ (*boar*-sah) *f* exchange; stock market, stock exchange

borsellino (boar-sayl-*lee*-noa) *m* purse

borsetta (boar-*sayt*-tah) *f* handbag, bag

boschetto (boa-*skayt*-toa) *m* grove

bosco (*bo*-skoa) *m* wood

boscoso (boa-$sk\overline{oa}$-soa) *adj* wooded

botanica (boa-*taa*-nee-kah) *f* botany

botola (*bo*-toa-lah) *f* hatch

botte (*boat*-tay) *f* cask, barrel

bottega (boat-$t\overline{ay}$-gah) *f* store

botteghino (boat-tay-*gee*-noa) *m* box office

bottiglia (boat-*tee*-l^{y}ah) *f* bottle

bottone (boat-$t\overline{oa}$-nay) *m* button

boutique (boo-*teek*) *f* boutique

braccetto: a ~ (ah braht-*chayt*-toa) arm-in-arm

braccialetto (braht-chah-*layt*-toa) *m* bracelet, bangle

braccio¹ (*braht*-choa) *m* (pl le braccia) arm

braccio² (*braht*-choa) *m* (pl bracci) arm; tributary

braciola (brah-*chaw*-lah) *f* chop

bramare (brah-*maa*-ray) *v* long for

bramosia (brah-moa-*zee*-ah) *f* longing

branchia (*brahng*-kyah) *f* gill

branda (*brahn*-dah) *f* camp bed

brano (*braa*-noa) *m* excerpt, passage

branzino (brahn-*dze*-noa) *m* bass

Brasile (brah-*zee*-lay) *m* Brazil

brasiliano (brah-zee-*l*^{y}*aa*-noa) *adj* Brazilian; *m*, **-a** *f* Brazilian

bravo (*braa*-voa) *adj* good

bretelle (bray-*tehl*-lay) *fpl* braces *pl*; suspenders *plAm*

breve (*br*$\overline{ay}$-vay) *adj* brief; concise; **tra ~** shortly

brevetto (bray-*vayt*-toa) *m* patent

brezza (*brayd*-dzah) *f* breeze

briciola (*bree*-choa-lah) *f* crumb

brillante (breel-*lahn*-tay) *adj* brilliant, bright

brillantina (breel-lahn-*tee*-nah) *f* hair cream

brillare (breel-*laa*-ray) *v* *shine

brindisi (*breen*-dee-zee) *m* toast

britannico (bree-*tahn*-nee-koa) *adj* British

britanno (bree-*tahn*-noa) *m* Briton

brivido (*bree*-vee-doa) *m* chill, shiver

brocca (*brok*-kah) *f* pitcher, jug

bronchite (broang-*kee*-tay) *f* bronchitis

brontolare (broan-toa-*laa*-ray) *v* grumble

bronzeo (*broan*-dzay-oa) *adj* bronze

bronzo (*broan*-dzoa) *m* bronze

bruciare (broo-*chaa*-ray) *v* *burn

bruciatura (broo-chah-$t\overline{oo}$-rah) *f* burn

brughiera (broo-$gy\overline{ay}$-rah) *f* moor

bruna (*br*$\overline{oo}$-nah) *f* brunette

brutale (broo-*taa*-lay) *adj* brutal

brutto (*broot*-toa) *adj* ugly; bad

buca (*bōō*-kah) *f* pit, hole; **~ delle lettere** letterbox, mailbox *Am*

bucato (boo-*kaa*-toa) *adj* punctured; *m* washing, laundry

bucatura (boo-kah-*tōō*-rah) *f* flat tyre, puncture

buccia (*boot*-chah) *f* skin, peel

buco (*bōō*-koa) *m* hole; gap; **~ della serratura** keyhole

budella (boo-*dehl*-lah) *fpl* bowels *pl*

bue (*bōō*-ay) *m* ox

buffet (boof-*feh*) *m* buffet

buffo (*boof*-foa) *adj* funny

bugia (boo-*dʒya*) *f* lie

bugiardo (boo-*dʒar*-doa) *m*, **-a** *f* liar

buio (*bōō*-yoa) *adj* obscure, dark; *m* dark

bulbo (*bool*-boa) *m* bulb

Bulgaria (bool-gah-*ree*-ah) *f* Bulgaria

bulgaro (*bool*-gah-roa) *adj* Bulgarian; *m*, **-a** *f* Bulgarian

bullone (bool-*lōa*-nay) *m* bolt

buon (bwawn) *adj* (buono)

buongustaio (bwon-goo-*staa*-yoa) *m* gourmet

buono (*bwaw*-noa) *adj* good; kind; nice; *m* voucher

burocrazia (boo-roa-krah-*tsee*-ah) *f* bureaucracy

burrasca (boor-*rah*-skah) *f* gale

burro (*boor*-roa) *m* butter

bussare (booss-*saa*-ray) *v* knock, tap

bussola (*booss*-soa-lah) *f* compass

busta (*boo*-stah) *f* envelope

busto (*boo*-stoa) *m* bust; corset, girdle

buttare (boot-*taa*-ray) *v* *throw

C

cabaret (kah-bah-*ray*) *m* cabaret

cabina (kah-*bee*-nah) *f* booth, cabin; **~ di coperta** deck cabin; **~ telefonica** telephone booth

caccia (*kaht*-chah) *f* chase, hunt

cacciare (kaht-*chaa*-ray) *v* hunt; chase; **~ di frodo** poach

cacciatore (kaht-chah-*tōā*-ray) *m* hunter

cacciavite (kaht-chah-*vee*-tay) *m* screwdriver

cachemire (kahsh-*meer*) *m* cashmere

cadavere (kah-*daa*-vay-ray) *m* corpse

cadere (kah-*dāy*-ray) *v* *fall; *far ~* drop

caduta (kah-*dōō*-tah) *f* fall

caffè (kahf-*feh*) *m* coffee; public house

caffeina (kahf-fay-*ee*-nah) *f* caffeine

caffettiera (kahf-fay-*ttyay*-rah) *f* coffee maker

calare (kah-*laa*-ray) *v* lower

calce (*kahl*-chay) *f* lime

calcestruzzo (kahl-chay-*stroot*-tsoa) *m* concrete

calcio (*kahl*-choa) *m* kick; soccer; calcium; **~ d'inizio** kickoff; **~ di rigore** penalty kick; *prendere a calci** kick

calcolare (kahl-koa-*laa*-ray) *v* calculate

calcolatrice (kahl-koa-laa-*tree*-chay) *f* calculator

calcolo (*kahl*-koa-loa) *m* calculation; **calcolo biliare** gallstone; *fare i calcoli** reckon

caldo (*kahl*-doa) *adj* warm, hot; *m* heat

calendario (kah-layn-*daa*-ryoa) *m* calendar

32

callo (*kahl*-loa) *m* corn

calma (*kahl*-mah) *f* calm

calmante (*kahl-maan-tay*) *m* tranquil(l)izer, sedative

calmare (kahl-*maa*-ray) *v* calm down; **calmarsi** calm down

calmo (*kahl*-moa) *adj* calm; serene, quiet

calore (kah-*lōa*-ray) *m* warmth, heat

caloria (kah-loa-*ree*-ah) *f* calorie

calunnia (kah-*loon*-ñah) *f* slander

calvo (*kahl*-voa) *adj* bald

calza (*kahl*-tsah) *f* sock; stocking

calzamaglia (kahl-tsah-*maa*-l'ah) *f* panty hose, tights *pl*

calzatura (kahl-tsah-*tōō*-rah) *f* footwear

calzino (kahl-*tsee*-noa) *m* sock

calzolaio (kahl-tsoa-*laa*-yoa) *m*, **-a** *f* shoemaker

calzoleria (kahl-tsoa-lay-*ree*-ah) *f* shoe shop

calzoncini (kahl-tsoan-*chee*-nee) *mpl* shorts *pl*; trunks *pl*

calzoni (kahl-*tsōa*-nee) *mpl* slacks *pl*; pants *plAm*; **~ da sci** ski pants

cambiamento (kahm-byah-*mayn*-toa) *m* alteration, change

cambiare (kahm-*byaa*-ray) *v* change; alter, vary; exchange, switch; **~ marcia** change gear; **cambiarsi** change (one's clothes)

cambio (*kahm*-byoa) *m* change; exchange; gearbox; **corso del ~** exchange rate; ***dare il ~** relieve

camera (*kaa*-may-rah) *f* room, chamber; **~ blindata** vault; **~ da letto** bedroom; **~ d'aria** inner tube; **~ degli ospiti** guest room; **~ dei bambini** nursery

cameriera (kah-may-*ryai*-rah) *f* waitress

cameriere (kah-may-*ryai*-ray) *m* valet; waiter

camerino (kah-may-*ree*-noa) *m* dressing room

camicetta (*kah-mee-tʃay*-tah) *f* blouse

camicia (kah-*mee*-chah) *f* shirt; **~ da notte** nightdress

caminetto (kah-mee-*nayt*-toa) *m* fireplace

camino (kah-*mee*-noa) *m* chimney; fireplace

camion (*kah*-myoan) *m* lorry; truck

camionetta (kah-myoa-*nayt*-tah) *f* pick-up van

cammello (kahm-*mehl*-loa) *m* camel

cammeo (kahm-*mai*-oa) *m* cameo

camminare (kahm-mee-*naa*-ray) *v* *go, walk; step; hike

camomilla (kah-moa-*meel*-lah) *f* camomile (tea)

camoscio (kah-*moa*-ʃoa) *m* chamois; suede

campagna (kahm-*paa*-ñah) *f* countryside, country; campaign

campana (kahm-*paa*-nah) *f* bell

campanello (kahm-pah-*nehl*-loa) *m* bell, doorbell

campanile (kahm-pah-*nee*-lay) *m* steeple

campeggiatore (kahm-payd-jah-*tōa*-ray) *m* camper

campeggio (kahm-*payd*-joa) *m* camping; camping site

camper (*kahm*-payr) *m* camper van

campione (kahm-*pyōa*-nay) *m* sample; *m*, **-essa** *f* champion

campo (*kahm*-poa) *m* field; camp; **~ da golf** golf course; **~ di grano** cornfield; **~ da tennis** tennis court

camposanto (kahm-poa-*sahn*-toa) *m* churchyard

Canadà (kah-nah-*dah*) *m* Canada

canadese (kah-nah-*dāy*-zay) *adj* Canadian; *m/f* Canadian

canale (kah-*naa*-lay) *m* canal; channel

canapa (*kah*-nah-pah) *f* hemp

canarino (kah-nah-*ree*-noa) m canary

cancellare (*kahn*-tʃayl-*lah*-ray) v delete; cancel; rub out

cancello (kahn-*chehl*-loa) m gate

cancro (*kahng*-kroa) m cancer

candela (kahn-*dāy*-lah) f candle; ~ **d'accensione** sparking plug

candidato (kahn-dee-*daa*-toa) m, **-a** f candidate

cane (*kaa*-nay) m dog; ~ **guida** guide dog

canguro (kahng-*gōō*-roa) m kangaroo

canile (kah-*nee*-lay) m kennel

canna (*kahn*-nah) f cane; ~ **da pesca** fishing rod

cannella (kahn-*nehl*-lah) f cinnamon

cannone (kahn-*nōā*-nay) m gun

cannuccia (kahn-*nōōt*-chah) f straw

canoa (kah-*nōā*-ah) f canoe

canottiera (kah-noat-*tyay*-rah) f vest

canotto (kah-*nōāt*-toa) m rowing boat

cantante (kahn-*tahn*-tay) m/f singer

cantare (kahn-*taa*-ray) v *sing

cantina (kahn-*tee*-nah) f cellar; wine cellar

canto (*kahn*-toa) m song

canzonare (kahn-tsoa-*naa*-ray) v mock

canzone (kahn-*tsōā*-nay) f song

caos (*kaa*-oass) m chaos

caotico (kah-*aw*-tee-koa) adj chaotic

C.A.P. (kap) m postcode, zip code Am

capace (kah-*paa*-chay) adj able; capable

capacità (kah-pah-chee-*tah*) f capacity; faculty

capanna (kah-*pahn*-nah) f hut; cabin

caparbio (kah-*pahr*-byoa) adj obstinate

capello (kah-*payl*-loa) m hair; **fissatore per capelli** setting lotion

capire (kah-*pee*-ray) v *understand, *see

capitale (kah-pee-*taa*-lay) m capital

capitalismo (kah-pee-tah-*lee*-zmoa) m capitalism

capitano (kah-pee-*taa*-noa) m captain

capitare (kah-pee-*taa*-ray) v occur

capitolazione (kah-pee-toa-lah-*tsyōā*-nay) f capitulation

capitolo (kah-*pee*-toa-loa) m chapter

capo (*kaa*-poa) m head; manager, boss, chieftain, chief; cape; ~ **di stato** head of state

capocameriere (kah-poa-kah-may-*ryai*-ray) m head waiter

capocuoco (kah-poa-*kwaw*-koa) m, **-a** f chef

capodanno (kah-poa-*dahn*-noa) f New Year's Day

capogiro (kah-poa-*jee*-roa) m dizziness

capolavoro (kah-poa-lah-*vōā*-roa) m masterpiece

capolinea (*kah*-poa-lee-nay-ah) m terminus

capomastro (kah-poa-*mah*-stroa) m foreman

capoverso (kah-poa-*vehr*-soa) m paragraph

***capovolgere** (kah-poa-*vol*-jay-ray) v turn over

cappella (kahp-*pehl*-lah) f chapel

cappellano (kahp-payl-*laa*-noa) m chaplain

cappello (kahp-*pehl*-loa) m hat

cappotto (kahp-*pot*-toa) m coat; ~ **di pelliccia** fur coat

cappuccio (kahp-*poot*-choa) m hood

capra (*kaa*-prah) f goat

capretto (kah-*prayt*-toa) m kid

capriccio (kah-*preet*-choa) m fancy, whim

capsula (*kah*-psoo-lah) f capsule

carabiniere (kah-rah-bee-*nyay*-ray) m police officer

caraffa (kah-*rahf*-fah) f jug

caramella (kah-rah-*mehl*-lah) f sweet;

candy *Am*; ~ **mou** toffee

carato (kah-*raa*-toa) *m* carat

carattere (kah-*raht*-tay-ray) *m* character

caratteristica (kah-raht-tay-*ree*-stee-kah) *f* feature, characteristic, quality

caratteristico (kah-raht-tay-*ree*-stee-koa) *adj* typical, characteristic

caratterizzare (kah-raht-tay-reed-*dzaa*-ray) *v* mark, characterize

carbone (kahr-*boa*-nay) *m* coal; ~ **di legno** charcoal

carburatore (kahr-boo-rah-*toa*-ray) *m* carburettor

carcere (*kahr*-chay-ray) *m* prison, jail

carciofo (kahr-*chaw*-foa) *m* artichoke

cardinale (kahr-dee-*naa*-lay) *m* cardinal; *adj* cardinal

cardine (*kahr*-dee-nay) *m* hinge

cardiologia (kahr-*dyoa*-loa-*jee*-ah) *f* cardiology

cardo (*kahr*-doa) *m* thistle

carenza (kah-*rehn*-tsah) *f* shortage

caricare (kah-ree-*kaa*-ray) *v* load, charge; *wind

carico (*kaa*-ree-koa) *m* cargo, load, freight, charge

carillon (kah-ree-*yoyah*) *m* music(al) box

carino (kah-*ree*-noa) *adj* nice; pretty

carità (kah-ree-*tah*) *f* charity

carnagione (kahr-nah-*joa*-nay) *f* complexion

carne (*kahr*-nay) *f* flesh; meat

carnevale (kahr-nay-*vaa*-lay) *m* carnival

caro (*kaa*-roa) *adj* dear; expensive; *m*, **-a** *f* darling

carota (kah-*raw*-tah) *f* carrot

carovana (kah-roa-*vah*-nah) *f* caravan

carpa (*kahr*-pah) *f* carp

carreggiata (kahr-rayd-*jaa*-tah) *f* roadway

carrello (kahr-rayl-loa) *m* trolley

carriera (kahr-*ryai*-rah) *f* career

carriola (kahr-*ryaw*-lah) *f* wheelbarrow

carro (*kahr*-roa) *m* cart

carrozza (kahr-*rot*-tsah) *f* coach, carriage

carrozzeria (kahr-roat-tsay-*ree*-ah) *f* motor body *Am*

carrozzina (kahr-roat-*tsee*-nah) *f* pram; baby carriage *Am*

carrucola (kahr-*roo*-koa-lah) *f* pulley

carta (*kahr*-tah) *f* paper; menu; ~ **assorbente** blotting paper; ~ **carbone** carbon paper; ~ **da gioco** playing-card; ~ **da imballaggio** wrapping paper; ~ **da lettere** writing paper; notepaper; ~ **da parati** wallpaper; ~ **di credito** credit card; charge plate *Am*; ~ **d'identità** identity card; ~ **igienica** toilet paper; ~ **nautica** chart; ~ **stradale** road map; ~ **verde** green card; ~ **vetrata** sandpaper; **di** ~ paper

cartella (kahr-*tehl*-lah) *f* briefcase; satchel

cartello (kahr-*tehl*-loa) sign; ~ **stradale** road sign

cartellone (kahr-tayl-*loa*-nay) *m* poster; placard

cartilagine (kahr-tee-*laa*-jee-nay) *f* cartilage

cartina (kahr-*tee*-nah) *f* map

cartoleria (kahr-toa-lay-*ree*-ah) *f* stationer's; stationery

cartolina (kahr-toa-*lee*-nah) *f* card, postcard; ~ **illustrata** picture postcard

cartoncino (kahr-toan-*chee*-noa) *m* card

cartone (kahr-*toa*-nay) *m* cardboard; ~ **animato** cartoon; **di** ~ cardboard

cartuccia (kahr-*toot*-chah) *f* cartridge

casa (*kaa*-sah) *f* house; home; **a** ~ home; ~ **di campagna** country house; **~ di riposo** rest home; **~ galleggiante** houseboat; **~ padronale** mansion; **in ~** at home

casalinga (kah-sah-*leeng*-gah) *f* housewife

casalingo (kah-sah-*leeng*-goa) *adj* domestic

cascata (kah-*skaa*-tah) *f* waterfall

cascina (kah-*shee*-nah) *f* farmhouse

casco (*kah*-skoa) *m* helmet

caseggiato (kah-sayd-*jaa*-toa) *m* block of flats

casello (kah-*sel*-loa) *m* toll booth

caserma (kah-*zehr*-mah) *f* barracks *pl*

casinò (kah-see-*noa*) *m* casino

caso *m* luck, chance; case, instance, event; **~ di emergenza** emergency; **in ~ di** in case of; **in ogni ~** anyway; **per ~** by chance

cassa (*kahss*-sah) *f* pay desk; **~ di risparmio** savings bank

cassaforte (kahss-sah-*for*-tay) *f* safe

casseruola (kahss-say-*rwaw*-lah) *f* saucepan

cassetta (kahss-*sayt*-tah) box; crate; cassette; **~ per le lettere** letterbox, mailbox *Am*

cassetto (kahss-*sayt*-toa) *m* drawer

cassettone (kahss-sayt-*tōa*-nay) *m* chest of drawers

cassiere (kahss-*syai*-ray) *m*, **-a** *f* cashier

castagna (kah-*staa*-ñah) *f* chestnut

castano (kah-*staa*-noa) *adj* brown

castello (kah-*stehl*-loa) *m* castle

casto (*kah*-stoa) *adj* chaste

castoro (kah-*staw*-roa) *m* beaver

catacomba (kah-tah-*koam*-bah) *f* catacomb

catalogo (kah-*taa*-loa-goa) *m* catalogue

catarro (kah-*tahr*-roa) *m* catarrh

catastrofe (kah-*tah*-stroa-fay) *f* catastrophe, disaster

categoria (kah-tay-goa-*ree*-ah) *f* category

categorico (kah-tay-*gaw*-ree-koa) *adj* explicit

catena (kah-*tāy*-nah) *f* chain; **~ di montagne** mountain range

catino (kah-*tee*-noa) *m* basin

catrame (kah-*traa*-may) *m* tar

cattedra (*kaht*-tay-drah) *f* pulpit

cattedrale (kaht-tay-*draa*-lay) *f* cathedral

cattivo (kaht-*tee*-voa) *adj* bad; ill, evil; naughty

cattolico (kaht-*taw*-lee-koa) *adj* Roman Catholic, catholic

cattura (kaht-*tōo*-rah) *f* capture

catturare (kaht-too-*raa*-ray) *v* capture

caucciù (kou-*choo*) *m* rubber

causa (*kou*-zah) *f* cause; reason; case; lawsuit; **a ~ di** owing to; because of, for, on account of

causare (kou-*zaa*-ray) *v* cause

cautela (kou-*tai*-lah) *f* caution

cauto (*kou*-toa) *adj* cautious

cauzione (kou-*tsyōa*-nay) *f* guarantee, security; bail

cava (*kaa*-vah) *f* quarry

cavalcare (kah-vahl-*kaa*-ray) *v* *ride

cavalcavia (kah-*vahl*-kah-*vyah*) flyover

cavaliere (kah-vah-*l'ai*-ray) *m* knight

cavalla (kah-*vahl*-lah) *f* mare

cavallerizzo (kah-vahl-lay-*reet*-tzoa) *m* rider, horseman

cavalletta (kah-vahl-*layt*-tah) *f* grasshopper

cavallo (kah-*vahl*-loa) *m* horse; **~ da corsa** race-horse; **~ vapore** horsepower

cavatappi (kah-vah-*tahp*-pee) *m* corkscrew

caverna (kah-*vehr*-nah) *f* cavern, cave

caviale (kah-*vyaa*-lay) *m* caviar

caviglia (kah-*vee*-l'ah) *f* ankle

cavità (kah-vee-*tah*) f cavity

cavo (*kaa*-voa) m cable; adj hole; ~ **elettrico** flex

cavolfiore (kah-voal-*fyōa*-ray) m cauliflower

cavolini di Bruxelles (kah-voa-*lee*-nee dee broo-*ksayl*) mpl sprouts pl

cavolo (*kaa*-voa-loa) m cabbage

CD (*chee-dee*) m CD; **lettore ~ CD** player

c'è (chay) (essere)

ceco (*chai*-koa) adj Czech; m, **-a** f Czech; **Repubblica ceca** (ray-*poob*-blee-kah *chai*-kah) f Czech Republic

cedere (*chai*-day-ray) v *give in, indulge

cedola (*chai*-doa-lah) f coupon

cedro (*chāy*-droa) m lime

ceffone (chayf-*fōa*-nay) m smack

celare (chay-*laa*-ray) v *hide

celebrare (chay-lay-*braa*-ray) v celebrate

celebrazione (chay-lay-brah-*tsyōa*-nay) f celebration

celebre (*chai*-lay-bray) adj famous

celebrità (chay-lay-bree-*tah*) f celebrity

celeste (chay-*lay*-stay) adj sky blue

celibe (*chai*-lee-bay) adj single; m bachelor

cella (*chehl*-lah) f cell

cellulare (chayl-loo-*lah*-ray) m mobile phone, cellular phone Am

cemento (chay-*mayn*-toa) m cement

cena (*chāy*-nah) f dinner, supper

cenare (chay-*nah*-ray) v *have supper; dine

cenere (*chāy*-nay-ray) f ash

cenno (*chayn*-noa) m sign

censura (chayn-*sōo*-rah) f censorship

centigrado (chayn-*tee*-grah-doa) adj centigrade

centimetro (chayn-*tee*-may-troa) m centimetre, centimeter Am

cento (*chehn*-toa) num hundred

centrale (chayn-*traa*-lay) adj central; ~ **elettrica** power station

centralinista (chayn-trah-lee-*nee*-stah) f/m operator

centralino (chayn-trah-*lee*-noa) m telephone exchange

centralizzare (chayn-trah-leed-*dzaa*-ray) v centralize

centro (*chehn*-troa) m centre, center Am; ~ **commerciale** shopping centre, mall Am; ~ **della città** town centre, downtown Am

ceppo (*chayp*-poa) m block; log

cera (*chāy*-rah) f wax

ceramica (chay-*raa*-mee-kah) f ceramics pl, pottery

cerbiatto (chayr-*byaht*-toa) m fawn

cercare (chayr-*kaa*-ray) v look for; *seek, search, hunt for; look up

cerchio (*chayr*-kyoa) m circle, ring

cerchione (chayr-*kyōa*-nay) m rim

cerimonia (chay-ree-*maw*-nee-ah) f ceremony

cerniera lampo (chayr-*nyay*-rah *laam*-poa) f zip, zipper Am

cerotto (chay-*rot*-toa) m plaster; adhesive tape

certamente (chayr-tah-*mayn*-tay) adv surely

certezza (chayr-*tayt*-tsah) f certainty

certificato (chayr-tee-fee-*kaa*-toa) m certificate

certo (*chehr*-toa) adj certain; adv of course

cervello (chayr-*vehl*-loa) m brain

cervo (*chehr*-voa) m deer

cespuglio (chay-*spōo*-lʸoa) m scrub, bush

cessare (chayss-*saa*-ray) v end; stop, discontinue, quit

cestino (chay-*stee*-noa) m wastepaper basket

ceto (*chai*-toa) m class; ~ **medio**

middle class

cetriolo (chay-*tryaw*-loa) *m* cucumber

chalet (shah-*lay*) *m* chalet

champagne (shahn8g-*pahñ*) *m* champagne

che (kay) *pron* that; who; which; how; *conj* that; as, than

chi (kee) *pron* who; **a ~** whom

chiacchierare (kyahk-kyay-*raa*-ray) *v* chat

chiacchierata (kyahk-kyay-*raa*-tah) *f* chat

chiacchierone (kyahk-kyay-*rōa*-nay) *m*, **-a** *f* chatterbox

chiamare (kyah-*maa*-ray) *v* call; **chiamarsi** *be called; **mi chiamo ...** my name is ...

chiamata (kyah-*maa*-tah) *f* telephone call; **~ urbana** local call

chiarire (kyah-*ree*-ray) *v* clarify, explain

chiaro (*kyaa*-roa) *adj* clear; pale, light; plain, distinct; **~ di luna** moonlight

chiasso (*kyahss*-soa) *m* noise, racket

chiave (*kyaa*-vay) *f* key; wrench *Am*; spanner

chiavistello (kyah-vee-*stehl*-loa) *m* bolt

chiazza (*keeaht*-tsah) *f* spot

*chiedere (*kyai*-day-ray) *v* ask; beg; ***chiedersi** wonder

chierico (*kyai*-ree-koa) *m* clergyman

chiesa (*kyai*-zah) *f* church

chiglia (*kee*-l⁷ah) *f* keel

chilo (*kee*-loa), **chilogrammo** (*kee*-loa-*graam*-moa) *m* kilogram

chilometraggio (*kee*-loa-may-*trahd*-joa) *m* distance in kilometres

chilometro (*kee*-*law*-may-troa) *m* kilometre, kilometer *Am*

chimica (*kee*-mee-kah) *f* chemistry

chimico (*kee*-mee-koa) *adj* chemical; *m*, **-a** *f* chemist

chinarsi (kee-*nahr*-see) *v* *bend down

chiocciola (*kyot*-choa-lah) snail

chiodo (*kyaw*-doa) *m* nail

chiosco (*kyo*-skoa) *m* kiosk

chirurgia (kee-*roor*-dʒee-ah) *f* surgery

chirurgo (kee-*roor*-goa) *m*, **-a** *f* surgeon

chissà (kees-*sah*) who knows

chitarra (kee-*tahr*-rah) *f* guitar

*chiudere (*kyōō*-day-ray) *v* close; fasten, *shut; turn off; **~ a chiave** lock; lock up

chiunque (kyoong-*kway*) *pron* anybody, whoever; anyone

chiusa (*kyōō*-sah) *f* sluice, lock

chiuso (*kyōō*-soa) *adj* closed, shut

chiusura (kyoo-*sōō*-rah) *f* closing; **~ lampo** zip, zipper *Am*

ci (chee) *pron* ourselves, us; it

ciabatta (chah-*baht*-tah) *f* slipper

cialda (*chahl*-dah) *f* waffle

ciao! (*chaa*-oa) hello!; bye!

ciarlatano (chahr-lah-*taa*-noa) *m* quack

ciascuno (chah-*skōō*-noa) *adj* every, each

cibo (*chee*-boa) *m* food**cicatrice** (chee-kah-*tree*-chay) *f* scar

ciclista (chee-*klee*-stah) *m/f* cyclist

ciclo (*chee*-kloa) *m* cycle

cicogna (chee-*kōā*-ñah) *f* stork

cieco (*chai*-koa) *adj* blind

cielo (*chai*-loa) *m* sky; heaven

cifra (*chee*-frah) *f* number, figure

ciglio (*chee*-l⁷oa) *m* (pl le ciglia) eyelash

cigno (*chee*-ñoa) *m* swan

cigolare (chee-goa-*laa*-ray) *v* creak

Cile (*chee*-lay) *m* Chile

cileno (chee-*lāy*-noa) *adj* Chilean; *m*

ciliegia (chee-l⁷*āy*-jah) *f* cherry

cilindro (chee-*leen*-droa) *m* cylinder

cima (*chee*-mah) *f* top; peak; **in ~ a** on top of

cimice (*chee*-mee-chay) *f* bug

cimitero (chee-mee-*tai*-roa) m
graveyard, cemetery

Cina (*chee*-nah) f China

cinema (*chee*-nay-mah) m cinema;
movie theater Am

cinepresa (chee-nay-*pray*-sah) f
camera

cinese (chee-*nay*-say) adj Chinese;
m/f Chinese

*cingere (*cheen*-jay-ray) v encircle

cinghia (*cheeng*-gyah) f strap; belt

cinquanta (cheeng-*kwahn*-tah) num
fifty

cinque (*cheeng*-kway) num five

cintura (cheen-*too*-rah) f belt

cinturino (cheen-too-*ree*-noa) m
watchstrap

ciò (cho) pron that, this

cioccolata (choak-koa-*laa*-tah) f
chocolate

cioccolatino (choak-koa-lah-*tee*-noa)
m chocolate

cioccolato (choak-koa-*laa*-toa) m
chocolate

cioè (choa-*ai*) adv namely

ciottolo (*chot*-toa-loa) m pebble

cipolla (chee-*poal*-lah) f onion

cipria (*chee*-pryah) f face-powder

circa (*cheer*-kah) adv approximately,
about; prep about

circo (*cheer*-koa) m circus

circolazione (cheer-koa-lah-*tsyoa*-
nay) f circulation; ~ **del sangue**
circulation

circolo (*cheer*-koa-loa) m circle; club;
~ **nautico** yacht club

circondare (cheer-koan-*daa*-ray) v
circle, encircle, surround

circonvallazione (cheer-koan-vahl-
lah-*tsyoa*-nay) f ring-road

circostante (cheer-koa-*stahn*-tay) adj
surrounding

circostanza (cheer-koa-*stahn*-tsah) f
circumstance, condition

cistifellea (chee-stee-*fehl*-lay-ah) f
gall bladder

cistite (chee-*stee*-tay) f cystitis

citare (chee-*taa*-ray) v quote

citazione (chee-tah-*tsyoa*-nay) f
mention, quotation

città (cheet-*tah*) f city, town

cittadina (cheet-tah-*dee*-nah) f town

cittadinanza (cheet-tah-dee-*nahn*-
tsah) f townspeople pl; citizenship

cittadino (cheet-tah-*dee*-noa) m, **-a** f
citizen

ciuccio (*choo*-choa) m dummy

civico (*chee*-vee-koa) adj civic

civile (chee-*vee*-lay) adj civilian, civil

civilizzato (chee-vee-leed-*dzaa*-toa)
adj civilized

civiltà (chee-veel-*tah*) f civilization

clacson (*klahk*-soan) m hooter

classe (*klahss*-say) f class; grade;
form; ~ **turistica** tourist class

classico (*klahss*-see-koa) adj classical

classificare (klahss-see-fee-*kaa*-ray)
v classify, grade; sort

clausola (*klou*-zoa-lah) f clause

clava (*klaa*-vah) f club

clavicembalo (klah-vee-*chaym*-bah-
loa) m harpsichord

clavicola (klah-*vee*-koa-lah) f
collarbone

clemenza (klay-*mehn*-tsah) f mercy

cliente (*klyehn*-tay) m/f client,
customer

clima (*klee*-mah) m climate

clinica (*klee*-nee-kah) f clinic

cloro (*klaw*-roa) m chlorine

cocaina (koa-kah-*ee*-nah) f cocaine

cocciuto (koat-*choo*-toa) adj
stubborn

coccodrillo (koak-koa-*dreel*-loa) m
crocodile

coda (*koa*-dah) f tail; queue; ***fare la ~**
queue; stand in line Am

codardo (koa-*dahr*-doa) m coward

codice (*kaw*-dee-chay) *m* code; ~
postale zip code *Am*

coerenza (koa-ay-*rehn*-tsah) *f*
coherence

cofano (*kaw*-fah-noa) *m* bonnet;
hood *Am*

***cogliere** (*kaw*-l*y*ay-ray) *v* pick; *catch

cognac (koa-*ñahk*) *m* cognac

cognata (koa-*ñaa*-tah) *f* sister-in-law

cognato (koa-*ñaa*-toa) *m* brother-in-
law

cognome (koa-*ñōa*-may) *m* surname;
~ **da nubile** maiden name

coincidenza (koa-een-chee-*dehn*-
tsah) *f* connection

***coincidere** (koa-een-*chee*-day-ray) *v*
coincide

***coinvolgere** (koa-een-*vol*-jay-ray) *v*
involve

colapasta (koa-lah-*pah*-stah) *m*
strainer

colazione (koa-lah-*tsyōa*-nay) *f*
breakfast; **prima** ~ breakfast

colla (*koal*-lah) *f* gum, glue

collaboratore (koal-lah-boa-rah-*tōa*-
ray) *m*, **-trice** *f* collaborator;
freelance

collaborazione (koal-lah-boa-rah-
tsyōa-nay) *f* collaboration

collana (koal-*laa*-nah) *f* beads *pl*,
necklace

collant (koal-*laant*) *mpl* tights *pl*,
pantyhose *Am*

collare (koal-*laa*-ray) *m* collar

collega (koal-*lai*-gah) *m/f* colleague

collegare (koal-lay-*gaa*-ray) *v*
connect, link

collera (*kol*-lay-rah) *f* anger, passion

collettivo (koal-layt-*tee*-voa) *adj*
collective

colletto (koal-*layt*-toa) *m* collar

collettore (koal-layt-*tōa*-ray) *m*
collector

collezione (koal-lay-*tsyōa*-nay) *f*
collection; ~ **d'arte** art collection

collezionista (koal-lay-tsyoa-*nee*-
stah) *m/f* collector

collina (koal-*lee*-nah) *f* hill

collisione (koal-lee-*zyōa*-nay) *f*
collision

collo (*kol*-loa) *m* neck

collocare (koal-loa-*kaa*-ray) *v* *lay,
*put

colmo (*koal*-moa) *adj* full up; *m*
height

Colombia (koa-*loam*-byah) *f*
Colombia

colombiano (koa-loam-*byaa*-noa) *adj*
Colombian; *m*, **-a** *f* Colombian

colonia (koa-*law*-ñah) *f* colony; camp

colonna (koa-*lon*-nah) *f* pillar,
column

colonnello (koa-loan-*nehl*-loa) *m*
colonel

colorare (koa-*loa*-rah-ray) *v* colo(u)r

colore (koa-*lōa*-ray) *m* paint; colo(u)r;
di ~ colo(u)red

colorito (koa-loa-*ree*-toa) *adj*
colo(u)rful

colpa (*koal*-pah) *f* guilt, fault, blame

colpetto (koal-*payt*-toa) *m* tap

colpevole (koal-*pāy*-voa-lay) *adj*
guilty; **dichiarare** ~ convict

colpire (koal-*pee*-ray) *v* *hit; *strike;
touch

colpo (*koal*-poa) *m* knock, blow;
stroke; ~ **di sole** sunstroke

coltello (koal-*tehl*-loa) *m* knife

coltivare (koal-tee-*vaa*-ray) *v*
cultivate; *grow, raise

colto (*koal*-toa) *adj* cultured

coltura (koal-*tōo*-rah) *f* culture

coma (*kaw*-mah) *m* coma

comandante (koa-mahn-*dahn*-tay) *m*
commander; captain

comandare (koa-mahn-*daa*-ray) *v*
command, order

comando (koa-*mahn*-doa) *m* order;

leadership

combattere (koam-*baht*-tay-ray) v combat, *fight, battle

combattimento (koam-baht-tee-*mayn*-toa) m combat, battle; fight, struggle

combinare (koam-bee-*naa*-ray) v combine

combinazione (koam-bee-nah-*tsyōā*-nay) f combination

combustibile (koam-boo-*stee*-bee-lay) m fuel

come (*kōā*-may) adv such as, like; how; conj as; ~ **pure** as well; as well as; ~ **se** as if

comico (*kaw*-mee-koa) adj comic, humorous; m, **-a** f comedian

cominciare (koa-meen-*chaa*-ray) v *begin, start

comitato (koa-mee-*taa*-toa) m committee, commission

commedia (koam-*mai*-dyah) f comedy; ~ **musicale** musical comedy, musical

commediante (koam-may-*dyahn*-tay) m/f comedian

commemorazione (koam-may-moa-rah-*tsyōā*-nay) f commemoration

commentare (koam-mayn-*taa*-ray) v comment

commento (koam-*mayn*-toa) m comment; note

commerciale (koam-mayr-*chaa*-lay) adj commercial

commerciante (koam-mayr-*chahn*-tay) m/f merchant, dealer; trader

commerciare (koam-mayr-*chaa*-ray) v trade

commercio (koam-*mehr*-choa) m trade, commerce, business; ~ **al minuto** retail trade

commessa (koam-*mayss*-sah) f salesgirl

commesso (koam-*mayss*-soa) m salesman, shop assistant

commestibile (koam-may-*stee*-bee-lay) adj edible

***commettere** (koam-*mayt*-tay-ray) v commit

commissione (koam-meess-*syōā*-nay) f committee, commission

commozione (koam-moa-*tsyōā*-nay) f emotion; ~ **cerebrale** concussion

***commuovere** (koam-*mwaw*-vay-ray) v move

comò (koa-*mo*) m (pl ~) bureau Am

comodino (koa-mo-dee-*noa*) m bedside table

comodità (koa-moa-dee-*tah*) f comfort

comodo (*kaw*-moa-doa) adj convenient; comfortable, easy; m leisure

compact disc (kom-pahkt deesk) m compact disc

compagnia (koam-pah-*ñee*-ah) f company; society

compagno (koam-*paa*-ñoa) m, **-a** f companion; partner; comrade; ~ **di scuola** classmate

***comparire** (koam-pah-*ree*-ray) v appear

compassione (koam-pahss-*syōā*-nay) f sympathy; **provare** ~ **per** pity

compatire (koam-pah-*tee*-ray) v pity

compatriota (koam-pah-*tryaw*-tah) m countryman

compatto (koam-*paht*-toa) adj compact

compensare (koam-payn-*saa*-ray) v compensate, *make good

compensazione (koam-payn-sah-*tsyōā*-nay) f compensation

compera (*koam*-pay-rah) f purchase

competente (koam-pay-*tehn*-tay) adj expert; qualified

competere (koam-*pai*-tay-ray) v compete

competizione (koam-pay-tee-*tsyōa*-nay) f contest

compiacente (koam-pyah-*chehn*-tay) adj willing

compiere (*koam*-pyay-ray) v accomplish; commit; perform

compilare (koam-pee-*laa*-ray) v compile; *make up; fill out Am

compitare (koam-pee-*taa*-ray) v *spell

compito (*koam*-pee-toa) m duty, task

compleanno (koam-play-*ahn*-noa) m birthday; **buon ~!** happy birthday!

complesso (koam-*plehss*-soa) adj complex; m complex

completamente (koam-play-tah-*mayn*-tay) adv wholly, completely, quite

completare (koam-play-*taa*-ray) v complete, finish; fill in; fill out Am

completo (koam-*plai*-toa) adj total, complete, whole, utter

complicato (koam-plee-*kaa*-toa) adj complicated

complice (*kom*-plee-chay) m/f accomplice

complimentarsi con (koam-plee-mayn-*taa*-ray) v compliment

complimento (koam-plee-*mayn*-toa) m compliment

complotto (koam-*plot*-toa) m plot

***comporre** (koam-*poar*-ray) v compose

comportamento (koam-poar-tah-*mayn*-toa) m behavio(u)r

comportare (koam-poar-*taa*-ray) v imply; **comportarsi** behave; **comportarsi male** misbehave

compositore (koam-poa-zee-*tōa*-ray) m, **-trice** f composer

composizione (koam-poa-zee-*tsyōa*-nay) f composition

comprare (koam-*praa*-ray) v *buy

compratore (koam-prah-*tōa*-ray) m,

-trice f buyer, purchaser

***comprendere** (koam-*prehn*-day-ray) v contain, include; conceive, *understand

comprensione (koam-prayn-*syōa*-nay) f understanding

comprensivo (koam-prayn-*see*-voa) adj comprehensive; sympathetic

compreso (koam-*prāy*-soa) adj inclusive

compromesso (koam-proa-*mayss*-soa) m compromise

computer (koam-*poo*-tayr) m computer; **~ portatile** notebook

comune (koa-*mōō*-nay) adj common; municipality; town hall

comunicare (koa-moo-nee-*kaa*-ray) v communicate, inform

comunicato (koa-moo-nee-*kaa*-toa) m communiqué

comunicazione (koa-moo-nee-kah-*tsyōa*-nay) f communication, information

comunione (koa-moo-*nyōa*-nay) f congregation; communion; sharing

comunismo (koa-moo-*nee*-zmoa) m communism

comunista (koa-moo-*nee*-stah) m/f communist

comunità (koa-moo-nee-*tah*) f community

comunque (koa-*moong*-kway) adv at any rate, any way; still; however

con (koan) prep with; by

***concedere** (koan-*chai*-day-ray) v grant

concentrare (koan-chayn-*traa*-ray) v concentrate

concentrazione (koan-chayn-trah-*tsyōa*-nay) f concentration

concepimento (koan-chay-pee-*mayn*-toa) m conception

concepire (koan-chay-*pee*-ray) v conceive

concernere (koan-*chehr*-nay-ray) *v* concern

concerto (koan-*chehr*-toa) *m* concert

concessione (koan-chayss-*syoā*-nay) *f* concession

concetto (koan-*cheht*-toa) *m* concept

concezione (koan-chay-*tsyoā*-nay) *f* conception

conchiglia (koang-*kee*-l^yah) *f* seashell, shell

concime (koan-*chee*-may) *m* manure

conciso (koan-*chee*-zoa) *adj* concise

***concludere** (koang-*kloō*-day-ray) *v* conclude

conclusione (koang-kloo-*zyoā*-nay) *f* conclusion, issue

concordanza (koang-koar-*dahn*-tsah) *f* agreement

concorrente (koang-koar-*rehn*-tay) *m/f* rival, competitor

concorrenza (koang-koar-*rehn*-tsah) *f* rivalry, competition

concorso (koang-*koar*-soa) *m* concurrence

concreto (koang-*krai*-toa) *adj* concrete

condanna (koan-*dahn*-nah) *f* conviction

condannare (koan-dahn-*naa*-ray) *v* sentence; condemn

condannato (koan-dahn-*naa*-toa) *m*, **-a** *f* convict

condire (koan-*dee*-ray) *v* flavo(u)r; dress

condito (koan-*dee*-toa) *adj* spiced

***condividere** (koan-dee-*vee*-day-ray) *v* share

condizionale (koan-dee-tsyoa-*naa*-lay) *adj* conditional

condizione (koan-dee-*tsyoā*-nay) *f* term, condition

condominio (koan-doa-*mee*-nyoa) *m* block of flats, condo *Am*

condotta (koan-*doat*-tah) *f* conduct

conducente (koan-doo-*chayn*-tay) *m/f* driver

***condurre** (koan-*door*-ray) *v* conduct, carry; *drive

conduttore (koan-doot-*tōā*-ray) *m*, **-trice** *f* presenter

confederazione (koan-fay-day-rah-*tsyoā*-nay) *f* union, federation

conferenza (koan-fay-*rehn*-tsah) *f* lecture; conference; ~ **stampa** press conference

conferma (koan-*fayr*-mah) *f* confirmation

confermare (koan-fayr-*maa*-ray) *v* confirm, acknowledge

confessare (koan-fayss-*saa*-ray) *v* confess

confessione (koan-fayss-*syoā*-nay) *f* confession

confezionare (koan-fay-tsyoa-*naa*-ray) *v* manufacture

confezionato (koan-fay-tsyoa-*naa*-toa) *adj* ready-made

confidente (koan-fee-*dehn*-tay) *adj* confident

confidenziale (koan-fee-dayn-*tsyaa*-lay) *adj* confidential; familiar

confine (koan-*fee*-nay) *m* border

confiscare (koan-fee-*skaa*-ray) *v* confiscate

conflitto (koan-*fleet*-toa) *m* conflict

***confondere** (koan-*foan*-day-ray) *v* *mistake, confuse

conformità (koan-foar-mee-*tah*): **in ~ con** in accordance with

confortevole (koan-foar-*tāy*-voa-lay) *adj* cosy, comfortable

conforto (koan-*for*-toa) *m* comfort

confronto (koan-*froan*-toa) *m* comparison; confrontation

confusione (koan-foo-*zyoā*-nay) *f* confusion, disorder

confuso (koan-*foō*-zoa) *adj* confused

congedare (koan-jay-*daa*-ray) *v*

dismiss

congedo (koan-*jai*-doa) *m* leave

congelarsi (koan-jay-*lahr*-see) *v* *freeze

congelato (koan-jay-*laa*-toa) *adj* frozen

congelatore (koan-jay-lah-*toa*-ray) *m* deep-freeze, freezer

congettura (koan-jayt-*too*-rah) *f* guess

congiunto (koan-*joon*-toa) *adj* joint; related

congiura (koan-*joo*-rah) *f* plot

congratularsi con (koang-grah-too-*lahr*-see) *v* congratulate

congratulazione (koang-grah-too-lah-tsyoa-nay) *f* congratulation

congregazione (koang-gray-gah-tsyoa-nay) *f* congregation

congresso (koang-*grehss*-soa) *m* congress

coniglio (koa-*nee*-lyoa) *m* rabbit

coniugi (*kaw*-ñoo-jee) *mpl* married couple

connessione (koan-nayss-*syoa*-nay) *f* connection

***connettere** (koan-*neht*-tay-ray) *v* connect; plug in

connotati (koan-noa-*taa*-tee) *mpl* description

cono (*koa*-noa) *m* cone; ice-cream cone

conoscenza (koa-noash-*shehn*-tsah) *f* knowledge; acquaintance

***conoscere** (koa-*noash*-shay-ray) *v* *know

conquista (koang-*kwee*-stah) *f* conquest

conquistare (koang-kwee-*staa*-ray) *v* conquer

conquistatore (koang-kwee-stah-*toa*-ray) *m* conqueror

consapevole (koan-sah-*pay*-voa-lay) *adj* aware

conscio (*kon*-shoa) *adj* conscious

consegna (koan-*say*-ñah) *f* delivery

consegnare (koan-say-*ñaa*-ray) *v* deliver; commit

conseguentemente (koan-say-gwayn-tay-*mayn*-tay) *adv* consequently

conseguenza (koan-say-*gwehn*-tsah) *f* result, consequence; issue; **in ~ di** because of, for

conseguibile (koan-say-*gwee*-bee-lay) *adj* attainable

conseguire (koan-say-*gwee*-ray) *v* obtain

consenso (koan-*sehn*-soa) *m* consent

consentire (koan-sayn-*tee*-ray) *v* allow

conservare (koan-sayr-*vaa*-ray) *v* preserve; *hold

conservatore (koan-sayr-vah-*toa*-ray) *adj* conservative

conservatorio (koan-sayr-vah-*taw*-ryoa) *m* music academy

conserve (koan-*sehr*-vay) *fpl* tinned food, canned food *Am*

considerare (koan-see-day-*raa*-ray) *v* consider, regard; count, reckon

considerato (koan-see-day-*raa*-toa) *prep* considering

considerazione (koan-see-day-rah-tsyoa-nay) *f* consideration

considerevole (koan-see-day-*rāy*-voa-lay) *adj* considerable

consigliare (koan-*see*-lʸaa-ray) *v* recommend, advise

consigliere (koan-see-lʸai-ray) *m*, **-a** *f* adviser; council(l)or

consiglio (koan-*see*-lʸoa) *m* board; advice; counsel, council

consistere in (koan-*see*-stay-ray) consist of

consolare (koan-soa-*laa*-ray) *v* comfort

consolato (koan-soa-*laa*-toa) *m*

consulate

consolazione (koan-soa-lah-*tsyōā*-nay) f comfort

console (*kon*-soa-lay) m consul

consorte (koan-*sor*-tay) f wife

constatare (koan-stah-*taa*-ray) v ascertain

consueto (koan-*swai*-toa) adj habitual

consulta (koan-*sool*-tah) f consultation

consultare (koan-sool-*taa*-ray) v consult

consultazione (koan-sool-tah-*tsyōā*-nay) f consultation

consultorio (koan-sool-*taw*-ryoa) m family planning clinic

consumare (koan-soo-*maa*-ray) v use up

consumato (koan-soo-*maa*-toa) adj worn

consumatore (koan-soo-mah-*tōā*-ray) m, **-trice** f consumer

consumazione (koan-soo-ma-*tsyōō*-nay) f food; drink

contadino (koan-tah-*dee*-noa) m, **-a** f peasant

contagiare (koan-tah-*jaa*-ray) v infect

contagioso (koan-tah-*jōā*-soa) adj contagious, infectious

contaminazione (koan-tah-mee-nah-*tsyōā*-nay) f pollution

contanti (koan-*tahn*-tee) mpl cash

contare (koan-*taa*-ray) v count; **~ su** rely on

contatore (koan-taa-*toa*-ray) m meter

contattare (koan-taht-*taa*-ray) v contact

contatto (koan-*taht*-toa) m touch, contact

conte (*koan*-tay) m count, earl

contea (koan-*tai*-ah) f county

contemporaneo (koan-taym-poa-*raa*-nay-oa) adj contemporary

*contenere (koan-tay-*nāy*-ray) v contain; comprise; restrain; hold

contento (koan-*tehn*-toa) adj content; glad, happy

contenuto (koan-tay-*nōō*-toa) m contents pl

contessa (koan-*tayss*-sah) f countess

contiguo (koan-*tee*-gwoa) adj neighbo(u)ring

continentale (koan-tee-nayn-*taa*-lay) adj continental

continente (koan-tee-*nehn*-tay) m continent

continuamente (koan-tee-nwah-*mayn*-tay) adv all the time, continually

continuare (koan-tee-*nwaa*-ray) v continue, carry on; *go on, *go ahead, *keep on, *keep

continuazione (koan-tee-nwah-*tsyōā*-nay) f sequel

continuo (koan-*tee*-nwoa) adj continuous, continual; **di ~** continually

conto (*koan*-toa) m account; bill; check Am; **~ bancario** bank account; **per ~ di** on behalf of; ***rendere ~ di** account for

contorno (koan-*toar*-noa) m outline, contour

contrabbandare (koan-trahb-bahn-*daa*-ray) v smuggle

*contraddire (koan-trahd-*dee*-ray) v contradict

contraddittorio (koan-trahd-deet-*taw*-ryoa) adj contradictory

contraffatto (koan-trahf-*faht*-toa) adj false

contralto (koan-*trahl*-toa) m alto

contrario (koan-*traa*-ryoa) adj contrary, opposite; m reverse, contrary; **al ~** on the contrary

*contrarre (koan-*trahr*-ray) v contract

contrasto (koan-*trah*-stoa) m contrast

contratto (koan-*traht*-toa) *m*
agreement, contract; **~ di affitto** lease

contravvenzione (koan-trahv-vayn-
tsy*oa*-nay) *f* ticket, fine

contribuire (koan-tree-*bwee*-ray) *v*
contribute

contributo (koan-tree-*boo*-toa) *m*
contribution

contribuzione (koan-tree-boo-tsy*oa*-
nay) *f* contribution

contro (*koan*-troa) *prep* against;
versus

controllare (koan-troal-*laa*-ray) *v*
control

controllo (koan-*trol*-loa) *m* control,
inspection; **~ passaporti** passport
control

controllore (koan-troal-*loa*-ray) *m*
controller; ticket inspector

controversia (koan-troa-*vehr*-syah) *f*
dispute

controverso (koan-troa-*vehr*-soa) *adj*
controversial

contusione (koan-too-zy*oa*-nay) *f*
bruise

conveniente (koan-vay-*ñehn*-tay) *adj*
convenient, proper

*convenire (koan-vay-*nee*-ray) *v* be
better; agree

convento (koan-*vehn*-toa) *m* convent;
nunnery

conversazione (koan-vayr-sah-tsy*oa*-
nay) *f* conversation, discussion, talk

convertire (koan-vayr-*tee*-ray) *v*
convert; cash

*convincere (koan-*veen*-chay-ray) *v*
convince, persuade

convinzione (koan-veen-tsy*oa*-nay) *f*
conviction, persuasion

convulsione (koan-vool-sy*oa*-nay) *f*
convulsion

cooperativa (koa-oa-pay-rah-*tee*-vah)
f co-operative

cooperativo (koa-oa-pay-rah-*tee*-voa)

adj co-operative

cooperatore (koa-oa-pay-rah-*toa*-ray)
adj co-operative

cooperazione (koa-oa-pay-rah-tsy*oa*-
nay) *f* cooperation

coordinare (koa-oar-dee-*naa*-ray) *v*
co-ordinate

coordinazione (koa-oar-dee-nah-
tsy*oa*-nay) *f* coordination

coperchio (koa-*pehr*-kyoa) *m* top,
cover, lid

coperta (koa-*pehr*-tah) *f* blanket; deck

copertina (koa-payr-*tee*-nah) *f* cover

coperto (koa-*pehr*-toa) *adj* overcast

copertone (koa-payr-*toa*-nay) *m* tyre

copia (*kaw*-pyah) *f* copy; **brutta ~**
draft

copiare (koa-*pyaa*-ray) *v* copy

coppa (*kop*-pah) *f* cup

coppia (*kop*-pyah) *f* couple

copriletto (koa-pree-*leht*-toa) *m*
bedspread

*coprire (koa-*pree*-ray) *v* cover

coraggio (koa-*rahd*-joa) *m* guts,
courage

coraggioso (koa-rahd-*joa*-soa) *adj*
courageous; plucky, brave, bold

corallo (koa-*rahl*-loa) *m* coral

corazza (koa-*raht*-tsah) *f* armour

corda (*kor*-dah) *f* cord, rope; string

cordiale (koar-*dyaa*-lay) *adj* cordial;
hearty, sympathetic

cordicella (koar-dee-*chehl*-lah) *f* line

cordoglio (koar-*daw*-l^{y}oa) *m* grief

cornacchia (koar-*nahk*-kyah) *f* crow

cornetta (koar-*nayt*-tah) *f* receiver

cornice (koar-*nee*-chay) *f* frame

corno[1] (*kor*-noa) *m* (pl le corna) horn

corno[2] (*kor*-noa) *m* (pl i corni) horn

coro (*kaw*-roa) *m* choir

corona (koa-*roa*-nah) *f* crown

coronare (koa-roa-*naa*-ray) *v* crown

corpo (*kor*-poa) *m* body

corpulento (koar-poo-*lehn*-toa) *adj*

corpulent, stout

corredo (koar-*rai*-doa) *m* kit

*****correggere** (koar-*rehd*-jay-ray) *v* correct

corrente (koar-*rehn*-tay) *adj* current; *f* current, stream; **con la ~** downstream; **contro ~** upstream; **~ alternata** alternating current; **~ continua** direct current; **~ d'aria** draught; *****mettere al ~** inform

*****correre** (*koar*-ray-ray) *v* *run; *speed; *****~ troppo** *speed

correttezza (koar-rayt-*tayt*-tsah) *f* correctness

corretto (koar-*reht*-toa) *adj* correct, right

correzione (koar-ray-*tsyoa*-nay) *f* correction

corrida (koar-*ree*-dah) *f* bullfight

corridoio (koar-ree-$\overline{doa}$-yoa) *m* corridor

corriera *f* coach

corrispondente (koar-ree-spoan-*dehn*-tay) *m/f* correspondent

corrispondenza (koar-ree-spoan-*dehn*-tsah) *f* correspondence

*****corrispondere** (koar-ree-*spoan*-day-ray) *v* correspond, agree; fit

*****corrompere** (koar-*roam*-pay-ray) *v* corrupt, bribe

corrotto (koar-*roat*-toa) *adj* corrupt; vicious

corruzione (koar-roo-*tsyoa*-nay) *f* corruption, bribery

corsa (*koar*-sah) *f* ride; race; **~ di cavalli** horserace

corsia (koar-*see*-ah) *f* lane

corso (*koar*-soa) *m* course; avenue; **~ intensivo** intensive course; **~ del cambio** exchange rate, rate of exchange

corte (*koar*-tay) *f* court

corteccia (koar-*tayt*-chah) *f* bark

corteo (koar-*tai*-oa) *m* procession

cortese (koar-*tay*-zay) *adj* civil, courteous, polite

cortile (koar-*tee*-lay) *m* yard; **~ della scuola** playground

corto (*koar*-toa) *adj* short; **~ circuito** short circuit

corvo (*kor*-voa) *m* raven

cosa (*kaw*-sah) *f* thing; **che ~** what; **qualunque ~** anything

coscia (*kosh*-shah) *f* thigh; leg

coscienza (koash-*shehn*-tsah) *f* consciousness; conscience

così (koa-*see*) *adv* so, thus, such; as; **~ che** so that; **e ~ via** and so on

cosiddetto (koa-seed-*dayt*-toa) *adj* so-called

cosmetici (koa-*zmai*-tee-chee) *mpl* cosmetics *pl*

cospirare (koa-spee-*raa*-ray) *v* conspire

costa (*ko*-stah) *f* coast

costante (koan-*stahn*-tay) *adj* constant

costare (koa-*staa*-ray) *v* *cost

costernato (koa-stayr-*naa*-toa) *adj* upset

costituire (koa-stee-*twee*-ray) *v* constitute

costituzione (koa-stee-too-*tsyoa*-nay) *f* constitution

costo (*ko*-stoa) *m* cost; charge

costola (*ko*-stoa-lah) *f* rib

costoletta (koa-stoa-*layt*-tah) *f* cutlet

costoso (koa-*stoa*-soa) *adj* expensive

*****costringere** (koa-*streen*-jay-ray) *v* compel, force

costruire (koa-*strwee*-ray) *v* construct, *build

costruzione (koa-stroo-*tsyoa*-nay) *f* construction

costume (koa-*stoo*-may) *m* custom; **~ da bagno** bathing suit, swimsuit; swimming trunks; **~ nazionale** national dress; **costumi** *mpl* morals

cotoletta (koa-toa-*layt*-tah) *f* chop

cotone (koa-*tōa*-nay) *m* cotton; **di ~** cotton

cozza (*koat*-tsah) *f* mussel

cozzare (koat-*tsaa*-ray) *v* collide, bump

crampo (*krahm*-poa) *m* cramp

cranio (*kraa*-ñoa) *m* skull

cratere (krah-*tai*-ray) *m* crater

cravatta (krah-*vaht*-tah) *f* tie, necktie; **~ a farfalla** bow tie

cravattino (krah-vaht-*tee*-noa) *m* bow tie

creare (kray-*aa*-ray) *v* create

creatura (kray-ah-*tōō*-rah) *f* creature

credenza (kray-*dehn*-tsah) *f* dresser

credere (*krāy*-day-ray) *v* believe; guess, reckon

credibile (kray-*dee*-bee-lay) *adj* credible

credito (*krāy*-dee-toa) *m* credit

creditore (kray-dee-*tōa*-ray) *m*, **-trice** *f* creditor

credulone (*krai*-doo-loa) *adj* credulous

crema (*krai*-mah) *f* cream; **~ da barba** shaving cream; **~ idratante** moisturizing cream; **~ per la notte** night cream; **~ per la pelle** skin cream; **~ per le mani** hand cream

cremare (kray-*maa*-ray) *v* cremate

cremazione (kray-mah-*tsyōa*-nay) *f* cremation

cremisi (*kray*-mee-*zee*) *adj* crimson

cremoso (kray-*mōa*-soa) *adj* creamy

crepa (*krai*-pah) *f* cleft

crepuscolo (kray-*poo*-skoa-loa) *m* twilight, dusk

*crescere (*kraysh*-shay-ray) *v* *grow

crescione (kraysh-*shōa*-nay) *m* watercress

crescita (*kraysh*-shee-tah) *f* growth

cresima (*kray*-see-mah) *f* confirmation

cresta (*kray*-stah) *f* ridge

creta (*krāy*-tah) *f* clay

cretino (*kray*-tee-noa) *adj* stupid

cric (*kreek*) *m* jack

criminale (kree-mee-*naa*-lay) *adj* criminal; *m/f* criminal

criminalità (kree-mee-nah-lee-*tah*) *f* criminality

crimine (*kree*-mee-nay) *m* crime

crisi (*kree*-zee) *f* crisis

cristallino (kree-stahl-*lee*-noa) *adj* crystal

cristallo (kree-*stahl*-loa) *m* crystal

cristiano (kree-*styaa*-noa) *adj* Christian; *m*, **-a** *f* Christian

Cristo (*kree*-stoa) *m* Christ

critica (*kree*-tee-kah) *f* criticism

criticare (kree-tee-*kaa*-ray) *v* criticize

critico (*kree*-tee-koa) *adj* critical; *m*, **-a** *f* critic

croccante (kroak-*kahn*-tay) *adj* crisp

croce (*krōa*-chay) *f* cross

crocevia (kroa-chay-*vee*-ah) *m* junction, crossing

crociata (kroa-*chaa*-tah) *f* crusade

crociera (kroa-*chai*-rah) *f* cruise

*crocifiggere (kroa-chee-*feed*-jay-ray) *v* crucify

crocifissione (kroa-chee-feess-*syōa*-nay) *f* crucifixion

crocifisso (kroa-chee-*feess*-soa) *m* crucifix

crollare (kroal-*laa*-ray) *v* collapse

cromo (*kraw*-moa) *m* chromium

cronaca (*kraw*-nah-kah) *f* chronicle; commentary; news

cronico (*kraw*-nee-koa) *adj* chronic

cronologico (kroa-noa-*law*-jee-koa) *adj* chronological

crosta (*kro*-stah) *f* crust

crostaceo (kroa-*staa*-chay-oa) *m* shellfish

crostino (kroa-*stee*-noa) *m* toast

crudele (kroo-*dai*-lay) *adj* cruel, harsh

crudo (*kroo*-doa) *adj* raw

cruscotto (kroo-*skot*-toa) *m* dashboard

cubo (*koo*-boa) *m* cube

cuccetta (koot-*chayt*-tah) *f* couchette; berth

cucchiaiata (kook-kyah-*yaa*-tah) *f* spoonful

cucchiaino (kook-kyah-*ee*-noa) *m* teaspoon; teaspoonful

cucchiaio (kook-*kyaa*-yoa) *m* spoon, tablespoon

cucina (koo-*chee*-nah) *f* kitchen; stove; ~ **a gas** gas cooker

cucinare (koo-chee-*naa*-ray) *v* cook; ~ **alla griglia** grill

cucire (koo-*chee*-ray) *v* sew

cucitura (koo-chee-*too*-rah) *f* seam; **senza** ~ seamless

cuculo (*koo*-koo-loa) *m* cuckoo

cuffia (*koof*-fyah) *f* swimming cap; shower cap; headphones *pl*; earphones *pl*

cugino (koo-*jee*-noa) *m*, **-a** *f* cousin

cui (*koo*-ee) *pron* whose; of which; whom; to which

culla (*kool*-lah) *f* cradle

culmine (*kool*-mee-nay) *m* height

culto (*kool*-toa) *m* worship

cultura (kool-*too*-rah) *f* culture

cumulo (*koo*-moo-loa) *m* heap

cuneo (*koo*-nay-oa) *m* wedge

cuocere (*kwaw*-chay-ray) *v* cook; bake

cuoco (*kwaw*-koa) *m*, **-a** *f* cook

cuoio (*kwaw*-yoa) *m* leather

cuore (*kwaw*-ray) *m* heart

cupidigia (koo-pee-*dee*-jah) *f* greed

cupo (*koo*-poa) *adj* gloomy

cupola (*koo*-poa-lah) *f* dome

cura (*koo*-rah) *f* care; cure; ***aver ~ di** *take care of; ~ **di bellezza** beauty treatment

curapipe (koo-rah-*pee*-pay) *m* pipe cleaner

curare (koo-*raa*-ray) *v* nurse; cure; ~ **le unghie** manicure

curato (koo-*raa*-toa) *adj* neat

curiosità (koo-ryoa-see-*tah*) *f* curiosity; sight

curioso (koo-*ryoa*-soa) *adj* curious

curva (*koor*-vah) *f* bend; curve

curvare (koor-*vaa*-ray) *v* *bend

curvatura (koor-vah-*too*-rah) *f* bend

curvo (*koor*-voa) *adj* curved

cuscinetto (koosh-shee-*nayt*-toa) *m* pad

cuscino (koosh-*shee*-noa) *m* cushion; pillow

custode (koo-*staw*-day) *m/f* warden; caretaker

custodia (koo-*staw*-dyah) *f* custody

custodire (koo-stoa-*dee*-ray) *v* guard

D

da (dah) *prep* out of, from; at, to; as from; since; by

dado (*daa*-doa) *m* nut

daltonico (dahl-*taw*-nee-koa) *adj* colo(u)r-blind

danese (dah-*nay*-say) *adj* Danish; *m/f* Dane

Danimarca (dah-nee-*mahr*-kah) *f* Denmark

danneggiare (dahn-nayd-*jaa*-ray) *v* damage

danno (*dahn*-noa) *m* damage;

mischief, harm

dannoso (dahn-*nōā*-soa) *adj* harmful

danza (*dahn*-tsa) *f* dance

dappertutto (dahp-payr-*toot*-toa) *adv* throughout

***dare** (*daa*-ray) *v* *give

data (*daa*-tah) *f* date

dati (*daa*-tee) *mpl* data *pl*

dattero (*daht*-tay-roa) *m* date

dattilografo (daht-tee-*law*-grah-fah) *m*, **-a** *f* typist

davanti (dah-*vahn*-tee) *prep* in front; before

davanzale (dah-vahn-*tsaa*-lay) *m* windowsill

davvero (dahv-*vāy*-roa) *adv* really

dazio (*daa*-tsyoa) *m* Customs duty, duty

dea (*dai*-ah) *f* goddess

debito (*dai*-bee-toa) *m* debt; debit

debole (*dāy*-boa-lay) *adj* weak; faint; dim

debolezza (day-boa-*layt*-tsah) *f* weakness

decaffeinato (day-kahf-fay-*na*-toa) *adj* decaffeinated

deceduto (day-chay-*dōo*-toa) *adj* dead

decente (day-*chehn*-tay) *adj* decent, proper

decenza (day-*chehn*-tsah) *f* decency

***decidere** (day-*chee*-day-ray) *v* decide

decimo (*dai*-chee-moa) *num* tenth

decisione (day-chee-*zyōa*-nay) *f* decision

deciso (day-*chee*-zoa) *adj* resolute

decollare (day-koal-*laa*-ray) *v* *take off

decollo (day-*kol*-loa) *m* take-off

decorazione (day-*ko*-rah-*tsyōa*-nay) *f* decoration

***decrescere** (day-*kraysh*-shay-ray) *v* decrease

dedicare (day-dee-*kaa*-ray) *v* dedicate; devote

***dedurre** (day-*door*-ray) *v* infer, deduce

deficienza (day-fee-*chehn*-tsah) *f* deficiency

deficit (*dai*-fee-cheet) *m* deficit

definire (day-fee-*nee*-ray) *v* define

definitivo (day-fee-nee-*tee*-voa) *adj* definitive

definizione (day-fee-nee-*tsyōa*-nay) *f* definition

deformato (day-foar-*maa*-toa) *adj* deformed

deforme (day-*foar*-may) *adj* deformed

degno di (*day*-ñoa dee) worthy of

delegato (day-lay-*gaa*-toa) *m*, **-a** *f* delegate

delegazione (day-lay-gah-*tsyōa*-nay) *f* delegation

deliberare (day-lee-bay-*raa*-ray) *v* deliberate

deliberazione (day-lee-bay-rah-*tsyōa*-nay) *f* deliberation

delicato (day-lee-*kaa*-toa) *adj* delicate; tender; gentle; mellow

delinquente (day-leeng-*kwehn*-tay) *m/f* criminal

delitto (day-*leet*-toa) *m* crime

delizia (day-*lee*-tsyah) *f* delight

delizioso (day-lee-*tsyōa*-soa) *adj* delicious, lovely, wonderful

deltaplano (dayl-*tah*-plaa-noa) *m* hang-glider

***deludere** (day-*lōo*-day-ray) *v* disappoint, *let down; *be disappointing

delusione (day-loo-*zyōa*-nay) *f* disappointment

democratico (day-moa-*kraa*-tee-koa) *adj* democratic

democrazia (day-moa-krah-*tsee*-ah) *f* democracy

demolire (day-moa-*lee*-ray) *v* demolish

demolizione (day-moa-lee-*tsyōa*-nay) *f* demolition

denaro (day-*naa*-roa) *m* money

denominazione (day-noa-mee-nah-*tsyōa*-nay) *f* denomination

denso (*dehn*-soa) *adj* dense, thick

dente (*dehn*-tay) *m* tooth

dentiera (dayn-*tyai*-rah) *f* denture, false teeth

dentifricio (dayn-tee-*free*-choa) *m* toothpaste

dentista (dayn-*tee*-stah) *m/f* dentist

dentro (*dayn*-troa) *adv* in, inside; *prep* inside, within, in

denuncia (day-*nōon*-chah) *f* denunciation; report

denutrizione (day-noo-tree-*tsyōa*-nay) *f* malnutrition

deodorante (day-oa-doa-*rahn*-tay) *m* deodorant

deperibile (day-pay-*ree*-bee-lay) *adj* perishable

depositare (day-poa-zee-*taa*-ray) *v* deposit, bank

deposito (day-*paw*-zee-toa) *m* deposit; depot, warehouse; ~ **bagagli** left luggage office; baggage deposit office *Am*, baggage check *Am*

depressione (day-prayss-*syōa*-nay) *f* depression

depresso (day-*prehss*-soa) *adj* depressed, blue

deprimente (day-pree-*mayn*-tay) *adj* depressing

*deprimere (day-*pree*-may-ray) *v* depress

deputato (day-poo-*taa*-toa) *m*, **-a** *f* Member of Parliament, Representative *Am*

derisione (day-ree-*zyōa*-nay) *f* mockery

derivare (day-ree-*vaa*-ray) *v* divert; ~ **da** derive from

dermatologo (dayr-mah-*tōa*-loa-goa) *m*, **-a** *f* dermatologist

*descrivere (day-*skree*-vay-ray) *v* describe

descrizione (day-skree-*tsyōa*-nay) *f* description

deserto (day-*zehr*-toa) *adj* desert; *m* desert

desiderabile (day-see-day-*raa*-bee-lay) *adj* desirable

desiderare (day-see-day-*raa*-ray) *v* want, desire, wish

desiderio (day-see-*dai*-ryoa) *m* desire, wish

desideroso (day-see-day-*rōa*-soa) *adj* eager

designare (day-see-*ñaa*-ray) *v* designate; appoint

desistere (day-*see*-stay-ray) *v* *give up

destinare (day-stee-*naa*-ray) *v* destine

destinatario (day-stee-nah-*taa*-ryoa) *m* addressee

destinazione (day-stee-nah-*tsyōa*-nay) *f* destination

destino (day-*stee*-noa) *m* fate, destiny, fortune

destra (*deh*-strah) *f* right; right-hand; **a** ~ on the right, to the right

destro (*deh*-stroa) *adj* right; right-hand; skilful

detenuto (day-tay-*nōo*-toa) *m*, **-a** *f* prisoner

detenzione (day-tayn-*tsyōa*-nay) *f* custody

detergente (day-tayr-*jehn*-tay) *m* detergent

determinare (day-tayr-mee-*naa*-ray) *v* define, determine

determinato (day-tayr-mee-*naa*-toa) *adj* definite

determinazione (day-tayr-mee-nah-*tsyōa*-nay) *f* determination

detersivo (day-tayr-*see*-voa) *m* washing powder

detestare (day-tay-*staa*-ray) *v* hate,

dislike

dettagliato (dayt-tah-*l*ⁱ*aa*-toa) *adj* detailed

dettaglio (dayt-*taa*-lⁱoa) *m* detail

dettare (dayt-*taa*-ray) *v* dictate

dettato (dayt-*taa*-toa) *m* dictation

deviare (day-*vyaa*-ray) *v* deviate

deviazione (day-vyah-*tsyōa*-nay) *f* detour, diversion

di (dee) *prep* of; *conj* than

diabete (dyah-*bai*-tay) *m* diabetes

diabetico (dyah-*bai*-tee-koa) *m*, **-a** *f* diabetic

diaframma (dyah-*fraam*-mah) *m* diaphragm

diagnosi (*dyaa*-ñoa-zee) *f* diagnosis

diagnosticare (dyah-ñoa-stee-*kaa*-ray) *v* diagnose

diagonale (dyah-goa-*naa*-lay) *adj* diagonal; *f* diagonal

diagramma (dyah-*grahm*-mah) *m* chart; diagram

dialetto (dyah-*leht*-toa) *m* dialect

dialogo (*dyaa*-loa-goa) *m* dialog(ue)

diamante (dyah-*mahn*-tay) *m* diamond

diapositiva (dyah-poa-zee-*tee*-vah) *f* slide

diario (*dyaa*-ryoa) *m* diary

diarrea (dyahr-*rai*-ah) *f* diarrh(o)ea

diavolo (*dyaa*-voa-loa) *m* devil

dibattere (dee-*baht*-tay-ray) *v* discuss

dibattito (dee-*baht*-tee-toa) *m* debate, discussion

dicembre (dee-*chehm*-bray) December

diceria (dee-chay-*ree*-ah) *f* rumo(u)r

dichiarare (dee-kyah-*raa*-ray) *v* declare

dichiarazione (dee-kyah-rah-*tsyōa*-nay) *f* declaration, statement

diciannove (dee-chahn-*naw*-vay) *num* nineteen

diciannovesimo (dee-chahn-noa-*vai*-zee-moa) *num* nineteenth

diciassette (dee-chahss-*seht*-tay) *num* seventeen

diciassettesimo (dee-chahss-sayt-*tai*-zee-moa) *num* seventeenth

diciottesimo (dee-choat-*tai*-zee-moa) *num* eighteenth

diciotto (dee-*chot*-toa) *num* eighteen

didietro (dee-*dyai*-troa) *m* bottom

dieci (*dyai*-chee) *num* ten

diesel (*dee*-zayl) *m* diesel

dieta (*dyai*-tah) *f* diet

dietro (*dyai*-troa) *prep* behind

***difendere** (dee-*fehn*-day-ray) *v* defend

difensore (dee-fayn-*sōa*-ray) *m* champion; defender

difesa (dee-*fāy*-sah) *f* defence, defense *Am*; plea

difetto (dee-*feht*-toa) *m* fault

difettoso (dee-fayt-*tōa*-soa) *adj* defective, faulty

differente (deef-fay-*rehn*-tay) *adj* different

differenza (deef-fay-*rehn*-tsah) *f* difference; distinction

differire (deef-fay-*ree*-ray) *v* differ, vary

difficile (deef-*fee*-chee-lay) *adj* difficult, hard

difficoltà (deef-fee-koal-*tah*) *f* difficulty

diffidare di (deef-fee-*daa*-ray) mistrust

***diffondere** (deef-*foan*-day-ray) *v* *shed

diffusione (deef-foo-*zyōa*-nay) *f* diffusion

difterite (deef-tay-*ree*-tay) *f* diphtheria

diga (*dee*-gah) *f* dike, dam

digeribile (dee-jay-*ree*-bee-lay) *adj* digestible

digerire (dee-jay-*ree*-ray) *v* digest

digestione (dee-jay-*styōa*-nay) *f*

digestion

digitale (dee-*jee*-taa-lay) *adj* digital

digiuno (dee-jōō-noa): **a ~** on an empty stomach

dignità (dee-ñee-*tah*) *f* dignity; rank

dignitoso (dee-ñee-*tōa*-soa) *adj* dignified

dilettevole (dee-layt-*tāy*-voa-lay) *adj* delightful

diletto (dee-*leht*-toa) *adj* dear; *m* delight, pleasure

diligente (dee-lee-*jehn*-tay) *adj* diligent

diligenza (dee-lee-*jehn*-tsah) *f* diligence

diluire (dee-*lwee*-ray) *v* dilute

diluito (dee-*lwee*-toa) *adj* weak

dimagrire (dee-mah-*gree*-ray) *v* slim

dimensione (dee-mayn-*syōa*-nay) *f* extent, size

dimenticare (dee-mayn-tee-*kaa*-ray) *v* *forget

*dimettersi (dee-*mayt*-tayr-see) *v* resign

dimezzare (dee-mayd-*dzaa*-ray) *v* halve

diminuire (dee-mee-*nwee*-ray) *v* reduce; decrease, lessen

diminuzione (dee-mee-noo-*tsyōa*-nay) *f* decrease

dimissioni (dee-meess-*syōa*-nee) *fpl* resignation

dimostrare (dee-moa-*straa*-ray) *v* demonstrate, prove, *show

dimostrazione (dee-moa-strah-*tsyōa*-nay) *f* demonstration; ***fare una ~** demonstrate

dinamo (*dee*-nah-moa) *f* dynamo

dinanzi a (dee-*nahn*-tsee ah) before

dintorni (deen-*toar*-nee) *mpl* environment, surroundings *pl*

dio (*dee*-oa) *m* (pl dei) god

dipendente (dee-payn-*dehn*-tay) *adj* dependant

dipendenza (dee-payn-*dehn*-tsah) *f* annex

*dipendere da (dee-*pehn*-day-ray) depend on; **dipende!** that depends!

diploma (dee-*plaw*-mah) *m* certificate; diploma

diplomarsi (dee-ploa-*mahr*-see) *v* graduate

diplomatico (dee-ploa-*maa*-tee-koa) *m*, **-a** *f* diplomat

diplomato (dee-ploa-*maa*-toa) *adj* qualified

*dire (*dee*-ray) *v* *say, *tell; ***voler ~** *mean

direttamente (dee-rayt-tah-*mayn*-tay) *adv* straight away

direttiva (dee-rayt-*tee*-vah) *f* directive

diretto (dee-*reht*-toa) *adj* direct; **~ a** bound for

direttore (dee-rayt-*tōa*-ray) *m*, **-trice** *f* director, manager; executive; **~ di scuola** head teacher, headmaster; **~ d'orchestra** conductor

direzione (dee-ray-*tsyōa*-nay) *f* way, direction; management; **indicatore di ~** trafficator; directional signal *Am*, blinker *Am*

dirigente (dee-ree-*jehn*-tay) *m/f* leader

*dirigere (dee-*ree*-jay-ray) *v* direct, head, *lead; conduct; manage

diritto (dee-*reet*-toa) *adj* erect, upright; *m* right; **~ amministrativo** administrative law; **~ civile** civil law; **~ commerciale** commercial law; **~ elettorale** franchise; **~ penale** criminal law; **sempre ~** straight ahead

dirottare (dee-roat-*taa*-ray) *v* hijack

dirottatore (dee-roat-tah-*tōa*-ray) *m*, **-trice** *f* hijacker

disabile (dee-*zah*-bee-lay) *adj* disabled

disabitato (dee-zah-bee-*taa*-toa) *adj*

uninhabited

disapprovare (dee-zahp-proa-*vaa*-ray) *v* disapprove

disastro (dee-*zah*-stroa) *m* disaster, calamity

disastroso (dee-zah-str$\overline{oa}$-soa) *adj* disastrous

discendente (deesh-shayn-*dehn*-tay) *m/f* descendant; *adj* descending

discendenza (deesh-shayn-*dehn*-tsah) *f* origin

discesa (deesh-*sh$\overline{ay}$*-sah) *f* descent; **in ~** downwards

dischetto (dee-*skayt*-toa) *m* diskette

disciplina (deesh-shee-*plee*-nah) *f* discipline

disco (*dee*-skoa) *m* disc; record; **~ fisso** hard disk; **~ orario** parking disc

discorso (dee-*skoar*-soa) *m* speech; conversation

discoteca (dee-skoa-tay-kah) *f* disco

discussione (dee-skooss-sy$\overline{oa}$-nay) *f* argument, discussion

*discutere (dee-sk$\overline{oo}$-tay-ray) *v* argue, discuss; dispute

disdegno (deez-*d$\overline{ay}$*-ñoa) *m* contempt

*disdire (deez-*dee*-ray) *v* cancel

disegnare (dee-say-*ñaa*-ray) *v* sketch, *draw

disegno (dee-*s$\overline{ay}$*-ñoa) *m* sketch, drawing; pattern; design; **puntina da ~** drawing pin; thumbtack *Am*

disertare (dee-zayr-*taa*-ray) *v* desert

*disfare (dee-*sfaa*-ray) *v* *undo; unwrap; **~ le valigie** unpack

disgelarsi (deez-jay-*lahr*-see) *v* thaw

disgelo (deez-*jai*-loa) *m* thaw

disgrazia (deez-*graa*-tsyah) *f* accident; disgrace

disgraziatamente (deez-grah-tsyah-tah-*mayn*-tay) *adv* unfortunately

disgustoso (deez-goo-st$\overline{oa}$-soa) *adj* revolting, disgusting

disimparare (dee-zeem-pah-*raa*-ray)

v unlearn

disinfettante (dee-zeen-fayt-*tahn*-tay) *m* disinfectant

disinfettare (dee-zeen-fayt-*taa*-ray) *v* disinfect

disinserire (dee-zeen-say-*ree*-ray) *v* disconnect

disinteressato (dee-zeen-tay-rayss-*saa*-toa) *adj* unselfish

disinvoltura (dee-zeen-voal-*t$\overline{oo}$*-rah) *f* ease

disoccupato (dee-zoak-koo-*paa*-toa) *adj* unemployed, jobless

disoccupazione (dee-zoak-koo-pah-tsy$\overline{oa}$-nay) *f* unemployment

disonesto (dee-zoa-*neh*-stoa) *adj* crooked, unfair, dishonest

disonore (dee-zoa-*n$\overline{oa}$*-ray) *m* disgrace, shame

disordinato (dee-zoar-dee-*naa*-toa) *adj* sloppy, untidy

disordine (dee-*zoar*-dee-nay) *m* mess, disorder; **in ~** in a mess; **disordini** riots

disossare (dee-zoass-*saa*-ray) *v* bone

dispari (*dee*-spah-ree) *adj* odd

dispensa (dee-*spehn*-sah) *f* larder

dispensare (dee-spayn-*saa*-ray) *v* exempt

disperare (dee-spay-*raa*-ray) *v* despair

disperato (dee-spay-*raa*-toa) *adj* desperate; hopeless

disperazione (dee-spay-rah-tsy$\overline{oa}$-nay) *f* despair

dispiacere (dee-spyah-*ch$\overline{ay}$*-ray) *m* sorrow

*dispiacere (dee-spyah-*ch$\overline{ay}$*-ray) *v* displease

disponibile (dee-spoa-*nee*-bee-lay) *adj* ..vailable; spare

*disporre (dee-*spoar*-ray) dispose

dispositivo (dee-spoa-zee-*tee*-voa) *m* apparatus

disposizione (dee-spoa-zee-*tsy$\overline{oa}$*-

nay) f disposal

disprezzare (dee-sprayt-*tsaa*-ray) v despise, scorn

disprezzo (dee-*spreht*-tsoa) m contempt, scorn

disputa (*dee*-spoo-tah) f argument, dispute

disputare (dee-spoo-*taa*-ray) v argue; dispute

dissentire (deess-sayn-*tee*-ray) v disagree

*dissuadere da (deess-swah-*day*-ray) v dissuade from

distante (dee-*stahn*-tay) adj far-away, remote

distanza (dee-*stahn*-tsah) f distance; space, way

distendersi (dee-*stayn*-dayr-see) v *lie down; relax

*distinguere (dee-*steeng*-gway-ray) v distinguish

distinto (dee-*steen*-toa) adj distinct; separate; distinguished

distinzione (dee-steen-*tsyōa*-nay) f distinction

distorsione (dee-stoar-*syōa*-nay) f sprain

distretto (dee-*strayt*-toa) m district

distribuire (dee-stree-*bwee*-ray) v *deal, distribute; issue

distributore (dee-stree-boo-*tōa*-ray) m distributor; petrol pump, gas pump Am; ~ **automatico** vending machine

distribuzione (dee-stree-boo-*tsyōa*-nay) f distribution; disposition

*distruggere (dee-*strood*-jay-ray) v destroy, wreck

distruzione (dee-stroo-*tsyōa*-nay) f destruction

disturbare (dee-stoor-*baa*-ray) v trouble, disturb; **disturbarsi** bother

disturbo (dee-*stoor*-boa) m disturbance

ditale (dee-*taa*-lay) m thimble

dito (*dee*-toa) m (pl le dita) finger; ~ **del piede** toe

ditta (*deet*-tah) f company, firm; business

dittafono (deet-*taa*-foa-noa) m dictaphone

dittatore (deet-tah-*tōa*-ray) m dictator

divano (dee-*vaa*-noa) m couch

*divenire (dee-vay-*nee*-ray) v *become

diventare (dee-vayn-*taa*-ray) v *grow, *go, *get

diversione (dee-vayr-*syōa*-nay) f diversion

diverso (dee-*vehr*-soa) adj different; unlike; **diversi** several

divertente (dee-vayr-*tehn*-tay) adj funny, entertaining, enjoyable, amusing

divertimento (dee-vayr-tee-*mayn*-toa) m pleasure, fun, entertainment, amusement

divertire (dee-vayr-*tee*-ray) v entertain, amuse; **divertirsi** enjoy oneself

*dividere (dee-*vee*-day-ray) v divide

divieto (dee-*vyai*-toa) m prohibition; ~ **di sorpasso** no overtaking; no passing Am; ~ **di sosta** no parking

divino (dee-*vee*-noa) adj divine

divisa estera (dee-*vee*-zah eh-*stay*-rah) foreign currency

divisione (dee-vee-*zyōa*-nay) f division; agency

divisorio (dee-vee-*zaw*-ryoa) m partition

divorziare da (dee-voar-*tsyaa*-ray) v divorce

divorziato (dee-vor-*tsyah*-toa) adj divorced

divorzio (dee-*vor*-tsyoa) m divorce

dizionario (dee-tsyoa-*naa*-ryoa) m dictionary

doccia (*doat*-chah) f shower

docente (doa-*chehn*-tay) *m/f* teacher

documento (doa-koo-*mayn*-toa) *m* document

dodicesimo (doa-dee-*chai*-zee-moa) *num* twelfth

dodici (*dōa*-dee-chee) *num* twelve

dogana (doa-*gaa*-nah) *f* Customs *pl*

doganiere (doa-gah-*ñai*-ray) *m* Customs officer

doglie (*daw*-ľ'ay) *fpl* labo(u)r

dolce (*doal*-chay) *adj* sweet; gentle, tender; mellow; *m* cake; dessert, sweet

dolciumi (doal-*chōo*-mee) *mpl* sweets; candy *Am*

*dolere (doa-*lāy*-ray) *v* ache, *hurt

dolore (doa-*lōa*-ray) *m* pain, ache; grief, sorrow

doloroso (doa-loa-*rōa*-soa) *adj* sorrowful, painful

domanda (doa-*mahn*-dah) *f* inquiry, query; question; request; demand

domandare (doa-mahn-*daa*-ray) *v* ask; query

domani (doa-*maa*-nee) *adv* tomorrow

domattina (doa-*maht*-tee-nah) *adv* tomorrow morning

domenica (doa-*māy*-nee-kah) *f* Sunday

domestica (doa-*meh*-stee-kah) *f* housemaid

domestico (doa-*meh*-stee-koa) *adj* domestic; *m* domestic; **faccende domestiche** housekeeping

domicilio (doa-mee-*chee*-lyoa) *m* domicile

dominante (doa-mee-*nahn*-tay) *adj* leading

dominare (doa-mee-*naa*-ray) *v* master; rule

dominazione (doa-mee-nah-*tsyōa*-nay) *f* domination

dominio (doa-*mee*-ño a) *m* rule, dominion

donare (doa-*naa*-ray) *v* donate

donatore (doa-nah-*tōa*-ray) *m*, **-trice** *f* donor

donazione (doa-nah-*tsyōa*-nay) *f* donation

dondolare (doan-doa-*laa*-ray) *v* rock, *swing

donna (*don*-nah) *f* woman

dono (*dōa*-noa) *m* gift, present

dopo (*daw*-poa) *prep* after; **~ che** after

dopobarba (doa-poa-*baar*-bah) *m* aftershave

dopodomani (*daw*-poa-doa-*mah*-nee) *adv* the day after tomorrow

dopopranzo (doa-poa-*praan*-tso) *m* afternoon

doppio (*doap*-pyoa) *adj* double

dorato (doa-*raa*-toa) *adj* gilt

dormire (doar-*mee*-ray) *v* *sleep

dormitorio (doar-mee-*taw*-ryoa) *m* dormitory

dorso (*dawr*-soa) *m* back

dose (*daw*-zay) *f* dose

dotato (doa-*taa*-toa) *adj* talented

dottore (doat-*tōa*-ray) *m*, **-essa** *f* doctor

dove (*dōa*-vay) *adv* where; *conj* where

dovere (doa-*vāy*-ray) *m* duty

*dovere (doa-*vāy*-ray) *v* need to, *have to, *be obliged to, *be bound to, *must, *ought to, *should, *shall; owe

dovunque (doa-*voong*-kway) *adv* anywhere; *conj* wherever

dovuto (doa-*vōo*-toa) *adj* due

dozzina (doad-*dzee*-nah) *f* dozen

drago (*draa*-goa) *m* dragon

dramma (*drahm*-mah) *m* drama

drammatico (drahm-*maa*-tee-koa) *adj* dramatic

drammaturgo (drahm-mah-*toor*-goa) *m*, **-a** *f* playwright, dramatist

drenare (dray-*naa*-ray) *v* drain

dritto (*dreet*-toa) *adj* straight; *adv*

straight
droga (*droa*-gah) *f* drug
drogheria (droa-gay-*ree*-ah) *f* grocer's
droghiere (droa-*gyai*-ray) *m* grocer
dubbio (*doob*-byoa) *m* doubt;
  *mettere in ~ query
dubbioso (doob-*byoa*-soa) *adj* doubtful
dubitare (doo-bee-*taa*-ray) *v* doubt
duca (*doo*-kah) *m* (pl duchi) duke
duchessa (doo-*kayss*-sah) *f* duchess
due (*doo*-ay) *num* two; **tutti e ~** either

duna (*doo*-nah) *f* dune
dunque (*doong*-kway) *conj* so; then
duomo (*dwaw*-moa) *m* cathedral
durante (doo-*rahn*-tay) *prep* for, during
durare (doo-*raa*-ray) *v* last
durata (doo-*raa*-tah) *f* duration
duraturo (doo-rah-*too*-roa) *adj* permanent, lasting
durevole (doo-*rāy*-voa-lay) *adj* lasting
duro (*doo*-roa) *adj* tough, hard

E

e (ay) *conj* and
è (*ay*) *v* is (pr esserci)
ebano (*ai*-bah-noa) *m* ebony
ebbene! (ayb-*bai*-nay) well!
ebraico (ay-*braa*-ee-koa) *adj* Jewish; *m* Hebrew
ebreo (ay-*brai*-oa) *m*, **-a** *f* Jew
eccedenza (ayt-chay-*dehn*-tsah) *f* surplus
eccedere (ayt-*chai*-day-ray) *v* exceed
eccellente (ayt-chayl-*lehn*-tay) *adj* excellent
*eccellere (ayt-*chehl*-lay-ray) *v* excel
eccentrico (ayt-*chehn*-tree-koa) *adj* eccentric
eccessivo (ayt-chayss-*see*-voa) *adj* excessive
eccesso (ayt-*chehss*-soa) *m* excess; **~ di velocità** speeding
eccetera (ayt-*chai*-tay-rah) etcetera
eccetto (ayt-*cheht*-toa) *prep* except
eccezionale (ayt-chayss-syoa-*naa*-lay) *adj* exceptional
eccezione (ayt-chayss-*syōa*-nay) *f* exception
eccitante (ayt-chee-*tahn*-tay) *adj*

exciting
eccitare (ayt-chee-*taa*-ray) *v* excite
eccitato (ayt-chee-*taa*-toa) *adj* excited
eccitazione (ayt-chee-tah-*tsyōa*-nay) *f* excitement
ecco (*ehk*-koa) here you are; *adv* here is
eclissi (ay-*kleess*-see) *f* eclipse
eco (*ai*-koa) *m/f* echo
ecografia (ay-koa-grah-*fyah*) *f* scan
economia (ay-koa-noa-*mee*-ah) *f* economy
economico (ay-koa-*naw*-mee-koa) *adj* economic; inexpensive, cheap, economical
economista (ay-koa-noa-*mee*-stah) *m/f* economist
economizzare (ay-koa-noa-meed-*dzaa*-ray) *v* economize
Ecuador (*ay*-kwah-doar) *m* Ecuador
eczema (ayk-*jai*-mah) *m* eczema
edera (*ai*-day-rah) *f* ivy
edicola (ay-*dee*-koa-lah) *f* newsstand, bookstand
edificare (ay-dee-fee-*kaa*-ray) *v* construct

edificio (ay-dee-*fee*-choa) *m*
  construction, building

editore (ay-dee-*tōa*-ray) *m* publisher

edizione (ay-dee-*tsyōa*-nay) *f* issue,
  edition; **~ del mattino** morning
  edition

educare (ay-doo-*kaa*-ray) *v* educate;
  *bring up

educato (*ay*-doo-kaa-toa) *adj* polite

educazione (ay-doo-kah-*tsyōa*-nay) *f*
  education

effervescenza (ayf-fayr-vaysh-*shehn*-tsah) *f* fizz

effettivamente (ayf-fayt-tee-vah-*mayn*-tay) *adv* as a matter of fact;
  indeed

effetto (ayf-*feht*-toa) *m* effect; **effetti personali** belongings *pl*

effettuare (ayf-fayt-*twaa*-ray) *v*
  implement, effect; achieve

efficace (ayf-fee-*kaa*-chay) *adj*
  effective

efficiente (ayf-fee-*chehn*-tay) *adj*
  efficient

Egitto (ay-*jeet*-toa) *m* Egypt

egiziano (ay-jee-*tsyaa*-noa) *adj*
  Egyptian; *m*, **-a** *f* Egyptian

egli (*āy*-l^yee) *pron* he

egocentrico (ay-goa-*chehn*-tree-koa)
  adj self-centred, self-centered *Am*

egoismo (ay-goa-*ee*-zmoa) *m*
  selfishness

egoista (ay-goa-*ee*-stah) *adj* selfish

egoistico (ay-goa-*ee*-stee-koa) *adj*
  ego(t)istic

elaborare (ay-lah-boa-*raa*-ray) *v*
  elaborate

elasticità (ay-lah-stee-chee-*tah*) *f*
  elasticity

elastico (ay-*lah*-stee-koa) *adj* elastic;
  m rubber band, elastic

elefante (ay-lay-*fahn*-tay) *m* elephant

elegante (ay-lay-*gahn*-tay) *adj* smart,
  elegant

eleganza (ay-lay-*gahn*-tsah) *f* elegance

*eleggere (ay-*lehd*-jay-ray) *v* elect

elementare (ay-lay-mayn-*taa*-ray) *adj*
  primary

elemento (ay-lay-*mayn*-toa) *m*
  element

elencare (ay-layng-*kaa*-ray) *v* list

elenco (ay-*lehng*-koa) *m* list; **~
telefonico** telephone directory;
  telephone book *Am*

elettricista (ay-layt-tree-*chee*-stah)
  m/f electrician

elettricità (ay-layt-tree-chee-*tah*) *f*
  electricity

elettrico (ay-*leht*-tree-koa) *adj* electric

elettrodomestici (*ay*-lehr-troa-doa-*may*-stee-chee) *mpl* household
  appliances

elettronico (ay-layt-*traw*-nee-koa) *adj*
  electronic

elevare (ay-lay-*vaa*-ray) *v* raise;
  elevate

elevato (*ay*-lay-vaa-toa) *adj* high; lofty

elevazione (ay-lay-vah-*tsyōa*-nay) *f*
  mound

elezione (ay-lay-*tsyōa*-nay) *f* election

elica (*ai*-lee-kah) *f* propeller

elicottero (*ay*-lee-*kōat*-tay-roa) *m*
  helicopter

eliminare (ay-lee-mee-*naa*-ray) *v*
  eliminate

ella (*ayl*-lah) *pron* she

elogio (ay-*law*-joa) *m* praise

emancipazione (ay-mahn-chee-pah-*tsyōa*-nay) *f* emancipation

emblema (aym-*blai*-mah) *m* emblem

emergenza (ay-mayr-*jehn*-tsah) *f*
  emergency

*emergere (ay-*mehr*-jay-ray) *v* appear,
  emerge; *stand out

*emettere (ay-*mayt*-tay-ray) *v* utter

emicrania (ay-mee-*kraa*-ñah) *f*
  migraine

emigrante (ay-mee-*grahn*-tay) *m/f*

emigrant

emigrare (ay-mee-*graa*-ray) *v* emigrate

emigrazione (ay-mee-grah-*tsyōa*-nay) *f* emigration

eminente (ay-mee-*nehn*-tay) *adj* outstanding

emissione (ay-meess-*syōa*-nay) *f* issue

emorragia (ay-moar-rah-*jee*-ah) *f* h(a)emorrhage

emorroidi (ay-moar-*raw*-ee-dee) *fpl* h(a)emorrhoids *pl*, piles *pl*

emozione (ay-moa-*tsyōa*-nay) *f* emotion

enciclopedia (ayn-chee-kloa-pay-*dee*-ah) *f* encyclop(a)edia

energia (ay-nayr-*jee*-ah) *f* energy; power; **~ nucleare** nuclear energy

energico (ay-*nehr*-jee-koa) *adj* energetic

enigma (ay-*neeg*-mah) *m* enigma, mystery; puzzle

enorme (ay-*nor*-may) *adj* tremendous, immense, enormous, huge

enoteca (ay-noa-*tay*-kah) *f* wine merchant's

ente (*ehn*-tay) *m* being; society

entrambi (ayn-*trahm*-bee) *adj* both

entrare (ayn-*traa*-ray) *v* *go in, enter

entrata (ayn-*traa*-tah) *f* way in, entry, entrance; **entrate** revenue

entro (*ayn*-troa) *prep* in, within

entusiasmo (ayn-too-*zyah*-zmoa) *m* enthusiasm

entusiastico (ayn-too-*zyah*-stee-koa) *adj* enthusiastic

epico (*ai*-pee-koa) *adj* epic

epidemia (ay-pee-day-*mee*-ah) *f* epidemic

epilessia (ay-pee-layss-*seeah*) *f* epilepsy

episodio (ay-pee-*zaw*-dyoa) *m* episode

epoca (*ai*-poa-kah) *f* period

eppure (ayp-*pōō*-ray) *conj* yet, however

equatore (ay-kwah-*tōa*-ray) *m* equator

equilibrio (ay-kwee-*lee*-bryoa) *m* balance

equipaggiamento (ay-kwee-pahd-jah-*mayn*-toa) *m* outfit, equipment

equipaggiare (ay-kwee-pahd-*jaa*-ray) *v* equip

equipaggio (ay-kwee-*pahd*-joa) *m* crew

equitazione (ay-kwee-tah-*tsyōa*-nay) *f* riding

equivalente (ay-kwee-vah-*lehn*-tay) *adj* equivalent

equivoco (ay-*kwee*-voa-koa) *adj* ambiguous

equo (*ai*-kwoa) *adj* right

era (*eh*-ra) *v* (pr essere)

erba (*ehr*-bah) *f* grass; **~ aromatica** herb; **~ cipollina** chives *pl*

erbaccia (ayr-*baht*-chah) *f* weed

erede (ay-*ray*-de) *m* heir, *f* heiress

eredità (ay-ray-dee-*tah*) *f* inheritance

ereditare (ay-ray-dee-*taa*-ray) *v* inherit

ereditario (ay-ray-dee-*taa*-ryoa) *adj* hereditary

erica (*ai*-ree-kah) *f* heather

*erigere (ay-*ree*-jay-ray) *v* erect

ermetico *adj* airtight

ernia (*ehr*-ñah) *f* hernia, slipped disc

eroe (ay-*raw*-ay) *m* hero

errare (ayr-*raa*-ray) *v* wander, err

erroneo (ayr-*raw*-nay-oa) *adj* mistaken, wrong

errore (ayr-*rōa*-ray) *m* mistake, error

erudito (ay-roo-*dee*-toa) *m* scholar

eruzione cutanea (ay-roo-*tsyōa*-nay koo-*taa*-nay-ah) *f* rash

esagerare (ay-zah-jay-*raa*-ray) *v* exaggerate

esame (ay-*zaa*-may) *m* examination; test

esaminare (ay-zah-mee-*naa*-ray) *v*

examine

esattamente (ay-_zaht_-tah-mayn-tay) *adv* just

esatto (ay-_zaht_-toa) *adj* exact, precise; correct, just

esaurire (ay-zou-_ree_-ray) *v* exhaust

esaurito (ay-_zou_-ree-toa) *adj* sold out

esausto (ay-_zous_-toa) *adj* overtired, overstrung

esca (_ay_-skah) *f* bait

esclamare (ay-sklah-_maa_-ray) *v* exclaim

esclamazione (ay-sklah-mah-_tsyoa_-nay) *f* exclamation

*****escludere** (ay-_sklōō_-day-ray) *v* exclude

escluso (ay-_sklōō_-zoa) *adj* excepted

esclusivamente (ay-skloo-zee-vah-_mayn_-tay) *adv* solely, exclusively

esclusivo (ay-skloo-_zee_-voa) *adj* exclusive

escogitare (ay-skoa-jee-_taa_-ray) *v* devise

escoriazione (ay-skoa-ryah-_tsyoa_-nay) *f* graze

escursione (ay-skoor-_syoa_-nay) *f* excursion

esecutivo (ay-zay-koo-tee-_voa_) *adj* executive

esecuzione (ay-zay-koo-_tsyoa_-nay) *f* execution

eseguire (ay-zay-_gwee_-ray) *v* execute, perform, carry out

esempio (ay-_zaym_-pyoa) *m* instance, example; **per ~** for instance, for example

esemplare (ay-zaym-_plaa_-ray) *m* specimen

esentare (ay-zayn-_taa_-ray) *v* exempt

esente (ay-_zehn_-tay) *adj* exempt; **~ da tassa** tax-free; **~ da dazio** duty-free

esenzione (ay-zayn-_tsyoa_-nay) *f* exemption

esercitare (ay-zayr-chee-_taa_-ray) *v*

exercise; **esercitarsi** practise

esercito (ay-_zehr_-chee-toa) *m* army

esercizio (ay-zayr-_chee_-tsyoa) *m* exercise

esibire (ay-zee-_bee_-ray) *v* exhibit; *show

esigente (ay-zee-_jehn_-tay) *adj* particular

esigenza (ay-zee-_jehn_-tsah) *f* demand; requirement

*****esigere** (ay-_zee_-jay-ray) *v* demand; require

esiguo (ay-_zee_-gwoa) *adj* minor

esilio (ay-_zee_-lᵞoa) *m* exile

esistenza (ay-zee-_stehn_-tsah) *f* existence

*****esistere** (ay-_zee_-stay-ray) *v* exist

esitare (ay-zee-_taa_-ray) *v* hesitate

esito (_ai_-zee-toa) *m* result; issue

esonerare da (ay-zoa-nay-_raa_-ray) discharge of

esotico (ay-_zaw_-tee-koa) *adj* exotic

*****espandere** (ay-_spahn_-day-ray) *v* expand

espansione (ay-spahn-_syoa_-nay) *f* expansion

*****espellere** (ay-_spehl_-lay-ray) *v* expel

esperienza (ay-spay-_ryehn_-tsah) *f* experience

esperimento (ay-spay-ree-_mayn_-toa) *m* experiment

esperto (ay-_spehr_-toa) *adj* experienced; skilful, skilled; *m*, **-a** *f* expert

espirare (ay-spee-_raa_-ray) *v* breathe out

esplicito (ay-_splee_-chee-toa) *adj* explicit; express, definite

*****esplodere** (ay-_splaw_-day-ray) *v* explode

esplorare (ay-sploa-_raa_-ray) *v* explore

esplosione (ay-sploa-_zyoa_-nay) *f* explosion, blast

esplosivo (ay-sploa-_zee_-voa) *adj*

explosive; *m* explosive

*esporre (ay-*spoar*-ray) *v* exhibit, display

esportare (ay-spoar-*taa*-ray) *v* export

esportazione (ay-spoar-tah-*tsyōa*-nay) *f* exports *pl*, exportation, export

esposizione (ay-spoa-zee-*tsyōa*-nay) *f* exposition, display, show; exposure

espressione (ay-sprayss-*syōa*-nay) *f* expression

espresso (ay-*sprehss*-soa) *adj* express; **per ~** special delivery

*esprimere (ay-*spree*-may-ray) *v* express

essa (*ayss*-sah) *pron* she

essenza (ayss-*sehn*-tsah) *f* essence

essenziale (ayss-sayn-*tsyaa*-lay) *adj* essential

essenzialmente (ayss-sayn-tsyahl-*mayn*-tay) *adv* essentially

esserci (*ehss-sayr*-chee) *v* be there; **c'è** there is; **ci sono** there are

essere (*ehss*-say-ray) *m* creature; being; **~ umano** human being

*essere (*ehss*-say-ray) *v* *be

essi (*ayss*-see) *pron* they

esso (*ayss*-soa) *pron* it; he

est (ehst) *m* east

estasi (*eh*-stah-zee) *f* ecstasy

estate (ay-*staa*-tay) *f* summer; **piena ~** midsummer

*estendere (ay-*stehn*-day-ray) *v* extend; expand

esteriore (ay-stay-*ryōa*-ray) *adj* external; *m* outside

esterno (ay-*stehr*-noa) *adj* outward, exterior; *m* outside, exterior

estero: all'~ (ahl-*leh*-stay-roa) abroad

esteso (ay-*stāy*-soa) *adj* broad

*estinguere (ay-*steeng*-gway-ray) *v* extinguish

estintore (ay-steen-*tōa*-ray) *m* fire extinguisher

*estorcere (ay-*stor*-chay-ray) *v* extort

estorsione (ay-stoar-*syōa*-nay) *f* extortion

estradare (ay-strah-*daa*-ray) *v* extradite

estraneo (ay-*straa*-nay-oa) *adj* foreign; *m*, **-a** *f* stranger

*estrarre (ay-*strahr*-ray) *v* extract

estremità (ay-stray-mee-*tah*) *f* end

estremo (ay-*strāy*-moa) *adj* extreme; very, utmost; *m* extreme

estuario (ay-*stwaa*-ryoa) *m* estuary

esuberante (ay-zoo-bay-*rahn*-tay) *adj* exuberant

esule (*ai*-zoo-lay) *m/f* exile

età (ay-*tah*) *f* age

etere (*ai*-tay-ray) *m* ether

eternità (ay-tayr-nee-*tah*) *f* eternity

eterno (ay-*tehr*-noa) *adj* eternal

eterosessuale (ay-tay-roa-sayss-swaa-lay) *adj* heterosexual

etichetta (ay-tee-*kayt*-tah) *f* label, tag

etichettare (ay-tee-kayt-*taa*-ray) *v* label

Etiopia (ay-*tyaw*-pyah) *f* Ethiopia

etto(grammo) (ayt-toa-*grahm*-moa) *m* hectogram

Eu (ay-*oo*) *f* EU

euro (*ay*^oo-raw) *m* euro

Europa (ay^oo-*raw*-pah) *f* Europe

europeo (ay^oo-roa-*pai*-oa) *adj* European; *m*, **-a** *f* European

evacuare (ay-vah-*kwaa*-ray) *v* evacuate

evaporare (ay-vah-poa-*raa*-ray) *v* evaporate

evasione (ay-vah-*zyōa*-nay) *f* escape

evento (ay-*vehn*-toa) *m* occurrence, event, happening

eventuale (ay-vayn-*twaa*-lay) *adj* possible

eventualmente (ay-vayn-*twaal-mayn*-tay) *adv* in case, if

evidente (ay-vee-*dehn*-tay) *adj* evident; noticeable

evidentemente (ay-vee-dehn-tay-*mayn*-tay) *adv* apparently

evitare (ay-vee-*taa*-ray) *v* avoid

evoluzione (ay-voa-loo-*tsyōa*-nay) *f* evolution

extracomunitario (ayk-strah-koa-moo-nee-*taa*-ryoa) *m*, **-a** *f* non-EU citizen

F

fa (fah) *adv* ago

fabbrica (*fahb*-bree-kah) *f* factory, mill, works *pl*

fabbricante (fahb-bree-*kahn*-tay) *m/f* manufacturer

fabbricare (fahb-bree-*kaa*-ray) *v* construct; manufacture

fabbricazione (fahb-bree-kah-*tsyōa*-nay) *f* construction

fabbro (*fahb*-broa) *m* smith, blacksmith

faccenda (faht-*chehn*-dah) *f* matter, concern; **faccende di casa** housekeeping

facchino (fahk-*kee*-noa) *m* porter

faccia (*faht*-chah) *f* face; **in ~ a** *prep* facing

facciata (faht-*chaa*-tah) *f* façade; front

facile (*faa*-chee-lay) *adj* easy

facilità (fah-chee-lee-*tah*) *f* ease

facoltà (fah-koal-*tah*) *f* faculty

facoltativo (fah-koal-tah-*tee*-voa) *adj* optional

faggio (*fahd*-joa) *m* beech

fagiano (fah-*jaa*-noa) *m* pheasant

fagiolo (fah-*jaw*-loa) *m* bean

fagotto (fah-*got*-toa) *m* bundle

falco (*fahl*-koa) *m* hawk

falegname (fah-lay-*ñaa*-may) *m* carpenter

fallimento (fahl-lee-*mayn*-toa) *m* failure

fallire (fahl-*lee*-ray) *v* fail

fallito (fahl-*lee*-toa) *adj* bankrupt

falsificare (fahl-see-fee-*kaa*-ray) *v* counterfeit, forge

falsificazione (fahl-see-fee-kah-*tsyōa*-nay) *f* fake

falso (*fahl*-soa) *adj* untrue; false

fama (*faa*-mah) *f* fame; reputation; **di ~ mondiale** world-famous

fame (*faa*-may) *f* hunger

famigerato (fah-mee-jay-*raa*-toa) *adj* notorious

famiglia (fah-*mee*-l^yah) *f* family

familiare (fah-mee-l^y*aa*-ray) *adj* familiar

famoso (fah-*mōa*-soa) *adj* famous

fanale (fah-*naa*-lay) *m* headlight

fanalino posteriore (fah-*naa*-lee-noa poa-stay-*ryōa*-ray) *m* rear light

fanatico (fah-naa-*tee*-koa) *adj* fanatical

fanciulla (fahn-*chool*-lah) *f* young girl

fanciullo (fahn-*chool*-loa) *m* boy

fanfara (fahn-*faa*-rah) *f* brass band

fango (*fahng*-goa) *m* mud

fangoso (fahng-*gōa*-soa) *adj* muddy

fantasia (fahn-tah-*zee*-ah) *f* fantasy

fantasma (fahn-*tah*-zmah) *m* spirit, phantom

fantastico (fahn-tah-*stee*-koa) *adj* fantastic

fante (*fahn*-tay) *m* knave

fanteria (fahn-tay-*ree*-ah) *f* infantry

fantino (fahn-*tee*-noa) *m* jockey

fard (fard) *m* blusher

*fare (*faa*-ray) *v* *do; *make; *have

farfalla (fahr-*fahl*-lah) *f* butterfly

farina (fah-*ree*-nah) *f* flour

farmacia (fahr-mah-*chee*-ah) *f* pharmacy, chemist's

farmacista (fahr-mah-*chee*-stah) *m/f* chemist, pharmacist *Am*

farmaco (*fahr*-mah-koa) *m* medicine

farmacologia (fahr-mah-koa-loa-*jee*-ah) *f* pharmacology

faro (*faa*-roa) *m* lighthouse; headlight

fascia (*fahsh*-shah) band; bandage; belt; ~ **elastica** piston ring

fasciare (fahsh-*shaa*-ray) *v* *bind up

fasciatura (fahsh-shah-*tōō*-rah) *f* bandage

fascino (*fahsh*-shee-noa) *m* glamour, charm

fascismo (fahsh-*shee*-zmoa) *m* fascism

fascista (fahsh-*shee*-stah) *m/f* fascist

fascistico (fahsh-*shee*-stee-koa) *adj* fascist

fase (*faa*-zay) *f* phase; stage

fastidio (fah-*stee*-dyoa) *m* bother, trouble

fastidioso (fah-stee-*dyōa*-soa) *adj* annoying

fata (*faa*-tah) *f* fairy

fatale (fah-*taa*-lay) *adj* fatal

fatica (fah-*tee*-kah) *f* fatigue; effort

faticare (fah-tee-*kaa*-ray) *v* labo(u)r

faticoso (fah-tee-*kōa*-soa) *adj* tiring

fato (*faa*-toa) *m* fate

fatto (*faht*-toa) *m* fact

fattore (faht-*tōa*-ray) *m* factor; farmer

fattoressa (faht-toa-*rayss*-sah) *f* farmer's wife

fattoria (faht-toa-*ree*-ah) *f* farm

fattorino d'albergo (faht-toa-*ree*-noa dahl-*behr*-goa) bellboy

fattura (faht-*tōō*-rah) *f* bill, invoice

fatturare (faht-toa-*raa*-ray) *v* bill

fauci (*fou*-chee) *fpl* mouth

favola (*fah*-voa-lah) *f* fable

favore (fah-*vōa*-ray) *m* favo(u)r; **a ~ di** on behalf of; **per ~** please

favorevole (fah-voa-*rāy*-voa-lay) *adj* favo(u)rable

favorire (fah-voa-*ree*-ray) *v* favo(u)r

favorito (fah-voa-*ree*-toa) *adj* pet; *m* favo(u)rite

fax (fahkss) *m* fax, telefax

fazzoletto (faht-tsoa-*layt*-toa) *m* handkerchief; ~ **di carta** paper tissue

febbraio (fayb-*braa*-yoa) February

febbre (*fehb*-bray) *f* fever; ~ **da fieno** hay fever

febbricitante (fayb-bree-chee-*tahn*-tay) *adj* feverish

fecondo (fay-*koan*-doa) *adj* fertile

fede (*fāy*-day) *f* belief, faith; wedding ring

fedele (fay-*dāy*-lay) *adj* true, faithful

federa (*fai*-day-rah) *f* pillowcase

federale (fay-day-*raa*-lay) *adj* federal

federazione (fay-day-rah-*tsyōa*-nay) *f* federation

fegato (*fāy*-gah-toa) *m* liver

felice (fay-*lee*-chay) *adj* happy

felicissimo (fay-lee-*cheess*-see-moa) *adj* delighted

felicità (fay-lee-chee-*tah*) *f* happiness

felicitarsi con (fay-lee-chee-*tahr*-see) compliment, congratulate

felicitazione (fay-lee-chee-tah-*tsyōa*-nay) *f* congratulation

felpa (*fayl*-pah) *f* sweatshirt

feltro (*fayl*-troa) *m* felt

femmina (*faym*-meé-nah) *f* female; girl

femminile (faym-mee-*nee*-lay) *adj* female; feminine

*fendere (*fayn*-day-ray) *v* *split

fendinebbia (fayn-dee-*nayb*-byah) *mpl* fog lamp

fenicottero (fay-nee-*kot*-tay-roa) *m* flamingo

fenomeno (fay-*naw*-may-noa) *m*

phenomenon

feriale (fay-*ree-ah*-lay) *adj* weekday

ferie (*fai*-ryay) *fpl* holiday; **in ~** on holiday

ferire (fay-*ree*-ray) *v* injure, wound, *hurt

ferita (fay-*ree*-tah) *f* injury, wound

ferito (fay-*ree*-toa) *adj* injured

fermaglio (fayr-*maa*-lʸoa) *m* fastener; **~ per capelli** bobby pin *Am*

fermare (fayr-*mah*-ray) stop; detain; **fermarsi** *v* halt, pull up; stay

fermata (fayr-*maa*-tah) *f* stop

fermentare (fayr-mayn-*taa*-ray) *v* ferment

fermo (*fayr*-moa) *adj* steadfast; **~ posta** poste restante

feroce (fay-*rōa*-chay) *adj* wild, fierce

ferragosto (fayr-rah-*goas*-toa) *m* August 15 public holiday

ferramenta (fayr-rah-*mayn*-tah) *fpl* hardware

ferro (*fehr*-roa) *m* iron; **di ~** iron; **~ da stiro** iron; **~ di cavallo** horseshoe

ferrovia (fayr-roa-*vee*-ah) *f* railway; railroad *Am*

fertile (*fehr*-tee-lay) *adj* fertile

fessura (fayss-*sōo*-rah) *f* crack,; slot

festa (*feh*-stah) *f* feast; party

festeggiare (fays-stayd-*dʒaa*-ray) *v* celebrate

festival (*fay*-stee-vahl) *m* festival

festivo (fay-*stee*-voa) *adj* festive

fetta (*fayt*-tah) *f* slice

feudale (fay͞-*daa*-lay) *adj* feudal

fiaba (*fyaa*-bah) *f* fairytale

fiacco (*fyahk*-koa) *adj* feeble, faint

fiamma (*fyahm*-mah) *f* flame

fiammifero (fyahm-*mee*-fay-roa) *m* match

fianco (*fyahng*-koa) *m* hip; side

fiato (*fyaa*-toa) *m* breath

fibbia (*feeb*-byah) *f* buckle

fibra (*fee*-brah) *f* fibre

fico (*fee*-koa) *m* fig

fidanzamento (fee-dahn-tsah-*mayn*-toa) *m* engagement

fidanzata (fee-dahn-*tsaa*-tah) *f* fiancée

fidanzato (fee-dahn-*tsaa*-toa) *adj* engaged; *m* fiancé

fidarsi di (fee-*dahr*-see) *v* trust

fidato (fee-*daa*-toa) *adj* trustworthy, reliable

fiducia (fee-*dōo*-chah) *f* faith, trust, confidence

fieno (*fyai*-noa) *m* hay

fiera (*fyai*-rah) *f* fair

fierezza (fyay-*rayt*-tsah) *f* pride

fiero (*fyai*-roa) *adj* proud

figlia (*fee*-lʸah) *f* daughter

figliastro (fee-*lʸah*-stroa) *m* stepchild

figliata (fee-*lʸaa*-tah) *f* litter

figlio (*fee*-lʸoa) *m* son

figliolo (fee-*lʸaw*-loa) *m* son; boy

figura (fee-*gōo*-rah) *f* figure; picture

figurarsi (fee-goo-*rahr*-see) *v* imagine; fancy

fila (*fee*-lah) *f* row, rank, file, line

filare (fee-*laa*-ray) *v* *spin

film (feelm) *m* (pl ~) film, movie

filmare (feel-*maa*-ray) *v* film

filo (*fee*-loa) *m* thread, wire, yarn

filosofia (fee-loa-zoa-*fee*-ah) *f* philosophy

filosofo (fee-*law*-zoa-foa) *m*, **-a** *f* philosopher

filtrare (feel-*traa*-ray) *v* strain

filtro (*feel*-troa) *m* filter; **~ dell'aria** air-filter; **~ dell'olio** oil filter

finale (fee-*naa*-lay) *adj* eventual, final

finalmente (fee-nahl-*mayn*-tay) *adv* at last

finanze (fee-*nahn*-tsay) *fpl* finances *pl*

finanziare (fee-nahn-*tsyaa*-ray) *v* finance

finanziario (fee-nahn-*tsyaa*-ryoa) *adj* financial

finanziatore (fee-nahn-tsyah-*tōa*-ray) *m*, **-trice** *f* investor

finché (feeng-*kay*) *conj* until, till; **~ non** till

fine (*fee*-nay) *f* ending, end; *m* purpose; **~ settimana** weekend

finestra (fee-*nay*-strah) *f* window

finestrino (fee-*nay*-stree-noa) *m* window

*fingere (*feen*-jay-ray) *v* pretend

finire (fee-*nee*-ray) *v* end, finish; expire

finito (fee-*nee*-toa) *adj* finished; over

finlandese (feen-lahn-*dāy*-say) *adj* Finnish; *m/f* Finn

Finlandia (feen-*lahn*-dyah) *f* Finland

fino (*fee*-noa) *adj* fine; sheer

fino a (*fee*-noa ah) *prep* until, to, till

finora (fee-*nōa*-rah) *adv* so far

finzione (feen-*tsyōa*-nay) *f* fiction

fioraio (fyoa-*raa*-yoa) *m*, **-a** *f* florist

fiore (*fyōa*-ray) *m* flower

fiorente (fyoa-*rehn*-tay) *adj* prosperous

Firenze (fee-*rayn*-tsay) *f* Florence

firma (*feer*-mah) *f* signature

firmare (feer-*maa*-ray) *v* sign

fischiare (fee-*skyaa*-ray) *v* whistle

fischio (*fee*-skyoa) *m* whistle

fisica (*fee*-zee-kah) *f* physics

fisico (*fee*-zee-koa) *adj* physical; *m*, **-a** *f* physicist

fisiologia (fee-zyoa-loa-*jee*-ah) *f* physiology

fissare (feess-*saa*-ray) *v* gaze, stare; settle

fisso (*feess*-soa) *adj* permanent, fixed

fitta (*feet*-tah) *f* stitch

fiume (*fyōō*-may) *m* river

flacone (flah-*kōa*-nay) *m* flask

flagello (flah-*jehl*-loa) *m* plague

flanella (flah-*nehl*-lah) *f* flannel

flash (flaysh) *m* flash

flauto (*flou*-toa) *m* flute

flessibile (flayss-*see*-bee-lay) *adj* supple, flexible, elastic

floscio (*flosh*-shoa) *adj* limp

flotta (*flot*-tah) *f* fleet

fluente (*flwehn*-tay) *adj* fluent

fluido (*flōō*-ee-doa) *adj* fluid; *m* fluid

flusso (*flooss*-soa) *m* flow

foca (*faw*-kah) *f* seal

foce (*faw*-chay) *f* mouth

fodera (*faw*-day-rah) *f* lining

foglia (*faw*-lᵞah) *f* leaf

foglio (*faw*-lᵞoa) *m* sheet

fogna (*fōa*-ñah) *f* sewer; gutter

folla (*fol*-lah) *f* crowd

folle (*fol*-lay) *adj* crazy, mad

folletto (foal-*layt*-toa) *m* elf

fondamentale (foan-dah-mayn-*taa*-lay) *adj* fundamental, essential, basic

fondamento (foan-dah-*mayn*-toa) *m* base; basis

fondare (foan-*daa*-ray) *v* found

fondato (foan-*daa*-toa) *adj* well-founded

fondazione (foan-dah-*tsyōa*-nay) *f* foundation

*fondere (*foan*-day-ray) *v* melt

fondo (*foan*-doa) *m* ground, bottom; **fondi** fund; **~ tinta** foundation cream

fonetico (foa-*nai*-tee-koa) *adj* phonetic

fontana (foan-*taa*-nah) *f* fountain

fonte (*foan*-tay) *f* spring; source

foratura (foa-rah-*tōō*-rah) *f* puncture, blowout

forbici (*for*-bee-chee) *fpl* scissors *pl*

forbicine (*for*-bee-*chee*-nay) *fpl* nail scissors *pl*

forca (*foar*-kah) *f* gallows *pl*

forchetta (foar-*kayt*-tah) *f* fork

forcina (foar-*chee*-nah) *f* hairpin, hairgrip

foresta (foa-*reh*-stah) *f* forest

forestiero (foa-ray-*styai*-roa) *m*, **-a** *f* foreigner

forfora (*foar*-foa-rah) *f* dandruff

forma (*foar*-mah) *f* form, shape; figure; condition

formaggio (foar-*mahd*-joa) *m* cheese

formale (foar-*maa*-lay) *adj* formal

formalità (foar-mah-lee-*tah*) *f* formality

formare (foar-*maa*-ray) *v* form, shape

formato (foar-*maa*-toa) *m* size

formazione (foar-mah-*tsyoa*-nay) *f* formation

formica (foar-*mee*-kah) *f* ant

formidabile (foar-mee-*daa*-bee-lay) *adj* terrific

formula (*for*-moo-lah) *f* formula

formulario (foar-moo-*laa*-ryoa) *m* form

fornace (foar-*naa*-chay) *f* furnace

fornello (foar-*nehl*-loa) *m* cooker; ~ **a gas** gas cooker; ~ **a spirito** spirit stove

fornire (foar-*nee*-ray) *v* furnish, provide, supply

fornitura (foar-nee-*too*-rah) *f* supply

forno (*foar*-noa) *m* oven; ~ **a microonde** microwave oven

forse (*foar*-say) *adv* maybe, perhaps

forte (*for*-tay) *adj* strong, powerful; loud

fortezza (foar-*tayt*-tsah) *f* fortress

fortuito (foar-*too*-ee-toa) *adj* accidental

fortuna (foar-*too*-nah) *f* luck

fortunato (foar-too-*naa*-toa) *adj* lucky, fortunate

foruncolo (foa-*roong*-koa-loa) *m* boil

forza (*for*-tsah) *f* energy, strength, force; ~ **di volontà** willpower; **forze militari** military force

forzare (foar-*tsaa*-ray) *v* force; strain

foschia (foa-*skee*-ah) *f* mist, haze

fosco (*foa*-skoa) *adj* hazy

fossato (foass-*saa*-toa) *m* ditch; moat

fosso (*foass*-soa) *m* ditch

foto (*faw*-toa) *f* photo; ~ **per passaporto** passport photograph

fotocopia (foa-toa-*kaw*-pyah) *f* photocopy

fotografare (foa-toa-grah-*faa*-ray) *v* photograph

fotografia (foa-toa-grah-*fee*-ah) *f* photography; photograph

fotografo (foa-*taw*-grah-foa) *m*, **-a** *f* photographer

fra (frah) *prep* among; amid

fragile (*fraa*-jee-lay) *adj* fragile

fragola (*fraa*-goa-lah) *f* strawberry

***fraintendere** (frah-een-*tehn*-day-ray) *v* *misunderstand

francese (frahn-*chay*-zay) *adj* French

Francia (*frahn*-chah) *f* France

franco (*frahng*-koa) *adj* open; ~ **di porto** postage paid

francobollo (frahng-koa-*boal*-loa) *m* postage stamp

frangia (*frahn*-jah) *f* fringe

frappé (frahp-*pay*) *m* milkshake

frase (*fraa*-zay) *f* sentence; phrase

fratello (frah-*tehl*-loa) *m* brother

frattanto (fraht-*tahn*-toa) *adv* meanwhile

frattempo (fraht-*tehm*-poa): **nel ~** in the meantime

frattura (fraht-*too*-rah) *f* fracture; break

fratturare (fraht-too-*raa*-ray) *v* fracture

frazione (frah-*tsyoa*-nay) *f* fraction; hamlet

freccia (*frayt*-chah) *f* arrow; indicator

freddino (frayd-*dee*-noa) *adj* chilly

freddo (*frayd*-doa) *adj* cold; *m* cold

frenare (fray-*nah*-ray) *v* brake; restrain

freno (*fray*-noa) *m* brake; ~ **a mano** handbrake; ~ **a pedale** foot brake

frequentare (fray-kwayn-*taa*-ray) *v* attend; frequent; associate with

frequente (fray-*kwehn*-tay) *adj*

frequent

frequenza (fray-*kwehn*-tsah) *f*
frequency; attendance

fresco (*fray*-skoa) *adj* fresh; cool

fretta (*frayt*-tah) *f* speed, haste, hurry;
in ~ in a hurry

frettoloso (frayt-toa-*lōa*-soa) *adj*
hasty

***friggere** (*freed*-jay-ray) *v* fry

frigorifero (free-goa-*ree*-fay-roa) *m*
refrigerator, fridge

fringuello (freeng-*gwehl*-loa) *m* finch

frittata (freet-*taa*-tah) *f* omelette

frizione (free-*tsyōa*-nay) *f* clutch

frode (*fraw*-day) *f* fraud

fronte (*froan*-tay) *f* forehead; **di ~ a** in
front of; opposite; ***far ~ a** face

frontiera (froan-*tyai*-rah) *f* frontier;
boundary

frontone (froan-*tōa*-nay) *m* gable

frullatore (frool-lah-*tōa*-ray) *m* mixer

frullino (frool-*lee*-noa) *m* whisk

frumento (froo-*mayn*-toa) *m* corn,
grain; wheat

frusta (*froo*-stah) *f* whip

frutta (*froot*-tah) *f* fruit

frutteto (froot-*tāy*-toa) *m* orchard

fruttivendolo (froot-tee-*vayn*-doa-
loa) *m*, **-a** *f* greengrocer; vegetable
merchant

frutto (*froot*-toa) *m* fruit

fruttuoso (froot-*twōa*-soa) *adj*
profitable

fucile (foo-*chee*-lay) *m* gun, rifle

fuga (*fōo*-gah) *f* flight; leak

fuggire (food-*jee*-ray) *v* escape

fuggitivo (food-jee-*tee*-voa) *m*

runaway

fulmine (*fōol*-mee-nay) *m* lightning

fumare (foo-*maa*-ray) *v* smoke

fumatore (foo-mah-*tōa*-ray) *m*
smoker; **compartimento per
fumatori** smoking compartment

fumo (*fōo*-moa) *m* smoke

funerale (foo-nay-*raa*-lay) *m* funeral

fungo (*foong*-goa) *m* toadstool,
mushroom

funzionamento (foon-tsyoa-nah-
mayn-toa) *m* working, operation

funzionare (foon-tsyoa-*naa*-ray) *v*
work, operate

funzionario (foon-tsyoa-*naa*-ryoa) *m*,
-a *f* civil servant

funzione (foon-*tsyōa*-nay) *f* function;
office

fuoco (*fwaw*-koa) *m* fire; focus

fuorché (fwawr-*kay*) *prep* except

fuori (*fwaw*-ree) *adv* out; outside; **al di
~** outwards; **~ di** outside, out of

furbo (*foor*-boa) *adj* cunning

furfante (foor-*fahn*-tay) *m* villain

furgone (foor-*gōa*-nay) *m* delivery
van, van

furibondo (foo-ree-*boan*-doa) *adj*
furious

furioso (foo-*ryōa*-soa) *adj* furious

furore (foo-*rōa*-ray) *m* rage

furto (*foor*-toa) *m* robbery, theft

fusibile (foo-*zee*-bee-lay) *m* fuse

fusione (foo-*zyōa*-nay) *f* merger

futile (*fōo*-tee-lay) *adj* insignificant

futuro (foo-*tōo*-roa) *m* future; *adj*
future

G

gabbia (*gahb*-byah) *f* cage

gabbiano (gahb-*byaa*-noa) *m* gull; seagull

gabinetto (gah-bee-*nayt*-toa) *m* toilet, bathroom, lavatory; cabinet

gaio (*gaa*-yoa) *adj* cheerful

galleggiante (gahl-layd-*jahn*-tay) *m* float

galleggiare (gahl-layd-*jaa*-ray) *v* float

galleria (gahl-lay-*ree*-ah) *f* tunnel; gallery; circle; ~ **d'arte** art gallery

gallina (gahl-*lee*-nah) *f* hen

gallo (*gahl*-loa) *m* cock

galoppo (gah-*lop*-poa) *m* gallop

gamba (*gahm*-bah) *f* leg

gamberetto (gahm-bay-*rayt*-toa) *m* shrimp

gambero (*gahm*-bay-roa) *m* prawn

gambo (*gahm*-boa) *m* stem

gancio (*gahn*-choa) *m* peg

gara (*gaa*-rah) *f* competition; race

garage (gaa-raaʒ) *m* garage

garantire (gah-rahn-*tee*-ray) *v* guarantee

garanzia (gah-rahn-*tsee*-ah) *f* guarantee

garza (*gahr*-dzah) *f* gauze

gas (gahz) *m* gas; ~ **di scarico** exhaust gases

gasolio (gah-z*ōā*-lyoa) *m* oil; diesel fuel

gastrico (*gah*-stree-koa) *adj* gastric

gatto (*gaht*-toa) *m* cat

gazza (*gahd*-dzah) *f* magpie

gelare (jay-*laa*-ray) *v* *freeze

gelateria (jay-lah-tay-*ree*-ah) *f* ice cream parlo(u)r

gelatina (jay-lah-*tee*-nah) *f* jelly

gelato (jay-*laa*-toa) *m* ice cream

gelo (*jai*-loa) *m* frost

gelosia (jay-loa-*see*-ah) *f* jealousy

geloso (jay-*lōā*-soa) *adj* envious, jealous

gemelli (jay-*mehl*-lee) *mpl* twins *pl*; cuff links *pl*

gemere (*jai*-may-ray) *v* groan, moan

gemma (*jehm*-mah) *f* gem

generale (jay-nay-*raa*-lay) *adj* general; universal, broad, public; *m* general; **in ~** in general

generalità (jay-nay-rah-lee-*tah*) *fpl* personal particulars

generalmente (jay-nay-rahl-*mayn*-tay) *adv* as a rule

generare (jay-nay-*raa*-ray) *v* generate

generatore (jay-nay-rah-*tōā*-ray) *m* generator

generazione (jay-nay-rah-tsy*ōā*-nay) *f* generation

genere (*jai*-nay-ray) *m* sort, kind; gender

genero (*jai*-nay-roa) *m* son-in-law

generosità (jay-nay-roa-see-*tah*) *f* generosity

generoso (jay-nay-*rōā*-soa) *adj* generous, liberal

gengiva (jayn-*jee*-vah) *f* gum

genio (*jai*-ñoa) *m* genius

genitale (jay-nee-*taa*-lay) *adj* genital

genitori (jay-nee-*tōā*-ree) *mpl* parents *pl*

gennaio (jayn-*naa*-yoa) January

Genova (*jayn*-noa-vah) *f* Genoa

gente (*jehn*-tay) *f* people *pl*

gentile (jayn-*tee*-lay) *adj* good-natured; kind; gentle

genuino (jay-*nwee*-noa) *adj* genuine

geografia (jay-oa-grah-*fee*-ah) *f* geography

geologia (jay-oa-loa-*jee*-ah) *f* geology

geometria (jay-oa-may-*tree*-ah) *f* geometry

gerarchia (jay-rahr-*kee*-ah) *f* hierarchy

Germania (jayr-*maa*-nyah) *f* Germany

germe (*jehr*-may) *m* germ

gesso (*jehss*-soa) *m* plaster; chalk

gesticolare (jay-stee-koa-*laa*-ray) *v* gesticulate

gestione (jay-sty*oā*-nay) *f* management

gesto (*jeh*-stoa) *m* sign

gettare (jayt-*taa*-ray) *v* toss, *throw, *cast

getto (*jeht*-toa) *m* spout, jet

gettone (jayt-*tōā*-nay) *m* token, chip

ghiacciaio (gyaht-*chaa*-yoa) *m* glacier

ghiaccio (*gyaht*-choa) *m* ice

ghiaia (*gyaa*-yah) *f* gravel

ghianda (*gyahn*-dah) *f* acorn

ghiandola (*gyahn*-doa-lah) *f* gland

ghiottoneria (gyoat-toa-nay-*ree*-ah) *f* delicacy

ghiribizzo (gee-ree-*beed*-dzoa) *m* whim

ghisa (*gee*-zah) *f* cast iron

già (jah) *adv* already

giacca (*jahk*-kah) *f* jacket; ~ **e pantaloni** pant suit; ~ **sportiva** blazer; ~ **a vento** windcheater

giacimento (jah-chee-*mayn*-toa) *m* deposit

giada (*jaa*-dah) *f* jade

giallo (*jahl*-loa) *adj* yellow

Giappone (jahp-*pōā*-nay) *m* Japan

giapponese (jahp-poa-*nāy*-say) *adj* Japanese; *m/f* Japanese

giardiniere (jahr-dee-*ñai*-ray) *m*, **-a** *f* gardener

giardino (jahr-*dee*-noa) *m* garden; ~ **pubblico** public garden; ~ **zoologico** zoological gardens, zoo

gigante (jee-*gahn*-tay) *m* giant

gigantesco (jee-gahn-*tay*-skoa) *adj* gigantic

giglio (*jee*-l'oa) *m* lily

ginecologo (jee-nay-*kaw*-loa-goa) *m*, **-a** *f* gyn(a)ecologist

ginnasta (jeen-*nah*-stah) *m/f* gymnast

ginnastica (jeen-*nah*-stee-kah) *f* gymnastics *pl*

ginocchio (jee-*nok*-kyoa) *m* (pl le ginocchia) knee

giocare (joa-*kaa*-ray) *v* play

giocatore (joa-kah-*tōā*-ray) *m*, **-trice** *f* player

giocattolo (joa-*kaht*-toa-loa) *m* toy

gioco (*jaw*-koa) *m* play; game; **carta da** ~ playing card; ~ **della dama** draughts, checkers *Am*

giogo (*jōā*-goa) *m* yoke

gioia (*jaw*-yah) *f* gladness, joy

gioielliere (joa-yayl-*l'ai*-ray) *m*, **-a** *f* jeweller

gioiello (joa-*yehl*-loa) *m* gem, jewel; **gioielli** jewel(l)ery

gioioso (joa-*yōā*-soa) *adj* joyful

Giordania (joar-*daa*-ñah) *f* Jordan

giornalaio (joar-nah-*laa*-yoa) *m*, **-a** *f* newsagent

giornale (joar-*naa*-lay) *m* paper, newspaper; journal; ~ **del mattino** morning paper

giornaliero (joar-nah-*l'ai*-roa) *adj* daily

giornalismo (joar-nah-*lee*-zmoa) *m* journalism

giornalista (joar-nah-*lee*-stah) *m/f* journalist

giornata (joar-*naa*-tah) *f* day

giorno (*joar*-noa) *m* day; **al** ~ per day; **di** ~ by day; ~ **feriale** weekday; ~ **festivo** holiday; ~ **lavorativo** working day; **quindici giorni** fortnight; **un** ~ some time; **un** ~ **o l'altro** some day

giostra (*jo*-strah) *f* merry-go-round

giovane (*jōā*-vah-nay) *adj* young; *m* lad; ~ **esploratore** boy scout; ~ **esploratrice** girl guide

giovanile (joa-vah-*nee*-lay) *adj* juvenile

giovanotto (joa-vah-*not*-toa) *m* youth

giovare (joa-*vaa*-ray) *v* *be of use

giovedì (joa-vay-*dee*) *m* Thursday

gioventù (joa-vayn-*too*) *f* youth

giovinezza (joa-vee-*nayt*-tsah) *f* youth

giradischi (jee-rah-*dee*-skee) *m* record player

girare (jee-*raa*-ray) *v* turn; endorse; *far ~ *spin; ~ intorno a by-pass

giro (*jee*-roa) *m* turn; day trip; detour; ~ d'affari turnover

gita (*jee*-tah) *f* trip, excursion; ~ turistica tour

giù (joo) *adv* beneath, below, down; downstairs; over; ~ da off; in ~ downwards, down

giudicare (joo-dee-*kaa*-ray) *v* judge

giudice (*jōō*-dee-chay) *m* judge

giudizio (jōō-*dee*-tsyoa) *m* judgment

giugno (*jōō*-ñoa) June

giunco (*joong*-koa) *m* reed; rush

*giungere (*joon*-jay-ray) *v* arrive

giungla (*joong*-glah) *f* jungle

giuramento (joo-rah-*mayn*-toa) *m* oath, vow

giurare (joo-*raa*-ray) *v* vow, *swear

giuria (joo-*ree*-ah) *f* jury

giuridico (joo-*ree*-dee-koa) *adj* legal

giurista (joo-*ree*-stah) *m/f* lawyer

giustamente (joo-stah-*mayn*-tay) *adv* rightly

giustificare (joo-stee-fee-*kaa*-ray) *v* justify

giustizia (joo-*stee*-tsyah) *f* justice

giusto (*joo*-stoa) *adj* righteous, right, fair, just; proper

glaciale (glah-*chaa*-lay) *adj* freezing

gli (l*ee) *pron* him

globale (gloa-*baa*-lay) *adj* global; global

globo (*glaw*-boa) *m* globe

gloria (*glaw*-ryah) *f* glory

glossario (gloass-*saa*-ryoa) *m* vocabulary

goccia (*goat*-chah) *f* drop

godere (goa-*dāy*-ray) *v* enjoy

goffo (*gof*-foa) *adj* clumsy, awkward

gola (*gōā*-lah) *f* throat; gorge

golf (goalf) *m* jumper; golf; campo da ~ golf links, golf course *Am*

golfo (*goal*-foa) *m* gulf

goloso (goa-*lōā*-soa) *adj* greedy

gomito (*gaw*-mee-toa) *m* elbow

gomma (*goam*-mah) *f* gum; ~ da masticare chewing gum; ~ per cancellare rubber, eraser

gommapiuma (goam-mah-*pyōō*-mah) *f* foam rubber

gommone (goam-*mōā*-nay) *m* rubber dinghy

gondola (*goan*-doa-lah) *f* gondola

gonfiabile (goan-*fyaa*-bee-lay) *adj* inflatable

gonfiare (goan-*fyaa*-ray) *v* inflate; *swell

gonfiore (goan-*fyōā*-ray) *m* swelling

gonna (*goan*-nah) *f* skirt

gotta (*goat*-tah) *f* gout

governante (goa-vayr-*nahn*-tay) *f* governess; housekeeper

governare (goa-vayr-*naa*-ray) *v* govern, rule; navigate

governatore (goa-vayr-nah-*tōā*-ray) *m* governor

governo (goa-*vehr*-noa) *m* government, rule

gradevole (grah-*dāy*-voa-lay) *adj* pleasing, pleasant, enjoyable, agreeable

gradire (grah-*dee*-ray) *v* fancy, like

grado (*graa*-doa) *m* degree; *essere in ~ di *be able to

graduale (grah-*dwaa*-lay) *adj* gradual

graffetta (grahf-*fayt*-tah) *f* staple

graffiare (grahf-*fyaa*-ray) *v* scratch

graffio (*grahf*-fyoa) *m* scratch

grafico (*graa*-fee-koa) *adj* graphic; *m* graph, diagram

grammatica (grahm-*maa*-tee-kah) f grammar

grammaticale (grahm-mah-tee-*kaa*-lay) adj grammatical

grammo (*grahm*-moa) m gram

grammofono (grahm-*maw*-foa-noa) m gramophone

granaio (grah-*naa*-yoa) m barn

Gran Bretagna (grahn bray-*taa*-ñah) Great Britain, Britain

granchio (*grahng*-kyoa) m crab

grande (*grahn*-day) adj big; great, large, major

grandezza (grahn-*dayt*-tsah) f size

grandine (*grahn*-dee-nay) f hail

grandioso (grahn-*dyoa*-soa) adj magnificent, superb

granello (grah-*nehl*-loa) m corn, grain

granito (grah-*nee*-toa) m granite

grano (*graa*-noa) m corn, grain

granoturco (grahn-*toor*-koa) m maize, corn Am; **pannocchia di ~** corn on the cob

grasso (*grahss*-soa) adj fat; corpulent; greasy; m grease, fat

grassottello (grahss-soat-*tehl*-loa) adj plump

grata (*graa*-tah) f grate

gratis (*graa*-teess) adj gratis

gratitudine (grah-tee-*too*-dee-nay) f gratitude

grato (*graa*-toa) adj grateful

grattacielo (graht-tah-*chai*-loa) m skyscraper

grattugia (graht-*too*-jah) f grater

grattugiare (graht-*too*-jah-ray) v grate

gratuito (grah-*too*-ee-toa) adj free of charge, free

grave (*graa*-vay) adj grave

gravidanza (grah-vee-*daan*-tsa) f pregnancy

gravità (grah-vee-*tah*) f gravity

grazia (*graa*-tsyah) f grace

grazie (*graa*-tsyay) thank you

grazioso (grah-*tsyoa*-soa) adj graceful

Grecia (*grai*-chah) f Greece

greco (*grai*-koa) adj (pl greci) Greek; m, **-a** f Greek

gregge (*grayd*-jay) m herd, flock

grembiule (graym-*byoo*-lay) m apron

gremito (gray-*mee*-toa) adj chock-full

gridare (gree-*daa*-ray) v cry; shout

grido (*gree*-doa) m cry, scream, shout

grigio (*gree*-joa) adj grey

griglia (*gree*-l^yah) f grill

grilletto (greel-*layt*-toa) m trigger

grillo (*greel*-loa) m cricket

grinza (*green*-tsah) f crease

grossa (*gross*-sah) f gross

grossista (groass-*see*-stah) m/f wholesale dealer

grosso (*gross*-soa) adj big, stout

grossolano (groass-soa-*laa*-noa) adj coarse; rude

grotta (*grot*-tah) f cavern, cave

gru (groo) f crane

gruccia (groot-*cha*) f hanger

grumo (*groo*-moa) m lump

grumoso (groo-*moa*-soa) adj lumpy

gruppo (*groop*-poa) m group, party, set; bunch

guadagnare (gwah-dah-*ñaa*-ray) v *make, earn; gain

guadagno (gwah-*daa*-ñoa) m profit

guadare (gwah-*daa*-ray) v wade

guaio (*gwaa*-yoa) m trouble

guancia (*gwahn*-chah) f cheek

guanto (*gwahn*-toa) m glove

guardare (gwahr-*daa*-ray) v look; watch, look at, view; **guardarsi** beware

guardaroba (gwahr-dah-*raw*-bah) m wardrobe; checkroom Am

guardia (*gwahr*-dyah) f attendant; **~ del corpo** bodyguard; **~ forestale** forester

guardiano (gwahr-*dyaa*-noa) m, **-a** f guard, warden

guardrail (gwahrd-*raayl*) *m* guardrail

guarigione (gwah-ree-*jōa*-nay) *f* recovery, cure

guarire (gwah-*ree*-ray) *v* heal; recover

guastare (gwah-*staa*-ray) *v* *spoil; **guastarsi** *break down

guasto (*gwah*-stoa) *adj* broken; *m* breakdown

guerra (*gwehr*-rah) *f* war; **~ mondiale** world war

gufo (*gōo*-foa) *m* owl

guglia (*gōo*-lᵞah) *f* spire

guida (*gwee*-dah) *f* lead; guide; guidebook

guidare (gwee-*daa*-ray) *v* guide, conduct; *drive

guinzaglio (gween-*tsaa*-lᵞoa) *m* leash, lead

guscio (*goosh*-shoa) *m* shell

gustare (goo-*staa*-ray) *v* enjoy

gusto (*goo*-stoa) *m* taste; flavo(u)r; zest

gustoso (goo-*stōa*-soa) *adj* enjoyable, tasty

H

ha (*ah*), **hai** (*ahy*) *v* (pr avere)

handiccapato (ahn-dee-kahp-*paa*- toa) *adj* disabled

hanno (*ahn*-noa), **ho** (*oa*) *v* (pr avere)

I

icona (ee-*kōa*-nah) *f* icon

idea (ee-*dai*-ah) *f* idea

ideale (ee-day-*aa*-lay) *adj* ideal; *m* ideal

identico (ee-*dehn*-tee-koa) *adj* identical

identificare (ee-dayn-tee-fee-*kaa*-ray) *v* identify

identificazione (ee-dayn-tee-fee-kah-*tsyōa*-nay) *f* identification

identità (ee-dayn-tee-*tah*) *f* identity

idillio (ee-*deel*-lᵞoa) *m* romance

idioma (ee-*dyaw*-mah) *m* idiom

idiomatico (ee-dyoa-*maa*-tee-koa) *adj* idiomatic

idiota (ee-*dyaw*-tah) *adj* idiotic; *m/f* idiot

idolo (*ee*-doa-loa) *m* idol

idoneo (ee-*daw*-nay-oa) *adj* adequate

idraulico (ee-*drou*-lee-koa) *m* plumber

idrogeno (ee-*draw*-jay-noa) *m* hydrogen

ieri (*yai*-ree) *adv* yesterday

igiene (ee-*jai*-nay) *f* hygiene

igienico (ee-*jai*-nee-koa) *adj* hygienic

ignorante (ee-ñoa-*rahn*-tay) *adj* ignorant

ignorare (ee-ñoa-*raa*-ray) *v* ignore

ignoto (ee-*ñaw*-toa) *adj* unknown

il (*eel*) *art* (f la; pl i, gli, le) the *art*

illecito (eel-*lāy*-chee-toa) *adj* unauthorized

illegale (eel-lay-*gaa*-lay) *adj* unlawful, illegal

illeggibile (eel-layd-*jee*-bee-lay) *adj*

illegible

illimitato (eel-lee-mee-*taa*-toa) *adj*
unlimited

illuminare (eel-loo-mee-*naa*-ray) *v*
illuminate

illuminazione (eel-loo-mee-nah-
tsyoa-nay) *f* lighting, illumination

illusione (eel-loo-*zyoa*-nay) *f* illusion

illustrare (eel-loo-*straa*-ray) *v*
illustrate

illustrazione (eel-loo-strah-*tsyoa*-nay)
f illustration; picture

illustre (eel-*loo*-stray) *adj* noted

imballaggio (eem-bahl-*lahd*-joa) *m*
packing

imballare (eem-bahl-*laa*-ray) *v* pack
up

imbarazzante (eem-bah-raht-*tsahn*-
tay) *adj* awkward, embarrassing;
puzzling

imbarazzare (eem-bah-raht-*tsaa*-ray)
v embarrass

imbarcare (eem-bahr-*kaa*-ray) *v*
embark

imbarco (eem-*bahr*-koa) *m*
embarkation

imbiancare (eem-byahng-*kaa*-ray) *v*
bleach

imboscata (eem-boa-*skaa*-tah) *f*
ambush

imbrogliare (eem-broa-*lʸaa*-ray) *v*
cheat

imbroglio (eem-*braw*-lʸoa) *m* swindle

imbronciato (eem-broan-*chaa*-toa)
adj cross

imbuto (eem-*boo*-toa) *m* funnel

imitare (ee-mee-*taa*-ray) *v* copy,
imitate

imitazione (ee-mee-tah-*tsyoa*-nay) *f*
imitation

immacolato (eem-mah-koa-*laa*-toa)
adj stainless, spotless

immagazzinare (eem-mah-gahd-
dzee-*naa*-ray) *v* store

immaginare (eem-mah-jee-*naa*-ray) *v*
fancy, imagine

immaginario (eem-mah-jee-*naa*-
ryoa) *adj* imaginary

immaginazione (eem-mah-jee-nah-
tsyoa-nay) *f* fancy, imagination

immagine (eem-*maa*-jee-nay) *f* image;
~ **riflessa** reflection

immangiabile (eem-mahn-*jaa*-bee-
lay) *adj* inedible

immatricolazione (eem-mahn-*tree*-
koa-lah-*tsyoa*-nay) *f* registration;
matriculation

immediatamente (eem-may-dyah-
tah-*mayn*-tay) *adv* instantly,
immediately

immediato (eem-may-*dyaa*-toa) *adj*
immediate

immenso (eem-*mehn*-soa) *adj* vast,
immense, huge

immigrare (eem-mee-*graa*-ray) *v*
immigrate

immigrato (eem-mee-*graa*-toa) *m*, **-a** *f*
immigrant

immigrazione (eem-mee-grah-*tsyoa*-
nay) *f* immigration

imminente (eem-mee-*nehn*-tay) *adj*
oncoming

immobile (eem-*maw*-bee-lay) *m*
house

immondizia (eem-moan-*dee*-tsyah) *f*
rubbish, refuse, garbage

immunità (eem-moo-nee-*tah*) *f*
immunity

immunizzare (eem-moo-need-*dzaa*-
ray) *v* immunize

impalcatura (eem-pahl-kah-*too*-rah) *f*
scaffolding

imparare (eem-pah-*raa*-ray) *v* *learn;
~ **a memoria** memorize

imparziale (eem-pahr-*tsyaa*-lay) *adj*
impartial

impasto (eem-*pah*-stoa) *m* batter

impaurito (eem-pou-*ree*-toa) *adj*

afraid

impaziente (eem-pah-*tsyehn*-tay) *adj* eager, impatient

impeccabile (eem-payk-*kaa*-bee-lay) *adj* faultless

impedimento (eem-pay-dee-*mayn*-toa) *m* impediment

impedire (eem-pay-*dee*-ray) *v* prevent; impede

impegnare (eem-pay-*ñaa*-ray) *v* pawn; **impegnarsi** engage

impegno (eem-*pāy*-ñoa) *m* engagement

imperatore (eem-pay-rah-*tōā*-ray) *m* emperor

imperatrice (eem-pay-rah-*tree*-chay) *f* empress

imperfetto (eem-payr-*feht*-toa) *adj* imperfect

imperfezione (eem-payr-fay-*tsyōā*-nay) *f* fault

imperiale (eem-pay-*ryaa*-lay) *adj* imperial

impermeabile (eem-payr-may-*aa*-bee-lay) *adj* waterproof, rainproof; *m* mackintosh, raincoat

impero (eem-*pai*-roa) *m* empire

impersonale (eem-payr-soa-*naa*-lay) *adj* impersonal

impertinente (eem-payr-tee-*nehn*-tay) *adj* insolent, impertinent

impertinenza (eem-payr-tee-*nehn*-tsah) *f* impertinence

impetuoso (eem-pay-*twōā*-soa) *adj* violent

impianto (eem-*pyahn*-toa) *m* plant

impiegare (eem-pyay-*gaa*-ray) *v* employ; *spend

impiegato (eem-pyay-*gaa*-toa) *m*, **-a** *f* clerk, employee

impiego (eem-*pyai*-goa) *m* job, post; employment; **domanda d'impiego** application

implicare (eem-plee-*kaa*-ray) *v* imply

imponente (eem-poa-*nehn*-tay) *adj* imposing, grand

impopolare (eem-poa-poa-*laa*-ray) *adj* unpopular

***imporre** (eem-*poar*-ray) *v* impose; order; ***imporsi** assert oneself

importante (eem-poar-*tahn*-tay) *adj* important, capital; big

importanza (eem-poar-*tahn*-tsah) *f* importance; ***avere ~** matter

importare (eem-poar-*taa*-ray) *v* import

importatore (eem-poar-tah-*tōā*-ray) *m*, **-trice** *f* importer

importazione (eem-poar-tah-*tsyōā*-nay) *f* import

importunare (eem-poar-too-*naa*-ray) *v* disturb, bother

impossibile (eem-poass-*see*-bee-lay) *adj* impossible

imposta[1](eem-*po*-stah) *f* shutter

imposta[2](eem-*poa*-stah) *f* taxation; **~ sul reddito** income tax

impostare (eem-poa-*staa*-ray) *v* mail, post

impostazione (eem-poa-stah-*tsyōā*-nay) *f* approach

impotente (eem-poa-*tehn*-tay) *adj* powerless; impotent

impotenza (eem-poa-*tehn*-tsah) *f* impotence

imprenditore (eem-prayn-dee-*tōā*-ray) *m*, **-trice** *f* contractor

impresa (eem-*prāy*-sah) *f* enterprise, concern, undertaking

impressionante (eem-prayss-syoa-*nahn*-tay) *adj* impressive; striking

impressionare (eem-prayss-syoa-*naa*-ray) *v* impress

impressione (eem-prayss-*syōā*-nay) *f* impression

imprigionare (eem-pree-joa-*naa*-ray) *v* imprison

improbabile (eem-proa-*baa*-bee-lay)

adj improbable, unlikely

improvvisamente (eem-proav-vee-zah-*mayn*-tay) *adv* suddenly

improvvisare (eem-proav-vee-*zaa*-ray) *v* improvise

improvviso (eem-proav-*vee*-zoa) *adj* sudden

impugnatura (eem-poo-ñah-*too*-rah) *f* handle

impulsivo (eem-pool-*see*-voa) *adj* impulsive

impulso (eem-*pool*-soa) *m* impulse; urge

in (een) *prep* in, into; at

inabitabile (ee-nah-bee-*taa*-bee-lay) *adj* uninhabitable

inaccessibile (ee-naht-chayss-*see*-bee-lay) *adj* inaccessible

inaccettabile (ee-naht-chayt-*taa*-bee-lay) *adj* unacceptable

inadatto (ee-nah-*daht*-toa) *adj* unsuitable; unfit

inadeguato (ee-nah-day-*gwaa*-toa) *adj* inadequate

inamidare (ee-nah-mee-*daa*-ray) *v* starch

inaspettato (ee-nah-spayt-*taa*-toa) *adj* unexpected

inaugurare (ee-nou-goo-*raa*-ray) *v* open, inaugurate

incantare (eeng-kahn-*taa*-ray) *v* bewitch

incantevole (eeng-kahn-*tay*-voa-lay) *adj* enchanting

incanto (eeng-*kahn*-toa) *m* spell, charm

incapace (eeng-kah-*paa*-chay) *adj* incapable, unable

incaricare (eeng-kah-ree-*kaa*-ray) *v* charge; **incaricarsi di** *take charge of; **incaricato di** in charge of

incarico (eeng-*kaa*-ree-koa) *m* assignment

incassare (eeng-kahss-*saa*-ray) *v* cash

incendio (een-*chehn*-dyoa) *m* fire

incenso (een-*chehn*-soa) *m* incense

incerto (een-*chehr*-toa) *adj* uncertain, doubtful

inchiesta (eeng-*kyeh*-stah) *f* enquiry, inquiry

inchiostro (eeng-*kyo*-stroa) *m* ink

inciampare (een-chahm-*paa*-ray) *v* stumble

incidentale (een-chee-dayn-*taa*-lay) *adj* incidental, casual

incidente (een-chee-*dehn*-tay) *m* accident; incident; **~ aereo** plane crash

***incidere** (een-*chee*-day-ray) *v* engrave

incinta (een-*cheen*-tah) *adj* pregnant

incisione (een-chee-*zyoa*-nay) *f* cut; engraving

incisore (een-chee-*zōa*-ray) *m* engraver

incitare (een-chee-*taa*-ray) *v* incite

inclinare (eeng-klee-*naa*-ray) *v* slant; **inclinato** slanting, sloping

inclinazione (eeng-klee-nah-*tsyōa*-nay) *f* inclination, tendency

***includere** (eeng-*kloo*-day-ray) *v* count, include

incollare (eeng-koal-*laa*-ray) *v* paste, *stick

incolto (eeng-*koal*-toa) *adj* waste, uncultivated

incolume (eeng-*kaw*-loo-may) *adj* unhurt

incombustibile (eeng-koam-boo-*stee*-bee-lay) *adj* fireproof

incompetente (eeng-koam-pay-*tehn*-tay) *adj* incompetent; unqualified

incompleto (eeng-koam-*plai*-toa) *adj* incomplete

inconcepibile (eeng-koan-chay-*pee*-bee-lay) *adj* inconceivable

incondizionato (eeng-koan-dee-tsyoa-*naa*-toa) *adj* unconditional

inconscio (eeng-*kon*-shoa) *adj*
unconscious

inconsueto (eeng-koan-*swai*-toa) *adj*
unusual

incontrare (eeng-koan-*traa*-ray) *v*
*meet; *come across, encounter; ~
per caso run into

incontro (eeng-*koan*-troa) *m* meeting,
encounter

inconveniente (eeng-koan-vay-*ñehn*-
tay) *m* inconvenience

incoraggiare (eeng-koa-rahd-*jaa*-ray)
v encourage

incoronare (eeng-koa-roa-*naa*-ray) *v*
crown

incosciente (eeng-koash-*shehn*-tay)
adj reckless; unconscious

incredibile (eeng-kray-*dee*-bee-lay)
adj incredible

incremento (eeng-kray-*mayn*-toa) *m*
increase

increscioso (eeng-kraysh-*shoā*-soa)
adj unpleasant

increspare (eeng-kray-*spaa*-ray) *v*
crease

incrinarsi (eeng-kree-*nahr*-see) *v*
crack

incrocio (eeng-*krōa*-choa) *m*
crossroads

incubo (*eeng*-koo-boa) *m* nightmare

incurabile (eengkoo-*raa*-bee-lay) *adj*
incurable

indaffarato (een-dahf-fah-*raa*-toa) *adj*
busy

indagare (een-dah-*gaa*-ray) *v* enquire;
inquire

indagine (een-*daa*-jee-nay) *f* inquiry;
examination

indecente (een-day-*chehn*-tay) *adj*
indecent

indefinito (een-day-fee-*nee*-toa) *adj*
indefinite

indemoniato (een-day-moa-*ñaa*-toa)
adj possessed

indennità (een-dayn-nee-*tah*) *f*
indemnity, compensation

indesiderabile (een-day-see-day-*raa*-
bee-lay) *adj* undesirable

India (*een*-dyah) *f* India

indiano (een-*dyaa*-noa) *adj* Indian

indicare (een-dee-*kaa*-ray) *v* point
out; indicate, declare

indicazione (een-dee-kah-*tsyōa*-nay) *f*
indication; direction

indice (*een*-dee-chay) *m* index finger;
index; table of contents

indietro (een-*dyai*-troa) *adv* behind;
back; **all'indietro** backwards

indifeso (een-dee-*fāy*-soa) *adj*
unprotected

indifferente (een-deef-fay-*rehn*-tay)
adj indifferent

indigeno (een-*dee*-jay-noa) *m* native

indigestione (een-dee-jay-*styōa*-nay)
f indigestion

indignazione (een-dee-ñah-*tsyōa*-
nay) *f* indignation

indipendente (een-dee-payn-*dehn*-
tay) *adj* independent

indipendenza (een-dee-payn-*dehn*-
tsah) *f* independence

indiretto (een-dee-*reht*-toa) *adj*
indirect

indirizzare (een-dee-reet-*tsaa*-ray) *v*
address

indirizzo (een-dee-*reet*-tsoa) *m*
address

indispensabile (een-dee-spayn-*saa*-
bee-lay) *adj* essential

indisposto (een-dee-*spoa*-stoa) *adj*
unwell

individuale (een-dee-vee-*dwaa*-lay)
adj individual

individuo (een-dee-*vee*-dwoa) *m*
individual

indiziato (een-dee-*tsyaa*-toa) *m*, **-a** *f*
suspect

indizio (een-*dee*-tsyoa) *m* indication

indole (*een*-doa-lay) *f* nature

indolenzito (een-doa-layn-*jee*-toa) *adj* sore

indolore (een-doa-*lōa*-ray) *adj* painless

Indonesia (een-doa-*nai*-zyah) *f* Indonesia

indossare (een-doass-*saa*-ray) *v* *put on; *wear

indossatrice (een-doass-sah-*tree*-chay) *f* model, mannequin

indovinare (een-doa-vee-*naa*-ray) *v* guess

indovinello (een-doa-vee-*nehl*-loa) *m* riddle

indubbiamente (een-doob-byah-*mayn*-tay) *adv* undoubtedly

indugio (een-*dōō*-joa) *m* delay

***indurre a** (een-*door*-ray) cause to

industria (een-*doo*-stryah) *f* industry; ~ **mineraria** mining

industriale (een-doo-*stryaa*-lay) *adj* industrial

inefficace (een-ayf-fee-*kaa*-chay) *adj* inefficient

ineguale (ee-nay-*gwaa*-lay) *adj* uneven, unequal

inesatto (ee-nay-*zaht*-toa) *adj* incorrect

inesperto (ee-nay-*spehr*-toa) *adj* inexperienced

inesplicabile (ee-nay-splee-*kaa*-bee-lay) *adj* unaccountable

inestimabile (ee-nay-stee-*maa*-bee-lay) *adj* priceless

inevitabile (ee-nay-vee-*taa*-bee-lay) *adj* inevitable, unavoidable

infarto (een-*faar*-toa) *m* infarct

infastidire (een-fah-stee-*dee*-ray) *v* annoy; bother

infatti (een-*faht*-tee) *conj* as a matter of fact, in fact

infedele (een-fay-*dai*-lay) *adj* unfaithful

infelice (een-fay-*lee*-chay) *adj* unhappy

inferiore (een-fay-*ryōa*-ray) *adj* inferior, bottom

infermeria (een-fayr-may-*ree*-ah) *f* infirmary

infermiere (een-fayr-*myai*-rah) *m*, **-a** *f* nurse

inferno (een-*fehr*-noa) *m* hell

inferriata (een-fayr-*ryaa*-tah) *f* railing

infettare (een-fayt-*taa*-ray) *v* infect

infezione (een-fay-*tsyōa*-nay) *f* infection

infiammabile (een-fyahm-*maa*-bee-lay) *adj* inflammable

infiammarsi (een-fyahm-*mahr*-see) *v* *become inflamed

infiammazione (een-fyahm-mah-*tsyōa*-nay) *f* inflammation

infierire (een-fyay-*ree*-ray) *v* rage

infilare (een-fee-*laa*-ray) *v* thread

infine (een-*fee*-nay) *adv* at last

infinito (een-fee-*nee*-toa) *adj* infinite, endless; *m* infinitive

inflazione (een-flah-*tsyōa*-nay) *f* inflation

influente (een-*flwehn*-tay) *adj* influential

influenza (een-*flwehn*-tsah) *f* influence; influenza, flu

influenzare (een-floo-ayn-*tsaa*-ray) *v* affect

influire (een-*flwee*-ray) *v* influence

informale (een-foar-*maa*-lay) *adj* informal, casual

informare (een-foar-*maa*-ray) *v* inform; **informarsi** enquire, inquire

informatica (een-foar-*maa*-tee-kah) *f* computer science; information technology

informazione (een-foar-mah-*tsyōa*-nay) *f* information, enquiry

infornare (een-foar-*naa*-ray) *v* bake

infrangibile (een-frahn-*jee*-bee-lay)

adj unbreakable

infrarosso (een-frah-*roass*-soa) *adj* infra-red

infruttuoso (een-froot-*twoa*-soa) *adj* unsuccessful

ingannare (eeng-gahn-*naa*-ray) *v* deceive, cheat

inganno (een-*gahn*-noa) *m* deceit

ingegnere (een-jay-*ñai*-ray) *m* engineer

ingenuo (een-*jai*-nwoa) *adj* simple, naïve

Inghilterra (eeng-geel-*tehr*-rah) *f* England

inghiottire (eeng-gyoat-*tee*-ray) *v* swallow

inginocchiarsi (een-jee-noak-*kyahr*-see) *v* *kneel

ingiuriare (een-joo-*ryaa*-ray) *v* call names

ingiustizia (een-joo-*stee*-tsyah) *f* injustice

ingiusto (een-*joo*-stoa) *adj* unjust, unfair

inglese (eeng-*glay*-say) *adj* English; British; *m/f* Englishman, Englishwoman, Briton

ingoiare (eeng-goa-*yaa*-ray) *v* swallow

ingorgo (eeng-*goar*-goa) *m* traffic jam; bottleneck

ingrandimento (eeng-grahn-dee-*mayn*-toa) *m* enlargement

ingrandire (eeng-grahn-*dee*-ray) *v* enlarge

ingrato (eeng-*graa*-toa) *adj* ungrateful

ingrediente (eeng-gray-*dyehn*-tay) *m* ingredient

ingresso (eeng-*grehss*-soa) *m* entry; entrance; admission; entrance fee

ingrosso (eeng-*gross*-soa) *m* wholesale

inguine (*eeng*-gwee-nay) *m* groin

iniettare (ee-ñayt-*taa*-ray) *v* inject

iniezione (ee-ñay-*tsyoa*-nay) *f* injection, shot

ininterrotto (ee-neen-tayr-*roat*-toa) *adj* continuous

iniziale (ee-nee-*tsyaa*-lay) *adj* initial; *f* initial

iniziare (ee-nee-*tsyaa*-ray) *v* *begin, commence

iniziativa (ee-nee-tsyah-*tee*-vah) *f* initiative

inizio (ee-*nee*-tsyoa) *m* beginning, start

innalzare (een-nahl-*tsaa*-ray) *v* erect

innamorarsi di (een-nah-moa-*raar*-see) *v* fall in love with

innamorato (een-nah-moa-*raa*-toa) *adj* in love

innanzi (een-*nahn*-tsee) *adv* forwards; before; ~ **a** before

innato (een-*naa*-toa) *adj* natural

inno (*een*-noa) *m* hymn; ~ **nazionale** national anthem

innocente (een-noa-*chehn*-tay) *adj* innocent

innocenza (een-noa-*chehn*-tsah) *f* innocence

innocuo (een-*naw*-kwoa) *adj* harmless

inoltrare (ee-noal-*traa*-ray) *v* forward

inoltre (ee-*noal*-tray) *adv* moreover, besides, furthermore

inondazione (ee-noan-dah-*tsyoa*-nay) *f* flood

inopportuno (ee-noap-poar-*too*-noa) *adj* misplaced

inquieto (eeng-kwee-*ai*-toa) *adj* restless, uneasy

inquietudine (eeng-kwee-ay-*too*-dee-nay) *f* unrest

inquilino (eeng-kwee-*lee*-noa) *m*, **-a** *f* tenant; lodger

inquinamento (eeng-kwee-nah-*mayn*-toa) *m* pollution

insalata (een-sah-*laa*-tah) *f* salad

insegnamento (een-say-ñah-*mayn*-

toa) *m* tuition; teachings *pl*

insegnante (een-say-*ñahn*-tay) *m/f*
teacher; master, schoolteacher

insegnare (een-say-*ñaa*-ray) *v* *teach

inseguire (een-say-*gwee*-ray) *v* chase

insenatura (een-say-nah-*tōō*-rah) *f*
creek, inlet

insensato (een-sayn-*saa*-toa) *adj*
senseless; meaningless

insensibile (een-sayn-*see*-bee-lay) *adj*
insensitive

inserire (een-say-*ree*-ray) *v* insert

inserzione (een-sayr-*tsyōa*-nay) *f*
advertisement

insetticida (een-sayt-tee-*chee*-dah) *m*
insecticide

insettifugo (een-sayt-tee-*fōō*-goa) *m*
insect repellent

insetto (een-*seht*-toa) *m* insect; bug
Am

insieme (een-*syai*-may) *adv* together;
jointly

insignificante (een-see-ñee-fee-*kahn*-
tay) *adj* unimportant, insignificant;
petty

insipido (een-*see*-pee-doa) *adj*
tasteless

insistere (een-*see*-stay-ray) *v* insist

insoddisfacente (een-soad-dee-sfah-
chehn-tay) *adj* unsatisfactory

insolente (een-soa-*lehn*-tay) *adj*
insolent

insolenza (een-soa-*lehn*-tsah) *f*
insolence

insolito (een-*saw*-lee-toa) *adj*
uncommon, unusual

insomma (een-*soam*-mah) *adv* in
short

insonne (een-*son*-nay) *adj* sleepless

insonnia (een-*son*-ñah) *f* insomnia

insonorizzato (een-soa-noa-reed-*jaa*-
toa) *adj* soundproof

insopportabile (een-soap-poar-*taa*-
bee-lay) *adj* unbearable

instabile (een-*staa*-bee-lay) *adj*
unstable

installare (een-stahl-*laa*-ray) *v* install

installazione (een-stahl-lah-*tsyōa*-
nay) *f* installation

insuccesso (een-soot-*chehss*-soa) *m*
failure

insufficiente (een-soof-fee-*chehn*-
tay) *adj* insufficient

insultante (een-sool-*tahn*-tay) *adj*
offensive

insultare (een-sool-*taa*-ray) *v* insult

insulto (een-*sool*-toa) *m* insult

insuperato (een-soo-pay-*raa*-toa) *adj*
unsurpassed

insurrezione (een-soor-ray-*tsyōa*-nay)
f rising

intagliare (een-tah-*lʸaa*-ray) *v* carve

intanto (een-*tahn*-toa) *adv* in the
meantime

intatto (een-*taht*-toa) *adj* unbroken,
whole, intact

intelletto (een-tayl-*leht*-toa) *m*
intellect

intellettuale (een-tayl-layt-*twaa*-lay)
adj intellectual

intelligente (een-tayl-lee-*jehn*-tay) *adj*
intelligent; clever, smart, bright

intelligenza (een-tayl-lee-*jehn*-tsah) *f*
intelligence; brain

***intendere** (een-*tehn*-day-ray) *v*
*mean; intend

intenditore (een-tayn-dee-*tōa*-ray) *m*,
-trice *f* connoisseur

intensità (een-tayn-see-*tah*) *f* intensity

intenso (een-*tehn*-soa) *adj* intense,
violent

intento (een-*tehn*-toa) *m* aim

intenzionale (een-tayn-tsyoa-*naa*-lay)
adj intentional

intenzione (een-tayn-*tsyōa*-nay) *f*
intention, purpose

interamente (een-tay-rah-*mayn*-tay)
adv completely, entirely, altogether,

quite

interessamento (een-tay-rayss-sah-*mayn*-toa) *m* interest

interessante (een-tay-rayss-*sahn*-tay) *adj* interesting

interessare (een-tay-rayss-*saa*-ray) *v* interest; **interessato** concerned

interesse (een-tay-*rehss*-say) *m* interest

interferenza (een-tayr-fay-*rehn*-tsah) *f* interference

interferire (een-tayr-fay-*ree*-ray) *v* interfere

interim (*een*-tay-reem) *m* interim

interiora (een-tay-*ryoa*-rah) *fpl* insides

interiore (een-tay-*ryoa*-ray) *m* interior

intermediario (een-tayr-may-*dyaa*-ryoa) *m* intermediary; ***fare da ~** mediate

intermezzo (een-tayr-*mehd*-dzoa) *m* interlude

internazionale (een-tayr-nah-tsyoa-*naa*-lay) *adj* international

Internet (*een-tayr*-nayt) *m* Internet

interno (een-*tehr*-noa) *adj* inner, internal, inside; resident; domestic; *m* inside; extension; **all'interno** within; **verso l'interno** inwards

intero (een-*tay*-roa) *adj* entire, whole

interpretare (een-tayr-pray-*taa*-ray) *v* interpret

interprete (een-*tehr*-pray-tay) *m/f* interpreter

interrogare (een-tayr-roa-*gaa*-ray) *v* interrogate

interrogativo (een-tayr-roa-gah-*tee*-voa) *adj* interrogative

interrogatorio (een-tayr-roa-gah-*taw*-ryoa) *m* interrogation

interrogazione (een-tayr-roa-gah-*tsyoa*-nay) *f* examination

*interrompere (een-tayr-*roam*-pay-ray) *v* interrupt; ***interrompersi** pause

interruttore (een-tayr-root-*toa*-ray) *m* switch

interruzione (een-tayr-roo-*tsyoa*-nay) *f* interruption

intersezione (een-tayr-say-*tsyoa*-nay) *f* intersection

interurbana (een-tayr-roor-*baa*-nah) *f* long-distance call

intervallo (een-tayr-*vahl*-loa) *m* interval; intermission, break; half time

*intervenire (een-tayr-vay-*nee*-ray) *v* intervene

intervista (een-tayr-*vee*-stah) *f* interview

intestino (een-tay-*stee*-noa) *m* gut, intestine; bowels *pl*

intimità (een-tee-mee-*tah*) *f* privacy

intimo (*een*-tee-moa) *adj* intimate; cosy

intirizzito (een-tee-reed-*dzee*-toa) *adj* numb

intollerabile (een-toal-lay-*raa*-bee-lay) *adj* intolerable

intonarsi con (een-toa-*nahr*-see) match

intorno (een-*toar*-noa) *adv* around; **~ a** around, round, about

intorpidito (een-toar-pee-*dee*-toa) *adj* numb

intossicazione (een-toass-see-kah-*tsyoa*-nay) *f* poisoning

*intraprendere (een-trah-*prehn*-day-ray) *v* *undertake

*intrattenere (een-traht-tay-*nāy*-ray) *v* entertain

*intravedere (een-trahv-vay-*dāy*-ray) *v* glimpse

intricato (een-tree-*kaa*-toa) *adj* complex

intrigo (een-*tree*-goa) *m* intrigue

*introdurre (een-troa-*door*-ray) *v* introduce

introduzione (een-troa-doo-*tsyoa*-

nay) f introduction
intromettersi: ~ in (een-troa-*mayt*-tayr-see) interfere with
intuire (een-*twee*-ray) v *understand
inumidire (ee-noo-mee-*dee*-ray) v moisten, damp
inutile (ee-*nōō*-tee-lay) adj useless; vain
inutilmente (ee-noo-teel-*mayn*-tay) adv in vain
***invadere** (een-*vaa*-day-ray) v invade
invalido (een-*vaa*-lee-doa) adj disabled, invalid; m, **-a** f invalid, handicapped Am
invano (een-*vaa*-noa) adv in vain
invasione (een-vah-*zyōa*-nay) f invasion
invece di (een-*vāy*-chay dee) instead of
inveire (een-vay-*ee*-ray) v scold
inventare (een-vayn-*taa*-ray) v invent
inventario (een-vayn-*taa*-ryoa) m inventory
inventivo (een-vayn-*tee*-voa) adj inventive
inventore (een-vayn-*tōa*-ray) m, **-trice** f inventor
invenzione (een-vayn-*tsyōa*-nay) f invention
inverno (een-*vehr*-noa) m winter
inverso (een-*vehr*-soa) adj reverse
invertire (een-vayr-*tee*-ray) v invert
investigare (een-vay-stee-*gaa*-ray) v investigate
investigatore (een-vay-stee-gah-*tōa*-ray) m, **-trice** f detective
investigazione (een-vay-stee-gah-*tsyōa*-nay) f enquiry, investigation
investimento (een-vay-stee-*mayn*-toa) m investment
investire (een-vay-*stee*-ray) v invest
inviare (een-*vyaa*-ray) v dispatch
inviato (een-*vyaa*-toa) m, **-a** f correspondent

invidia (een-*vee*-dyah) f envy
invidiare (een-vee-*dyaa*-ray) v grudge, envy
invidioso (een-vee-*dyōa*-soa) adj envious
invio (een-*vee*-oa) m expedition
invisibile (een-vee-*zee*-bee-lay) adj invisible
invitare (een-vee-*taa*-ray) v ask, invite
invitato (een-*vee*-taa-toa) m, **-a** f guest
invito (een-*vee*-toa) m invitation
invocare (een-voa-*kaa*-ray) v invoke
involontario (een-voa-loan-*taa*-ryoa) adj unintentional
inzuppare (een-tsoop-*paa*-ray) v soak
io (*ee*-oa) pron I; **~ stesso** myself
iodio (*yaw*-dyoa) m iodine
ipocrisia (ee-poa-kree-*see*-ah) f hypocrisy
ipocrita (ee-*paw*-kree-tah) m/f hypocrite; adj hypocritical
ipoteca (ee-poa-*tai*-kah) f mortgage
ipotesi (ee-*paw*-tay-zee) f supposition
ippodromo (eep-*paw*-droa-moa) m racecourse
ippoglosso (eep-poa-*gloss*-soa) m halibut
ira (*ee*-rah) f anger
iracheno (ee-rah-*kāy*-noa) adj Iraqi; m, **-a** f Iraqi
Iran (*ee*-rahn) m Iran
iraniano (ee-rah-*nyaa*-noa) adj Iranian; m, **-a** f Iranian
Iraq (*ee*-rahk) m Iraq
irascibile (ee-rahsh-*shee*-bee-lay) adj hot-tempered, quick-tempered
Irlanda (eer-*lahn*-dah) f Ireland
irlandese (eer-lahn-*dāy*-say) adj Irish
ironia (ee-roa-*nee*-ah) f irony
ironico (ee-*raw*-nee-koa) adj ironical
irragionevole (eer-rah-joa-*nāy*-voa-lay) adj unreasonable
irreale (eer-ray-*aa*-lay) adj unreal
irregolare (eer-ray-goa-*laa*-ray) adj

irregular; uneven

irreparabile (eer-ray-pah-*raa*-bee-lay) *adj* irreparable

irrequieto (eer-ray-kwee-*ai*-toa) *adj* restless

irrestringibile (eer-ray-streen-*jee*-bee-lay) *adj* shrinkproof

irrevocabile (eer-ray-voa-*kaa*-bee-lay) *adj* irrevocable

irrilevante (eer-ree-lay-*vahn*-tay) *adj* insignificant

irritabile (eer-ree-*taa*-bee-lay) *adj* irritable

irritare (eer-ree-*taa*-ray) *v* irritate

irruzione (eer-roo-*tsyoa*-nay) *f* invasion; raid

***iscrivere** (ee-*skree*-vay-ray) *v* enter; **per iscritto** in writing, written; **iscriversi** enrol(l) at; register; join

iscrizione (ee-skree-*tsyoa*-nay) *f* inscription

Islanda (ee-*zlahn*-dah) *f* Iceland

islandese (ee-zlahn-*day*-say) *adj* Icelandic; *m/f* Icelander

isola (*ee*-zoa-lah) *f* island

isolamento (ee-zoa-lah-*mayn*-toa) *m* isolation; insulation

isolare (ee-zoa-*laa*-ray) *v* isolate; insulate

isolato (ee-zoa-*laa*-toa) *adj* isolated; *m* house block *Am*

ispessire (ee-spayss-*see*-ray) *v* thicken

ispettore (ee-spayt-*tōa*-ray) *m*, **-trice** *f* inspector; supervisor

ispezionare (ee-spay-tsyoa-*naa*-ray) *v* inspect

ispezione (ee-spay-*tsyōa*-nay) *f* inspection

ispirare (ee-spee-*raa*-ray) *v* inspire

Israele (ee-zrah-*ai*-lay) *m* Israel

israeliano (ee-zrah-ay-*lʸaa*-noa) *adj* Israeli; *m*, **-a** *f* Israeli

issare (eess-*saa*-ray) *v* hoist

istantanea (ee-stahn-*taa*-nay-ah) *f* snapshot

istante (ee-*stahn*-tay) *m* instant, second; while; **all'istante** instantly

istanza (ee-*stahn*-tsah) *f* petition, application

isterico (ee-*stai*-ree-koa) *adj* hysterical

istigare (ee-stee-*gah*-ray) *v* stir up

istinto (ee-*steen*-toa) *m* instinct

istituire (ee-stee-*twee*-ray) *v* institute; found

istituto (ee-stee-*tōo*-toa) *m* institute; institution

istituzione (ee-stee-too-*tsyoa*-nay) *f* institution, institute

istruire (ee-*strwee*-ray) *v* instruct; educate

istruttivo (ee-stroot-*tee*-voa) *adj* instructive

istruttore (ee-stroot-*tōa*-ray) *m*, **-trice** *f* instructor

istruzione (ee-stroo-*tsyōa*-nay) *f* instruction; background; **istruzioni per l'uso** directions for use

Italia (ee-*taa*-lʸah) *f* Italy

italiano (ee-tah-lʸaa-noa) *adj* Italian; *m*, **-a** *f* Italian

itinerario (ee-tee-nay-*raa*-ryoa) *m* itinerary

itterizia (eet-tay-*ree*-tsyah) *f* jaundice

K

kaki (*kaa*-kee) *m* khaki

Kenia (*kai*-nyah) *m* Kenya

L

la (lah) *pron* her; it

là (lah) *adv* there; **al di ~** beyond; **al di ~ di** past; **di ~** there

labbro (*lahb*-broa) *m* (pl le labbra) lip

labirinto (lah-bee-*reen*-toa) *m* labyrinth

laboratorio (lah-boa-rah-*taw*-ryoa) *m* laboratory; **~ linguistico** language laboratory

laborioso (lah-boa-*ryōā*-soa) *adj* industrious

lacca (*lahk*-kah) *f* lacquer; varnish; hair spray

laccio (*laht*-choa) *m* lace

lacrima (*laa*-kree-mah) *f* tear

ladro (*laa*-droa) *m*, **-a** *f* robber, thief

laggiù (lahd-*joo*) *adv* over there

lagnanza (lah-*ñahn*-tsah) *f* complaint

lagnarsi (lah-*ñahr*-see) *v* complain

lago (*laa*-goa) *m* lake

laguna (lah-*gōō*-nah) *f* lagoon

lama (*laa*-mah) *f* blade

lamentarsi di (lah-mayn-*tāyr*-see) *v* complain about

lametta (*laa*-mayt-tah) *f* razor blade

lamiera (lah-*myai*-rah) *f* plate

lamina (*laa*-mee-nah) *f* sheet

lampada (*lahm*-pah-dah) *f* lamp; **~ da tavolo** reading lamp

lampadario (lahm-pah-*daa*-ryoa) *m* chandelier

lampadina (lahm-pah-*dee*-nah) *f* light bulb; **~ tascabile** torch

lampante (lahm-*pahn*-tay) *adj* self-evident

lampione (lahm-*pyōā*-nay) *m* lamppost

lampo (*lahm*-poa) *m* lightning

lampone (lahm-*pōā*-nay) *m* raspberry

lana (*laa*-nah) *f* wool; **di ~** wool(l)en; **~ da rammendo** darning wool

lancia (*lahn*-chah) *f* spear

lanciare (lahn-*chaa*-ray) *v* *throw, *cast; launch

lancio (*lahn*-choa) *m* cast

lanterna (lahn-*tehr*-nah) *f* lantern

lanugine (lah-*nōō*-jee-nay) *f* down

lapide (*laa*-pee-day) *f* gravestone

lardo (*lahr*-doa) *m* bacon

larghezza (lahr-*gayt*-tsah) *f* width, breadth

largo (*lahr*-goa) *adj* wide, broad; *farsi ~** push

laringite (lah-reen-*jee*-tay) *f* laryngitis

lasca (*lah*-skah) *f* roach

lasciare (lahsh-*shaa*-ray) *v* desert, *leave; *leave behind; allow to, *let

lassativo (lahss-sah-*tee*-voa) *m* laxative

lassù (lahss-*soo*) *adv* up there

lastricare (lah-stree-*kaa*-ray) *v* pave

lateralmente (lah-tay-rahl-*mayn*-tay) *adv* sideways

laterizio (lah-tay-*ree*-tsyoa) *m* brick

latino americano (lah-*tee*-noa ah-may-ree-*kaa*-noa) Latin-American

latitudine (lah-tee-*tōō*-dee-nāy) *f* latitude

lato (*laa*-toa) *m* way, side

latrare (lah-*traa*-ray) *v* bay

lattaio (laht-*taa*-yoa) *m*, **-a** *f* milkman

latte (*laht*-tay) *m* milk

latteria (laht-tay-*ree*-ah) *f* dairy

lattina (laht-*tee*-nah) *f* tin, can

lattuga (laht-*tōō*-gah) *f* lettuce

lavabile (lah-*vaa*-bee-lay) *adj* washable

lavaggio (lah-*vahd*-joa) *m* washing

lavagna (lah-*vaa*-ñah) *f* blackboard

lavanderia (lah-vahn-day-*ree*-ah) *f* laundry; **~ automatica** launderette

lavandino (lah-vahn-*dee*-noa) *m* washbasin

lavare (lah-*vaa*-ray) *v* wash; **~ i piatti**

wash up

lavatrice (lah-vah-*tree*-chay) f washing machine

lavastoviglie (lah-vah-stoa-*vee*-l^yay) f dishwasher

lavello (lah-*vehl*-loa) m sink

lavorare (lah-voa-*raa*-ray) v work; ~ **all'uncinetto** crochet; ~ **a maglia** *knit; ~ **sodo** labo(u)r; ~ **troppo** overwork

lavoratore (lah-voa-rah-*tōa*-ray) m worker

lavoro (lah-*vōa*-roa) m work; labo(u)r; job; **datore di** ~ employer; **lavori di casa** housework; ~ **fatto a mano** handwork; ~ **manuale** handicraft

Le (lay) *pron* you

le (lay) *pron* her; it

leale (lay-*aa*-lay) *adj* true, loyal

lebbra (*layb*-brah) f leprosy

leccare (layk-*kaa*-ray) v lick

leccornia (layk-*koar*-ñah) f delicatessen

lega (*lāy*-gah) f union, league

legale (lay-*gaa*-lay) *adj* lawful, legal; **procuratore** ~ solicitor

legalizzazione (lay-gah-leed-dzah-*tsyōa*-nay) f legalization

legame (lay-*gaa*-may) m link

legare (lay-*gaa*-ray) v *bind, tie; ~ **insieme** bundle

legato (lay-*gaa*-toa) m legacy

legatura (lay-gah-*tōō*-rah) f binding

legazione (lay-gah-*tsyōa*-nay) f legation

legge (*lehd*-jay) f law

leggenda (layd-*jehn*-dah) f legend; caption

***leggere** (*lehd*-jay-ray) v *read

leggero (layd-*jai*-roa) *adj* light; slight; gentle

leggibile (layd-*jee*-bee-lay) *adj* legible

leggio (layd-*jee*-oa) m desk

legittimo (lay-*jeet*-tee-moa) *adj* legitimate, legal

legname (lay-*ñaa*-may) m timber

legno (*lāy*-ñoa) m wood; **di** ~ wooden

Lei (*lai*-ee) *pron* you; ~ **stesso** yourself

lente (*lehn*-tay) f lens; ~ **d'ingrandimento** magnifying glass; **lenti a contatto** contact lenses

lento (*lehn*-toa) *adj* slack, slow

lenza (*lehn*-tsah) f fishing line

lenzuolo (layn-*tswaw*-loa) m sheet

leone (lay-*ōa*-nay) m lion

lepre (*lai*-pray) f hare

lesione (lay-*zyōa*-nay) f injury

letale (lay-*taa*-lay) *adj* mortal

letamaio (lay-tah-*maa*-yoa) m dunghill

letame (lay-*taa*-may) m dung

lettera (*leht*-tay-rah) f letter; **carta da lettere** notepaper; ~ **di credito** letter of credit; ~ **di raccomandazione** letter of recommendation

letterario (layt-tay-*raa*-ryoa) *adj* literary

letteratura (layt-tay-rah-*tōō*-rah) f literature

lettino (*leht*-tee-noa) m bed; cot; couch; ~ **da campeggio** camp bed; cot *Am*

letto (*leht*-toa) m bed

lettore (layt-*tōa*-ray) m, **-trice** f reader; lecturer in a foreign language; disk drive

lettura (layt-*tōō*-rah) f reading

leva (*lāy*-vah) f lever, draft *Am*; ~ **del cambio** gear lever

levare (lay-*vaa*-ray) v *take away

levata (lay-*vaa*-tah) f collection

levigato (lay-vee-*gaa*-toa) *adj* smooth

levriere (lay-*vryai*-ray) m greyhound

lezione (lay-*tsyōa*-nay) f lesson, lecture

li (lee) *pron* (f le) them

lì (lee) *adv* there

libanese (lee-bah-*nāy*-say) *adj* Lebanese; *m/f* Lebanese

Libano (*lee*-bah-noa) *m* Lebanon

libbra (*leeb*-brah) *f* pound

liberale (lee-bay-*raa*-lay) *adj* liberal

liberare (lee-bay-*raa*-ray) *v* deliver

liberazione (lee-bay-rah-*tsyoa*-nay) *f* liberation; delivery

Liberia (lee-*bai*-ryah) *f* Liberia

liberiano (lee-bay-*ryaa*-noa) *adj* Liberian; *m*, **-a** *f* Liberian

libero (*lee*-bay-roa) *adj* free

libertà (lee-bayr-*tah*) *f* freedom, liberty

libraio (lee-*braa*-yoa) *m*, **-a** *f* bookseller

libreria (lee-bray-*ree*-ah) *f* bookstore

libretto (lee-*brayt*-toa) *m* booklet; **~ degli assegni** chequebook; **~ di circolazione** registration document

libro (*lee*-broa) *m* book; **~ di cucina** cookery book; cookbook *Am*; **~ di testo** textbook; **~ tascabile** paperback

licenza (lee-*chehn*-tsah) *f* permission, licence, license *Am*

licenziare (lee-chayn-*tsyaa*-ray) *v* fire; **licenziarsi** resign

liceo (lee-*chay*-oa) *m* high school

lido (*lee*-doa) *m* beach; Lido

lieto (*ľai*-toa) *adj* pleased, glad

lieve (*ľai*-vay) *adj* light

lievito (*ľai*-vee-toa) *m* yeast

lilla (*leel*-lah) *adj* mauve

lima (*lee*-mah) *f* file

limetta (lee-*mayt*-tah) *f* nail file

limitare (lee-mee-*taa*-ray) *v* limit

limite (*lee*-mee-tay) *m* boundary, bound; limit; **~ di velocità** speed limit

limonata (lee-moa-*naa*-tah) *f* lemonade

limone (lee-*mōa*-nay) *m* lemon

limpido (*leem*-pee-doa) *adj* limpid

lindo (*leen*-doa) *adj* neat

linea (*lee*-nayah) *f* line; **~ aerea** airline; **~ di navigazione** shipping line; **~ principale** main line

lineetta (lee-nay-*ayt*-tah) *f* dash; hyphen

lingua (*leeng*-gwah) *f* tongue; language

linguaggio (leeng-*gwahd*-joa) *m* speech

lino (*lee*-noa) *m* linen

liquido (*lee*-kwee-doa) *adj* liquid

liquirizia (lee-kwee-*ree*-tsyah) *f* liquorice

liquore (lee-*kwaw*-ray) *m* liqueur; **spaccio di liquori** off-licence, liquor store *Am*

lisca (*lee*-skah) *f* fishbone

liscio (*leesh*-shoa) *adj* smooth

lista (*lee*-stah) *f* strip; list; **~ dei vini** wine list; **~ di attesa** waiting list

listino (lee-*stee*-noa) *f* price list

lite (*lee*-tay) *f* row, dispute, quarrel

litigare (lee-tee-*gaa*-ray) *v* quarrel

litigio (lee-*tee*-joa) *m* quarrel

litorale (lee-toa-*raa*-lay) *m* seacoast

litro (*lee*-troa) *m* litre, liter *Am*

livella (lee-*vehl*-lah) *f* level

livellare (lee-vayl-*laa*-ray) *v* level

livello (lee-*vehl*-loa) *m* level; **~ di vita** standard of living

livido (*lee*-vee-doa) *m* bruise

lo (loa) *pron* him; it

locale (loa-*kaa*-lay) *adj* local

località (loa-kah-lee-*tah*) *f* spot, locality

localizzare (loa-kah-leed-*dzaa*-ray) *v* locate

locanda (loa-*kahn*-dah) *f* inn, roadhouse; roadside restaurant

locomotiva (loa-koa-moa-*tee*-vah) *f* locomotive

lodare (loa-*daa*-ray) *v* praise

lode (*law*-day) *f* glory

loggione (load-*jōa*-nay) *m* gallery

logica (*law*-jee-kah) *f* logic

logico (*law*-jee-koa) *adj* logical

logorare (loa-goa-*raa*-ray) *v* wear out

lombaggine (loam-*bahd*-jee-nay) *f* lumbago

longitudine (loan-jee-*tōo*-dee-nay) *f* longitude

lontano (loan-*taa*-noa) *adj* far-off, far, distant

loquace (loa-*kwaa*-chay) *adj* talkative

lordo (*loar*-doa) *adj* gross

loro (*lōa*-roa) *adj* their; *pron* them; they

lotta (*lot*-tah) *f* combat, fight, battle; contest, struggle

lottare (loat-*taa*-ray) *v* *fight, struggle

lotteria (loat-tay-*ree*-ah) *f* lottery

lozione (loa-*tsyōa*-nay) *f* lotion

lubrificante (loo-bree-fee-*kahn*-tay) *m* lubrication oil

lubrificare (loo-bree-fee-*kaa*-ray) *v* grease, lubricate

lubrificazione (loo-bree-fee-kah-*tsyōa*-nay) *f* lubrication

lucchetto (look-*kayt*-toa) *m* padlock

luccio (*loot*-choa) *m* pike

luce (*lōo*-chay) *f* light; ~ **del giorno** daylight; ~ **del sole** sunshine, sunlight; ~ **laterale** sidelight; ~ **posteriore** taillight; **luci di arresto** brake lights; **luci di posizione** parking light

lucentezza (loo-chayn-*tayt*-tsah) *f* gloss

lucertola (loo-*chayr*-toa-lah) *f* lizard

lucidare (loo-chee-*daa*-ray) *v* polish

lucido (*lōo*-chee-doa) *adj* bright; glossy

luglio (*lōo*-l'oa) July

lui (looæ*h*) *pron* him; he

lumaca (loo-*maa*-kah) *f* snail

lume (*lōo*-may) *m* light; lamp

luminoso (loo-mee-*nōa*-soa) *adj* luminous

luna (*lōo*-nah) *f* moon; ~ **di miele** honeymoon

lunedì (loo-nay-*dee*) *m* Monday

lunghezza (loong-*gayt*-tsah) *f* length; ~ **d'onda** wavelength

lungo (*loong*-goa) *adj* long; tall; *prep* along, past; **di gran lunga** by far; **per** ~ lengthways

lungomare (loong-goa-*maa*-ray) *m* sea front

luogo (*lwaw*-goa) *m* spot; ***aver** ~ *take place; **in nessun** ~ nowhere; ~ **di nascita** place of birth; ~ **di villeggiatura** holiday resort

lupo (*lōo*-poa) *m* wolf

luppolo (*loop*-poa-loa) *m* hop

lusso (*looss*-soa) *m* luxury

lussuoso (looss-*swōa*-soa) *adj* luxurious

lutto (*loot*-toa) *m* mourning

M

macchia (*mahk*-kyah) *f* stain, spot, blot

macchiare (mahk-*kyaa*-ray) *v* stain

macchina (*mahk*-kee-nah) *f* engine, machine; car; ~ **da cucire** sewing machine; ~ **da scrivere** typewriter; ~ **fotografica** camera; ~ **sportiva** sports car

macchinario (mahk-kee-*naa*-ryoa) *m* machinery

macelleria (mah-chayl-*lay-ree*-ah) *m* butcher's shop

macinare (mah-chee-*naa*-ray) *v* *grind

macinino (mah-chee-*nee*-noa) *m* mill

madre (*maa*-dray) *f* mother

madrelingua (*maa*-dray-*leeng*-gwah) *f* mother tongue

madreperla (mah-dray-*pehr*-lah) *f* mother - of pearl

madrina (mah-*dree*-nah) *f* godmother

maestro (mah-*eh*-stroa) *m*, **-a** *f* master; schoolmaster, teacher

magari (mah-*gaa*-ree) *adv* even; *conj* even if

magazzinaggio (mah-gahd-dzee-*nahd*-joa) *m* storage

magazzino (mah-gahd-*dzee*-noa) *m* depository, warehouse, store house; **grande ~** department store; *****tenere in ~** stock

maggio (*mahd*-joa) May

maggioranza (mahd-joa-*rahn*-tsah) *f* majority

maggiore (mahd-*jōa*-ray) *adj* major, main, superior; elder; eldest; *m* major

maggiorenne (mahd-joa-*rehn*-nay) *adj* of age

magia (mah-*jee*-ah) *f* magic

magico (*maa*-jee-koa) *adj* magic

magistrato (mah-jee-*straa*-toa) *m* magistrate

maglia (*maa*-lᵞah) *f* mesh; vest

maglietta (mah-lᵞ*ayt*-tah) *f* undershirt

maglione (mah-lᵞ*ōa*-nay) *m* jersey, pullover, sweater

magnete (mah-*ñai*-tay) *m* magneto

magnetico (mah-*ñai*-tee-koa) *adj* magnetic

magnifico (mah-*ñee*-fee-koa) *adj* gorgeous, splendid, magnificent, swell

magro (*maa*-groa) *adj* thin, lean

mai (migh) *adv* ever; **non ... ~** never

maiale (mah-*yaa*-lay) *m* pig

maiuscola (mah-*yoo*-skoa-lah) *f* capital letter

malaria (mah-*laa*-ryah) *f* malaria

malato (mah-*laa*-toa) *adj* ill

malattia (mah-laht-*tee*-ah) *f* disease, ailment, illness; **~ venerea** venereal disease

male (*maa*-lay) *m* mischief, evil, harm; sickness; **mal d'aria** airsickness; **mal di denti** toothache; **mal di gola** sore throat; **mal di mare** seasickness; **mal di pancia** stomachache; **mal di schiena** backache; **mal di stomaco** stomach-ache; **mal di testa** headache; **mal d'orecchi** earache; **far ~** hurt

*****maledire** (mah-lay-*dee*-ray) *v* curse

Malesia (mah-*lai*-zyah) *f* Malaysia

malessere (mah-*lehss*-say-ray) *m* hangover

malevolo (mah-*lāy*-voa-loa) *adj* spiteful, malicious

malfermo (mahl-*fayr*-moa) *adj* unsteady

malgrado (mahl-*graa*-doa) *prep* in spite of, despite; *conj* although

maligno (mah-*lee*-ñoa) *adj* malignant

malinconia (mah-leeng-koa-*nee*-ah) *f* melancholy

malinconico (mah-leeng-*kaw*-nee-koa) *adj* sad

malinteso (mah-leen-*tāy*-soa) *m* misunderstanding

malizia (mah-*lee*-tsyah) *f* malice

malizioso (mah-lee-tsy*ōa*-soa) *adj* malicious

malsano (mahl-*saa*-noa) *adj* unhealthy

malsicuro (mahl-see-*kōō*-roa) *adj* unsafe

malvagio (mahl-*vaa*-joa) *adj* evil, ill

mamma (*mahm*-mah) *f* mum

mammifero (mahm-*mee*-fay-roa) *m*

mammal

mammut (mahm-*moot*) *m* mammoth

mancante (mahng-*kahn*-tay) *adj* missing

mancanza (mahng-*kahn*-tsah) *f* want, lack, shortage; fault

mancare (mahng-*kaa*-ray) *v* lack; fail

mancia (*mahn*-chah) *f* gratuity, tip

manciata (mahn-*chaa*-tah) *f* handful

mancino (mahn-*chee*-noa) *adj* left-handed

mandare (mahn-*daa*-ray) *v* *send

mandarino (mahn-dah-*ree*-noa) *m* mandarin, tangerine

mandato (mahn-*daa*-toa) *m* mandate

mandorla (*mahn*-doar-lah) *f* almond

maneggevole (mah-nayd-*jāy*-voa-lay) *adj* handy

maneggiabile (mah-nayd-*jaa*-bee-lay) *adj* manageable

maneggiare (mah-nayd-*jaa*-ray) *v* handle

manette (mah-*nayt*-tay) *fpl* handcuffs *pl*

mangiare (mahn-*jaa*-ray) *v* *eat; *m* food

mangiatoia (mahn-jah-*tōā*-yah) *f* manger

mania (mah-*nee*-ah) *f* craze

manica (*maa*-nee-kah) *f* sleeve; **La Manica** English Channel

manico (*maa*-nee-koa) *m* handle

manicure (mah-nee-*kōō*-ray) *f* manicure

maniera (mah-*nāy*-rah) *f* way, manner; **maniere** manners *pl*

manifestare (mah-nee-fay-*staa*-ray) *v* express

manifestazione (mah-nee-fay-stah-*tsyōā*-nay) *f* expression

maniglia (mah-*nee*-l'ah) *m* handle; strap

mano (*maa*-noa) *f* hand; **fatto a ~** hand-made

manopola (mah-*naw*-poa-lah) *f* knob

manoscritto (mah-noa-*skreet*-toa) *m* manuscript

mansueto (mahn-*swai*-toa) *adj* tame

mantella (mahn-*tehl*-lah) *f* cape

mantello (mahn-*tehl*-loa) *m* cloak

*mantenere (mahn-tay-*nāy*-ray) *v* maintain; *keep

mantenimento (mahn-tay-nee-*mayn*-toa) *m* upkeep

manuale (mah-*nwaa*-lay) *adj* manual; *m* handbook, textbook; **~ di conversazione** phrase book

manutenzione (mah-noo-tayn-*tsyōā*-nay) *f* maintenance

manzo (*mahn*-dzoa) *m* beef

mappa (*mahp*-pah) *f* map

marca (*mahr*-kah) *f* brand

marcare (mahr-*kaa*-ray) *v* mark

marchio (*mahr*-kyoa) *m* brand; **~ di fabbrica** trademark

marcia (*mahr*-chah) *f* march; gear; ***far ~ indietro** reverse; **~ indietro** reverse

marciapiede (mahr-chah-*pyai*-day) *m* pavement; sidewalk *Am*

marciare (mahr-*chaa*-ray) *v* march

marcio (*mahr*-choa) *adj* rotten

mare (*maa*-ray) *m* sea; **riva del ~** seaside

marea (mah-*rai*-ah) *f* tide; **alta ~** high tide; **bassa ~** low tide

margarina (mahr-gah-*ree*-nah) *f* margarine

margine (*mahr*-jee-nay) *m* edge; margin; **~ della strada** wayside, roadside

marina (mah-*ree*-nah) *f* navy; seascape

marinaio (mah-ree-*naa*-yoa) *m* sailor, seaman

marito (mah-*ree*-toa) *m* husband

marittimo (mah-*reet*-tee-moa) *adj* maritime

marmellata (mahr-mayl-*laa*-tah) *f* marmalade, jam

marmitta (mahr-*meet*-tah) *f* silencer, muffler *Am*

marmo (*mahr*-moa) *m* marble

marocchino (mah-roak-*kee*-noa) *adj* Moroccan; *m*, **-a** *f* Moroccan

Marocco (mah-*rok*-koa) *m* Morocco

marrone (mahr-*roa*-nay) *adj* brown

martedì (mahr-tay-*dee*) *m* Tuesday

martello (mahr-*tehl*-loa) *m* hammer

martire (*mahr*-tee-ray) *m* martyr

marzo (*mahr*-tsoa) March

mascella (mahsh-*shehl*-lah) *f* jaw

maschera (*mah*-skay-rah) *f* mask; usherette; ~ **di bellezza** face pack

maschile (mah-*skee*-lay) *adj* masculine, male

maschio (*mah*-skyoa) *adj* male

massa (*mahss*-sah) *f* lot, bulk; mass, crowd

massaggiare (mahss-sahd-*jaa*-ray) *v* massage

massaggiatore (mahss-sahd-jah-*tōā*-ray) *m*, **-trice** *f* masseur

massaggio (mahss-*sahd*-joa) *m* massage; ~ **facciale** face massage

massiccio (mahss-*seet*-choa) *adj* solid, massive

massimo (*mahss*-see-moa) *adj* greatest; **al** ~ at most

masso (*mahss*-soa) *m* boulder

masticare (mah-stee-*kaa*-ray) *v* chew

matematica (mah-tay-*maa*-tee-kah) *f* mathematics

matematico (mah-tay-*maa*-tee-koa) *adj* mathematical

materassino (mah-tay-rahss-*see*-noa) *m* airbed

materasso (mah-tay-*rahss*-soa) *m* mattress

materia (mah-*tai*-ryah) *f* matter; ~ **prima** raw material

materiale (mah-tay-*ryaa*-lay) *adj* material, substantial; *m* material

matita (mah-*tee*-tah) *f* pencil; ~ **per gli occhi** eyebrow pencil

matrice (mah-*tree*-chay) *f* stub

matrigna (mah-*tree*-ñah) *f* stepmother

matrimonio (mah-tree-*maw*-ñoa) *m* marriage; matrimony; wedding

mattina (maht-*tee*-nah) *f* morning

mattino (maht-*tee*-noa) *m* morning

matto (*maht*-toa) *adj* mad

mattone (maht-*tōā*-nay) *m* brick

mattonella (maht-toa-*nehl*-lah) *f* tile

maturità (mah-too-ree-*tah*) *f* maturity

maturo (mah-*tōō*-roa) *adj* ripe, mature

mausoleo (mou-zoa-*lai*-oa) *m* mausoleum

mazza (*maht*-tsah) *f* club; ~ **da golf** golfclub

mazzo (*maht*-tsoa) *m* bunch, bouquet

me (may) *pron* me

meccanico (mayk-*kaa*-nee-koa) *adj* mechanical; *m* mechanic

meccanismo (mayk-kah-*nee*-zmoa) *m* mechanism, machinery

medaglia (may-*daa*-lʸah) *f* medal

medesimo (may-*dāy*-zee-moa) *adj* same

media (*mai*-dyah) *f* average, mean; **in** ~ on the average

mediante (may-*dyahn*-tay) *prep* by means of

mediatore (may-dyah-*tōā*-ray) *m*, **-trice** *f* mediator; broker

medicina (may-dee-*chee*-nah) *f* medicine

medico (*mai*-dee-koa) *adj* medical; *m* physician, doctor; ~ **generico** general practitioner

medievale (may-dyay-*vaa*-lay) *adj* mediaeval

medio (*mai*-dyoa) *adj* medium; average

mediocre (may-*dyaw*-kray) *adj* ordinary; poor

medioevo (may-dyoa-*ai*-voa) *m*

Middle Ages

meditare (may-dee-*taa*-ray) *v* meditate

Mediterraneo (may-dee-tayr-*raa*-nay-oa) *m* Mediterranean

medusa (may-*doo*-zah) *f* jellyfish

meglio (*mai*-l*y*oa) *adv* better; best

mela (*may*-lah) *f* apple

melanzana (may-lahn-*tsaa*-nah) *f* eggplant

melma (*mayl*-mah) *f* muck

melodia (may-loa-*dee*-ah) *f* tune, melody

melodioso (may-loa-*dyoa*-soa) *adj* tuneful

melodramma (may-loa-*drahm*-mah) *m* melodrama

melone (may-*loa*-nay) *m* melon

membrana (maym-*braa*-nah) *f* membrane

membro(*mehm*-broa) *m* (pl i membri) member; **qualità di ~** membership

memorabile (may-moa-*raa*-bee-lay) *adj* memorable

memoria (may-*maw*-ryah) *f* memory; **a ~** by heart

ménage (may-*naazh*) *m* household

mendicante (mayn-dee-*kahn*-tay) *m* beggar

mendicare (mayn-dee-*kaa*-ray) *v* beg

meno (*may*-noa) *adv* less; minus; **a ~ che** unless; ***fare a ~ di** spare

mensa (*mayn*-sah) *f* canteen

mensile (mayn-*see*-lay) *adj* monthly

menta (*mayn*-tah) *f* mint; **~ piperita** peppermint

mentale (mayn-*taa*-lay) *adj* mental

mente (*mayn*-tay) *f* mind

mentire (mayn-*tee*-ray) *v* lie

mento (*mayn*-toa) *m* chin

mentre (*mayn*-tray) *conj* whilst, while

menu, menù (may-*noo*) *m* menu

menzionare (mayn-tsyoa-*naa*-ray) *v* mention

menzogna (mayn-*tsoa*-ñah) *f* lie

meraviglia (may-rah-*vee*-l*y*ah) *f* surprise; marvel

meravigliarsi (may-rah-vee-l*y*ahr-see) *v* marvel

meraviglioso (may-rah-vee-l*y*oa-soa) *adj* marvel(l)ous, fine, wonderful

mercante (mayr-*kahn*-tay) *m* merchant; **~ di vini** wine merchant

mercanteggiare (mayr-kahn-tayd-jaa-ray) *v* bargain

mercanzia (mayr-kahn-*tsee*-ah) *f* merchandise

mercato (mayr-*kaa*-toa) *m* market; **a buon ~** cheap; **~ nero** black market

merce (*mehr*-chay) *f* merchandise; **merci** goods *pl*, wares *pl*

merceria (mayr-chay-*ree*-ah) *f* haberdashery

mercoledì (mayr-koa-lay-*dee*) *m* Wednesday

mercurio (mayr-*koo*-ryoa) *m* mercury

merenda (may-*rehn*-dah) *f* tea; snack

meridionale (may-ree-dyoa-*naa*-lay) *adj* southern, southerly

meritare (may-ree-*taa*-ray) *v* deserve, merit

merito (*mai*-ree-toa) *m* merit

merletto (mayr-*layt*-toa) *m* lace

merlo (*mehr*-loa) *m* blackbird

merluzzo (mayr-*loot*-tsoa) *m* cod; **~ affumicato** haddock

meschino (may-*skee*-noa) *adj* mean; narrow-minded

mescolare (may-skoa-*laa*-ray) *v* mix; stir; shuffle

mese (*may*-say) *m* month

messa (*mayss*-sah) *f* Mass

messaggero (mayss-sahd-*jai*-roa) *m*, **-a** *f* messenger

messaggio (mayss-*sahd*-joa) *m* message

messicano (mayss-see-*kaa*-noa) *adj*

Mexican; *m*, **-a** *f* Mexican

Messico (*mehss*-see-koa) *m* Mexico

mestiere (may-*styai*-ray) *m* trade; business

mestruazione (may-strwah-*tsyoa*-nay) *f* menstruation

metà (may-*tah*) *f* half; **a ~** half

metallico (may-*tahl*-lee-koa) *adj* metal

metallo (may-*tahl*-loa) *m* metal

meticoloso (may-tee-koa-*loa*-soa) *adj* precise

metodico (may-*taw*-dee-koa) *adj* methodical

metodo (*mai*-toa-doa) *m* method

metrico (*mai*-tree-koa) *adj* metric

metro (*mai*-troa) *m* metre, meter *Am*

metropolitana (may-troa-poa-lee-*taa*-nah) *f* underground; subway *Am*

***mettere** (*mayt*-tay-ray) *v* *set, *put; *lay; **~ in imbarazzo** embarrass

mezzanotte (mayd-dzah-*not*-tay) *f* midnight

mezzo (*mehd*-dzoa) *adj* half; middle; *m* midst, middle; means; medium; **in ~ a** amid; among

mezzogiorno (mayd-dzoa-*joar*-noa) *m* midday, noon

mi (mee) *pron* me; myself

mica (*mee*-kah) (not) at all

miccia (*meet*-chah) *f* fuse

micia (*mee*-chah) *f* pussy-cat

microfono (mee-*kraw*-foa-noa) *m* microphone

midollo (mee-*doal*-loa) *m* marrow

miele (*myai*-lay) *m* honey

miglio (*mee*-lʸoa) *m* (pl le miglia) mile

miglioramento (mee-lʸoa-rah-*mayn*-toa) *m* improvement

migliorare (mee-lʸoa-*raa*-ray) *v* improve

migliore (mee-lʸ*oa*-ray) *adj* better; superior

mignolo (*mee*-ñoa-loa) *m* little finger

Milano (mee-*laa*-noa) *f* Milan

milionario (mee-lʸoa-*naa*-ryoa) *m*, **-a** *f* millionaire

milione (mee-lʸ*oa*-nay) *m* million

militare (mee-lee-*taa*-ray) *adj* military; *m* soldier

mille (*meel*-lay) *num* thousand

minaccia (mee-*naht*-chah) *f* threat

minacciare (mee-naht-*chaa*-ray) *v* threaten

minaccioso (mee-naht-*choa*-soa) *adj* threatening

minatore (mee-nah-*toa*-ray) *m* miner

minerale (mee-nay-*raa*-lay) *m* mineral; ore

minestra (mee-*neh*-strah) *f* soup

miniatura (mee-ñah-*too*-rah) *f* miniature

miniera (mee-*ñai*-rah) *f* mine, pit; **~ d'oro** goldmine

minimo (*mee*-nee-moa) *adj* least; *m* minimum

ministero (mee-nee-*stai*-roa) *m* ministry

ministro (mee-*nee*-stroa) *m* minister; **primo ~** Prime Minister, premier

minoranza (mee-noa-*rahn*-tsah) *f* minority

minore (mee-*noa*-ray) *adj* minor; junior

minorenne (mee-noa-*rehn*-nay) *adj* under age; *m* minor

minuscolo (mee-*noo*-skoa-loa) *adj* tiny

minuto (mee-*noo*-toa) *m* minute

minuzioso (mee-noo-*tsyoa*-soa) *adj* thorough

mio (*mee*-oa) *adj* (f mia; pl miei, mie) my

miope (*mee*-oa-pay) *adj* short-sighted

miracolo (mee-*raa*-koa-loa) *m* miracle

miracoloso (mee-rah-koa-*loa*-soa) *adj* miraculous

mirare a (mee-*raa*-ray) aim at

mirino (mee-*ree*-noa) *m* viewfinder

miscuglio (mee-*skoo*-l^{y}oa) *m* mixture

miserabile (mee-zay-*raa*-bee-lay) *adj* miserable

miseria (mee-*zai*-ryah) *f* misery

misericordia (mee-zay-ree-*kor*-dyah) *f* mercy

misericordioso (mee-zay-ree-koar-*dyoa*-soa) *adj* merciful

misero (mee-zay-roa) *adj* miserable; poor

missione (meess-*syoa*-nay) *f* mission

misterioso (mee-stay-*ryoa*-soa) *adj* mysterious

mistero (mee-*stai*-roa) *m* mystery

misto (mee-stoa) *adj* mixed

misura (mee-*zoo*-rah) *f* measure; size; **fatto su ~** made to order, tailor-made

misurare (mee-zoo-*raa*-ray) *v* measure

misuratore (mee-zoo-rah-*toa*-ray) *m* gauge

mite (mee-tay) *adj* mild

mitigare (mee-tee-*gaa*-ray) *v* relieve

mito (mee-toa) *m* myth

mittente (meet-*tayn*-tay) *m/f* sender

mobile (*maw*-bee-lay) *adj* mobile; movable; *m* a piece of furniture; **mobili** *pl* furniture

moda (*maw*-dah) *f* fashion; **alla ~** fashionable; **fuori ~** out of date

modellare (moa-dayl-*laa*-ray) *v* model

modella (moa-*dehl*-lah) *f* model

modello (moa-*dehl*-loa) *m* model

modem (*moa*-dem) *m* modem

moderato (moa-day-*raa*-toa) *adj* moderate

moderno (moa-*dehr*-noa) *adj* modern

modestia (moa-*deh*-styah) *f* modesty

modesto (moa-*deh*-stoa) *adj* modest

modifica (moa-*dee*-fee-kah) *f* alteration

modificare (moa-dee-fee-*kaa*-ray) *v* modify, change, alter

modo (*maw*-doa) *m* way, fashion, manner; **ad ogni ~** at any rate; **in nessun ~** by no means; **in ogni ~** anyhow; **nello stesso ~** likewise

modulo (*moa*-doo-loa) *m* form

moglie (*moa*-l^{y}ay) *f* wife

molare (moa-*laa*-ray) *m* molar

molesto (moa-*leh*-stoa) *adj* troublesome

molla (*mol*-lah) *f* spring

molleggio (moal-*layd*-joa) *m* suspension

molo (*maw*-loa) *m* pier, jetty; wharf, quay

moltiplicare (moal-tee-plee-*kaa*-ray) *v* multiply

moltiplicazione (moal-tee-plee-kah-*tsyoa*-nay) *f* multiplication

molto (*moal*-toa) *adj* much; *adv* very, quite; far, much; **molti** *adj* many

momentaneo (moa-mayn-*taa*-nay-oa) *adj* momentary

momento (moa-*mayn*-toa) *m* moment; **a momenti** presently

monaca (*maw*-nah-kah) *f* nun

monaco (*maw*-nah-koa) *m* monk

monarca (moa-*nahr*-kah) *m* monarch

monarchia (moa-nahr-*kee*-ah) *f* monarchy

monastero (moa-nah-*stai*-roa) *m* cloister, monastery

mondiale (moan-*dyaa*-lay) *adj* world-wide

mondo (*moan*-doa) *m* world

monello (moa-*nehl*-loa) *m*, **-a** *f* rascal

moneta (moa-*nāy*-tah) *f* coin

monetario (moa-nay-*taa*-ryoa) *adj* monetary

monologo (moa-*naw*-loa-goa) *m* monologue

monopattino (moa-noa-*paht*-tee-noa) *m* scooter

monopolio (moa-noa-*paw*-lyoa) *m*

monopoly

monotono (moa-*naw*-toa-noa) *adj*
monotonous, dull

montagna (moan-*taa*-ñah) *f* mountain

montagnoso (moan-tah-*ñoa*-soa) *adj*
mountainous

montare (moan-*taa*-ray) *v* mount; *get
on; assemble

montatura (moan-tah-*too*-rah) *f*
frame

monte (*moan*-tay) *m* mount

montone (moan-*toa*-nay) *m* mutton

monumento (moa-noo-*mayn*-toa) *m*
monument; ~ **commemorativo**
memorial

mora (*maw*-rah) *f* blackberry

morale (moa-*raa*-lay) *adj* moral; *f*
moral; *m* spirits

moralità (moa-rah-lee-*tah*) *f* morality

morbido (*mor*-bee-doa) *adj* soft,
smooth

morbillo (moar-*beel*-loa) *m* measles

*****mordere** (*mor*-day-ray) *v* *bite

morfina (moar-*fee*-nah) *f* morphine

*****morire** (moa-*ree*-ray) *v* die

mormorare (moar-moa-*raa*-ray) *v*
whisper

morsa (*mor*-sah) *f* clamp

morsetto (moar-*sayt*-toa) *m* clamp

morso (*mor*-soa) *m* bite

mortale (moar-*taa*-lay) *adj* fatal;
mortal

morte (*mor*-tay) *f* death

morto (*mor*-toa) *adj* dead

mosaico (moa-*zaa*-ee-koa) *m* mosaic

mosca (*moa*-skah) *f* fly

moschea (moa-*skai*-ah) *f* mosque

mossa (*moss*-sah) *f* move

mostra (*moa*-strah) *f* display;
exhibition; *****mettere in** ~ display; ~
d'arte *art* exhibition

mostrare (moa-*straa*-ray) *v* display,
*show; **mostrarsi** prove

motel (moa-*tayl*) *m* motel

motivo (moa-*tee*-voa) *m* cause,
occasion

moto (*maw*-toa) *m* motion

motocicletta (moa-toa-chee-*klayt*-
tah) *f* motorcycle

motonave (moa-toa-*naa*-vay) *f* launch

motore (moa-*toa*-ray) *m* motor,
engine

motorino (moa-toa-*ree*-noa) *m*
moped; motorbike *Am*

motoscafo (moa-toa-*skaa*-foa) *m*
motorboat

motto (*mot*-toa) *m* motto, slogan

movente (moa-*vehn*-tay) *m* motive

movimento (moa-vee-*mayn*-toa) *m*
movement

mozione (moa-*tsyoa*-nay) *f* motion

mucca (*mook*-ka) *f* cow

mucchio (*mook*-kyoa) *m* heap; **un ~
di** a lot of

muffa (*moof*-fah) *f* mildew

muffole (*moof*-foa-lay) *fpl* mittens *pl*

mugghiare (moog-*gyaa*-ray) *v* roar

mugnaio (moo-*ñaa*-yoa) *m* miller

mulino (moo-*lee*-noa) mill; ~ **a vento**
windmill

mulo (*moo*-loa) *m* mule

multa (*mool*-tah) *f* fine; parking ticket

municipale (moo-nee-chee-*paa*-lay)
adj municipal

municipio (moo-nee-*chee*-pyoa) *m*
town hall

munifico (moo-*nee*-fee-koa) *adj*
generous

*****muovere** (*mwaw*-vay-ray) *v* move,
stir

murare (moo-*raa*-ray) *v* *lay bricks

muratore (moo-rah-*toa*-ray) *m*
bricklayer

muro (*moo*-roa) *m* wall

muschio (*moo*-skyoa) *m* moss

muscolo (*moo*-skoa-loa) *m* muscle

muscoloso (moo-skoa-*loa*-soa) *adj*
muscular

museo (moo-*zai*-oa) *m* museum; ~ **delle cere** waxworks *pl*

musica ($m\overline{oo}$-zee-kah) *f* music

musicale (moo-zee-*kaa*-lay) *adj* musical

musicista (moo-zee-*chee*-stah) *m/f* musician

muso ($m\overline{oo}$-zoa) *m* snout

mutamento (moo-tah-*mayn*-toa) *m* variation

mutande (moo-*tahn*-day) *fpl* drawers; panties *pl*, pants *pl*; shorts *plAm*

mutandine (moo-tahn-*dee*-nay) *fpl* panties *pl*, briefs *pl*; underpants *plAm*

mutare (moo-*taa*-ray) *v* change

muto ($m\overline{oo}$-toa) *adj* mute, dumb; speechless

mutuo ($m\overline{oo}$-twoa) *adj* mutual

N

nafta (*nahf*-tah) *f* fuel oil

nailon (*nigh*-loan) *m* nylon

nano (*naa*-noa) *m* dwarf

Napoli (*naa*-poa-lee) *f* Naples

narciso (nahr-*chee*-zoa) *m* daffodil

narcosi (nahr-*kaw*-zee) *f* narcosis

narcotico (nahr-*kaw*-tee-koa) *m* narcotic, drug

narice (nah-*ree*-chay) *f* nostril

***nascere** (*nahsh*-shay-ray) *v* *be born

nascita (*nahsh*-shee-tah) *f* birth

***nascondere** (nah-*skoan*-day-ray) *v* *hide; conceal

naso (*naa*-soa) *m* nose

nastro (*nah*-stroa) *m* ribbon; tape; ~ **adesivo** adhesive tape

Natale (nah-*taa*-lay) Xmas, Christmas

natica (*naa*-tee-kah) *f* buttock

nativo (nah-*tee*-voa) *adj* native

nato (*naa*-toa) *adj* born

natura (nah-$t\overline{oo}$-rah) *f* nature

naturale (nah-too-*raa*-lay) *adj* natural

naturalmente (nah-too-rahl-*mayn*-tay) *adv* of course, naturally

nausea (*nou*-zay-ah) *f* nausea, sickness

nauseante (nou-zay-*ahn*-tay) *adj* disgusting

nauseato (nou-zay-*aa*-toa) *adj* sick

navale (nah-*vaa*-lay) *adj* naval; **cantiere** ~ shipyard

nave (*naa*-vay) *f* ship; vessel; ~ **da guerra** man-of-war; ~ **di linea** liner

navigabile (nah-vee-*gaa*-bee-lay) *adj* navigable

navigare (nah-vee-*gaa*-ray) *v* sail, navigate

navigazione (nah-vee-gah-*tsyoa*-nay) *f* navigation

nazionale (nah-tsyoa-*naa*-lay) *adj* national

nazionalità (nah-tsyoa-nah-lee-*tah*) *f* nationality

nazionalizzare (nah-tsyoa-nah-leed-*dzaa*-ray) *v* nationalize

nazione (nah-*tsyoa*-nay) *f* nation

ne (nay) *pron* of it; about him; it

né ... né (nay) neither ... nor

neanche (nay-*ahng*-kay) *adv* not even; *conj* nor

nebbia (*nayb*-byah) *f* mist, fog

nebbioso (nayb-*byoa*-soa) *adj* misty, hazy, foggy

necessario (nay-chayss-*saa*-ryoa) *adj* necessary

necessità (nay-chayss-see-*tah*) *f*

necessity; need

necroscopia (nay-kroa-skoa-*pee*-ah) *f* autopsy

negare (nay-*gaa*-ray) *v* deny

negativa (nay-gah-*tee*-vah) *f* negative

negativo (nay-gah-*tee*-voa) *adj* negative

negligente (nay-glee-*jehn*-tay) *adj* neglectful

negligenza (nay-glee-*jehn*-tsah) *f* neglect

negoziante (nay-goa-*tsyahn*-tay) *m/f* dealer; shopkeeper

negoziare (nay-goa-*tsyaa*-ray) *v* negotiate

negozio (nay-*gaw*-tsyoa) *m* shop; **~ di ferramenta** hardware store; **~ di fiori** flower shop; **~ di giocattoli** toyshop

nemico (nay-*mee*-koa) *m*, **-a** *f* enemy

nemmeno (naym-*māy*-noa) *adv* not even; *conj* nor

neon (*nai*-oan) *m* neon

neonato (nay-oa-*naa*-toa) *m* infant

neppure (nayp-*pōō*-ray) *adv* not even; *conj* nor

nero (*nāy*-roa) *adj* black

nervo (*nehr*-voa) *m* nerve

nervoso (nayr-*vōa*-soa) *adj* nervous

nessuno (nayss-*sōō*-noa) *adj* no; *pron* none, nobody, no one

netto (*nayt*-toa) *adj* net

neutrale (nay⁻*traa*-lay) *adj* neutral

neutro (*neh⁰⁰*-troa) *adj* neuter

neve (*nāy*-vay) *f* snow; **~ fangosa** slush

nevicare (nay-vee-*kaa*-ray) *v* snow

nevoso (nay-*vōa*-soa) *adj* snowy

nevralgia (nay-vrahl-*jee*-ah) *f* neuralgia

nevrosi (nay-*vraw*-zee) *f* neurosis

nichelio (nee-*kai*-lʸoa) *m* nickel

nicotina (nee-koa-*tee*-nah) *f* nicotine

nido (*nee*-doa) *m* nest

niente (*ñehn*-tay) *pron* nothing

Nigeria (nee-*jai*-ryah) *f* Nigeria

nigeriano (nee-jay-*ryaa*-noa) *adj* Nigerian; *m*, **-a** *f* Nigerian

nipote (nee-*pōa*-tay) *m* grandson; nephew; *f* granddaughter; niece; *m/f* grandchild

no (no) no

nobile (*naw*-bee-lay) *adj* noble

nobiltà (noa-beel-*tah*) *f* nobility

nocca (*nok*-kah) *f* knuckle

nocciola (noat-*chaw*-lah) *f* hazelnut

nocciolo (*not*-choa-loa) *m* stone; essence, heart

noce (*nōa*-chay) *f* nut; walnut; **~ di cocco** coconut; **~ moscata** nutmeg

nocivo (noa-*chee*-voa) *adj* harmful, hurtful

nodo (*naw*-doa) *m* knot; lump; **~ scorsoio** loop

nodulo (*naw*-doo-loa) *m* lump

noi (noi) *pron* we; **~ stessi** ourselves

noia (*naw*-yah) *f* annoyance; bother

noioso (noa-*yōa*-soa) *adj* annoying, dull, boring

noleggiare (noa-layd-*jaa*-ray) *v* hire

noleggio (noa-*layd*-dʒoa) *m* hire

nolo: a ~ (ah *naw*-loa) for hire

nome (*nōa*-may) *m* name; first name; denomination; noun; **a ~ di** in the name of; **~ di battesimo** Christian name

nomina (*naw*-mee-nah) *f* appointment, nomination

nominale (noa-mee-*naa*-lay) *adj* nominal

nominare (noa-mee-*naa*-ray) *v* mention, name; appoint, nominate

non (noan) not; **~ ... mai** never; **~ ... più** no longer

nonché (noang-*kay*) *conj* as well as

noncurante (noang-koo-*rahn*-tay) *adj* careless

nonna (*non*-nah) *f* grandmother

nonno (*non*-noa) *m* grandfather,

granddad; **nonni** grandparents *pl*

nono (*naw*-noa) *num* ninth

nonostante (noa-noa-*stahn*-tay) *prep* in spite of

nord (nord) *m* north; **polo Nord** North Pole

nord-est (nor-*dehst*) *m* northeast

nordico (*nor*-dee-koa) *adj* northern

nord-ovest (nor-*daw*-vayst) *m* northwest

norma (*nor*-mah) *f* standard; **di ~** as a rule

normale (noar-*maa*-lay) *adj* normal; standard, regular

norvegese (noar-vay-*jāy*-say) *adj* Norwegian; *m/f* Norwegian

Norvegia (noar-*vāy*-jah) *f* Norway

nostalgia (noa-stahl-*jee*-ah) *f* homesickness

nostro (*no*-stroa) *adj* our

nota (*naw*-tah) *f* memo; tone

notaio (noa-*taa*-yoa) *m* notary

notare (noa-*taa*-ray) *v* note; notice

notevole (noa-*tāy*-voa-lay) *adj* considerable, remarkable, noticeable, striking

notificare (noa-tee-fee-*kaa*-ray) *v* notify

notizia (noa-*tee*-tsyah) *f* notice; **notizie** news

notiziario (noa-tee-*tsyaa*-ryoa) *m* news

noto (*naw*-toa) *adj* well-known

notte (*not*-tay) *f* night; **di ~** by night; overnight

notturno (noat-*toor*-noa) *adj* nightly; **locale ~** nightclub

novanta (noa-*vahn*-tah) *num* ninety

nove (*naw*-vay) *num* nine

novembre (noa-*vehm*-bray) November

novità (noa-vee-*tah*) *f* news

nozione (noa-*tsyoā*-nay) *f* notion

nozze (*noat*-tse) *fpl* wedding

nubile (*nōō*-bee-lay) *adj* unmarried

nuca (*nōō*-kah) *f* nape of the neck

nucleare (noo-klay-*aa*-ray) *adj* nuclear

nucleo (*nōō*-klay-oa) *m* core, nucleus

nudo (*nōō*-doa) *adj* nude, bare, naked; *m* nude

nulla (*nool*-lah) *m* nothing

nullo (*nool*-loa) *adj* invalid, void

numerale (noo-may-*raa*-lay) *m* numeral

numero (*nōō*-may-roa) *m* number; digit; quantity; act; **~ di targa** registration number; license number *Am*

numeroso (noo-may-*roā*-soa) *adj* numerous

***nuocere** (*nwaw*-chay-ray) *v* harm

nuora (*nwaw*-rah) *f* daughter-in-law

nuotare (nwoa-*taa*-ray) *v* *swim

nuotatore (nwoa-tah-*tōā*-ray) *m*, **-trice** *f* swimmer

nuoto (*nwaw*-toa) *m* swimming; **~ a farfalla** butterfly stroke; **~ a rana** breaststroke

nuovamente (nwaw-vah-*mayn*-tay) *adv* again

Nuova Zelanda (*nwaw*-vah tsay-*lahn*-dah) New Zealand

nuovo (*nwaw*-voa) *adj* new; **di ~** again; **~ fiammante** brand-new

nutriente (noo-*tryehn*-tay) *adj* nutritious

nutrire (noo-*tree*-ray) *v* *feed

nuvola (*nōō*-voa-lah) *f* cloud

nuvoloso (noo-voa-*lōā*-soa) *adj* cloudy

O

o (oa) *conj* or; **~ ... o** either ... or

oasi (*aw*-ah-zee) *f* oasis

obbligare (oab-blee-*gaa*-ray) *v* oblige

obbligatorio (oab-blee-gah-*taw*-ryoa) *adj* compulsory, obligatory

obbligazione (oab-blee-gah-*tsyoa*-nay) *f* bond

obbligo (*ob*-blee-goa) *m* obligation

obeso (oa-*bai*-zoa) *adj* corpulent, stout

obiettare (oa-byayt-*taa*-ray) *v* object

obiettivo (oa-byayt-*tee*-voa) *m* objective, object

obiezione (oa-byay-*tsyoa*-nay) *f* objection; ***fare ~ a** mind

obliquo (oa-*blee*-kwoa) *adj* slanting

oca (*aw*-kah) *f* goose

occasionalmente (oak-kah-zyoa-nahl-*mayn*-tay) *adv* occasionally

occasione (oak-kah-*zyoa*-nay) *f* chance, occasion, opportunity

occhiali (oak-*kyaa*-lee) *mpl* spectacles, glasses; **~ da sole** sunglasses *pl*; **~ di protezione** goggles *pl*

occhiata (oak-*kyaa*-tah) *f* glimpse, glance, look; ***dare un'occhiata** glance

occhio (*ok*-kyoa) *m* eye; ***tenere d'occhio** watch

occidentale (oat-chee-dayn-*taa*-lay) *adj* western; westerly

occidente (oat-chee-*dehn*-tay) *m* west

*occorrere (oak-*koar*-ray-ray) *v* need

occupante (oak-koo-*pahn*-tay) *m/f* occupant

occupare (oak-koo-*paa*-ray) *v* occupy, *take up; **occuparsi di** attend to, look after, see to, *take care of; **occupato** *adj* busy, engaged; occupied

occupazione (oak-koo-pah-*tsyoa*-nay) *f* occupation; employment

oceano (oa-*chai*-ah-noa) *m* ocean

oculista (oa-koo-*lee*-stah) *m/f* oculist

odiare (oa-*dyaa*-ray) *v* hate

odio (*aw*-dyoa) *m* hatred, hate

odorare (oa-doa-*raa*-ray) *v* *smell

odore (oa-*doa*-ray) *m* odo(u)r, smell

*offendere (oaf-*fehn*-day-ray) *v* injure, offend, wound, *hurt

offensiva (oaf-fayn-*see*-vah) *f* offensive

offensivo (oaf-fayn-*see*-voa) *adj* offensive

offerta (oaf-*fehr*-tah) *f* offer; supply

offesa (oaf-*fāy*-sah) *f* offence, offense *Am*

officina (oaf-feet-*chee*-nah) *f* workshop; garage

*offrire (oaf-*free*-ray) *v* offer

offuscato (oaf-foo-*skaa*-toa) *adj* dim

oggettivo (oad-jayt-*tee*-voa) *adj* objective

oggetto (oad-*jeht*-toa) *m* object; **oggetti smarriti** lost and found

oggi (*od*-jee) *adv* today

oggigiorno (oad-jee-*joar*-noa) *adv* nowadays

ogni (*ōa*-ñee) *adj* every, each; **~ volta che** whenever

ognuno (oa-*ñōō*-noa) *pron* everyone, everybody

Olanda (oa-*lahn*-dah) *f* Holland

olandese (oa-lahn-*dāy*-say) *adj* Dutch

oleoso (oa-lay-*ōa*-soa) *adj* oily

olio (*aw*-lʲoa) *m* oil; **~ abbronzante** suntan oil; **~ da tavola** salad oil; **~ d'oliva** olive oil

oliva (oa-*lee*-vah) *f* olive

olmo (*oal*-moa) *m* elm

oltraggio (oal-*trahd*-joa) *m* outrage

oltre (*oal*-tray) *prep* beyond; over; **~ a** besides

oltremare (oal-tray-*mah*-ray) *adj* overseas

omaggio (oa-*mahd*-joa) *m* tribute, homage

ombelico (oam-bay-*lee*-koa) *m* navel

ombra (*oam*-brah) *f* shadow, shade

ombreggiato (oam-brayd-*jaa*-toa) *adj* shady

ombrello (oam-*brehl*-loa) *m* umbrella

ombrellone (oam-brayl-*lōa*-nay) *m* beach umbrella

ombretto (oam-*brayt*-toa) *m* eye shadow

***omettere** (oa-*mayt*-tay-ray) *v* omit, *leave out; skip

omicidio (oa-mee-*chee*-dyoa) *m* murder

omosessuale (oa-moa-sayss-*swaa*-lay) *adj* homosexual

onda (*oan*-dah) *f* wave

ondulare (oan-doo-*laa*-ray) *v* curl

ondulato (oan-doo-*laa*-toa) *adj* wavy

onestà (oa-nay-*stah*) *f* honesty

onesto (oa-*neh*-stoa) *adj* honest; fair, straight; hono(u)rable

onice (*aw*-nee-chay) *f* onyx

onnipotente (oan-nee-poa-*tehn*-tay) *adj* omnipotent

onorare (oa-noa-*raa*-ray) *v* hono(u)r

onorario (oa-noa-*raa*-ryoa) *m* fee

onore (oa-*nōa*-ray) *m* glory, hono(u)r

onorevole (oa-noa-*rāy*-voa-lay) *adj* hono(u)rable

opaco (oa-*paa*-koa) *adj* dim, mat

opale (oa-*paa*-lay) *m* opal

opera (*aw*-pay-rah) *f* opera

operaio (oa-pay-*raa*-yoa) *m*, **-a** *f* worker

operare (oa-pay-*rah*-ray) *v* operate

operazione (oa-pay-rah-*tsyōa*-nay) *f* surgery, operation

operetta (oa-pay-*rayt*-tah) *f* operetta

opinione (oa-pee-*nōa*-nay) *f* view, opinion

***opporsi** (oap-*poar*-see) *v* oppose; **~ a** object to

opportunità (oap-poar-too-nee-*tah*) *f* chance, opportunity

opportuno (oap-poar-*tōō*-noa) *adj* opportune

opposizione (oap-poa-zee-*tsyōa*-nay) *f* opposition

opposto (oap-*poa*-stoa) *adj* opposite

***opprimere** (oap-*pree*-may-ray) *v* oppress

oppure (oap-*pōō*-ray) *conj* or

opuscolo (oa-*poo*-skoa-loa) *m* brochure

ora (*ōa*-rah) *f* hour; *adv* now; **~ d'arrivo** time of arrival; **~ di partenza** time of departure; **~ di punta** rush hour, peak hour; **ore d'ufficio** office hours, business hours; **quarto d'ora** quarter of an hour

orale (oa-*raa*-lay) *adj* oral

orario (oa-*raa*-ryoa) *m* timetable, schedule; **~ di apertura** business hours; **~ delle visite** visiting hours; **~ di ricevimento** consultation hours; **~ estivo** summer time

orchestra (oar-*keh*-strah) *f* orchestra

ordinare (oar-dee-*naa*-ray) *v* arrange; order

ordinario (oar-dee-*naa*-ryoa) *adj* ordinary

ordinato (oar-dee-*naa*-toa) *adj* tidy

ordinazione (oar-dee-nah-*tsyōa*-nay) *f* order; **modulo di ~** order form

ordine (*oar*-dee-nay) *m* order; method; command; **in ~** in order; ***mettere in ~** arrange

orecchino (oa-rayk-*kee*-noa) *m* earring

orecchio (oa-*rayk*-kyoa) *m* ear

orecchioni (oa-rayk-*kyōa*-nee) *mpl* mumps

orefice (oa-*rāy*-fee-chay) *m* goldsmith

orfano (*or*-fah-noa) *m* orphan

organico (oar-*gaa*-nee-koa) *adj* organic

organismo (oar-gah-*nee*-zmoa) *m* organism

organizzare (oar-gah-need-*dza*-ray) *v* organize; arrange

organizzazione (oar-gah-need-dzah-*tsyoa*-nay) *f* organization

organo (*or*-gah-noa) *m* organ

orgoglio (oar-*gaw*-lʲoa) *m* pride

orgoglioso (oar-goa-lʲoa-soa) *adj* proud

orientale (oa-ryayn-*taa*-lay) *adj* eastern; easterly; oriental

orientarsi (oa-ryayn-*tahr*-see) *v* orientate

oriente (oa-*ryehn*-tay) *m* east; Orient

originale (oa-ree-jee-*naa*-lay) *adj* original

originariamente (oa-ree-jee-nah-ryah-*mayn*-tay) *adv* originally

origine (oa-*ree*-jee-nay) *f* origin

origliare (oa-ree-lʲ*aa*-ray) *v* eavesdrop

orizzontale (oa-reed-dzoan-*taa*-lay) *adj* horizontal

orizzonte (oa-reed-*dzoan*-tay) *m* horizon

orlo (*oar*-loa) *m* rim, brim; hem

ormai (oar-*mah*-ee) *adv* by now; by then

ornamentale (oar-nah-mayn-*taa*-lay) *adj* ornamental

ornamento (oar-nah-*mayn*-toa) *m* ornament

oro (*aw*-roa) *m* gold; ~ **laminato** gold leaf

orologiaio (oa-roa-loa-*jaa*-yoa) *m*, -a *f* watchmaker

orologio (oa-roa-*law*-joa) *m* watch; clock; ~ **da polso** wristwatch

orrendo (oar-*rehn*-doa) *adj* hideous

orribile (oar-*ree*-bee-lay) *adj* horrible

orrore (oar-*roa*-ray) *m* horror

orso (*oar*-soa) *m* bear

orticaria (oar-*tee*-kaa-rya) *f* nettle rash

orto (*or*-toa) *m* kitchen garden

ortodosso (oar-toa-*doss*-soa) *adj* orthodox

ortografia (oar-toa-grah-*fee*-ah) *f* spelling

orzo (*or*-dzoa) *m* barley

osare (oa-*zaa*-ray) *v* dare

osceno (oash-*shai*-noa) *adj* obscene

oscurità (oa-skoo-ree-*tah*) *f* gloom, dark

oscuro (oa-*skoo*-roa) *adj* dim, dark; obscure

ospedale (oa-spay-*daa*-lay) *m* hospital

ospitale (oa-spee-*taa*-lay) *adj* hospitable

ospitalità (oa-spee-tah-lee-*tah*) *f* hospitality

ospitare (oa-spee-*taa*-ray) *v* entertain

ospite (*o*-spee-tay) *f* hostess, host; *m* guest; **camera degli ospiti** spare room

ospizio (oa-*spee*-tsyoa) *m* old folk's home

osservare (oass-sayr-*vaa*-ray) *v* observe; watch, regard; remark, note

osservatorio (oass-sayr-vah-*toa*-ryoa) *m* observatory

osservazione (oass-sayr-vah-*tsyoa*-nay) *f* observation; remark

ossessione (oass-sayss-*syoa*-nay) *f* obsession

ossia (oass-*see*-ah) *conj* that is; or rather

ossigeno (oass-*see*-jay-noa) *m* oxygen

osso (*oss*-soa) *m* (pl le ossa) bone

ostacolare (oa-stah-koa-*laa*-ray) *v* hinder; handicap

ostacolo (oa-*staa*-koa-loa) *m* obstacle

ostaggio (oa-*stahd*-joa) *m* hostage

ostello (oa-*stehl*-loa) *m* hostel; ~ **della gioventù** youth hostel

osteria (oa-stay-*ree*-ah) *f* inn

ostetrica (*o-stay*-tree-kah) *f* obstetrician

ostia (*o*-styah) *f* wafer; host

ostile (oa-*stee*-lay) *adj* hostile

ostinato (oa-stee-*naa*-toa) *adj* obstinate, dogged

ostrica (*o*-stree-kah) *f* oyster

ostruire (oa-strwee-ray) *v* block

otite (oa-*tee*-tay) *f* ear infection

ottanta (oat-*tahn*-tah) *num* eighty

ottavo (oat-*taa*-voa) *num* eighth

*ottenere (oat-tay-*nāy*-ray) *v* *get, obtain; acquire

ottico (*ot*-tee-koa) *m*, **-a** *f* optician

ottimismo (oat-tee-*mee*-zmoa) *m* optimism

ottimista (oat-tee-*mee*-stah) *m* optimist

ottimistico (oat-tee-*mee*-stee-koa) *adj* optimistic

ottimo (*ot*-tee-moa) *adj* excellent, first-rate, fine; best

otto (*ot*-toa) *num* eight

ottobre (oat-*tōā*-bray) October

ottone (oat-*tōā*-nay) *m* brass

otturazione (oat-too-rah-*tsyōā*-nay) *f* filling

ottuso (oat-*tōō*-zoa) *adj* blunt; dumb

ovale (oa-*vaa*-lay) *adj* oval

ovatta (oa-*vaht*-tah) *f* cotton wool

ovest (*aw*-vayst) *m* west

ovunque (oa-*voong*-kway) *adv* anywhere, everywhere

ovvio (*ov*-vyoa) *adj* obvious, apparent

ozioso (oa-*tsyōā*-soa) *adj* idle

ozono (oa-*dzōā*-noa) *m* ozone

P

pacchetto (pahk-*kayt*-toa) *m* parcel, packet

pacco (*pahk*-koa) *m* parcel, package

pace (*paa*-chay) *f* peace

pachistano (pah-kee-*staa*-noa) *adj* Pakistani; *m*, **-a** *f* Pakistani

pacifico (pah-*chee*-fee-koa) *adj* peaceful

pacifismo (pah-chee-*fee*-zmoa) *m* pacifism

pacifista (pah-chee-*fee*-stah) *m/f* pacifist; *adj* pacifist

padella (pah-*dehl*-lah) *f* frying pan

padiglione (pah-dee-*lʸōā*-nay) *m* pavilion

padre (*paa*-dray) *m* father; dad

padrino (pah-*dree*-noa) *m* godfather

padrona (pah-*drōā*-nah) *f* mistress

padrone (pah-*drōā*-nay) *m* master, boss; ~ **di casa** landlord

paesaggio (pahᵃʸ-*zahd*-joa) *m* landscape, scenery

paese (pah-*āy*-zay) *m* country; village; region; ~ **natio** native country

Paesi Bassi (pah-*āy*-zee *bahss*-see) the Netherlands

paga (*paa*-gah) *f* pay

pagamento (pah-gah-*mayn*-toa) *m* payment

pagano (pah-*gaa*-noa) *adj* pagan, heathen; *m*, **-a** *f* pagan, heathen

pagare (pah-*gaa*-ray) *v* *pay; ***far ~** charge; ~ **a rate** *pay on account; **pagato in anticipo** prepaid

pagina (*paa*-jee-nah) *f* page

paglia (*paa*-lʸah) *f* straw

pagliaccio (pah-*lʸaht*-choa) *m* clown

pagnotta (pah-*ñot*-tah) *f* loaf

paio (*paa*-yoa) *m* (pl le paia) pair

Pakistan (pah-kee-*stahn*) *m* Pakistan

pala (*paa*-lah) *f* shovel

palazzo (pah-*laht*-tsoa) *m* palace; mansion

palco (*pahl*-koa) *m* stage

palestra (pah-*leh*-strah) *f* gymnasium, gym

palla (*pahl*-lah) *f* ball

pallacanestro (*pahl*-lah-cah-*nay*-stroa) *f* basketball

pallavolo (*pahl*-lah-*vōa*-loa) *f* volley ball

pallido (*pahl*-lee-doa) *adj* pale; dim, mat

pallina (pahl-*lee*-nah) *f* marble

pallino (pahl-*lee*-noa) *m* hobbyhorse

palloncino (pahl-loan-*chee*-noa) *m* balloon

pallone (pahl-*lōa*-nay) *m* football

pallottola (pahl-*lot*-toa-lah) *f* bullet

palma (*pahl*-mah) *f* palm

palo (*paa*-loa) *m* pole, post

palpare (pahl-*paa*-ray) *v* *feel

palpebra (*pahl*-pay-brah) *f* eyelid

palpitazione (pahl-pee-tah-*tsyōa*-nay) *f* palpitation

palude (pah-*lōō*-day) *f* marsh, swamp, bog

pancia (*pahn*-chah) *f* belly

panciotto (pahn-*chot*-toa) *m* waistcoat; vest *Am*

pane (*paa*-nay) *m* bread; **~ integrale** wholemeal bread

panettiere (pah-nayt-*tyai*-ray) *m* baker

panificio (pah-nee-*fee*-choa) *f* bakery

paninoteca (pah-nee-noa-*tay*-kah) *f* sandwich shop

panfilo (*pahn*-fee-loa) *m* yacht

panico (*paa*-nee-koa) *m* panic

paniere (pah-*ñai*-ray) *m* hamper, basket

panino (pah-*nee*-noa) *m* roll, bun

panna (*pahn*-nah) *f* cream

pannello (pahn-*nehl*-loa) *m* panel; **rivestimento a pannelli** panelling

panno (*pahn*-noa) *m* cloth

pannolino (pahn-noa-*lee*-noa) *m* nappy; diaper *Am*; **~ igienico** sanitary towel

pantaloncini (pahn-tah-loan-*chee*-nee) *mpl* shorts

pantaloni (pahn-tah-*lōa*-nee) *mpl* trousers *pl*

pantofola (pahn-*taw*-foa-lah) *f* slipper

Papa (*paa*-pah) *m* pope

papà (pah-*pah*) *m* daddy

papavero (pah-*paa*-vay-roa) *m* poppy

pappagallo (pahp-pah-*gahl*-loa) *m* parrot

parabrezza (pah-rah-*brayd*-dzah) *m* windscreen; windshield *Am*

parafango (pah-rah-*fahng*-goa) *m* wing; fender *Am*

paragonare (pah-rah-goa-*naa*-ray) *v* compare

paragone (pah-rah-*gōa*-nay) *m* comparison

paragrafo (pah-*raa*-grah-foa) *m* paragraph

paralitico (pah-rah-*lee*-tee-koa) *adj* lame

paralizzare (pah-rah-leed-*dzaa*-ray) *v* paralyse

parallela (pah-rahl-*lai*-lah) *f* parallel

parallelo (pah-rahl-*lai*-loa) *adj* parallel

paralume (pah-rah-*lōō*-may) *m* lampshade

parata (pah-*raa*-tah) *f* parade

paraurti (pah-rah-*oor*-tee) *m* bumper

parcheggiare (pahr-kayd-*dʒah*-ray) *v* park

parcheggio (pahr-*kehd*-joa) *m* parking; car park; parking lot *Am*

parchimetro (pahr-*kee*-may-troa) *m* parking meter

parco (*pahr*-koa) *m* park; ~ **giochi** playground; ~ **nazionale** national park

parecchi (pah-*rayk*-kee) *adj* several

pareggiare (pah-rayd-*jaa*-ray) *v* level; equalize

parente (pah-*rehn*-tay) *m/f* relative

parere (pah-*rāy*-ray) *m* view, opinion

*parere (pah-*rāy*-ray) *v* seem

parete (pah-*rāy*-tay) *f* wall

pari (*paa*-ree) *adj* even

parlamentare (pahr-lah-mayn-*taa*-ray) *adj* parliamentary

parlamento (pahr-lah-*mayn*-toa) *m* parliament

parlare (pahr-*laa*-ray) *v* *speak, talk

parola (pah-*raw*-lah) *f* word; speech; ~ **d'ordine** password

parrocchia (pahr-*rok*-kyah) *f* parish

parrucca (pahr-*rook*-kah) *f* wig

parrucchiere (pahr-rook-*kyai*-ray) *m*, **-a** *f* hairdresser

parsimonioso (pahr-see-moa-*nyōa*-soa) *adj* thrifty, economical

parte (*pahr*-tay) *f* part; share; side; **a ~** apart, separately; **dall'altra ~** across; **dall'altra ~ di** across; **da ~** aside; **in ~** partly; **una ~** some

partecipante (pahr-tay-chee-*pahn*-tay) *m/f* participant

partecipare (pahr-tay-chee-*paa*-ray) *v* participate

partenza (pahr-*tehn*-tsah) *f* departure

particolare (pahr-tee-koa-*laa*-ray) *adj* particular, special, peculiar; *m* detail; **in ~** in particular

particolareggiato (pahr-tee-koa-lah-rayd-*jaa*-toa) *adj* detailed

particolarmente (pahr-tee-koa-lahr-*mayn*-tay) *adv* specially

partire (pahr-*tee*-ray) *v* depart, *leave; *set out; pull out; **a ~ da** as from

partita (pahr-*tee*-tah) *f* batch; match; ~ **di calcio** football match

partito (pahr-*tee*-toa) *m* party

parto (*pahr*-toa) *m* delivery, childbirth

parziale (pahr-*tsyaa*-lay) *adj* partial

pascolare (pah-skoa-*laa*-ray) *v* graze

pascolo (*pah*-skoa-loa) *m* pasture

Pasqua (*pah*-skwah) Easter

passaggio (pahss-*sahd*-joa) *m* passage; aisle; ~ **a livello** level crossing; ~ **pedonale** crossing, pedestrian crossing; crosswalk *Am*

passante (pahss-*sahn*-tay) *m/f* passer-by

passaporto (pahss-sah-*por*-toa) *m* passport

passare (pahss-*saa*-ray) *v* pass; *go through; ~ **accanto** pass by

passatempo (pahss-sah-*tehm*-poa) *m* entertainment, amusement; hobby

passato (pahss-*saa*-toa) *adj* past; *m* past

passeggero (pahss-sayd-*jāy*-roa) *m*, **-a** *f* passenger

passeggiare (pahss-sayd-*jaa*-ray) *v* walk, stroll

passeggiata (pahss-sayd-*jaa*-tah) *f* walk, stroll

passeggino (pahss-sayd-*jee*-noa) *m* pushchair

passero (*pahss*-say-roa) *m* sparrow

passione (pahss-*syōa*-nay) *f* passion

passivo (pahss-*see*-voa) *adj* passive

passo (*pahss*-soa) *m* pace, step; mountain pass; extract; *stare al ~ **con** *keep up with; ~ **carraio**, ~ **carrabile** driveway

pasta (*pah*-stah) *f* dough; paste

pasticca (pah-*steek*-kah) *f* tablet

pasticceria (pah-steet-chay-*ree*-ah) *f* pastry shop, sweetshop; candy store *Am*

pasticciere (pah-steet-*chai*-ray) *m*, **-a** *f* confectioner

pasticcino (pah-steet-*chee*-noa) *m* pastry

pasticcio (pah-*steet*-choa) *m* muddle

pasto (*pah*-stoa) *m* meal

pastore (pah-*stōa*-ray) *m* shepherd; clergyman, parson, minister, rector

patata (pah-*taa*-tah) *f* potato

patatine fritte (pah-*taa*-tee-nay *freet*-tay) chips, French fries *Am*

patente (pah-tayn-tay) *f* driving licence, driver's license *Am*

patria (*paa*-tryah) *f* native country

patrigno (pah-*tree*-ño) *m* stepfather

patriota (pah-*tryaw*-tah) *m* patriot

patrocinatore (pah-troa-chee-nah-*tōa*-ray) *m* advocate

pattinaggio (paht-tee-*nahd*-joa) *m* skating; ~ **a rotelle** roller-skating

pattinare (paht-tee-*naa*-ray) *v* skate

pattino (*paht*-tee-noa) *m* skate

patto (*paht*-toa) *m* agreement; term

pattuglia (paht-*tōō*-l'ah) *f* patrol

pattugliare (paht-too-l'*aa*-ray) *v* patrol

pattumiera (paht-too-*myai*-rah) *f* rubbish bin, dustbin; trash can *Am*

paura (pah-*ōō*-rah) *f* fear, fright; ***aver ~** *be afraid

pausa (*pou*-zah) *f* pause

pavimentare (pah-vee-mayn-*taa*-ray) *v* pave

pavimento (pah-vee-*mayn*-toa) *m* floor

pavone (pah-*vōa*-nay) *m* peacock

paziente (pah-*tsyehn*-tay) *adj* patient; *m/f* patient

pazienza (pah-*tsyehn*-tsah) *f* patience

pazzia (paht-*tsee*-ah) *f* madness, lunacy

pazzo (*paht*-tsoa) *adj* crazy, mad, lunatic; insane; *m* lunatic

peccato (payk-*kaa*-toa) *m* sin; **peccato!** what a pity!

pecora (*pai*-koa-rah) *f* sheep

pedaggio (pay-*dahd*-joa) *m* toll

pedale (pay-*daa*-lay) *m* pedal

pedata (pay-*daa*-tah) *f* kick

pediatra (*pay*-dyaa-trah) *m/f* p(a)ediatrician

pedina (pay-*dee*-nah) *f* pawn

pedone (pay-*dōa*-nay) *m* pedestrian

peggio (*pehd*-joa) *adv* worse; worst

peggiore (payd-*jōa*-ray) *adj* worse

pelle (*pehl*-lay) *f* skin; hide; leather; **di ~** leather; ~ **di vitello** calf skin; ~ **d'oca** goose flesh; ~ **scamosciata** suede

pellegrinaggio (payl-lay-gree-*nahd*-joa) *m* pilgrimage

pellegrino (payl-lay-*gree*-noa) *m* pilgrim

pellicano (payl-lee-*kaa*-noa) *m* pelican

pelliccia (payl-*leet*-chah) *f* fur

pellicola (payl-*lee*-koa-lah) *f* film; ~ **a colori** colo(u)r film

pelo (*pay*-loa) *m* hair, coat

peloso (pay-*lōa*-soa) *adj* hairy

peltro (*payl*-troa) *m* pewter

pena (*pāy*-nah) *f* trouble, pains; penalty; ~ **di morte** death penalty; ***valer la ~** *be worth-while

pendente (payn-*dehn*-tay) *adj* slanting; *m* pendant

pendere (*pehn*-day-ray) *v* *hang; slope

pendio (payn-*dee*-oa) *m* hillside, slope

pendolare (payn-doa-*laa*-ray) *m/f* commuter

penetrare (pay-nay-*traa*-ray) *v* penetrate

penicillina (pay-nee-cheel-*lee*-nah) *f* penicillin

penisola (pay-*nee*-zoa-lah) *f* peninsula

penna (*payn*-nah) *f* feather; pen; ~ **a sfera** Biro®, ballpoint-pen; ~ **stilografica** fountain pen

pennello (payn-*nehl*-loa) *m* brush; paintbrush; ~ **da barba** shaving brush

penoso (pay-*nōa*-soa) *adj* painful

pensare (payn-*saa*-ray) *v* *think; ~ **a** *think of

pensiero (payn-*syai*-roa) *m* thought, idea

pensieroso (payn-syay-*rōa*-soa) *adj* thoughtful

pensionante (payn-syoa-*nahn*-tay) *m/f* boarder

pensionato (payn-syoa-*naa*-toa) *adj* retired

pensione (payn-*syōa*-nay) *f* board; guesthouse, pension, boardinghouse; ~ **completa** full board

Pentecoste (payn-tay-*ko*-stay) *f* Whitsun, Pentecost *Am*

pentimento (payn-tee-*mayn*-toa) *m* repentance

pentirsi (payn-*teer*-see) *v* repent; regret

pentola (*pehn*-toa-lah) *f* pot; ~ **a pressione** pressure cooker

penuria (pay-*nōō*-ryah) *f* scarcity

pepe (*pāy*-pay) *m* pepper

per (payr) *prep* for; to; with; times

pera (*pāy*-rah) *f* pear

percento (payr-*chehn*-toa) *m* percent

percentuale (payr-chayn-*twaa*-lay) *f* percentage

percepire (payr-chay-*pee*-ray) *v* perceive, sense

percettibile (payr-chayt-*tee*-bee-lay) *adj* perceptible

percezione (payr-chay-*tsyōa*-nay) *f* perception

perché (payr-*kay*) *adv* what for, why; *conj* because

perciò (payr-*cho*) *conj* therefore

*percorrere (payr-*koar*-ray-ray) *v* cover; *walk; *drive

*percuotere (payr-*kwaw*-tay-ray) *v* thump

perdere (*pehr*-day-ray) *v* *lose; **che perde** leaky; **perdersi** get lost

perdita (*pehr*-dee-tah) *f* loss; leak

perdonare (payr-doa-*naa*-ray) *v* *forgive

perdono (payr-*dōa*-noa) *m* pardon

perfetto (payr-*feht*-toa) *adj* perfect; faultless

perfezione (payr-fay-*tsyōa*-nay) *f* perfection

perfido (*pehr*-fee-doa) *adj* foul

perfino (payr-*fee*-noa) *adv* even

perforare (payr-foa-*raa*-ray) *v* pierce

pericolo (pay-*ree*-koa-loa) *m* danger; risk, peril; distress

pericoloso (pay-ree-koa-*lōa*-soa) *adj* perilous, dangerous

periodico (pay-*ryaw*-dee-koa) *adj* periodical; *m* periodical

periodo (pay-*ree*-oa-doa) *m* period, term

perire (pay-*ree*-ray) *v* perish

perito (pay-*ree*-toa) *m* expert

perla (*pehr*-lah) *f* pearl

perlina (payr-*lee*-nah) *f* bead

perlustrare (payr-loo-*straa*-ray) *v* search

permanente (payr-mah-*nehn*-tay) *adj* permanent; *f* permanent wave

permesso (payr-*mayss*-soa) *m* permission; permit; ***avere il ~ di** *be allowed to; ~ **di lavoro** work permit; labor permit *Am*; ~ **di pesca** fishing licence, fishing license *Am*; ~ **di soggiorno** residence permit; **permesso?** may I?

*permettere (payr-*mayt*-tay-ray) *v* allow, permit; ***permettersi** afford

pernice (payr-*nee*-chay) *f* partridge

però (pay-*roa*) *conj* but; only; yet; though

perorare (pay-roa-*raa*-ray) *v* plead

perpendicolare (payr-payn-dee-koa-*laa*-ray) *adj* perpendicular

perquisire (payr-kwee-*zee*-ray) *v* search

perseguire (payr-say-*gwee*-ray) *v*
pursue

perseverare (payr-say-vay-*raa*-ray) *v*
*keep up

persiana (payr-*syaa*-nah) *f* shutter,
blind

persiano (payr-*syaa*-noa) *adj* Persian;
m, **-a** *f* Persian

persistere (payr-*see*-stay-ray) *v* insist

persona (payr-*soa*-nah) *f* person; **a ~**
per person; **di ~** personally

personaggio (payr-soa-*nahd*-joa) *m*
personality; character

personale (payr-soa-*naa*-lay) *adj*
personal, private; *m* staff, personnel

personalità (payr-soa-nah-lee-*tah*) *f*
personality

perspicace (payr-spee-*kaa*-chay) *adj*
clever

*persuadere (payr-swah-*day*-ray) *v*
persuade

pesante (pay-*sahn*-tay) *adj* heavy

pesare (pay-*saa*-ray) *v* weigh

pesca[1] (*peh*-skah) *f* peach

pesca[2] (*pay*-skah) *f* fishing industry

pescare (pay-*skaa*-ray) *v* fish; **~ con
l'amo** angle

pescatore (pay-skah-*toa*-ray) *m*
fisherman

pesce (*paysh*-shay) *m* fish; **~ persico**
perch

pescecane (paysh-shay-*kaa*-nay) *m*
shark

pescheria (pay-skay-*ree*-ah) *f* fish
shop

peso (*pay*-soa) *m* weight; load,
burden

pessimismo (payss-see-*mee*-zmoa) *m*
pessimism

pessimista (payss-see-*mee*-stah) *m/f*
pessimist

pessimistico (payss-see-*mee*-stee-
koa) *adj* pessimistic

pessimo (*pehss*-see-moa) *adj* worst

pestare (pay-*staa*-ray) *v* stamp

petalo (*pai*-tah-loa) *m* petal

petizione (pay-tee-*tsyoa*-nay) *f*
petition

petroliera (pay-troa-*l'ai*-rah) *f* tanker

petrolio (pay-*traw*-l'oa) *m* petroleum;
oil

pettegolezzo (payt-tay-goa-*layt*-tsoa)
m gossip

pettinare (payt-tee-*naa*-ray) *v* comb;
pettinarsi comb one's hair

pettine (*peht*-tee-nay) *m* comb

pettirosso (payt-tee-*roass*-soa) *m*
robin

petto (*peht*-toa) *m* chest, bosom

pezzetto (payt-*tsayt*-toa) *m* bit; scrap

pezzo (*peht*-tsoa) *m* piece; part, lump;
fragment; **in due pezzi** two-piece; **~
di ricambio** spare part

piacere (pyah-*chay*-ray) *m* pleasure;
con ~ gladly

*piacere (pyah-*chay*-ray) *v* please

piacevole (pyah-*chay*-voa-lay) *adj*
pleasant, enjoyable, nice

piacevolissimo (pyah-chay-voa-*leess*-
see-moa) *adj* delightful

piaga (*pyaa*-gah) *f* sore

pianeta (pyah-*nay*-tah) *m* planet

*piangere (*pyahn*-jay-ray) *v* *weep,
cry

pianista (pyah-*nee*-stah) *m/f* pianist

piano (*pyaa*-noa) *adj* plane, smooth,
even, flat, level; *m* floor, stor(e)y;
project; **primo ~** foreground

pianoforte (pyah-noa-*for*-tay) *m*
piano; **~ a coda** grand piano

pianta (*pyahn*-tah) *f* plant; map, plan

piantagione (pyahn-tah-*joa*-nay) *f*
plantation

piantare (pyahn-*taa*-ray) *v* plant

pianterreno (pyahn-tayr-*ray*-noa) *m*
ground floor

pianura (pyah-*noo*-rah) *f* plain

piattino (pyaht-*tee*-noa) *m* saucer

piatto (*pyaht*-toa) *adj* even, flat, level; *m* plate, dish

piazza (*pyaht*-tsah) *f* square; **~ del mercato** marketplace

piazzale (*pyaht*-tsaa-lay) *m* large square; toll-booth area

piccante (peek-*kahn*-tay) *adj* savo(u)ry; spicy

picchiare (peek-*kyaa*-ray) *v* *strike, *beat; smack

piccino (peet-*chee*-noa) *m*, **-a** *f* baby

piccione (peet-*choa*-nay) *m* pigeon

piccolo (*peek*-koa-loa) *adj* small, little; minor, petty

picnic (*peek*-neek) *m* picnic

pidocchio (pee-*dok*-kyoa) *m* louse

piede (*pyai*-day) *m* foot; **a piedi** walking, on foot; **in piedi** upright; **~ di porco** crowbar

piega (*pyai*-gah) *f* fold; crease

piegare (pyay-*gaa*-ray) *v* fold

pieghevole (pyay-*gay*-voa-lay) *adj* flexible, supple

pieno (*pyai*-noa) *adj* full; ***fare il ~** fill up; **~ zeppo** chock-full

pietà (pyay-*tah*) *f* pity

pietanza (pyay-*tahn*-tsah) *f* dish

pietra (*pyai*-trah) *f* stone; **di ~** stone; **~ miliare** milestone; landmark; **~ pomice** pumice stone; **~ preziosa** stone

pietrina (pyay-*tree*-nah) *f* flint

pigiama (pee-*jaa*-mah) *m* pyjamas *pl*

pigliare (pee-*ly̆aa*-ray) *v* *take

pigro (*pee*-groa) *adj* lazy; idle

pila (*pee*-lah) *f* stack; flashlight; torch

pilastro (pee-*lah*-stroa) *m* pillar

pillola (*peel*-loa-lah) *f* pill

pilota (pee-*law*-tah) *m/f* pilot

pinguino (peeng-*gwee*-noa) *m* penguin

pinze (*peen*-tsay) *fpl* pliers *pl*, tongs *pl*

pinzette (peen-*tsayt*-tay) *fpl* tweezers *pl*

pio (*pee*-oa) *adj* pious

pioggerella (pyoad-jay-*rehl*-lah) *f* drizzle

pioggia (*pyod*-jah) *f* rain

piombo (*pyoam*-boa) *m* lead; **senza ~** unleaded

pioniere (pyoa-*ñai*-ray) *m* pioneer

*piovere (*pyaw*-vay-ray) *v* rain

piovoso (pyoa-*voa*-soa) *adj* rainy

pipa (*pee*-pah) *f* pipe

pirata (pee-*raa*-tah) *m* pirate

piroscafo (pee-*raw*-skah-foa) *m* steamer

piscina (peesh-*shee*-nah) *f* swimming pool

pisello (pee-*sehl*-loa) *m* pea

pisolino (pee-zoa-*lee*-noa) *m* nap

pista (*pee*-stah) *f* track; ring; **~ da corsa** racecourse, racetrack; **~ di decollo** runway; **~ di pattinaggio** skating rink

pistola (pee-*staw*-lah) *f* pistol

pittore (peet-*toa*-ray) *m*, **-trice** *f* painter

pittoresco (peet-toa-*ray*-skoa) *adj* picturesque, scenic

pittura (peet-*too*-rah) *f* painting, picture; **~ ad olio** oil painting

pitturare (peet-too-*raa*-ray) *v* paint

più (pyoo) *adv* more; *prep* plus; **il ~** most; **per lo ~** mostly; **~ ... più** the ... the; **~ in là di** beyond; **~ lontano** further; **sempre ~** more and more; **tutt'al ~** at most

piuttosto (pee^{t-}to-stoa) *adv* sooner, rather; fairly, pretty, quite

pizzeria (peet-tsay-*rya*) f pizza parlo(u)r

pizzicare (peet-tsee-*kaa*-ray) *v* pinch

planetario (plah-nay-*taa*-ryoa) *m* planetarium

plasmare (plah-*zmaa*-ray) *v* model

plastica (*plah*-stee-kah) *f* plastic

plastico (*plah*-stee-koa) *adj* plastic

platino (*plaa*-tee-noa) *m* platinum

plurale (ploo-*raa*-lay) *m* plural

pneumatico (pnay⁰⁰-*maa*-tee-koa) *adj* pneumatic; *m* tire; **~ di scorta** spare tyre

po': **un ~ (di)** (oon poa dee) a little, some

poco (*paw*-koa) *adj* little; *m* bit; **pochi** *adj* few; **press'a ~** about; **tra ~** soon

poderoso (poa-day-*rōa*-soa) *adj* mighty, powerful

poema (poa-*ai*-mah) *m* poem; **~ epico** epic

poesia (poa-ay-*zee*-ah) *f* poetry

poeta (poa-*ai*-tah) *m*, **-essa** *f* poet

poi (poi) *adv* then; afterwards

poiché (poay-*kay*) *conj* as, since, because; for

polacco (poa-*lahk*-koa) *adj* Polish; *m*, **-a** *f* Pole

policlinico (*paw*-lee-*klee*-nee-koa) *m* general hospital

polio (*paw*-lˡoa) *f* polio

polipo (*paw*-lee-poa) *m* octopus

politica (poa-*lee*-tee-kah) *f* politics

politico (poa-*lee*-tee-koa) *adj* political

polizia (poa-lee-*tsee*-ah) *f* police *pl*

poliziotto (poa-lee-*tsyot*-toa) *m* policeman, **-a** *f* policewoman

polizza (poa-*leet*-tsah) *f* policy; **~ di assicurazione** insurance policy

pollame (poal-*laa*-may) *m* fowl; poultry

pollice (*pol*-lee-chay) *m* thumb

pollivendolo (poal-lee-*vayn*-doa-loa) *m* poulterer

pollo (*poal*-loa) *m* chicken

polmone (poal-*mōa*-nay) *m* lung

polmonite (poal-moa-*nee*-tay) *f* pneumonia

Polonia (poa-*law*-ñah) *f* Poland

polpaccio (poal-*paht*-choa) *m* calf

polsino (poal-*see*-noa) *m* cuff

polso (*poal*-soa) *m* pulse; wrist

poltrona (poal-*trōa*-nah) *f* armchair, easy chair; **~ in platea** orchestra seat *Am*; stall

polvere (*poal*-vay-ray) *f* dust; powder; **~ da sparo** gunpowder

polveroso (poal-vay-*rōa*-soa) *adj* dusty

pomeriggio (poa-may-*reed*-joa) *m* afternoon; **oggi ~** this afternoon

pomodoro (poa-moa-*daw*-roa) *m* tomato

pompa (*poam*-pah) *f* pump; **~ dell'acqua** water pump

pompare (poam-*paa*-ray) *v* pump

pompelmo (poam-*pehl*-moa) *m* grapefruit

pompieri (poam-*pyai*-ree) *mpl* fire brigade

ponderare (poan-day-*raa*-ray) *v* consider

ponte (*poan*-tay) *m* bridge; **~ di coperta** main deck; **~ levatoio** drawbridge; **~ sospeso** suspension bridge

pontefice (poan-*tāy*-fee-chay) *m* pontiff

popolare (poa-poa-*laa*-ray) *adj* popular; **danza ~** folk dance

popolazione (poa-poa-lah-*tsyōa*-nay) *f* population

popolo (*paw*-poa-loa) *m* people; nation, folk

porcellana (poar-chayl-*laa*-nah) *f* porcelain, china

porcellino (poar-chayl-*lee*-noa) *m* piglet; **~ d'India** guinea pig

porco (*por*-koa) *m* (pl porci) pig

porcospino (poar-koa-*spee*-noa) *m* porcupine

*porgere (*por*-jay-ray) *v* hand, *give

*porre (*poar*-ray) *v* place; *put

porta (*por*-tah) *f* door; **~ girevole** revolving door; **~ scorrevole** sliding door

portabagagli (poar-tah-bah-*gaa*-l^yee) *m* luggage rack

portacarte (poar-tah-*kahr*-tay) *m* attaché case

portacenere (poar-tah-*chay*-nay-ray) *m* ashtray

portacipria (poar-tah-*chee*-pryah) *m* powder compact

portafoglio (poar-tah-*fōa*-l^yoa) *m* wallet

portafortuna (poar-tah-foar-*tōo*-nah) *m* lucky charm

portare (poar-*taa*-ray) *v* *bring; carry, *bear; **portar via** *take away

portasigarette (poar-tah-see-gah-*rayt*-tay) *m* cigarette case

portata (poar-*taa*-tah) *f* course; reach, range

portatile (poar-*taa*-tee-lay) *adj* portable

portatore (poar-tah-*tōa*-ray) *m* bearer

portauovo (poar-tah-*waw*-voa) *m* eggcup

portico (*por*-tee-koa) *m* arcade

portiera (*por*-tyay-rah) *f* door

portiere (poar-*tyai*-ray) *m* porter; goalkeeper

portinaio (poar-tee-*naa*-yoa) *m*, **-a** *f* concierge, janitor; doorkeeper

porto (*por*-toa) *m* harbo(u)r, port; **~ di mare** seaport

Portogallo (poar-toa-*gahl*-loa) *m* Portugal

portoghese (poar-toa-*gay*-say) *adj* Portuguese; *m/f* Portuguese

portuale (poar-*twaa*-lay) *m* docker

porzione (poar-*tsyōa*-nay) *f* portion, helping

posare (poa-*saa*-ray) *v* *lay; *put; place

posate (poa-*saa*-tay) *fpl* cutlery

positiva (poa-zee-*tee*-vah) *f* positive, print

positivo (poa-zee-*tee*-voa) *adj* positive

posizione (poa-zee-*tsyōa*-nay) *f* position; site, location

*possedere (poass-say-*day*-ray) *v* possess, own

possedimenti (poass-say-dee-*mayn*-tee) *mpl* possessions

possesso (poass-*sehss*-soa) *m* possession

possibile (poass-*see*-bee-lay) *adj* possible

possibilità (poass-see-bee-lee-*tah*) *f* possibility

posta (*po*-stah) *f* post, mail; bet; **~ aerea** airmail

posteggiare (poa-stayd-*jaa*-ray) *v* park

posteggio (poa-*stayd*-joa) *m* carpark

posteriore (poa-stay-*ryōa*-ray) *adj* rear; later

postino (poa-*stee*-noa) *m* postman

posto (*poa*-stoa) *m* place; seat; station; **in qualche ~** somewhere; ***mettere a ~** *put away; **~ di polizia** police station; **~ di pronto soccorso** first-aid post; **~ libero** vacancy

potabile (poa-*taa*-bee-lay) *adj* for drinking

potente (poa-*tehn*-tay) *adj* powerful

potenza (poa-*tehn*-tsah) *f* might; power; capacity

potere (poa-*tay*-ray) *m* power; faculty

*potere (poa-*tay*-ray) *v* *can, *be able to; *might, *may

povero (*paw*-vay-roa) *adj* poor

povertà (poa-vayr-*tah*) *f* poverty

pozzanghera (poat-*tsahng*-gay-rah) *f* puddle

pozzo (*poat*-tsoa) *m* well; **~ petrolifero** oil well

pranzare (prahn-*dzaa*-ray) *v* dine; have lunch

pranzo (*prahn*-dzoa) *m* dinner; lunch; **~ a prezzo fisso** set menu

pratica (*praa*-tee-kah) *f* practice

praticamente (prah-tee-kah-*mayn*-tay) *adv* practically

praticare (prah-tee-*kaa*-ray) *v* practise

pratico (*praa*-tee-koa) *adj* practical

prato (*praa*-toa) *m* meadow; lawn

precario (pray-*kaa*-ryoa) *adj* critical, precarious

precauzione (pray-kou-*tsyoa*-nay) *f* precaution

precedente (pray-chay-*dehn*-tay) *adj* previous, former, preceding

precedentemente (pray-chay-dayn-tay-*mayn*-tay) *adv* before

precedenza (pray-chay-*dehn*-tsah) *f* right of way; priority

precedere (pray-*chai*-day-ray) *v* precede

precettore (pray-chayt-*toa*-ray) *m* tutor

precipitare (pray-chee-pee-*taa*-ray) *v* crash; **precipitarsi** dash

precipitazione (pray-chee-pee-tah-*tsyoa*-nay) *f* shower; precipitation

precipizio (pray-chee-*pee*-tsyoa) *m* precipice

precisamente (pray-chee-zah-*mayn*-tay) *adv* exactly

precisare (pray-chee-*zaa*-ray) *v* specify

precisione (pray-chee-*zyoa*-nay) *f* precision

preciso (pray-*chee*-zoa) *adj* very, precise

predecessore (pray-day-chayss-*soa*-ray) *m* predecessor

predicare (pray-dee-*kaa*-ray) *v* preach

*predire (pray-*dee*-ray) *v* predict

preferenza (pray-fay-*rehn*-tsah) *f* preference

preferibile (pray-fay-*ree*-bee-lay) *adj* preferable

preferire (pray-fay-*ree*-ray) *v* prefer; **preferito** favo(u)rite

prefisso (pray-*feess*-soa) *m* prefix; area code

pregare (pray-*gaa*-ray) *v* pray

preghiera (pray-*gyai*-rah) *f* prayer

pregiudizio (pray-joo-*dee*-tsyoa) *m* prejudice

prego! (*pray*-goa) you are welcome!

preliminare (pray-lee-mee-*naa*-ray) *adj* preliminary

prematuro (pray-mah-*too*-roa) *adj* premature

premeditato (pray-may-dee-*taa*-toa) *adj* deliberate

premere (*prai*-may-ray) *v* press

premio (*prai*-myoa) *m* award, prize; premium; **~ di consolazione** consolation prize

premura (pray-*moo*-rah) *f* haste

premuroso (pray-moo-*roa*-soa) *adj* thoughtful

*prendere (*prehn*-day-ray) *v* *take; *catch; capture; **andare a ~** pick up

prenotare (pray-noa-*taa*-ray) *v* reserve, book

prenotazione (pray-noa-tah-*tsyoa*-nay) *f* reservation, booking

preoccuparsi (pray-oak-koo-*pahr*-see) *v* worry; **~ di** care about

preoccupato (pray-oak-koo-*paa*-toa) *adj* concerned, anxious, worried

preoccupazione (pray-oak-koo-pah-*tsyoa*-nay) *f* worry; trouble, care

preparare (pray-pah-*raa*-ray) *v* prepare; cook

preparazione (pray-pah-rah-*tsyoa*-nay) *f* preparation

preposizione (pray-poa-zee-*tsyoa*-nay) *f* preposition

presa (*prai*-sah) *f* grip; capture

presbiterio (pray-zbee-*tai*-ryoa) *m* parsonage, rectory, vicarage

prescindere (pray-*sheen*-day-ray): **a ~ da** apart from

*prescrivere (pray-*skree*-vay-ray) *v*

prescribe

presentare (pray-zayn-*taa*-ray) v offer, present; introduce; **presentarsi** report; appear

presentazione (pray-zayn-tah-*tsyōa*-nay) f introduction

presente (pray-*zehn*-tay) adj present; m present

presenza (pray-*zehn*-tsah) f presence

preservativo (pray-*sayr*-vah-tee-voa) m condom

preservazione (pray-zayr-vah-*tsyōa*-nay) f preservation

preside (*prai*-see-day) m/f headmaster, principal

presidente (pray-see-*dehn*-tay) m, **-essa** f president

pressante (prayss-*sahn*-tay) adj pressing

pressione (prayss-*syōa*-nay) f pressure; **~ atmosferica** atmospheric pressure; **~ dell'olio** oil pressure; **~ delle gomme** tyre pressure; **~ sanguigna** blood pressure

presso (*prehss*-soa) prep with

prestare (pray-*staa*-ray) v *lend

prestazione (pray-stah-*tsyōa*-nay) f feat

prestigiatore (pray-stee-jah-*tōa*-ray) m magician

prestigio (pray-*stee*-joa) m prestige

prestito (*preh*-stee-toa) m loan; *****prendere in ~** borrow

presto (*preh*-stoa) adv soon, shortly

*****presumere** (pray-*zōō*-may-ray) v assume

presuntuoso (pray-zoon-*twōa*-soa) adj conceited, presumptuous

prete (*prai*-tay) m priest

*****pretendere** (pray-*tehn*-day-ray) v pretend

pretesa (pray-*tāy*-sah) f pretence; claim

pretesto (pray-*teh*-stoa) m pretext

*****prevedere** (pray-vay-*dāy*-ray) v forecast; anticipate

*****prevenire** (pray-vay-*nee*-ray) v anticipate, prevent

preventivo (pray-vayn-*tee*-voa) adj preventive; m estimate

previo (*prai*-vyoa) adj previous

previsione (pray-vee-*zyōa*-nay) f forecast; **previsioni del tempo** weather forecast

prezioso (pray-*tsyōa*-soa) adj valuable, precious

prezzare (prayt-*tsaa*-ray) v price

prezzemolo (prayt-*tsāy*-moa-loa) m parsley

prezzo (*preht*-tsoa) m price; cost, rate; **~ del biglietto** fare; **~ del coperto** cover charge

prigione (pree-*jōa*-nay) m jail, prison

prigioniero (pree-joa-*ñai*-roa) m, **-a** f prisoner; *****far ~** capture

prima (*pree*-mah) adv at first; before; **~ che** before; **~ di** before

primario (pree-*maa*-ryoa) adj primary

primato (pree-*maa*-toa) m record

primavera (pree-mah-*vāy*-rah) f springtime, spring

primitivo (pree-mee-*tee*-voa) adj primitive

primo (*pree*-moa) num first, foremost, primary, chief

principale (preent-shee-*paa*-lay) adj leading, main, cardinal, principal, primary, chief

principalmente (preen-chee-pahl-*mayn*-tay) adv mainly

principe (*preen*-chee-pay) m prince

principessa (preen-chee-*payss*-sah) f princess

principiante (preen-chee-*pyahn*-tay) m/f beginner, learner

principio (preen-*chee*-pyoa) m beginning; principle; **al ~** at first

priorità (pryoa-ree-*tah*) f priority

privare: ~ **di** (pree-*vaa*-ray) deprive of

privato (pree-*vaa*-toa) adj private

privilegiare (pree-vee-lay-*jaa*-ray) v favo(u)r

privilegio (pree-vee-*lai*-joa) m privilege

probabile (proa-*baa*-bee-lay) adj probable, likely

probabilmente (proa-bah-beel-*mayn*-tay) adv probably

problema (proa-*blai*-mah) m problem, question

procedere (proa-*chai*-day-ray) v proceed

procedimento (proa-chay-dee-*mayn*-toa) m procedure; process

processione (proa-chayss-*syoa*-nay) f procession

processo (proa-*chehss*-soa) m trial, lawsuit; process

proclamare (proa-klah-*maa*-ray) v proclaim

procurare (proa-koo-*raa*-ray) v furnish

prodigo (*praw*-dee-goa) adj lavish; liberal

prodotto (proa-*doat*-toa) m product; produce

*produrre (proa-*door*-ray) v produce

produttore (proa-doot-*toa*-ray) m, **-trice** f producer

produzione (proa-doo-*tsyoa*-nay) f production, output; ~ **in serie** mass production

profano (proa-*faa*-noa) m layman

professare (proa-fayss-*saa*-ray) v confess

professionale (proa-fayss-syoa-*naa*-lay) adj professional

professione (proa-fayss-*syoa*-nay) f profession

professionista (*proa-fayss-syoa-nee-stah*) m/f professional; **libero ~** self-employed person

professore (proa-fayss-*soa*-ray) m, **-essa** f master; professor; teacher

profeta (proa-*fai*-tah) m prophet

profitto (proa-*feet*-toa) m benefit, gain; profit

profondità (proa-foan-dee-*tah*) f depth

profondo (proa-*foan*-doa) adj deep; profound

profugo (*proa-foo*-goa) m, **-a** f refugee

profumeria (proa-*foo*-may-*ryah*) f perfume shop

profumo (proa-*fōō*-moa) m scent; perfume

progettare (proa-jayt-*taa*-ray) v plan; design

progetto (proa-*jeht*-toa) m plan, scheme; project

programma (proa-*grahm*-mah) m programme

programmare (proa-grahm-*maa*-ray) v program; plan

programmatore (proa-grahm-mah-*tōa*-ray) m, **-trice** f programmer

progredire (proa-gray-*dee*-ray) v *get on

progressista (proa-grayss-*see*-stah) adj progressive

progressivo (proa-grayss-*see*-voa) adj progressive

progresso (proa-*grehss*-soa) m progress

proibire (proa-ee-*bee*-ray) v *forbid, prohibit; **proibito passare** no entry

proibitivo (proa-ee-bee-*tee*-voa) adj prohibitive

proiettore (proa-yayt-*tōa*-ray) m projektor

prolunga (proa-*loong*-gah) f extension cord

prolungamento (proa-loong-gah-*mayn*-toa) m extension

promessa (proa-*mayss*-sah) f

promise; vow

*promettere (proa-*mayt*-tay-ray) *v* promise

promontorio (proa-moan-*taw*-ryoa) *m* headland

promozione (proa-moa-*tsyōa*-nay) *f* promotion

*promuovere (proa-*mwaw*-vay-ray) *v* promote

pronome (proa-*nōa*-may) *m* pronoun

pronto (*proan*-toa) *adj* ready; prompt; **pronto!** hello!

pronuncia (proa-*noon*-chah) *f* pronunciation

pronunciare (proa-noon-*chaa*-ray) *v* pronounce

propaganda (proa-pah-*gahn*-dah) *f* propaganda

propenso (proa-*pehn*-soa) *adj* inclined

*proporre (proa-*poar*-ray) *v* propose

proporzionale (proa-poar-tsyoa-*naa*-lay) *adj* proportional

proporzione (proa-poar-*tsyōa*-nay) *f* proportion

proposito (proa-*paw*-zee-toa) *m* purpose; **a ~** by the way

proposta (proa-*poa*-stah) *f* proposition, proposal

proprietà (proa-pryay-*tah*) *f* property; estate

proprietario (proa-pryay-*taa*-ryoa) *m*, **-a** *f* proprietor, owner

proprio (*pro*-pryoa) *adj* own

prosaico (proa-*zigh*-koa) *adj* matter-of-fact

prosciugare (proash-shoo-*gaa*-ray) *v* drain

prosciutto (proash-*shoot*-toa) *m* ham

proseguire (proa-say-*gwee*-ray) *v* continue, carry on

prosperità (proa-spay-ree-*tah*) *f* prosperity

prospettiva (proa-spayt-*tee*-vah) *f*

perspective; prospect, outlook

prospetto (proa-*speht*-toa) *m* prospectus

prossimamente (proass-see-mah-*mayn*-tay) *adv* shortly

prossimità (proass-see-mee-*tah*) *f* vicinity

prossimo (*pross*-see-moa) *adj* next

prostituta (proa-stee-*tōō*-tah) *f* prostitute

protagonista (proa-tah-goa-*nee*-stah) *m/f* protagonist

*proteggere (proa-*tehd*-jay-ray) *v* protect

proteina (proa-tay-*ee*-nah) *f* protein

protesta (proa-*teh*-stah) *f* protest

protestante (proa-tay-*stahn*-tay) *adj* Protestant

protestare (proa-tay-*staa*-ray) *v* protest

protezione (proa-tay-*tsyōa*-nay) *f* protection

prova (*praw*-vah) *f* trial, experiment, test; evidence, token, proof; rehearsal; ***fare le prove** rehearse; **mettere alla ~** test; **in ~** on approval

provare (proa-*vaa*-ray) *v* attempt; prove; experience; try on

provenienza (proa-vay-*ñehn*-tsah) *f* origin

*provenire da (proa-vay-*nee*-ray) *v* *come from; originate from

proverbio (proa-*vehr*-byoa) *m* proverb

provincia (proa-*veen*-chah) *f* province

provinciale (proa-veen-*chaa*-lay) *adj* provincial

provocare (proa-voa-*kaa*-ray) *v* cause

*provvedere (proav-vay-*dāy*-ray) *v* provide

provvedimento (proav-vay-dee-*mayn*-toa) *m* measure

provvisorio (proav-vee-*zaw*-ryoa) *adj* provisional, temporary

provvista (proav-*vee*-stah) *f* supply;
provviste *fpl* provisions *pl*

prudente (proo-*dehn*-tay) *adj* wary

prudere (*prōo*-day-ray) *v* itch

prugna (*prōo*-ñah) *f* plum

prurito (proo-*ree*-toa) *m* itch

psichiatra (psee-*kyaa*-trah) *m/f*
psychiatrist

psichico (*psee*-kee-koa) *adj* psychic

psicoanalista (psee-koa-ah-nah-*lee*-
stah) *m/f* psychoanalyst

psicologia (psee-koa-loa-*jee*-ah) *f*
psychology

psicologico (psee-koa-*law*-jee-koa)
adj psychological

psicologo (psee-*kaw*-loa-goa) *m*, **-a** *f*
psychologist

pubblicare (poob-blee-*kaa*-ray) *v*
publish

pubblicazione (poob-blee-kah-tsy*ōa*-
nay) *f* publication

pubblicità (poob-blee-chee-*tah*) *f*
advertising, publicity; commercial

pubblico (*poob*-blee-koa) *adj* public;
m public

pudore (poo-*dōa*-ray) *m* shame

pugno (*pōo*-ñoa) *m* fist; punch;
sferrare pugni punch

pulce (pool-*chay*) *f* flea

pulcino (pool-*chee*-noa) *m* chick

pulire (poo-*lee*-ray) *v* clean; ~ **a secco**
dry-clean

pulito (poo-*lee*-toa) *adj* clean

pulitura (poo-lee-*tōo*-rah) *f* cleaning

pulizia (poo-lee-*tsee*-ah) *f* cleaning

pulpito (*pool*-pee-toa) *m* pulpit

pulsante (pool-*sahn*-tay) *m* push
button

*pungere (*poon*-jay-ray) *v* *sting,
prick

punire (poo-*nee*-ray) *v* punish

punizione (poo-nee-*tsyōa*-nay) *f*
punishment; penalty

punta (*poon*-tah) *f* point, tip

puntare su (poon-*taa*-ray) aim at

punteggio (poon-*tehd*-joa) *m* score

punto (*poon*-toa) *m* point; period, full
stop; item, issue; stitch; ~ **d'incontro**
meeting place; ~ **di partenza** starting
point; ~ **di riferimento** landmark; ~
di vista point of view, outlook; ~ **e
virgola** semicolon; ~ **interrogativo**
question mark

puntuale (poon-*twaa*-lay) *adj*
punctual

puntura (poon-*tōo*-rah) *f* bite, sting

purché (poor-*kay*) *conj* provided that

pure (*pōo*-ray) *adv* as well, also

puro (*pōo*-roa) *adj* clean, pure; neat,
sheer

purtroppo (poor-*trōop*-poa) *adv*
unfortunately

pus (pooss) *m* pus

pustoletta (poo-stoa-*layt*-tah) *f*
pimple

puttana (poot-*taa*-nah) *f* whore

puzzare (poot-*tsaa*-ray) *v* *smell,
*stink

puzzle (pahzl) jigsaw puzzle

puzzolente (poot-tsoa-*lehn*-tay) *adj*
smelly

Q

qua (kwah) *adv* here

quaderno (kwah-*dayr*-noa) *m*
exercise book

quadrato (kwah-*draa*-toa) *adj* square;

m square

quadretto (kwah-*drayt*-toa) *m* check; **a quadretti** chequered

quadro (*kwaa*-droa) *m* picture; cadre; painting

quaglia (*kwaa*-l^yah) *f* quail

qualche (*kwahl*-kay) *adj* some

qualcosa (kwahl-*kaw*-sah) *pron* something

qualcuno (kwahl-$k\overline{oo}$-noa) *pron* someone, somebody

quale (*kwaa*-lay) *pron* which

qualifica (kwah-*lee*-fee-kah) *f* qualification

qualificato (kwah-lee-fee-*kaa*-toa) *adj* qualified; **non ~** unskilled

qualità (kwah-lee-*tah*) *f* quality; **di prima ~** first-rate, first-class

qualora (kwah-$l\overline{oa}$-rah) *conj* when, in case

qualsiasi (kwahl-*see*-ah-see) *adj* whatever; whichever

quando (*kwahn*-doa) *adv* when; *conj* when; **da ~** since

quantità (kwahn-tee-*tah*) *f* amount, quantity; number; lot

quanto (*kwahn*-toa) *adj* how much, how many

quantunque (kwahn-*toong*-kway) *conj* though

quaranta (kwah-*rahn*-tah) *num* forty

quarantena (kwah-rahn-*tai*-nah) *f* quarantine

quartiere (kwahr-*tyai*-ray) *m* district, quarter; **quartier generale** headquarters *pl*; **~ povero** slum

quarto (*kwahr*-toa) *num* fourth; *m* quarter

quasi (*kwaa*-zee) *adv* almost, nearly

quattordicesimo (kwaht-toar-dee-*chai*-zee-moa) *num* fourteenth

quattordici (kwaht-*tor*-dee-chee) *num* fourteen

quattro (*kwaht*-troa) *num* four

quello[1] (*kwayl*-loa) *pron* that; **quelli** those; **~ che** what

quello[2] (*kwayl*-loa) *adj* that; **quei** *adj* those

quercia (*kwehr*-chah) *f* oak

questione (kway-$sty\overline{oa}$-nay) *f* matter, issue, question

questo (*kway*-stoa) *adj* this; **questi** these

qui (kwee) *adv* here

quiete (kwee-*ai*-tay) *f* quiet

quieto (kwee-*ai*-toa) *adj* quiet

quindi (*kween*-dee) *conj* therefore

quindicesimo (kween-dee-*chai*-zee-moa) *num* fifteenth

quindici (*kween*-dee-chee) *num* fifteen

quintale (kween-*tah*-lay) *m* quintal

quinto (*kween*-toa) *num* fifth

quota (*kwaw*-tah) *f* quota

quotidiano (kwoa-tee-*dyaa*-noa) *adj* daily; everyday; *m* daily

R

rabarbaro (rah-*bahr*-bah-roa) *m* rhubarb

rabbia (*rahb*-byah) *f* anger, rage; rabies

rabbioso (rahb-$by\overline{oa}$-soa) *adj* mad

rabbrividire (rahb-bree-vee-*dee*-ray) *v* shiver

raccapricciante (rahk-kahp-preet-*chahn*-tay) *adj* creepy

raccapriccio (rahk-kahp-*preet*-choa)

m horror

racchetta (rahk-*kayt*-tah) *f* racket; bat

*raccogliere (rahk-*kaw*-lʸay-ray) *v* pick up; gather; collect;
   *raccogliersi gather

raccolta (rahk-*kol*-tah) *f* crop

raccolto (rahk-*kol*-toa) *m* harvest

raccomandare (rahk-koa-mahn-*daa*-ray) *v* recommend; register

raccomandata (rahk-koa-mahn-*daa*-tah) *f* registered letter

raccomandazione (rahk-koa-mahn-dah-*tsyoa*-nay) *f* recommendation

raccontare (rahk-koan-*taa*-ray) *v* relate, *tell

racconto (rahk-*koan*-toa) *m* story, tale; **~ a fumetti** comics *pl*

raccordo (rahk-*koar*-doa) *m* slip road; junction

*radersi (*raa*-dayr-see) *v* shave

radiatore (rah-dyah-*toa*-ray) *m* radiator

radicale (rah-dee-*kaa*-lay) *adj* radical

radice (rah-*dee*-chay) *f* root

radio (*raa*-dyoa) *f* radio

radiografare (rah-dyoa-grah-*faa*-ray) *v* X-ray

radiografia (rah-dyoa-grah-*fee*-ah) *f* X-ray

raduno (rah-*doo*-noa) *m* rally

radura (rah-*doo*-rah) *f* clearing

rafano (*raa*-fah-noa) *m* horseradish

raffermo (rahf-*fayr*-moa) *adj* stale

raffica (*rahf*-fee-kah) *f* gust, blow

raffigurare (rahf-fee-goo-*raa*-ray) *v* represent

raffineria (rahf-fee-nay-*ree*-ah) *f* refinery; oil refinery

raffreddarsi (rahf-frayd-*daar*-see) *v* cool down; catch cold

raffreddore (rahf-frayd-*doa*-ray) *m* cold; ***prendere un ~** catch a cold

ragazza (rah-*gaht*-tsah) *f* girl; girlfriend

ragazzo (rah-*gaht*-tsoa) *m* lad, boy; boyfriend

raggio (*rahd*-joa) *m* beam, ray; radius; spoke

*raggiungere (rahd-*joon*-jay-ray) *v* attain, achieve, reach

raggiungibile (rahd-joon-*jee*-bee-lay) *adj* attainable

ragionamento (rah-joa-nah-*mayn*-toa) *m* reasoning

ragionare (rah-joa-*naa*-ray) *v* reason

ragione (rah-*joa*-nay) *f* reason, wits *pl*, sense; cause; ***avere ~** *be right

ragionevole (rah-joa-*nāy*-voa-lay) *adj* reasonable; sensible

ragioniere (rah-joa-*nyay*-ray) *m*, **-a** *f* accountant

ragnatela (rah-ñah-*tāy*-lah) *f* spider's web

ragno (*raa*-ñoa) *m* spider

rallegrare (rahl-lay-*graa*-ray) *v* cheer up

rallentare (rahl-layn-*taa*-ray) *v* slow down

rame (*raa*-may) *m* copper

rammendare (rahm-mayn-*daa*-ray) *v* mend, darn

rammentare (rahm-mayn-*taa*-ray) *v* remind of; **rammentarsi** remember

ramo (*raa*-moa) *m* branch

ramoscello (rah-moash-*shehl*-loa) *m* twig

rampa (*rahm*-pah) *f* ramp

rana (*raa*-nah) *f* frog

rancido (*rahn*-chee-doa) *adj* rancid

rapida (*raa*-pee-dah) *f* rapids *pl*

rapidità (rah-pee-dee-*tah*) *f* speed

rapido (*raa*-pee-doa) *adj* fast; swift, rapid

rapimento (rah-pee-*mayn*-toa) *m* kidnap(p)ing

rapina (rah-*pee*-nah) *f* robbery, hold-up

rappezzare (rahp-payt-*tsaa*-ray) *v*

patch

rapporto (rahp-*por*-toa) *m* report; affair, intercourse

rappresentante (rahp-pray-zayn-*tahn*-tay) *m/f* agent

rappresentanza (rahp-pray-zayn-*tahn*-tsah) *f* representation

rappresentare (rahp-pray-zayn-*taa*-ray) *v* represent

rappresentativo (rahp-pray-zayn-tah-*tee*-voa) *adj* representative

rappresentazione (rahp-pray-zayn-tah-*tsyōa*-nay) *f* performance, show; ~ **teatrale** play

raramente (rah-rah-*mayn*-tay) *adv* seldom, rarely

raro (*raa*-roa) *adj* uncommon, rare

raschiare (rah-*skyaa*-ray) *v* scrape

raso (*raa*-soa) *m* satin

rasoio (rah-*sōa*-yoa) *m* razor; ~ **elettrico** electric razor; shaver

rassegna (rahss-*sāy*-ñah) *f* festival; exhibition

rassomiglianza (rahss-soa-mee-*l'ahn*-tsah) *f* similarity

rastrello (rah-*strehl*-loa) *m* (pl ~n) rake

rata (*raa*-tah) *f* instal(l)ment

ratto (*raht*-toa) *m* rat

rauco (*rou*-koa) *adj* hoarse

ravanello (rah-vah-*nehl*-loa) *m* radish

razione (rah-*tsyōa*-nay) *f* ration

razza (*raht*-tsah) *f* breed, race

razziale (raht-*tsyaa*-lay) *adj* racial

razzo (*raht*-tsoa) *m* rocket

re (ray) *m* (pl ~) king

reale (ray-*aa*-lay) *adj* true, factual, actual, real; royal

realizzabile (ray-ah-leed-*dzaa*-bee-lay) *adj* feasible, realizable

realizzare (ray-ah-leed-*dzaa*-ray) *v* realize

realtà (ray-ahl-*tah*) *f* reality; **in** ~ actually, in effect; really

reato (ray-*aa*-toa) *m* offence, offense *Am*

reazione (ray-ah-*tsyōa*-nay) *f* reaction

recapitare (ray-kah-pee-*taa*-ray) *v* deliver

recare (ray-*kaa*-ray) *v* *bring; cause; **recarsi** *go

recensione (ray-chayn-*syōa*-nay) *f* review

recente (ray-*chehn*-tay) *adj* recent; **di** ~ recently

recentemente (ray-chayn-tay-*mayn*-tay) *adv* lately, recently

recessione (ray-chayss-*syōa*-nay) *f* recession

recinto (ray-*cheen*-toa) *m* fence

recipiente (ray-chee-*pyehn*-tay) *m* container, vessel

reciproco (ray-*chee*-proa-koa) *adj* mutual

recital (ray-see-*tahl*) *m* recital

recitare (ray-chee-*taa*-ray) *v* act

reclamare (ray-klah-*maa*-ray) *v* claim

reclamo (ray-*klaa*-moa) *m* complaint

reclusione (ray-kloo-*zyōa*-nay) *m* imprisonment

recluta (*ray*-kloo-tah) *f* recruit

recuperare (ray-koo-pay-*raa*-ray) *v* recover

redattore (ray-daht-*tōa*-ray) *m*, **-trice** *f* editor

reddito (*rehd*-dee-toa) *m* revenue, income; earnings *pl*

*redigere (ray-*dee*-jay-ray) *v* *draw up

*redimere (ray-*dee*-may-ray) *v* redeem

refe (*rāy*-fay) *m* thread

referenza (ray-fay-*rehn*-tsah) *f* reference

regalare (ray-gah-*lah*-ray) *v* *give, make a present

regalo (ray-*gaa*-loa) *m* gift, present

regata (ray-*gaa*-tah) *f* regatta

*reggersi (*rehd*-jayr-see) *v* *hold on

reggipetto (rayd-jee-*peht*-toa) *m* bra

reggiseno (rayd-jee-*say*-noa) *m* bra

regia (ray-*jee*-ah) *f* direction

regime (ray-*jee*-may) *m* rule, régime

regina (ray-*jee*-nah) *f* queen

regionale (ray-joa-*naa*-lay) *adj* regional

regione (ray-*joa*-nay) *f* region; country, district

regista (ray-*jee*-stah) *m/f* director

registrare (ray-jee-*straa*-ray) *v* record, book; **registrarsi** register, check in

registratore (ray-jee-*straa*-toa-ray) *m* recorder

registrazione (ray-jee-strah-*tsyoa*-nay) *f* registration; record, entry; recording

regnare (ray-*ñaa*-ray) *v* reign

regno (*ray*-ñoa) *m* kingdom; reign

regola (*rai*-goa-lah) *f* rule

regolamentazione (ray-goa-lah-mayn-tah-*tsyoa*-này) *f* regulation

regolamento (ray-goa-lah-*mayn*-toa) *m* regulation

regolare (ray-goa-*laa*-ray) *adj* regular; *v* regulate; adjust; **regolato** regular

relativo (ray-lah-*tee*-voa) *adj* relative; comparative

relazione (ray-lah-*tsyoa*-nay) *f* relation; reference, connection; report; **in ~ a** regarding

religione (ray-lee-*joa*-nay) *f* religion

religioso (ray-lee-*joa*-soa) *adj* religious

reliquia (ray-lee-*kwee*-ah) *f* relic

relitto (ray-*leet*-toa) *m* wreck

remare (ray-*maa*-ray) *v* row

remo (*rai*-moa) *m* oar; paddle

remoto (ray-*maw*-toa) *adj* remote

*rendere (*rehn*-day-ray) *v* reimburse; **~ conto di** account for; **~ omaggio** hono(u)r

rene (*rai*-nay) *m* kidney

renna (*rehn*-nah) *f* reindeer

reparto (ray-*pahr*-toa) *m* section,

division; department

repellente (ray-payl-*lehn*-tay) *adj* repellent

repertorio (ray-payr-*taw*-ryoa) *m* repertory

*reprimere (ray-*pree*-may-ray) *v* suppress

repubblica (ray-*poob*-blee-kah) *f* republic

repubblicano (ray-poob-blee-*kaa*-noa) *adj* republican

reputare (ray-poo-*taa*-ray) *v* consider

reputazione (ray-poo-tah-*tsyoa*-nay) *f* fame, reputation

resa (*ray*-sah) *f* surrender

residente (ray-see-*dehn*-tay) *adj* resident; *m/f* resident

residenza (ray-see-*dehn*-tsah) *f* residence

residuo (ray-*see*-dwoa) *m* remnant, remainder

resina (*rai*-zee-nah) *f* resin

resistenza (ray-see-*stehn*-tsah) *f* resistance; strength

resistere (ray-*see*-stay-ray) *v* resist

resoconto (ray-soa-*koan*-toa) *m* account

*respingere (ray-*speen*-jay-ray) *v* turn down, reject

respirare (ray-spee-*raa*-ray) *v* breathe

respiratore (ray-spee-rah-*toa*-ray) *m* snorkel

respirazione (ray-spee-rah-*tsyoa*-nay) *f* respiration, breathing

respiro (ray-*spee*-roa) *m* breath

responsabile (ray-spoan-*saa*-bee-lay) *adj* responsible; liable

responsabilità (ray-spoan-sah-bee-lee-*tah*) *f* responsibility; liability

restare (ray-*staa*-ray) *v* remain

restauro (ray-*stou*-roa) *m* repair

restio (ray-*stee*-oa) *adj* unwilling

resto (*reh*-stoa) *m* rest; remnant, remainder

*restringersi (ray-*streen*-jayr-see) *v* *shrink; tighten

restrizione (ray-stree-tsy$\overline{oa}$-nay) *f* restriction, qualification

rete (*r$\overline{ay}$*-tay) *f* net; network; goal; ~ **da pesca** fishing net; ~ **stradale** road system

retina (*rai*-tee-nah) *f* retina

rettangolare (rayt-tahng-goa-*laa*-ray) *adj* rectangular

rettangolo (rayt-*tahng*-goa-loa) *m* rectangle, oblong

rettifica (rayt-*tee*-fee-kah) *f* correction

rettile (*reht*-tee-lay) *m* reptile

retto (*reht*-toa) *adj* right; *m* rectum

reumatismo (ray^{oo}-mah-*tee*-zmoa) *m* rheumatism

revisionare (ray-vee-zyoa-*naa*-ray) *v* revise, overhaul

revisione (ray-vee-zy$\overline{oa}$-nay) *f* revision

revocare (ray-voa-*kaa*-ray) *v* recall

rialzo (*ryahl*-tsoa) *m* rise

riassunto (ryahss-*soon*-toa) *m* résumé

ribassare (ree-bahss-*saa*-ray) *v* lower

ribasso (ree-*bahss*-soa) *m* reduction

ribellione (ree-bayl-l'*$\overline{oa}$*-nay) *f* revolt, rebellion

ribes (*ree*-bayss) *m* currant; ~ **nero** blackcurrant

ricamare (ree-kah-*maa*-ray) *v* embroider

ricambio (ree-*kahm*-byoa) *m* refill

ricamo (ree-*kaa*-moa) *m* embroidery

ricchezza (reek-*kayt*-tsah) *f* riches *pl*, wealth, fortune

riccio (*reet*-choa) *m* hedgehog; ~ **di mare** sea urchin

ricciolo (*reet*-choa-loa) *m* curl; wave

ricciuto (reet-*ch$\overline{oo}$*-toa) *adj* curly

ricco (*reek*-koa) *adj* rich, wealthy

ricerca (ree-*chehr*-kah) *f* research; search

ricetta (ree-*cheht*-tah) *f* prescription; recipe

ricevere (ree-*ch$\overline{ay}$*-vay-ray) *v* receive

ricevimento (ree-chay-vee-*mayn*-toa) *m* reception, receipt

ricevitore (ree-chay-vee-*t$\overline{oa}$*-ray) *m* receiver

ricevuta (ree-chay-*v$\overline{oo}$*-tah) *f* receipt; voucher

richiamare (ree-kyah-*maa*-ray) *v* recall

richiamo (ree-*ki$\ae$ha*-moa) *m* recall *m*; allurement; cross-reference

*richiedere (ree-*kyai*-day-ray) *v* request; demand

richiesta (ree-*kyeh*-stah) *f* request; application

richiesto (ree-*keeeh*-stoa) *adj* requisite

riciclabile (ree-chee-*klah*-bee-lay) *adj* recyclable

riciclare (ree-chee-*klah*-ray) *v* recycle

ricominciare (ree-koa-meen-*chaa*-ray) *v* recommence

ricompensa (ree-koam-*pehn*-sah) *f* reward, prize

ricompensare (ree-koam-payn-*saa*-ray) *v* reward

riconciliazione (ree-koan-chee-lyah-tsy$\overline{oa}$-nay) *f* reconciliation

riconoscente (ree-koa-noash-*shehn*-tay) *adj* grateful, thankful

*riconoscere (ree-koa-*noash*-shay-ray) *v* recognize; acknowledge; admit, confess

riconoscimento (ree-koa-noash-shee-*mayn*-toa) *m* recognition

ricordare (ree-koar-*daa*-ray) *v* remember; *think of; *far ~ remind; **ricordarsi (di)** recollect, remember, recall

ricordo (ree-*kor*-doa) *m* memory, remembrance; souvenir

*ricorrere (ree-*koar*-ray-ray) *v* recur;

appeal; ~ **a** apply to

ricostruire (ree-koa-*strwee*-ray) v *rebuild; reconstruct

ricreazione (ree-kray-ah-*tsyoa*-nay) f recreation

ridacchiare (ree-dahk-*kyaa*-ray) v giggle

ridere (*ree*-day-ray) v laugh

ridicolizzare (ree-dee-koa-leed-*dzaa*-ray) v ridicule

ridicolo (ree-*dee*-koa-loa) adj ridiculous, ludicrous

ridondante (ree-doan-*dahn*-tay) adj redundant

ridotto (ree-*doat*-toa) m lobby, foyer

ridurre (ree-*door*-ray) v reduce, *cut

riduzione (ree-doo-*tsyoa*-nay) f discount, reduction, rebate

rieducazione (ryay-doo-kah-*tsyoa*-nay) f rehabilitation

riempire (ryaym-*pee*-ray) v fill

rientrare (rɪæ*h*yn-*traa*-ray) v return; ~ **in** *be part of

riferimento (ree-fay-ree-*mayn*-toa) m reference

riferire (ree-fay-*ree*-ray) v report

rifiutare (ree-fyoo-*taa*-ray) v deny, refuse; reject

rifiuto (ree-*fyoo*-toa) m refusal; **rifiuti** litter

riflessione (ree-flayss-*syoa*-nay) f deliberation

riflesso (ree-*flehss*-soa) m reflection

***riflettere*[1]** (ree-*fleht*-tay-ray) v (pp riflesso) reflect

***riflettere*[2]** (ree-*fleht*-tay-ray) v (pp riflettuto) *think

riflettore (ree-flayt-*toa*-ray) m searchlight; reflector

riforma (ree-*foar*-mah) f reformation

rifornimento (ree-foar-nee-*mayn*-toa) m supply

rifugiarsi (ree-foo-*jahr*-see) v *seek refuge

rifugiato (ree-foo-*jaa*-toa) m, **-a** f refugee

rifugio (ree-*foo*-joa) m cover, shelter

riga (*ree*-gah) f line; ruler

rigettare (ree-jayt-*taa*-ray) v reject; vomit

rigido (*ree*-jee-doa) adj stiff; bleak; strict

rigirarsi (ree-jee-*rahr*-see) v turn round

rigoroso (ree-goa-*roa*-soa) adj severe

riguardare (ree-gwahr-*daa*-ray) v concern, affect; **per quanto riguarda** as regards; **riguardante** concerning

riguardo (ree-*gwahr*-doa) m regard, consideration; ~ **a** regarding; concerning, with reference to

riguardoso (ree-gwahr-*doa*-soa) adj considerate

rilassamento (ree-lahss-sah-*mayn*-toa) m relaxation

rilassarsi (ree-lahss-*sahr*-see) v relax

rilevante (ree-lay-*vahn*-tay) adj important

rilevare (ree-lay-*vaa*-ray) v notice; collect; *take over

rilievo (ree-*lʲ ai*-voa) m relief; importance

rima (*ree*-mah) f rhyme

rimandare (ree-mahn-*daa*-ray) v postpone; ~ **a** refer to

rimanente (ree-mah-*nehn*-tay) adj remaining

rimanenza (ree-mah-*nehn*-tsah) f remnant

rimanere (ree-mah-*nay*-ray) v stay, remain

rimborsare (reem-boar-*saa*-ray) v reimburse, refund, *repay

rimborso (reem-*boar*-soa) m refund, repayment

rimedio (ree-*may*-dyoa) m remedy

rimessa (ree-*mayss*-sah) f remittance

rimettere (ree-*mayt*-tay-ray) v remit

rimmel ® (*reem*-mayl) *m* mascara

rimorchiare (ree-moar-*kyaa*-ray) *v* tug

rimorchiatore (ree-moar-kyah-*tōa*-ray) *m* tug

rimorchio (ree-*mor*-kyoa) *m* trailer

*rimpiangere (reem-*pyahn*-jay-ray) *v* regret

rimpianto (reem-*pyahn*-toa) *m* regret

rimproverare (reem-proa-vay-*raa*-ray) *v* reproach, reprimand; blame

rimprovero (reem-*praw*-vay-roa) *m* reproach

rimunerare (ree-moo-nay-*raa*-ray) *v* remunerate

rimunerativo (ree-moo-nay-rah-*tee*-voa) *adj* paying

rimunerazione (ree-moo-nay-rah-*tsyōa*-nay) *f* remuneration

rincasare (reeng-kah-*saa*-ray) *v* *go home

*rinchiudere (reeng-*kyōō*-day-ray) *v* *shut in

rinfrescare (reen-fray-*skaa*-ray) *v* refresh

rinfresco (reen-*fray*-skoa) *m* refreshment

ringhiera (reeng-*gyai*-rah) *f* rail

ringraziare (reeng-grah-*tsyaa*-ray) *v* thank

rinnovare (reen-noa-*vaa*-ray) *v* renew

rinoceronte (ree-noa-chay-*roan*-tay) *m* rhinoceros

rinomato (ree-noa-*mah*-toa) *adj* well-known

rintracciare (reen-traht-*chaa*-ray) *v* trace

rinviare (reen-*vyaa*-ray) *v* *send back; adjourn, *put off

rinvio (reen-*vee*-oa) *m* delay

riordinare (ryoar-dee-*naa*-ray) *v* tidy up

riparare (ree-pah-*raa*-ray) *v* shelter; mend, repair, fix

riparazione (ree-pah-rah-*tsyōa*-nay) *f* reparation

riparo (ree-*paa*-roa) *m* shelter; screen

ripartire (ree-pahr-*tee*-ray) *v* divide

ripensare (ree-payn-*saa*-ray) *v* *think over

ripetere (ree-*pai*-tay-ray) *v* repeat

ripetizione (ree-pay-tee-*tsyōa*-nay) *f* repetition

ripetutamente (ree-pay-too-tah-*mayn*-tay) *adv* again and again

ripido (*ree*-pee-doa) *adj* steep

ripieno (ree-*pyai*-noa) *adj* stuffed; *m* filling; stuffing

riportare (ree-poar-*taa*-ray) *v* *bring back

riposante (ree-poa-*sahn*-tay) *adj* restful

riposarsi (ree-poa-*sahr*-see) *v* rest

riposo (ree-*paw*-soa) *m* rest

*riprendere (ree-*prehn*-day-ray) *v* resume

ripresa (ree-*prāy*-sah) *f* round

ripristino (ree-pree-*stee*-noa) *m* revival

*riprodurre (ree-proa-*door*-ray) *v* reproduce

riproduzione (ree-proa-doo-*tsyōa*-nay) *f* reproduction

riprovare (ree-proa-*vaa*-ray) *v* try again

ripugnante (ree-poo-*ñahn*-tay) *adj* repellent

ripugnanza (ree-poo-*ñahn*-tsah) *f* dislike

risarcimento (ree-sahr-chee-*mayn*-toa) *m* indemnity

risata (ree-*saa*-tah) *f* laughter

riscaldamento (ree-skahl-dah-*mayn*-toa) *m* heating

riscatto (ree-*skaht*-toa) *m* ransom

rischiare (ree-*skyaa*-ray) *v* risk

rischio (*ree*-skyoa) *m* risk; chance, hazard

rischioso (ree-*skyoa*-soa) *adj* risky

*riscuotere (ree-*skwaw*-tay-ray) *v* cash

risentirsi per (ree-sayn-*teer*-see) resent

riserva (ree-*sehr*-vah) *f* reserve; store; qualification; **di ~** spare

riservare (ree-sayr-*vaa*-ray) *v* reserve, engage

riservato (ree-sayr-*vaa*-toa) *adj* reserved

riso¹ (*ree*-soa) *m* laugh

riso² (*ree*-soa) *m* rice

risoluto (ree-soa-*loo*-toa) *adj* determined, resolute

*risolvere (ree-*sol*-vay-ray) *v* solve

risparmi (ree-*spahr*-mee) *mpl* savings *pl*

risparmiare (ree-spahr-*myaa*-ray) *v* save

rispedire (ree-spay-*dee*-ray) *v* *send back

rispettabile (ree-spayt-*taa*-bee-lay) *adj* respectable

rispettare (ree-spayt-*taa*-ray) *v* respect

rispettivo (ree-spayt-*tee*-voa) *adj* respective

rispetto (ree-*speht*-toa) *m* esteem, respect

rispettoso (ree-spayt-*toa*-soa) *adj* respectful

risplendere (ree-*splehn*-day-ray) *v* *shine

*rispondere (ree-*spoan*-day-ray) *v* answer; reply

risposta (ree-*spoa*-stah) *f* answer, reply; **in ~** in reply; **senza ~** unanswered

ristorante (ree-stoa-*rahn*-tay) *m* restaurant

risultare (ree-sool-*taa*-ray) *v* result; appear

risultato (ree-sool-*taa*-toa) *m* result;

issue, effect, outcome

ritardare (ree-tahr-*daa*-ray) *v* delay

ritardo (ree-*tahr*-doa) *m* delay; **in ~** late

*ritenere (ree-tay-*nay*-ray) *v* consider

ritirare (ree-tee-*raa*-ray) *v* *withdraw; *draw

ritmo (*reet*-moa) *m* rhythm

ritornare (ree-toar-*naa*-ray) *v* turn back, return

ritorno (ree-*toar*-noa) *m* return; way back; **andata e ~** round trip *Am*

ritratto (ree-*traht*-toa) *m* portrait

ritrovare (ree-troa-*vaa*-ray) *v* recover, *find back

riunione (ryoo-*nyoa*-nay) *f* assembly, meeting

riunire (ryoo-*nee*-ray) *v* reunite; assemble; join

*riuscire (ryoosh-*shee*-ray) *v* manage, succeed; *make; **riuscito** successful

riva (*ree*-vah) *f* bank, shore; **~ del mare** seashore

rivale (ree-*vaa*-lay) *m* rival

rivaleggiare (ree-vah-layd-*jaa*-ray) *v* rival

rivalità (ree-vah-lee-*tah*) *f* rivalry

*rivedere (ree-vay-*day*-ray) *v* check

rivelare (ree-vay-*laa*-ray) *v* reveal

rivelazione (ree-vay-lah-*tsyoa*-nay) *f* revelation

rivendicare (ree-vayn-dee-*kaa*-ray) *v* claim

rivendicazione (ree-vayn-dee-kah-*tsyoa*-nay) *f* claim

rivenditore (ree-vayn-dee-*toa*-ray) *m* retailer

riviera (ree-*vyay*-rah) *f* coast

rivista (ree-*vee*-stah) *f* magazine, review; revue; **~ mensile** monthly magazine

*rivolgersi a (ree-*vol*-jayr-see) apply to

rivolgimento (ree-voal-jee-*mayn*-toa)

m reverse

rivolta (ree-*vol*-tah) *f* revolt, rebellion

rivoltante (ree-voal-*tahn*-tay) *adj* revolting

rivoltarsi (ree-voal-*tahr*-see) *v* revolt

rivoltella (ree-voal-*tehl*-lah) *f* revolver

rivoluzionario (ree-voa-loo-tsyoa-*naa*-ryoa) *adj* revolutionary

rivoluzione (ree-voa-loo-*tsyoa*-nay) *f* revolution

roba (*raw*-bah) *f* stuff

robaccia (roa-*baht*-chah) *f* trash

robusto (roa-*boo*-stoa) *adj* robust, solid

roccaforte (roak-kah-*for*-tay) *f* stronghold

rocchetto (roak-*kayt*-toa) *m* spool

roccia (*rot*-chah) *f* rock

roccioso (roat-*choa*-soa) *adj* rocky

roco (*raw*-koa) *adj* hoarse

Roma (*roa*-mah) *f* Rome

Romania (roa-mah-*nee*-ah) *f* Rumania

romantico (roa-*mahn*-tee-koa) *adj* romantic

romanziere (roa-mahn-*dzyai*-ray) *m* novelist

romanzo (roa-*mahn*-dzoa) *m* novel; ~ **a puntate** serial; ~ **poliziesco** detective story

rombo¹ (*roam*-boa) *m* roar

rombo² (*roam*-boa) *m* brill

romeno (roa-*mai*-noa) *adj* Rumanian; *m*, **-a** *f* Rumanian

*rompere (*roam*-pay-ray) *v* *break

rompicapo (roam-pee-*kaa*-poa) *m* puzzle

rondine (*roan*-dee-nay) *f* swallow

rosa (*raw*-zah) *f* rose; *adj* rose, pink

rosario (roa-*zaa*-ryoa) *m* rosary, beads *pl*

rosolia (roa-*zoa*-lee-ah) *f* German measles

rospo (*ro*-spoa) *m* toad

rossetto (roass-*sayt*-toa) *m* lipstick

rosso (*roass*-soa) *adj* red

rosticceria (roa-steet-chay-*ree*-ah) *f* grillroom

rotolare (roa-toa-*laa*-ray) *v* roll

rotolo (*raw*-toa-loa) *m* roll

rotonda (roa-*toan*-dah) *f* roundabout

rotondo (roa-*toan*-doa) *adj* round

rotta (*roat*-tah) *f* route; course

rotto (*roat*-toa) *adj* broken

rottura (roat-*too*-rah) *f* breaking; break-up

rotula (*raw*-too-lah) *f* kneecap

roulette (roo-*leht*) *f* roulette

roulotte (roo-*lōat*) *f* caravan; trailer *Am*

rovesciare (roa-vaysh-*shaa*-ray) *v* *spill, knock over; *overthrow; turn inside out; **rovesciarsi** overturn

rovescio (roa-*vehsh*-shoa) *m* reverse; **alla rovescia** the other way round; inside out

rovina (roa-*vee*-nah) *f* ruin; **rovine** ruins

rovinare (roa-vee-*naa*-ray) *v* ruin

rozzo (*road*-dzoa) *adj* gross

rubare (roo-*baa*-ray) *v* *steal; rob

rubinetto (roo-bee-*nayt*-toa) *m* tap; faucet *Am*

rubino (roo-*bee*-noa) *m* ruby

rubrica (roo-*bree*-kah) *f* column

ruga (*rōo*-gah) *f* wrinkle

ruggine (*rood*-jee-nay) *f* rust

ruggire (rood-*jee*-ray) *v* roar

ruggito (rood-*jee*-toa) *m* roar

rugiada (roo-*jaa*-dah) *f* dew

rullino (rool-*lee*-noa) *m* film

rumore (roo-*mōa*-ray) *m* noise

rumoroso (roo-moa-*rōa*-soa) *adj* noisy

ruolo (rwaw-loa) *m* role; **di ~** on the staff

ruota (*rwaw*-tah) *f* wheel; **~ di scorta** spare wheel

rurale (roo-*raa*-lay) *adj* rural
ruscello (roosh-*shehl*-loa) *m* brook, stream
russare (rooss-*saa*-ray) *v* snore
Russia (*rooss*-syah) *f* Russia

russo (*rooss*-soa) *adj* Russian; *m*, **-a** *f* Russian
rustico (*roo*-stee-koa) *adj* rustic
ruvido (*rōō*-vee-doa) *adj* uneven

S

sabato (*saa*-bah-toa) *m* Saturday
sabbia (*sahb*-byah) *f* sand
sabbioso (sahb-*byōa*-soa) *adj* sandy
sacchetto (sahk-*kayt*-toa) *m* paper bag; pouch
sacco (*sahk*-koa) *m* bag, sack; **~ a pelo** sleeping bag
sacerdote (sah-chayr-*daw*-tay) *m* priest
sacrificare (sah-kree-fee-*kaa*-ray) *v* sacrifice
sacrificio (sah-kree-*fee*-choa) *m* sacrifice
sacrilegio (sah-kree-*lai*-joa) *m* sacrilege
sacro (*saa*-kroa) *adj* sacred
saggezza (sahd-*jayt*-tsah) *f* wisdom
saggio (*sahd*-joa) *adj* wise; *m* essay
sala (*saa*-lah) *f* hall; **~ da ballo** ballroom; **~ concerti** concert hall; **~ da pranzo** dining room; **~ d'aspetto** waiting room; **~ da tè** tea-shop; **~ di lettura** reading room; **~ per fumatori** smoking room
salario (sah-*laa*-ryoa) *m* salary, pay
salassare (sah-lahss-*saa*-ray) *v* *bleed
salato (sah-*laa*-toa) *adj* salty
saldare (sahl-*daa*-ray) *v* weld; *pay off
saldatura (sahl-dah-*tōō*-rah) *f* joint
saldo (*sahl*-doa) *adj* firm; *m* balance; **saldi** sales
sale (*saa*-lay) *m* salt; **sali da bagno** bath salts

saliera (sah-*lʸai*-rah) *f* salt cellar, salt shaker *Am*
***salire** (sah-*lee*-ray) *v* ascend; *rise, increase
salita (sah-*lee*-tah) *f* slope; climb
saliva (sah-*lee*-vah) *f* spit
salmone (sahl-*mōa*-nay) *m* salmon
salone (sah-*lōa*-nay) *m* salon; lounge; hall
salotto (sah-*lot*-toa) *m* living room
salsa (*sahl*-sah) *f* sauce
salsiccia (sahl-*seet*-chah) *f* sausage
saltare (sahl-*taa*-ray) *v* jump
saltellare (sahl-tayl-*laa*-ray) *v* skip, hop
saltello (sahl-*tehl*-loa) *m* hop
salto (*sahl*-toa) *m* leap, jump
salubre (sah-*lōō*-bray) *adj* wholesome
salutare (sah-loo-*taa*-ray) *v* greet; salute; say hello to
salute (sah-*lōō*-tay) *f* health
saluto (sah-*lōō*-toa) *m* greeting
salvagente (sahl-vah-*dʒayn*-tay) *m* lifebelt; ring; traffic island
salvare (sahl-*vaa*-ray) *v* save, rescue
salvataggio (sahl-vah-*tahd*-joa) *m* rescue; **cintura di ~** lifebelt
salvatore (sahl-vah-*tōa*-ray) *m* savio(u)r
salve! (*sahl*-vay) hello!
salvo (*sahl*-voa) *prep* except
sanatorio (sah-nah-*taw*-ryoa) *m* sanatorium

sandalo (*sahn*-dah-loa) *m* sandal

sangue (*sahng*-gway) *m* blood; **~ dal naso** nosebleed

sanguinare (sahng-gwee-*naa*-ray) *v* *bleed

sanitario (sah-nee-*taa*-ryoa) *adj* sanitary

sano (*saa*-noa) *adj* healthy; well

santo (*sahn*-toa) *adj* holy; *m* saint

santuario (sahn-*twaa*-ryoa) *m* shrine

***sapere** (sah-*pāy*-ray) *v* taste; *know; *be able to

sapone (sah-*pōa*-nay) *m* soap; **~ da barba** shaving soap

sapore (sah-*pōa*-ray) *m* taste

saporito (sah-poa-*ree*-toa) *adj* savo(u)ry, tasty

sardina (sahr-*dee*-nah) *f* sardine

sarta (*sahr*-tah) *f* dressmaker

sarto (*sahr*-toa) *m* tailor

sasso (*sahss*-soa) *m* stone

satellite (sah-*tehl*-lee-tay) *m* satellite

saudita (sou-*dee*-tah) *adj* Saudi Arabian

sauna (*sou*-nah) *f* sauna

sbadigliare (zbah-dee-*lʸaa*-ray) *v* yawn

sbagliarsi (zbah-*lʸahr*-see) *v* *be mistaken

sbagliato (zbah-*lʸaa*-toa) *adj* false, wrong; misplaced

sbagliarsi (*zbah-lʸahr*-see) *v* make a mistake

sbaglio (*zbaa*-lʸoa) *m* mistake, error

sbalordire (zbah-loar-*dee*-ray) *v* astonish

sbarcare (zbahr-*kaa*-ray) *v* land, disembark

sbarra (*zbahr*-rah) *f* bar

sbattere (*zbaht*-tay-ray) *v* slam; whip; **andare a ~ contro** hit

sbiadire (zbyah-*dee*-ray) *v* fade

sbottonare (zboat-toa-*naa*-ray) *v* unbutton

sbucciare (zboot-*chaa*-ray) *v* peel

scacchi (*skahk*-kee) *mpl* chess

scacchiera (skahk-*kyai*-rah) *f* draughtboard; checkerboard *Am*

scacciare (skaht-*chaa*-ray) *v* chase

scacco! (*skahk*-koa) check!

scadente (skah-*dehn*-tay) *adj* poor

scadenza (skah-*dehn*-tsah) *f* expiry; deadline

***scadere** (skah-*dāy*-ray) *v* expire

scaffale (skahf-*faa*-lay) *m* shelf

scala (*skaa*-lah) *f* stairs *pl*, staircase; ladder; scale; **~ antincendio** fire escape; **~ mobile** escalator

scaldare (skahl-*daa*-ray) *v* warm, heat

scalfire (skahl-*fee*-ray) *v* scratch

scalfittura (skahl-feet-*tōō*-rah) *f* scratch

scalino (skah-*lee*-noa) *m* step

scalo (*skaa*-loa) *m* dock

scalpello (skahl-*pehl*-loa) *m* chisel

scalpore (skahl-*pōa*-ray) *m* fuss

scambiare (skahm-*byaa*-ray) *v* exchange

scambio (*skahm*-byoa) *m* exchange; points *pl*

scandalo (*skahn*-dah-loa) *m* scandal; offence, offense *Am*

Scandinavia (skahn-dee-*naa*-vyah) *f* Scandinavia

scandinavo (skahn-dee-*naa*-voa) *adj* Scandinavian; *m*, **-a** *f* Scandinavian

scapolo (*skaa*-poa-loa) *adj* unmarried

scappamento (skahp-pah-*mayn*-toa) *m* exhaust

scappare (skahp-*paa*-ray) *v* escape; slip

scaricare (skah-ree-*kaa*-ray) *v* discharge, unload

scarlattina (sskahr-laht-*tee*-nah) *f* scarlet fever

scarlatto (skahr-*laht*-toa) *adj* scarlet

scarpa (*skahr*-pah) *f* shoe; **lucido per**

scarpe shoe polish; **scarpe da ginnastica** gym shoes, plimsolls *pl*; sneakers *plAm*; **scarpe da tennis** tennis shoes

scarpone (*skahr-pōa-nay*) *m* boot

scarrozzata (skahr-roat-*tsaa*-tah) *f* drive

scarsamente (skahr-sah-*mayn*-tay) *adv* scarcely

scarsezza (skahr-*sayt*-tsah) *f* want

scarso (*skahr*-soa) *adj* scarce; small

scartare (skahr-*taa*-ray) *v* discard

scassinare (skahss-see-*naa*-ray) *v* burgle

scassinatore (skahss-see-nah-*tōa*-ray) *m* burglar

scatola (*skaa*-toa-lah) *f* box; ~ **di colori** paintbox; ~ **di fiammiferi** matchbox

scatolone (skah-toa-*lōa*-nay) *m* carton

scavare (skah-*vaa*-ray) *v* *dig

scavo (*skaa*-voa) *m* excavation

*scegliere (*shai-l'ay*-ray) *v* *choose; pick, select; elect

scelta (*shayl*-tah) *f* choice; pick, selection

scelto (*shayl*-toa) *adj* select

scena (*shai*-nah) *f* scene; stage

scenario (shay-*naa*-ryoa) *m* setting

*scendere (*shayn*-day-ray) *v* descend; *get off

scheda (*skay*-dah) *f* card; form

scheggia (*skayd*-jah) *f* splinter, chip

scheggiare (skayd-*jaa*-ray) *v* chip

scheletro (*skai*-lay-troa) *m* skeleton

schema (*skai*-mah) *m* scheme; diagram

schermo (*skayr*-moa) *m* screen

scherno (*skayr*-noa) *m* scorn

scherzare (skayr-*tsaa*-ray) *v* joke

scherzo (*skayr*-tsoa) *m* joke; fun

schiaccianoci (skyaht-chah-*nōa*-chee) *m* nutcrackers *pl*

schiacciare (skyaht-*chaa*-ray) *v* mash; press; overwhelm

schiaffeggiare (skyahf-fayd-*jaa*-ray) *v* slap

schiaffo (*skyahf*-foa) *m* slap

schiavo (*skyaa*-voa) *m* slave

schiena (*skyay*-nah) *f* back

schioccare (skyoak-*kaa*-ray) *v* crack

schiocco (*skyok*-koa) *m* crack

schiuma (*skyōo*-mah) *f* lather, foam, froth

schivo (*skee*-voa) *adj* shy

schizzare (skeet-*tsaa*-ray) *v* splash

schizzo (*skeet*-tsoa) *m* sketch

sci (shee) *m* ski; skiing; **scarponi da ~** ski boots; **~ d'acqua** water ski

sciacquare (shahk-*kwaa*-ray) *v* rinse

sciagura (shah-*gōo*-rah) *f* disaster

scialle (*shahl*-lay) *m* scarf, shawl

sciare (*shyaa*-ray) *v* ski

sciarpa (*shahr*-pah) *f* scarf

sciatore (shyah-*tōa*-ray) *m*, **-trice** *f* skier

sciatto (*shaht*-toa) *adj* slovenly

scientifico (shayn-*tee*-fee-koa) *adj* scientific

scienza (*shehn*-tsah) *f* science

scienziato (shayn-*tsyaa*-toa) *m*, **-a** *f* scientist

scimmia (*sheem*-myah) *f* monkey

scintilla (sheen-*teel*-lah) *f* spark

scintillante (sheen-teel-*lahn*-tay) *adj* sparkling

scintillare (sheen-teel-*laa*-ray) *v* *shine

sciocchezza (shoak-*kayt*-tsah) *f* nonsense

sciocco (*shok*-koa) *adj* crazy, foolish silly; *m* fool

*sciogliere (*shaw-l'ay*-ray) *v* dissolve melt; **sciogliersi** melt

scioperare (shoa-pay-*raa*-ray) *v* *strike

sciopero (*shaw*-pay-roa) *m* strike

sciroppo (shee-*rop*-poa) *m* syrup

scivolare (shee-voa-*laa*-ray) *v* glide, slip; skid

scivolata (shee-voa-*laa*-tah) *f* slide

scivolo (*shee*-voa-loa) *m* slide

scodella (skoa-*dehl*-lah) *f* bowl

scogliera (skoa-*l^yay*-rah) *f* cliff

scoglio (*skaw*-l^yoa) *m* cliff

scoiattolo (skoa-*yaht*-toa-loa) *m* squirrel

scolara (skoa-*laa*-rah) *f* schoolgirl

scolaro (skoa-*laa*-roa) *m* schoolboy; pupil

scolo (*skōa*-loa) *m* drain

scolorirsi (skoa-loa-*reer*-see) *v* fade, discolo(u)r

scommessa (skoam-*mayss*-sah) *f* bet

*scommettere (skoam-*mayt*-tay-ray) *v* *bet

scomodo (*skaw*-moa-doa) *adj* uncomfortable; inconvenient

*scomparire (skoam-pah-*ree*-ray) *v* disappear

scompartimento (skoam-pahr-tee-*mayn*-toa) *m* compartment

*sconfiggere (skoan-*feed*-jay-ray) *v* defeat

sconfinato (skoan-fee-*naa*-toa) *adj* unlimited

sconfitta (skoan-*feet*-tah) *f* defeat

sconosciuto (skoa-noash-*shōo*-toa) *adj* unfamiliar

sconsiderato (skoan-see-day-*raa*-toa) *adj* rash

scontentare (skoan-tayn-*taa*-ray) *v* displease

scontento (skoan-*tehn*-toa) *adj* dissatisfied, discontented

sconto (*skoan*-toa) *m* discount, rebate; **tasso di ~** bank rate

scontrarsi (skoan-*trahr*-see) *v* crash

scontrino (skoan-*tree*-noa) *m* receipt

scontro (*skoan*-troa) *m* collision, crash

scopa (*skōa*-pah) *f* broom

scopare (skoa-*paa*-ray) *v* *sweep

scoperta (skoa-*pehr*-tah) *f* discovery

scopo (*skaw*-poa) *m* design; **allo ~ di** to, in order to

scoppiare (skoap-*pyaa*-ray) *v* *burst

scoppio (*skop*-pyoa) *m* outbreak

*scoprire (skoa-*pree*-ray) *v* uncover; detect, discover

*scorgere (*skor*-jay-ray) *v* perceive

*scorrere (*skoar*-ray-ray) *v* flow, stream

scorretto (skoar-*reht*-toa) *adj* incorrect

scorso (*skoar*-soa) *adj* past, last

scorta (*skor*-tah) *f* escort; stock

scortare (skoar-*taa*-ray) *v* escort

scortese (skoar-*tāy*-zay) *adj* unkind, impolite

scossa (*skoss*-sah) *f* shock

scottare (skoat-*taa*-ray) *v* burn

scottatura (skoat-tah-*too*-rah) *f* burn

Scozia (*skaw*-tsyah) *f* Scotland

scozzese (skoat-*tsāy*-say) *adj* Scottish, Scotch; *m/f* Scot

scritto (*skreet*-toa) *m* writing

scrittoio (skreet-*tōa*-yoa) *m* bureau

scrittore (skreet-*tōa*-ray) *m*, **-trice** *f* writer

scrittura (skreet-*tōō*-rah) *f* handwriting

scrivania (skree-vah-*nee*-ah) *f* desk

*scrivere (*skree*-vay-ray) *v* *write; **~ a macchina** type

scrupoloso (skroo-poa-*lōa*-soa) *adj* careful

sculacciata (skoo-laht-*chaa*-tah) *f* spanking

scultore (skool-*tōa*-ray) *m*, **-trice** *f* sculptor

scultura (skool-*tōō*-rah) *f* sculpture; **~ in legno** carving

scuola (*skwaw*-lah) *f* school; **~ di equitazione** riding school; **~ media**

secondary school; **~ materna** kindergarten

*scuotere (skwaw-tay-ray) v shock

scuro (skoo-roa) adj obscure

scusa (skoo-zah) f apology, excuse

scusare (skoo-zaa-ray) v excuse; **scusa!** sorry!; **scusarsi** apologize

sdraiarsi (zdrah-yahr-see) v *lie down

sdrucciolevole (zdroot-choa-lay-voa-lay) adj slippery

se (say) conj if; whether; **se … o** whether … or

sé (say) pron oneself

sebbene (sayb-bai-nay) conj though, although

seccatore (sayk-kah-toa-ray) m bore

seccatura (sayk-kah-too-rah) f trouble, bother

secchio (sayk-kyoa) m pail, bucket

secolo (sai-koa-loa) m century

secondario (say-koan-daa-ryoa) adj secondary, subordinate

secondo¹ (say-koan-doa) num second; **di seconda mano** second-hand

secondo² (say-koan-doa) prep according to

secondo³ (say-koan-doa) m second

sedano (sai-dah-noa) m celery

sedativo (say-dah-tee-voa) m sedative

sede (sai-day) f seat; headquarters

sedere (say-day-ray) m bottom

*sedere (say-day-ray) v *sit; *sedersi *sit down

sedia (sai-dyah) f chair, seat; **~ a rotelle** wheelchair; **~ a sdraio** deckchair

sedicesimo (say-dee-chai-zee-moa) num sixteenth

sedici (say-dee-chee) num sixteen

sedile (say-dee-lay) m seat

sedimento (say-dee-mayn-toa) m deposit

*sedurre (say-door-ray) v seduce

seduta (say-doo-tah) f session

sega (say-gah) f saw

segatura (say-gah-too-rah) f sawdust

seggio (sehd-joa) m chair

seggiolino (sehd-joa-lee-noa) m child's seat

seggiolone (sehd-joa-loa-nay) m high chair

seggiovia (sehd-joa-vyah) f chair lift

segheria (say-gay-ree-ah) f sawmill

segmento (sayg-mayn-toa) m segment

segnalare (say-ñah-laa-ray) v signal; indicate

segnale (say-ñaa-lay) m signal; **~ di soccorso** distress signal

segnare (say-ñaa-ray) v mark; score

segno (say-ñoa) m sign; mark; token signal

segretaria (say-gray-taa-ryah) f secretary

segretario (say-gray-taa-ryoa) m clerk, secretary

segreteria (say-gray-tay-ryah) f administrative office; **~ telefonica** answering maschine

segreto (say-gray-toa) adj secret; m secret

seguente (say-gwehn-tay) adj following

seguire (say-gwee-ray) v follow; **in seguito** then, afterwards

seguitare (say-gooæ*h*-taa-ray) v continue

sei (say) num six

selezionare (say-lay-tsyoa-naa-ray) v select; **selezionato** select

selezione (say-lay-tsyoa-nay) f selection; choice

sella (sehl-lah) f saddle

selvaggina (sayl-vahd-jee-nah) f game

selvaggio (sayl-vahd-joa) adj fierce, savage

selvatico (sayl-vaa-tee-koa) adj wild

semaforo (say-maa-foa-roa) m traffic

light

sembrare (saym-*braa*-ray) v appear, seem, look

seme ($\overline{say}$-may) m pip

semenza (say-*mehn*-tsah) f seed

semi- (say-mee) semi-

semicerchio (say-mee-*chehr*-kyoa) m semicircle

seminare (say-mee-*naa*-ray) v *sow

seminterrato (say-meen-tayr-*raa*-toa) m basement

semplice (*saym*-plee-chay) adj simple; plain; mere

sempre (*sehm*-pray) adv always, ever; ~ **diritto** straight ahead; **per** ~ forever, for ever

senape (*sai*-nah-pay) f mustard

senato (say-*naa*-toa) m senate

senatore (say-nah-*tōa*-ray) m, **-trice** f senator

senile (say-*nee*-lay) adj senile

seno ($\overline{say}$-noa) m breast, bosom

sensato (sayn-*saa*-toa) adj down-to-earth

sensazionale (sayn-sah-tsyoa-*naa*-lay) adj sensational

sensazione (sayn-sah-*tsyōa*-nay) f feeling; sensation

sensibile (sayn-*see*-bee-lay) adj sensitive

sensibilità (sayn-see-bee-lee-*tah*) f sensibility

senso (*sehn*-soa) m sense; reason; ~ **unico** one-way traffic

sentenza (sayn-*tehn*-tsah) f sentence, verdict

sentiero (sayn-*tyai*-roa) m trail, path, lane, footpath

sentimentale (sayn-tee-mayn-*taa*-lay) adj sentimental

sentimento (sayn-tee-*mayn*-toa) m feeling

sentire (sayn-*tee*-ray) v *feel; listen

senza (*sehn*-tsah) prep without;

senz'altro without fail

separare (say-pah-*raa*-ray) v part, separate, divide; **separato** separate

separatamente (say-pah-rah-tah-*mayn*-tay) adv apart

sepoltura (say-poal-*tōo*-rah) f burial

seppellimento (sayp-payl-lee-*mayn*-toa) m burial

seppellire (sayp-payl-*lee*-ray) v bury

sequenza (say-*kwehn*-tsah) f shot

sequestrare (say-kway-*straa*-ray) v confiscate

sera ($\overline{say}$-rah) f evening; night

serata (say-*raa*-tah) f evening

serbatoio (sayr-bah-*tōo*-yoa) m reservoir; tank; ~ **di benzina** petrol tank, gas tank Am

sereno (say-*rāy*-noa) adj serene

serie (*sai*-ryay) f (pl ~) series, sequence

serietà (say-ryay-*tah*) f seriousness; gravity

serio (*sai*-ryoa) adj serious

sermone (sayr-*mōa*-nay) m sermon

serpeggiante (sayr-payd-*jahn*-tay) adj winding

serpente (sayr-*pehn*-tay) m snake

serra (*sehr*-rah) f greenhouse

serrare (sayr-*raa*-ray) v tighten

serratura (sayr-rah-*tōo*-rah) f lock

servire (sayr-*vee*-ray) v attend on, serve, wait on

servitore (sayr-vee-*tōa*-ray) m servant

servizievole (sayr-vee-*tsyāy*-voa-lay) adj obliging, helpful

servizio (sayr-*vee*-tsyoa) m service; service charge; ~ **da tè** tea set; ~ **in camera** room service; ~ **postale** postal service

servo (*sehr*-voa) m, **-a** f servant

servosterzo (sehr-voa-stayr-*tsoa*) m power steering

sessanta (sayss-*sahn*-tah) num sixty

sessione (sayss-*syōa*-nay) f session

sesso (*sehss*-soa) *m* sex

sessuale (sayss-*swaa*-lay) *adj* sexual

sessualità (sayss-swah-lee-*tah*) *f* sexuality

sesto (*seh*-stoa) *num* sixth

seta (*say*-tah) *f* silk

setacciare (say-taht-*chaa*-ray) *v* sieve

setaccio (say-*taht*-choa) *m* sieve

sete (*say*-tay) *f* thirst

settanta (sayt-*tahn*-tah) *num* seventy

sette (*seht*-tay) *num* seven

settembre (sayt-*tehm*-bray) September

settentrionale (sayt-tayn-tryoa-*naa*-lay) *adj* northerly, north

settentrione (sayt-tayn-*tryoa*-nay) *m* north

setticemia (sayt-tee-chay-*mee*-ah) *f* blood poisoning

settimana (sayt-tee-*maa*-nah) *f* week

settimanale (sayt-tee-mah-*naa*-lay) *adj* weekly

settimo (*seht*-tee-moa) *num* seventh

settore (sayt-*toa*-ray) *m* field

severo (say-*vai*-roa) *adj* harsh, strict, severe

sezione (say-*tsyoa*-nay) *f* department; section

sfacciato (sfaht-*chaa*-toa) *adj* bold

sfavorevole (sfah-voa-*ray*-voa-lay) *adj* unfavo(u)rable

sfera (*sfai*-rah) *f* sphere

sfida (*sfee*-dah) *f* challenge

sfidare (sfee-*daa*-ray) *v* challenge, dare

sfilacciarsi (sfee-laht-*chahr*-see) *v* fray

sfiorare (sfyoa-*raa*-ray) *v* skim over; touch on

sfondo (*sfoan*-doa) *m* background

sfortuna (sfoar-*too*-nah) *f* bad luck, misfortune

sfortunato (sfoar-too-*naa*-toa) *adj* unfortunate, unlucky

sforzarsi (sfoar-*tsahr*-see) *v* try hard

sforzo (*sfor*-tsoa) *m* effort; strain

sfrontato (sfroan-*taa*-toa) *adj* bold

sfruttare (sfroot-*taa*-ray) *v* exploit

sfuggire (sfood-*jee*-ray) *v* escape

sfumatura (sfoo-mah-*too*-rah) *f* nuance

sgangerato (zgahng-gay-*raa*-toa) *adj* ramshackle

sgarbato (zgahr-*baa*-toa) *adj* unkind

sgomberare (zgoam-*bay*-raa-ray) *v* vacate

sgombro (*zgoam*-broa) *m* mackerel

sgradevole (zgrah-*day*-voa-lay) *adj* disagreeable, unpleasant, nasty

sguardo (*zgwahr*-doa) *m* look

si (see) *pron* himself; herself; themselves

sì (see) yes

sia ... sia (*see*-ah) both ... and

siamese (syah-*may*-zay) *adj* Siamese *m/f* Siamese

siccità (seet-chee-*tah*) *f* drought

siccome (seek-*koa*-may) *conj* as

sicurezza (see-koo-*rayt*-tsah) *f* safety; security; **cintura di ~** safety belt, seat belt

sicuro (see-*koo*-roa) *adj* safe, secure; sure

siepe (*syai*-pay) *f* hedge

siero (*syai*-roa) *m* serum

sigaretta (see-gah-*rayt*-tah) *f* cigarette

sigaro (*see*-gah-roa) *m* cigar

sigillo (see-*jeel*-loa) *m* seal

significare (see-ñee-fee-*kaa*-ray) *v* *mean

significativo (see-ñee-fee-kah-*tee*-voa) *adj* significant

significato (see-ñee-fee-*kaa*-toa) *m* meaning, sense

signora (see-*ñoa*-rah) *f* lady; mistress; madam

signore (see-*ñoa*-ray) *m* gentleman; mister; sir

signorina (see-ñoa-*ree*-nah) *f* miss

silenziatore (see-layn-tsyah-*tōa*-ray) *m* silencer; muffler *Am*

silenzio (see-*lehn*-tsyoa) *m* silence

silenzioso (see-layn-*tsyōa*-soa) *adj* silent

sillaba (*seel*-lah-bah) *f* syllable

simbolo (*seem*-boa-loa) *m* symbol

simile (*see*-mee-lay) *adj* alike, like; such; similar

simpatia (seem-pah-*tee*-ah) *f* sympathy

simpatico (seem-*paa*-tee-koa) *adj* nice

simulare (see-moo-*laa*-ray) *v* simulate

simultaneo (see-mool-*taa*-nay-oa) *adj* simultaneous

sinagoga (see-nah-*gaw*-gah) *f* synagogue

sincero (seen-*chai*-roa) *adj* honest, sincere

sindacato (seen-dah-*kaa*-toa) *m* trade union

sindaco (*seen*-dah-koa) *m* mayor

sinfonia (seen-foa-*nee*-ah) *f* symphony

singhiozzo (seeng-*geeot*-tsoa) *m* hiccup

singolare (seeng-goa-*laa*-ray) *adj* queer; *m* singular

singolarità (seeng-goa-lah-ree-*tah*) *f* peculiarity

singolo (*seeng*-goa-loa) *adj* individual, single; *m* individual

sinistra (see-*nee*-strah) *f* left; left-hand; **a ~** on the left, to the left

sinistro (see-*nee*-stroa) *adj* left; ominous, sinister

sino a (*see*-noa ah) as far as, till

sinonimo (see-*naw*-nee-moa) *m* synonym

sintetico (seen-*tai*-tee-koa) *adj* synthetic

sintomo (*seen*-toa-moa) *m* symptom

sintonizzare (seen-toa-need-*dzaa*-ray) *v* tune in

sipario (see-*paa*-ryoa) *m* curtain

sirena (see-*rai*-nah) *f* siren

Siria (*see*-ryah) *f* Syria

siriano (see-*ryaa*-noa) *adj* Syrian; *m*, **-a** *f* Syrian

siringa (see-*reeng*-gah) *f* syringe

sistema (see-*stai*-mah) *m* system; **~ decimale** decimal system; **~ lubrificante** lubrication system

sistemare (see-stay-*maa*-ray) *v* settle; **sistemarsi** settle down

sistematico (see-stay-*maa*-tee-koa) *adj* systematic

sistemazione (see-stay-mah-*tsyōa*-nay) *f* accommodation

sito (*see*-toa) *m* site

situato (see-*twaa*-toa) *adj* situated

situazione (see-twah-*tsyōa*-nay) *f* situation; position

slacciare (zlaht-*chaa*-ray) *v* unfasten, untie

sleale (zlay-*ah*-lay) *adj* unfair; untrustworthy

slegare (zlay-*gaa*-ray) *v* loosen; **slegato** loose

slip (zleep) *mpl* briefs *pl*

slitta (*zleet*-tah) *f* sleigh, sledge

slittare (zleet-*taa*-ray) *v* *slide

slogato (zloa-*gaa*-toa) *adj* dislocated

smacchiatore (zmahk-kyah-*tōa*-ray) *m* stain remover, cleaning fluid

smaltare (zmahl-*taa*-ray) *v* glaze; **smaltato** enamelled

smalto (*zmahl*-toa) *m* enamel; **~ per unghie** nail polish

smarrire (zmahr-*ree*-ray) *v* *lose; *mislay; **smarrito** lost

smemorato (zmay-moa-*raa*-toa) *adj* forgetful

smeraldo (zmay-*rahl*-doa) *m* emerald

*smettere (*zmayt*-tay-ray) *v* cease, stop, quit

smisurato (zmee-zoo-*raa*-toa) *adj* immense

smoking (*zmo*-keeng) *m* dinner jacket; tuxedo *Am*

smorfia (*zmoar*-fyah) *f* grin

smorto (*zmor*-toa) *adj* dull

smussato (zmooss-*saa*-toa) *adj* dull

snello (*znehl*-loa) *adj* slim, slender

sobborgo (soab-*boar*-goa) *m* suburb; outskirts *pl*

sobrio (*saw*-bryoa) *adj* sober

soccombere (soak-*koam*-bay-ray) *v* succumb

soccorso (soak-*koar*-soa) *m* assistance, aid; **cassetta del pronto ~** first-aid kit; **pronto ~** first aid

sociale (soa-*chaa*-lay) *adj* social

socialismo (soa-chah-*lee*-zmoa) *m* socialism

socialista (soa-chah-*lee*-stah) *adj* socialist; *m/f* socialist

società (soa-chyay-*tah*) *f* community; society; company

socio (*saw*-choa) *m*, **-a** *f* associate; partner

*soddisfare (soad-dee-*sfaa*-ray) *v* satisfy

soddisfazione (soad-dee-sfah-tsy*ōā*-nay) *f* satisfaction

sofà (soa-*fah*) *m* sofa

sofferenza (soaf-fay-*rehn*-tsah) *f* suffering

soffiare (soaf-*fyaa*-ray) *v* *blow

soffione (soaf-*fyōā*-nay) *m* dandelion

soffitta (soaf-*feet*-tah) *f* attic

soffitto (soaf-*feet*-toa) *m* ceiling

soffocare (soaf-foa-*kaa*-ray) *v* choke

*soffrire (soaf-*free*-ray) *v* suffer

software (*sōāft*-uea) *m* software

soggetto (soad-*jeht*-toa) *m* topic, subject; **soggetto a** subject to, liable to

soggiornare (soad-joar-*naa*-ray) *v* stay

soggiorno (soad-*joar*-noa) *m* stay; sitting room, living room

soglia (*saw*-l'ah) *f* threshold

sogliola (*saw*-l'oa-lah) *f* sole

sognare (soa-*ñaa*-ray) *v* *dream

sogno (*sōā*-ñoa) *m* dream

solamente (soa-lah-*mayn*-tay) *adv* only

solco (*soal*-koa) *m* groove

soldato (soal-*daa*-toa) *m*, **-essa** *f* soldier

soldi (*sōāl*-dee) *mpl* money

sole (*sōā*-lay) *m* sun

soleggiato (soa-layd-*jaa*-toa) *adj* sunny

solenne (soa-*lehn*-nay) *adj* solemn

solido (soa-*lee*-doa) *adj* sound, solid, firm; *m* solid

solitario (soa-lee-*taa*-ryoa) *adj* lonely

solito (*saw*-lee-toa) *adj* customary, usual, ordinary

solitudine (soa-lee-*tōō*-dee-nay) *f* loneliness

sollecito (soal-*lāy*-chee-toa) *adj* prompt

solleticare (soal-lay-tee-*kaa*-ray) *v* tickle

sollevare (soal-lay-*vaa*-ray) *v* lift, raise; *bring up

sollievo (soal-*l'ai*-voa) *m* relief

solo (*sōā*-loa) *adj* only; *adv* only, alone

soltanto (soal-*tahn*-toa) *adv* only, merely

solubile (soa-*lōō*-bee-lay) *adj* soluble

soluzione (soa-loo-tsy*ōā*-nay) *f* solution

somiglianza (soa-mee-l'*ahn*-tsah) *f* resemblance

somma (*soam*-mah) *f* amount, sum; **~ globale** lump sum

sommario (soam-*maa*-ryoa) *m* summary

somministrare (soam-mee-nee-*straa*-ray) *v* administer

sommo (*soam*-moa) *adj* top

sommossa (soam-*moss*-sah) *f* riot

sonnifero (soan-*nee*-fay-roa) *m*
sleeping pill

sonno (*soan*-noa) *m* sleep

sono (*soa*-noa) *v* (pr essere)

sonoro (soa-*naw*-roa) *adj* noisy

sopportare (soap-poar-*taa*-ray) *v*
*bear, sustain, endure

sopra (*soa*-prah) *prep* over; *adv* above;
al di ~ over; **di ~** upstairs

soprabito (soa-*praa*-bee-toa) *m* coat;
overcoat

sopracciglio (soa-praht-*chee*-lʲoa) *m*
eyebrow

*sopraffare (soa-prahf-*faa*-ray) *v*
overwhelm

soprannome (soa-prahn-*nōa*-may) *m*
nickname

soprattutto (soa-praht-*toot*-toa) *adv*
most of all, especially

sopravvivenza (soa-prahv-vee-*vehn*-
tsah) *f* survival

*sopravvivere (soa-prahv-*vee*-vay-
ray) *v* survive

sordo (*soar*-doa) *adj* deaf

sorella (soa-*rehl*-lah) *f* sister

sorgente (soar-*jehn*-tay) *f* source,
spring, fountain

*sorgere (*sor*-jay-ray) *v* *rise; *arise

sorpassare (soar-pahss-*saa*-ray) *v*
pass; *overtake

sorpasso (soar-*pahs*-soa) *m* passing

sorprendente (soar-prayn-*dehn*-tay)
adj astonishing

*sorprendere (soar-*prehn*-day-ray) *v*
surprise

sorpresa (soar-*prāy*-sah) *f*
astonishment, surprise

*sorridere (soar-*ree*-day-ray) *v* smile

sorriso (soar-*ree*-soa) *m* smile

sorso (*soar*-soa) *m* sip

sorte (*sor*-tay) *f* destiny, lot

sorteggio (soar-*tayd*-joa) *m* draw

sorveglianza (soar-vay-lʲ*ahn*-tsah) *f*
supervision

sorvegliare (soar-vay-lʲ*aa*-ray) *v*
patrol

*sospendere (soa-*spehn*-day-ray) *v*
discontinue, suspend

sospensione (soa-spayn-*syōa*-nay) *f*
suspension

sospettare (soa-spayt-*taa*-ray) *v*
suspect

sospetto (soa-*speht*-toa) *adj*
suspicious; *m* suspicion

sospettoso (soa-spayt-*tōa*-soa) *adj*
suspicious

sostanza (soa-*stahn*-tsah) *f* substance

sostanziale (soa-stahn-*tsyaa*-lay) *adj*
substantial

sosta (*soas*-tah) *f* stop; break

sostare (soa-*staa*-ray) *v* stop

sostegno (soa-*stāy*-ñoa) *m* support

*sostenere (soa-stay-*nāy*-ray) *v* *hold
up, support

sostituire (soa-stee-*twee*-ray) *v*
replace, substitute

sostituto (soa-stee-*tōo*-toa) *m*, **-a** *f*
deputy, substitute

sottaceti (soat-tah-*chāy*-tee) *mpl*
pickles *pl*

sottacqua (soat-*tahk*-kwah) *adj*
underwater

sotterraneo (soa-tayr-*raa*-nay-oa) *adj*
underground

sottile (soat-*tee*-lay) *adj* thin, sheer;
subtle

sotto (*soat*-toa) *prep* beneath, below,
under; *adv* underneath; **di ~**
downstairs

sottolineare (soat-toa-lee-nay-*aa*-ray)
v underline; stress, emphasize

*sottomettere (soat-toa-*mayt*-tay-ray)
v subject; ***sottomettersi** submit

*sottoporre (soat-toa-*poar*-ray) *v*
subject; submit; **~ a un test** test

sottoscritto (soat-toa-*skreet*-toa) *m*

undersigned

*sottoscrivere (soat-toa-*skree*-vay-ray) *v* sign

sottosopra (soat-toa-*sōa*-prah) upside down

sottotitolo (soat-toa-*tee*-toa-loa) *m* subtitle

sottovalutare (soat-toa-vah-loo-*taa*-ray) *v* underestimate

*sottrarre (soat-*trahr*-ray) *v* subtract; deduct

sovrano (soa-*vraa*-noa) *m* sovereign; ruler

sovrappeso (soa-vrahp-*pāy*-soa) *m* overweight

sovrintendenza (soa-vreen-tayn-*dehn*-tsah) *f* supervision

*sovrintendere (soa-vreen-*tehn*-day-ray) *v* supervise

sovvenzione (soav-vayn-*tsyōa*-nay) *f* subsidy

spaccare (spahk-*kaa*-ray) *v* crack; chop; **spaccarsi** *burst

spada (*spaa*-dah) *f* sword

Spagna (*spaa*-ñah) *f* Spain

spagnolo (spah-*ñōa*-loa) *adj* Spanish

spago (*spaa*-goa) *m* twine, cord, string

spalancare (spah-lahng-*kaa*-ray) *v* open wide

spalla (*spahl*-lah) *f* shoulder

*spandere (*spahn*-day-ray) *v* *spill

sparare (spah-*raa*-ray) *v* fire, *shoot

*spargere *v* *strew; *shed, spill; *spread

sparire (spah-*ree*-ray) *v* disappear, vanish

sparo (*spaa*-roa) *m* shot

sparpagliare (spahr-pah-*lʸaa*-ray) *v* scatter

spaventare (spah-vayn-*taa*-ray) *v* scare, frighten; **spaventarsi** *be frightened

spavento (spah-*vehn*-toa) *m* scare, fright

spaventoso (spah-vayn-*tōa*-soa) *adj* dreadful, terrible; horrible, terrifying

spaziare (spah-*tsyaa*-ray) *v* space

spazio (*spaa*-tsyoa) *m* room, space; gap

spazioso (spah-*tsyōa*-soa) *adj* roomy, spacious, large

spazzare (spaht-*tsaa*-ray) *v* *sweep

spazzatura (spaht-tsah-*tōo*-rah) *f* junk, garbage

spazzola (*spaht*-tsoa-lah) *f* brush; hairbrush

spazzolare (spaht-tsoa-*laa*-ray) *v* brush

spazzolino (spaht-tsoa-*lee*-noa) *m* brush; ~ **da denti** toothbrush

specchietto (spehk-*kyayt*-toa) *m* hand mirror; ~ **retrovisore** rear-view mirror

specchio (*spehk*-kyoa) *m* mirror

speciale (spay-*chaa*-lay) *adj* particular, special, peculiar

specialista (spay-chah-*lee*-stah) *m/f* specialist

specialità (spay-chah-lee-*tah*) *f* speciality

specializzarsi (spay-chah-leed-*dzahr*-see) *v* specialize

specialmente (spay-chahl-*mayn*-tay) *adv* especially

specie (*spai*-chay) *f* (pl ~) species, breed; sort

specifico (spay-*chee*-fee-koa) *adj* specific

speculare (spay-koo-*laa*-ray) *v* speculate

spedire (spay-*dee*-ray) *v* despatch, dispatch, *send off, *send; ship

spedizione (spay-dee-*tsyōa*-nay) *f* shipment; expedition

*spegnere (*spai*-ñay-ray) *v* extinguish; *put out, switch off

*spendere (*spehn*-day-ray) *v* *spend

spensierato (spayn-syay-*raa*-toa) *adj*

carefree

speranza (spay-*rahn*-tsah) f hope

speranzoso (spay-rahn-*tsōa*-soa) adj hopeful

sperare (spay-*raa*-ray) v hope

spergiuro (spayr-*jōo*-roa) m perjury

sperimentare (spay-ree-mayn-*taa*-ray) v experiment; experience

spesa (*spāy*-sah) f expense, expenditure; ***fare la ~** shop; **spese** expenses pl, expenditure; **spese di viaggio** fare; travelling expenses

spesso (*spayss*-soa) adj thick; adv often

spessore (spayss-*sōa*-ray) m thickness

spettacolo (spayt-*taa*-koa-loa) m spectacle, show; sight

spettatore (spayt-tah-*tōa*-ray) m, **-trice** f spectator

spettro (*speht*-troa) m spook, ghost

spezie (*spai*-tsyay) fpl spices

spezzare (spayt-*tsaa*-ray) v *break; interrupt

spia (*spee*-ah) f spy

spiacente (spyah-*chehn*-tay) adj sorry

spiacevole (spyah-*chāy*-voa-lay) adj unpleasant

spiaggia (*spyahd*-jah) f beach; **~ per nudisti** nudist beach

spianato (spyah-*naa*-toa) adj level

spiare (*spyaa*-ray) v peep

spicciarsi (speet-*chahr*-see) v hurry

spiccioli (*speet*-choa-lee) mpl change

spiedo (*spyai*-doa) m spit

spiegabile (spyay-*gaa*-bee-lay) adj explicable

spiegare (spyay-*gaa*-ray) v unfold; explain

spiegazione (spyay-gah-*tsyōa*-nay) f explanation

spietato (spyay-*taa*-toa) adj heartless

spilla (*speel*-lah) f brooch; **~ da balia** safety pin

spillo (*speel*-loa) m pin

spina (*spee*-nah) f thorn; plug; **~ di pesce** fishbone; **~ dorsale** spine, backbone

spinaci (spee-*naa*-chee) mpl spinach

*spingere (*speen*-jay-ray) v push

spinta (*speen*-tah) f push

spirito (*spee*-ree-toa) m spirit; soul; ghost

spiritoso (spee-ree-*tōa*-soa) adj witty, humorous

spirituale (spee-ree-*twaa*-lay) adj spiritual

splendido (*splehn*-dee-doa) adj splendid; glorious, magnificent, lovely

splendore (splayn-*dōa*-ray) m glare; splendo(u)r

spogliarsi (spoa-*l'ahr*-see) v undress

spogliatoio (spoa-l'ah-*tōa*-yoa) m dressing room

spoglio (*spaw*-l'oa) adj bare, naked

sponda (*spoan*-dah) f shore

sporcare (spoar-*kaa*-ray) v dirty

sporco (*spor*-koa) adj dirty, foul

*sporgere (*spor*-jay-ray) v *put out; protrude

sport (sport) m sport; **~ invernali** winter sports; **~ velico** yachting

sportivo (spoar-*tee*-voa) m sportsman

sportello (spor-*tehl*-loa) m door; **~ automatico** cash dispenser, automatic teller machine

sposa (*spaw*-zah) f bride

sposare (spoa-*zaa*-ray) v marry

sposarsi (spoa-*zaar*-see) v get married

sposato (spoa-*zaa*-toa) adj married

sposo (*spaw*-zoa) m bridegroom

spostamento (spoa-stah-*mayn*-toa) m shift

spostare (spoa-*staa*-ray) v move

sprecare (spray-*kaa*-ray) v waste

spreco (*sprai*-koa) m waste

spruzzatore (sproot-tsah-*tōā*-ray) *m* atomizer

spugna (*spōō*-ñah) *f* sponge

spumante (spoo-*mahn*-tay) *adj* sparkling

spumare (spoo-*maa*-ray) *v* foam

spuntato (spoon-*taa*-toa) *adj* blunt

spuntino (spoon-*tee*-noa) *m* snack

sputare (spoo-*taa*-ray) *v* *spit

sputo (*spōō*-toa) *m* spit

squadra (*skwaa*-drah) *f* team; gang; soccer team

squalo (*skwaa*-loa) *m* shark

squama (*skwaa*-mah) *f* scale

squattrinato (skwaht-tree-*naa*-toa) *adj* broke

squisito (skwee-*zee*-toa) *adj* exquisite, delicious

stabile (*staa*-bee-lay) *adj* steady, stable, permanent; *m* premises *pl*

stabilire (stah-bee-*lee*-ray) *v* establish; determine

staccare (stahk-*kaa*-ray) *v* detach

stadio (*staa*-dyoa) *m* stadium; stage

stagione (stah-*jōā*-nay) *f* season; **alta ~** peak season, high season; **bassa ~** low season; **fuori ~** off season

stagno (*staa*-ñoa) *m* tin; pond

stagnola (stah-*ñaw*-lah) *f* tinfoil

stalla (*stahl*-lah) *f* stable

stamattina (stah-*maat*-tee-nah) *adv* this morning

stampa (*stahm*-pah) *f* press; picture, print, engraving; **stampe** printed matter

stampante (stahm-*paan*-tay) *f* printer

stampare (stahm-*paa*-ray) *v* print

stampella (stahm-*pehl*-lah) *f* crutch

stancare (stahng-*kaa*-ray) *v* tire

stanco (*stahng*-koa) *adj* weary, tired

stanotte (stah-*not*-tay) *adv* tonight

stantio (stahn-*tee*-oa) *adj* stuffy

stantuffo (stahn-*toof*-foa) *m* piston

stanza (*stahn*-tsah) *f* room

stappare (stahp-*paa*-ray) *v* uncork

*stare (*staa*-ray) *v* stay; **lasciar ~** *keep off; ***star disteso** *lie; **~ attento a** *pay attention to; **~ in guardia** watch out; **~ in piedi** *stand

starnutire (stahr-noo-*tee*-ray) *v* sneeze

stasera (stah-*sai*-rah) *adv* tonight

statale (stah-*taa*-lay) *adj* national

statistica (stah-*tee*-stee-kah) *f* statistics *pl*

Stati Uniti (*staa*-tee oo-*nee*-tee) United States, the States

stato (*staa*-toa) *m* state; condition; **~ di emergenza** emergency

statua (*staa*-twah) *f* statue

stavolta (stah-*vōal*-tah) *adv* this time

stazionario (stah-tsyoa-*naa*-ryoa) *adj* stationary

stazione (stah-*tsyōā*-nay) *f* station; depot *Am*; **~ balneare** seaside resort; **~ centrale** central station; **~ termale** spa

stecca (*stayk*-kah) *f* rod; splint; carton

steccato (stayk-*kaa*-toa) *m* fence

stella (*stayl*-lah) *f* star

stendardo (stayn-*dahr*-doa) *m* banner

*stendere (*stehn*-day-ray) *v* *spread

stenografia (stay-noa-grah-*fee*-ah) *f* shorthand

sterile (*stai*-ree-lay) *adj* sterile

sterilizzare (stay-ree-leed-*dzaa*-ray) *v* sterilize

sterzo (*stayr*-tsoa) *m* steering

stesso (*stayss*-soa) *adj* same; **se ~** himself; **se stessa** herself; **io ~** myself

stile (*stee*-lay) *m* style

stima (*stee*-mah) *f* esteem, respect; ***fare la ~** estimate

stimare (stee-*maa*-ray) *v* esteem

stimolante (stee-moa-*lahn*-tay) *m* stimulant

stimolare (stee-moa-*laa*-ray) *v* stimulate, urge

stimolo (*stee*-moa-loa) *m* impulse

stipendio (stee-*pehn*-dyoa) *m* salary, wages *pl*

stipulare (stee-poo-*laa*-ray) *v* stipulate

stipulazione (stee-poo-lah-*tsyoa*-nay) *f* stipulation

stirare (stee-*raa*-ray) *v* iron, press; **non si stira** wash and wear, drip-dry

stitichezza (stee-tee-*kayt*-tsah) *f* constipation

stitico (*stee*-tee-koa) *adj* constipated

stiva (*stee*-vah) *f* hold

stivale (stee-*vaa*-lay) *m* boot

stizza (*steet*-tsah) *f* temper

stoffa (*stof*-fah) *f* cloth, fabric, material

stola (*staw*-lah) *f* stole

stolto (*stoal*-toa) *adj* foolish

stomachevole (stoa-mah-*kay*-voa-lay) *adj* revolting

stomaco (*staw*-mah-koa) *m* stomach; **bruciore di ~** heartburn

stop (*stoap*) *m* brake light; stop sign

*storcere (*stor*-chay-ray) *v* wrench; sprain

stordito (stoar-*dee*-toa) *adj* giddy, dizzy

storia (*staw*-ryah) *f* history; tale; **~ dell'arte** art history

storico (*staw*-ree-koa) *adj* historical, historic; *m* historian

stornello (stoar-*nehl*-loa) *m* starling

storpio (*stor*-pyo) *adj* crippled

storta (*stor*-tah) *f* wrench

storto (*stor*-toa) *adj* crooked

stoviglie (stoa-*vee*-lʸay) *fpl* pottery; **canovaccio per ~** tea cloth, kitchen towel *Am*

strabico (*straa*-bee-koa) *adj* cross-eyed

straccio (*straht*-choa) *m* rag

strada (*straa*-dah) *f* road, street; drive; **a metà ~** halfway; **~ a pedaggio**

turnpike *Am*; **~ in riparazione** road up; **~ maestra** thoroughfare

strangolare (strahng-goa-*laa*-ray) *v* strangle

straniero (strah-*ñai*-roa) *adj* alien, foreign; *m*, **-a** *f* alien, stranger, foreigner

strano (*straa*-noa) *adj* strange; odd, curious, peculiar, queer, singular, funny

straordinario (strah-oar-dee-*naa*-ryoa) *adj* extraordinary, exceptional

strappare (strahp-*paa*-ray) *v* rip, *tear

strappo (*strahp*-poa) *m* tear

strato (*straa*-toa) *m* layer

strattone (straht-*toa*-nay) *m* tug

stravagante (strah-vah-*gahn*-tay) *adj* extravagant

strega (*stray*-gah) *f* witch

stregare (stray-*gaa*-ray) *v* bewitch

stretta (*strayt*-tah) *f* clutch, grip, grasp; **~ di mano** handshake

strettamente (strayt-tah-*mayn*-tay) *adv* tight

stretto (*strayt*-toa) *adj* narrow; tight

striato (*stryaa*-toa) *adj* striped

strillare (streel-*laa*-ray) *v* scream, yell, shriek

strillo (*streel*-loa) *m* scream, yell, shriek

*stringere (*streen*-jay-ray) *v* tighten

striscia (*streesh*-shah) *f* strip

strisciare (streesh-*shaa*-ray) *v* *creep

strofa (*straw*-fah) *f* stanza

strofinare (stroa-fee-*naa*-ray) *v* rub, scrub; wipe

strozzare (stroat-*tsaa*-ray) *v* choke

strumento (stroo-*mayn*-toa) *m* implement; instrument; **~ musicale** musical instrument

struttura (stroot-*too*-rah) *f* fabric, structure, texture

struzzo (*stroot*-tsoa) *m* ostrich

stucco (*stook*-koa) *m* plaster

studente (stoo-*dehn*-tay) *m*, **-essa** *f* student

studiare (stoo-*dyaa*-ray) *v* study

studio (*stoo*-dyoa) *m* study

stufa (*stoo*-fah) *f* stove; **~ a gas** gas stove

stufo di (*stoo*-foa dee) tired of; bored with

stuoia (*stwaw*-yah) *f* mat

*stupefare (stoo-pay-*faa*-ray) *v* amaze

stupendo (stoo-*pehn*-doa) *adj* wonderful

stupidaggini (stoo-pee-*dahd*-jee-nee) *fpl* rubbish: ***dire ~** talk rubbish

stupido (*stoo*-pee-doa) *adj* stupid; foolish, dumb

stupire (stoo-*pee*-ray) *v* amaze, surprise

stupore (stoo-*poa*-ray) *m* amazement, wonder

stuzzicadenti (stoot-tsee-kah-*dehn*-tee) *m* toothpick

stuzzicare (stoot-tsee-*kaa*-ray) *v* kid, tease

stuzzichino (stoot-tsee-*kee*-noa) *m* appetizer

su (soo) *prep* on, upon, in; above; about; *adv* up; upstairs; **in ~** upwards, up; overhead

subacqueo (soo-*bahk*-kway-oa) *adj* underwater

subalterno (soo-bahl-*tehr*-noa) *adj* subordinate

subire (soo-*bee*-ray) *v* suffer

subito (*soo*-bee-toa) *adv* at once, instantly, straight away, presently, immediately

subordinato (soo-boar-dee-*naa*-toa) *adj* minor

suburbano (soo-boor-*baa*-noa) *adj* suburban

*succedere (soot-*chai*-day-ray) *v* succeed; happen, occur

successione (soot-chayss-*syoa*-nay) *f* sequence

successivo (soot-chayss-*see*-voa) *adj* following, subsequent

successo (soot-*chehss*-soa) *m* success; hit

succhiare (sook-*kyaa*-ray) *v* suck

succo (*sook*-koa) *m* juice

succoso (sook-*koa*-soa) *adj* juicy

succursale (sook-koor-*saa*-lay) *f* branch

sud (sood) *m* south; **polo Sud** South Pole

sudare (soo-*daa*-ray) *v* perspire, sweat

suddito (*sood*-dee-toa) *m* subject

sud-est (soo-*dehst*) *m* southeast

sudicio (*soo*-dee-choa) *adj* dirty; filthy

sudiciume (soo-dee-*choo*-may) *m* dirt

sudore (soo-*doa*-ray) *m* perspiration, sweat

sud-ovest (sood-*aw*-vayst) *m* southwest

sufficiente *adj* enough, sufficient

suffragio (soof-*fraa*-joa) *m* suffrage

suggerimento (sood-jay-ree-*mayn*-toa) *m* suggestion

suggerire (sood-jay-*ree*-ray) *v* suggest

sughero (*soo*-gay-roa) *m* cork

sugo (*soo*-goa) *m* gravy

suicidio (swee-*chee*-dyoa) *m* suicide

sunto (*soon*-toa) *m* summary

suo (*soo*-oa) *adj* (f sua; pl suoi, sue) his; her; **Suo** *adj* your

suocera (*swaw*-chay-rah) *f* mother-in-law

suocero (*swaw*-chay-roa) *m* father-in-law; **suoceri** parents-in-law *pl*

suola (*swaw*-lah) *f* sole

suolo (*swaw*-loa) *m* soil, earth

suonare (swoa-*naa*-ray) *v* sound; *ring; play; **~ il clacson** hoot, honk *Am*

suono (*swaw*-noa) *m* sound

suora (*swaw*-rah) *f* nun; sister

superare (soo-pay-*raa*-ray) v exceed, *outdo

superbo (soo-*pehr*-boa) adj superb

superficiale (soo-payr-fee-*chaa*-lay) adj superficial

superficie (soo-payr-*fee*-chay) f surface

superfluo (soo-*pehr*-flwoa) adj unnecessary, superfluous

superiore (soo-pay-*ryoa*-ray) adj upper, superior

superlativo (soo-payr-lah-*tee*-voa) adj superlative; m superlative

supermercato (soo-payr-mayr-*kaa*-toa) m supermarket

superstizione (soo-payr-stee-*tsyoa*-nay) f superstition

superstrada (soo-payr-*straa*-dah) f motorway, highway Am

supplementare (soop-play-mayn-*taa*-ray) adj extra, additional

supplemento (soop-play-*mayn*-toa) m supplement; surcharge

supplicare (soop-plee-*kaa*-ray) v beg

*supporre (soop-*poar*-ray) v suppose; suspect; **supposto che** supposing that

supposta (soop-*poa*-stah) f suppository

surf (*soorf*) m surfboard

surgelati (soor-jay-*lah*-tee) mpl frozen food

suscitare (soosh-shee-*taa*-ray) v stir up

susina (soo-*see*-nah) f plum

sussidio (sooss-*see*-dyoa) m grant

sussurro (sooss-*soor*-roa) m whisper

suturare (soo-too-*raa*-ray) v sew up

svago (*zvaa*-goa) m recreation

svalutare (zvah-loo-*taa*-ray) v devalue

svalutazione (zvah-loo-tah-*tsyoa*-nay) f devaluation

svantaggio (zvahn-*tahd*-joa) m disadvantage

svedese (zvay-*day*-zay) adj Swedish; m/f Swede

sveglia (*zvay*-lʸah) f alarm clock

svegliare (zvay-*lʸaa*-ray) v *awake, *wake; **svegliarsi** wake up

sveglio (*zvay*-lʸoa) adj awake; clever, smart, bright

svelare (zvay-*laa*-ray) v reveal

svelto (*zvehl*-toa) adj quick

svendita (*zvayn*-dee-tah) f clearance sale

*svenire (zvay-*nee*-ray) v faint

sventolare (zvayn-toa-*laa*-ray) v wave

Svezia (*zvai*-tsyah) f Sweden

sviluppare (zvee-loop-*paa*-ray) v develop

sviluppo (zvee-*loop*-poa) m development

svista (*zvee*-stah) f slip, oversight

svitare (zvee-*taa*-ray) v unscrew

Svizzera (*zveet*-tsay-rah) f Switzerland

svizzero (*zveet*-tsay-roa) adj Swiss; m, **-a** f Swiss

*svolgere (*zvol*-jay-ray) v *unwind; treat; carry out

svolta (*zvol*-tah) f turning, curve

T

tabaccaio (tah-bahk-*kaa*-yoa) m tobacconist

tabaccheria (tah-bahk-kay-*ree*-ah) f tobacconist's, cigar shop

tabacco (tah-*bahk*-koa) *m* tobacco; ~ **da pipa** pipe tobacco

tabella (tah-*behl*-lah) *f* chart, table; ~ **di conversione** conversion chart

tabù (tah-*boo*) *m* taboo

taccagno (tahk-*kaa*-ñoa) *adj* stingy

tacchino (tahk-*kee*-noa) *m* turkey

tacco (*tahk*-koa) *m* heel

taccuino (tahk-*kwee*-noa) *m* notebook

*tacere (tah-*chāy*-ray) *v* *keep quiet, *be silent; ***far ~** silence

tachimetro (tah-*kee*-may-troa) *m* speedometer

taglia (*tah*-lᵛah) *f* size

tagliacarte (tah-lᵛah-*kahr*-tay) *m* paper knife, letter opener *Am*

tagliando (tah-lᵛ*ahn*-doa) *m* coupon

tagliare (tah-lᵛ*aa*-ray) *v* *cut; *cut off, carve, chip

taglio (*taa*-lᵛoa) *m* cut; ~ **di capelli** haircut

tailandese (tigh-lahn-*dāy*-say) *adj* Thai; *m/f* Thai

Tailandia (tigh-*lahn*-dyah) *f* Thailand

talco (*tahl*-koa) *m* talc powder; ~ **per piedi** foot powder

tale (*taa*-lay) *adj* such

talento (tah-*lehn*-toa) *m* gift, talent; **di ~** gifted

talloncino (tahl-loan-*cheenoa*) *m* counterfoil

tallone (tahl-*lōā*-nay) *m* heel

talmente (tahl-*mayn*-tay) *adv* so

taluni (tah-*lōō*-nee) *pron* some

talvolta (tahl-*vol*-tah) *adv* sometimes

tamburo (tahm-*bōō*-roa) *m* drum; ~ **del freno** brake drum

tamponamento (tahm-poa-nah-*mayn*-toa) *m* collision

tampone (tahm-*pōā*-nay) *m* tampon

tana (*taa*-nah) *f* den

tangenziale (*than*-jayn-tsyaa-lay) *f* ring road

tangibile (tahn-*jee*-bee-lay) *adj* tangible

tanto (*tahn*-toa) *adv* as much; **di ~ in tanto** now and then; **ogni ~** occasionally

tappa (*tahp*-pah) *f* stage

tappeto (tahp-*pāy*-toa) *m* carpet; rug

tappezzare (tahp-payt-*tsaa*-ray) *v* upholster

tappezzeria (tahp-payt-tsay-*ree*-ah) *f* wallpaper

tappo (*tahp*-poa) *m* cork, stopper

tardi (*tahr*-dee) *adv* late

tardo (*tahr*-doa) *adj* late; slow

targa (*tahr*-gah) *f* numberplate; nameplate

tariffa (tah-*reef*-fah) *f* tariff, rate; ~ **del parcheggio** parking fee; ~ **doganale** Customs duty; ~ **notturna** night rate

tarma (*tahr*-mah) *f* moth

tartaruga (tahr-tah-*rōō*-gah) *f* turtle

tasca (*tah*-skah) *f* pocket

tassa (*tahss*-sah) *f* tax

tassametro (tahss-*saa*-may-troa) *m* taximeter

tassare (tahss-*saa*-ray) *v* tax

tassì (tahss-*see*) *m* cab, taxi

tassista (tahss-*see*-stah) *m* cab driver, taxi driver

tasto (*tahs*-toa) *m* key

tattica (*taht*-tee-kah) *f* tactics *pl*

tatto (*taht*-toa) *m* touch

taverna (tah-*vehr*-nah) *f* public house, pub; tavern

tavola (*taa*-voa-lah) *f* table; ~ **calda** snack bar, cafeteria; ~ **da surf** surfboard

tavoletta (tah-voa-*layt*-tah) *f* board

tavolo (*taa*-voa-loa) *m* table

tazza (*taht*-tsah) *f* cup; mug

tazzina (*taht*-tsee-nah) *f* cup; ~ **da tè** teacup

te (tay) *pron* you

tè (teh) *m* tea

teatro (tay-*aa*-troa) *m* theatre, theater *Am*; drama; ~ **dell'opera** opera house

tecnica (*tehk*-nee-kah) *f* technique

tecnico (*tehk*-nee-koa) *adj* technical; *m*, **-a** *f* technician

tecnologia (tayk-noa-loa-*jee*-ah) *f* technology

tedesco (tay-*day*-skoa) *adj* German; *m*, **-a** *f* German

tegame (tay-*gaa*-may) *m* pan

tegola (*tay*-goa-lah) *f* tile

teiera (tay-*yai*-rah) *f* teapot

telaio (tay-*laa*-yoa) *m* chassis

telecomando (tay-lay-koa-*maan*-doa) *m* remote control

telefonare (tay-lay-foa-*naa*-ray) *v* ring up, phone, call; call up *Am*

telefonata (tay-lay-foa-*naa*-tah) *f* call

telefonino (tay-lay-foa-*nee*-noa) *m* mobile phone, cellular phone *Am*

telefonista (tay-lay-foa-*nee*-stah) *m/f* telephonist, telephone operator

telefono (tay-*lai*-foa-noa) *m* phone, telephone

telegiornale (tay-lay-joar-naa-lay) *m* news *pl*

telegrafare (tay-lay-grah-*faa*-ray) *v* cable, telegraph

telegramma (tay-lay-*grahm*-mah) *m* cable, telegram

telemetro (tay-*lai*-may-troa) *m* range finder

televisione (tay-lay-vee-*zyoa*-nay) *f* television; ~ **via cavo** cable television; ~ **via satellite** satellite television

televisore (tay-lay-vee-*zoa*-ray) *m* television set

telex (tay-*lehks*) *m* telex

tema (*tai*-mah) *m* theme; essay

temere (tay-*may*-ray) *v* fear, dread

temperamatite (taym-pay-rah-mah-*tee*-tay) *m* pencil sharpener

temperatura (taym-pay-rah-*too*-rah) *f* temperature; ~ **ambientale** room temperature

temperino (taym-pay-*ree*-noa) *m* pocketknife, penknife

tempesta (taym-*peh*-stah) *f* storm, tempest

tempestoso (taym-pay-*stoa*-soa) *adj* stormy

tempia (*tehm*-pyah) *f* temple

tempio (*tehm*-pyoa) *m* temple

tempo (*tehm*-poa) *m* time; weather; **in** ~ in time; ~ **libero** spare time; **un** ~ formerly

temporale (taym-poa-*raa*-lay) *m* thunderstorm

temporalesco (taym-poa-rah-*lay*-skoa) *adj* thundery

temporaneo (taym-poa-*raa*-nay-oa) *adj* temporary

tenace (tay-*naa*-chay) *adj* tough

tenaglie (tay-*naa*-lʸay) *fpl* pincers *pl*

tenda (*tehn*-dah) *f* curtain; tent; awning

tendenza (tayn-*dehn*-tsah) *f* tendency

*tendere (*tehn*-day-ray) *v* stretch; *be inclined to; ~ **a** tend to

tendine (tayn-*dee*-nay) *m* sinew, tendon

*tenere (tay-*nay*-ray) *v* *keep; *hold

tenero (*tai*-nay-roa) *adj* tender

tennis (*tehn*-neess) *m* tennis; **campo da** ~ tennis court

tensione (tayn-*syoa*-nay) *f* tension; stress, pressure

tentare (tayn-*taa*-ray) *v* try, attempt; tempt

tentativo (tayn-tah-*tee*-voa) *m* try, attempt, effort

tentazione (tayn-tah-*tsyoa*-nay) *f* temptation

teologia (tay-oa-loa-*jee*-ah) *f* theology

teoria (tay-oa-*reeah*) *f* theory

teorico (tay-*aw*-ree-koa) *adj*

theoretical

terapia (tay-rah-*pee*-ah) f therapy

tergicristallo (tayr-jee-kree-*stahl*-loa) m windscreen wiper; windshield wiper Am

terminal (*tayr*-mee-*nah*l) m terminal

terminare (tayr-mee-*naa*-ray) v finish; stop

termine (*tehr*-mee-nay) m term; finish, end

termometro (tayr-*maw*-may-troa) m thermometer

termos (*tehr*-moass) m vacuum flask, thermos flask

termosifone (tayr-moa-see-*foa*-nay) m radiator

termostato (tayr-*mo*-stah-toa) m thermostat

terra (*tehr*-rah) f earth; land; ground, soil; **a ~** ashore; down

terracotta (tayr-rah-*kot*-tah) f terracotta

terraferma (tayr-rah-*fayr*-mah) f mainland

terrazza (tayr-*raht*-tsah) f terrace

terremoto (tayr-ray-*maw*-toa) m earthquake

terreno (tayr-*rāy*-noa) m soil; grounds, terrain

terribile (tayr-*ree*-bee-lay) adj terrible; awful, dreadful, frightful

territorio (tayr-ree-*taw*-ryoa) m territory

terrore (tayr-*rōa*-ray) m terror

terrorismo (tayr-roa-*ree*-zmoa) m terrorism

terrorista (tayr-roa-*ree*-stah) m/f terrorist

terzo (*tehr*-tsoa) num third

tesi (*tai*-zee) f thesis

teso (*tāy*-soa) adj tense

tesoriere (tay-zoa-*ryai*-ray) m treasurer

tesoro (tay-*zaw*-roa) m treasure;

Ministero del Tesoro m Treasury

tessera (*tehss*-say-rah) f card; pass; ticket

tessere (*tehss*-say-ray) v *weave

tessitore (tayss-see-*tōa*-ray) m weaver

tessuto (tayss-*sōo*-toa) m tissue; textile

testa (*teh*-stah) f head; **in ~ a** ahead of

testamento (tay-stah-*mayn*-toa) m will

testardo (tay-*stahr*-doa) adj pig-headed, headstrong

testimone (tay-stee-*maw*-nay) m/f witness; **~ oculare** eyewitness

testimoniare (tay-stee-moa-*ñaa*-ray) v testify

testo (*teh*-stoa) m text

tetro (*tai*-troa) adj sombre, somber Am

tetto (*tayt*-toa) m roof; **~ di paglia** thatched roof

ti (tee) pron you; yourself

tiepido (*tyai*-pee-doa) adj lukewarm, tepid

tifo (*tee*-foa) m typhus

tifoso (tee-*fōa*-soa) m, **-a** f fan; supporter

tiglio (*tee*-lʸoa) m limetree, lime

tigre (*tee*-gray) f tiger

timbro (*teem*-broa) m stamp; tone

timidezza (tee-mee-*dayt*-tsah) f timidity, shyness

timido (*tee*-mee-doa) adj timid, shy

timo (*tee*-moa) m thyme

timone (tee-*mōa*-nay) m rudder, helm

timoniere (tee-moa-*ñai*-ray) m steersman, helmsman

timore (tee-*mōa*-ray) m fear, dread

timpano (*teem*-pah-noa) m eardrum

tinta (*teen*-tah) f shade; dye

tintoria (teen-toa-*ree*-ah) f dry cleaner's

tintura (teen-*tōo*-rah) f dye

*tingere (*teen*-jay-ray) v dye

tipico (tee-pee-koa) *adj* typical, characteristic

tipo (tee-poa) *m* type; guy, fellow

tiranno (tee-rahn-noa) *m* tyrant

tirare (tee-raa-ray) *v* *draw, pull; *blow; ~ **di scherma** fence

tiro (tee-roa) *m* throw; trick

titolo (tee-toa-loa) *m* title; headline, heading; degree; **titoli** stocks and shares

tizio (tee-tsyoa) *m* chap

toccare (toak-kaa-ray) *v* touch

tocco (toak-koa) *m* touch

***togliere** (taw-l'ay-ray) *v* *take out, *take away

toilette (toa-leht) *f* dressing table; washroom *Am*; ~ **delle signore** ladies' room; ~ **dei signori** men's room

tollerabile (toal-lay-raa-bee-lay) *adj* tolerable

tollerare (toal-lay-raa-ray) *v* *bear

tomba (toam-bah) *f* grave, tomb

tonico (taw-nee-koa) *m* tonic

tonnellata (toan-nayl-laa-tah) *f* ton

tonno (toan-noa) *m* tuna

tono (taw-noa) *m* tone; note

tonsille (toan-seel-lay) *fpl* tonsils *pl*

tonsillite (toan-seel-lee-tay) *f* tonsilitis

topo (taw-poa) *m* mouse

torace (toa-raa-chay) *m* chest

***torcere** (tor-chay-ray) *v* twist

torcia (tor-chah) *f* torch

tordo (toar-doa) *m* thrush

Torino (toa-ree-noa) *f* Turin

tormenta (toar-mayn-tah) *f* blizzard, snowstorm

tormentare (toar-mayn-taa-ray) *v* torment

tormento (toar-mayn-toa) *m* torment

tornante (toar-nahn-tay) *m* hairpin bend

tornare (toar-naa-ray) *v* *go back, *get back

torneo (toar-nai-oa) *m* tournament

toro (taw-roa) *m* bull

torre (toar-ray) *f* tower

torrone (toar-rōa-nay) *m* nougat

torsione (toar-syōa-nay) *f* twist

torsolo (toar-soa-loa) *m* core

torta (toar-tah) *f* cake

torto (tor-toa) *m* wrong; ***avere** ~ *be wrong; ***fare un** ~ wrong

tortuoso (toar-twōa-soa) *adj* crooked

tortura (toar-tōō-rah) *f* torture

torturare (toar-too-raa-ray) *v* torture

tosse (toass-say) *f* cough

tossico (toss-see-koa) *adj* toxic

tossire (toass-see-ray) *v* cough

totale (toa-taa-lay) *adj* total; utter; *m* whole; total

totalitario (toa-tah-lee-taa-ryoa) *adj* totalitarian

totalmente (toa-tahl-mayn-tay) *adv* completely

toupet (too-pay) *m* hair piece

tovaglia (toa-vaa-l'ah) *f* tablecloth

tovagliolo (toa-vah-l'aw-loa) *m* napkin, serviette; ~ **di carta** paper napkin

tra (trah) *prep* between; among, amid

traccia (traht-chah) *f* trail, trace

tradimento (trah-dee-mayn-toa) *m* treason

tradire (trah-dee-ray) *v* betray; *give away

traditore (trah-dee-tōa-ray) *m*, **-trice** *f* traitor

tradizionale (trah-dee-tsyoa-naa-lay) *adj* traditional

tradizione (trah-dee-tsyōa-nay) *f* tradition

***tradurre** (trah-door-ray) *v* translate

traduttore (trah-doot-tōa-ray) *m*, **-trice** *f* translator

traduzione (trah-doo-tsyōa-nay) *f* translation, version

traffico (trahf-fee-koa) *m* traffic

tragedia (trah-*jai*-dyah) f tragedy; drama

traghetto (trah-*gayt*-toa) m ferry-boat

tragico (*traa*-jee-koa) adj tragic

traguardo (trah-*gwahr*-doa) m finish; goal

trainare (trigh-*naa*-ray) v tow, haul

tralasciare (trah-lahsh-*shaa*-ray) v *leave out

tram (trahm) m tram; streetcar Am

trama (*traa*-mah) f plot

trambusto (trahm-*boo*-stoa) m fuss

tramezzino (trah-mayd-*dzee*-noa) m sandwich

tramonto (trah-*moan*-toa) m sunset

tranne (*trahn*-nay) prep but

tranquillante (trahng-kweel-*lahn*-tay) m tranquillizer

tranquillità (trahng-kweel-lee-*tah*) f quiet

tranquillizzare (trahng-kweel-leed-*dzaa*-ray) v reassure

tranquillo (trahng-*kweel*-loa) adj calm; still, tranquil, quiet

transatlantico (trahn-saht-*lahn*-tee-koa) adj transatlantic

transazione (trahn-sah-*tsyoa*-nay) f transaction

transizione (trahn-see-*tsyoa*-nay) f transition

trapanare (trah-pah-*naa*-ray) v drill, bore

trapano (*traa*-pah-noa) m drill

trapassare (trah-pahss-*saa*-ray) v depart

trappola (*trahp*-poa-lah) f trap

trapunta (trah-*poon*-tah) f quilt

***trarre** (*trahr*-ray) v *draw

trascinare (trahsh-shee-*naa*-ray) v drag

***trascorrere** (trah-*skoar*-ray-ray) v pass

trascurare (trah-skoo-*raa*-ray) v neglect; overlook; **trascurato** careless

trasferire (trah-sfay-*ree*-ray) v transfer

trasformare (trah-sfoar-*maa*-ray) v transform

trasformatore (trah-sfoar-mah-*toa*-ray) m transformer

trasgredire (trahz-gray-*dee*-ray) v trespass, offend

trasgressore (trah-zgrayss-*soa*-ray) m trespasser

traslocare (trah-zloa-*kaa*-ray) v move

trasloco (trah-*zlaw*-koa) m move

***trasmettere** (trah-*zmayt*-tay-ray) v transmit, *broadcast

trasmettitore (trah-zmayt-tee-*toa*-ray) m transmitter

trasmissione (trah-zmeess-*syoa*-nay) f transmission; broadcast

trasparente (trah-spah-*rehn*-tay) adj transparent, sheer

traspirare (trah-spee-*raa*-ray) v perspire

traspirazione (trah-spee-rah-*tsyoa*-nay) f perspiration

trasportare (trah-spoar-*taa*-ray) v transport

trasporto (trah-*spor*-toa) m transportation, transport

trattamento (traht-tah-*mayn*-toa) m treatment

trattare (traht-*taa*-ray) v handle, treat; ~ **con** *deal with

trattativa (traht-tah-*tee*-vah) f negotiation

trattato (traht-*taa*-toa) m essay; treaty

***trattenere** (traht-tay-*nay*-ray) v restrain; ***trattenersi** stay

tratto (*traht*-toa) m line; feature, trait; ~ **del carattere** characteristic

trattore (traht-*toa*-ray) m tractor

trattoria (traht-toa-*ree*-ah) f restaurant

trave (*traa*-vay) f beam

traversa (trah-*vehr*-sah) f side street

traversata (trah-vayr-*saa*-tah) f

passage, crossing

travestimento (trah-vay-stee-*maynt*-toa) *m* disguise

travestirsi (trah-vay-*steer*-see) *v* disguise

tre (tray) *num* three; **~ quarti** three-quarter

tredicesimo (tray-dee-*chai*-zee-moa) *num* thirteenth

tredici (*trāy*-dee-chee) *num* thirteen

tremare (tray-*maa*-ray) *v* tremble, shiver

tremendo (tray-*mehn*-doa) *adj* terrible

trementina (tray-mayn-*tee*-nah) *f* turpentine

treno (*trai*-noa) *m* train; **~ diretto** through train; **~ locale** local train; **~ merci** goods train; freight train *Am*; **~ notturno** night train; **~ passeggeri** passenger train; **~ rapido** express train

trenta (*trayn*-tah) *num* thirty

trentesimo (trayn-*tai*-zee-moa) *num* thirtieth

triangolare (tryahng-goa-*laa*-ray) *adj* triangular

triangolo (*tryahng*-goa-loa) *m* triangle

tribordo (tree-*boar*-doa) *m* starboard

tribù (tree-*boo*) *f* tribe

tribuna (tree-*bōō*-nah) *f* stand

tribunale (tree-boo-*naa*-lay) *m* law court

trifoglio (tree-*faw*-lʸoa) *m* clover; shamrock

triglia (*tree*-lʸah) *f* mullet

trimestrale (tree-may-*straa*-lay) *adj* quarterly

trimestre (tree-*meh*-stray) *m* quarter

trinciato (treen-*chaa*-toa) *m* cigarette tobacco

trionfante (tryoan-*fahn*-tay) *adj* triumphant

trionfare (tryoan-*faa*-ray) *v* triumph

trionfo (*tryoan*-foa) *m* triumph

triste (*tree*-stay) *adj* sad

tristezza (tree-*stayt*-tsah) *f* sadness, sorrow

tritare (tree-*taa*-ray) *v* *grind, mince

triviale (tree-*vyaa*-lay) *adj* vulgar

tromba (*troam*-bah) *f* trumpet

troncare (troang-*kaa*-ray) *v* *cut off

tronco (*troang*-koa) *m* trunk

trono (*traw*-noa) *m* throne

tropicale (troa-pee-*kaa*-lay) *adj* tropical

tropici (*traw*-pee-chee) *mpl* tropics *pl*

troppo (*trop*-poa) *adv* too

trota (*traw*-tah) *f* trout

trovare (troa-*vaa*-ray) *v* *find, *come across; **trovarsi** *be; *feel; *meet

trovata (troa-*vaa*-tah) *f* idea

truccarsi (*trook*-kaar-see) *v* put on one's make-up

trucco (*trook*-koa) *m* make-up; trick

truffa (*troof*-fah) *f* swindle

truffare (troof-*faa*-ray) *v* swindle

truffatore (troof-fah-*tōa*-ray) *m* swindler

truppe (*troop*-pay) *fpl* troops *pl*

tu (too) *pron* you; **~ stesso** yourself

tubatura (too-bah-*tōō*-rah) *f* pipe

tubercolosi (too-bayr-koa-*law*-zee) *f* tuberculosis

tubetto (too-*bayt*-toa) *m* tube

tubo (*tōō*-boa) *m* tube

tuffarsi (toof-*faa*-ray) *v* dive

tulipano (too-lee-*paa*-noa) *m* tulip

tumore (too-*mōā*-ray) *m* tumo(u)r; cancer

tumulto (too-*mool*-toa) *m* disturbance

tunica (*tōō*-nee-kah) *f* tunic

Tunisia (too-nee-*zee*-ah) *f* Tunisia

tunisino (too-nee-*zee*-noa) *adj* Tunisian; *m*, **-a** *f* Tunisian

tuo (*tōō*-oa) *adj* (f tua; pl tuoi, tue)

your

tuonare (twoa-*naa*-ray) v thunder

tuono (*twaw*-noa) m thunder

tuorlo (*twor*-loa) m egg yolk

turbare (toor-*baa*-ray) v upset

turbina (toor-*bee*-nah) f turbine

turbolento (toor-boa-*lehn*-toa) adj rowdy

Turchia (toor-*kee*-ah) f Turkey

turco (*toor*-koa) adj Turkish; m, **-a** f Turk

turismo (too-*ree*-zmoa) m tourism

turista (too-*ree*-stah) m/f tourist

turno (*toor*-noa) m turn; shift

tuta ($\overline{oo}$-tah) f overalls pl

tutela (too-*tai*-lah) f custody

tutore (too-*t$\overline{oa}$*-ray) m, **-trice** f guardian, tutor

tuttavia (toot-tah-*vee*-ah) adv however, nevertheless

tutto (*toot*-toa) adj all; entire; pron everything; **in ~** altogether; **~ compreso** all in

tuttora (toot-*t$\overline{oa}$*-rah) adv still

tweed (tweed) m tweed

U

ubbidiente (oob-bee-*dyehn*-tay) adj obedient

ubbidienza (oob-bee-*dyehn*-tsah) f obedience

ubbidire (oob-bee-*dee*-ray) v obey

ubicazione (oo-bee-kah-tsy$\overline{oa}$-nay) f situation

ubriaco (oo-*bryaa*-koa) adj intoxicated, drunk

uccello (oot-*chehl*-loa) m bird; **~ marino** seabird

***uccidere** (oot-*chee*-day-ray) v kill

udibile (oo-*dee*-bee-lay) adj audible

udienza (oo-*dyehn*-tsah) f audience

***udire** (oo-*dee*-ray) v *hear

udito (oo-*dee*-toa) m hearing

ufficiale (oof-fee-*chaa*-lay) adj official; m officer

ufficio (oof-*fee*-choa) m office; **~ cambi** money exchange, exchange office; **~ di collocamento** employment agency; **~ informazioni** inquiry office, information bureau; **~ oggetti smarriti** lost property; **~ postale** post office

ufficioso (oof-fee-*ch$\overline{oa}$*-soa) adj unofficial

uguaglianza (oo-gwah-*l^yahn*-tsah) f equality

uguagliare (oo-gwah-*l^yaa*-ray) v equal

uguale (oo-*gwaa*-lay) adj even, equal; alike

ulcera (*ool*-chay-rah) f ulcer; **~ gastrica** gastric ulcer

ulteriore (ool-tay-*ry$\overline{oa}$*-ray) adj further

ultimamente (ool-tee-mah-*mayn*-tay) adv lately

ultimo (*ool*-tee-moa) adj last, ultimate

ultravioletto (ool-trah-vyoa-*layt*-toa) adj ultraviolet

umanità (oo-mah-nee-*tah*) f humanity, mankind

umano (oo-*maa*-noa) adj human

umidità (oo-mee-dee-*tah*) f moisture, humidity, damp

umido ($\overline{oo}$-mee-doa) adj wet, moist, humid, damp

umile ($\overline{oo}$-mee-lay) adj humble

umore (oo-*m$\overline{oa}$*-ray) m spirit, mood; **di buon ~** good-tempered, good-humo(u)red

umorismo (oo-*moa-ree*-zmoa) *m* humo(u)r

un (oon) *art* (uno; f una) a *art*

unanime (oo-*naa*-nee-may) *adj* unanimous

uncino (oon-*chee*-noa) *m* hook

undicesimo (oon-dee-*chai*-zee-moa) *num* eleventh

undici (*oon*-dee-chee) *num* eleven

ungherese (oong-gay-*rāy*-zay) *adj* Hungarian; *m/f* Hungarian

Ungheria (oong-gay-*ree*-ah) *f* Hungary

unghia (*oong*-gyah) *f* nail

unguento (oong-*gwehn*-toa) *m* salve, ointment

unicamente (oo-nee-kah-*mayn*-tay) *adv* exclusively

unico (*ōō*-nee-koa) *adj* sole; unique

uniforme (oo-nee-*foar*-may) *adj* uniform; *f* uniform

unilaterale (oo-nee-lah-tay-*raa*-lay) *adj* one-sided

unione (oo-*ñōa*-nay) *f* union; **Unione europea** European Union

unire (oo-*nee*-ray) *v* join; unite; combine; **unirsi a** join

unità (oo-nee-*tah*) *f* unity; unit; ~ **monetaria** monetary unit

unito (oo-*nee*-toa) *adj* joint

universale (oo-nee-vayr-*saa*-lay) *adj* universal; all-round

università (oo-nee-vayr-see-*tah*) *f* university

universo (oo-nee-*vehr*-soa) *m* universe

uno (*ōō*-noa) *num* one; *pron* one

unto (*oon*-toa) *adj* greasy

uomo (*waw*-moa) *m* (pl uomini) man; ~ **d'affari** businessman; ~ **di stato** statesman; ~ **politico** politician

uovo (*waw*-voa) *m* (pl le uova) egg;

uova di pesce roe

uragano (oo-rah-*gaa*-noa) *m* hurricane

urbano (oor-*baa*-noa) *adj* urban

urgente (oor-*jehn*-tay) *adj* urgent, pressing

urgenza (oor-*jehn*-tsah) *f* urgency

urina (oo-*ree*-nah) *f* urine

urlare (oor-*laa*-ray) *v* scream, shout

urlo (*oor*-loa) *m* cry

urtante (oor-*tahn*-tay) *adj* irritating, annoying

urtare (oor-*taa*-ray) *v* bump

urto (*oor*-toa) *m* bump; push

uruguaiano (oo-roo-gwah-*yaa*-noa) *adj* Uruguayan; *m*, **-a** *f* Uruguayan

Uruguay (oo-roo-*gwaa*-ee) *m* Uruguay

usabile (oo-*zaa*-bee-lay) *adj* usable

usa e getta (oo-*zaa*-ay-*jeht*-tah) *adj* disposable

usanza (oo-*zahn*-tsah) *f* usage

usare (oo-*zaa*-ray) *v* use; **usato** worn-out

*uscire (oosh-*shee*-ray) *v* *go out

uscita (oosh-*shee*-tah) *f* way out, exit; issue; ~ **di sicurezza** emergency exit

usignolo (oo-zee-*ñōa*-loa) *m* nightingale

uso (*ōō*-zoa) *m* use; **fuori** ~ out of order

usuale (oo-*zwaa*-lay) *adj* customary

utensile (oo-tayn-*see*-lay) *m* utensil, implement

utente (oo-*tehn*-tay) *m/f* user

utero (*ōō*-tay-roa) *m* womb

utile (*ōō*-tee-lay) *adj* useful

utilità (oo-tee-lee-*tah*) *f* utility, use

utilizzare (oo-tee-leed-*dzaa*-ray) *v* utilize, employ; exploit

uva (*ōō*-vah) *f* grapes *pl*; ~ **spina** gooseberry

uvetta (oo-*vayt*-tah) *f* raisin

V

vacante (vah-*kahn*-tay) *adj* unoccupied, vacant

vacanza (vah-*kahn*-tsah) *f* vacation

vacca (*vahk*-kah) *f* cow

vaccinare (vaht-chee-*naa*-ray) *v* vaccinate; inoculate

vaccinazione (vaht-chee-nah-*tsyōa*-nay) *f* vaccination; inoculation

vacillante (vah-cheel-*lahn*-tay) *adj* shaky; unsteady

vacillare (vah-cheel-*laa*-ray) *v* falter

vagabondare (vah-gah-boan-*daa*-ray) *v* roam, tramp

vagabondo (vah-gah-*boan*-doa) *m* tramp

vagare (vah-*gaa*-ray) *v* wander

vaglia (*vaa*-lʸah) *m* money order; ~ **postale** postal order; money order *Am*

vagliare (vah-lʸ*aa*-ray) *v* sift

vago (*vaa*-goa) *adj* faint, vague

vagone (vah-*gōa*-nay) *m* coach, carriage; wag(g)on; passenger car *Am*; ~ **letto** sleeping car; ~ **ristorante** dining car

vaiolo (vah-*yaw*-loa) *m* smallpox

valanga (vah-*lahng*-gah) *f* avalanche

*valere (vah-*lāy*-ray) *v* *be worth

valido (*vaa*-lee-doa) *adj* valid

valigia (vah-*lee*-jah) *f* bag, case, suitcase; **fare le valigie** pack

valle (*vahl*-lay) *f* valley

valore (vah-*lōa*-ray) *m* value, worth; **senza** ~ worthless; **valori** valuables *pl*

valoroso (vah-loa-*rōa*-soa) *adj* courageous

valuta (vah-*lōō*-tah) *f* currency

valutare (vah-loo-*taa*-ray) *v* evaluate, estimate, appreciate, value

valutazione (vah-loo-tah-*tsyōa*-nay) *f* estimate

valvola (*vahl*-voa-lah) *f* valve; ~ **dell'aria** choke

valzer (*vahl*-tsayr) *m* waltz

vanga (*vahng*-gah) *f* spade

vangelo (vahn-*jai*-loa) *m* gospel

vaniglia (vah-*nee*-lʸah) *f* vanilla

vanità (vah-nee-*tah*) *f* vanity

vano (*vaa*-noa) *adj* vain, idle; *m* room

vantaggio (vahn-*tahd*-joa) *m* benefit, advantage; profit; lead

vantaggioso (vahn-tahd-*jōa*-soa) *adj* advantageous

vantarsi (vahn-*tahr*-see) *v* boast

vapore (vah-*pōa*-ray) *m* steam, vapo(u)r

vaporetto (vah-poa-*rayt*-toa) *m* water bus

vaporizzatore (vah-poa-reed-dzah-*tōa*-ray) *m* atomizer

vari (*vaa*-ree) *adj* various

variabile (vah-*ryaa*-bee-lay) *adj* variable

variare (vah-*ryaa*-ray) *v* vary

variazione (vah-ryah-*tsyōa*-nay) *f* variation

varicella (vah-ree-*chehl*-lah) *f* chickenpox

varietà (vah-ryay-*tah*) *f* variety

varo (*vaa*-roa) *m* launching

vasca (*vaas*-kah) *f* tank; ~ **da bagno** bath, tub

vaschetta (*vaas-kayt*-tah) *f* tub

vascello (vahsh-*shehl*-loa) *m* vessel

vasellame (vah-zayl-*laa*-may) *m* crockery

vaselina (vah-zay-*lee*-nah) *f* vaseline

vaso (*vaa*-zoa) *m* vase; bowl; ~ **sanguigno** blood vessel

vassoio (vahss-*sōa*-yoa) *m* tray

vasto (*vah*-stoa) *adj* vast; extensive, wide

Vaticano (vah-tee-*kah*-noa) *m* the

Vatican

vecchiaia (vayk-*kyaa*-yah) *f* old age

vecchio (*vehk*-keeoa) *adj* old; ancient

*vedere (vay-*dāy*-ray) *v* *see; notice; ***far ~** *show

vedova (*vāy*-doa-vah) *f* widow

vedovo (*vāy*-doa-voa) *m* widower

veduta (vay-*dōō*-tah) *f* sight

veemente (vay-ay-*mayn*-tay) *adj* fierce, intense

vegetariano (vay-jay-tah-*ryaa*-noa) *m*, **-a** *f* vegetarian

vegetazione (vay-jay-tah-*tsyōā*-nay) *f* vegetation

veicolo (vay-*ee*-koa-loa) *m* vehicle

vela (*vāy*-lah) *f* sail

veleno (vay-*lāy*-noa) *m* poison

velenoso (vay-lay-*nōā*-soa) *adj* poisonous

velivolo (vay-*lee*-voa-loa) *m* aircraft

velluto (vayl-*lōō*-toa) *m* velvet; **~ a coste** corduroy

velo (*vāy*-loa) *m* veil

veloce (vay-*lōā*-chay) *adj* fast, rapid

velocità (vay-loa-chee-*tah*) *f* speed; pace, rate; **limite di ~** speed limit; **~ di crociera** cruising speed

vena (*vāy*-nah) *f* vein; **~ varicosa** varicose vein

vendemmia (vayn-*daym*-myah) *f* vintage

vendere (*vayn*-day-ray) *v* *sell; **~ al minuto** retail

vendetta (vayn-*dayt*-tah) *f* revenge

vendibile (vayn-*dee*-bee-lay) *adj* saleable

vendita (*vayn*-dee-tah) *f* sale; **in ~** for sale; **~ al minuto** retail

venerabile (vay-nay-*raa*-bee-lay) *adj* venerable

venerare (vay-nay-*raa*-ray) *v* worship

venerdì (vay-nayr-*dee*) *m* Friday

Venezia (vay-*nay*-tsya) *f* Venice

venezuelano (vay-nay-tsoo-ay-*laa*-noa) *adj* Venezuelan; *m*, **-a** *f* Venezuelan

Venezuela (vay-nay-*tswai*-lah) *m* Venezuela

*venire (vay-*nee*-ray) *v* *come; ***far ~** *send for

ventaglio (vayn-*taa*-lʸoa) *m* fan

ventesimo (vayn-*tai*-zee-moa) *num* twentieth

venti (*vayn*-tee) *num* twenty

ventilare (vayn-tee-*laa*-ray) *v* ventilate

ventilatore (vayn-tee-lah-*tōā*-ray) *m* fan, ventilator

ventilazione (vayn-tee-lah-*tsyōā*-nay) *f* ventilation

vento (*vehn*-toa) *m* wind

ventoso (vayn-*tōā*-soa) *adj* gusty, windy

veramente (vay-rah-*mayn*-tay) *adv* really

veranda (vay-*rahn*-dah) *f* veranda

verbale (vayr-*baa*-lay) *adj* verbal; *m* minutes

verbo (*vehr*-boa) *m* verb

verde (*vayr*-day) *adj* green

verdetto (vayr-*dayt*-toa) *m* verdict

verdura (vayr-*dōō*-rah) *f* greens *pl*, vegetable

vergine (*vehr*-jee-nay) *f* virgin

vergogna (vayr-*gōā*-ñah) *f* shame; ***aver ~** *be ashamed; **vergogna!** shame!

vergognarsi (vayr-goa-*ñaar*-see) *v* be ashamed; be shy

verificare (vay-ree-fee-*kaa*-ray) *v* check, verify

verità (vay-ree-*tah*) *f* truth

veritiero (vay-ree-*tyai*-roa) *adj* truthful

verme (*vehr*-may) *m* worm

vernice (vayr-*nee*-chay) *f* varnish

verniciare (vayr-nee-*chaa*-ray) *v* varnish, paint

vero (*vāy*-roa) *adj* true; very

versamento (vayr-sah-*mayn*-toa) *m* deposit

versare (vayr-*saa*-ray) *v* pour; *shed

versione (vayr-*syoa*-nay) *f* version

verso[1](*vehr*-soa) *prep* to; at, towards

verso[2] (*vehr*-soa) *m* verse

verticale (vayr-tee-*kaa*-lay) *adj* vertical

vertigine (vayr-*tee*-jee-nay) *f* giddiness

vescica (vaysh-*shee*-kah) *f* bladder

vescovo (*vāy*-skoa-voa) *m* bishop

vespa (*vay*-spah) *f* wasp

vestaglia (vay-*staa*-l*y*ah) *f* negligee; dressing gown

veste (*veh*-stay) *f* frock; robe

vestire (vay-*stee*-ray) *v* dress; *wear; **vestirsi** get dressed; dress

vestiti (vayss-*tee*-tee) *mpl* clothes *pl*; ~ **da uomo** men's wear; **vestito da donna** dress; **vestito da uomo** *m* suit

veterinario (vay-tay-ree-*naa*-ryoa) *m* veterinary surgeon

vetrina (vay-*tree*-nah) *f* shopwindow

vetro (*vāy*-troa) *m* glass; pane; **di** ~ glass; ~ **colorato** stained glass

vetta (*vayt*-tah) *f* peak, summit

vi (vee) *pron* you; yourselves

via[1](*vee*-ah) *f*; ~ **principale** main street; ~ **selciata** causeway

via[2](*vee*-ah) *adv* away, gone, off; *prep* via

viadotto (vyah-*doat*-toa) *m* viaduct

viaggiare (veeahd-*jaa*-ray) *v* travel

viaggiatore (vyahd-jah-*tōa*-ray) *m*, **-trice** *f* travel(l)er

viaggio (*vyahd*-joa) *m* journey; trip; voyage; ~ **d'affari** business trip; ~ **di ritorno** return journey

viale (*vyaa*-lay) *m* avenue

vibrare (vee-*braa*-ray) *v* tremble, vibrate

vibrazione (vee-brah-*tsyoa*-nay) *f* vibration

vicenda (vee-*chehn*-dah) *f* vicissitude; event

vicepresidente (vee-chay-pray-see-*dehn*-tay) *m* vice president

vicinanza (vee-chee-*nahn*-tsah) *f* vicinity

vicinato (vee-chee-*naa*-toa) *m* neighbo(u)rhood

vicino (vee-*chee*-noa) *adj* close, nearby, near; *m* neighb(o)ur; ~ **a** near; beside, next to, by

vicolo (*vee*-koa-loa) *m* lane, alley; ~ **cieco** cul-de-sac

video (*vee*-day-oa) *m* screen

videocamera (vee-day-oa-*kaa*-may-rah) *f* video camera

videocassetta (*vee*-day-oa-kahss-*sayt*-tah) *f* video cassette

videoregistratore (*vee*-day-oa-ray-jee-straa-*toa*-ray) *m* video recorder

vietato (vyay-*taa*-toa) *adj* prohibited; ~ **ai pedoni** no pedestrians; ~ **fumare** no smoking; ~ **l'ingresso** no admittance

vigile (*vee*-dʒee-lay) *adj* vigilant; ~ **urbano** traffic policeman; ~ **del fuoco** fireman; **vigili del fuoco** fire brigade

vigilia (vee-*dʒee*-lee-ay) *f* eve

vigna (*vee*-ñah) *f* vineyard

vile (*vee*-lay) *adj* cowardly

villa (*veel*-lah) *f* villa

villaggio (veel-*lahd*-joa) *m* village

villino (veel-*lee*-noa) *m* cottage

***vincere** (*veen*-chay-ray) *v* conquer, *overcome; *win

vincita (*veen*-chee-tah) *f* winnings *pl*

vincitore (veen-chee-*tōa*-ray) *m*, **-trice** *f* winner

vino (*vee*-noa) *m* wine

viola (*vyoa*-lah) *adj* purple

violazione (vyoa-lah-*tsyoa*-nay) *f* violation

violentare (vyoa-layn-*taa*-ray) *v* rape
violento (vyoa-*lehn*-toa) *adj* violent
violenza (vyoa-*lehn*-tsah) *f* violence
violetta (vyoa-*layt*-tah) *f* violet
violetto (vyoa-*layt*-toa) *adj* violet
violino (vyoa-*lee*-noa) *m* violin
virgola (*veer*-goa-lah) *f* comma
virgolette (veer-goa-*layt*-tay) *fpl* quotation marks
virtù (veer-*too*) *f* virtue
viscido (*veesh*-shee-doa) *adj* slippery
visibile (vee-*zee*-bee-lay) *adj* visible
visibilità (vee-zee-bee-lee-*tah*) *f* visibility
visione (vee-z*yoa*-nay) *f* vision
visita (*vee*-zee-tah) *f* visit, call; **~ medica** medical examination
visitare (vee-zee-*taa*-ray) *v* visit
visitatore (vee-zee-tah-*toa*-ray) *m*, **-trice** *f* visitor
viso (*vee*-zoa) *m* face
visone (vee-*zoa*-nay) *m* mink
vista (*vee*-stah) *f* sight; view
visto (*vee*-stoa) *m* visa
vistoso (vee-*stoa*-soa) *adj* striking
vita (*vee*-tah) *f* life; waist
vitale (vee-*taa*-lay) *adj* vital
vitamina (vee-tah-*mee*-nah) *f* vitamin
vite (*vee*-tay) *f* screw; vine
vitello (vee-*tehl*-loa) *m* calf; veal
vittima (*veet*-tee-mah) *f* victim; casualty
vitto (*veet*-toa) *m* fare, food; **~ e alloggio** room and board, bed and board, board and lodging
vittoria (veet-*taw*-ryah) *f* victory
vivace (vee-*vaa*-chay) *adj* active, brisk, lively; gay
vivaio (vee-*vaa*-yoa) *m* nursery
vivente (vee-*vehn*-tay) *adj* alive
*vivere (*vee*-vay-ray) *v* live
vivido (*vee*-vee-doa) *adj* vivid
vivo (*vee*-voa) *adj* alive, live
viziare (vee-*tsyaa*-ray) *v* *spoil

vizio (*vee*-ts ɪæ*h*) *m* vice
vocabolario (voa-kah-boa-*laa*-ryoa) *m* vocabulary
vocale (voa-*kaa*-lay) *adj* vocal; *f* vowel
voce (*voa*-chay) *f* voice; **ad alta ~** aloud
voglia (*vaw*-lʸah) *f* fancy; ***aver ~ di** fancy, *feel like
voi (*voa*-ee) *pron* you; **~ stessi** yourselves
volante (voa-*lahn*-tay) *m* steering wheel
volare (voa-*laa*-ray) *v* *fly
volentieri (voa-layn-*tyai*-ree) *adv* gladly, willingly
*volere (voa-*lay*-ray) *v* *will, want; ***voler bene** like
volgare (vol-*gaa*-ray) *adj* coarse, vulgar
*volgere (*vol*-jay-ray) *v* turn
volo (*voa*-loa) *m* flight; **~ charter** charter flight; **~ di ritorno** return flight; **~ notturno** night flight
volontà (voa-loan-*tah*) *f* will
volontario (voa-loan-*taa*-ryoa) *adj* voluntary; *m*, **-a** *f* volunteer
volpe (*voal*-pay) *f* fox
volt (voalt) *m* volt
volta (*vol*-tah) *f* time; vault; **ancora una ~** once more; **due volte** twice; **qualche ~** sometimes; **una ~** once
voltaggio (voal-*tahd*-joa) *m* voltage
voltare (voal-*taa*-ray) *v* turn; turn round
volume (voa-*loo*-may) *m* volume
voluminoso (voa-loo-mee-*noa*-soa) *adj* big, bulky
vomitare (voa-mee-*taa*-ray) *v* vomit
vostro (*vo*-stroa) *adj* your
votare (voa-*taa*-ray) *v* vote
votazione (voa-tah-*tsyoa*-nay) *f* vote
voto (*voa*-toa) *m* vote; mark
vulcano (vool-*kaa*-noa) *m* volcano
vulnerabile (vool-nay-*raa*-bee-lay) *adj*

vulnerable
vuotare (vwo-*taa*-ray) *v* empty

vuoto (*vwaw*-toa) *adj* empty; hollow; unoccupied; *m* vacuum

Z

zaffiro (dzahf-*fee*-roa) *m* sapphire

zaino (*dzigh*-noa) *m* rucksack, knapsack

zampa (*tsahm*-pah) *f* paw

zampillo (tsahm-*peel*-loa) *m* squirt

zanzara (dzahn-*dzaa*-rah) *f* mosquito

zanzariera (dzahn-dzah-*ryai*-rah) *f* mosquito net

zappa (*tsahp*-pah) *f* spade

zattera (*tsaht*-tay-rah) *f* raft

zebra (*dzai*-brah) *f* zebra

zelante (dzay-*lahn*-tay) *adj* diligent, zealous

zelo (*dzai*-loa) *m* diligence, zeal

zenit (*dzai*-neet) *m* zenith

zenzero (*dzehn*-dzay-roa) *m* ginger

zero (*dzai*-roa) *m* nought, zero; nil

zia (*tsee*-ah) *f* aunt

zigomo (*dzee*-goa-moa) *m* cheekbone

zigzagare (dzeeg-dzah-*gaa*-ray) *v* *wind

zinco (*dzeeng*-koa) *m* zinc

zio (*tsee*-oa) *m* uncle

zitella (tsee-*tehl*-lah) *f* spinster

zitto (*tseet*-toa) *adj* silent

zoccolo (*tsok*-koa-loa) *m* wooden shoe; hoof

zodiaco (dzoa-*dee*-ah-koa) *m* zodiac

zona (*dzōa*-nah) *f* zone; area; ~ **di parcheggio** parking zone; ~ **industriale** industrial area

zoologia (dzoa-oa-loa-*jee*-ah) *f* zoology

zoom (z$\overline{oo}$m) *m* zoom lens

zoppicante (tsoap-pee-*kahn*-tay) *adj* lame

zoppicare (tsoap-pee-*kaa*-ray) *v* limp

zoppo (*tsop*-poa) *adj* lame

zuccherare (tsook-kay-*raa*-ray) *v* sweeten

zucchero (*tsook*-kay-roa) *m* sugar; **zolletta di** ~ lump of sugar

Menu Reader
Food

abbacchio grilled lamb

~ alla cacciatora pieces of lamb, often braised with garlic, rosemary, white wine, anchovy paste and hot peppers

abbrustolito roasted

(all') abruzzese Abruzzi style; with red peppers and sometimes ham

acciughe anchovies

~ al limone fresh anchovies served with a sauce of lemon, oil, breadcrumbs and oregano

(all')aceto (in) vinegar

acetosella sorrel

acquacotta soup of bread and vegetables, sometimes with eggs and cheese

affettati sliced cold meat, ham and salami (US cold cuts)

affumicato smoked

agliata garlic sauce; garlic mashed with breadcrumbs

aglio garlic

agnello lamb

agnolotti kind of ravioli with savoury filling of vegetables, chopped meats, sometimes with garlic and herbs

(all')agro dressing of lemon juice and oil

agrodolce sweet-sour dressing of caramelized sugar, vinegar and flour to which capers, raisins or lemon may be added

al, all', alla in the style of: with

ala wing

albicocca apricot

alice anchovy

allodola lark

alloro bay leaf

amarena sour black cherry

ananas pineapple

anatra duck

~ selvatica wild duck

anguilla eel

~ alla veneziana braised with tunny (tuna) and lemon sauce

anguria watermelon

anice aniseed

animelle (di vitello) (veal) sweetbreads

annegati slices of meat in white wine or Marsala wine

antipasto hors-d'œuvre

~ di mare seafood

~ a scelta to one's own choosing

arachide peanuts

aragosta spiny lobster

arancia orange

aranciata orangeade

aringa herring

arista loin of pork

arrosto roast(ed)

aromatico aromatic

arsella kind of mussel

asiago cheese made of skimmed milk, semi hard to hard, sweet when young

asparago asparagus

assortito assorted

astice lobster

attorta flaky pastry filled with fruit and almonds

babbaluci snails in olive-oil sauce with tomatoes and onions

baccalà stockfish, dried cod

~ alla fiorentina floured and fried in oil

~ alla vicentina poached in milk with onion, garlic, parsley, anchovies and cinnamon

(con) bagna cauda simmering sauce

of butter, olive oil, garlic and chopped anchovies, into which raw vegetables and bread are dipped

barbabietola beetroot

basilico basil

beccaccia woodcock

Bel Paese smooth cheese with delicate taste

ben cotto well-done

(alla) besciamella (with) white sauce

bigoli in salsa noodles with an anchovy or sardine sauce

biscotto rusk, biscuit (US zwieback, cookie)

bistecca steak, usually beef, but may be another kind of meat

~ **di manzo** beef steak

~ **(alla) pizzaiola** with tomatoes, basil and sometimes garlic

~ **di vitello** veal scallop

bocconcini diced meat with herbs

bollente boiling hot

bollito 1) boiled 2) meat or fish stew

(alla) bolognese in a sauce of tomatoes and meat or ham and cheese

(alla) brace on charcoal

bovino bovine

braciola di maiale pork chop

bracioletta small slice of meat

~ **a scottadito** charcoal-grilled lamb chops

braciolone alla napoletana breaded rumpsteak with garlic, parsley, ham and currants; rolled, sautéed and stewed

branzino bass

brasato braised

broccoletti strascinati brocoli sautéed with pork fat and garlic

brodetto fish soup with onions and tomato pulp

brodo bouillon, broth, soup

~ **vegetale** vegetable broth

bruschetta a thick slice of countrystyle bread, grilled, rubbed with garlic and sprinkled with olive oil

budino pudding

bue beef

burrida fish casserole strongly flavoured with spices and herbs

burro butter

~ **maggiordomo** with lemon juice and parsley

busecca thick tripe and vegetable soup

cacciagione game

(alla) cacciatora often with mushrooms, herbs, shallots, wine, tomatoes, strips of ham and tongue

cacciucco spicy fish soup, usually with onions, green pepper, garlic and red wine topped with garlic flavoured croutons

caciocavallo firm, slightly sweet cheese from cow's or sheep's milk

calamaretto young squid

calamaro squid

caldo hot

calzone pizza dough envelope with ham, cheese, herbs and baked

(alla) campagnola with vegetables, especially onions and tomatoes

canditi candied fruit

canederli dumplings made from ham, sausage and breadcrumbs

cannella cinnamon

cannelloni tubular dough stuffed with meat, cheese or vegetables, covered with a white sauce and baked

~ **alla Barbaroux** with chopped ham, veal, cheese and covered with white sauce

~ **alla laziale** with meat and onion filling and baked in tomato sauce

~ **alla napoletana** with cheese and ham filling in tomato and herb sauce

cannolo rolled pastry filled with sweet, white cheese, sometimes nougat and crystallized fruit

capitone large eel

apocollo smoked salt pork

caponata aubergine, green pepper, tomato, vegetable marrow, garlic, oil and herbs; usually served cold

cappelletti small ravioli filled with meat, herbs, cheese and eggs

cappero caper

appon magro pyramid of cooked vegetables and fish salad

cappone capon

capretto kid

~ **ripieno al forno** stuffed with herbs and roasted

caprino a soft goat's cheese

~ **romano** hard goat's milk cheese

capriolo roebuck, venison

caramellato caramelized

(alla) carbonara *pasta* with smoked ham, cheese, eggs and olive oil

arbonata 1) grilled pork chop 2) beef stew in red wine

arciofo artichoke

~ **alla romana** stuffed, sautéed in oil, garlic and white wine

arciofino small artichoke

cardo cardoon

arne meat

~ **a carrargiu** spit-roasted

arota carrot

arpa, carpione carp

della) casa chef's speciality

alla) casalinga home-made

al) cartoccio baked in tinfoil

assata ice-cream with a crystallized fruit filling

~ **(alla) siciliana** sponge cake garnished with sweet cream cheese, chocolate and crystallized fruit

in) casseruola (in a) casserole

astagnaccio chestnut cake with pine

kernels, raisins, nuts, cooked in oil

castagne chestnuts

caviale caviar

cavolfiore cauliflower

cavolino di Bruxelles brussels sprout

cavolo cabbage

cazzoeula a casserole of pork, celery, onions, cabbage and spices

cece chick-pea

cena dinner, supper

cerfoglio chervil

cervella brains

cervo stag

cetriolino gherkin (US pickle)

cetriolo cucumber

chiodo di garofano cloves

ciambella ringshaped bun

cicoria endive (US chicory)

ciliegia cherry

cima cold, stuffed veal

~ **alla genovese** stuffed with eggs, sausage and mushrooms

cinghiale (wild) boar

cioccolata chocolate

cipolla onion

cipollina pearl onion

ciuppin thick fish soup

cocomero watermelon

coda di bue oxtail

colazione breakfast

composta stewed fruit

condimento 1) seasoning 2) dressing

confetto sugared almond

confettura jam

coniglio rabbit

~ **all'agro** stewed in red wine, with the addition of lemon juice

contorno garnish

copata small wafer of honey and nuts

coppa kind of raw ham, usually smoked

corda lamb tripes roasted or braised in tomato sauce with peas

cornetti 1) string beans 2) crescent

rolls

cornetto 1) croissant 2) cone, cornet

cosce di rana frogs' legs

coscia leg, thigh

cosciotto leg

costata beef steak or chop, entre-côte

~ **alla fiorentina** grilled over an olive-wood fire, served with lemon juice and parsley

~ **alla pizzaiola** braised in sauce with tomatoes, marjoram, parsley and *mozzarella* cheese

~ **al prosciutto** with ham, cheese and truffles; breaded and fried

costoletta cutlet, chop (veal or pork)

~ **alla bolognese** breaded veal cutlet topped with a slice of ham, cheese and tomato sauce

~ **alla milanese** veal cutlet, breaded, then fried

~ **alla parmigiana** breaded and baked with parmesan cheese

~ **alla valdostana** with ham and *fontina* cheese

~ **alla viennese** breaded veal scallop, wiener schnitzel

cotechino spiced pork sausage, served hot in slices

cotogna quince

cotto cooked, baked

ben ~ well-done

~ **a puntino** medium (done)

cozza mussel

cozze alla marinara mussels cooked in white wine with parsley and garlic

crauti sauerkraut

crema cream, custard

cremino 1) soft cheese 2) type of ice-cream bar

cren horseradish

crescione watercress

crespolino spinach-filled pancake baked in cheese sauce

crocchetta potato or rice croquette

crostaceo shellfish

crostata pie, flan, tart

crostini small pieces of toast, croutons

~ **in brodo** broth with croutons

~ **alla provatura** diced bread and *provatura* cheese toasted on a spit

crostino alla napoletana small toast with anchovies and melted cheese

crudo raw

crusca bran

cubetto di ghiaccio ice cube

culatello type of raw ham, cured in white wine

cuore heart

~ **di sedano** celery heart

cuscusu di Trapani fish soup with semolina flakes

dattero date

datteri di mare mussels, small clams

dentice dentex (Mediterranean fish, similar to sea bream)

dessert dessert

(alla) diavola usually grilled with a lavish amount of pepper, chili pepper or pimento

digestivo digestif

diverso varied

dolce sweet, dessert

dolci pastries, cakes

(alla) Doria with cucumbers

dragoncello tarragon

fagiano pheasant

fagiolino French bean (US green bean)

fagiolo haricot bean

faraona guinea hen

farcire 1) stuff 2) fill

farcito 1) stuffed 2) filled

farsumagru rolled beef or veal stuffed with bacon, ham, eggs, cheese, parsley and onions; braised with tomatoes

fatto in casa home-made

fava broad bean

'avata casserole of beans, bacon, sausage and seasoning

'egatelli di maiale alla Fiorentina pork liver grilled on a skewer with bay leaves and diced, fried croutons

'egato liver

~ **alla veneziana** slices of calf's liver fried with onions

ai) ferri on the grill, grilled

'esa round cut taken from leg of veal

~ **in gelatina** roast veal in aspic jelly

'ettina small slice

'ettuccine flat narrow noodles

~ **verdi** green noodles

'ico fig

'iletto fillet

'ilone French stick

'inocchio fennel

~ **in salsa bianca** in white sauce

alla) fiorentina with herbs, oil and often spinach

'ocaccia 1) flat bread, sprinkled with olive oil, sometimes with fried chopped onions or cheese 2) sweet ring-shaped cake

~ **di vitello** veal patty

'ondo di carciofo artichoke heart (US bottom)

'onduta melted cheese with egg-yolk, milk and truffles

'ontina a soft, creamy cheese from Piedmont, chiefly used in cooking

'ormaggio cheese

al) forno baked

'orte hot, spicy

'ra diavolo with a spicy tomato sauce

'ragola strawberry

~ **di bosco** wild

'rattaglie giblets

'regula soup with semolina and saffron dumplings

'resco cool, fresh, uncooked

'rittata omelet

~ **semplice** plain

frittatina di patate potato omelet

frittella fritter, pancake, often filled with ham and cheese or with an apple

fritto deep-fried

~ **alla milanese** breaded

~ **misto** deep-fried bits of seafood, vegetables or meat

~ **alla napoletana** fried fish, vegetables and cheese

~ **alla romana** sweetbread, artichokes and cauliflower

~ **di verdura** fried vegetables

frullare 1) liquidize 2) whisk

frullato milk-shake

frutta fruit

~ **candita** crystallized (US candied)

~ **cotta** stewed

frutti di mare shellfish

fungo mushroom

galantina tartufata truffles in aspic jelly

gallina hen

gallinaccio 1) chanterelle mushroom 2) woodcock

gallinella water-hen

gallo cedrone grouse

gamberetto shrimp

gambero crayfish, crawfish

garofolato beef stew with cloves

(in) gelatina (in) aspic jelly

gelato ice-cream; iced dessert

(alla) genovese with basil and other herbs, pine kernels, garlic and oil

ghiacciato iced, chilled

ghiacciolo ice lolly

ginepro juniper (berry)

girello round steak from the leg

glassa icing

gnocchi potato dumplings

gorgonzola most famous of the Italian blue-veined cheese, rich with a tangy flavour

grana hard cheese; also known as *parmigiano(-reggiano)*

granchio crab

granita crushed ice with coffee or fruit syrup

grasso rich with fat or oil

(alla) graticola grilled

gratinata sprinkled with breadcrumbs and grated cheese and oven-browned

grattugiato grated

(alla) griglia from the grill

grissino bread stick

gruviera mild cheese with holes, Italian version of Swiss *gruyère*

guazzetto meat stew with garlic, rosemary, tomatoes and pimentos

incasciata layers of dough, meat sauce, hard-boiled eggs and grated cheese

indivia chicory (US endive)

infarinare flour

insalata salad

~ **all'americana** mayonnaise and shrimps

~ **russa** diced boiled vegetables in mayonnaise

~ **verde** green

~ **di verdura cotta** boiled vegetables

involtino stuffed meat or ham roll

lampone raspberry

lampreda lamprey

lardo bacon

lasagne thin layers of generally green noodle dough alternating with tomato, sausage meat, ham, white sauce and grated cheese; baked in the oven

latte alla portoghese baked custard with liquid caramel

lattuga lettuce

lauro bay leaf

(alla) laziale with onions

legumi peas and beans

lenticchia lentil

lepre hare

~ **al lardo con funghi** with bacon

and mushrooms

~ **in salmì** jugged

leprotto leveret

lesso 1) boiled 2) meat or fish stew

limone lemon

lingua tongue

linguine flat noodles

lista dei vini wine list

lodigiano kind of parmesan cheese

lombata loin

lombo loin

luganega pork sausage

lumaca snail

lupo di mare sea perch

maccheroni macaroni

macedonia (di frutta) fruit salad

maggiorana marjoram

magro 1) lean 2) dish without meat

maiale pork

~ **al latte** cooked in milk

~ **ubriaco** cooked in red wine

maionese mayonnaise

mandarino mandarin

mandorla almond

manzo beef

~ **arrosto ripieno** stuffed roast

~ **lesso** boiled

~ **salato** corned beef

(alla) marinara sauce of tomatoes, olives, garlic, clams and mussels

marinato marinated

maritozzo soft roll

marmellata jam

~ **d'arance** marmalade

marrone chestnut

mascarpone soft, butter-coloured cheese, often served as a sweet dish

medaglione round fillet of beef or veal

mela apple

~ **cotogna** quince

melagrana pomegranate

melanzana aubergine (US eggplant)

melanzane alla parmigiana

aubergines baked with tomatoes, parmesan cheese and spices

elanzane ripiene stuffed with various ingredients and gratinéed

elone melon

~ **con prosciutto** with cured ham

enta mint

eringa meringue

erlano whiting

erluzzo cod

essicani veal scallops rolled around a meat, cheese or herb stuffing

idollo marrow (bone)

iele honey

(alla) milanese 1) Milanese style of cooking 2) breaded (of meat)

illefoglie custard slice (US napoleon)

inestra soup

~ **in brodo** bouillon with noodles or rice and chicken liver

~ **di funghi** cream of mushroom

inestrone thick vegetable soup

~ **alla genovese** with spinach, basil, macaroni

~ **verde** with French beans and herbs

irtillo bilberry (US blueberry)

isto mixed

itilo mussel

(alla) montanara with different root vegetables

ontone mutton

ora blackberry, mulberry

ortadella bologna (sausage)

ostarda mustard

~ **di frutta** spiced crystallized fruits (US candied fruits) in a sweet-sour syrup

ozzarella soft, unripened cheese with a bland, slightly sweet flavour, made from buffalo's milk in southern Italy, elsewhere with cow's milk

(alla) napoletana with cheese, tomatoes, herbs and sometimes

anchovies

nasello whiting, hake

naturale plain, without sauce or filling

navone yellow turnip

nocciola hazelnut

noce nut

~ **di cocco** coconut

~ **moscata** nutmeg

nostrano local, home-grown

oca goose

olio oil

~ **d'arachide** peanut oil

~ **di semi** seed oil

olive agrodolci olives in vinegar and sugar

olive ripiene stuffed olives (e.g. with meat, cheese, pimento)

ombrina umbrine (fish)

orata John Dory, gilthead bream (fish)

origano oregano

osso bone

~**buco** veal shanks cooked in various ways depending on the region

ostrica oyster

ovalina small *mozzarella* cheese from buffalo's milk

ovolo egg mushroom

(alla) paesana with bacon, potatoes, carrots, vegetable marrow and other root vegetables

pagliarino medium-soft cheese from Piedmont

palomba wood-pigeon, ring-dove

pan di Genova almond cake

pan di Spagna sponge cake

pan tostato toasted Italian bread

pancetta bacon

pandolce heavy cake with dried fruit and pine kernels

pane bread

~ **casareccio** home-made

~ **scuro** dark

~ **di segale** rye

~ **integrale** wholemeal

panettone tall light cake with a few raisins and crystallized fruit

panforte di Siena flat round slab made mostly of spiced crystallized fruit

pangrattato breadcrumbs

panicielli d'uva passula grapes wrapped in citron leaves and baked

panino roll

~ **imbottito** sandwich

panna cream

~ **montata** whipped

pannocchia cob

panzarotti fried or baked large dough envelopes often with a filling of pork, eggs, cheese, anchovies and tomatoes

pappardelle long, broad noodles

~ **con la lepre** garnished with spiced hare

parmigiano(-reggiano) parmesan, a hard cheese generally grated for use in hot dishes

passatelli pasta made from a mixture of egg, parmesan cheese, breadcrumbs, often with a pinch of nutmeg

passato purée, creamed

~ **di verdura** mashed vegetable soup, generally with croutons

pasta the traditional Italian first course; essentially a dough consisting of flour, water, oil (or butter) and eggs; produced in a variety of shapes and sizes (e.g. spaghetti, macaroni, broad noodles, ravioli, shell- and star-shaped *pasta*); may be eaten on its own, in a bouillon, seasoned with butter or olive oil, stuffed or accompanied by a savoury sauce, sprinkled with grated cheese

~**sciutta** any pasta not eaten in a bouillon; served with any of various dressings

pasticcino tart, cake, small pastry

pasticcio 1) pie 2) type of *pasta* like *lasagne*

pastina small *pasta* in various shape used principally as a bouillon or soup ingredient

pasto meal

patate potatoes

~ **fritte** chips (*US* French fries)

~ **lesse** boiled

~ **novelle** new

~ **in padella** fried in a pan

~ **rosolate** roasted

~ **saltate** sliced and sautéed

patatine 1) small, new potatoes 2) crisps (*US* chips)

pecorino a hard cheese made from sheep's milk

pepato peppered

pepe pepper

peperonata stew of peppers, tomatoe and sometimes onions

peperoncino chilli

peperone green or red sweet pepper

~ **arrostito** roasted sweet pepper

~ **ripieno** stuffed, usually with rice and chopped meat

pera pear

pernice partridge

pesca peach

~ **melba** peach-halves poached in syrup over vanilla ice-cream, toppe with raspberry sauce and whipped cream

pescatrice angler fish, frog fish

pesce fish

~ **spada** swordfish

pesto sauce of basil leaves, garlic, cheese, olice oil and pine kernels; used in *minestrone* or with *pasta*

petto breast

(a) piacere to your own choosing

piatto dish

~ **del giorno** the day's speciality

~ **principale** main course

~rimo ~ first course

~iccante highly seasoned

~iccata thin veal scallop

  ~ al marsala braised in Marsala sauce

~iccione pigeon (US squab)

~iede trotter (US foot)

~alla) piemontese Piedmontese style; with truffles and rice

~ignoli pine kernels

~inoccate pine kernel and almond cake

~isello pea

~istacchi pistachio nuts

~iviere plover (bird)

~izza flat, open(-faced) pie, tart, flan; bread dough bottom with any of a wide variety of toppings

~izzetta small *pizza*

~olenta pudding of maizemeal (US cornmeal)

  ~ pasticciata *polenta*, sliced and served with meat sauce, mushrooms, white sauce, butter and cheese

  ~ e uccelli small birds spitroasted and served with *polenta*

~ollame fowl

~ollo chicken

  ~ alla diavola highly spiced and grilled

  ~ novello spring chicken

~olpa 1) flesh 2) meat

polpetta di carne meatball

~olpettone meat loaf of seasoned beef or veal

~olpo octopus

  ~ in purgatorio sautéed in oil with tomatoes, parsley, garlic and peppers

salsa di) pommarola tomato sauce for *pasta*

~omodoro tomato

~ompelmo grapefruit

~opone melon

~orchetta roast suck(l)ing pig

porcini boletus mushrooms

porro leek

pranzo lunch or dinner

precotto pre-cooked

prezzemolo parsley

prezzo price

  ~ fisso fixed price

prima colazione breakfast

primizie spring fruit or vegetables

profiterole filled cream puff

  ~ alla cioccolata with chocolate frosting

prosciutto ham

  ~ affumicato cured, smoked

  ~ di cinghiale smoked wild boar

  ~ di Parma cured ham from Parma

provatura soft, mild and slightly sweet cheese made from buffalo's milk

provolone white, medium-hard cheese

prugna plum

  ~ secca prune

punte di asparagi asparagus tips

purè di patate mashed potatoes

quaglia quail

rabarbaro rhubarb

rafano horse-radish

ragù meat sauce for *pasta*

ragusano hard and slightly sweet cheese

rapa turnip

ravanello radish

raviggiolo cheese made from sheep's or goat's milk

razza ray

ribes currants

  ~ neri blackcurrants

  ~ rossi redcurrants

riccio di mare sea urchin

ricotta soft cow's or sheep's milk cheese

rigaglie giblets

rigatoni 1) type of *pasta* similar to *cannelloni* 2) type of macaroni

ripieno stuffing, stuffed

risi e bisi rice and peas cooked in chicken bouillon

riso rice

~ in bianco white rice with butter

risotto dish made of boiled rice served as a first course, with various ingredients according to the region

(brodo) ristretto consommé

robiola soft, rich and sweet sheep's milk cheese

robiolina goat's or sheep's milk cheese

rognoni kidneys

(alla) romana with vegetables, particularly onions, mint and sometimes anchovies

rombo turbot, brill

rosbif roast beef

rosmarino rosemary

rotolo rolled, stuffed meat

salame salami

(in) salamoia in brine

 salato salted

sale salt

salmone salmon

salsa sauce

salsiccia any spiced pork sausage to be served cooked

saltimbocca veal slices with ham, sage, herbs and wine

~ alla romana veal cutlet flavoured with ham and sage, sautéed in butter and white wine

salvia sage

sambuco elder

 (al) sangue underdone (US rare)

sarda pilchard, sardine

sardina small sardine

sardo sheep's milk cheese, hard, pungent and aromatic

sartù oven-baked rice with tomatoes, meat balls, chicken giblets, mushrooms and peas

scalogno shallot

scaloppa, scaloppina escalope

~ alla fiorentina with spinach and white sauce

scamorza aged *mozzarella*, firmer and saltier

scampi Dublin Bay prawns

scapece fried fish preserved in white vinegar with saffron

(allo) sciroppo in syrup

scorfano rascasse, a Mediterranean fish, used for fish soup

scorzonera salsify

scremato skimmed

 parzialmente ~ semi-skimmed

sedano celery

selvaggina game

senape mustard

seppia cuttlefish, squid

servizio (non) compreso service (not) included

sfogliatelle puff pastry with custard or fruit-preserve filling

sformato soufflé sgombro mackerel

silvano chocolate meringue or tart

soffritto sautéed

sogliola sole

~ arrosto baked in olive oil, herbs and white wine

~ dorata breaded and fried

~ ai ferri grilled

~ alla mugnaia sautéed in butter with lemon juice and parsley

soppressata 1) sausage 2) preserved pig's head with pistachio nuts

sottaceti pickled vegetables

sottaceto pickled

spaghetti spaghetti

~ aglio e olio with olive oil and fried garlic

~ all'amatriciana with tomato sauce, garlic and parmesan cheese

~ alla carbonara with oil, cheese, bacon and eggs

~ **pomodoro e basilico** fresh tomatoes and basil leaves

~ **alle vongole** with clam or mussel sauce, tomatoes, garlic and pimento

spalla shoulder

specialità speciality

spezzatino meat or fowl stew

  spicchio section ~ **d'aglio** clove of garlic

  spiedino pieces of meat grilled or roasted on a skewer

~ **di mare** pieces of fish and seafood skewered and roasted

(allo) spiedo (on a) spit

spigola sea bass

spinaci spinach

spugnola morel mushroom

spumone foamy ice-cream dessert with crystallized fruit, whipped cream and nuts

(di) stagione (in) season

stellette star-shaped *pasta*

stinco knuckle (of veal), shin (of beef)

stoccafisso stockfish, dried cod

storione sturgeon

stracchino creamy, soft to medium-soft cheese

stracciatella 1) consommé with semolina or breadcrumbs, eggs and grated cheese 2) chocolate chip

stracotto meat stew, slowly cooked for several hours

strascinati shell-shaped fresh *pasta* with different sauces

strutto lard

stufato 1) stew 2) beef stew

succu tunnu soup with semolina and saffron dumplings

sufflé soufflé

sugo sauce, gravy

(carne di) suino pork

suppli rice croquettes with *mozzarella* cheese and meat sauce

suprema di pollo in gelatina chicken breast in aspic jelly

susina plum

tacchino turkey

tagliatelle flat noodles

tagliolini thin flat noodles

taleggio medium-hard cheese with a mild flavour

tartaruga turtle

tartina open(-faced) sandwich, canapé

tartufo truffle

tartufi di mare cockles or small clams

(al) tegame sautéed

(alla) teglia fried in a pan

testa di vitello calf's head

timo thyme

tinca tench (fish)

tonnato in tunny (tuna) sauce

tonno tunny (US tuna)

topinambur Jerusalem artichoke

tordo thrush

torrone nougat

torta pie, tart, flan

tortelli small fritters

tortellini ringlets of dough filled with seasoned minced meat

tortiglione almond cake

tortino savoury tart filled with cheese and vegetables

~ **di carciofi** fried artichokes mixed with beaten eggs

(alla) toscana with tomatoes, celery and herbs

tostato toasted

totano young squid

tramezzino small sandwich

trenette noodles

triglia red mullet

trippe alla fiorentina slowly braised tripe and minced beef with tomato sauce, marjoram, parmesan cheese

trippe alla milanese tripe stewed with onions, leek, carrots, tomatoes, beans, sage and nutmeg

trippe alla romana cooked in sweet-

and-sour sauce with cheese

tritato minced

trota trout

~ **alle mandorle** stuffed, seasoned, baked in cream and topped with almonds

~ **di ruscello** river trout

tutto compreso everything included

uccelletti, uccelli small birds, usually spit-roasted

~ **in umido** stewed

uovo egg

~ **affogato nel vino** poached in wine

~ **al burro** fried in butter

~ **in camicia** poached

~ **alla coque** boiled

~ **alla fiorentina** fried, served on a bed of spinach

~ **(al) forno** baked

~ **fritto** fried

~ **molle** soft-boiled

~ **ripieno** stuffed

~ **sodo** hard-boiled

~ **strapazzato** scrambled

uva grape

vaniglia vanilla

vario assorted

(alla) veneziana with onions or shallots, white wine and mint

verdura green vegetables

vermicelli thin noodles

verza green cabbage, savoy cabbage

vitello veal

~ **all'uccelletto** diced veal, sage, simmered in wine

vongola small clam

yogurt yoghurt

zaba(gl)ione dessert of egg-yolks, sugar and Marsala wine; served warm

zafferano saffron

zampone pig's trotter filled with seasoned pork, boiled and served in slices

zèppola fritter, doughnut

zimino fish stew

zucca pumpkin, gourd

zucchero sugar

zucchino small vegetable marrow (US zucchini)

zuppa soup

~ **fredda** cold

~ **di frutti di mare** seafood

~ **di pesce** fish soup

~ **inglese** sponge cake steeped in rum with candied fruit and custard or whipped cream, trifle

~ **alla pavese** consommé with poached egg, croutons and grated cheese

~ **di verdure** vegetable soup

~ **di vongole** clam soup with white wine

Drinks

abboccato medium dry (wine)

acqua water

~ **fredda** ice-cold

~ **gas(s)ata** soda water

acquavite brandy, spirits

Aleatico a dessert wine made from muscat grapes

amabile slightly sweet (wine)

Americano a popular aperitif made with *Campari*, vermouth, angostura and lemon peel

aperitivo aperitif

aranciata orangeade

asciutto dry (wine)

Asti Spumante the renowned sparkling white wine from Piedmont

Aurum an orange liqueur

Barbaresco a red wine from Piedmont resembling *Barolo*, but lighter and slightly drier

Barbera a dark red, full-bodied wine from Piedmont and Lombardy with a rich bouquet

Bardolino a very pale red wine, from the Lago di Garda near Verona

Barolo a high quality red wine from Piedmont, can be compared to wines from the Rhone Valley

bibita beverage, drink

birra beer
  ~ **di barile** draught (US draft)
  ~ **chiara** lager, light
  ~ **scura** dark
  ~ **alla spina** draught (US draft)

caffè coffee
  ~ **corretto** espresso laced with a shot of liquor or brandy
  ~ **decaffeinato** decaffeinated
  ~ **hag** decaffeinated
  ~ **freddo** iced
  ~ **macchiato** with a few drops of milk
  ~ **nero** black
  ~ **ristretto** small and concentrated

caffellatte coffee with milk

Campania the region around Naples is noted for its fine red and white wines like *Capri*, *Falerno* and *Lacrima Christi*

Campari a reddish bitter aperitif with a quinine taste

cappuccino black coffee and whipped milk, sometimes with grated chocolate

caraffa carafe

Castelli Romani a common dry white wine from south-east of Rome

Centerbe a strong, green herb liqueur

Cerasella a cherry liqueur

Certosino a yellow or green herb liqueur

Chianti the renowned red and white table wines of Tuscany, traditionally bottled in a *fiasco*; there are many different qualities depending on the vineyards

Chiaretto one of Italy's most famous rosé wines; best when drunk very young; produced south of Lago di Garda

Cortese a dry white wine from Piedmont with limited production

degustazione vini wine tasting

dolce sweet (wine)

Emilia-Romagna the region around Bologna produces chiefly red wine like *Lambrusco*, which is sparkling and has a certain tang, and *Sangiovese*, a still type

Est! Est! Est! a semi-sweet white wine from the region north of Rome

Etna wines from the west slopes of Mount Etna (Sicily)

Falerno red and white dry wines produced in Campagnia

Fernet-Branca a bitter digestive

fiasco a straw-covered flask

frappè milk shake

Frascati a *Castelli Romani* white wine which can be dry or slightly sweet

Freisa red wines from Piedmont; one type is dry and fruity, the other is lighter and can be slightly sweet or semi-sparkling; one of Italy's best red wines produced south-west of Lago Maggiore

frizzante semi-sparkling (wine); fizzy

Gattinara a red, high-quality fullbodied wine from Piedmont, south-east of Lago Maggiore

granatina, granita fruit syrup or coffee served over crushed ice

grappa spirit distilled from grape

mash

Grignolino good quality red wine with a special character and scent; often with a high alcoholic content

Lacrima Christi the most well-known wine from the Vesuvian slopes (Campania); the white wine is the best, but there are also red and rosé versions

Lago di Caldaro light red wine produced in the Italian Tyrol

Lagrein Rosato a good rosé from the region around Bolzano in the Italian Tyrol

Lambrusco a sparkling and tingling red wine from Emilia-Romagna

latte milk

~ al cacao chocolate drink

Lazio Latium; the region principally to the south of Rome produces chiefly white wine like *Castelli Romani, Est! Est! Est!* and *Frascati*

limonata lemonade

Lombardia Lombardy; the region around Milan produces various red wines like the *Bonarda, Inferno, Spanna* and *Valtellina,* the rosé *Chiaretto* and the white *Lugana*

Lugana a good dry white wine from the region of Lago di Garda

Marsala the renowned red dessert wine from Sicily

Martini a brand-name of white and red vermouth

Millefiori a liqueur distilled from herbs and alpine flowers

Moscatello, Moscato muscatel; name for different dessert and table wines produced from the muscat grapes; there are some red, but most are white

mosto must, unfermented grape juice

Orvieto light, white wine from Umbria; three versions exist: dry,

slightly sweet and sweet

Piemonte Piedmont; the north-western region of Italy reputedly produces the highest quality wine in the country and is best known for its sparkling wine *Asti Spumante;* among its red wines are *Barbaresco, Barbera, Barolo, Dolcetto, Freisa, Gattinara, Grignolino, Nebbiolo; Cortese* is a light white wine

porto port (wine)

Puglia Apulia; at the south-eastern tip of Italy, this region produces the greatest quantity of the nation's wine, mainly table wine and some dessert wine

Punt e Mès a brand-name vermouth

Sangiovese a red table wine from Emilia-Romagna

Santa Giustina a good red table wine from the Italian Tyrol

Santa Maddalena a good quality red wine from the Italian Tyrol, light in colour and rather fruity

sciroppo fruit syrup diluted with water

secco dry (wine)

Sicilia Sicily; this island is noted for its dessert wine, particularly the celebrated *Marsala;* among many table wines the red, white and rosé *Etna* wines are the best known

sidro cider

Silvestro a herb and mint liqueur

Soave very good dry white wine, which is best when drunk young (from the east ov Verona)

spremuta fresh fruit juice

~ di limone lemon juice

~ d'arancia orange juice

spumante sparkling

Stock a wine-distilled brandy

Strega a strong herb liqueur

succo juice

tè tea
~ **al latte** with milk
~ **al limone** with lemon
Terlano Tyrolean white wine, renowned, well balanced, greenish yellow in colour and with a delicate taste
Toscana Tuscany; the region around Florence is particularly noted for its red and white *Chianti*, a good table wine, and the dessert wines *Aleatico* and *Vin Santo*
Traminer a Tyrolean white wine from the region which gave the grape and the name to the renowned Alsatian *Traminer* and *Gewürztraminer* white wines
Trentino-Alto Adige the alpine region produces red wines like *Lago di Caldaro, Santa Giustina, Santa Maddalena; Terlano* and *Traminer* are notable white wines; *Lagrein Rosato* is a rosé to remember while *Vin Santo* is a good dessert wine

Valpolicella a light red wine with a rich cherry colour and a trace of bitterness; it is best when drunk young
Valtellina region near the Swiss border which produces good, dark red wine
Vecchia Romagna a wine-distilled brandy
Veneto the north-eastern region of Italy produces high quality wines; among its red wines are *Amarone, Bardolino, Merlot, Pinot Nero, Valpolicella*; among the whites, *Pinot Grigio, Soave, Recioto* is a sparkling red wine
Vin Santo (Vinsanto) a fine dessert wine produced chiefly in Tuscany but also in Trentino, the Italian Tyrol
vino wine
~ **aperto** open
~ **bianco** white
~ **del paese** local
~ **rosatello, rosato** rosé
~ **rosso** red

Mini-Grammar

Articles

There are two genders in Italian—masculine (masc.) and feminine (fem.).

1. Definite article (the):

	singular	plural
masc.	**l'** before a vowel	**gli**
	lo before **z** or **s** + consonant	**gli**
	il before all other consonants	**i**
	l'amico (the friend)	**gli amici** (the friends)
	lo studente (the student)	**gli studenti** (the students)
	il treno (the train)	**i treni** (the trains)
fem.	**l'** before a vowel	**le**
	la before a consonant	**le**
	l'arancia (the orange)	**le arance** (the oranges)
	la casa (the house)	**le case** (the houses)

2. Indefinite article (a/an):

masc.	**un** (**uno** before **z** or **s** + consonant*)
	un piatto (a plate)
	uno specchio (a mirror)
fem.	**una** (**un'** before a vowel)
	una strada (a street)
	un'amica (a girl friend)

3. Partitive (some/any)

In affirmative sentences and some interrogatives, **some** and **any** are expressed by **di** + **definite article,** which has the following contracted forms:

masc.	**dell'** before a vowel	**degli**
	dello before **z** or **s** + consonant	**degli**
	del before other consonants	**dei**
fem.	**dell'** before a vowel	**delle**
	della before a consonant	**delle**

Desidero del vino.	I want some wine.
Vorrei delle sigarette.	I'd like some cigarettes.
Ha degli amici a Roma?	Have you any friends in Rome?

Nouns

Nouns ending in **o** are generally masculine. To form the plural, change **o** to **i**.

---

* When **s** is followed by a vowel, the masculine articles are **il/i** (definite) and **un** (indefinite).

il tavolo (the table)   **i tavoli** (the tables)

Nouns ending in **a** are usually feminine. To form the plural, change **a** to **e**.

la casa (the house)   **le case** (the houses)

Nouns ending in **e**—no rule as to gender. Learn each noun individually. Plurals are formed by changing the **e** to **i**.

il piede (the foot) **i piedi** (the feet) **la notte** (the night) **le notti** (the nights)

Adjectives

They agree with the noun and they modify in number and gender. There are two basic types—ending in **o** and ending in **e**.

	singular	plural		singular	plural
masc.	**leggero** light (in weight)	**leggeri**	fem.	**leggera**	**leggere**
	grande big	**grandi**		**grande**	**grandi**

They usually follow the noun but certain common adjectives precede the noun.

un caro amico (a dear friend)   **una strada lunga** (a long street)

Demonstratives

this	**questo/questa** (contracted to **quest'** before a vowel)
these	**questi/queste** (no contraction)
that	**quell', quello, quel** (masc.)/**quell', quella*** (fem.)
those	**quegli, quei** (masc.)/**quelle** (fem.)

Possessive adjectives and pronouns

These agree in number and gender *with the nouns they modify* (or replace).

	masculine		feminine	
	singular	plural	singular	plural
my, mine	**il mio**	**i miei**	**la mia**	**le mie**
your, yours	**il tuo**	**i tuoi**	**la tua**	**le tue**
his, her, hers, its	**il suo**	**i suoi**	**la sua**	**le sue**
our, ours	**il nostro**	**i nostri**	**la nostra**	**le nostre**
your, yours	**il vostro**	**i vostri**	**la vostra**	**le vostre**
their, theirs	**il loro**	**i loro**	**la loro**	**le loro**
**your, yours (sing.)	**il suo**	**i suoi**	**la sua**	**le sue**
**your, yours (plur.)	**il loro**	**i loro**	**la loro**	**le loro**

Thus, depending on the context, **il suo cane** can mean *his, her* or *your dog.*

---

* These forms follow the same system as **dell'/dello/della**, etc. (see p. 167).

** This is the formal form—used in addressing people you do not know well.

Personal pronouns

	Subject	Direct Object	Indirect Object	After a Preposition
I	**io**	**mi**	**mi**	**me**
you	**tu**	**ti**	**ti**	**te**
he, it (masc.)	**lui/egli**	**lo**	**gli**	**lui**
she, it (fem.)	**lei/ella**	**la**	**le**	**lei**
we	**noi**	**ci**	**ci**	**noi**
you	**voi**	**vi**	**vi**	**voi**
they (masc.)	**loro/essi**	**li**	**loro**	**loro**
they (fem.)	**loro/esse**	**le**	**loro**	**loro**

Note: There are two forms for "you" in Italian: **tu** (singular) is used when talking to relatives, close friends and children (and between young people); the plural of **tu** is **voi**. **Lei** (singular) and **Loro** (plural) are used in all other cases (with the 3rd person singular/plural of the verb).

Italian verbs

Below is a list of Italian verbs in three regular conjugations, grouped by families according to their infinitive endings, *-are*, *-ere* and *-ire*. Within the *-ire* group is one category that lengthens its stem by the addition of *-isc-* in the singular and the third person plural of the present tense (e.g. *fiorire — fiorisco*). Verbs which do not follow the conjugations below are considered irregular (see irregular verb list). Note that there are some verbs which follow the regular conjugation of the category they belong to, but present some minor changes in spelling. Examples: *mangiare, mangerò; cominciare, comincerò; navigare, navigherò*. The personal pronoun is not generally expressed since the verb endings clearly indicate the person.

		1st conj.	2nd conj.	3rd conj.
Infinitive		**am are**	**tem ere**	**vest ire**
		(*love*)	(*fear*)	(*dress*)
Present	(io)	am **o**	tem **o**	vest **o**
	(tu)	am **i**	tem **i**	vest **i**
	(egli)	am **a**	tem **e**	vest **e**
	(noi)	am **iamo**	tem **iamo**	vest **iamo**
	(voi)	am **ate**	tem **ete**	vest **ite**
	(essi)	am **ano**	tem **ono**	vest **ono**
Imperfect	(io)	am **avo**	tem **evo**	vest **ivo**
	(tu)	am **avi**	tem **evi**	vest **ivi**
	(egli)	am **ava**	tem **eva**	vest **iva**
	(noi)	am **avamo**	tem **evamo**	vest **ivamo**
	(voi)	am **avate**	tem **evate**	vest **ivate**

	(essi)	am **avano**	tem **evano**	vest **ivano**
Past Definit	(io)	am **ai**	tem **ei**	vest **ii**
	(tu)	am **asti**	tem **esti**	vest **isti**
	(egli)	am **ò**	tem **è**	vest **ì**
	(noi)	am **ammo**	tem **emmo**	vest **immo**
	(voi)	am **aste**	tem **este**	vest **iste**
	(essi)	am **arono**	tem **erono**	vest **irono**
Future	(io)	am **erò**	tem **erò**	vest **irò**
	(tu)	am **erai**	tem **erai**	vest **irai**
	(egli)	am **erà**	tem **erà**	vest **irà**
	(noi)	am **eremo**	tem **eremo**	vest **iremo**
	(voi)	am **erete**	tem **erete**	vest **irete**
	(essi)	am **eranno**	tem **eranno**	vest **iranno**
Conditional	(io)	am **erei**	tem **erei**	vest **irei**
	(tu)	am **eresti**	tem **eresti**	vest **iresti**
	(egli)	am **erebbe**	tem **erebbe**	vest **irebbe**
	(noi)	am **eremmo**	tem **eremmo**	vest **iremmo**
	(voi)	am **ereste**	tem **ereste**	vest **ireste**
	(essi)	am **erebbero**	tem **erebbero**	vest **irebbero**
Pres. subj.	(io)	am **i**	tem **a**	vest **a**
	(tu)	am **i**	tem **a**	vest **a**
	(egli)	am **i**	tem **a**	vest **a**
	(noi)	am **iamo**	tem **iamo**	vest **iamo**
	(voi)	am **iate**	tem **iate**	vest **iate**
	(essi)	am **ino**	tem **ano**	vest **ano**
Pres. part./ gerund		am **ando**	tem **endo**	vest **endo**
Past. part.		am **ato**	tem **uto**	vest **ito**

Auxiliary verbs

	avere (*to have*)		**essere** (*to be*)	
	Present	*Imperfect*	*Present*	*Imperfect*
(io)	ho	avevo	sono	ero
(tu)	hai	avevi	sei	eri
(egli)	ha	aveva	è	era
(noi)	abbiamo	avevamo	siamo	eravamo
(voi)	avete	avevate	siete	eravate
(essi)	hanno	avevano	sono	erano
	Future	*Conditional*	*Future*	*Conditional*
(io)	avrò	avrei	sarò	sarei

(tu)	avrai	avresti	sarai	saresti
(egli)	avrà	avrebbe	sarà	sarebbe
(noi)	avremo	avremmo	saremo	saremmo
(voi)	avrete	avreste	sarete	sareste
(essi)	avranno	avrebbero	saranno	sarebbero

	Pres. subj.	*Pres. perf.*	*Pres. subj.*	*Pres. perf.*
(io)	abbia	ho avuto	sia	sono stato/stata
(tu)	abbia	hai avuto	sia	sei stato/stata
(egli)	abbia	ha avuto	sia	è stato/stata
(noi)	abbiamo	abbiamo avuto	siamo	siamo stati/state
(voi)	abbiate	avete avuto	siate	siete stati/state
(essi)	abbiano	hanno avuto	siano	sono stati/state

	Past definit		*Past definit*	
(io)	ebbi		fui	
(tu)	avesti		fosti	
(egli)	ebbe		fu	
(noi)	avemmo		fummo	
(voi)	aveste		foste	
(essi)	ebbero		furono	

Irregular verbs

Below is a list of the verbs and tenses commonly used in spoken Italian. In the listing, a) stands for the present tense, b) for the past definit, c) for the future, d) for the conditional and e) for the past participle. Certain verbs are considered irregular although often only their past participles have an irregular form while, for the rest, they are conjugated like regular verbs. A few verbs are conjugated irregularly in the present tense. Such cases are shown below in all persons, the first person singular only is given for all other tenses. Unless otherwise indicated, the verbs with prefixes like *ac-*, *am-*, *ap-*, *as-*, *at-*, *av-*, *co-*, *com-*, *con-*, *cor-*, *de-*, *di-*, *dis-*, *e-*, *es-*, *im-*, *in-*, *inter-*, *intra-*, *ot-*, *per-*, *pro-*, *re-*, *ri-*, *sopra-*, *sup-*, *tra(t)-*, etc. are conjugated like the stem verb.

accendere a) accendo; b) accesi; c) accenderò; d) accenderei; e) acceso
ight

accludere a) accludo; b) acclusi; c) accluderò; d) accluderei; e) accluso
nclose

accorgersi a) mi accorgo, ti accorgi, si accorge, ci accorgiamo, vi accorgete,
erceive si accorgono; b) mi accorsi; c) mi accorgerò; d) mi accorgerei; e) accorto

addurre a) adduco; b) addussi; c) addurrò; d) addurrei; e) addotto
ring, result in

affliggere a) affliggo; b) afflissi; c) affliggerò; d) affliggerei; e) afflitto
afflict, upset

alludere a) alludo; b) allusi; c) alluderò; d) alluderei; e) alluso
allude

andare a) vado, vai, va, andiamo, andate, vanno; b) andai; c) andrò; d)
go andrei; e) andato

annettere a) annetto; b) annettei; c) annetterò; d) annetterei; e) annesso
annex

apparire a) appaio, apparisci, appare, appariamo, apparite, appaiono; b)
appear apparsi; c) apparirò; d) apparirei; e) apparso

appendere a) appendo; b) appesi; c) appenderò; d) appenderei; e) appeso
hang

aprire a) apro; b) aprii; c) aprirò; d) aprirei; e) aperto
open

ardere a) ardo; b) arsi; c) arderò; d) arderei; e) arso
burn

assistere a) assisto; b) assistei; c) assisterò; d) assisterei; e) assistito
assist

assolvere a) assolvo; b) assolsi; c) assolverò; d) assolverei; e) assolto
absolve

assumere a) assumo; b) assunsi; c) assumerò; d) assumerei; e) assunto
employ; assume

avere a) ho, hai, ha, abbiamo, avete, hanno; b) ebbi; c) avrò; d) avrei; e)
have avuto

bere a) bevo, bevi, beve, beviamo, bevete, bevono; b) bevvi; c) berrò
drink d) berrei; e) bevuto

cadere a) cado; b) caddi; c) cadrò; d) cadrei; e) caduto
fall

capire a) capisco, capisci, capisce, capiamo, capite, capiscono; b) capii
understand c) capirò; d) capirei; e) capito

chiedere a) chiedo; b) chiesi; c) chiederò; d) chiederei; e) chiesto
ask

chiudere a) chiudo; b) chiusi; c) chiuderò; d) chiuderei; e) chiuso
close

cingere a) cingo; b) cinsi; c) cingerò; d) cingerei; e) cinto
gird

cogliere a) colgo, cogli, coglie, cogliamo, cogliete, colgono; b) colsi; c)
pick coglierò; d) coglierei; e) colto

compiere a) compio, compi, compie, compiamo, compiete, compiono; b)
complete, do compiei; c) compierò; d) compierei; e) compiuto

comprimere a) comprimo; b) compressi; c) comprimerò; d) comprimerei; e)
squeeze; press compresso

concludere *conclude*	→ chiudere
condurre *escort, drive*	a) conduco; b) condussi; c) condurrò; d) condurrei; e) condotto
connetere *connect, join*	a) connetto; b) connessi; c) connetterò; d) connetterei; e) connesso
conoscere *know, be aware of*	a) conosco; b) conobbi; c) conoscerò; d) conoscerei; e) conosciuto
coprire *cover*	a) copro; b) coprii; c) coprirò; d) coprirei; e) coperto
correre *run*	a) corro; b) corsi; c) correrò; d) correrei; e) corso
costruire *construct*	→ capire
crescere *grow*	a) cresco; b) crebbi; c) crescerò; d) crescerei; e) cresciuto
cucire *sew*	a) cucio, cuci, cuce, cuciamo, cucite, cuciono; b) cucii; c) cucirò; d) cucirei; e) cucito
cuocere *cook*	a) cuocio, cuoci, cuoce, cuociamo, cuocete, cuociono; b) cossi; c) cuocerò; d) cuocerei; e) cotto
dare *give*	a) do, dai, dà, diamo, date, danno; b) diedi; c) darò; d) darei; e) dato
decidere *decide*	a) decido; b) decisi; c) deciderò; d) deciderei; e) deciso
dedurre *deduct*	→ condurre
deludere *disappoint*	→ alludere
deprimere *depress*	→ comprimere
difendere *defend*	a) difendo; b) difesi; c) difenderò; d) difenderei; e) difeso
dipendere *depend*	→ appendere
dipingere *paint*	a) dipingo; b) dipinsi; c) dipingerò; d) dipingerei; e) dipinto
dire *say, tell*	a) dico, dici, dice, diciamo, dite, dicono; b) dissi; c) dirò; d) direi; e) detto
dirigere *manage; conduct*	a) dirigo; b) diressi; c) dirigerò; d) dirigerei; e) diretto
discutere *discuss*	a) discuto; b) discussi; c) discuterò; d) discuterei; e) discusso

dissuadere a) dissuado; b) dissuasi; c) dissuaderò; d) dissuaderei; e) dissuaso
dissuade

distinguere a) distinguo; b) distinsi; c) distinguerò; d) distinguerei; e) distinto
distinguish

dividere a) divido; b) divisi; c) dividerò; d) divederei; e) diviso
divide

dolere a) dolgo, duoli, duole, dogliamo, dolete, dolgono; b) dolsi; c)
hurt; ache dorrò; d) dorrei; e) doluto

dovere a) devo, devi, deve, dobbiamo, dovete, debbono (devono); b)
have to, dovetti; c) dovrò; d) dovrei; e) dovuto
ought to

eccellere a) eccello; b) eccelsi; c) eccellerò; d) eccellerei; e) eccelso
excel, outshine

emergere a) emergo; b) emersi; c) emergerò; d) emergerei; e) emerso
rise; distinguish
oneself

erigere a) erigo; b) eressi; c) erigerò; d) erigerei; e) eretto
erect, build

escludere → alludere
exclude

esigere a) esigo; b) esigei; c) esigerò; d) esigerei; e) esatto
demand, require

esistere a) esisto; b) esistei; c) esisterò; d) esisterei; e) esistito
exist, live

espellere a) espello; b) espulsi; c) espellerò; d) espellerei; d) espulso
expel

esplodere a) esplodo; b) esplosi; c) esploderò; d) esploderei; e) esploso
explode

esprimere → comprimere
express

essere a) sono, sei, è, siamo, siete, sono; b) fui; c) sarò; d) sarei; e) stato
be

estinguere → distinguere
extinguish

fare a) faccio, fai, fa, facciamo, fate, fanno; b) feci; c) farò; d) farei; e)
do, make fatto

fendere a) fendo; b) fendei; c) fenderò; d) fenderei; e) fesso
split

ferire → capire
wound, hurt

fingere a) fingo; b) finsi; c) fingerò; d) fingerei; e) finto
pretend

flettere	a) fletto; b) flettei; c) fletterò; d) fletterei; e) flesso
bend	
fondere	a) fondo; b) fusi; c) fonderò; d) fonderei; e) fuso
melt	
frangere	a) frango; b) fransi; c) frangerò; d) frangerei; e) franto
break	
friggere	→ affliggere
fry	
giacere	a) giaccio, giaci, giace, giaciamo, giacete, giacciono; b) giacqui;
lie, rest	c) giacerò; d) giacerei; e) giaciuto
giungere	a) giungo; b) giunsi; c) giungerò; d) giungerei; e) giunto
arrive	
immergere	a) immergo; b) immersi; c) immergerò; d) immergerei; e)
dip, immerse	immerso
incidere	a) incido; b) incisi; c) inciderò; d) inciderei; e) inciso
engrave; record;	
have influence	
includere	→ alludere
include	
indurre	→ condurre
induce	
introdurre	→ condurre
insert, introduce	
invadere	a) invado; b) invasi; c) invaderò; d) invaderei; e) invaso
invade	
leggere	a) leggo; b) lessi; c) leggerò; d) leggerei; e) letto
read	
mettere	a) metto; b) misi; c) metterò; d) metterei; e) messo
put	
mordere	a) mordo; b) morsi; c) morderò; d) morderei; e) morso
bite	
morire	a) muoio, muori, muore, moriamo, morite, muoiono; b) morii; c)
die	morirò; d) morirei; e) morto
muovere	→ mordere; e) mosso
move	
nascere	→ conoscere; e) nato
be born	
nascondere	→ mordere; e) nascosto
hide	
nuocere	a) nuoccio, nuoci, nuoce, nociamo, nocete, nuociono; b) nocqui;
harm, damage	c) nocerò; d) nocerei; e) nuociuto
nutrire	→ capire
nourish	

offendere   a) offendo; b) offesi; c) offenderò; d) offenderei; e) offeso
offend

offrire   a) offro; b) offrii; c) offrirò; d) offrirei; e) offerto
offer

opprimere   → comprimere
oppress

parere   a) paio, pari, pare, paiamo, parete, paiono; b) parvi; c) parrò; d)
seem   parrei; e) parso

percuotere   a) percuoto; b) percossi; c) percuoterò; d) percuoterei; e)
hit, strike   percosso

perdere   a) perdo; b) persi; c) perderò; d) perderei; e) perso
lose

persuadere   → dissuadere
persuade

piacere   a) piaccio, piaci, piace, piacciamo, piacete, piacciono; b) piacqui
like; please   c) piacerò; d) piacerei; e) piaciuto

piangere   a) piango; b) piansi; c) piangerò; d) piangerei; e) pianto
cry

piovere   a) piove; b) piovve; c) pioverà; d) pioverebbe; e) piovuto
rain

porgere   → leggere; e) porto
hand over, offer

porre   a) pongo, poni, pone, poniamo, ponete, pongono; b) posi; c)
place, put   porrò; d) porrei; e) posto

potere   a) posso, puoi, può, possiamo, potete, possono; b) potei; c) potrò
be able to   d) potrei; e) potuto

prendere   a) prendo; b) presi; c) prenderò; d) prenderei; e) preso
take

presumere   → assumere
presume

produrre   → condurre
produce

proteggere   a) proteggo; b) protessi; c) proteggerò; d) proteggerei; e)
protect   protetto

pungere   a) pungo; b) punsi; c) pungerò; d) pungerei; e) punto
sting

radere   a) rado; b) rasi; c) raderò; d) raderei; e) raso
shave, raze

redigere   a) redigo; b) redassi; c) redigerò; d) redigerei; e) redatto
edit, write

redimere   a) redimo; b) redensi; c) redimerò; d) redimerei; e) redento
redeem

reggere	→ leggere
uphold, support	
rendere	→ prendere
render, give up	
reprimere	→ comprimere
repress	
retrocedere	a) retrocedo; b) retrocedei; c) retrocederò; d) retrocederei; e)
retreat	retroceduto
ridere	→ prendere
laugh	
ridurre	→ condurre
reduce	
rimanere	a) rimango, rimani, rimane, rimaniamo, rimanete, rimangono;
remain	b) rimasi; c) rimarrò; d) rimarrei; e) rimasto
riprodurre	→ condurre
reproduce	
risolvere	→ assolvere
resolve	
rispondere	a) rispondo; b) risposi; c) risponderò; d) risponderei; e) risposto
answer	
rompere	a) rompo; b) ruppi; c) romperò; d) romperei; e) rotto
break	
salire	a) salgo, sali, sale, saliamo, salite, salgono; b) salii; c) salirò; d)
go up, climb	salirei; e) salito
sapere	a) so, sai, sa, sappiamo, sapete, sanno; b) seppi; c) saprò; d)
know	saprei; e) saputo
scegliere	a) scelgo, scegli, sceglie, scegliamo, scegliete, scelgono; b) scelsi;
choose	c) sceglierò; d) sceglierei; e) scelto
scendere	a) scendo; b) scesi; c) scenderò; d) scenderei; e) sceso
get down	
sciogliere	→ cogliere
solve	
scomparire	→ apparire
disappear	
scoprire	→ coprire
dis-,	
uncover	
scorgere	a) scorgo; b) scorsi; c) scorgerò; d) scorgerei; e) scorto
notice, see	
scrivere	→ leggere
write	
scuotere	→ percuotere
shake	

sedere	a) siedo, siedi, siede, sediamo, sedete, siedono; b) sedei; c)
sit	sederò; d) sederei; e) seduto
sedurre	→ condurre
seduce	
smettere	→ mettere
put a stop to	
soffrire	→ offrire
suffer	
solere	a) soglio, suoli, suole, sogliamo, solete, sogliono; b) solei; c) —;
be used to	d) —; e) solito
sommergere	→ immergere
flood, sink	
sopprimere	→ comprimere
suppress, abolish	
sorgere	→ leggere; e) sorto
rise, ascend;	
be due to	
sospendere	→ appendere
suspend	
spandere	a) spando; b) spansi; c) spanderò; d) spanderei; e) spanto
spread	
spargere	a) spargo; b) sparsi; c) spargerò; d) spargerei; e) sparso
scatter, strew	
spegnere	a) spengo, spegni, spegne, spegniamo, spegnete, spengono; b)
extinguish	spensi; c) spegnerò; d) spegnerei; e) spento
spendere	a) spendo; b) spesi; c) spenderò; d) spenderei; e) speso
spend;	
make use of	
spingere	a) spingo; b) spinsi; c) spingerò; d) spingerei; e) spinto
push	
stare	a) sto, stai, sta, stiamo, state, stanno; b) stetti; c) starò; d) starei;
stand, remain	e) stato
stendere	→ tendere
stretch	
stringere	a) stringo; b) strinsi; c) stringerò; d) stringerei; e) stretto
press, tighten	
struggere	a) struggo; b) strussi; c) struggerò; d) struggerei; e) strutto
melt; torment	
succedere	a) succedo; b) successi; c) succederò; d) succederei; e) successo
happen, succeed	
tacere	a) taccio, taci, tace, tacciamo, tacete, tacciono; b) tacqui; c)
be silent	tacerò; d) tacerei; e) taciuto

tendere *stretch*	a) tendo; b) tesi; c) tenderò; d) tenderei; e) teso
tenere *keep*	a) tengo, tieni, tiene, teniamo, tenete, tengono; b) tenni; c) terrò; d) terrei; e) tenuto
tingere *dye*	a) tingo; b) tinsi; c) tingerò; d) tingerei; e) tinto
togliere *take away*	→ cogliere
torcere *wring*	a) torco; b) torsi; c) torcerò; d) torcerei; e) torto
tradurre *translate*	→ condurre
trarre *draw, haul in*	a) traggo, trai, trae, traiamo, traete, traggono; b) trassi; c) trarrò; d) trarrei; e) tratto
uccidere *kill*	a) uccido; b) uccisi; c) ucciderò; d) ucciderei; e) ucciso
udire *hear, listen to*	a) odo, odi, ode, udiamo, udite, odono; b) udii; c) udirò; d) udirei; e) udito
uscire *go, come out*	a) esco, esci, esce, usciamo, uscite, escono; b) uscii; c) uscirò; d) uscirei; e) uscito
valere *be worth*	a) valgo, vali, vale, valiamo, valete, valgono; b) valsi; c) varrò; d) varrei; e) valuto (valso)
vedere *see*	a) vedo; b) vidi; c) vedrò; d) vedrei; e) visto
venire *come, arrive*	a) vengo, vieni, viene, veniamo, venite, vengono; b) venni; c) verrò; d) verrei; e) venuto
vincere *win, conquer*	a) vinco; b) vinsi; c) vincerò; d) vincerei; e) vinto
vivere *live*	a) vivo; b) vissi; c) vivrò; d) vivrei; e) vissuto (vivuto)
volere *want*	a) voglio, vuoi, vuole, vogliamo, volete, vogliono; b) volli; c) vorrò; d) vorrei; e) voluto
volgere *turn*	a) volgo; b) volsi; c) volgerò; d) volgerei; e) volto

Italian Abbreviations

ab.	*abitanti*	inhabitants, population
abb.	*abbonamento*	subscription
a. C.	*avanti Cristo*	B.C.
A.C.I.	*Automobile Club d'Italia*	Italian Automobile Association
A.D.	*anno Domini*	Anno Domini
A.G.I.P.	*Azienda Generale Italiana Petroli*	Italian National Oil Company
all.	*allegato*	enclosure, enclosed
A.N.A.S.	*Azienda Nazionale Autonoma della Strada*	National Road Board
A.N.S.A.	*Azienda Nazionale Stampa Associata*	Italian News Agency
Avv.	*Avvocato*	lawyer, solicitor, barrister
C.A.I.	*Club Alpino Italiano*	Italian Alpine Club
cat.	*categoria*	category
Cav.	*Cavaliere*	title of nobility corresponding to knight
C.C.I.	*Camera di Commercio Internazionale*	International Chamber of Commerce
cfr.	*confronta*	compare
C.I.T.	*Compagnia Italiana Turismo*	Italian Tourist Information Office
c. m.	*corrente mese*	instant, of this month
Com. in Prov.	*Comune in provincia di...*	township in the province of...
C.O.N.I.	*Comitato Olimpico Nazionale Italiano*	Italian Olympic Games Committee
C.P.	*casella postale*	post office box
C.so	*Corso*	main street
c. c.	*conto corrente*	current account
d. C.	*dopo Cristo*	A.D.
dott., dr.	*dottore*	doctor
dott.ssa	*dottoressa*	lady doctor
dozz.	*dozzina*	dozen
ecc.	*eccetera*	and so on
Ed.	*editore*	publisher
EE	*Escursionisti Esteri*	licence plate for foreigners temporarily living in Italy
Fed.	*federale*	federal
F.S.	*Ferrovie dello Stato*	Italian State Railways
I.C.E.	*Istituto Italiano per il Commercio Estero*	Italian Institute for Foreign Trade
I.V.A.	*Imposta sul Valore Aggiunto*	VAT, value added tax
L., Lit.	*Lira italiana*	lira

mod.	*modulo*	form
n/, ns.	*nostro*	our(s)
p.	*pagina*	page
P.T.	*Poste & Telecomunicazioni*	Post and Telecommunications
P.za	*piazza*	square
racc.	*raccomandata*	registered (letter)
R.A.I.	*Radio Audizioni Italiane*	Italian Broadcasting Corporation
Rep.	*Repubblica*	republic
Rev.	*Reverendo*	reverend
S.	*Santo*	saint
S.E.	*Sua Eccellenza*	His/Her Excellency
sec.	*secolo*	century
Sig.	*Signor*	Mr.
Sig.na	*Signorina*	Miss
Sig.a	*Signora*	Mrs.
S. p. A.	*Società per Azioni*	Ltd., Inc.
s. r. l.	*Società a responsabilità limitata*	limited liability company
S.S.	*Sua Santità*	His Holiness
T.C.I.	*Touring Club Italiano*	Italian Touring Club
U.e.	*Unione europea*	European Union
v/, vs.	*vostro*	your(s)
V.le	*Viale*	boulevard, avenue
v. p.	*vedi pagina*	see page
v. r.	*vedi retro*	P.T.O., please turn over

Numerals

Cardinal numbers		Ordinal numbers	
0	zero	1°	primo
1	uno	2°	secondo
2	due	3°	terzo
3	tre	4°	quarto
4	quattro	5°	quinto
5	cinque	6°	sesto
6	sei	7°	settimo
7	sette	8°	ottavo
8	otto	9°	nono
9	nove	10°	decimo
10	dieci	11°	undicesimo
11	undici	12°	dodicesimo
12	dodici	13°	tredicesimo
13	tredici	14°	quattordicesimo
14	quattordici	15°	quindicesimo
15	quindici	16°	sedicesimo
16	sedici	17°	diciassettesimo
17	diciassette	18°	diciottesimo
18	diciotto	19°	diciannovesimo
19	diciannove	20°	ventesimo
20	venti	21°	ventunesimo
21	ventuno	22°	ventiduesimo
22	ventidue	23°	ventitreesimo
28	ventotto	24°	ventiquattresimo
30	trenta	30°	trentesimo
31	trentuno	31°	trentunesimo
32	trentadue	32°	trentaduesimo
40	quaranta	33°	trentatreesimo
50	cinquanta	40°	quarantesimo
60	sessanta	50°	cinquantesimo
70	settanta	60°	sessantesimo
80	ottanta	70°	settantesimo
90	novanta	80°	ottantesimo
100	cento	90°	novantesimo
101	centuno	100°	centesimo
230	duecentotrenta	101°	centunesimo
1.000	mille	102°	centoduesimo
1.001	milleuno	230°	duecentotrentesimo
2.000	duemila	1.000°	millesimo
1.000.000	un milione	1.001°	milleunesimo

Time

In everyday conversation the 12-hour clock is generally used, but you will notice that the 24-hour system is employed elsewhere (e.g., 14.00 = 2 p.m.).

If you have to indicate that it is a.m. or p.m., add *del mattino*, *del pomeriggio* or *di sera*.

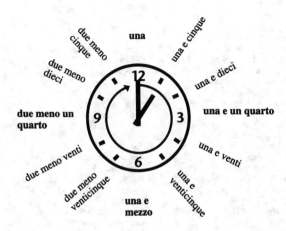

otto del mattino	8 a.m.	
due del pomeriggio	2 p.m.	
otto di sera	8 p.m.	

Days of the Week

domenica	Sunday	*giovedì*	Thursday
lunedì	Monday	*venerdì*	Friday
martedì	Tuesday	*sabato*	Saturday
mercoledì	Wednesday		

Some Basic Phrases

Please.
Thank you very much.
Don't mention it.
Good morning.
Good afternoon.
Good evening.
Good night.
Good-bye.
See you later.
Where is/Where are…?
What do you call this?
What does that mean?
Do you speak English?
Do you speak German?
Do you speak French?
Do you speak Spanish?
Do you speak Italian?
Could you speak more slowly, please?
I don't understand.
Can I have…?
Can you show me…?
Can you tell me…?
Can you help me, please?
I'd like…
We'd like…
Please give me…
Please bring me…
I'm hungry.
I'm thirsty.
I'm lost.
Hurry up!
There is/There are…
There isn't/There aren't…

Arrival

Your passport, please.
Have you anything to declare?
No, nothing at all.
Can you help me with my luggage,
please?

Alcune espressioni utili

Per favore.
Mille grazie.
Prego.
Buongiorno.
Buongiorno.
Buona sera.
Buona notte.
Arrivederci.
A più tardi.
Dov'è/Dove sono…?
Come si chiama questo?
Cosa significa?
Parla inglese?
Parla tedesco?
Parla francese?
Parla spagnolo?
Parla italiano?
Può parlare più adagio, per piacere?
Non capisco.
Posso avere…?
Può indicarmi…?
Può dirmi…?
Può aiutarmi, per piacere?
Vorrei…
Vorremmo…
Per favore, mi dia…
Per favore, mi porti…
Ho fame.
Ho sete.
Mi sono perso/persa.
Si affretti!
C'è/Ci sono…
Non c'è/Non ci sono…

L'arrivo

Il passaporto, per favore.
Ha qualcosa da dichiarare?
No, non ho nulla.
Può prendere le mie valige, per favore?

Where's the bus to the centre of town, please?	Dov'è l'autobus per il centro della città, per favore?
This way, please.	Da questa parte, per piacere.
Where can I get a taxi?	Dove posso trovare un taxi?
What's the fare to…?	Quanto costa la corsa per…?
Take me to this address, please.	Mi porti a questo indirizzo, per favore.
I'm in a hurry.	Ho fretta.

Hotel

L'albergo

My name is…	Mi chiamo…
Have you a reservation?	Ha fatto la prenotazione?
I'd like a room with a bath.	Vorrei una camera con bagno.
What's the price per night?	Qual è il prezzo per una notte?
May I see the room?	Posso vedere la camera?
What's my room number, please?	Qual è il numero della mia camera?
There's no hot water.	Non c'è acqua calda.
May I see the manager, please?	Posso vedere il direttore, per piacere?
Did anyone telephone me?	Mi ha telefonato qualcuno?
Is there any mail for me?	C'è posta per me?
May I have my bill (check), please?	Posso avere il conto, per favore?

Eating out

Al ristorante

Do you have a fixed-price menu?	Avete un menù a prezzo fisso?
May I see the menu?	Posso vedere il menù?
May we have an ashtray, please?	Possiamo avere un portacenere, per favore?
Where's the toilet, please?	Dove sono i gabinetti, per favore?
I'd like an hors d'uvre (starter).	Vorrei degli antipasti.
Have you any soup?	Ha un brodo?
I'd like some fish.	Vorrei del pesce.
What kind of fish do you have?	Che pesce ha?
I'd like a steak.	Vorrei una bistecca.
What vegetables have you got?	Quali verdure ha?
Nothing more, thanks.	Nient'altro. Grazie.
What would you like to drink?	Cosa desidera bere?
I'll have a beer, please.	Mi dia una birra, per piacere.
I'd like a bottle of wine.	Vorrei una bottiglia di vino.
May I have the bill (check), please?	Posso avere il conto, per piacere?
Is service included?	È compreso il servizio?
Thank you, that was a very good meal.	Grazie. Abbiamo mangiato molto bene.

Travelling

English	In viaggio
Where's the railway station, please?	Dove si trova la stazione, per favore?
Where's the ticket office, please?	Dove si trova lo sportello dei biglietti, per favore?
I'd like a ticket to...	Vorrei un biglietto per...
First or second class?	Di prima o di seconda classe?
First class, please.	Di prima classe, per piacere.
Single or return (one way or round-trip)?	Andata o andata e ritorno?
Do I have to change trains?	Devo cambiare treno?
What platform does the train for... leave from?	Da che binario parte il treno per...?
Where's the nearest underground (subway) station?	Dov'è la stazione della metropolitana più vicina?
Where's the bus station, please?	Dov'è la stazione degli autobus, per piacere?
When's the first bus to...?	Quando passa il primo autobus per...?
Please let me off at the next stop.	Mi faccia scendere alla prossima fermata, per piacere.

Relaxing — Gli svaghi

English	Gli svaghi
What's on at the cinema (movies)?	Cosa danno al cinema?
What time does the film begin?	A che ora incomincia il film?
Are there any tickets for tonight?	Ci sono ancora posti liberi per questa sera?
Where can we go dancing?	Dove possiamo andare a ballare?

Meeting people — Incontri

English	Incontri
How do you do.	Buongiorno.
How are you?	Come sta?
Very well, thank you. And you?	Molto bene. Grazie. E lei?
May I introduce...?	Posso presentarle...?
My name is...	Mi chiamo...
I'm very pleased to meet you.	Sono molto lieto di fare la sua conoscenza.
How long have you been here?	Da quanto tempo è qui?
It was nice meeting you.	Sono lieto di aver fatto la sua conoscenza.
Do you mind if I smoke?	Le disturba se fumo?
Do you have a light, please?	Mi fa accendere, per piacere?
May I get you a drink?	Posso offrirle da bere?
May I invite you for dinner tonight?	Posso invitarla a cena questa sera?
Where shall we meet?	Dove possiamo incontrarci?

Shops, stores and services

Where's the nearest bank, please?
Where can I cash some travellers' cheques?
Can you give me some small change, please?
Where's the nearest chemist's (pharmacy)?

How do I get there?
Is it within walking distance?
Can you help me, please?
How much is this? And that?
It's not quite what I want.
I like it.
Can you recommend something for sunburn?
I'd like a haircut, please.
I'd like a manicure, please.

Street directions

Can you show me on the map where I am?
You are on the wrong road.
Go/Walk straight ahead.
It's on the left/on the right.

Emergencies

Call a doctor quickly.
Call an ambulance.
Please call the police.

Negozi, grandi magazzini e altro

Dov'è la banca più vicina, per favore?
Dove posso incassare dei travellers' cheque?
Potrebbe darmi della moneta spicciola, per favore?
Dov'è la farmacia più vicina?

Come ci si può arrivare?
Ci si può andare anche a piedi?
Può aiutarmi, per piacere?
Quanto costa questo? E quello?
Non è quello che volevo.
Questo mi piace.
Può consigliarmi qualcosa per una scottatura?
Vorrei tagliarmi i capelli, per favore.
Vorrei una manicure, per favore.

Indicazioni stradali

Può indicarmi sulla cartina dove mi trovo?
È sulla strada sbagliata.
Continui diritto.
È a sinistra/a destra.

Urgenze

Chiami subito un medico.
Chiami un'ambulanza.
Per piacere, chiami la polizia.

Inglese-Italiano

English-Italian

Introduzione

Questo dizionario è stato compilato in modo da rispondere il megli
possibile a necessità di ordine pratico. Sono state volontariament
omesse informazioni linguistiche ritenute non indispensabili. Le vo
sono collocate in ordine alfabetico, siano esse costituite da una parol
sola, o da più parole separate o no tra loro da una lineetta. Come unic
eccezione a questa regola, alcune espressioni idiomatiche sono stal
classificate come voci principali nella posizione alfabetica della parol
più significativa nell'espressione stessa. Quando ad una voc
susseguono accezioni varie come espressioni e locuzioni particolar
esse sono egualmente collocate in ordine alfabetico.

Ad ogni vocabolo fa seguito la trascrizione fonetica (vedasi la Guida
pronuncia) la quale a sua volta precede, salvo eccezioni, la definizion
della categoria grammaticale del vocabolo (nome, verbo, aggettivo
ecc.). Quando un vocabolo rappresenta più di una categoria, le vari
traduzioni sono raggruppate dopo le rispettive categorie.

Quando irregolare, la forma plurale di un nome è generalment
indicata, com'è pure indicata nei casi in cui il lettore possa avere u
dubbio.

La tilde (~) è usata per rappresentare una voce ogni qualvolta essa
ripeta, in forme irregolari o in accezioni varie.

Nei plurali irregolari dei nomi composti, è scritta per intero solo la part
che cambia, mentre quella che rimane immutata è rappresentata da un
lineetta.

Un verbo irregolare è segnalato da un asterisco (*) posto dinnanzi. Pe
dettagli, ci si può riferire all'elenco dei verbi irregolari.

Il dizionario segue le norme dell'ortografia britannica. Ogni vocabolo
significato di esso che sia prevalentemente americano è stat
contrassegnato come tale (vedasi l'elenco delle abbreviazioni usat
nel testo).

Abbreviazioni

adj	aggettivo	*num*	numerale
adv	avverbio	*p*	passato
Am	Americano	*pl*	plurale
art	articolo	*plAm*	plurale (Americano)
conj	congiunzione	*pp*	participio passato
f	femminile	*pr*	presente
fpl	femminile plurale	*pref*	prefisso
m	maschile	*prep*	preposizione
mpl	maschile plurale	*pron*	pronome
n	nome	*v*	verbo
nAm	nome (Americano)	*vAm*	verbo (Americano)

Guida della pronuncia

Ogni lemma di questa parte del dizionario è accompagnato da un trascrizione fonetica che ne indica la pronuncia e che si deve legger come l'italiano. Diamo spiegazioni (sotto) solo per le lettere e i simbo ambigui o particolarmente difficili da comprendere.
Le lineette indicano le divisioni fra le sillabe, che sono stampate i *corsivo* quando si devono pronunciare accentuate.
Certo, i suoni delle due lingue non coincidono mai perfettamente, m seguendo alla lettera le nostre indicazioni, potrete pronunciare l parole straniere in modo da farvi comprendere. Per facilitarvi compito, talvolta le nostre trascrizioni semplificano leggermente sistema fonetico della lingua pur riflettendo le differenze di suon essenziali.

Consonanti

ð	una **s** blesa come in rosa; mettete la punta della lingua contro denti incisivi centrali superiori e soffiate leggermente facend vibrare le corde vocali come per pronunciare **d**
gh	come in **gh**iro
h	come **c** nella pronuncia toscana di **c**asa (**h**asa); espirate udibilmente, come se aveste appena fatto una corsa
ng	come **ng** in lu**ng**o, ma senza pronunciare la **g** finale
r	mettete la lingua nella posizione come per pronunciare ʒ (ve sotto), poi aprite leggermente la bocca e abbassate la lingu
s	sempre sonora, come in rosa, mai come in si
∫	come **sc** in **sc**i
θ	come **ð**, ma senza far vibrare le corde vocali
ʒ	il suono dolce della **g** toscana; come **g** in **g**iro, ma senza far sentire la **d** che compone all'inizio tale suono

Vocali e dittonghi

æ	fra **a** in c**a**so ed **e** in b**e**lla
ê	come **e** in b**e**lla (aperta)
o	come in p**o**rta (aperta)
ô	come **o** in s**o**le (chiusa)
ö	un suono neutro, come la vocale di f**uo**co nei dialetti settentrionali ("f**oech**")

1) Le vocali lunghe sono stampate doppie.
2) Le lettere rialzate (es. **"i, u"**) si devono pronunciare rapidamente.
3) Alcune parole inglesi derivanti dal francese hanno vocali nasali, che abbiamo trascritto col simbolo della vocale più **ng** (es. **ang**). Questo **ng** *non* si deve pronunciare: serve unicamente a indicare il suono nasale della vocale da pronunciare simultaneamente attraverso la bocca e il naso.

Pronuncia americana

La nostra trascrizione fonetica segue le norme usuali della pronunzia britannica. Benchè vi siano numerose variazioni secondo le regioni, l'inglese parlato in America presenta un certo numero di differenze generali. Eccone alcune:
1) La **r**, sia essa posta dinnanzi a consonante o in fine di parola, si pronunzia sempre (contrariamente all'usanza britannica).
2) In numerose parole (quali ad es. *ask*, *castle*, *laugh*, ecc.) **aa** diventa **ææ**.
3) Il suono britannico **o** si pronunzia **a**, spesso anche **oo**.
4) In vocaboli come *duty*, *tune*, *new*, ecc., **'uu** diventa sovente una sola **uu**.
5) Infine, talune parole sono accentuate diversamente.

a (ei, ö) *art* (an) un, uno, un', una

abbey (æ-bi) *n* abbazia *f*

abbreviation (ö-brii-vi-*ei*-ʃön) *n* abbreviazione *f*

ability (ö-*bi*-lö-ti) *n* abilità *f*

able (*ei*-böl) *adj* capace; abile; ***be ~ to** *essere in grado di; *sapere, *potere

aboard (ö*bood*) *adv* a bordo

abolish (ö-*bo*-liʃ) *v* abolire

abortion (ö-*boo*-ʃön) *n* aborto *m*

about (ö-*baut*) *prep* su; circa; intorno a; *adv* pressappoco, circa; attorno

above (ö-*bav*) *prep* su; *adv* sopra

abroad (ö-*brood*) *adv* all'estero

abscess (*æb*-ssèss) *n* ascesso *m*

absence (*æb*-ssönss) *n* assenza *f*

absent (*æb*-ssönt) *adj* assente

absolutely (*æb*-ssö-luut-li) *adv* assolutamente

abstain from (öb-*sstein*) *astenersi da

abstract (*æb*-sstrækt) *adj* astratto

absurd (öb-*ssööd*) *adj* assurdo

abundance (ö-*ban*-dönss) *n* abbondanza *f*

abundant (ö-*ban*-dönt) *adj* abbondante

abuse (ö-*bʲuuss*) *n* abuso *m*

abyss (ö-*biss*) *n* abisso *m*

academy (ö-*kæ*-dö-mi) *n* accademia *f*

accelerate (ök-*ssê*-lö-reit) *v* accelerare

accelerator (ök-*ssê*-lö-rei-tö) *n* acceleratore *m*

accent (*æk*-ssönt) *n* accento *m*

accept (ök-*ssêpt*) *v* accettare; *accogliere

access (*æk*-ssèss) *n* accesso *m*

accessible (ök-*ssê*-ssö-böl) *adj* accessibile

accessories (ök-*ssê*-ssö-ris) *pl* accessori *mpl*

accident (*æk*-ssi-dönt) *n* incidente *m*

accidental (æk-ssi-*dên*-töl) *adj* fortuito

accommodate (ö-*ko*-mö-deit) *v* alloggiare

accommodation (ö-ko-mö-*dei*-ʃön) *n* sistemazione *f*, alloggio *m*

accompany (ö-*kam*-pö-ni) *v* accompagnare

accomplish (ö-*kam*-pliʃ) *v* compiere; adempiere

accordance: in ~ with (in ö-*koo*-dönss ⁱið) in conformità con

according to (ö-*koo*-ding tuu) secondo

account (ö-*kaunt*) *n* conto *m*; resoconto *m*; **~ for** *rendere conto di; **on ~ of** a causa di

accountable (ö-*kaun*-tö-böl) *adj* responsabile

accurate (*æ*-kⁱu-röt) *adj* accurato

accuse (ö-*kʲuus*) *v* accusare

accused (ö-*kʲuusd*) *n* imputato *m*, -a *f*

accustom (ö-*ka*-sstöm) *v* abituare

ache (eik) *v* *dolere; *n* dolore *m*

achieve (ö-*tʃiiv*) *v* *raggiungere; effettuare

achievement (ö-*tʃiiv*-mönt) *n* adempimento *m*

acid (*æ*-ssid) *n* acido *m*

acknowledge (ök-*no*-lidʒ) *v* *riconoscere; *ammettere; confermare

acne (*æk*-ni) *n* acne *f*

acorn (*ei*-koon) *n* ghianda *f*

acquaintance (ö-*kʷein*-tönss) *n* conoscenza *f*

acquire (ö-*kʷaiᵒ*) *v* *ottenere

acquisition (æ-kʷⁱi-*si*-ʃön) *n* acquisizione *f*

acquittal (ö-*kʷi*-töl) *n* assoluzione *f*

acre (*ei*-kö) *n* acro *m*

across (ö-*kross*) *prep* attraverso;

dall'altra parte di; *adv* dall'altra parte

act (ækt) *n* atto *m*; numero *m*; *v* agire; comportarsi; recitare

action (æk-ʃön) *n* azione *f*

active (æk-tiv) *adj* attivo; vivace

activity (æk-*ti*-vö-ti) *n* attività *f*

actor (æk-tö) *n* attore *m*

actress (æk-triss) *n* attrice *f*

actual (æk-tʃu-öl) *adj* reale

actually (æk-tʃu-ö-li) *adv* in realtà

acute (ö-*k'uut*) *adj* acuto

adapt (ö-*dæpt*) *v* adattare

adaptor (ö-*dæp*-tö) *n* adattatore *m*

add (æd) *v* addizionare; *aggiungere

addition (ö-*di*-ʃön) *n* addizione *f*; aggiunta *f*

additional (ö-*di*-ʃo-nöl) *adj* supplementare; accessorio

address (ö-*drêss*) *n* indirizzo *m*; *v* indirizzare; *rivolgersi a

addressee (æ-drê-*ssii*) *n* destinatario *m*, -a *f*

adequate (æ-di-k^uöt) *adj* adeguato; idoneo

adjective (æ-dʒik-tiv) *n* aggettivo *m*

adjourn (ö-*dʒöön*) *v* rinviare

adjust (ö-*dʒasst*) *v* regolare; adattare

administer (öd-*mi*-ni-sstö) *v* somministrare

administration (öd-mi-ni-*sstrei*-ʃön) *n* amministrazione *f*

administrative (öd-*mi*-ni-sströ-tiv) *adj* amministrativo; ~ **law** diritto amministrativo

admiration (æd-mö-*rei*-ʃön) *n* ammirazione *f*

admire (öd-*mai*^ö) *v* ammirare

admission (öd-*mi*-ʃön) *n* ingresso *m*; ammissione *f*

admit (öd-*mit*) *v* *ammettere; *riconoscere

admittance (öd-*mi*-tönss) *n* ammissione *f*; **no** ~ vietato l'ingresso

adopt (ö-*dopt*) *v* adottare

adorable (ö-*doo*-rö-böl) *adj* adorabil

adult (æ-dalt) *n* adulto *m*; *adj* adult

advance (öd-*vaanss*) *n* avanzamento *m*; anticipo *m*; *v* avanzare; **in** ~ anticipatamente, in anticipo

advanced (öd-*vaansst*) *adj* avanzato

advantage (öd-*vaan*-tidʒ) *n* vantaggi *m*

advantageous (æd-vön-*tei*-dʒöss) *ad* vantaggioso

adventure (öd-*vên*-tʃö) *n* avventura

adverb (æd-vööb) *n* avverbio *m*

advertise (öd-vöö-tais) *v* mettere un annuncio (per); reclamizzare; fare pubblicità**advertisement** (öd-*vöö*-tiss-mönt) *n* inserzione *f*, annuncio *n*

advertising (æd-vö-tai-sing) *n* pubblicità *f*

advice (öd-*vaiss*) *n* consiglio *m*

advise (öd-*vais*) *v* consigliare

advocate (æd-vö-köt) *n* patrocinatore *m*, -trice *f*

aerial (ê^ö-ri-öl) *n* antenna *f*

aeroplane (ê^ö-rö-plein) *n* aeroplano *n*

affair (ö-*fê*^ö) *n* affare *m*; rapporto *m*

affect (ö-*fêkt*) *v* influenzare; riguardare

affected (ö-*fêk*-tid) *adj* affettato

affection (ö-*fêk*-ʃön) *n* affezione *f*; affetto *m*

affectionate (ö-*fêk*-ʃö-nit) *adj* affettuoso

affiliated (ö-*fi*-li-ei-tid) *adj* associato

affirm ((ö-*fööm*)) *v* affermare

affirmative (ö-*föö*-mö-tiv) *adj* affermativo

afford (ö-*food*) *v* *permettersi

afraid (ö-*freid*) *adj* impaurito; *be* ~ *aver paura

Africa (æ-fri-kö) Africa *f*

African (æ-fri-kön) *adj* africano

after (*aaf*-tö) *prep* dopo; *conj* dopo che

afternoon (aaf-tö-*nuun*) *n* pomeriggi *m*; **this** ~ oggi pomeriggio

afterwards (*aaf*-tö-ᵘöds) *adv* poi; in seguito

again (ö-*ghên*) *adv* ancora; di nuovo; **~ and again** ripetutamente

against (ö-*ghênsst*) *prep* contro

age (eidʒ) *n* età *f*; vecchiaia *f*; **of ~** maggiorenne; **under ~** minorenne

aged (*ei*-dʒid) *adj* attempato; anziano

agency (*ei*-dʒön-ssi) *n* agenzia *f*; divisione *f*

agenda (ö-*dʒên*-dö) *n* ordine del giorno

agent (*ei*-dʒönt) *n* agente *m/f*, rappresentante *m/f*

aggressive (ö-*ghrê*-ssiv) *adj* aggressivo

ago (ö-*ghou*) *adv* fa

agree (ö-*ghrii*) *v* accordarsi; acconsentire; *corrispondere

agreeable (ö-*ghrii*-ö-böl) *adj* gradevole

agreement (ö-*ghrii*-mönt) *n* contratto *m*; accordo *m*; concordanza *f*

agriculture (*æ*-ghri-kal-tʃö) *n* agricoltura *f*

ahead (ö-*hêd*) *adv* avanti; **~ of** in testa a; ***go ~** continuare; **straight ~** sempre diritto

aid (eid) *n* soccorso *m*; *v* *assistere, aiutare

aim (eim) *n* intento *m*; **~ at** puntare su, mirare a; aspirare a

air (ê*ᵒ*) *n* aria *f*; *v* arieggiare; **~ conditioning** aria condizionata

air-conditioned (ê*ᵒ*-kön-di-ʃönd) *adj* ad aria condizionata

aircraft (ê*ᵒ*-kraaft) *n* (pl **~**) velivolo *m*; aereo *m*

airfield (ê*ᵒ*-fiild) *n* aerodromo *m*

air-filter (ê*ᵒ*-fil-tö) *n* filtro dell'aria

airline (ê*ᵒ*-lain) *n* linea aerea

airmail (ê*ᵒ*-meil) *n* posta aerea

airplane (ê*ᵒ*-plein) *nAm* aeroplano *m*

airport (ê*ᵒ*-poot) *n* aeroporto *m*

airsickness (ê*ᵒ*-ssik-nöss) *n* mal d'aria

airtight (ê*ᵒ*-tait) *adj* ermetico

airy (ê*ᵒ*-ri) *adj* arioso

aisle (ail) *n* navata laterale; passaggio *m*

alarm (ö-*laam*) *n* allarme *m*; *v* allarmare; **~ clock** sveglia *f*

album (*æl*-böm) *n* album *m*

alcohol (*æl*-kö-hol) *n* alcol *m*

alcoholic (æl-kö-*ho*-lik) *adj* alcolico

ale (eil) *n* birra *f*

algebra (*æl*-dʒi-brö) *n* algebra *f*

Algeria (æl-*dʒiᵒ*-ri-ö) Algeria *f*

Algerian (æl-*dʒiᵒ*-ri-ön) *adj* algerino

alien (*ei*-li-ön) *n* straniero *m*, -a *f*; *adj* straniero

alike (ö-*laik*) *adj* uguale; simile; *adv* ugualmente

alive (ö-*laiv*) *adj* vivo, vivente

all (ool) *adj* tutto; **~ in** tutto compreso; **~ right!** va bene!; **at ~** affatto

allergy (*æ*-lö-dʒi) *n* allergia *f*

alley (*æ*-li) *n* vicolo *m*

alliance (ö-*lai*-önss) *n* alleanza *f*

allow (ö-*lau*) *v* *permettere; **~ to** lasciare; ***be allowed** *essere permesso; ***be allowed to** *avere il permesso di

allowance (ö-*lau*-önss) *n* assegno *m*

all-round (ool-*raund*) *adj* completo

ally (*æ*-lai) *n* alleato *m*

almond (*aa*-mönd) *n* mandorla *f*

almost (*ool*-mousst) *adv* quasi

alone (ö-*loun*) *adv* solo

along (ö-*long*) *prep* lungo

aloud (ö-*laud*) *adv* ad alta voce

alphabet (*æl*-fö-bêt) *n* alfabeto *m*

already (ool-*rê*-di) *adv* già

also (*ool*-ssou) *adv* anche, pure

altar (*ool*-tö) *n* altare *m*

alter (*ool*-tö) *v* cambiare, modificare

alteration (ool-tö-*rei*-ʃön) *n* cambiamento *m*, modifica *f*

alternate (ool-*töö*-nöt) *adj* alternato

alternative (ool-*töö*-nö-tiv) *n* alternativa *f*

although (ool-*ðou*) *conj* benché, sebbene

altitude (*æl*-ti-t'uud) *n* altitudine *f*

alto (*æl*-tou) *n* (pl ⁓s) contralto *m*

altogether (ool-tö-*ghê*-ðö) *adv* interamente; in tutto

always (*ool*-ᴸeis) *adv* sempre

am (æm) *v* (pr be)

amaze (ö-*meis*) *v* stupire, *stupefare

amazement (ö-*meis*-mönt) *n* stupore *m*

amazing (ö-*mei*-sing) *adj* sorprendente; incredibile

ambassador (æm-*bæ*-ssö-dö) *n* ambasciatore *m*, -trice *f*

amber (*æm*-bö) *n* ambra *f*

ambiguous (æm-*bi*-gh'u-öss) *adj* ambiguo; equivoco

ambition (æm-*bi*-ʃön) *n* ambizione *f*

ambitious (æm-*bi*-ʃöss) *adj* ambizioso

ambulance (*æm*-b'u-lönss) *n* ambulanza *f*

ambush (*æm*-buʃ) *n* imboscata *f*

America (ö-*mê*-ri-kö) America *f*

American (ö-*mê*-ri-kön) *adj* americano

amethyst (*æ*-mi-θisst) *n* ametista *f*

amid (ö-*mid*) *prep* fra; tra, in mezzo a

ammonia (ö-*mou*-ni-ö) *n* ammoniaca *f*

amnesty (*æm*-ni-ssti) *n* amnistia *f*

among (ö-*mang*) *prep* tra; fra, in mezzo a; ⁓ **other things** tra l'altro

amount (ö-*maunt*) *n* quantità *f*; ammontare *m*, somma *f*; ⁓ **to** ammontare a

amuse (ö-*m'uus*) *v* divertire

amusement (ö-*m'uus*-mönt) *n* passatempo *m*, divertimento *m*

amusing (ö-*m'uu*-sing) *adj* divertente

anaemia (ö-*nii*-mi-ö) *n* anemia *f*

anaesthesia (æ-niss-*θii*-si-ö) *n* anestesia *f*

anaesthetic (æ-niss-*θê*-tik) *n* anestetico *m*

analyse (*æ*-nö-lais) *v* analizzare

analysis (ö-*næ*-lö-ssiss) *n* (pl -ses) analisi *f*

analyst (*æ*-nö-lisst) *n* analista *m/f*; psicoanalista *m/f*

anarchy (*æ*-nö-ki) *n* anarchia *f*

anatomy (ö-*næ*-tö-mi) *n* anatomia *f*

ancestor (*æn*-ssê-sstö) *n* antenato *m* -a *f*

anchor (*æng*-kö) *n* ancora *f*

anchovy (*æn*-tʃö-vi) *n* acciuga *f*

ancient (*ein*-ʃönt) *adj* vecchio, antico antiquato

and (ænd, önd) *conj* e, ed

angel (*ein*-dʒöl) *n* angelo *m*

anger (*æng*-ghö) *n* collera *f*, rabbia *f* ira *f*

angle (*æng*-ghöl) *v* pescare con l'amo *n* angolo *m*

angry (*æng*-ghri) *adj* arrabbiato

animal (*æ*-ni-möl) *n* animale *m*

ankle (*æng*-köl) *n* caviglia *f*

annex¹ (*æ*-nêkss) *n* dipendenza *f*; allegato *m*

annex² (ö-*nêkss*) *v* *annettere

anniversary (æ-ni-*vöö*-ssö-ri) *n* anniversario *m*

announce (ö-*naunss*) *v* annunciare

announcement (ö-*naunss*-mönt) *n* annuncio *m*, avviso *m*

annoy (ö-*noi*) *v* infastidire

annoyance (ö-*noi*-önss) *n* seccatura

annoying (ö-*noi*-ing) *adj* seccante

annual (*æ*-n'u-öl) *adj* annuale; *n* annuario *m*

annum (*æ*-nöm): **per ⁓** all'anno

anonymous (ö-*no*-ni-möss) *adj* anonimo

another (ö-*na*-ðö) *adj* un altro

answer (*aan*-ssö) *v* *rispondere a; *n* risposta *f*

ant (ænt) n formica f

antibiotic (æn-ti-bai-*o*-tik) n antibiotico m

anticipate (æn-*ti*-ssi-peit) v *prevedere, anticipare; *prevenire

antifreeze (æn-ti-friis) n antigelo m

antipathy (æn-*ti*-pö-θi) n antipatia f

antique (æn-*tiik*) adj antico; n oggetto antico; ~ **dealer** antiquario m, -a f

antiquity (æn-*ti*-kᵘö-ti) n Antichità f; **antiquities** pl antichità fpl

anxiety (æng-*sai*-ö-ti) n ansietà f

anxious (æng-∫öss) adj ansioso; preoccupato

any (ê-ni) adj qualche; nessuno; (uno) qualunque

anybody (ê-ni-bo-di) pron chiunque; nessuno; qualcuno

anyhow (ê-ni-hau) adv in ogni modo

anyone (ê-ni-ᵘan) pron chiunque; nessuno; qualcuno

anything (ê-ni-θing) pron qualunque cosa; niente; qualcosa

anyway (ê-ni-ᵘei) adv in ogni caso

anywhere (ê-ni-ᵘêᵒ) adv dovunque; da nessuna parte; da qualche parte

apart (ö-paat) adv a parte, separatamente; ~ **from** a prescindere da

apartment (ö-*paat*-mönt) nAm appartamento m, alloggio m; ~ **house** Am caseggiato m

aperitif (ö-pê-rö-tiv) n aperitivo m

apologize (ö-*po*-lö-dʒais) v scusarsi

apology (ö-*po*-lö-dʒi) n scusa f

apparatus (æ-pö-*rei*-töss) n dispositivo m, apparecchio m

apparent (ö-*pæ*-rönt) adj apparente; ovvio

apparently (ö-*pæ*-rönt-li) adv apparentemente; evidentemente

appeal (ö-*piil*) n appello m

appear (ö-*pi*ᵒ) v sembrare; risultare; *apparire; presentarsi

appearance (ö-*pi*ᵒ-rönss) n apparenza f; aspetto m; ingresso m

appendicitis (ö-pên-di-*ssai*-tiss) n appendicite f

appendix (ö-*pên*-dikss) n (pl -dices, -dixes) appendice f

appetite (æ-pö-tait) n appetito m

appetizer (æ-pö-tai-sö) n stuzzichino m

appetizing (æ-pö-tai-sing) adj appetitoso

applaud (ö-*plood*) v applaudire

applause (ö-*ploos*) n applauso m

apple (æ-pöl) n mela f

appliance (ö-*plai*-önss) n apparecchio m

application (æ-pli-*kei*-∫ön) n applicazione f; richiesta f; domanda d'impiego

apply (ö-*plai*) v applicare; inoltrare una domanda d'impiego; applicarsi

appoint (ö-*point*) v designare, nominare

appointment (ö-*point*-mönt) n appuntamento m; nomina f

appreciate (ö-*prii*-∫i-eit) v valutare; apprezzare

appreciation (ö-prii-∫i-*ei*-∫ön) n apprezzamento m

apprentice (ö-pren-tis) n apprendista m/f

approach (ö-*prout∫*) v avvicinare; n impostazione f; accesso m

appropriate (ö-*prou*-pri-öt) adj adatto, appropriato

approval (ö-*pruu*-völ) n approvazione f; accordo m; **on ~** in prova

approve (ö-*pruuv*) v approvare

approximate (ö-*prok*-ssi-möt) adj approssimativo

approximately (ö-*prok*-ssi-möt-li) adv circa, approssimativamente

apricot (*ei*-pri-kot) n albicocca f

April (*ei*-pröl) aprile

apron (*ei*-prön) *n* grembiule *m*

Arab (*æ*-röb) *adj* arabo

arbitrary (*aa*-bi-trö-ri) *adj* arbitrario

arcade (*aa*-keid) *n* portico *m*, arcata *f*

arch (aat∫) *n* arco *m*; arcata *f*

archaeologist (aa-ki-*o*-lö-dʒisst) *n* archeologo *m*, -a *f*

archaeology (aa-ki-*o*-lö-dʒi) *n* archeologia *f*

archbishop (aat∫-*bi*-∫öp) *n* arcivescovo *m*

arched (aat∫t) *adj* arcato

architect (*aa*-ki-têkt) *n* architetto *m*

architecture (*aa*-ki-têk-t∫ö) *n* architettura *f*

archives (*aa*-kaivs) *pl* archivio *m*

are (aa) *v* (pr be)

area (*e*⁰-ri-ö) *n* area *f*; zona *f*; ~ **code** prefisso *m*

Argentina (aa-dʒön-*tii*-nö) Argentina *f*

Argentinian (aa-dʒön-*ti*-ni-ön) *adj* argentino

argue (*aa*-gh¹uu) *v* argomentare, *discutere; litigare

argument (*aa*-gh¹u-mönt) *n* argomento *m*; discussione *f*; lite *f*

***arise** (ö-*rais*) *v* *sorgere

arithmetic (ö-*ri*θ-mö-tik) *n* aritmetica *f*

arm (aam) *n* braccio *m*; arma *f*; *v* armare

armchair (*aam*-t∫ê⁰) *n* poltrona *f*

armed (aamd) *adj* armato; ~ **forces** forze armate

armour (*aa*-mö) *n* corazza *f*

army (*aa*-mi) *n* esercito *m*

around (ö-*raund*) *prep* intorno a; *adv* intorno

arrange (ö-*reindʒ*) *v* ordinare, *mettere in ordine; organizzare

arrangement (ö-*reindʒ*-mönt) *n* accomodamento *m*

arrest (ö-*rêsst*) *v* arrestare; *n* arresto *m*

arrival (ö-*rai*-völ) *n* arrivo *m*

arrive (ö-*raiv*) *v* arrivare

arrow (*æ*-rou) *n* freccia *f*

art (aat) *n* arte *f*; abilità *f*; ~ **collection** collezione d'arte; ~ **exhibition** mostra d'arte; ~ **gallery** galleria d'arte; ~ **history** storia dell'arte; **arts and crafts** arti e mestieri; ~ **school** accademia di belle arti

artery (*aa*-tö-ri) *n* arteria *f*

artichoke (*aa*-ti-t∫ouk) *n* carciofo *m*

article (*aa*-ti-köl) *n* articolo *m*

artificial (aa-ti-*fi*-∫öl) *adj* artificiale

artist (*aa*-tisst) *n* artista *m/f*

artistic (aa-*ti*-sstik) *adj* artistico

as (æs) *conj* come; così; che; poiché, siccome; ~ **from** a partire da; da; ~ **if** come se

asbestos (æs-*bê*-sstoss) *n* amianto *m*

ascend (ö-*ssênd*) *v* *salire; *ascendere

ascent (ö-*ssênt*) *n* ascensione *f*; ascesa *f*

ascertain (æs-ssö-*tein*) *v* constatare; accertarsi di, accertare

ash (æ∫) *n* cenere *f*

ashamed (ö-*∫eimd*) *adj* vergognoso; *be ~ vergognarsi

ashore (ö-*∫oo*) *adv* a terra

ashtray (*æ∫*-trei) *n* portacenere *m*

Asia (*ei*-∫ö) Asia *f*

Asian (*ei*-∫ön) *adj* asiatico

aside (ö-*ssaid*) *adv* da parte

ask (aassk) *v* domandare; *chiedere; invitare

asleep (ö-*ssliip*) *adj* addormentato

asparagus (ö-*sspæ*-rö-ghöss) *n* asparago *m*

aspect (*æ*-sspêkt) *n* aspetto *m*

asphalt (*æss*-fælt) *n* asfalto *m*

aspire (ö-*sspai*⁰) *v* aspirare

aspirin (*æ*-sspö-rin) *n* aspirina *f*

assassination (ö-ssæ-ssi-*nei*-∫ön) *n* assassinio *m*

assault (ö-*ssoolt*) *v* attaccare;

aggredire

assemble (ö-*ssêm*-böl) *v* riunire; montare

assembly (ö-*ssêm*-bli) *n* riunione *f*, assemblea *f*

assignment (ö-*ssain*-mönt) *n* incarico *m*

assign to (ö-*ssain*) assegnare a; attribuire a

assist (ö-*ssisst*) *v* *assistere

assistance (ö-*ssi*-sstönss) *n* aiuto *m*; soccorso *m*, assistenza *f*

assistant (ö-*ssi*-sstönt) *n* assistente *m/f*

associate (ö-*ssou*-ʃi-öt) *n* socio *m*, -a *f*; alleato *m*, -a *f*; *v* associare; ~ **with** frequentare

association (ö-ssou-ssi-*ei*-ʃön) *n* associazione *f*

assort (ö-*ssoot*) *v* assortire

assortment (ö-*ssoot*-mönt) *n* assortimento *m*

assume (ö-ss*i'uum*) *v* *assumere; *presumere

assure (ö-*ʃu*ᵒ) *v* assicurare

asthma (*æss*-mö) *n* asma *f*

astonish (ö-*ssto*-niʃ) *v* sbalordire

astonishing (ö-*ssto*-ni-ʃing) *adj* sorprendente

astonishment (ö-*ssto*-niʃ-mönt) *n* sorpresa *f*

astronaut (*ö*-sstro-nöt) *n* astronauta *m/f*

astronomy (ö-*sstro*-nö-mi) *n* astronomia *f*

asylum (ö-*ssai*-löm) *n* asilo politico; ospizio *m*

at (æt) *prep* in, da, a; verso

ate (êt) *v* (p eat)

atheist (*ei*-θi-isst) *n* ateo *m*

athlete (*æθ*-liit) *n* atleta *m/f*

athletics (æθ-*lê*-tikss) *pl* atletica *f*

Atlantic (öt-*læn*-tik) Atlantico *m*

atmosphere (*æt*-möss-fiᵒ) *n*

atmosfera *f*

atom (*æ*-töm) *n* atomo *m*

atomic (ö-*to*-mik) *adj* atomico

atomizer (*æ*-tö-mai-sö) *n* atomizzatore *m*; spruzzatore *m*, vaporizzatore *m*

attach (ö-*tætʃ*) *v* attaccare; *annettere; **attached to** affezionato a

attack (ö-*tæk*) *v* *assalire; *n* attacco *m*

attain (ö-*tein*) *v* *raggiungere

attainable (ö-*tei*-nö-böl) *adj* raggiungibile; conseguibile

attempt (ö-*têmpt*) *v* tentare; provare; *n* tentativo *m*

attend (ö-*tênd*) *v* *assistere a; ~ **on** servire; ~ **to** accudire a, occuparsi di; prestare attenzione a

attendance (ö-*tên*-dönss) *n* frequenza *f*

attendant (ö-*tên*-dönt) *n* guardia *f*

attention (ö-*tên*-ʃön) *n* attenzione *f*; *pay ~ *fare attenzione

attentive (ö-*tên*-tiv) *adj* attento

attic (*æ*-tik) *n* soffitta *f*

attitude (*æ*-ti-t'uud) *n* attitudine *f*

attorney (ö-*töö*-ni) *n* avvocato *m*

attract (ö-*trækt*) *v* *attrarre

attraction (ö-*træk*-ʃön) *n* attrattiva *f*; attrazione *f*

attractive (ö-*træk*-tiv) *adj* attraente

auction (*ook*-ʃön) *n* asta *f*

audible (*oo*-di-böl) *adj* udibile

audience (*oo*-di-önss) *n* pubblico *m*; udienza *f*

auditor (*oo*-di-tö) *n* revisore contabile; uditore *m*, -trice *f*

auditorium (oo-di-*too*-ri-öm) *n* auditorium *m*

August (*oo*-ghösst) agosto

aunt (aant) *n* zia *f*

Australia (o-*sstrei*-li-ö) Australia *f*

Australian (o-*sstrei*-li-ön) *adj* australiano

Austria (*o*-sstri-ö) Austria *f*

Austrian (*o*-sstri-ön) *adj* austriaco
authentic (oo-*θ*én-tik) *adj* autentico
author (*oo*-*θ*ö) *n* autore *m*, -trice *f*
authoritarian (oo-*θ*o-ri-*tê*ᵒ-ri-ön) *adj*
  autoritario
authority (oo-*θ*o-rö-ti) *n* autorità *f*;
  potere *m*
authorize (*oo*-*θ*ö-rais) *v* autorizzare;
  be authorized to essere autorizzato
  a
authorization (oo-*θ*ö-rai-sei-ʃön) *n*
  autorizzazione *f*; permesso *m*
automatic (oo-tö-*mæ*-tik) *adj*
  automatico; **~ teller** *Am* sportello
  automatico *f*
automation (oo-tö-*mei*-ʃön) *n*
  automazione *f*
automobile (*oo*-tö-mö-biil) *n*
  automobile *f*; **~ club** automobile club
autonomous (oo-*to*-nö-möss) *adj*
  autonomo
autopsy (*oo*-to-pssi) *n* autopsia *f*
autumn (*oo*-töm) *n* autunno *m*

available (ö-*vei*-lö-böl) *adj*
  disponibile
avalanche (æ-vö-laanʃ) *n* valanga *f*
avenue (æ-vö-n¹uu) *n* viale *m*
average (æ-vö-ridჳ) *adj* medio; *n*
  media *f*; **on the ~** in media
aversion (ö-*vöö*-ʃön) *n* avversione *f*
avert (ö-*vööt*) *v* *distogliere
avoid (ö-*void*) *v* evitare
await (ö-ᵘ*eit*) *v* aspettare
awake (ö-ᵘ*eik*) *adj* sveglio
***awake** (ö-ᵘ*eik*) *v* svegliare
award (ö-ᵘ*ood*) *n* premio *m*; *v*
  aggiudicare
aware (ö-ᵘ*êᵒ*) *adj* consapevole
away (ö-ᵘ*ei*) *adv* via; ***go ~** *andarsene
awful (*oo*-föl) *adj* terribile
awkward (*oo*-kᵘöd) *adj* imbarazzante;
  goffo
awning (*oo*-ning) *n* tenda di riparo
axe (ækss) *n* ascia *f*
axle (æk-ssöl) *n* asse *m*

B

baby (*bei*-bi) *n* bebè *m*; **~ carriage**
  Am carrozzina *f*
babysitter (*bei*-bi-ssi-tö) *n* babysitter *f*
bachelor (*bæ*-tʃö-lö) *n* celibe *m*
back (bæk) *n* schiena *f*; *adv* indietro;
  ***go ~** tornare
backache (*bæ*-keik) *n* mal di schiena
backbone (*bæk*-boun) *n* spina dorsale
background (*bæk*-ghraund) *n* sfondo
  m; istruzione *f*
backwards (*bæk*-ᵘöds) *adv*
  all'indietro
bacon (*bei*-kön) *n* lardo *m*
bacterium (bæk-*tii*-ri-öm) *n* (pl -ria)
  batterio *m*

bad (bæd) *adj* cattivo; brutto
bag (bægh) *n* sacco *m*; borsetta *f*,
  borsa *f*; valigia *f*
baggage (*bæ*-ghidჳ) *n* bagaglio *m*; **~
  deposit office** *Am*, **~ check** *Am*
  deposito bagagli; **hand ~** *Am*
  bagaglio a mano
bail (beil) *n* cauzione *f*
bait (beit) *n* esca *f*
bake (beik) *v* cuocere in forno
baker (*bei*-kö) *n* panettiere *m*
bakery (*bei*-kö-ri) *n* panetteria *f*
balance (*bæ*-lönss) *n* equilibrio *m*;
  bilancio *m*; saldo *m*
balcony (*bæl*-kö-ni) *n* balcone *m*;

galleria *f*

bald (boold) *adj* calvo

ball (bool) *n* palla *f*; ballo *m*

ballet (*bæ*-lei) *n* balletto *m*

balloon (bö-*luun*) *n* palloncino *m*

ballpoint pen (*bool*-point-pên) *n* penna a sfera

ballroom (*bool*-ruum) *n* sala da ballo

bamboo (bæm-*buu*) *n* (pl ~s) bambù *m*

banana (bö-*naa*-nö) *n* banana *f*

band (bænd) *n* banda *f*; benda *f*

bandage (*bæn*-didȝ) *n* fasciatura *f*

bandit (*bæn*-dit) *n* bandito *m*

bangle (*bæng*-ghöl) *n* braccialetto *m*

bank (bængk) *n* riva *f*; banca *f*; *v* depositare; ~ **account** conto bancario; ~ **rate** tasso di sconto

banknote (*bængk*-nout) *n* banconota *f*

bankrupt (*bængk*-rapt) *adj* fallito

banner (*bæ*-nö) *n* stendardo *m*

banquet (*bæng*-k^{u}it) *n* banchetto *m*

baptism (*bæp*-ti-söm) *n* battesimo *m*

baptize (bæp-*tais*) *v* battezzare

bar (baa) *n* bar *m*; sbarra *f*

barbecue (*baa*-bee-k^{u}uu) *n* barbecue *m*; *v* cuocere al barbecue

barbed wire (*baa*-böd ^{u}ai^ö) n filo spinato

barber (*baa*-bö) *n* barbiere *m*

bare (bê^ö) *adj* nudo; spoglio

barely (*bê^ö*-li) *adv* appena

bargain (*baa*-ghin) *n* affare *m*; *v* mercanteggiare

baritone (*bæ*-ri-toun) *n* baritono *m*

bark (baak) *n* corteccia *f*; *v* abbaiare

barley (*baa*-li) *n* orzo *m*

barmaid (*baa*-meid) *n* barista *f*

barman (*baa*-mön) *n* (pl -men) barista *m*

barn (baan) *n* granaio *m*

barometer (bö-*ro*-mi-tö) *n* barometro *m*

baroque (bö-*rok*) *adj* barocco

barracks (*bæ*-rökss) *pl* caserma *f*

barrel (*bæ*-röl) *n* botte *f*, barile *m*

barrier (*bæ*-ri-ö) *n* barriera *f*

barrister (*bæ*-ri-sstö) *n* avvocato *m*

bartender (*baa*-tên-dö) *n* barista *m*

base (beiss) *n* base *f*; fondamento *m*; *v* basare

baseball (*beiss*-bool) *n* baseball *m*

basement (*beiss*-mönt) *n* seminterrato *m*

basic (*bei*-ssik) *adj* fondamentale; *npl* **the basics** i rudimenti; **get down to basics** venire al sodo

basilica (bö-*si*-li-kö) *n* basilica *f*

basin (*bei*-ssön) *n* bacino *m*, catino *m*

basis (*bei*-ssiss) *n* (pl bases) fondamento *m*, base *f*

basket (*baa*-sskit) *n* paniere *m*

bass[1] (beiss) *n* basso *m*

bass[2] (bæss) *n* (pl ~) branzino *m*

bastard (*baa*-sstöd) *n* bastardo *m*

batch (bætʃ) *n* partita *f*

bath (baaθ) *n* bagno *m*; ~ **salts** sali da bagno; ~ **towel** asciugamano *m*

bathe (beið) *v* *fare il bagno

bathing cap (*bei*-ðing-kæp) *n* cuffia da bagno

bathing suit (*bei*-ðing-ssuut) *n* costume da bagno

bathing trunks (*bei*-ðing-trangkss) *n* calzoncini da bagno

bathrobe (*baaθ*-roub) *n* accappatoio *m*

bathroom (*baaθ*-ruum) *n* bagno; gabinetto *m*

batter (*bæ*-tö) *n* impasto *m*

battery (*bæ*-tö-ri) *n* batteria *f*; accumulatore *m*

battle (*bæ*-töl) *n* battaglia *f*; lotta *f*, combattimento *m*; *v* combattere

bay (bei) *n* baia *f*; *v* latrare

*be (bii) *v* *essere

beach (biitʃ) *n* spiaggia *f*; **nudist** ~ spiaggia per nudisti

bead (biid) *n* perlina *f*; **beads** *pl* collana *f*; rosario *m*

beak (biik) *n* becco *m*

beam (biim) *n* raggio *m*; trave *f*

bean (biin) *n* fagiolo *m*

bear (bê⁰) *n* orso *m*

***bear** (bê⁰) *v* portare; tollerare; sopportare

beard (bi⁰d) *n* barba *f*

bearer (bê⁰-rö) *n* portatore *m*, -trice *f*

beast (biisst) *n* animale *m*; ~ **of prey** animale da preda

***beat** (biit) *v* picchiare; battere

beautiful (b'uu-ti-föl) *adj* bello

beauty (b'uu-ti) *n* bellezza *f*; ~ **parlour** salone di bellezza; ~ **salon** salone di bellezza; ~ **treatment** cura di bellezza

beaver (bii-vö) *n* castoro *m*

because (bi-kos) *conj* perché; poiché; ~ **of** a causa di

***become** (bi-kam) *v* *diventare; *addirsi

bed (bêd) *n* letto *m*; ~ **and board** vitto e alloggio, pensione completa; ~ **and breakfast** pensione familiare, bed and breakfast; **bunk** ~ letto a castello; **double** ~ letto matrimoniale; **single** ~ letto singolo

bedding (bê-ding) *n* biancheria da letto

bedroom (bêd-ruum) *n* camera da letto

bee (bii) *n* ape *f*

beech (bii-tʃ) *n* faggio *m*

beef (biif) *n* manzo *m*

beefburger (biif-bö-gö) *n* hamburger *m*

beehive (bii-haiv) *n* alveare *m*

been (biin) *v* (pp be)

beer (bi⁰) *n* birra *f*

beet (biit) *n* barbabietola *f*

beetle (bii-töl) *n* scarabeo *m*

beetroot (biit-ruut) *n* barbabietola *f*

before (bi-foo) *prep* prima di; davanti; *conj* prima che; *adv* prima; precedentemente

beg (bêgh) *v* mendicare; supplicare; *chiedere

beggar (bê-ghö) *n* mendicante *m/f*

***begin** (bi-ghin) *v* cominciare, iniziare

beginner (bi-ghi-nö) *n* principiante *m*

beginning (bi-ghi-ning) *n* inizio *m*, principio *m*

behalf (bi-haaf): **on** ~ **of** a nome di, per conto di; a favore di; **on my** ~ a nome mio

behave (bi-heiv) *v* comportarsi

behavio(u)r (bi-hei-v'ö) *n* comportamento *m*

behind (bi-haind) *prep* dietro; *adv* indietro

beige (beiȝ) *adj* beige

being (bii-ing) *n* essere *m*

Belgian (bêl-dȝön) *adj* belga

Belgium (bêl-dȝöm) Belgio *m*

belief (bi-liif) *n* fede *f*

believe (bi-liiv) *v* credere

bell (bêl) *n* campana *f*; campanello *m*

bellboy (bêl-boi) *n* fattorino d'albergo

belly (bê-li) *n* pancia *f*

belong (bi-long) *v* *appartenere

belongings (bi-long-ings) *pl* effetti personali

beloved (bi-lavd) *adj* amato

below (bi-lou) *prep* sotto; *adv* giù

belt (bêlt) *n* cinghia *f*; **garter** ~ *Am* reggicalze *m*

bench (bêntʃ) *n* banco *m*

bend (bênd) *n* curva *f*; curvatura *f*

***bend** (bênd) *v* curvare; ~ **down** chinarsi

beneath (bi-niiθ) *prep* sotto; *adv* giù

benefit (bê-ni-fit) *n* profitto *m*, beneficio *m*; vantaggio *m*; *v* approfittare

bent (bênt) *adj* (pp bend) curvato

beret (bê-rei) *n* berretto *m*

berry (*bê*-ri) *n* bacca *f*

beside (bi-*ssaid*) *prep* vicino a

besides (bi-*ssaids*) *adv* inoltre; d'altronde; *prep* oltre a

best (bêsst) *adj* ottimo

bet (bêt) *n* scommessa *f*; posta *f*

*bet (bêt) *v* *scommettere

betray (bi-*trei*) *v* tradire

better (*bê*-tö) *adj* migliore

between (bi-*tⁱiin*) *prep* tra

beverage (*bê*-vö-ridʒ) *n* bevanda *f*

beware (bi-ᵘ*ê°*) *v* guardarsi, *fare attenzione

bewitch (bi-ᵘ*itʃ*) *v* stregare, incantare

beyond (bi-ⁱ*ond*) *prep* più in là di; oltre; in aggiunta a; *adv* al di là

bible (*bai*-böl) *n* bibbia *f*

bicycle (*bai*-ssi-köl) *n* bicicletta *f*

bid (bid) *n* offerta *f*; tentativo *m*; *v* offrire

big (bigh) *adj* grande; voluminoso; grosso; importante

bike (baik) *n* bici *f*; *v* andare in bici; **I biked here** sono venuto in bici

bile (bail) *n* bile *f*

bilingual (bai-*ling*-ghᵘöl) *adj* bilingue

bill (bil) *n* fattura *f*; conto *m*; *v* fatturare

billiards (*bil*-ⁱöds) *pl* biliardo *m*

billion (*bi*-liön) *n* miliardo *m*

*bind (baind) *v* legare

binding (*bain*-ding) *n* legatura *f*

binoculars (bi-*no*-kⁱö-lös) *pl* binocolo *m*

biology (bai-*o*-lö-dʒi) *n* biologia *f*

birch (böötʃ) *n* betulla *f*

bird (bööd) *n* uccello *m*

Biro (*bai*-rou) *n* penna a sfera

birth (bööθ) *n* nascita *f*

birthday (*bööθ*-dei) *n* compleanno *m*

biscuit (*biss*-kit) *n* biscotto *m*

bishop (*bi*-ʃöp) *n* vescovo *m*

bit (bit) *n* pezzetto *m*; poco *m*

bitch (bitʃ) *n* cagna *f*

bite (bait) *n* boccone *m*; morso *m*; puntura *f*

*bite (bait) *v* *mordere

bitter (*bi*-tö) *adj* amaro

black (blæk) *adj* nero; **~ market** mercato nero

blackberry (*blæk*-bö-ri) *n* mora *f*

blackbird (*blæk*-bööd) *n* merlo *m*

blackboard (*blæk*-bood) *n* lavagna *f*

blackcurrant (blæk-*ka*-rönt) *n* ribes nero

blackmail (*blæk*-meil) *n* ricatto *m*; *v* ricattare

blacksmith (*blæk*-ssmiθ) *n* fabbro *m*

bladder (*blæ*-dö) *n* vescica *f*

blade (bleid) *n* lama *f*; **~ of grass** filo d'erba

blame (bleim) *n* colpa *f*; biasimo *m*; *v* biasimare; rimproverare

blank (blængk) *adj* in bianco

blanket (*blæng*-kit) *n* coperta *f*

blast (blaasst) *n* esplosione *f*

blazer (*blei*-sö) *n* giacca sportiva

bleach (bliitʃ) *v* imbiancare

bleak (bliik) *adj* rigido

*bleed (bliid) *v* sanguinare; salassare

bless (blêss) *v* *benedire

blessing (*blê*-ssing) *n* benedizione *f*

blind (blaind) *n* avvolgibile *m*, persiana *f*; *adj* cieco; *v* abbagliare

blinker (*blin*-kö) *nAm* freccia *f*

blister (*bli*-sstö) *n* bolla *f*

blizzard (*bli*-söd) *n* tormenta *f*

block (blok) *v* ostruire, bloccare; *n* ceppo *m*; **~ of flats** caseggiato *m*

blond (blond) *adj* biondo

blonde (blond) *n* bionda *f*

blood (blad) *n* sangue *m*; **~ pressure** pressione sanguigna; **~ poisoning** setticemia *f*; **~ vessel** vaso sanguigno

bloody (*bla*-di) *adj* insanguinato; sanguinoso; maledetto; **~ hell!** porca miseria!

blossom (*blo*-söm) *n* fiori *mpl*; *v*

fiorire

blot (blot) *n* macchia *f*

blotting paper (blot-ting *pei*-pö) *n* carta assorbente

blouse (blaus) *n* camicetta *f*

blow (blou) *n* colpo *m*; raffica *f*

***blow** (blou) *v* soffiare,tirare; ***~ up** *v* far saltare; gonfiare; ingrandire; esplodere

blowout (*blou*-aut) *n* foratura *f*

blue (bluu) *adj* blu; depresso

blunt (blant) *adj* spuntato

blush (blaʃ) *v* arrossire; *n* fard *m*

board (bood) *n* asse *f*; tavoletta *f*; pensione *f*; comitato *m*; **~ and lodging** pensione completa, vitto e alloggio

boarder (*boo*-dö) *n* pensionante *m*

boardinghouse (*boo*-ding-hauss) *n* pensione *f*

boarding school (*boo*-ding-sskuul) *n* convitto *m*

boast (bousst) *v* vantarsi

boat (bout) *n* battello *m*, barca *f*

body (*bo*-di) *n* corpo *m*

bodyguard (*bo*-di-ghaad) *n* guardia del corpo

bog (bogh) *n* palude *f*

boil (boil) *v* bollire; *n* foruncolo *m*

bold (bould) *adj* coraggioso; sfrontato, sfacciato

Bolivia (bö-*li*-vi-ö) Bolivia *f*

Bolivian (bö-*li*-vi-ön) *adj* boliviano

bolt (boult) *n* chiavistello *m*; bullone *m*

bomb (bom) *n* bomba *f*; *v* bombardare

bond (bond) *n* obbligazione *f*

bone (boun) *n* osso *m*; lisca *f*; *v* disossare

bonnet (*bo*-nit) *n* cofano *m*

book (buk) *n* libro *m*; *v* prenotare; registrare

booking (*bu*-king) *n* prenotazione *f*

bookmaker (*buk*-mei-kö) *n*

allibratore *m*

bookseller (*buk*-ssê-lö) *n* libraio *m*, -a *f*

bookstand (*buk*-sstænd) *n* edicola *f*

bookstore (*buk*-sstoo) *n* libreria *f*

boot (buut) *n* stivale *m*; bagagliaio *m*

booth (buuð) *n* bancarella *f*; cabina *f*

booze (buuz) *n* alcolici *mpl*

border (*boo*-dö) *n* confine *m*; bordo *m*

bore[1] (boo) *v* annoiare; trapanare; *n* seccatore *m*

bore[2] (boo) *v* (p bear)

boring (*boo*-ring) *adj* noioso

born (boon) *adj* nato

borrow (*bo*-rou) *v* *prendere in prestito

bosom (*bu*-söm) *n* petto *m*, seno *m*

boss (boss) *n* capo *m*, padrone *m*, -a *f*

botany (*bo*-tö-ni) *n* botanica *f*

both (bouθ) *adj* entrambi; **both … and** sia … ma

bother (*bo*-ðö) *v* infastidire, importunare; disturbarsi; *n* noia *f*

bottle (*bo*-töl) *n* bottiglia *f*; **~ opener** apribottiglie *m*; **hot-water ~** borsa dell'acqua calda

bottleneck (*bo*-töl-nêk) *n* ingorgo *m*

bottom (*bo*-töm) *n* fondo *m*; didietro *m*, sedere *m*; *adj* inferiore

bought (boot) *v* (p, pp buy)

boulder (*boul*-dö) *n* masso *m*

bound (baund) *n* limite *m*; ***be ~ to** *dovere; **~ for** diretto a

boundary (*baun*-dö-ri) *n* limite *m*; frontiera *f*

bouquet (bu-*kei*) *n* mazzo *m*

bourgeois (buⁿ-ʒ*aa*) *adj* borghese

boutique (bu-*tiik*) *n* boutique *f*

bow[1] (bau) *v* chinare

bow[2] (bou) *n* arco *m*; **~ tie** cravattino *m*, cravatta a farfalla

bowels (bauⁿls) *pl* intestino *m*, budella *fpl*

bowl (boul) *n* vaso *m*

bowling (*bou*-ling) *n* bowling *m*; ~ **alley** pista da bowling

box[1] (bokss) *v* *fare del pugilato; **boxing match** partita di pugilato

box[2] (bokss) *n* scatola *f*; ~ **office** botteghino *m*, biglietteria *f*

boy (boi) *n* ragazzo *m*; ragazzino *m*, fanciullo *m*; ~ **scout** giovane esploratore

boyfriend (*boi*-frênd) *n* ragazzo *m*; amico *m*

bra (braa) *n* reggipetto *m*, reggiseno *m*

bracelet (*breiss*-lit) *n* braccialetto *m*

braces (*brei*-ssis) *pl* bretelle *fpl*

brain (brein) *n* cervello *m*; intelligenza *f*; ~ **wave** lampo di genio

brake (breik) *n* freno *m*; ~ **drum** tamburo del freno; ~ **lights** luci di arresto

branch (braantʃ) *n* ramo *m*; succursale *f*

brand (brænd) *n* marca *f*; marchio *m*

brand-new (brænd-*n'uu*) *adj* nuovo fiammante

brass (braass) *n* ottone *m*; ~ **band** *n* fanfara *f*

brave (breiv) *adj* audace, coraggioso

Brazil (brö-*sil*) Brasile *m*

Brazilian (brö-*sil*-[1]ön) *adj* brasiliano

breach (briitʃ) *n* rottura *f*

bread (brêd) *n* pane *m*; **wholemeal** ~ pane integrale

breadth (brêdθ) *n* larghezza *f*

break (breik) *n* frattura *f*; intervallo *m*

*break (breik) *v* *rompere; ~ **down** guastarsi; analizzare; arenarsi; scoppiare in lacrime; avere un esaurimento; buttare giù

breakdown (*breik*-daun) *n* guasto *m*, avaria *f*

breakfast (*brêk*-fösst) *n* colazione

breast (brêsst) *n* seno *m*

breaststroke (*brêsst*-sstrouk) *n* nuoto a rana

breath (brêθ) *n* respiro *m*; fiato *m*

breathe (briið) *v* respirare

breathing (*brii*-ðing) *n* respirazione *f*

breed (briid) *n* razza *f*; specie *f*

*breed (briid) *v* allevare

breeze (briis) *n* brezza *f*

brew (bruu) *v* *fare la birra

brewery (*bruu*-ö-ri) *n* birreria *f*

bribe (braib) *v* *corrompere

bribery (*brai*-bö-ri) *n* corruzione *f*

brick (brik) *n* laterizio *m*, mattone *m*

bricklayer (*brik*-lei[0]) *n* muratore *m*

bride (braid) *n* sposa *f*

bridegroom (*braid*-ghruum) *n* sposo *m*

bridge (bridʒ) *n* ponte *m*; bridge *m*

brief (briif) *adj* breve

briefcase (*briif*-keiss) *n* cartella *f*

briefs (briifss) *pl* slip *mpl*, mutandine *fpl*

bright (brait) *adj* brillante; lucido; sveglio, intelligente

brill (bril) *n* rombo *m*

brilliant (*bril*-[1]önt) *adj* brillante

brim (brim) *n* orlo *m*

*bring (bring) *v* portare; ~ **back** riportare; ~ **up** educare; sollevare

brisk (brissk) *adj* vivace

Britain (*bri*-tön) Gran Bretagna

British (*bri*-tiʃ) *adj* britannico; inglese

Briton (*bri*-tön) *n* britanno *m*; inglese *m*

broad (brood) *adj* largo; ampio, esteso; generale

broadcast (*brood*-kaasst) *n* trasmissione *f*

*broadcast (*brood*-kaasst) *v* *trasmettere

brochure (brou-ʃu[0]) *n* opuscolo *m*

broke[1] (brouk) *v* (p break)

broke[2] (brouk) *adj* squattrinato

broken (*brou*-kön) *adj* (pp break) guasto, rotto

broker (*brou*-kö) *n* mediatore *m*,

-trice *f*

bronchitis (brong-*kai*-tiss) *n* bronchite *f*

bronze (brons) *n* bronzo *m; adj* bronzeo

brooch (brout∫) *n* spilla *f*

brook (bruk) *n* ruscello *m*

broom (bruum) *n* scopa *f*

brothel (*bro*-θöl) *n* bordello *m*

brother (*bra*-öö) *n* fratello *m*

brother-in-law (*bra*-öö-rin-loo) *n* (pl brothers-) cognato *m*

brought (broot) *v* (p, pp bring)

brown (braun) *adj* marrone; castano

bruise (bruus) *n* livido *m*, contusione *f; v* ammaccare

brunette (bruu-*nêt*) *n* bruna *f*

brush (bra∫) *n* spazzola *f;* pennello *m; v* spazzolare

brutal (*bruu*-töl) *adj* brutale

bubble (*ba*-böl) *n* bolla *f*

buck (bak) *n Am* dollaro *m*

bucket (*ba*-kit) *n* secchio *m*

buckle (*ba*-köl) *n* fibbia *f*

bud (bad) *n* bocciolo *m*

buddy (badi) *n* amico *m*, amica *f*

budget (*ba*-dʒit) *n* bilancio *m*, budget *m*

buffet (*bu*-fei) *n* buffet *m*

bug (bagh) *n* cimice *f; Am* insetto *m*

***build** (bild) *v* costruire

building (*bil*-ding) *n* edificio *m*

bulb (balb) *n* bulbo *m;* **light ~** lampadina *f*

Bulgaria (bal-*ghê*ᵒ-ri-ö) Bulgaria *f*

Bulgarian (bal-*ghê*ᵒ-ri-ön) *adj* bulgaro

bulk (balk) *n* massa *f;* maggior parte

bulky (*bal*-ki) *adj* voluminoso

bull (bul) *n* toro *m*

bullet (*bu*-lit) *n* pallottola *f*

bulletin (*bu*-li-tin) *n* bollettino *m*

bullfight (*bul*-fait) *n* corrida *f*

bullring (*bul*-ring) *n* arena *f*

bump (bamp) *v* urtare; cozzare; *n* urto *m*

bumper (*bam*-pö) *n* paraurti *m*

bumpy (*bam*-pi) *adj* accidentato

bun (ban) *n* panino *m*

bunch (bant∫) *n* mazzo *m;* gruppo *m*

bundle (*ban*-döl) *n* fagotto *m; v* legare insieme

bunk (bangk) *n* cuccetta *f*

buoy (boi) *n* boa *f*

burden (*böö*-dön) *n* peso *m*

bureau (*b*ᵗ*u*ᵒ-rou) *n* (pl ~x, ~s) scrittoio *m; Am* comò *m*

bureaucracy (*b*ᵗ*u*ᵒ-*ro*-krö-ssi) *n* burocrazia *f*

burglar (*böö*-ghlö) *n* scassinatore *m*, -trice *f*

burgle (*böö*-ghöl) *v* scassinare

burial (*bê*-ri-öl) *n* seppellimento *m*, sepoltura *f*

burn (böön) *n* bruciatura *f*

***burn** (böön) *v* *ardere; bruciare

***burst** (bööst) *v* scoppiare; spaccarsi

bury (*bê*-ri) *v* seppellire

bus (bass) *n* autobus *m*

bush (bu∫) *n* cespuglio *m*

business (*bis*-nöss) *n* affari; commercio *m;* azienda *f*, ditta *f;* mestiere *m;* affare *m;* **~ hours** orario di apertura, ore d'ufficio; **~ trip** viaggio d'affari; **on ~** per affari

businessman (*bis*-nöss-mön) *n* (pl -men) uomo d'affari

bust (basst) *n* busto *m*

bustle (*ba*-ssöl) *n* andirivieni *m*

busy (*bi*-si) *adj* occupato, indaffarato; animato

but (bat) *conj* ma, però; *prep* tranne

butcher (*bu*-t∫ö) *n* macellaio *m*, -a *f*

butter (*ba*-tö) *n* burro *m*

butterfly (*ba*-tö-flai) *n* farfalla *f;* **~ stroke** nuoto a farfalla

buttock (*ba*-tök) *n* natica *f*

button (*ba*-tön) *n* bottone *m; v* abbottonare

buttonhole (*ba*-tön-houl) *n* asola *f*
*buy (bai) *v* comprare, acquistare
buyer (*bai*-ö) *n* compratore *m*, -trice *f*
buzz (baz) *n* ronzio *m*; emozione *f*; *v* ronzare; suonare; chiamare

by (bai) *prep* da; con; vicino a
bye-bye! (*bai*-bai) ciao!
bypass (*bai*-paass) *n* circonvallazione *f*; *v* girare intorno a

C

cab (kæb) *n* tassì *m*; **~ driver** tassista *m/f*
cabaret (*kæ*-bö-rei) *n* cabaret *m*
cabbage (*kæ*-bidʒ) *n* cavolo *m*
cabin (*kæ*-bin) *n* cabina *f*; capanna *f*
cabinet (*kæ*-bi-nöt) *n* gabinetto *m*
cable (*kei*-böl) *n* cavo *m*; telegramma *m*; *v* telegrafare
cadre (*kaa*-dö) *n* quadro *m*
café (*kæ*-fei) *n* bar *m*
cafeteria (kæ-fö-*ti*⁰-ri-ö) *n* tavola calda
caffeine (*kæ*-fiin) *n* caffeina *f*
cage (keidʒ) *n* gabbia *f*
cake (keik) *n* dolce *m*; torta *f*
calamity (kö-*læ*-mö-ti) *n* calamità *f*, disastro *m*
calcium (*kæl*-ssi-öm) *n* calcio *m*
calculate (*kæl*-kⁱu-leit) *v* calcolare
calculation (kæl-kⁱu-*lei*-ʃön) *n* calcolo *m*
calculator (*kæl*-kⁱu-*lei*-tö) *n* calcolatrice *f*
calendar (*kæ*-lön-dö) *n* calendario *m*
calf (kaaf) *n* (pl calves) vitello *m*; polpaccio *m*; **~ skin** pelle di vitello
call (kool) *v* chiamare; telefonare; *n* appello *m*; visita *f*; telefonata *f*; ***be called** chiamarsi; **~ names** ingiuriare; **~ on** andare a trovare; **~ up** *Am* telefonare
calm (kaam) *adj* tranquillo, calmo; **~ down** calmare

calorie (*kæ*-lö-ri) *n* caloria *f*
Calvinism (*kæl*-vi-ni-söm) *n* calvinismo *m*
came (keim) *v* (p come)
camel (*kæ*-möl) *n* cammello *m*
camera (*kæ*-mö-rö) *n* macchina fotografica; cinepresa *f*; **~ shop** negozio di articoli fotografici
camp (kæmp) *n* campo *m*; *v* accamparsi; **~ bed** lettino da campeggio, branda *f*
campaign (kæm-*pein*) *n* campagna *f*
camper (*kæm*-pö) *n* campeggiatore *m*
camping (*kæm*-ping) *n* campeggio *m*; **~ site** campeggio *m*
can (kæn) *n* lattina *f*; scatola *f*; **~ opener** apriscatole *m*
*can (kæn) *v* *potere
Canada (*kæ*-nö-dö) Canadà *m*
Canadian (kö-*nei*-di-ön) *adj* canadese
canal (kö-*næl*) *n* canale *m*
canary (kö-*nê*⁰-ri) *n* canarino *m*
cancel (*kæn*-ssöl) *v* annullare, *disdire
cancellation (kæn-ssö-*lei*-ʃön) *n* annullamento *m*
cancer (*kæn*-ssö) *n* cancro *m*
candidate (*kæn*-di-döt) *n* candidato *m*, -a *f*
candle (*kæn*-döl) *n* candela *f*
candy (*kæn*-di) *nAm* caramella *f*; dolciumi *mpl*; **~ store** *Am* pasticceria *f*

cane (kein) *n* canna *f*; bastone *m*

canister (*kæ*-ni-sstö) *n* barattolo *m*

canned food (kænd-fuud) *nAm* cibo in scatola

canoe (kö-*nuu*) *n* canoa *f*

canteen (kæn-*tiin*) *n* mensa *f*

canvas (*kæn*-vöss) *n* tela di canapa

cap (kæp) *n* berretto *m*

capable (*kei*-pö-böl) *adj* capace

capacity (kö-*pæ*-ssö-ti) *n* capacità *f*; potenza *f*; abilità *f*

cape (keip) *n* mantella *f*; capo *m*

capital (*kæ*-pi-töl) *n* capitale *f*; capitale *m*; *adj* importante, capitale; ~ **letter** maiuscola *f*

capitalism (*kæ*-pi-tö-li-söm) *n* capitalismo *m*

capitulation (kö-pi-t^{i}u-*lei*-∫ön) *n* capitolazione *f*

capsule (*kæp*-ss^{i}uul) *n* capsula *f*

captain (*kæp*-tin) *n* capitano *m*; comandante *m*

capture (*kæp*-t∫ö) *v* *far prigioniero, catturare; *prendere; *n* cattura *f*; presa *f*

car (kaa) *n* macchina *f*, auto(mobile) *f*; ~ **hire** autonoleggio *m*; ~ **park** parcheggio *m*; ~ **rental** *Am* autonoleggio *m*

caramel (*kæ*-rö-möl) *n* caramella mou

carat (*kæ*-röt) *n* carato *m*

caravan (*kæ*-rö-væn) *n* carovana *f*; carrozzone *m*; roulotte *f*

carburettor (kaa-b^{i}u-*rê*-tö) *n* carburatore *m*

card (kaad) *n* cartoncino *m*; cartolina *f*

cardboard (*kaad*-bood) *n* cartone *m*; *adj* di cartone

cardigan (*kaa*-di-ghön) *n* cardigan *m*

cardinal (*kaa*-di-nöl) *n* cardinale *m*; *adj* cardinale, principale

care (kê^ö) *n* cura *f*; preoccupazione *f*; ~ **about** preoccuparsi di; ~ **for** provvedere a; ***take** ~ **of** *aver cura

di, occuparsi di

career (kö-*ri^ö*) *n* carriera *f*

carefree (*kê^ö*-frii) *adj* spensierato

careful (*kê^ö*-föl) *adj* attento; scrupoloso, accurato

careless (*kê^ö*-löss) *adj* noncurante, trascurato

caretaker (*kê^ö*-tei-kö) *n* custode *m/f*

cargo (*kaa*-ghou) *n* (pl ~es) carico *m*

carnival (*kaa*-ni-völ) *n* carnevale *m*

carp (kaap) *n* (pl ~) carpa *f*

carpenter (*kaa*-pin-tö) *n* falegname *m/f*

carpet (*kaa*-pit) *n* tappeto *m*

carriage (*kæ*-rid3) *n* vagone *m*; carrozza *f*

carriageway (*kæ*-rid3-^{u}ei) *n* carreggiata *f*

carrot (*kæ*-röt) *n* carota *f*

carry (*kæ*-ri) *v* portare; *condurre; ~ **on** continuare; proseguire; ~ **out** eseguire

carrycot (*kæ*-ri-kot) *n* porte-enfant *m*

cart (kaat) *n* carro *m*

cartilage (*kaa*-ti-lid3) *n* cartilagine *f*

carton (*kaa*-tön) *n* scatolone *m*; stecca *f*

cartoon (kaa-*tuun*) *n* cartone animato

cartridge (*kaa*-trid3) *n* cartuccia *f*

carve (kaav) *v* tagliare; intagliare

carving (*kaa*-ving) *n* scultura in legno

case (keiss) *n* caso *m*; causa *f*; valigia *f*; astuccio *m*; **attaché** ~ portacarte *m*; **in** ~ qualora; **in** ~ **of** in caso di

cash (kæ∫) *n* contanti *mpl*; *v* convertire, *riscuotere, incassare; ~ **dispenser** sportello Bancomat® *f*

cashier (kæ-*fi^ö*) *n* cassiere *m*, -a *f*

cashmere (*kæf*-mi^ö) *n* cachemire *m*

casino (kö-*ssii*-nou) *n* (pl ~s) casinò *m*

cask (kaassk) *n* barile *m*, botte *f*

cassette (ka-*set*) *n* cassetta *f*

cast (kaasst) *n* lancio *m*

***cast** (kaasst) *v* lanciare, gettare; **cast**

iron ghisa *f*

castle (*kaa*-ssöl) *n* castello *m*

casual (*kæ*-ʒu-öl) *adj* informale; incidentale, fortuito

casualty (*kæ*-ʒu-öl-ti) *n* vittima *f*

cat (kæt) *n* gatto *m*

catacomb (*kæ*-tö-koum) *n* catacomba *f*

catalogue (*kæ*-tö-logh) *n* catalogo *m*

catarrh (kö-*taa*) *n* catarro *m*

catastrophe (kö-*tæ*-sströ-fi) *n* catastrofe *f*

*catch (kætʃ) *v* acchiappare; afferrare; *cogliere

category (*kæ*-ti-ghö-ri) *n* categoria *f*

cathedral (kö-*θi*-dröl) *n* duomo *m*, cattedrale *f*

catholic (*kæ*-θö-lik) *adj* cattolico

cattle (*kæ*-töl) *pl* bestiame *m*

caught (koot) *v* (p, pp catch)

cauliflower (*ko*-li-flauᵒ) *n* cavolfiore *m*

cause (koos) *v* causare; provocare; *n* causa *f*; ragione *f*, motivo *m*; ~ **to** *indurre a

causeway (*koos*-ᵘei) *n* via selciata

caution (*koo*-ʃön) *n* cautela *f*; *v* ammonire

cautious (*koo*-ʃöss) *adj* cauto

cave (keiv) *n* grotta *f*

cavern (*kæ*-vön) *n* caverna *f*

caviar (*kæ*-vi-aa) *n* caviale *m*

cavity (*kæ*-vö-ti) *n* cavità *f*

CD(-ROM) *f* cd (rom) *m*, CD(-ROM) *m*

cease (ssiiss) *v* *smettere

cease-fire (ssiiss faiᵒ) *n* cessate il fuoco

ceiling (*ssii*-ling) *n* soffitto *m*

celebrate (*ssê*-li-breit) *v* celebrare

celebration (ssê-li-*brei*-ʃön) *n* celebrazione *f*

celebrity (ssi-*lê*-brö-ti) *n* celebrità *f*

celery (*ssê*-lö-ri) *n* sedano *m*

cell (ssêl) *n* cella *f*

cellar (*ssê*-lö) *n* cantina *f*

cement (ssi-*mênt*) *n* cemento *m*

cemetery (*ssê*-mi-tri) *n* cimitero *m*

censorship (*ssên*-ssö-ʃip) *n* censura *f*

center (*ssên*-tö) *nAm* centro *m*

centigrade (*ssên*-ti-ghreid) *adj* centigrado

centimeter Am, **centimetre** (*ssên*-ti-mii-tö) *n* centimetro *m*

central (*ssên*-tröl) *adj* centrale; ~ **heating** riscaldamento centrale; ~ **station** stazione centrale

centralize (*ssên*-trö-lais) *v* centralizzare

centre (*ssên*-tö) *n* centro *m*

century (*ssên*-tʃö-ri) *n* secolo *m*

ceramics (ssi-*ræ*-mikss) *pl* ceramica *f*

ceremony (*ssê*-rö-mö-ni) *n* cerimonia *f*

certain (*ssöö*-tön) *adj* certo

certainly (*ssöö*-tön-li) *adv* certamente; ~ **not!** certo che no!

certificate (ssö-*ti*-fi-köt) *n* attestato *m*; certificato *m*, atto *m*, diploma *m*

chain (tʃein) *n* catena *f*

chair (tʃêᵒ) *n* sedia *f*; seggio *m*

chairman (*tʃêᵒ*-mön) *n* (pl -men) presidente *m*

chalet (*ʃæ*-lei) *n* chalet *m*

chalk (tʃook) *n* gesso *m*

challenge (*tʃæ*-löndʒ) *v* sfidare; *n* sfida *f*

chamber (*tʃeim*-bö) *n* camera *f*

champagne (ʃæm-*pein*) *n* champagne *m*

champion (*tʃæm*-pi̇ön) *n* campione *m*, -essa *f*; difensore *m*

chance (tʃaanss) *n* caso *m*; opportunità *f*, occasione *f*; rischio *m*; azzardo *m*; **by** ~ per caso

change (tʃeindʒ) *v* modificare, cambiare; cambiarsi; *n* cambiamento *m*, cambio *m*; spiccioli *mpl*

channel (*tʃæ*-nöl) *n* canale *m*;
  English Channel La Manica

chaos (*kei*-oss) *n* caos *m*

chaotic (kei-*o*-tik) *adj* caotico

chap (tʃæp) *n* tizio *m*

chapel (*tʃæ*-pöl) *n* cappella *f*

chaplain (*tʃæ*-plin) *n* cappellano *m*

character (*kæ*-rök-tö) *n* carattere *m*

characteristic (kæ-rök-tö-*ri*-sstik) *adj*
  tipico, caratteristico; *n* caratteristica
  f; tratto del carattere

characterize (*kæ*-rök-tö-rais) *v*
  caratterizzare

charcoal (*tʃaa*-koul) *n* carbone di
  legno

charge (tʃaadʒ) *v* *far pagare;
  incaricare; accusare; caricare; *n* costo
  m; carica *f*; accusa *f*; ~ **plate** *Am* carta
  di credito; **free of** ~ gratuito; **in** ~ **of**
  incaricato di; ***take** ~ **of** incaricarsi di

charity (*tʃæ*-rö-ti) *n* carità *f*

charm (tʃaam) *n* incanto *m*, fascino *m*;
  amuleto *m*

charming (*tʃaa*-ming) *adj*
  affascinante

chart (tʃaat) *n* tabella *f*; diagramma *m*;
  carta nautica; **conversion** ~ tabella
  di conversione

chase (tʃeiss) *v* inseguire; scacciare,
  cacciare; *n* caccia *f*

chasm (*kæ*-söm) *n* baratro *m*

chassis (*ʃæ*-ssi) *n* (pl ~) telaio *m*

chaste (tʃeisst) *adj* casto

chat (tʃæt) *v* chiacchierare, ciarlare; *n*
  ciancia *f*, ciarlata *f*, chiacchierata *f*

chatterbox (*tʃæ*-tö-bokss) *n*
  chiacchierone *m*

chauffeur (*ʃou*-fö) *n* autista *m/f*

cheap (tʃiip) *adj* a buon mercato,
  economico

cheat (tʃiit) *v* ingannare; imbrogliare

check (tʃêk) *v* verificare, *rivedere; *n*
  quadretto *m*; *Am* conto *m*; assegno
  m; **check!** scacco!; ~ **in** registrarsi;

fare il check-in; ~ **out** pagare il conto
  e andarsene

checkbook (*tʃêk*-buk) *nAm* libretto
  degli assegni

checkerboard (*tʃê*-kö-bood) *nAm*
  scacchiera *f*

checkers (*tʃê*-kös) *plAm* gioco della
  dama

checkroom (*tʃêk*-ruum) *nAm*
  guardaroba *m*

checkup (*tʃê*-kap) *n* visita medica,
  checkup *m*

cheek (tʃiik) *n* guancia *f*

cheekbone (*tʃiik*-boun) *n* zigomo *m*

cheeky (*tʃii*-ki) *adj* sfacciato

cheer (tʃi⁶) *v* acclamare; ~ **up**
  rallegrare

cheerful (*tʃi⁶*-föl) *adj* gaio, allegro

cheese (tʃiis) *n* formaggio *m*

chef (ʃêf) *n* capocuoco *m*, -a *f*

chemical (*kê*-mi-köl) *adj* chimico

chemist (*kê*-misst) *n* farmacista *m/f*;
  chemist's farmacia *f*

chemistry (*kê*-mi-sstri) *n* chimica *f*

cheque (tʃêk) *n* assegno *m*

chequebook (*tʃêk*-buk) *n* libretto
  degli assegni

chequered (*tʃê*-köd) *adj* a quadretti

cherry (*tʃê*-ri) *n* ciliegia *f*

chess (tʃêss) *n* scacchi *mpl*

chest (tʃêsst) *n* petto *m*, torace *m*;
  baule *m*; ~ **of drawers** cassettone *m*

chestnut (*tʃêss*-nat) *n* castagna *f*

chew (tʃuu) *v* masticare

chewing gum (*tʃuu*-ing-gham) *n*
  gomma da masticare

chicken (*tʃi*-kin) *n* pollo *m*

chickenpox (*tʃi*-kin-pokss) *n* varicella
  f

chief (tʃiif) *n* capo *m*; *adj* primo,
  principale

chieftain (*tʃiif*-tön) *n* capo *m*

child (tʃaild) *n* (pl children) bambino
  m

childbirth (*tʃaild*-bööθ) *n* parto *m*

childhood (*tʃaild*-hud) *n* infanzia *f*

Chile (*tʃi*-li) Cile *m*

Chilean (*tʃi*-li-ön) *adj* cileno

chill (tʃil) *n* brivido *m*

chilly (*tʃi*-li) *adj* freddino

chimney (*tʃim*-ni) *n* camino *m*

chin (tʃin) *n* mento *m*

China (*tʃai*-nö) Cina *f*

china (*tʃai*-nö) *n* porcellana *f*

Chinese (*tʃai-niis*) *adj* cinese

chip (tʃip) *n* scheggia *f*; gettone *m*; chip *m*; *v* tagliare, scheggiare; **chips** patatine fritte

chisel (*tʃi*-söl) *n* scalpello *m*

chives (tʃaivs) *pl* erba cipollina *f*

chlorine (*kloo*-riin) *n* cloro *m*

chock-full (tʃok-*ful*) *adj* gremito, pieno zeppo

chocolate (*tʃo*-klöt) *n* cioccolata *f*; cioccolatino *m*

choice (tʃoiss) *n* scelta *f*; selezione *f*

choir (kᵘaiᵒ) *n* coro *m*

choke (tʃouk) *v* soffocare; strozzare; *n* valvola dell'aria

*choose (tʃuus) *v* *scegliere

chop (tʃop) *n* cotoletta *f*, braciola *f*; *v* spaccare

Christ (kraisst) Cristo *m*

christen (*kri*-ssön) *v* battezzare

christening (*kri*-ssö-ning) *n* battesimo *m*

Christian (*kriss*-tʃön) *adj* cristiano; ~ **name** nome di battesimo

Christmas (*kriss*-möss) Natale

chromium (*krou*-mi-öm) *n* cromo *m*

chronic (*kro*-nik) *adj* cronico

chronological (kro-nö-*lo*-dʒi-köl) *adj* cronologico

chuckle (*tʃa*-köl) *v* ridacchiare

chunk (tʃangk) *n* grosso pezzo

church (tʃöötʃ) *n* chiesa *f*

churchyard (*tʃöötʃ*-ⁱaad) *n* camposanto *m*

cigar (ssi-*ghaa*) *n* sigaro *m*; ~ **shop** tabaccheria *f*

cigarette (ssi-ghö-*rêt*) *n* sigaretta *f*; ~ **case** portasigarette *m*; ~ **holder** bocchino *m*; ~ **lighter** accendino *m*; ~ **tobacco** trinciato *m*

cinema (*ssi*-nö-mö) *n* cinema *m*

cinnamon (*ssi*-nö-mön) *n* cannella *f*

circle (*ssöö*-köl) *n* cerchio *m*; circolo *m*; galleria *f*; *v* accerchiare, circondare

circulation (ssöö-kⁱu-*lei*-ʃön) *n* circolazione *f*; circolazione del sangue

circumstance (*ssöö*-köm-sstænss) *n* circostanza *f*

circus (*ssöö*-köss) *n* circo *m*

citizen (*ssi*-ti-sön) *n* cittadino *m*, -a *f*

citizenship (*ssi*-ti-sön-ʃip) *n* cittadinanza *f*

city (*ssi*-ti) *n* città *f*

civic (*ssi*-vik) *adj* civico

civil (*ssi*-völ) *adj* civile; cortese; ~ **law** diritto civile; ~ **servant** funzionario *m*

civilian (ssi-*vil*-ⁱön) *adj* civile; *n* borghese *m/f*

civilization (ssi-vö-lai-*sei*-ʃön) *n* civiltà *f*

civilized (*ssi*-vö-laisd) *adj* civilizzato

claim (kleim) *v* rivendicare, reclamare; asserire; *n* rivendicazione *f*, pretesa *f*

clamp (klæmp) *n* morsa *f*, morsetto *m*

clap (klæp) *v* battere le mani, applaudire

clarify (*klæ*-ri-fai) *v* chiarire, chiarificare

class (klaass) *n* classe *f*

classical (*klæ*-ssi-köl) *adj* classico

classify (*klæ*-ssi-fai) *v* classificare

classmate (*klaass*-meit) *n* compagno,-a di scuola

classroom (*klaass*-ruum) *n* aula *f*

clause (kloos) n clausola f

claw (kloo) n artiglio m

clay (klei) n argilla f

clean (kliin) adj puro, pulito; v pulire

cleaning (klii-ning) n pulizia f, pulitura f; ~ fluid smacchiatore m

clear (kli⁰) adj chiaro; v sgombrare

clearing (kli⁰-ring) n radura f

cleft (klêft) n crepa f

clergyman (klöö-dʒi-mön) n (pl -men) pastore m; chierico m

clerk (klaak) n impiegato m, -a f; segretario m, -a f; commesso m, -a f

clever (klê-vö) adj intelligente; perspicace, sveglio .

click (klik) n clic m; v scattare

client (klai-önt) n cliente m/f

cliff (klif) n scoglio m, scogliera f

climate (klai-mit) n clima m

climb (klaim) v arrampicarsi; arrampicare

cling (kling) v essere attillato

clinic (kli-nik) n clinica f

cloak (klouk) n mantello m

cloakroom (klouk-ruum) n guardaroba m

clock (klok) n orologio m; at ... o'clock alle ...

cloister (kloi-sstö) n monastero m

close¹ (klous) v *chiudere

close² (klouss) adj vicino

closet (klo-sit) n armadio a muro

cloth (kloθ) n stoffa f; panno m

clothes (klouðs) pl abiti, vestiti mpl

clothing (klou-ðing) n vestiti mpl

cloud (klaud) n nuvola f

cloudy (klau-di) adj nuvoloso

clover (klou-vö) n trifoglio m

clown (klaun) n pagliaccio m

club (klab) n circolo m; associazione f; clava f, mazza f

clumsy (klam-si) adj goffo

clutch (klatʃ) n frizione f; stretta f

coach (koutʃ) n autobus m; vagone m, carrozza f; allenatore m, -trice f

coal (koul) n carbone m

coarse (kooss) adj grossolano; volgare

coast (kousst) n costa f

coat (kout) n cappotto m, soprabito m; ~ hanger gruccia f

coatstand (kout-sstænd) n attaccapanni m

cocaine (kou-kein) n cocaina f

coc (kok) n gallo m

cocktail (kok-teil) n cocktail m

coconut (kou-kö-nat) n noce di cocco

cod (kod) n (pl ~) merluzzo m

code (koud) n codice m

coffee (ko-fi) n caffè m

cognac (ko-niæk) n cognac m

coherence (kou-hiᵒ-rönss) n coerenza f

coin (koin) n moneta f

coincide (kou-in-ssaid) v *coincidere

cold (kould) adj freddo; n freddo m; raffreddore m; catch a ~ *prendere un raffreddore

collaborate (kö-læ-bö-reit) v collaborare

collapse (kö-læpss) v crollare

collar (ko-lö) n collare m; colletto m; ~ stud bottoncino per colletto

collarbone (ko-lö-boun) n clavicola f

colleague (ko-liigh) n collega m

collect (kö-lêkt) v *raccogliere; rilevare, *andare a prendere; *fare una colletta

collection (kö-lêk-ʃön) n collezione f; levata f

collective (kö-lêk-tiv) adj collettivo

collector (kö-lêk-tö) n collezionista m/f; collettore m

college (ko-lidʒ) n college m; Am università f

collide (kö-laid) v cozzare

collision (kö-li-ʒön) n scontro m, collisione f

Colombia (kö-lom-bi-ö) Colombia f

Colombian (kö-*lom*-bi-ön) *adj*
colombiano

colonel (*köö*-nöl) *n* colonnello *m*

colony (*ko*-lö-ni) *n* colonia *f*

colo(u)r (*ka*-lö) *n* colore *m*; *v* colorare;
~ **film** pellicola a colori

colo(u)r-blind (*ka*-lö-blaind) *adj*
daltonico

colo(u)red (*ka*-löd) *adj* di colore

colo(u)rful (*ka*-lö-föl) *adj* pieno di
colore, colorito

column (*ko*-löm) *n* colonna *f*; rubrica *f*

coma (*kou*-mö) *n* coma *m*

comb (koum) *v* pettinare; *n* pettine *m*

combat (*kom*-bæt) *n* lotta *f*,
combattimento *m*; *v* combattere

combination (kom-bi-*nei*-ʃön) *n*
combinazione *f*

combine (köm-*bain*) *v* combinare;
unire

*****come** (kam) *v* *venire; ~ **across**
incontrare; trovare

comedian (kö-*mii*-di-ön) *n*
commediante *m/f*; comico *m*, -a *f*

comedy (*ko*-mö-di) *n* commedia *f*;
musical ~ commedia musicale

comfort (*kam*-föt) *n* agio *m*, comodità
f, conforto *m*, consolazione *f*; *v*
consolare

comfortable (*kam*-fö-tö-böl) *adj*
confortevole, comodo

comic (*ko*-mik) *adj* comico

comics (*ko*-mikss) *pl* racconto a
fumetti

coming (*ka*-ming) *n* venuta *f*

comma (*ko*-mö) *n* virgola *f*

command (kö-*maand*) *v* comandare;
n ordine *m*

commander (kö-*maan*-dö) *n*
comandante *m*

commemoration (kö-mê-mö-*rei*-ʃön)
n commemorazione *f*

commence (kö-*mênss*) *v* iniziare

comment (*ko*-mênt) *n* commento *m*; *v*
commentare

commerce (*ko*-mööss) *n* commercio
m

commercial (kö-*möö*-ʃöl) *adj*
commerciale; *n* annuncio
pubblicitario; ~ **law** diritto
commerciale

commission (kö-*mi*-ʃön) *n* comitato
m

commit (kö-*mit*) *v* affidare,
consegnare; *commettere, compiere

committee (kö-*mi*-ti) *n* commissione
f, comitato *m*

common (*ko*-mön) *adj* comune;
abituale

commune (*ko*-m'uun) *n* comune *f*

communicate (kö-*m'uu*-ni-keit) *v*
comunicare

communication (kö-m'uu-ni-*kei*-ʃön)
n comunicazione *f*

communism (*ko*-m'u-ni-söm) *n*
comunismo *m*

communist (*ko*-m'u-nisst) *n*
comunista *m*

community (kö-*m'uu*-nö-ti) *n* società
f, comunità *f*

commuter (kö-*m'uu*-tö) *n* pendolare
m/f

compact (*kom*-pækt) *adj* compatto

compact disc (*kom*-pækt dissk) *n*
compact disc *m*; ~ **player** lettore CD
m

companion (köm-*pæ*-n'ön) *n*
compagno *m*, -a *f*

company (*kam*-pö-ni) *n* compagnia *f*;
ditta *f*, società *f*

comparative (köm-*pæ*-rö-tiv) *adj*
relativo

compare (köm-*pêᵒ*) *v* paragonare

comparison (köm-*pæ*-ri-ssön) *n*
paragone *m*

compartment (köm-*paat*-mönt) *n*
scompartimento *m*

compass (*kam*-pöss) *n* bussola *f*

compel (köm-*pêl*) v *costringere
compensate (*kom*-pön-sseit) v compensare
compensation (kom-pön-*ssei*-ʃön) n compensazione f; indennità f
compete (köm-*piit*) v competere
competition (kom-pö-*ti*-ʃön) n gara f; concorrenza f
competitor (köm-*pê*-ti-tör) n concorrente m
compile (köm-*pail*) v compilare
complain (köm-*plein*) v lagnarsi
complaint (köm-*pleint*) n lagnanza f; **complaints book** libro dei reclami
complete (köm-*pliit*) adj completo; v completare
completely (köm-*pliit*-li) adv interamente, totalmente, completamente
complex (*kom*-plêkss) n complesso m; adj intricato, complesso
complexion (köm-*plêk*-ʃön) n carnagione f
complicated (*kom*-pli-kei-tid) adj complicato
compliment (*kom*-pli-mönt) n complimento m; v complimentarsi con, felicitarsi con
compose (köm-*pous*) v *comporre
composer (köm-*pou*-sö) n compositore m, -trice f
composition (kom-pö-*si*-ʃön) n composizione f
comprehensive (kom-pri-*hên*-ssiv) adj comprensivo
comprise (köm-*prais*) v *comprendere, *contenere
compromise (*kom*-prö-mais) n compromesso m
compulsory (köm-*pal*-ssö-ri) adj obbligatorio
computer (kom-*p'uu*-tö) n computer m
conceal (kön-*ssiil*) v *nascondere

conceited (kön-*ssii*-tid) adj presuntuoso
conceive (kön-*ssiiv*) v concepire, *comprendere
concentrate (*kon*-ssön-treit) v concentrare
concentration (kon-ssön-*trei*-ʃön) n concentrazione f
conception (kön-*ssêp*-ʃön) n concezione f; concepimento m
concern (kön-*ssöön*) v riguardare, concernere; n ansietà f; faccenda f; azienda f, impresa f
concerned (kön-*ssööni*) adj preoccupato; interessato
concerning (kön-*ssöö*-ning) prep riguardo a, riguardante
concert (*kon*-ssöt) n concerto m; ~ **hall** sala concerti
concession (kön-*ssê*-ʃön) n concessione f
concierge (koñg-ssi-*êʲ*ʒ) n portinaio m
concise (kön-*ssaiss*) adj conciso, breve
conclusion (köng-*kluu*-ʒön) n conclusione f
concrete (*kong*-kriit) adj concreto; n calcestruzzo m
concussion (köng-*ka*-ʃön) n commozione cerebrale
condition (kön-*di*-ʃön) n condizione f; stato m, forma f; circostanza f
conditional (kön-*di*-ʃö-nöl) adj condizionale
conditioner (kön-*di*-ʃö-nö) n balsamo m
condom (*kön*-döm) n preservativo n
conduct[1] (*kon*-dakt) n condotta f
conduct[2] (kön-*dakt*) v *condurre; guidare; *dirigere
conductor (kön-*dak*-tö) n conduttore m, -trice f; direttore d'orchestra
confectioner (kön-*fêk*-ʃö-nö) n

pasticciere *m*, -a *f*

conference (*kon*-fö-rönss) *n*
conferenza *f*

confess (kön-*fêss*) *v* *riconoscere;
confessare; professare

confession (kön-*fê*-ʃön) *n*
confessione *f*

confidence (*kon*-fi-dönss) *n* fiducia *f*

confident (*kon*-fi-dönt) *adj*
confidente

confidential (kon-fi-*dên*-ʃöl) *adj*
confidenziale

confirm (kön-*fööm*) *v* confermare

confirmation (kon-fö-*mei*-ʃön) *n*
conferma *f*

confiscate (*kon*-fi-sskeit) *v*
sequestrare, confiscare

conflict (*kon*-flikt) *n* conflitto *m*

confuse (kön-*f'uus*) *v* *confondere;
confused *adj* confuso

confusion (kön-*f'uu*-ʒön) *n*
confusione *f*

congratulate (köng-*ghræ*-tʃu-leit) *v*
congratularsi con, felicitarsi con

congratulation (köng-ghræ-tʃu-*lei*-ʃön) *n* congratulazione *f*,
felicitazione *f*

congregation (kong-ghri-*ghei*-ʃön) *n*
comunione *f*, congregazione *f*

congress (*kong*-ghrêss) *n* congresso *m*

connect (kö-*nêkt*) *v* *connettere;
collegare

connection (kö-*nêk*-ʃön) *n* relazione *f*; connessione *f*; coincidenza *f*

connoisseur (ko-nö-*ssöö*) *n*
intenditore *m*

connotation (ko-nö-*tei*-ʃön) *n*
significato secondario

conquer (*kong*-kö) *v* conquistare;
*vincere

conqueror (*kong*-kö-rö) *n*
conquistatore *m*

conquest (*kong*-k^uêsst) *n* conquista *f*

conscience (*kon*-ʃönss) *n* coscienza *f*

conscious (*kon*-ʃöss) *adj* conscio

consciousness (*kon*-ʃöss-nöss) *n*
coscienza *f*

consent (kön-*ssênt*) *v* acconsentire; *n*
consenso *m*

consequence (*kon*-ssi-k^uönss) *n*
conseguenza *f*

consequently (*kon*-ssi-k^uönt-li) *adv*
conseguentemente

conservative (kön-*ssöö*-vö-tiv) *adj*
conservatore

consider (kön-*ssi*-dö) *v* considerare;
reputare, *ritenere

considerable (kön-*ssi*-dö-rö-böl) *adj*
considerevole; notevole

considerate (kön-*ssi*-dö-röt) *adj*
riguardoso

consideration (kön-ssi-dö-*rei*-ʃön) *n*
considerazione *f*; riguardo *m*,
attenzione *f*

considering (kön-*ssi*-dö-ring) *prep*
considerato

consignment (kön-*ssain*-mönt) *n*
consegna *f*

consist of (kön-*ssisst*) consistere in

conspire (kön-*sspai°*) *v* cospirare

constant (*kon*-sstönt) *adj* costante

constipation (kon-ssti-*pei*-ʃön) *n*
stitichezza *f*

constituency (kön-*ssti*-tʃu-ön-ssi) *n*
circoscrizione elettorale

constitution (kon-ssti-*t'uu*-ʃön) *n*
costituzione *f*

construct (kön-*sstrakt*) *v* costruire;
edificare, fabbricare

construction (kön-*sstrak*-ʃön) *n*
costruzione *f*; fabbricazione *f*,
edificio *m*

consul (*kon*-ssöl) *n* console *m*

consulate (*kon*-ssⁱu-löt) *n* consolato *m*

consult (kön-*ssalt*) *v* consultare

consultation (kon-ssöl-*tei*-ʃön) *n*

consultazione f; consulta f; ~ **hours** n orario di ricevimento

consume (kön-ss⎮uum) v consumare

consumer (kön-ss⎮uu-mö) n consumatore m, -trice f

contact (kon-tækt) n contatto m; accensione f; v contattare; ~ **lenses** lenti a contatto

contagious (kön-tei-dӡöss) adj contagioso

contain (kön-tein) v *contenere; *comprendere

container (kön-tei-nö) n recipiente m; container m

contemporary (kön-têm-pö-rö-ri) adj contemporaneo; n contemporaneo m

contempt (kön-têmpt) n disprezzo m, disdegno m

content (kön-tênt) adj contento

contents (kon-têntss) pl contenuto m

contest (kon-têsst) n lotta f; competizione f

continent (kon-ti-nönt) n continente m

continental (kon-ti-nên-töl) adj continentale

continual (kön-ti-n⎮u-öl) adj continuo

continue (kön-ti-n⎮uu) v continuare; proseguire

continuous (kön-ti-n⎮u-öss) adj continuo, ininterrotto

contour (kon-tuó) n contorno m

contraceptive (kon-trö-ssêp-tiv) n anticoncezionale m

contract[1] (kon-trækt) n contratto m

contract[2] (kön-trækt) v *contrarre

contractor (kön-træk-tö) n imprenditore m, -trice f

contradict (kon-trö-dikt) v *contraddire

contradictory (kon-trö-dik-tö-ri) adj contraddittorio

contrary (kon-trö-ri) n contrario m; adj contrario; **on the** ~ al contrario

contrast (kon-traasst) n contrasto m

contribution (kon-tri-b⎮uu-ʃön) n contribuzione f

control (kön-troul) n controllo m; v controllare

controversial (kon-trö-vöö-ʃöl) adj controverso

convenience (kön-vii-n⎮önss) n comodità f

convenient (kön-vii-n⎮önt) adj comodo; conveniente

convent (kon-vönt) n convento m

conversation (kon-vö-ssei-ʃön) n discorso m, conversazione f

convert (kön-vööt) v convertire

convict[1] (kön-vikt) v dichiarare colpevole

convict[2] (kon-vikt) n condannato m

conviction (kön-vik-ʃön) n convinzione f; condanna f

convince (kön-vinss) v *convincere

convulsion (kön-val-ʃön) n convulsione f

cook (kuk) n cuoco m; v cucinare; preparare

cookbook (kuk-buk) nAm libro di cucina

cooker (ku-kö) n fornello m; **gas** ~ cucina a gas

cookery book (ku-kö-ri-buk) n libro di cucina

cookie (ku-ki) nAm biscotto m

cool (kuul) adj fresco

cooperation (kou-o-pö-rei-ʃön) n cooperazione f

co-operative (kou-o-pö-rö-tiv) adj cooperativo; cooperatore; n cooperativa f

coordinate (kou-oo-di-neit) v coordinare

coordination (kou-oo-di-nei-ʃön) n coordinazione f

cope (koup) v farcela

copper (ko-pö) n rame m

copy (*ko*-pi) *n* copia *f*; *v* copiare; imitare; **carbon ~** copia *f*

coral (*ko*-röl) *n* corallo *m*

cord (kood) *n* corda *f*, spago *m*

cordial (*koo*-di-öl) *adj* cordiale

corduroy (*koo*-dö-roi) *n* velluto a coste

core (koo) *n* nucleo *m*; torsolo *m*

cork (kook) *n* sughero *m*; tappo *m*

corkscrew (*kook*-sskruu) *n* cavatappi *m*

corn (koon) *n* granello *m*; frumento *m*, grano *m*; callo *m*; granoturco *m*; **~ on the cob** pannocchia di granoturco

corner (*koo*-nö) *n* angolo *m*

cornfield (*koon*-fiild) *n* campo di grano

corpse (koopss) *n* cadavere *m*

corpulent (*koo*-p'u-lönt) *adj* corpulento; grasso, obeso

correct (kö-*rêkt*) *adj* esatto, corretto; *v* *corﾞeggere

correction (kö-*rêk*-ʃön) *n* correzione *f*; rettifica *f*

correctness (kö-*rêkt*-nöss) *n* correttezza *f*

correspond (ko-ri-*sspond*) *v* *corrispondere

correspondence (ko-ri-*sspon*-dönss) *n* corrispondenza *f*

correspondent (ko-ri-*sspon*-dönt) *n* corrispondente *m/f*

corridor (*ko*-ri-doo) *n* corridoio *m*

corrupt (kö-*rapt*) *adj* corrotto; *v* *corrompere

corruption (kö-*rap*-ʃön) *n* corruzione *f*

corset (*koo*-ssit) *n* busto *m*

cosmetics (kos-*mê*-tikss) *pl* cosmetici *mpl*

cost (kosst) *n* costo *m*; prezzo *m*

***cost** (kosst) *v* costare

cosy (*kou*-si) *adj* intimo, confortevole

cot (kot) *nAm* lettino da campeggio

cottage (*ko*-tidӡ) *n* villino *m*

cotton (*ko*-tön) *n* cotone *m*; *adj* di cotone; **~ wool** ovatta *f*

couch (kautʃ) *n* divano *m*

cough (kof) *n* tosse *f*; *v* tossire

could (kud) *v* (p can)

council (*kaun*-ssöl) *n* consiglio *m*

councillor (*kaun*-ssö-lö) *n* consigliere *m*, -a *f*

counsel (*kaun*-ssöl) *n* consiglio *m*

counsellor (*kaun*-ssö-lö) *n* consigliere *m*

count (kaunt) *v* contare; addizionare; *includere; considerare; *n* conte *m*

counter (*kaun*-tö) *n* banco *m*

counterfeit (*kaun*-tö-fiit) *v* falsificare

counterfoil (*kaun*-tö-foil) *n* talloncino *m*

countess (*kaun*-tiss) *n* contessa *f*

country (*kan*-tri) *n* paese *m*; campagna *f*; regione *f*; **~ house** casa di campagna

countryman (*kan*-tri-mön) *n* (pl -men) compatriota *m*

countryside (*kan*-tri-ssaid) *n* campagna *f*

county (*kaun*-ti) *n* contea *f*

couple (*ka*-pöl) *n* coppia *f*

coupon (*kuu*-pon) *n* cedola *f*, tagliando *m*

courage (*ka*-ridӡ) *n* audacia *f*, coraggio *m*

courageous (kö-*rei*-dӡöss) *adj* valoroso, coraggioso

course (kooss) *n* rotta *f*; portata *f*; corso *m*; **intensive ~** corso intensivo; **of ~** naturalmente

court (koot) *n* tribunale *m*; corte *f*

courteous (*köö*-ti-öss) *adj* cortese

cousin (*ka*-sön) *n* cugina *f*, cugino *m*

cover (*ka*-vö) *v* *coprire; *n* rifugio *m*; coperchio *m*; copertina *f*; **~ charge** prezzo del coperto

cow (kau) *n* vacca *f*, mucca *f*

coward (*kau*-öd) *n* codardo *m*

cowardly (*kau*-öd-li) *adj* vile

crab (kræb) *n* granchio *m*

crack (kræk) *n* schiocco *m*; fessura *f*; *v* schioccare; spaccare, incrinarsi

cracker (*kræ*-kö) *nAm* cracker *m*

cradle (*krei*-döl) *n* culla *f*

cramp (kræmp) *n* crampo *m*

crane (krein) *n* gru *f*

crash (kræʃ) *n* scontro *m*; *v* scontrarsi; precipitare; **~ barrier** guardrail *m*

crate (kreit) *n* cassetta *f*

crater (*krei*-tö) *n* cratere *m*

crawl (krool) *v* *andare carponi; *n* crawl *m*

craze (kreis) *n* mania *f*

crazy (*krei*-si) *adj* pazzo; sciocco, folle

creak (kriik) *v* cigolare

cream (kriim) *n* crema *f*; panna *f*; *adj* color crema

creamy (*krii*-mi) *adj* cremoso

crease (kriiss) *v* increspare; *n* piega *f*; grinza *f*

create (kri-*eit*) *v* creare

creative (kri-*ei*-tiv) *adj* creativo

creature (*krii*-tʃö) *n* creatura *f*; essere *m*

credible (*krê*-di-böl) *adj* credibile

credit (*krê*-dit) *n* credito *m*; *v* accreditare; **~ card** carta di credito

creditor (*krê*-di-tö) *n* creditore *m*

credulous (*krê*-d¹u-löss) *adj* credulone

creek (kriik) *n* insenatura *f*

***creep** (kriip) *v* strisciare

creepy (*krii*-pi) *adj* raccapricciante

cremate (kri-*meit*) *v* cremare

cremation (kri-*mei*-ʃön) *n* cremazione *f*

crew (kruu) *n* equipaggio *m*

cricket (*kri*-kit) *n* cricket *m*; grillo *m*

crime (kraim) *n* crimine *m*

criminal (*kri*-mi-nöl) *n* delinquente *m/f*, criminale *m/f*; *adj* criminale; **~**

law diritto penale

criminality (kri-mi-*næ*-lö-ti) *n* criminalità *f*

crimson (*krim*-sön) *adj* cremisi

crippled (*kri*-pöld) *adj* storpio

crisis (*krai*-ssiss) *n* (pl crises) crisi *f*

crisp (krissp) *adj* croccante

critic (*kri*-tik) *n* critico *m*, -a *f*

critical (*kri*-ti-köl) *adj* critico; precario

criticism (*kri*-ti-ssi-söm) *n* critica *f*

criticize (*kri*-ti-ssais) *v* criticare

crochet (*krou*-ʃei) *v* lavorare all'uncinetto

crockery (*kro*-kö-ri) *n* vasellame *m*

crocodile (*kro*-kö-dail) *n* coccodrillo *m*

crooked (*kru*-kid) *adj* tortuoso, storto; disonesto

crop (krop) *n* raccolta *f*

cross (kross) *v* attraversare; *adj* arrabbiato, imbronciato; *n* croce *f*

cross-eyed (*kross*-aid) *adj* strabico

crossing (*kro*-ssing) *n* traversata *f*; crocevia *m*; passaggio pedonale; passaggio a livello

crossroads (*kross*-rouds) *n* incrocio *m*

crosswalk (*kross*-ᵁook) *nAm* passaggio pedonale

crow (krou) *n* cornacchia *f*

crowbar (*krou*-baa) *n* piede di porco

crowd (kraud) *n* massa *f*, folla *f*

crowded (*krau*-did) *adj* affollato

crown (kraun) *n* corona *f*; *v* incoronare; coronare

crucifix (*kruu*-ssi-fikss) *n* crocifisso *m*

crucifixion (kruu-ssi-*fik*-ʃön) *n* crocifissione *f*

crucify (*kruu*-ssi-fai) *v* *crocifiggere

cruel (kru⁰l) *adj* crudele

cruise (kruus) *n* crociera *f*

crumb (kram) *n* briciola *f*

crusade (kruu-*sseid*) *n* crociata *f*

crust (krasst) *n* crosta *f*

crutch (kratʃ) *n* stampella *f*

cry (krai) *v* *piangere; gridare; *n* urlo *m*, grido *m*

crystal (*kri*-sstöl) *n* cristallo *m*; *adj* cristallino

Cuba (kⁱuu-bö) Cuba *f*

Cuban (kⁱuu-bön) *adj* cubano

cube (kⁱuub) *n* cubo *m*

cuckoo (ku-kuu) *n* cuculo *m*

cucumber (kⁱuu-köm-bö) *n* cetriolo *m*

cuddle (ka-döl) *v* coccolare

cuff (kaf) *n* polsino *m*

cuff links (kaf-lingkss) *pl* gemelli *mpl*

cul-de-sac (kal-dö-ssæk) *n* vicolo cieco

cultivate (kal-ti-veit) *v* coltivare

culture (kal-tʃö) *n* cultura *f*; coltura *f*

cultured (kal-tʃöd) *adj* colto

cunning (ka-ning) *adj* furbo

cup (kap) *n* tazza *f*; coppa *f*

cupboard (ka-böd) *n* armadio *m*

curb (kööb) *n* bordo del marciapiede; *v* frenare

cure (kⁱu^ö) *v* curare; *n* cura *f*; guarigione *f*

curiosity (kⁱu^ö-ri-*o*-ssö-ti) *n* curiosità *f*

curious (kⁱu^ö-ri-öss) *adj* curioso; strano

curl (kööl) *v* ondulare; arricciare; *n* ricciolo *m*

curler (köö-lö) *n* bigodino *m*

curly (köö-li) *adj* ricciuto

currant (ka-rönt) *n* uva passa; ribes *m*

currency (ka-rön-ssi) *n* valuta *f*;

foreign ~ divisa estera

current (ka-rönt) *n* corrente *f*; *adj* corrente; **alternating** ~ corrente alternata; **direct** ~ corrente continua

curry (ka-ri) *n* curry *m*

curse (kööss) *v* bestemmiare; *maledire; *n* bestemmia *f*

curtain (köö-tön) *n* tenda *f*; sipario *m*

curve (kööv) *n* curva *f*; svolta *f*

curved (köövd) *adj* curvo

cushion (ku-ʃön) *n* cuscino *m*

custody (ka-sstö-di) *n* custodia tutelare; custodia *f*, tutela *f*

custom (ka-sstöm) *n* costume *m*; abitudine *f*

customary (ka-sstö-mö-ri) *adj* usuale, solito, abituale

customer (ka-sstö-mö) *n* cliente *m*/*f*; avventore *m*

Customs (ka-sstöms) *pl* dogana *f*; ~ **duty** dazio *m*; ~ **officer** doganiere *m*

cut (kat) *n* incisione *f*; taglio *m*

***cut** (kat) *v* tagliare; *ridurre; ~ **off** tagliare; troncare

cutlery (kat-lö-ri) *n* posate *fpl*

cutlet (kat-löt) *n* costoletta *f*

cycle (ssai-köl) *n* ciclo *m*; bicicletta *f*

cyclist (ssai-klisst) *n* ciclista *m*/*f*

cylinder (ssi-lin-dö) *n* cilindro *m*

cystitis (ssi-*sstai*-tiss) *n* cistite *f*

Czech (tʃêk) *adj* ceco

Czech Republic (tʃêk ri-*pa*-blik) Repubblica Ceca *f*

D

dad (dæd) *n* papà *m*

daddy (dæ-di) *n* papà *m*

daffodil (dæ-fö-dil) *n* narciso *m*

daily (dei-li) *adj* giornaliero,

quotidiano; *n* quotidiano *m*

dairy (dê^ö-ri) *n* latteria *f*

dam (dæm) *n* argine *m*; diga *f*

damage (dæ-midʒ) *n* danno *m*; *v*

danneggiare

damn (dæm) accidenti; adj maledetto; adv incredibilmente; v maledire

damp (dæmp) adj umido; bagnato; n umidità f; v inumidire

dance (daanss) v ballare; n ballo m

dandelion (dæn-di-lai-ön) n soffione m

dandruff (dæn-dröf) n forfora f

danger (dein-dʒö) n pericolo m

dangerous (dein-dʒö-röss) adj pericoloso

Danish (dei-niʃ) adj danese

dare (dê°) v osare; sfidare

daring (dê°-ring) adj temerario

dark (daak) adj buio, oscuro; n oscurità f, buio m

darling (daa-ling) n amore m, caro m

darn (daan) v rammendare

dash (dæʃ) v precipitarsi; n lineetta f

dashboard (dæʃ-bood) n cruscotto m

data (dei-tö) pl dati mpl

date¹ (deit) n data f; appuntamento m; v datare; **out of ~** fuori moda

date² (deit) n dattero m

daughter (doo-tö) n figlia f

daughter-in-law (doo-tö in loo) n (pl daughters-in-law) nuora f

dawn (doon) n alba f, aurora f

day (dei) n giorno m; **by ~** di giorno; **~ trip** giro m; **per ~** al giorno; **the ~ before yesterday** avant'ieri

daybreak (dei-breik) n aurora f

daylight (dei-lait) n luce del giorno

dead (dêd) adj morto; deceduto

deaf (dêf) adj sordo

deal (diil) n accordo m, affare m

***deal** (diil) v distribuire; **~ with** v trattare con; *fare affari con

dealer (dii-lö) n negoziante m/f, commerciante m/f

dear (di°) adj caro; diletto

death (dêθ) n morte f; **~ penalty** pena di morte

debate (di-beit) n dibattito m

debit (dê-bit) n debito m

debt (dêt) n debito m

decaffeinated (dii-kæ-fi-nei-tid) adj decaffeinato

deceit (di-ssiit) n inganno m

deceive (di-ssiiv) v ingannare

December (di-ssêm-bö) dicembre

decency (dii-ssön-ssi) n decenza f

decent (dii-ssönt) adj decente

decide (di-ssaid) v *decidere

decision (di-ssi-ʒön) n decisione f

deck (dêk) n coperta f; **~ cabin** cabina di coperta;

deckchair (dêk tʃê°) n sedia a sdraio

declaration (dê-klö-rei-ʃön) n dichiarazione f

declare (di-klê°) v dichiarare; indicare

decorate (dê-kö-reit) v imbiancare; tappezzare; decorare

decoration (dê-kö-rei-ʃön) n decorazione f

decrease (dii-kriiss) v diminuire; *decrescere; n diminuzione f

dedicate (dê-di-keit) v dedicare

deduce (di-dᵘuss) v *dedurre

deduct (di-dakt) v *sottrarre

deed (diid) n azione f, atto m

deep (diip) adj profondo

deep-freeze (diip-friis) n congelatore m

deer (di°) n (pl ~) cervo m

defeat (di-fiit) v *sconfiggere; n sconfitta f

defective (di-fêk-tiv) adj difettoso

defence (di-fênss) n difesa f

defend (di-fênd) v *difendere

defense (di-fênss) nAm difesa f

deficiency (di-fi-ʃön-ssi) n deficienza f

deficit (dê-fi-ssit) n deficit m

define (di-fain) v definire, determinare

definite (dê-fi-nit) adj determinato;

esplícito

definition (dê-fi-*ni*-ʃön) n definizione f

deformed (di-*foomd*) adj deformato, deforme

degree (di-*ghrii*) n grado m; titolo m

delay (di-*lei*) v ritardare; n indugio m, ritardo m; rinvio m

delegate (*dê*-li-ghöt) n delegato m

delegation (dê-li-*ghei*-ʃön) n delegazione f

deliberate[1] (di-*li*-bö-reit) v ponderare

deliberate[2] (di-*li*-bö-röt) adj premeditato

deliberation (di-li-bö-*rei*-ʃön) n riflessione f

delicacy (*dê*-li-kö-ssi) n ghiottoneria f

delicate (*dê*-li-köt) adj delicato

delicatessen (dê-li-kö-*tê*-ssön) n leccornia f; negozio di specialità gastronomiche

delicious (di-*li*-ʃöss) adj squisito, delizioso

delight (di-*lait*) n diletto m, delizia f; v deliziare; **delighted** felicissimo, lieto

delightful (di-*lait*-föl) adj dilettevole, piacevolissimo

deliver (di-*li*-vö) v recapitare, consegnare; liberare

delivery (di-*li*-vö-ri) n consegna f; parto m; liberazione f; ~ **van** furgone m

demand (di-*maand*) v *richiedere, *esigere; n esigenza f; domanda f

democracy (di-*mo*-krö-ssi) n democrazia f

democratic (dê-mö-*kræ*-tik) adj democratico

demolish (di-*mo*-liʃ) v demolire

demolition (dê-mö-*li*-ʃön) n demolizione f

demonstrate (*dê*-mön-sstreit) v dimostrare; *fare una dimostrazione

demonstration (dê-mön-*sstrei*-ʃön) n dimostrazione f

den (dên) n tana f

Denmark (*dên*-maak) Danimarca f

denomination (di-no-mi-*nei*-ʃön) n denominazione f

dense (dênss) adj denso

dent (dênt) n ammaccatura f

dentist (*dên*-tisst) n dentista m

denture (*dên*-tʃö) n dentiera f

deny (di-*nai*) v negare; rifiutare

deodorant (dii-*ou*-dö-rönt) n deodorante m

depart (di-*paat*) v *andarsene, partire; trapassare

department (di-*paat*-mönt) n sezione f, reparto m; ~ **store** grande magazzino

departure (di-*paa*-tʃö) n partenza f

dependant (di-*pên*-dönt) adj dipendente

depend (di-*pênd*) *dipendere; **that depends** dipende; **it depends on the weather** dipende dal tempo; **I am depending on you** conto su di te

deposit (di-*po*-sit) n versamento m; deposito m; sedimento m, giacimento m; v depositare

depository (di-*po*-si-tö-ri) n magazzino m

depot (*dê*-pou) n deposito m; Am stazione f

depress (di-*prêss*) v *deprimere

depression (di-*prê*-ʃön) n depressione f

deprive of (di-*praiv*) privare di

depth (dêpθ) n profondità f

deputy (*dê*-pʼu-ti) n sostituto m, -a f

descend (di-*ssênd*) v *scendere

descendant (di-*ssên*-dönt) n discendente m/f

descent (di-*ssênt*) n discesa f

describe (di-*sskraib*) v *descrivere

description (di-*sskrip*-ʃön) n descrizione f

desert[1] (*dê*-söt) *n* deserto *m; adj* deserto

desert[2] (di-*sööt*) *v* disertare; lasciare

deserve (di-*sööv*) *v* meritare

design (di-*sain*) *v* progettare; *n* disegno *m*; scopo *m*

designate (*dê*-sigh-neit) *v* designare

desirable (di-*sai*ᵒ-rö-böl) *adj* desiderabile

desire (di-*sai*ᵒ) *n* desiderio *m; v* desiderare

desk (dêssk) *n* scrivania *f*; leggio *m*; banco di scuola

despair (di-*sspê*ᵒ) *n* disperazione *f; v* disperare

despatch (di-*sspætʃ*) *v* spedire

desperate (*dê*-sspö-röt) *adj* disperato

despise (di-*sspais*) *v* disprezzare

despite (di-*sspait*) *prep* malgrado

dessert (di-*sööt*) *n* dolce *m*

destination (dê-ssti-*nei*-ʃön) *n* destinazione *f*

destine (*dê*-sstin) *v* destinare

destiny (*dê*-ssti-ni) *n* destino *m*, sorte *f*

destroy (di-*sstroi*) *v* *distruggere

destruction (di-*sstrak*-ʃön) *n* distruzione *f*

detach (di-*tætʃ*) *v* staccare

detail (*dii*-teil) *n* particolare *m*, dettaglio *m*

detailed (*dii*-teild) *adj* particolareggiato, dettagliato

detect (di-*têkt*) *v* *scoprire

detective (di-*têk*-tiv) *n* investigatore *m*, -trice *f*; ~ **story** romanzo poliziesco

detergent (di-*töö*-dʒönt) *n* detergente *m*

determine (di-*töö*-min) *v* stabilire, determinare

determined (di-*töö*-mind) *adj* risoluto

detest (*dii*-têsst) *v* detestare

detour (*dii*-tuᵒ) *n* giro *m*; deviazione *f*

devaluation (dii-væl-ᵘu-*ei*-ʃön) *n* svalutazione *f*

devalue (dii-*væl*-ᵢuu) *v* svalutare

develop (di-*vê*-löp) *v* sviluppare

development (di-*vê*-löp-mönt) *n* sviluppo *m*

deviate (*dii*-vi-eit) *v* deviare

devil (*dê*-völ) *n* diavolo *m*

devise (di-*vais*) *v* escogitare

devote (di-*vout*) *v* dedicare

dew (dᵢuu) *n* rugiada *f*

diabetes (dai-ö-*bii*-tiis) *n* diabete *m*

diabetic (dai-ö-*bê*-tik) *n* diabetico *m*, -a *f*

diagnose (dai-ögh-*nous*) *v* diagnosticare

diagnosis (dai-ögh-*nou*-ssiss) *n* (pl -ses) diagnosi *f*

diagonal (dai-*æ*-ghö-nöl) *n* diagonal *f; adj* diagonale

diagram (*dai*-ö-ghræm) *n* diagramma *m*; schema *m*, grafico *m*

dial (*dai*-öl) *n* quadrante *m*; disco *m* combinatore; *v* comporre (il numero)

dialect (*dai*-ö-lêkt) *n* dialetto *m*

diamond (*dai*-ö-mönd) *n* diamante *m*

diaper (*dai*-ö-pö) *nAm* pannolino *m*

diaphragm (*dai*-ö-fræm) *n* diaframma *m*

diarr(o)ea (dai-ö-*ri*-ö) *n* diarrea *f*

diary (*dai*-ö-ri) *n* agenda *f*; diario *m*

dictaphone (*dik*-tö-foun) *n* dittafono *m*

dictate (dik-*teit*) *v* dettare

dictation (dik-*tei*-ʃön) *n* dettato *m*

dictator (dik-*tei*-tö) *n* dittatore *m*

dictionary (*dik*-ʃö-nö-ri) *n* dizionario *m*

did (did) *v* (p do)

die (dai) *v* *morire

diesel (*dii*-söl) *n* diesel *m*

diet (*dai*-öt) *n* dieta *f*

differ (*di*-fö) *v* differire

difference (*di*-fö-rönss) *n* differenza *f*

different (*di*-fö-rönt) *adj* differente;

altro

difficult (*di*-fi-költ) *adj* difficile

difficulty (*di*-fi-köl-ti) *n* difficoltà *f*

*dig (digh) *v* scavare

digest (di-dʒêsst) *v* digerire

digestible (di-dʒê-sstö-böl) *adj* digeribile

digestion (di-dʒêss-tʃön) *n* digestione *f*

digit (*di*-dʒit) *n* numero *m*

digital (*di*-dʒi-töl) *adj* digitale

dignity (*di*-gnö-ti) *n* dignitá *f*

dike (daik) *n* diga *f*; argine *m*

dilapidated (di-*læ*-pi-dei-tid) *adj* malandato

diligence (*di*-li-dʒönss) *n* zelo *m*, diligenza *f*

diligent (*di*-li-dʒönt) *adj* zelante, diligente

dilute (dai-*l'uut*) *v* allungare, diluire

dim (dim) *adj* pallido, opaco; oscuro, debole, offuscato

dine (dain) *v* pranzare; cenare

dinghy (*ding*-ghi) *n* barchetta *f*

dining car (*dai*-ning-kaa) *n* vagone ristorante

dining room (*dai*-ning-ruum) *n* sala da pranzo

dinner (*di*-nö) *n* pranzo *m*; cena *f*; ~ **jacket** smoking *m*; ~ **service** servizio da tavola

diphtheria (dif-θ*i°*-ri-ö) *n* difterite *f*

diploma (di-*plou*-mö) *n* diploma *m*

diplomat (*di*-plö-mæt) *n* diplomatico *m*, -a *f*

direct (di-*rêkt*) *adj* diretto; *v* *dirigere

direction (di-*rêk*-ʃön) *n* direzione *f*; indicazione *f*; regia *f*; amministrazione *f*; **directions for use** istruzioni per l'uso

directional signal (di-*rêk*-ʃö-nal signal) *nAm* frecce *fpl*

directive (di-*rêk*-tiv) *n* direttiva *f*

director (di-*rêk*-tö) *n* direttore *m*,

-trice *f*; regista *m/f*

directory (di-*rêk*-tö-ri) *n* elenco *m*; guida *f* telefonica

dirt (dööt) *n* sudiciume *m*

dirty (*döö*-ti) *adj* sudicio, sporco

disabled (di-*ssei*-böld) *adj* invalido

disadvantage (di-ssöd-*vaan*-tidʒ) *n* svantaggio *m*

disagree (di-ssö-*ghrii*) *v* non *essere d'accordo

disagreeable (di-ssö-*ghrii*-ö-böl) *adj* sgradevole

disappear (di-ssö-*pi°*) *v* sparire

disappoint (di-ssö-*point*) *v* *deludere

disappointment (di-ssö-*point*-mönt) *n* delusione *f*

disapprove (di-ssö-*pruuv*) *v* disapprovare

disaster (di-*saa*-sstö) *n* disastro *m*; catastrofe *f*, sciagura *f*

disastrous (di-*saa*-sströss) *adj* disastroso

disc (dissk) *n* disco *m*; **slipped** ~ ernia *f*

discard (di-*sskaad*) *v* scartare

discharge (diss-tʃaadʒ) *v* scaricare; ~ **of** esonerare da

discipline (*di*-ssi-plin) *n* disciplina *f*

discolo(u)r (di-*sska*-lö) *v* scolorirsi

disconnect (di-sskö-*nêkt*) *v* *scollegare; disinserire

discontented (di-sskön-*tên*-tid) *adj* scontento

discontinue (di-sskön-*ti*-n'uu) *v* *sospendere, cessare

discount (*di*-sskaunt) *n* sconto *m*, riduzione *f*

discourage (diss-*ka*-ridʒ) *v* scoraggiare

discover (di-*sska*-vö) *v* *scoprire

discovery (di-*sska*-vö-ri) *n* scoperta *f*

discuss (di-*sskass*) *v* *discutere; dibattere

discussion (di-*sska*-ʃön) *n*

discussione *f*; conversazione *f*,
dibattito *m*

disease (di-*siis*) *n* malattia *f*

disembark (di-ssim-*baak*) *v* sbarcare

disgrace (diss-*ghreiss*) *n* disonore *m*

disguise (diss-*ghais*) *v* travestirsi; *n*
travestimento *m*

disgust (diss-*ghasst*) *n* disgusto *m*; **in
~** disgustato; *v* disgustare

disgusting (diss-*gha*-ssting) *adj*
nauseante, disgustoso

dish (diʃ) *n* piatto *m*; pietanza *f*

dishonest (di-*sso*-nisst) *adj* disonesto

dishwasher (diʃ-*uo*-ʃö) *n*
lavastoviglie *f*; lavapiatti *m/f*

disinfect (di-ssin-*fêkt*) *v* disinfettare

disinfectant (di-ssin-*fêk*-tönt) *n*
disinfettante *m*

dislike (di-*sslaik*) *v* detestare, non
piacere; *n* ripugnanza *f*, avversione *f*,
antipatia *f*

dislocated (*di*-sslö-kei-tid) *adj* slogato

dismiss (diss-*miss*) *v* congedare

disorder (di-*ssoo*-dö) *n* disordine *m*;
confusione *f*

dispatch (di-*sspætʃ*) *v* inviare, spedire

display (di-*ssplei*) *v* *mettere in
mostra, *esporre; mostrare; *n*
esposizione *f*, mostra *f*

displease (di-*sspliis*) *v* scontentare:
*dispiacere

disposable (di-*sspou*-sö-böl) *adj* usa
e getta

disposal (di-*sspou*-söl) *n* disposizione
f

dispose (di-*sspous*) *disporre

dispute (di-*sspⁱuut*) *n* disputa *f*; lite *f*,
controversia *f*; *v* *discutere, disputare

dissatisfied (di-*ssæ*-tiss-faid) *adj*
scontento

dissolve (di-*solv*) *v* *sciogliere

dissuade from (di-*ssᵘeid*) *dissuadere
da

distance (*di*-sstönss) *n* distanza *f*; **~ in**

kilometres chilometraggio *m*

distant (*di*-sstönt) *adj* lontano

distinct (di-*sstingkt*) *adj* chiaro;
distinto

distinction (di-*sstingk*-ʃön) *n*
distinzione *f*, differenza *f*

distinguish (di-*ssting*-ghᵘiʃ) *v*
*distinguere

distinguished (di-*ssting*-ghᵘiʃt) *adj*
distinto

distress (di-*sstrêss*) *n* pericolo *m*; **~
signal** segnale di soccorso

distribute (di-*sstri*-bⁱuut) *v* distribuire

distributor (di-*sstri*-bⁱu-tö) *n*
distributore *m*

district (*di*-sstrikt) *n* distretto *m*;
regione *f*; quartiere *m*

disturb (di-*sstööb*) *v* importunare,
disturbare

disturbance (di-*sstöö*-bönss) *n*
disturbo *m*; tumulto *m*

ditch (ditʃ) *n* fosso *m*, fossato *m*

dive (daiv) *v* tuffarsi

diversion (dai-*vöö*-ʃön) *n* deviazione
f; diversione *f*

divide (di-*vaid*) *v* *dividere; ripartire
separare

divine (di-*vain*) *adj* divino

division (di-*vi*-ʒön) *n* divisione *f*;
reparto *m*

divorce (di-*vooss*) *n* divorzio *m*; *v*
divorziare da

dizziness (*di*-si-nöss) *n* capogiro *m*

dizzy (*di*-si) *adj* stordito

***do** (duu) *v* *fare; bastare

dock (dok) *n* bacino *m*; scalo *m*; *v*
attraccare

docker (*do*-kö) *n* portuale *m/f*

doctor (*dok*-tö) *n* medico *m*, dottore
m, -essa *f*

document (*do*-kⁱu-mönt) *n*
documento *m*

dog (dogh) *n* cane *m*

dogged (*do*-ghid) *adj* ostinato

doll (dol) *n* bambola *f*

dollar (*do*-lö) n dollaro *m*

dome (doum) *n* cupola *f*

domestic (dö-*mê*-sstik) *adj*
domestico; interno; *n* domèstico *m*

domicile (*do*-mi-ssail) *n* domicilio *m*

domination (do-mi-*nei*-ʃön) *n*
dominazione *f*

dominion (dö-*mi*-nⁱön) *n* dominio *m*

donate (dou-*neit*) *v* donare

donation (dou-*nei*-ʃön) *n* donazione *f*

done (dan) *v* (pp do)

donkey (*dong*-ki) *n* asino *m*

donor (*dou*-nö) *n* donatore *m*

door (doo) *n* porta *f*; **revolving ~**
porta girevole; **sliding ~** porta
scorrevole

doorbell (*doo*-bêl) *n* campanello *m*

doorkeeper (*doo*-kii-pö) *n* portinaio
m, -a *f*

doorman (*doo*-mön) *n* (pl -men)
portinaio *m*

dormitory (*doo*-mi-tri) *n* dormitorio
m

dose (douss) *n* dose *f*

dot (dot) *n* punto *m*

double (*da*-böl) *adj* doppio

doubt (daut) *v* dubitare di, dubitare; *n*
dubbio *m*; **without ~** senza dubbio

doubtful (*daut*-föl) *adj* dubbioso;
incerto

dough (dou) *n* pasta *f*

down¹ (daun) *adv* giù; in giù, a terra;
adj abbattuto; *prep* lungo, giù da; **~**
payment acconto *m*

down² (daun) *n* lanugine *f*

downpour (*daun*-poo) *n* acquazzone
m

downstairs (daun-*sstê°s*) *adv* giù, di
sotto

downstream (daun-*sstriim*) *adv* con la
corrente

down-to-earth (daun-tu-*ööθ*) *adj*
sensato

downwards (*daun*-ᵘöds) *adv* in giù, in
discesa

dozen (*da*-sön) *n* (pl ~, ~s) dozzina *f*

draft (draaft) *n* brutta copia

drag (drægh) *v* trascinare

dragon (*dræ*-ghön) *n* drago *m*

drain (drein) *v* prosciugare; drenare; *n*
scolo *m*

drama (*draa*-mö) *n* dramma *m*;
tragedia *f*; teatro *m*

dramatic (drö-*mæ*-tik) *adj*
drammatico

dramatist (*dræ*-mö-tisst) *n*
drammaturgo *m*

drank (drængk) *v* (p drink)

drapery (*drei*-pö-ri) *n* stoffa *f*

draught (draaft) *n* corrente d'aria;
draughts gioco della dama

draw (droo) *n* sorteggio *m*

*draw (droo) *v* disegnare; tirare;
ritirare; **~ up** *redigere

drawbridge (*droo*-bridʒ) *n* ponte
levatoio

drawer (*droo*-ö) *n* cassetto *m*;
drawers mutande *fpl*

drawing (*droo*-ing) *n* disegno *m*; **~ pin**
puntina da disegno; **~ room** salotto
m

dread (drêd) *v* temere; *n* timore *m*

dreadful (*drêd*-föl) *adj* terribile,
spaventoso

dream (driim) *n* sogno *m*

*dream (driim) *v* sognare

dress (drêss) *v* vestire; vestirsi;
abbigliare; bendare; *n* abito
femminile, vestito da donna

dressing (*drê*-ssing) condimento per
l'insalata; benda *f*; **~ gown** vestaglia
f; **~ room** camerino *m*; **~ table** toilette
f

dressmaker (*drêss*-mei-kö) *n* sarto *m*,
-a *f*

drill (dril) *v* trapanare; addestrare; *n*
trapano *m*

drink (dringk) *n* aperitivo *m*, bibita *f*

***drink** (dringk) *v* *bere

drinking water (*dring-king-*^{u}oo-tö) *n* acqua potabile

drip-dry (drip-*drai*) *adj* non si stira, senza stiratura

drive (draiv) *n* strada *f*; scarrozzata *f*

***drive** (draiv) *v* guidare; *condurre

driver (*drai*-vö) *n* autista *m/f*

drizzle (*dri*-söl) *n* pioggerella *f*

drop (drop) *v* *far cadere; *n* goccia *f*

drought (draut) *n* siccità *f*

drown (draun) *v* affogare

drug (dragh) *n* narcotico *m*

drugstore (*dragh*-sstoo) *nAm* drugstore *m*, emporio *m*

drum (dram) *n* tamburo *m*

drunk (drangk) *adj* (pp drink) ubriaco

dry (drai) *adj* asciutto; *v* asciugare; **~ cleaner's** tintoria *f*

dry-clean (drai-*kliin*) *v* pulire a secco

dryer (*drai*-ö) *n* asciugabiancheria *f*

duchess (da-t∫iss) *n* duchessa *f*

duck (dak) *n* anatra *f*

due (d^{i}uu) *adj* in arrivo; dovuto

dues (d^{i}uus) *pl* tributo *m*

dug (dagh) *v* (p, pp dig)

duke (d^{i}uuk) *n* duca *m*

dull (dal) *adj* monotono, noioso; smorto, pallido; smussato

dumb (dam) *adj* muto; ottuso, stupido

dune (d^{i}uun) *n* duna *f*

dung (dang) *n* letame *m*

dunghill (*dang*-hil) *n* letamaio *m*

duration (d^{i}u-*rei*-∫ön) *n* durata *f*

during (*d^{u}ö*-ring) *prep* durante

dusk (dassk) *n* crepuscolo *m*

dust (dasst) *n* polvere *f*

dustbin (*dasst*-bin) *n* pattumiera *f*

dusty (*da*-ssti) *adj* polveroso

Dutch (dat∫) *adj* olandese

duty (d^{i}uu-ti) *n* dovere *m*; compito *m*; dazio *m*; **Customs ~** tariffa doganale

duty-free (d^{i}uu-ti-*frii*) *adj* esente da dazio, duty free

dwarf (d^{u}oof) *n* nano *m*

dye (dai) *v* *tingere; *n* tintura *f*

dynamo (*dai*-nö-mou) *n* (pl ~s) dinamo *f*

E

each (iit∫) *adj* ogni, ciascuno; **~ other** l'un l'altro

eager (*ii*-ghö) *adj* desideroso, ansioso, impaziente

eagle (*ii*-ghöl) *n* aquila *f*

ear (i^ö) *n* orecchio *m*; orecchia *f*

earache (*i^ö*-reik) *n* mal d'orecchi

eardrum (*i^ö*-dram) *n* timpano *m*

earl (ööl) *n* conte *m*

early (*öö*-li) *adj* presto

earn (öön) *v* guadagnare

earnest (*öö*-nisst) *n* serietà *f*

earnings (*öö*-nings) *pl* reddito *m*, guadagno *m*

earring (*i^ö*-ring) *n* orecchino *m*

earth (ööθ) *n* terra *f*; suolo *m*

earthquake (*ööθ*-k^{u}eik) *n* terremoto *m*

ease (iis) *n* disinvoltura *f*, facilità *f*; agio *m*

east (iist) *n* oriente *m*; est *m*

Easter (*ii*-sstö) Pasqua

easterly (*ii*-sstö-li) *adj* orientale

eastern (*ii*-sstön) *adj* orientale

easy (*ii*-si) *adj* facile; comodo; **~ chair** poltrona *f*

easy-going (ii-si-ghou-ing) *adj* calmo

eat (iit) *v* mangiare

eavesdrop (iivs-drop) *v* origliare

ebony (*ê*-bö-ni) *n* ebano *m*

eccentric (ik-*ssên*-trik) *adj* eccentrico

echo (*ê*-kou) *n* (pl ~es) eco *m/f*

eclipse (i-*klipss*) *n* eclissi *f*

economic (ii-kö-*no*-mik) *adj* economico

economical (ii-kö-*no*-mi-köl) *adj* parsimonioso; economico

economist (i-*ko*-nö-misst) *n* economista *m/f*

economize (i-*ko*-nö-mais) *v* economizzare

economy (i-*ko*-nö-mi) *n* economia *f*

ecstasy (*êk*-sstö-si) *n* estasi *f*

Ecuador (*ê*-k^{u}ö-doo) Ecuador *m*

Ecuadorian (ê-k^{u}ö-*doo*-ri-ön) *n* ecuadoriano *m*

eczema (*êk*-si-mö) *n* eczema *m*

edge (êd$_3$) *n* bordo *m*, margine *m*

edible (*ê*-di-böl) *adj* commestibile

edit (*ê*-dit) *v* rivedere; curare; dirigere; montare; editare

edition (i-*di*-ʃön) *n* edizione *f*; **morning** ~ edizione del mattino

editor (*ê*-di-tö) *n* redattore *m*

educate (*ê*-d$_3$u-keit) *v* istruire, educare

education (ê-d$_3$u-*kei*-ʃön) *n* educazione *f*

eel (iil) *n* anguilla *f*

effect (i-*fêkt*) *n* risultato *m*, effetto *m*; *v* effettuare; **in** ~ in realtà

effective (i-*fêk*-tiv) *adj* efficace

efficient (i-*fi*-ʃönt) *adj* efficiente

effort (*ê*-föt) *n* sforzo *m*; tentativo *m*

egg (êgh) *n* uovo *m*; ~ **yolk** tuorlo *m*

eggcup (*êgh*-kap) *n* portauovo *m*

eggplant (*êgh*-plaant) *n* melanzana *f*

ego(t)istic (ê-ghou-*i*-sstik) *adj* egoistico

Egypt (*ii*-d$_3$ipt) Egitto *m*

Egyptian (i-*d$_3$ip*-ʃön) *adj* egiziano

eiderdown (*ai*-dö-daun) *n* trapunta di piume *m*

eight (eit) *num* otto

eighteen (ei-*tiin*) *num* diciotto

eighteenth (ei-*tiinθ*) *num* diciottesimo

eighth (eitθ) *num* ottavo

eighty (*ei*-ti) *num* ottanta

either (*ai*-ðö) *pron* l'uno o l'altro; **either ... or** o... o

elaborate (i-*læ*-bö-reit) *v* elaborare

elastic (i-*læ*-sstik) *adj* elastico; flessibile; elastico *m*

elasticity (ê-læ-*ssti*-ssö-ti) *n* elasticità *f*

elbow (*êl*-bou) *n* gomito *m*

elder (*êl*-dö) *adj* maggiore

elderly (*êl*-dö-li) *adj* anziano

eldest (*êl*-disst) *adj* maggiore

elect (i-*lêkt*) *v* *scegliere, *eleggere

election (i-*lêk*-ʃön) *n* elezione *f*

electric (i-*lêk*-trik) *adj* elettrico; ~ **razor** rasoio elettrico; ~ **cord** cordone elettrico

electrician (i-lêk-*tri*-ʃön) *n* elettricista *m/f*

electricity (i-lêk-*tri*-ssö-ti) *n* elettricità *f*

electronic (i-lêk-*tro*-nik) *adj* elettronico

elegance (*ê*-li-ghönss) *n* eleganza *f*

elegant (*ê*-li-ghönt) *adj* elegante

element (*ê*-li-mönt) *n* elemento *m*

elephant (*ê*-li-fönt) *n* elefante *m*

elevator (*ê*-li-vei-tö) *nAm* ascensore *m*

eleven (i-*lê*-vön) *num* undici

eleventh (i-*lê*-vönθ) *num* undicesimo

elf (êlf) *n* (pl elves) folletto *m*

eliminate (i-*li*-mi-neit) *v* eliminare

elm (êlm) *n* olmo *m*

else (êlss) *adv* altrimenti

elsewhere (êl-*ss^{u}ê^ö*) *adv* altrove

elucidate (i-*luu*-ssi-deit) *v* spiegare

e-mail (*ii*-meil) *n* e-mail *m*; *v* mandare un e-mail a; mandare per e-mail

emancipation (i-mæn-ssi-*pei*-ʃön) *n* emancipazione *f*

embankment (im-*bængk*-mönt) *n* argine *m*

embargo (êm-*baa*-ghou) *n* (pl ~es) embargo *m*

embark (im-*baak*) *v* imbarcarsi; imbarcare

embarkation (êm-baa-*kei*-ʃön) *n* imbarco *m*

embarrass (im-*bæ*-röss) *v* imbarazzare, *mettere in imbarazzo

embarrassment (im-bæ-*röss*-mönt) *n* imbarazzo *m*

embassy (*êm*-bö-ssi) *n* ambasciata *f*

emblem (*êm*-blöm) *n* emblema *m*

embrace (im-*breiss*) *v* abbracciare; *n* abbraccio *m*

embroider (im-*broi*-dö) *v* ricamare

embroidery (im-*broi*-dö-ri) *n* ricamo *m*

emerald (*ê*-mö-röld) *n* smeraldo *m*

emergency (i-*möö*-dʒön-ssi) *n* caso di emergenza, emergenza *f*; stato di emergenza; ~ exit uscita di sicurezza

emigrant (*ê*-mi-ghrönt) *n* emigrante *m*/*f*

emigrate (*ê*-mi-ghreit) *v* emigrare

emigration (ê-mi-*ghrei*-ʃön) *n* emigrazione *f*

emotion (i-*mou*-ʃön) *n* commozione *f*; emozione *f*

emotional (i-*mou*-ʃö-nal) *adj* emozionale; commovente; commosso

emperor (*êm*-pö-rö) *n* imperatore *m*

emphasize (*êm*-fö-ssais) *v* sottolineare

empire (*êm*-pai⁰) *n* impero *m*

employ (im-*ploi*) *v* impiegare; utilizzare

employee (êm-ploi-*ii*) *n* impiegato *m*, -a *f*

employer (im-*ploi*-ö) *n* datore, -trice di lavoro

employment (im-*ploi*-mönt) *n* impiego *m*, occupazione *f*; ~ agency ufficio di collocamento

empress (*êm*-priss) *n* imperatrice *f*

empty (*êmp*-ti) *adj* vuoto; *v* vuotare

enable (i-*nei*-böl) *v* permettere

enamel (i-*næ*-möl) *n* smalto *m*

enamelled (i-*næ*-möld) *adj* smaltato

enchanting (in-*tʃaan*-ting) *adj* affascinante, incantevole

encircle (in-*ssöö*-köl) *v* *cingere, circondare; accerchiare

enclose (ing-*klous*) *v* *accludere, allegare

enclosure (ing-*klou*-ʒö) *n* allegato *n*

encounter (ing-*kaun*-tö) *v* incontrare *n* incontro *m*

encourage (ing-*ka*-ridʒ) *v* incoraggiare

encyclop(a)edia (ên-ssai-klö-*pii*-di-ö) *n* enciclopedia *f*

end (ênd) *n* fine *f*, estremità *f*; termine *m*; *v* finire; cessare

ending (*ên*-ding) *n* fine *f*

endless (*ênd*-löss) *adj* infinito

endorse (in-*dooss*) *v* vistare, girare

endure (in-*d'u⁰*) *v* sopportare

enemy (*ê*-nö-mi) *n* nemico *m*, -a *f*

energetic (ê-nö-*dʒê*-tik) *adj* energico

energy (*ê*-nö-dʒi) *n* energia *f*; forza *f*

engage (in-*gheidʒ*) *v* *assumere; riservare; impegnarsi; engaged fidanzato; occupato

engagement (ing-*gheidʒ*-mönt) *n* fidanzamento *m*; impegno *m*; ~ ring anello di fidanzamento

engine (*ên*-dʒin) *n* motore *m*

engineer (ên-dʒi-*ni⁰*) *n* ingegnere *m*

England (*ing*-ghlönd) Inghilterra *f*

English (*ing*-ghliʃ) *adj* inglese

engrave (ing-*ghreiv*) *v* *incidere

engraving (ing-*ghrei*-ving) *n* stampa *f*; incisione *f*

enigma (i-*nigh*-mö) *n* enigma *m*

enjoy (in-*dʒoi*) *v* godere, gustare

enjoyable (in-*dʒoi*-ö-böl) *adj* piacevole, gradevole, divertente; gustoso

enjoyment (in-*dʒoi*-mönt) *n* piacere *m*

enlarge (in-*laadʒ*) *v* ingrandire; ampliare

enlargement (in-*laadʒ*-mönt) *n* ingrandimento *m*

enormous (i-*noo*-möss) *adj* enorme

enough (i-*naf*) *adv* abbastanza; *adj* sufficiente

enquire (ing-*k*ᵘ*ai*ᵒ) *v* informarsi; indagare

enquiry (ing-*k*ᵘ*ai*ᵒ-ri) *n* informazione *f*; investigazione *f*; inchiesta *f*

enter (*ên*-tö) *v* entrare; *iscrivere

enterprise (*ên*-tö-prais) *n* impresa *f*

entertain (ên-tö-*tein*) *v* divertire, *intrattenere; ospitare

entertaining (ên-tö-*tei*-ning) *adj* divertente

entertainment (ên-tö-*tein*-mönt) *n* divertimento *m*, passatempo *m*

enthusiasm (in-*θuu*-si-æ-söm) *n* entusiasmo *m*

enthusiastic (in-θ'uu-si-æ-sstik) *adj* entusiastico

entire (in-*tai*ᵒ) *adj* tutto, intero

entirely (in-*tai*ᵒ-li) *adv* interamente

entrance (*ên*-trönss) *n* entrata *f*; accesso *m*; ingresso *m*; ~ **fee** ingresso *m*

entry (*ên*-tri) *n* entrata *f*; ingresso *m*; registrazione *f*; **no** ~ proibito passare

envelop (*ên*-vö-lop) *v* avvolgere

envelope (*ên*-vö-loup) *n* busta *f*

envious (*ên*-vi-öss) *adj* invidioso, geloso

environment (in-*vai*ᵒ-rön-mönt) *n* ambiente *m*; dintorni *mpl*

envoy (*ên*-voi) *n* inviato *m*

envy (*ên*-vi) *n* invidia *f*; *v* invidiare

epic (*ê*-pik) *n* poema epico; *adj* epico

epidemic (ê-pi-*dê*-mik) *n* epidemia *f*

epilepsy (*ê*-pi-lêp-ssi) *n* epilessia *f*

episode (*ê*-pi-ssoud) *n* episodio *m*

equal (*ii*-k*ᵘöl) *adj* uguale; *v* uguagliare

equality (i-k*ᵘo-lö-ti) *n* uguaglianza *f*

equalize (*ii*-k*ᵘö-lais) *v* pareggiare

equally (*ii*-k*ᵘö-li) *adv* ugualmente

equator (i-k*ᵘei-tö) *n* equatore *m*

equip (i-k*ᵘip) *v* equipaggiare

equipment (i-k*ᵘip-mönt) *n* equipaggiamento *m*

equivalent (i-k*ᵘi-vö-lönt) *adj* equivalente

eraser (i-*rei*-sö) *n* gomma per cancellare

erect (i-*rêkt*) *v* innalzare, *erigere; *adj* diritto

err (öö) *v* errare

error (*ê*-rö) *n* sbaglio *m*, errore *m*

escalator (*ê*-sskö-lei-tö) *n* scala mobile

escape (i-*sskeip*) *v* scappare; fuggire, sfuggire; *n* evasione *f*

escort[1] (*ê*-sskoot) *n* scorta *f*

escort[2] (i-*sskoot*) *v* scortare

especially (i-*sspê*-ʃö-li) *adv* soprattutto, specialmente

essay (*ê*-ssei) *n* saggio *m*; trattato *m*; tema *m*

essence (*ê*-ssönss) *n* essenza *f*; nocciolo *m*

essential (i-*ssên*-ʃöl) *adj* indispensabile; fondamentale, essenziale

essentially (i-*ssên*-ʃö-li) *adv* essenzialmente

establish (i-*sstæ*-bliʃ) *v* stabilire

estate (i-*ssteit*) *n* proprietà *f*

esteem (i-*sstiim*) *n* rispetto *m*, stima *f*; *v* stimare

estimate¹ (*ê*-ssti-meit) *v* *fare la stima, valutare

estimate² (*ê*-ssti-möt) *n* valutazione *f*; preventivo *m*

estuary (*êss*-tʃu-ö-ri) *n* estuario *m*

etcetera (êt-ssê-tö-rö) eccetera

etching (*ê*-tʃing) *n* acquaforte *f*

eternal (i-*töö*-nöl) *adj* eterno

eternity (i-*töö*-nö-ti) *n* eternità *f*

ether (*ii*-Öö) *n* etere *m*

Ethiopia (i-θi-*ou*-pi-ö) Etiopia *f*

Ethiopian (i-θi-*ou*-pi-ön) *adj* etiopico

EU (ii-*iuu*) *n* Ue *f*

Euro (ᵘoᵒ-röu) *n* euro *m*

Europe (ᵘoᵒ-röp) Europa *f*

European (ᵘoᵒ-rö-*pii*-ön) *adj* europeo

evacuate (i-væ-kᶦu-eit) *v* evacuare

evade (i-*veid*) *v* eludere; evadere

evaluate (i-*væl*-ᶦu-eit) *v* valutare

evaporate (i-*væ*-pö-reit) *v* evaporare

even (*ii*-vön) *adj* piano, piatto, uguale; costante; pari; *adv* perfino

evening (*iiv*-ning) *n* sera *f*; ~ **dress** abito da sera

event (i-*vênt*) *n* evento *m*; caso *m*

eventual (i-*vên*-tʃu-öl) *adj* infine

eventually (i-*vên*-tʃu-öl-li) *adv* alla fine

ever (*ê*-vö) *adv* mai; sempre

every (*êv*-ri) *adj* ogni

everybody (*êv*-ri-bo-di) *pron* ognuno

everyday (*êv*-ri-dei) *adj* quotidiano

everyone (*êv*-ri-ᵘan) *pron* ognuno

everything (*êv*-ri-θing) *pron* tutto

everywhere (*êv*-ri-ᵘêᵒ) *adv* ovunque

evidence (*ê*-vi-dönss) *n* prova *f*

evident (*ê*-vi-dönt) *adj* evidente

evil (*ii*-völ) *n* male *m*; *adj* cattivo, malvagio

evolution (ii-vö-*luu*-ʃön) *n* evoluzione *f*

exact (igh-*sækt*) *adj* esatto

exactly (igh-*sækt*-li) *adv* precisamente

exaggerate (igh-*sæ*-dʒö-reit) *v* esagerare

exam (igh-*sæm*) *n* esame *m*; **sit an ~** dare un esame; **pass an ~** superare un esame; **fail an ~** essere bocciato a un esame

examination (igh-sæ-mi-*nei*-ʃön) *n* esame *m*; indagine *f*; interrogazione

examine (igh-*sæ*-min) *v* esaminare

example (igh-*saam*-pöl) *n* esempio *m*; **for ~** per esempio

excavation (êkss-kö-*vei*-ʃön) *n* scavo *m*

exceed (ik-*ssiid*) *v* eccedere; superare

excel (ik-*ssêl*) *v* *eccellere

excellent (*êk*-ssö-lönt) *adj* ottimo, eccellente

except (ik-*ssêpt*) *prep* eccetto, salvo

exception (ik-*ssêp*-ʃön) *n* eccezione

exceptional (ik-*ssêp*-ʃö-nöl) *adj* straordinario, eccezionale

excerpt (*êk*-ssööpt) *n* brano *m*

excess (ik-*ssêss*) *n* eccesso *m*

excessive (ik-*ssê*-ssiv) *adj* eccessivo

exchange (ikss-*tʃeindʒ*) *v* scambiare cambiare; *n* cambio *m*; borsa *f*; ~ **office** ufficio di cambio; ~ **rate** corso del cambio

excite (ik-*ssait*) *v* eccitare

excited (ik-*ssai*-töd) *adj* eccitato, agitato; **get ~** (**about**) eccitarsi (per

excitement (ik-*ssait*-mönt) *n* agitazione *f*, eccitazione *f*

exciting (ik-*ssai*-ting) *adj* eccitante

exclaim (ik-*sskleim*) *v* esclamare

exclamation (êk-ssklö-*mei*-ʃön) *n* esclamazione *f*

exclude (ik-*sskluud*) *v* *escludere

exclusive (ik-*sskluu*-ssiv) *adj* esclusivo

exclusively (ik-*sskluu*-ssiv-li) *adv* esclusivamente, unicamente

excursion (ik-*ssköö*-ʃön) *n* gita *f*, escursione *f*

excuse¹ (ik-*ssk*ᶦ*uuss*) *n* scusa *f*

excuse² (ik-*ssk*ⁱ*uus*) v scusare

execute (*êk*-ssi-k*ⁱuut*) v eseguire

execution (êk-ssi-k*ⁱuu*-ʃön) n
esecuzione f

executioner (êk-ssi-k*ⁱuu*-ʃö-nö) n
boia m

executive (igh-*sê*-kⁱu-tiv) adj
esecutivo; in potere esecutivo;
direttore m, -trice f

exempt (igh-ȝêmpt) v dispensare,
esentare; adj esente

exemption (igh-*sêm*-p-ʃön) n
esenzione f

exercise (*êk*-ssö-ssais) n esercizio m; v
esercitare

exhale (êkss-*heil*) v espirare

exhaust (igh-*soosst*) n scappamento
m; v esaurire; ~ **gases** gas di scarico

exhibit (igh-*si*-bit) v *esporre; esibire

exhibition (êk-ssi-*bi*-ʃön) n mostra f,
esposizione f

exile (*êk*-ssail) n esilio m; esule m

exist (igh-*sisst*) v *esistere

existence (igh-*si*-sstönss) n esistenza f

exit (*êk*-ssit) n uscita f

exotic (igh-*so*-tik) adj esotico

expand (ik-*sspænd*) v *espandere;
*estendere; allargare

expansion (ik-*sspæn*-ȝön) n
espansione f; dilatazione f

expect (ik-*sspêkt*) v aspettare

expectation (êk-sspêk-*tei*-ʃön) n
aspettativa f

expedition (êk-sspö-*di*-ʃön) n invio m;
spedizione f

expel (ik-*sspêl*) v *espellere

expenditure (ik-*sspên*-di-tʃö) n spesa
f

expense (ik-*sspênss*) n spesa f

expensive (ik-*sspên*-ssiv) adj caro;
costoso

experience (ik-*sspi*ⁱ-ri-önss) n
esperienza f; v provare,
sperimentare; **experienced** esperto

experiment (ik-*sspê*-ri-mönt) n prova
f, esperimento m; v sperimentare

expert (*êk*-sspööt) n perito m, esperto
m; adj competente

expire (ik-*sspai*ⁱ) v spirare, finire,
*scadere; espirare; **expired** scaduto

explain (ik-*ssplein*) v chiarire, spiegare

explanation (êk-ssplö-*nei*-ʃön) n
chiarimento m, spiegazione f

explicit (ik-*sspli*-ssit) adj esplicito

explode (ik-*ssploud*) v *esplodere

exploit (ik-*ssploit*) v sfruttare,
utilizzare

explore (ik-*ssploo*) v esplorare

explosion (ik-*ssplou*-ȝön) n
esplosione f

explosive (ik-*ssplou*-ssiv) adj
esplosivo; n esplosivo m

export¹ (ik-*sspoot*) v esportare

export² (*êk*-sspoot) n esportazione f

exportation (êk-sspoo-*tei*-ʃön) n
esportazione f

exports (*êk*-sspootss) pl esportazione
f

expose (ikss-*pous*) v scoprire;
denunciare; ~ **to** esporre a

exposition (êk-sspö-*si*-ʃön) n
esposizione f

exposure (ik-*sspou*-ȝö) n esposizione
f

express (ik-*ssprêss*) v *esprimere;
manifestare; adj espresso; esplicito; ~
train treno rapido

expression (ik-*ssprê*-ʃön) n
espressione f; manifestazione f

exquisite (ik-*ssk*ᵘ*i*-sit) adj squisito

extend (ik-*sstênd*) v *estendere;
allargare; accordare

extension (ik-*sstên*-ʃön) n
prolungamento m; ampliamento m;
interno m; ~ **cord** prolunga f

extensive (ik-*sstên*-ssiv) adj ampio;
vasto

extent (ik-*sstênt*) n dimensione f

exterior (êk-ssti*ö*-ri-ö) *adj* esterno; *n* esterno *m*

external (êk-sstöö-nöl) *adj* esteriore

extinguish (ik-ssting-gh*u*iʃ) *v* *spegnere; *estinguere

extort (ik-sstoot) *v* *estorcere

extortion (ik-sstoo-ʃön) *n* estorsione *f*

extra (êk-sströ) *adj* supplementare

extract[1] (ik-sstrækt) *v* *estrarre

extract[2] (êk-sstrækt) *n* passo *m*

extradite (êk-sströ-dait) *v* estradare

extraordinary (ik-sstroo-dön-ri) *adj* straordinario

extravagant (ik-sstræ-vö-ghönt) *adj* stravagante

extreme (ik-sstriim) *adj* estremo; *n* estremo *m*

exuberant (igh-s*uu*-bö-rönt) *adj* esuberante

eye (ai) *n* occhio *m*; ~ **shadow** ombretto *m*

eyebrow (*ai*-brau) *n* sopracciglio *m*; ~ **pencil** matita per gli occhi

eyelash (*ai*-læʃ) *n* ciglio *m*

eyelid (*ai*-lid) *n* palpebra *f*

eyewitness (*ai*-*u*it-nöss) *n* testimone oculare

F

fable (*fei*-böl) *n* favola *f*

fabric (*fæ*-brik) *n* stoffa *f*; struttura *f*

façade (fö-ssaad) *n* facciata *f*

face (feiss) *n* faccia *f*; *v* *far fronte a; ~ **cream** crema per il viso; ~ **massage** massaggio facciale; ~ **pack** maschera di bellezza

face-powder (*feiss*-pau-dö) *n* cipria *f*

facilities (fei-*si*-lö-teez) *pl* servizi *mpl*, strutture *fpl*

facing (*fei*-ssing) *prep* in faccia a

fact (fækt) *n* fatto *m*; **in** ~ infatti

factor (*fæk*-tö) *n* fattore *m*

factory (*fæk*-tö-ri) *n* fabbrica *f*

factual (*fæk*-tʃu-öl) *adj* reale

faculty (*fæ*-köl-ti) *n* potere *m*; capacità *f*, facoltà *f*

fade (feid) *v* scolorirsi, sbiadire

fail (feil) *v* fallire; mancare; bocciare; essere bocciato; **without** ~ senz'altro

failure (*feil*-*i*ö) *n* insuccesso *m*; fallimento *m*

faint (feint) *v* *svenire; *adj* fiacco, vago, debole

fair (fê*ö*) *n* fiera *f*; *adj* giusto, onesto; biondo; bello

fairly (*fê*ö-li) *adv* alquanto, piuttosto, abbastanza

fairy (*fê*ö-ri) *n* fata *f*

fairytale (*fê*ö-ri-teil) *n* fiaba *f*

faith (feiθ) *n* fede *f*; fiducia *f*

faithful (*fei*θ-ful) *adj* fedele

fake (feik) *n* falsificazione *f*

fall (fool) *n* caduta *f*; *Am* autunno *m*

*fall (fool) *v* *cadere

false (foolss) *adj* falso; sbagliato, contraffatto; ~ **teeth** dentiera *f*

falter (*fool*-tö) *v* vacillare; balbettare

fame (feim) *n* fama *f*; reputazione *f*

familiar (fö-*mil*-*i*ö) *adj* familiare; confidenziale

family (*fæ*-mö-li) *n* famiglia *f*; ~ **name** cognome *m*

famous (*fei*-möss) *adj* famoso

fan (fæn) *n* ventilatore *m*; ventaglio *m* tifoso *m*, -a *f*; ammiratore *m*, -trice *f*

fanatical (fö-*næ*-ti-köl) *adj* fanatico

fancy (*fæn*-ssi) *v* gradire, *aver voglia

di; figurarsi, immaginare; n capriccio m; immaginazione f

fantastic (fæn-tæ-sstik) adj fantastico

fantasy (fæn-tö-si) n fantasia f

far (faa) adj lontano; adv molto; **by ~** di gran lunga; **so ~** finora; **~ away** distante

fare (fê°) n spese di viaggio, prezzo del biglietto; vitto m, cibo m

farm (faam) n fattoria f

farmer (faa-mö) n fattore m; **farmer's wife** fattoressa f

farmhouse (faam-hauss) n cascina f

far-off (faa-rof) adj lontano

farther (faar-ðö) adv più lontano

fascinate (fæ-ssi-neit) v affascinare

fascism (fæ-ʃi-söm) n fascismo m

fascist (fæ-ʃisst) adj fascistico; n fascista m/f

fashion (fæ-ʃön) n moda f; modo m

fashionable (fæ-ʃö-nö-böl) adj alla moda

fast (faasst) adj rapido, veloce; fisso

fasten (faa-ssön) v allacciare; *chiudere

fastener (faa-ssö-nö) n fermaglio m

fat (fæt) adj grasso; n grasso m

fatal (fei-töl) adj fatale, mortale

fate (feit) n fato m, destino m

father (faa-ðö) n padre m

father-in-law (faa-ðö-rin-loo) n (pl fathers-) suocero m

fatty (fæ-ti) adj unto

faucet (foo-ssit) nAm rubinetto m

fault (foolt) n colpa f; imperfezione f, difetto m, mancanza f

faultless (foolt-löss) adj impeccabile; perfetto

faulty (fool-ti) adj difettoso

favo(u)r (fei-vö) n favore m; v privilegiare, favorire

favo(u)rite (fei-vö-rit) n favorito m, -a f; adj preferito

fawn (foon) n cerbiatto m

fax (fæks) n fax m; v mandare un fax

fear (fi°) n timore m, paura f; v temere

feasible (fii-sö-böl) adj realizzabile

feast (fiisst) n festa f

feat (fiit) n prestazione f

feather (fê-ðö) n penna f

feature (fii-tʃö) n caratteristica f; tratto m

February (fê-bru-ö-ri) febbraio

federal (fê-dö-röl) adj federale

federation (fê-dö-rei-ʃön) n federazione f; confederazione f

fee (fii) n onorario m

feeble (fii-böl) adj fiacco

*feed (fiid) v nutrire; **fed up with** stufo di

*feel (fiil) v sentire; palpare; **~ like** *aver voglia di

feeling (fii-ling) n sensazione f

feet n (pl foot)

fell (fêl) v (p fall)

fellow (fê-lou) n tipo m

felt¹ (fêlt) n feltro m

felt² (fêlt) v (p, pp feel)

female (fii-meil) adj femminile

feminine (fê-mi-nin) adj femminile

fence (fênss) n recinto m; steccato m; v tirare di scherma

ferment (föö-mênt) v fermentare

ferry (fê-ri) n traghetto m

fertile (föö-tail) adj fertile

festival (fê-ssti-völ) n festival m

festive (fê-sstiv) adj festivo

fetch (fêtʃ) v *andare a prendere

feudal (fʹuu-döl) adj feudale

fever (fii-vö) n febbre f

feverish (fii-vö-riʃ) adj febbricitante

few (fʹuu) adj pochi

fiancé (fi-ang-ssei) n fidanzato m

fiancée (fi-ang-ssei) n fidanzata f

fibre (fai-bö) n fibra f

fiction (fik-ʃön) n finzione f

field (fiild) n campo m; settore m; **~ glasses** binocolo m

fierce (fi⁰ss) *adj* feroce; selvaggio, veemente

fifteen (fif-*tiin*) *num* quindici

fifteenth (fif-*tiinθ*) *num* quindicesimo

fifth (fifθ) *num* quinto

fifty (*fif*-ti) *num* cinquanta

fig (figh) *n* fico *m*

fight (fait) *n* combattimento *m*, lotta *f*

***fight** (fait) *v* combattere, lottare

figure (*fi*-ghö) *n* forma *f*, figura *f*; cifra *f*

file (fail) *n* lima *f*; raccolta di documenti; fila *f*

fill (fil) *v* riempire; ~ **in** compilare; ~ **out** *Am* completare, compilare; ~ **up** *fare il pieno

filling (*fi*-ling) *n* otturazione *f*; ripieno *m*; ~ **station** distributore di benzina

film (film) *n* film *m*; pellicola *f*; *v* filmare

filter (*fil*-tö) *n* filtro *m*

filthy (*fil*-θi) *adj* sordido, sudicio

final (*fai*-nöl) *adj* finale

finally (*fai*-nöl-li) *adv* infine; finalmente

finance (fai-*nænss*) *v* finanziare

finances (fai-*næn*-ssis) *pl* finanze *fpl*

financial (fai-*næn*-ʃöl) *adj* finanziario

finch (fintʃ) *n* fringuello *m*

***find** (faind) *v* trovare

fine (fain) *n* multa *f*; *adj* fino; bello; ottimo, meraviglioso; ~ **arts** belle arti

finger (*fing*-ghö) *n* dito *m*; **little** ~ mignolo *m*

fingerprint (*fing*-ghö-print) *n* impronta digitale

finish (*fi*-niʃ) *v* completare, finire; terminare; *n* termine *m*; traguardo *m*

Finland (*fin*-lönd) Finlandia *f*

Finn (fin) *n* finlandese *m/f*

Finnish (*fi*-niʃ) *adj* finlandese

fire (fai⁰) *n* fuoco *m*; incendio *m*; *v* sparare; licenziare; ~ **alarm** allarme antincendio; ~ **brigade** pompieri

mpl; ~ **escape** scala antincendio; ~ **extinguisher** estintore *m*

firefighter (*fai⁰*-*fai*-tö) *n* pompiere *m*

fireplace (*fai⁰*-pleiss) *n* caminetto *m*

fireproof (*fai⁰*-pruuf) *adj* incombustibile

firm (fööm) *adj* saldo; solido; *n* ditta *f*

first (föösst) *num* primo; **at** ~ prima; al principio; ~ **name** nome *m*

first aid (föösst-*eid*) *n* pronto soccorso; ~ **kit** cassetta del pronto soccorso; ~ **post** posto di pronto soccorso

first-class (föösst-*klaass*) *adj* di prima qualità

first-rate (föösst-*reit*) *adj* ottimo, di prima qualità

fir tree (*föö*-trii) *n* abete *m*

fish¹ (fiʃ) *n* (pl ~, ~es) pesce *m*; ~ **shop** pescheria *f*

fish² (fiʃ) *v* pescare; pescare con l'amo

fishbone (*fiʃ*-boun) *n* lisca *f*, spina di pesce

fisherman (*fi*-ʃö-mön) *n* (pl -men) pescatore *m*

fishing (*fi*-ʃing) *n* pesca *f*; ~ **gear** attrezzi da pesca; ~ **hook** amo *m*; ~ **industry** pesca *f*; ~ **licence** permesso di pesca; ~ **line** lenza *f*; ~ **net** rete da pesca; ~ **rod** canna da pesca; ~ **tackle** attrezzi da pesca

fist (fisst) *n* pugno *m*

fit (fit) *adj* adatto; *n* attacco *m*; *v* *corrispondere

five (faiv) *num* cinque

fix (fikss) *v* riparare

fixed (fiksst) *adj* fisso

fizz (fis) *n* effervescenza *f*

flag (flægh) *n* bandiera *f*

flame (fleim) *n* fiamma *f*

flamingo (flö-*ming*-ghou) *n* (pl ~s, ~es) fenicottero *m*

flannel (*flæ*-nöl) *n* flanella *f*

flash (flæʃ) *n* baleno *m*

flashlight (*flæʃ*-lait) n pila f

flask (flaassk) n flacone m; **thermos ~** termos m

flat (flæt) adj piano, piatto; n appartamento m; **~ tyre** bucatura f

flavo(u)r (*flei*-vö) n gusto m; v condire

flea (flii) n pulce f

flee (flii) v scappare

fleet (fliit) n flotta f

flesh (flêʃ) n carne f

flew (fluu) v (p fly)

flex (flêkss) n cavo elettrico m

flexible (*flêk*-ssi-böl) adj flessibile; pieghevole

flight (flait) n volo m; **charter ~** volo charter

float (flout) v galleggiare; n galleggiante m

flock (flok) n gregge m

flood (flad) n inondazione f; fiume m

floor (floo) n pavimento m; piano m

Florence (*flo*-röns) Firenze f

florist (*flo*-risst) n fioraio m, -a f

flour (flau⁰) n farina f

flow (flou) v *scorrere

flower (flau⁰) n fiore m; **~ shop** negozio di fiori

flowerbed (*flau⁰*-bêd) n aiola f

flown (floun) v (pp fly)

flu (fluu) n influenza f

fluent (*fluu*-önt) adj fluente

fluid (*fluu*-id) adj fluido; n fluido m

flute (fluut) n flauto m

fly (flai) n mosca f; patta f

***fly** (flai) v volare

foam (foum) n schiuma f; v spumare; **~ rubber** gommapiuma f

focus (*fou*-köss) n fuoco m

fog (fogh) n nebbia f

foggy (*fo*-ghi) adj nebbioso

foglamp (*fogh*-læmp) n fendinebbia mpl

fold (fould) v piegare; n piega f

folk (fouk) n popolo m; **~ dance** danza popolare; **~ song** canzone popolare

folklore (*fouk*-loo) n folklore m

follow (*fo*-lou) v seguire

following (*fo*-lou-ing) adj successivo, seguente

fond (fond): ***be ~ of** amare

food (fuud) n cibo m; mangiare m, vitto m; **~ poisoning** intossicazione alimentare

foodstuffs (*fuud*-sstafss) pl alimentari mpl

fool (fuul) n idiota m, sciocco m; v beffare

foolish (*fuu*-liʃ) adj stolto, stupido; sciocco

foot (fut) n (pl feet) piede m; **~ brake** freno a pedale; **~ powder** talco per piedi; **on ~** a piedi

football (*fut*-bool) n pallone m; **~ match** partita di calcio

footpath (*fut*-paaθ) n sentiero m

footwear (*fut*-ᵘê⁰) n calzatura f

for (foo, fö) prep per; durante; a causa di, in conseguenza di; conj poiché

***forbid** (fö-*bid*) v proibire

force (fooss) v *costringere, forzare; n forza f; **by ~** per forza; **driving ~** forza motrice

forecast (*foo*-kaasst) n previsione f; v *prevedere

foreground (*foo*-ghraund) n primo piano

forehead (*fo*-rêd) n fronte f

foreign (*fo*-rin) adj straniero; estraneo

foreigner (*fo*-ri-nö) n straniero m, -a f

foreman (*foo*-mön) n (pl -men) capomastro m

foremost (*foo*-mousst) adj primo

forest (*fo*-risst) n foresta f

forester (*fo*-ri-sstö) n guardia forestale

forever (fö-ê-*vö*) adv per sempre; di continuo

forge (foodʒ) v falsificare

*forget (fö-*ghêt*) v dimenticare

forgetful (fö-*ghêt*-föl) *adj* smemorato

*forgive (fö-*ghiv*) v perdonare

fork (fook) n forchetta *f*; bivio *m*; v biforcarsi

form (foom) n forma *f*; formulario *m*; classe *f*; v formare

formal (*foo*-möl) *adj* formale

formality (foo-*mæ*-lö-ti) n formalità *f*

former (*foo*-mö) *adj* antico; precedente

formerly *adv* in passato, un tempo

formula (*foo*-m^{i}u-lö) n (pl ~e, ~s) formula *f*

fortnight (*foot*-nait) n quindici giorni

fortress (*foo*-triss) n fortezza *f*

fortunate (*foo*-t$\int$ö-nöt) *adj* fortunato

fortunately (*foo*-t$\int$ö-nöt-li) *adv* fortunatamente

fortune (*foo*-t$\int$uun) n ricchezza *f*; futuro *m*; fortuna *f*

forty (*foo*-ti) *num* quaranta

forward (*foo*-^{u}öd) *adv* in avanti, avanti; v inoltrare

fought (foot) v (p, pp fight)

foul (faul) *adj* sporco; perfido

found¹ (faund) v (p, pp find)

found² (faund) v fondare, istituire

foundation (faun-*dei*-$\int$ön) n fondazione *f*; ~ **cream** fondo tinta

fountain (*faun*-tin) n fontana *f*; sorgente *f*; ~ **pen** penna stilografica

four (foo) *num* quattro

fourteen (foo-*tiin*) *num* quattordici

fourteenth (foo-*tiin*θ) *num* quattordicesimo

fourth (fooθ) *num* quarto

fowl (faul) n (pl ~s, ~) pollame *m*

fox (fokss) n volpe *f*

foyer (*foi*-ei) n ridotto *m*

fraction (*fræk*-$\int$ön) n frazione *f*

fracture (*fræk*-t$\int$ö) v fratturare; n frattura *f*

fragile (*fræ*-d$_3$ail) *adj* fragile

fragment (*frægh*-mönt) n frammento *m*; pezzo *m*

frame (freim) n cornice *f*; montatura *f*

France (fraanss) Francia *f*

franchise (*fræn*-t$\int$ais) n diritto elettorale

fraud (frood) n frode *f*

fray (frei) v sfilacciarsi

free (frii) *adj* libero; gratuito; ~ **of charge** gratuito; ~ **ticket** biglietto gratuito

freedom (*frii*-döm) n libertà *f*

*freeze (friis) v gelare; congelarsi

freezer (*frii*-sö) n congelatore *m*; freezer *m*

freezing (*frii*-sing) *adj* glaciale; ~ **point** punto di congelamento

freight (freit) n carico *m*; ~ **train** *Am* treno merci

French (frênt$\int$) *adj* francese; ~ **fries** *Am* patatine fritte

frequency (*frii*-k^{u}ön-ssi) n frequenza *f*

frequent (*frii*-k^{u}önt) *adj* frequente

fresh (frê$\int$) *adj* fresco; ~ **water** acqua dolce

friction (*frik*-$\int$ön) n attrito *m*

Friday (*frai*-di) venerdì *m*

fridge (frid$_3$) n frigorifero *m*

friend (frênd) n amico *m*, -a *f*

friendly (*frênd*-li) *adj* affabile; amichevole

friendship (*frênd*-$\int$ip) n amicizia *f*

fright (frait) n paura *f*, spavento *m*

frighten (*frai*-tön) v spaventare

frightened (*frai*-tönd) *adj* spaventato; ***be ~** spaventarsi

frightful (*frait*-föl) *adj* terribile

fringe (frind$_3$) n frangia *f*

frock (frok) n veste *f*

frog (frogh) n rana *f*

from (from) *prep* da

front (frant) n facciata *f*; **in ~ of** di fronte a

frontier (*fran*-ti^ö) n frontiera *f*

frost (frosst) *n* gelo *m*
froth (froθ) *n* schiuma *f*
frozen (*frou*-sön) *adj* congelato; ~ **food** cibo surgelato
fruit (fruut) *n* frutta *f*; frutto *m*
fry (frai) *v* *friggere
frying pan (*frai*-ing-pæn) *n* padella *f*
fuel (fᵘuu-öl) *n* combustibile *m*; benzina *f*; ~ **pump** *Am* pompa di alimentazione
full (ful) *adj* pieno; ~ **board** pensione completa; ~ **stop** punto *m*; ~ **up** colmo
fun (fan) *n* divertimento *m*; scherzo *m*
function (*fangk*-ʃön) *n* funzione *f*
fund (fand) *n* fondi *mpl*
fundamental (fan-dö-*mên*-töl) *adj* fondamentale
funeral (fᵘuu-nö-röl) *n* funerale *m*

funnel (*fa*-nöl) *n* imbuto *m*
funny (*fa*-ni) *adj* buffo, divertente; strano
fur (föö) *n* pelliccia *f*; ~ **coat** cappotto di pelliccia
furious (fᵘuᵒ-ri-öss) *adj* furibondo, furioso
furnace (*föö*-niss) *n* fornace *f*
furnish (*föö*-niʃ) *v* fornire, procurare; arredare, ammobiliare
furniture (*föö*-ni-tʃö) *n* mobili *mpl*
further (*föö*-ðö) *adj* più lontano; ulteriore
furthermore (*föö*-ðö-moo) *adv* inoltre
furthest (*föö*-ðisst) *adj* il più lontano
fuse (fᵘuus) *n* fusibile *m*; miccia *f*
fuss (fass) *n* trambusto *m*; scalpore *m*
future (fᵘuu-tʃö) *n* futuro *m*; *adj* futuro

G

gable (*ghei*-böl) *n* frontone *m*
gadget (*ghæ*-dʒit) *n* aggeggio *m*
gain (ghein) *v* guadagnare; *n* profitto *m*
gale (gheil) *n* burrasca *f*
gall (ghool) *n* bile *f*; ~ **bladder** cistifellea *f*
gallery (*ghæ*-lö-ri) *n* loggione *m*; galleria *f*
gallon (*ghæ*-lon) *n* gallone *m* (*GB* 4,55 l; *Am* 3,79 l); **gallons of tea** litri di tè
gallop (*ghæ*-löp) *n* galoppo *m*
gallows (*ghæ*-lous) *pl* forca *f*
gallstone (*ghool*-sstoun) *n* calcolo biliare
game (gheim) *n* gioco *m*; selvaggina *f*; ~ **reserve** riserva per la selvaggina
gang (ghæng) *n* banda *f*; squadra *f*
gangway (*ghæng*-ᵘei) *n* passerella *f*

gap (ghæp) *n* spazio *m*, buco *m*
garage (*ghæ*-raaʒ) *n* garage *m*; officina *f*
garbage (*ghaa*-bidʒ) *n* spazzatura *f*, immondizia *f*
garden (*ghaa*-dön) *n* giardino *m*; **public** ~ giardino pubblico; **zoological gardens** giardino zoologico
gardener (*ghaa*-dö-nö) *n* giardiniere *m*, -a *f*
gargle (*ghaa*-ghöl) *v* fare i gargarismi
garlic (*ghaa*-lik) *n* aglio *m*
gas (ghæss) *n* gas *m*; *Am* benzina *f*; ~ **cooker** fornello a gas; ~ **pump** *Am* pompa di benzina; ~ **station** *Am* distributore; ~ **stove** stufa a gas; ~ **tank** *Am* serbatoio *m*
gasoline (*ghæ*-ssö-liin) *nAm* benzina *f*

gastric (*ghǽ-sstrik*) *adj* gastrico; ~ **ulcer** ulcera gastrica

gate (*gheit*) *n* cancello *m*

gather (*ghǽ-ðö*) *v* *raccogliere; *raccogliersi

gauge (*gheidʒ*) *n* misuratore *m*

gave (*gheiv*) *v* (p give)

gay (*ghei*) *adj* allegro; vivace

gaze (*gheis*) *v* fissare

gear (*ghiᵒ*) *n* marcia *f*; attrezzatura *f*; **change ~** cambiare marcia; **~ lever, ~ shift** leva del cambio

gearbox (*ghiᵒ-bokss*) *n* cambio *m*

geese (*ghiis*) *n* (pl goose)

gem (*dʒēm*) *n* gioiello *m*, gemma *f*

gender (*dʒēn-dö*) *n* genere *m*

general (*dʒē-nö-röl*) *adj* generale; *n* generale *m*; **~ practitioner** medico generico; **in ~** in generale

generate (*dʒē-nö-reit*) *v* generare

generation (dʒē-nö-*rei*-ʃön) *n* generazione *f*

generator (*dʒē-nö-rei-tör*) *n* generatore *m*

generosity (dʒē-nö-*ro*-ssö-ti) *n* generosità *f*

generous (*dʒē-nö-röss*) *adj* munifico, generoso

genital (*dʒē-ni-töl*) *adj* genitale

genius (*dʒii-ni-öss*) *n* genio *m*

Genoa (*dʒē-nö-uö*) Genova *f*

gentle (*dʒēn-töl*) *adj* dolce, leggero; gentile; delicato

gentleman (*dʒēn-töl-mön*) *n* (pl -men) signore *m*

genuine (*dʒē-nⁱu-in*) *adj* genuino

geography (dʒi-*o*-ghrö-fi) *n* geografia *f*

geology (dʒi-*o*-lö-dʒi) *n* geologia *f*

geometry (dʒi-*o*-mö-tri) *n* geometria *f*

germ (dʒööm) *n* germe *m*

German (*dʒöö-mön*) *adj* tedesco

Germany (*dʒöö-mö-ni*) Germania *f*

gesticulate (dʒi-*ssti*-kⁱu-leit) *v* gesticolare

***get** (*ghêt*) *v* *ottenere; *andare a prendere; diventare; **~ back** tornare; **~ off** *scendere; **~ on** montare; avanzare, progredire; **~ up** alzarsi

ghost (*ghousst*) *n* spettro *m*; spirito *m*

giant (*dʒai-önt*) *n* gigante *m*

giddiness (*ghi-di-nöss*) *n* vertigine *f*

giddy (*ghi-di*) *adj* stordito

gift (*ghift*) *n* regalo *m*, dono *m*; talento *m*

gifted (*ghif-tid*) *adj* di talento

gigantic (dʒai-*ghæn*-tik) *adj* gigantesco

giggle (*ghi-ghöl*) *v* ridacchiare

gill (*ghil*) *n* branchia *f*

gilt (*ghilt*) *adj* dorato

ginger (*dʒin-dʒö*) *n* zenzero *m*

girdle (*ghöö-döl*) *n* busto *m*

girl (*ghööl*) *n* ragazza *f*; **~ guide** giovane esploratrice

girlfriend (*ghööl-frênd*) *n* ragazza *f*; amica *f*

***give** (*ghiv*) *v* *dare; *porgere; **~ away** tradire; **~ in** cedere; **~ up** desistere

glacier (*ghlæ-ssi-ö*) *n* ghiacciaio *m*

glad (*ghlæd*) *adj* lieto, contento; **gladly** con piacere, volentieri

gladness (*ghlæd-nöss*) *n* gioia *f*

glamorous (*ghlæ-mö-röss*) *adj* affascinante

glamour (*ghlæ-mö*) *n* fascino *m*

glance (*ghlaanss*) *n* occhiata *f*; *v* *dare un'occhiata

gland (*ghlænd*) *n* ghiandola *f*

glare (*ghlêᵒ*) *n* bagliore *m*; splendore *m*

glaring (*ghlêᵒ-ring*) *adj* abbagliante

glass (*ghlaass*) *n* bicchiere *m*; vetro *m*; di vetro; **glasses** occhiali *mpl*; **magnifying ~** lente d'ingrandimento

glaze (*ghleis*) *v* smaltare

glide (*ghlaid*) *v* scivolare

glider (*ghlai-dö*) *n* aliante *m*

glimpse (ghlimpss) *n* occhiata *f*; *v* *intravedere

global (*ghlou*-böl) *adj* globale

globe (ghloub) *n* globo *m*

gloom (ghluum) *n* oscurità *f*

gloomy (*ghluu*-mi) *adj* cupo

glorious (*ghloo*-ri-öss) *adj* splendido

glory (*ghloo*-ri) *n* gloria *f*; onore *m*; lode *f*

gloss (ghloss) *n* lucentezza *f*

glossy (*ghlo*-ssi) *adj* lucido

glove (ghlav) *n* guanto *m*

glow (ghlou) *v* *ardere; *n* bagliore *m*; colorito *m*; brillare *m*

glue (ghluu) *n* colla *f*

*go (ghou) *v* *andare; camminare; diventare; ~ **ahead** continuare; ~ **away** *andarsene; ~ **back** tornare; ~ **home** rincasare; ~ **in** entrare; ~ **on** continuare; ~ **out** *uscire; ~ **through** passare

goal (ghoul) *n* traguardo *m*; rete *f*

goalkeeper (*ghoul*-kii-pö) *n* portiere *m*

goat (ghout) *n* capra *f*

god (ghod) *n* dio *m*

goddess (*gho*-diss) *n* dea *f*

godfather (*ghod*-faa-ðö) *n* padrino *m*

goggles (*gho*-ghöls) *pl* occhiali di protezione

gold (ghould) *n* oro *m*; ~ **leaf** oro laminato

golden (*ghoul*-dön) *adj* d'oro

goldmine (*ghould*-main) *n* miniera d'oro

goldsmith (*ghould*-ssmiθ) *n* orefice *m/f*

golf (gholf) *n* golf *m*; ~ **course**, ~ **links** campo da golf

golfclub (*gholf*-klab) *n* mazza da golf

gondola (*ghon*-dö-lö) *n* gondola *f*

gone (ghon) *adv* (pp go) via

good (ghud) *adj* buono; bravo

goodbye! (ghud-*bai*) arrivederci!

good-humo(u)red (ghud-*hʲuu*-mod) *adj* di buon umore

good-looking (ghud-*lu*-king) *adj* di bell'aspetto, bello

good-natured (ghud-*nei*-tʃöd) *adj* gentile

goods (ghuds) *pl* merci; ~ **train** treno merci

good-tempered (ghud-*têm*-pöd) *adj* di buon umore

goodwill (ghud-ʷ*il*) *n* benevolenza *f*

goose (ghuuss) *n* (pl geese) oca *f*; ~ **flesh** pelle d'oca

gooseberry (*ghus*-bö-ri) *n* uva spina

gorge (ghoodʒ) *n* gola *f*

gorgeous (*ghoo*-dʒöss) *adj* magnifico

gospel (*gho*-sspöl) *n* vangelo *m*

gossip (*gho*-ssip) *n* pettegolezzo *m*; *v* pettegolare

got (ghot) *v* (p, pp get)

gourmet (*ghuº*-mei) *n* buongustaio *m*,-a *f*

gout (ghaut) *n* gotta *f*

govern (*gha*-vön) *v* governare

government (*gha*-vön-mönt) *n* governo *m*

governor (*gha*-vö-nö) *n* governatore *m*

gown (ghaun) *n* vestito *m*

grace (ghreiss) *n* grazia *f*

graceful (*ghreiss*-föl) *adj* grazioso

grade (ghreid) *n* classe *f*; *v* classificare

gradient (*ghrei*-di-önt) *n* pendenza *f*

gradual (*ghræ*-dʒu-öl) *adj* graduale

graduate (*ghræ*-dʒu-eit) *v* diplomarsi

grain (ghrein) *n* granello *m*, frumento *m*, grano *m*

gram (ghræm) *n* grammo *m*

grammar (*ghræ*-mö) *n* grammatica *f*

grammatical (ghrö-*mæ*-ti-köl) *adj* grammaticale

grand (ghrænd) *adj* imponente

grandchild (*ghræn*-tʃaild) *n* (pl -children) *n* nipote *m/f*

granddad (*ghræn*-dæd) *n* nonno *m*

granddaughter (*ghræn*-doo-tö) *n* nipote *f*

grandfather (*ghræn*-faa-ðö) *n* nonno *m*

grandmother (*ghræn*-ma-ðö) *n* nonna *f*

grandparents (*ghræn*-pê°-röntss) *pl* nonni *mpl*

grandson (*ghræn*-ssan) *n* nipote *m*

granite (*ghræ*-nit) *n* granito *m*

grant (ghraant) *v* accordare; *concedere; *n* sussidio *m*; borsa di studio

grape (ghreip) *n* acino d'uva; **grapes** uva *f*

grapefruit (*ghreip*-fruut) *n* pompelmo *m*

grapes (ghreipss) *pl* uva *f*

graph (ghræf) *n* grafico *m*

graphic (*ghræ*-fik) *adj* grafico

grasp (ghraassp) *v* afferrare; *n* stretta *f*

grass (ghraass) *n* erba *f*

grasshopper (*ghraass*-ho-pö) *n* cavalletta *f*

grate (ghreit) *n* grata *f*; *v* grattugiare

grateful (*ghreit*-föl) *adj* grato, riconoscente

grater (*ghrei*-tö) *n* grattugia *f*

gratis (*ghræ*-tiss) *adj* gratis

gratitude (*ghræ*-ti-t'uud) *n* gratitudine *f*

gratuity (ghrö-*t'uu*-ö-ti) *n* mancia *f*

grave (ghreiv) *n* tomba *f*; *adj* grave

gravel (*ghræ*-völ) *n* ghiaia *f*

gravestone (*ghreiv*-sstoun) *n* lapide *f*

graveyard (*ghreiv*-¹aad) *n* cimitero *m*

gravity (*ghræ*-vö-ti) *n* gravità *f*; serietà *f*

gravy (*ghrei*-vi) *n* sugo dell'arrosto

graze (ghreis) *v* pascolare; *n* escoriazione *f*

grease (ghriiss) *n* grasso *m*; *v* lubrificare

greasy (*ghrii*-ssi) *adj* grasso, unto

great (ghreit) *adj* grande; **Great Britain** Gran Bretagna

Greece (ghriiss) Grecia *f*

greed (ghriid) *n* cupidigia *f*

greedy (*ghrii*-di) *adj* avido; goloso

Greek (ghriik) *adj* greco

green (ghriin) *adj* verde; **~ card** carta verde

greengrocer (*ghriin*-ghrou-ssö) *n* fruttivendolo *m*, -a *f*

greenhouse (*ghriin*-hauss) *n* serra *f*

greens (ghriins) *pl* verdura *f*

greet (ghriit) *v* salutare

greeting (*ghrii*-ting) *n* saluto *m*

grey (ghrei) *adj* grigio

greyhound (*ghrei*-haund) *n* levriere *m*

grief (ghriif) *n* cordoglio *m*; afflizione *f*, dolore *m*

grieve (ghriiv) *v* *affliggersi

grill (ghril) *n* griglia *f*; *v* cucinare alla griglia

grillroom (*ghril*-ruum) *n* rosticceria *f*

grim (ghrim) *adj* cupo; accanito

grin (ghrin) *v* fare un sorrisone; *n* smorfia *f*

*grind (ghraind) *v* macinare; tritare

grip (ghrip) *v* stringere; *n* presa *f*, stretta *f*; *Am* valigetta *f*

groan (ghroun) *v* gemere

grocer (*ghrou*-ssö) *n* droghiere *m*; **grocer's** drogheria *f*

groceries (*ghrou*-ssö-ris) *pl* alimentari *mpl*

grocery (*ghrou*-ssö-ri) *m* drogheria *f*

groin (ghroin) *n* inguine *m*

groom (ghruum) *n* sposo *m*; stalliere *m*; *v* strigliare; preparare; **well groomed** ben curato

groove (ghruuv) *n* solco *m*

gross[1] (ghrouss) *n* (pl ~) grossa *f*

gross[2] (ghrouss) *adj* rozzo; lordo

grotto (*ghro*-tou) *n* (pl ~es, ~s) grotta *f*

ground[1] (ghraund) *n* fondo *m*, terra *f*;

~ **floor** pianterreno *m*; **grounds** terreno *m*

ground² (ghraund) *v* (p, pp grind)

group (ghruup) *n* gruppo *m*

grove (ghrouv) *n* boschetto *m*

***grow** (ghrou) *v* *crescere; coltivare; diventare

growl (ghraul) *v* ringhiare

grown-up (*ghroun*-ap) *adj* adulto; *n* adulto *m*, -a *f*

growth (ghrouθ) *n* crescita *f*; tumore *m*

grudge (ghradʒ) *v* invidiare

grumble (*ghram*-böl) *v* brontolare

guarantee (ghæ-rön-*tii*) *n* garanzia *f*; cauzione *f*; *v* garantire

guard (ghaad) *n* guardiano *m*, -a *f*; *v* custodire

guardian (*ghaa*-di-ön) *n* tutore *m*, tutrice *f*

guess (ghêss) *v* indovinare; credere; *n* congettura *f*

guest (ghêsst) *n* ospite *m*; ~ **room** camera degli ospiti

guesthouse (*ghêsst*-hauss) *n* pensione *f*

guide (ghaid) *n* guida *f*; *v* guidare; ~ **dog** cane guida

guidebook (*ghaid*-buk) *n* guida *f*

guidelines (*ghaid*-lains) *pl* norme *fpl*

guilt (ghilt) *n* colpa *f*

guilty (*ghil*-ti) *adj* colpevole

guinea pig (*ghi*-ni-pigh) *n* porcellino d'India

guitar (ghi-*taa*) *n* chitarra *f*

gulf (ghalf) *n* golfo *m*

gull (ghal) *n* gabbiano *m*

gum (gham) *n* gengiva *f*; gomma *f*; colla *f*

gun (ghan) *n* fucile *m*; rivoltella *f*; cannone *m*

gunpowder (*ghan*-pau-dö) *n* polvere da sparo

gust (ghasst) *n* raffica *f*

gusty (*gha*-ssti) *adj* ventoso

gut (ghat) *n* intestino *m*; **guts** coraggio *m*

gutter (*gha*-tö) *n* fogna *f*

guy (ghai) *n* tipo *m*

gym (dʒim) *n* palestra *f*; ginnastica *f*

gymnasium (dʒim-*nei*-si-öm) *n* (pl ~s, -sia) palestra *f*

gymnast (*dʒim*-næsst) *n* ginnasta *m/f*

gymnastics (dʒim-*næ*-sstikss) *pl* ginnastica *f*

gynaecologist (ghai-nö-*ko*-lö-dʒisst) *n* ginecologo *m*, -a *f*

H

habit (*hæ*-bit) *n* abitudine *f*

habitable (*hæ*-bi-tö-böl) *adj* abitabile

habitual (hö-*bi*-tʃu-öl) *adj* consueto

had (hæd) *v* (p, pp have)

haddock (*hæ*-dök) *n* (pl ~) merluzzo affumicato

h(a)emorrhage (*hê*-mö-ridʒ) *n* emorragia *f*

h(a)emorrhoids (*hê*-mö-roids) *pl*

emorroidi *fpl*

hail (heil) *n* grandine *f*

hair (hê°) *n* capello *m*; capelli *mpl*; pelo *m*; ~ **cream** brillantina *f*; ~ **gel** gel *m*; ~ **piece** toupet *m*; ~ **rollers** bigodini *mpl*; ~ **spray** lacca per capelli

hairbrush (*hê°*-braʃ) *n* spazzola per capelli

haircut (*hê⁰*-kat) *n* taglio di capelli

hairdo (*hê⁰*-duu) *n* pettinatura *f*, acconciatura *f*

hairdresser (*hê⁰*-drê-ssö) *n* parrucchiere *m*, -a *f*

hairdrier, hairdryer (*hê⁰*-drai-ö) *n* asciugacapelli *m*

hairgrip (*hê⁰*-ghrip) *n* molletta *f*

hairpin (*hê⁰*-pin) *n* forcina *f*

hairy (*hê⁰*-ri) *adj* peloso

half¹ (haaf) *adj* mezzo; *adv* a metà; ~ **time** intervallo *m*

half² (haaf) *n* (pl halves) metà *f*

halfway (haaf-*u*ei) *adv* a metà strada

halibut (*hæ*-li-böt) *n* (pl ~) ippoglosso *m*

hall (hool) *n* sala *f*, salone *m*; atrio *m*

halt (hoolt) *v* fermarsi

halve (haav) *v* dimezzare

ham (hæm) *n* prosciutto *m*

hamlet (*hæm*-löt) *n* frazione *f*, paese *m*

hammer (*hæ*-mö) *n* martello *m*

hammock (*hæ*-mök) *n* amaca *f*

hamper (*hæm*-pö) *n* paniere *m*

hand (hænd) *n* mano *f*; *v* *porgere; ~ **cream** crema per le mani

handbag (*hænd*-bægh) *n* borsetta *f*

handbook (*hænd*-buk) *n* manuale *m*

handbrake (*hænd*-breik) *n* freno a mano

handcuffs (*hænd*-kafss) *pl* manette *fpl*

handful (*hænd*-ful) *n* manciata *f*

handicap (*hæn*-di-kæp) *n* handicap *m*; *v* ostacolare; **handicapped** *adj* Am invalido

handicraft (*hæn*-di-kraaft) *n* lavoro manuale; artigianato *m*

handkerchief (*hæng*-kö-tʃif) *n* fazzoletto *m*

handle (*hæn*-döl) *n* manico *m*, impugnatura *f*; *v* maneggiare; trattare

hand-made (hænd-*meid*) *adj* fatto a

mano

handshake (*hænd*-ʃeik) *n* stretta di mano

handsome (*hæn*-ssöm) *adj* bello

handwork (*hænd*-*u*öök) *n* lavoro fatto a mano

handwriting (*hænd*-rai-ting) *n* scrittura *f*

handy (*hæn*-di) *adj* maneggevole

***hang** (hæng) *v* *appendere; pendere

hanger (*hæng*-ö) *n* gruccia *f*

hangover (*hæng*-ou-vö) *n* postumi di una sbronza

happen (*hæ*-pön) *v* *accadere, *succedere

happening (*hæ*-pö-ning) *n* evento *m*

happiness (*hæ*-pi-nöss) *n* felicità *f*

happy (*hæ*-pi) *adj* contento, felice

harbo(u)r (*haa*-bö) *n* porto *m*

hard (haad) *adj* duro; difficile; ~ **disk** disco fisso, hard disk

hardly appena

hardware (haad-*u*ê⁰) *n* ferramenta *fpl*; ~ **store** negozio di ferramenta

hare (hê⁰) *n* lepre *f*

harm (haam) *n* danno *m*; male *m*; *v* *nuocere

harmful (*haam*-föl) *adj* dannoso, nocivo

harmless (*haam*-löss) *adj* innocuo

harmony (*haa*-mö-ni) *n* armonia *f*

harp (haap) *n* arpa *f*

harpsichord (*haap*-ssi-kood) *n* clavicembalo *m*

harsh (haaʃ) *adj* aspro; severo; crudele

harvest (*haa*-visst) *n* raccolto *m*

has (hæs) *v* (pr have)

haste (heisst) *n* premura *f*, fretta *f*

hasten (*hei*-ssön) *v* affrettarsi

hasty (*hei*-ssti) *adj* frettoloso

hat (hæt) *n* cappello *m*; ~ **rack** attaccapanni *m*

hatch (hætʃ) *n* botola *f*

hate (heit) *v* detestare; odiare; *n* odio *m*

hatred (*hei*-trid) *n* odio *m*

haughty (*hoo*-ti) *adj* altezzoso

haul (hool) *v* trainare

*have (hæv) *v* *avere; *fare; ~ **to** *dovere

hawk (hook) *n* falco *m*

hay (hei) *n* fieno *m*; ~ **fever** febbre da fieno

hazard (*hæ*-söd) *n* rischio *m*

haze (heis) *n* foschia *f*

hazelnut (*hei*-söl-nat) *n* nocciola *f*

hazy (*hei*-si) *adj* fosco; nebbioso

he (hii) *pron* egli, lui

head (hêd) *n* testa *f*; capo *m*; *v* *dirigere; ~ **of state** capo di stato; ~ **teacher** direttore, -trice della scuola, preside *m/f*; ~ **waiter** capocameriere *m*, -a *f*

headache (*hê*-deik) *n* mal di testa

heading (*hê*-ding) *n* titolo *m*

headlamp (*hêd*-læmp) *n* fanale *m*

headland (*hêd*-lönd) *n* promontorio *m*

headlight (*hêd*-lait) *n* faro *m*

headline (*hêd*-lain) *n* titolo *m*

headmaster (hêd-*maa*-sstö) *n* direttore, -trice della scuola; preside *m/f*

headquarters (hêd-k"oo-tös) *pl* quartier generale; sede *f*

headstrong (*hêd*-sstrong) *adj* testardo

heal (hiil) *v* guarire

health (hêlθ) *n* salute *f*; ~ **centre** poliambulatorio *m*; ~ **certificate** certificato di sanità

healthy (*hêl*-θi) *adj* sano

heap (hiip) *n* cumulo *m*, mucchio *m*

*hear (hi°) *v* *udire

hearing (*hi°*-ring) *n* udito *m*

heart (haat) *n* cuore *m*; nocciolo *m*; **by** ~ a memoria; ~ **attack** attacco cardiaco

heartburn (*haat*-böön) *n* bruciore di stomaco

heartless (*haat*-löss) *adj* spietato

hearty (*haa*-ti) *adj* cordiale

heat (hiit) *n* calore *m*, caldo *m*; *v* scaldare

heater (*hii*-tö) *n* stufa elettrica; **immersion** ~ bollitore ad immersione

heath (hiiθ) *n* brughiera *f*

heathen (*hii*-ðön) *n* pagano *m*

heather (*hê*-ðö) *n* erica *f*

heating (*hii*-ting) *n* riscaldamento *m*; ~ **pad** cuscino elettrico

heaven (*hê*-vön) *n* cielo *m*

heavy (*hê*-vi) *adj* pesante

Hebrew (*hii*-bruu) *n* ebraico *m*

hedge (hêdʒ) *n* siepe *f*

hedgehog (*hêdʒ*-hogh) *n* riccio *m*

heel (hiil) *n* tallone *m*; tacco *m*

height (hait) *n* altezza *f*; colmo *m*, culmine *m*

heir (êö), **heiress** *n* erede *m/f*

helicopter (*he*-li-cop-tö) *n* elicottero *m*

hell (hêl) *n* inferno *m*

hello (hê-*lou*) ciao; buongiorno; buonasera; pronto; **say** ~ **to** salutare

helm (hêlm) *n* timone *m*

helmet (*hêl*-mit) *n* casco *m*

helmsman (*hêlms*-mön) *n* timoniere *m*

help (hêlp) *v* aiutare; *n* aiuto *m*

helper (*hêl*-pö) *n* aiutante *m/f*

helpful (*hêlp*-föl) *adj* servizievole

helping (*hêl*-ping) *n* porzione *f*

hem (hêm) *n* orlo *m*

hemp (hêmp) *n* canapa *f*

hen (hên) *n* gallina *f*

her (höö) *pron* la, le; *adj* suo

herb (hööb) *n* erba aromatica

herd (hööd) *n* gregge *m*

here (hi°) *adv* qui; ~ **you are** ecco

hereditary (hi-*rê*-di-tö-ri) *adj*

eredítario
hernia (*höö*-ni-ö) *n* ernia *f*
hero (*hi*ᵒ-rou) *n* (pl ~es) eroe *m*
heron (*hê*-rön) *n* airone *m*
herring (*hê*-ring) *n* (pl ~, ~s) aringa *f*
herself (höö-*ssêlf*) *pron* si; lei stessa
hesitate (*hê*-si-teit) *v* esitare
heterosexual (hê-tö-rö-*ssêk*-ʃu-öl) *adj* eterosessuale
hiccup (*hi*-kap) *n* singhiozzo *m*
hide (haid) *n* pelle *f*
***hide** (haid) *v* *nascondere; celare
hideous (*hi*-di-öss) *adj* orrendo
hierarchy (*hai*ᵒ-raa-ki) *n* gerarchia *f*
high (hai) *adj* alto
highway (*hai*-ᵘei) *n* strada maestra *f*; *Am* autostrada *f*, superstrada *f*
hijack (*hai*-dʒæk) *v* dirottare
hijacker (*hai*-dʒæ-kö) *n* dirottatore *m*
hike (haik) *v* camminare
hill (hil) *n* collina *f*
hillside (*hil*-ssaid) *n* pendio *m*
hilltop (*hil*-top) *n* vetta *f*
hilly (*hi*-li) *adj* collinoso
him (him) *pron* lo, gli
himself (him-*ssêlf*) *pron* si; lui stesso
hinder (*hin*-dö) *v* ostacolare
hinge (hindʒ) *n* cardine *m*
hint (hint) *n* accenno *m*; consiglio *m*; allusione *f*; punta *f*
hip (hip) *n* fianco *m*
hire (hai ᵒ) *v* noleggiare; **for ~** a nolo; **~ purchase** vendita a rate
his (his) *adj* suo
historian (hi-*sstoo*-ri-ön) *n* storico *m*, -a *f*
historic (hi-*ssto*-rik) *adj* storico
historical (hi-*ssto*-ri-köl) *adj* storico
history (*hi*-sstö-ri) *n* storia *f*
hit¹ (hit) *n* successo *m*
***hit**² (hit) *v* colpire; andare a sbattere contro
hitchhike (*hitʃ*-haik) *v* *fare l'autostop

hitchhiker (*hitʃ*-hai-kö) *n* autostoppista *m/f*
hoarse (hooss) *adj* roco, rauco
hobby (*ho*-bi) *n* passatempo *m*, hobby *m*
hobbyhorse (*ho*-bi-hooss) *n* pallino *m*
hockey (*ho*-ki) *n* hockey *m*
hoist (hoisst) *v* issare
hold (hould) *n* stiva *f*
***hold** (hould) *v* *tenere; *contenere; **~ on** restare in linea; reggersi; **~ up** *sostenere
hold-up (*houl*-dap) *n* rapina *f*
hole (houl) *n* buca *f*, buco *m*
holiday (*ho*-lö-di) *n* ferie *fpl*; giorno festivo; **~ camp** colonia di vacanze; **~ resort** luogo di villeggiatura; **on ~** in ferie
Holland (*ho*-lönd) Olanda *f*
hollow (*ho*-lou) *adj* vuoto; cavo
holy (*hou*-li) *adj* santo
homage (*ho*-midʒ) *n* omaggio *m*
home (houm) *n* casa *f*; ospizio *m*, abitazione *f*; *adv* a casa; **at ~** in casa
home-made (houm-*meid*) *adj* fatto in casa
homesickness (*houm*-ssik-nöss) *n* nostalgia di casa
homework (*houm*-ᵘöök) *n* compiti per casa
homosexual (hou-mö-*ssêk*-ʃu-öl) *adj* omosessuale
honest (*o*-nisst) *adj* onesto; sincero
honesty (*o*-ni-ssti) *n* onestà *f*
honey (*ha*-ni) *n* miele *m*
honeymoon (*ha*-ni-muun) *n* luna di miele
honk (hangk) *vAm* suonare il clacson
hono(u)r (*o*-nö) *n* onore *m*; *v* onorare, *rendere omaggio
hono(u)rable (*o*-nö-rö-böl) *adj* onorevole; onesto
hood (hud) *n* cappuccio *m*; *Am*

cofano *m*

hoof (huuf) *n* zoccolo *m*

hook (huk) *n* uncino *m*

hoot (huut) *v* suonare il clacson

hooter (*huu*-tö) *n* clacson *m*

hoover (*huu*-vö) *v* passare l'aspirapolvere

hop[1] (hop) *v* saltellare; *n* saltello *m*

hop[2] (hop) *n* luppolo *m*

hope (houp) *n* speranza *f*; *v* sperare

hopeful (*houp*-föl) *adj* speranzoso

hopeless (*houp*-löss) *adj* disperato

horizon (hö-*rai*-sön) *n* orizzonte *m*

horizontal (ho-ri-*son*-töl) *adj* orizzontale

horn (hoon) *n* corno *m*

horrible (*ho*-ri-böl) *adj* orribile; atroce; spaventoso

horror (*ho*-rö) *n* orrore *m*

hors d'œuvre (oo-*döövr*) *n* antipasto *m*

horse (hooss) *n* cavallo *m*

horseman (*hooss*-mön) *n* (pl -men) cavallerizzo *m*

horsepower (*hooss*-pau⁶) *n* cavallo vapore

horserace (*hooss*-reiss) *n* corsa di cavalli

horseradish (*hooss*-ræ-diʃ) *n* rafano *m*

horseshoe (*hooss*-ʃuu) *n* ferro di cavallo

horticulture (*hoo*-ti-kal-tʃö) *n* orticoltura *m*

hospitable (ho-*sspi*-tö-böl) *adj* ospitale

hospital (ho-*sspi*-töl) *n* ospedale *m*

hospitality (ho-sspi-*tæ*-lö-ti) *n* ospitalità *f*

host (housst) *n* ospite *m*

hostage (*ho*-sstidʒ) *n* ostaggio *m*

hostel (*ho*-sstöl) *n* ostello *m*

hostess (*hou*-sstiss) *n* ospite *f*

hostile (*ho*-sstail) *adj* ostile

hot (hot) *adj* caldo

hotel (hou-*têl*) *n* albergo *m*

hot-tempered (hot-*têm*-pöd) *adj* irascibile

hour (au⁶) *n* ora *f*

hourly (*au⁶*-li) *adj* ogni ora

house (hauss) *n* casa *f*; abitazione *f*; immobile *m*; ~ **agent** agente immobiliare; ~ **block** *Am* isolato *m*; **public** ~ caffè *m*

household (*hauss*-hould) *n* ménage *m*

housekeeper (*hauss*-kii-pö) *n* governante *f*

housekeeping (*hauss*-kii-ping) *n* faccende domestiche, faccende di casa

housemaid (*hauss*-meid) *n* domestica *f*

housewife (*hauss*-ᵘaif) *n* casalinga *f*

housework (*hauss*-ᵘöök) *n* lavori di casa

how (hau) *adv* come; che; ~ **many** quanto; ~ **much** quanto

however (hau-ê-vö) *conj* tuttavia, eppure; comunque

hug (hagh) *v* abbracciare; *n* abbraccio *m*

huge (hⁱuudʒ) *adj* immenso, enorme

hum (ham) *v* canticchiare

human (*hⁱuu*-mön) *adj* umano; ~ **being** essere umano

humanity (hⁱu-*mæ*-nö-ti) *n* umanità *f*

humble (*ham*-böl) *adj* umile

humid (*hⁱuu*-mid) *adj* umido

humidity (hⁱu-*mi*-dö-ti) *n* umidità *f*

humorous (*hⁱuu*-mö-röss) *adj* comico, spiritoso

humo(u)r (*hⁱuu*-mö) *n* umorismo *m*

hundred (*han*-dröd) *n* cento

Hungarian (hang-*ghê⁶*-ri-ön) *adj* ungherese

Hungary (*hang*-ghö-ri) Ungheria *f*

hunger (*hang*-ghö) *n* fame *f*

hungry (*hang*-ghri) *adj* affamato

hunt (hant) *v* cacciare; *n* caccia *f*; ~ **for** cercare

hunter (*han*-tö) *n* cacciatore *m*, -trice *f*

hurricane (*ha*-ri-kön) *n* uragano *m*

hurry (*ha*-ri) *v* spicciarsi, affrettarsi; *n* fretta *f*; **in a** ~ in fretta

*hurt (hööt) *v* *far male a, ferire; far male; *offendere

hurtful (*hööt*-föl) *adj* nocivo

husband (*has*-bönd) *n* marito *m*

hut (hat) *n* capanna *f*

hydrogen (*hai*-drö-dʒön) *n* idrogeno *m*

hygiene (*hai*-dʒiin) *n* igiene *f*

hygienic (hai-*dʒii*-nik) *adj* igienico

hymn (him) *n* inno *m*

hyphen (*hai*-fön) *n* lineetta *f*

hypocrisy (hi-*po*-krö-ssi) *n* ipocrisia *f*

hypocrite (*hi*-pö-krit) *n* ipocrita *m*

hypocritical (hi-pö-*kri*-ti-köl) *adj* ipocrita

hysterical (hi-*sstê*-ri-köl) *adj* isterico

I

I (ai) *pron* io

ice (aiss) *n* ghiaccio *m*; ~ **bag** borsa del ghiaccio; ~ **cream** gelato *m*

Iceland (*aiss*-lönd) Islanda *f*

Icelander (*aiss*-lön-dö) *n* islandese *m/f*

Icelandic (aiss-*læn*-dik) *adj* islandese

icon (*ai*-kon) *n* icona *f*

idea (ai-*di^o*) *n* idea *f*; trovata *f*, pensiero *m*

ideal (ai-*di^o*l) *adj* ideale; *n* ideale *m*

identical (ai-*dên*-ti-köl) *adj* identico

identification (ai-dên-ti-fi-*kei*-ʃön) *n* identificazione *f*

identify (ai-*dên*-ti-fai) *v* identificare

identity (ai-*dên*-tö-ti) *n* identità *f*; ~ **card** carta d'identità

idiomatic (i-di-ö-*mæ*-tik) *adj* idiomatico

idiot (*i*-di-öt) *n* idiota *m*

idiotic (i-di-*o*-tik) *adj* idiota

idle (*ai*-döl) *adj* ozioso; pigro; vano

idol (*ai*-döl) *n* idolo *m*

if (if) *conj* se

ignition (igh-*ni*-ʃön) *n* accensione *f*

ignorant (*igh*-nö-rönt) *adj* ignorante; ignaro

ignore (igh-*noo*) *v* ignorare

ill (il) *adj* ammalato; cattivo; malvagio

illegal (i-*lii*-ghöl) *adj* illegale

illegible (i-*lê*-dʒö-böl) *adj* illeggibile

illiterate (i-*li*-tö-röt) *n* analfabeta *m/f*

illness (*il*-nöss) *n* malattia *f*

illuminate (i-*luu*-mi-neit) *v* illuminare

illumination (i-luu-mi-*nei*-ʃön) *n* illuminazione *f*

illusion (i-*luu*-ʒön) *n* illusione *f*

illustrate (*i*-lö-sstreit) *v* illustrare

illustration (i-lö-*sstrei*-ʃön) *n* illustrazione *f*

image (*i*-midʒ) *n* immagine *f*

imaginary (i-*mæ*-dʒi-nö-ri) *adj* immaginario

imagination (i-mæ-dʒi-*nei*-ʃön) *n* immaginazione *f*

imagine (i-*mæ*-dʒin) *v* immaginare; figurarsi

imitate (*i*-mi-teit) *v* imitare

imitation (i-mi-*tei*-ʃön) *n* imitazione *f*

immediate (i-*mii*-d'öt) *adj* immediato

immediately (i-*mii*-d'öt-li) *adv* subito, immediatamente

immense (i-*mênss*) *adj* smisurato,

enorme, immenso

immigrant (*i*-mi-ghrönt) *n* immigrante m/f

immigrate (*i*-mi-ghreit) *v* immigrare

immigration (i-mi-*ghrei*-∫ön) *n* immigrazione f

immunity (i-*m'uu*-nö-ti) *n* immunità f

immunize (i-m'u-nais) *v* immunizzare

impartial (im-*paa*-∫öl) *adj* imparziale

impatient (im-*pei*-∫önt) *adj* impaziente

impede (im-*piid*) *v* impedire

impediment (im-*pê*-di-mönt) *n* impedimento m

imperfect (im-*pöö*-fikt) *adj* imperfetto

imperial (im-*pi⁰*-ri-öl) *adj* imperiale

impersonal (im-*pöö*-ssö-nöl) *adj* impersonale

impertinence (im-*pöö*-ti-nönss) *n* impertinenza f

impertinent (im-*pöö*-ti-nönt) *adj* impertinente, insolente

implement¹ (*im*-pli-mönt) *n* utensile m, strumento m

implement² (*im*-pli-mênt) *v* effettuare

imply (im-*plai*) *v* implicare; comportare

impolite (im-pö-*lait*) *adj* scortese

import¹ (im-*poot*) *v* importare

import² (*im*-poot) *n* importazione f; ~ **duty** dazio m

importance (im-*poo*-tönss) *n* rilievo m, importanza f

important (im-*poo*-tönt) *adj* rilevante, importante

importer (im-*poo*-tö) *n* importatore m, -trice f

imposing (im-*pou*-sing) *adj* imponente

impossible (im-*po*-ssö-böl) *adj* impossibile

impotence (*im*-pö-tönss) *n* impotenza f

impotent (*im*-pö-tönt) *adj* impotente

impress (im-*prêss*) *v* impressionare

impression (im-*prê*-∫ön) *n* impressione f

impressive (im-*prê*-ssiv) *adj* impressionante

imprison (im-*pri*-sön) *v* imprigionare

imprisonment (im-*pri*-sön-mönt) *n* reclusione f

improbable (im-*pro*-bö-böl) *adj* improbabile

improper (im-*pro*-pö) *adj* inadeguato

improve (im-*pruuv*) *v* migliorare

improvement (im-*pruuv*-mönt) *n* miglioramento m

improvise (*im*-prö-vais) *v* improvvisare

impulse (*im*-palss) *n* impulso m; stimolo m

impulsive (im-*pal*-ssiv) *adj* impulsivo

in (in) *prep* in; entro, su; *adv* dentro

inaccessible (i-næk-*ssê*-ssö-böl) *adj* inaccessibile

inaccurate (i-*næ*-k'u-röt) *adj* inesatto

inadequate (i-*næ*-di-kᵘöt) *adj* inadeguato

incapable (ing-*kei*-pö-böl) *adj* incapace

incense (*in*-ssênss) *n* incenso m

inch (*int*∫) *n* pollice m (2,54 cm)

incident (*in*-ssi-dönt) *n* avvenimento m

incidental (in-ssi-*dên*-töl) *adj* incidentale

incite (in-*ssait*) *v* incitare

inclination (ing-kli-*nei*-∫ön) *n* inclinazione f

incline (ing-*klain*) *n* pendio m

inclined (ing-*klaind*) *adj* propenso, tendente; ***be ~ to** *v* *tendere a

include (ing-*kluud*) *v* *comprendere, *includere

inclusive (ing-*kluu*-ssiv) *adj* compreso

income (*ing*-köm) *n* reddito m; ~ **tax** imposta sul reddito

incompetent (ing-*kom*-pö-tönt) *adj*
incompetente

incomplete (in-köm-*pliit*) *adj*
incompleto

inconceivable (ing-kön-*ssii*-vö-böl)
adj inconcepibile

inconspicuous (ing-kön-*sspi*-kʲu-öss)
adj che non dà nell'occhio

inconvenience (ing-kön-*vii*-nʲönss) *n*
seccatura *f*; inconveniente *m*

inconvenient (ing-kön-*vii*-nʲönt) *adj*
scomodo; fastidioso

incorrect (ing-kö-*rêkt*) *adj* inesatto,
scorretto

increase¹ (ing-*kriiss*) *v* aumentare;
*salire, *accrescere

increase² (*ing*-kriiss) *n* aumento *m*;
incremento *m*

incredible (ing-*krê*-dö-böl) *adj*
incredibile

incurable (ing-*kʲuᵒ*-rö-böl) *adj*
incurabile

indecent (in-*dii*-ssönt) *adj* indecente

indeed (in-*diid*) *adv* effettivamente

indefinite (in-*dê*-fi-nit) *adj* indefinito

indemnity (in-*dêm*-nö-ti) *n*
risarcimento *m*, indennità *f*

independence (in-di-*pên*-dönss) *n*
indipendenza *f*

independent (in-di-*pên*-dönt) *adj*
indipendente; autonomo

index (*in*-dêkss) *n* indice *m*; **~ finger**
indice *m*

India (*in*-di-ö) India *f*

Indian (*in*-di-ön) *adj* indiano

indicate (*in*-di-keit) *v* segnalare,
indicare

indication (in-di-*kei*-ʃön) *n* indizio *m*,
indicazione *f*

indicator (*in*-di-kei-tö) *n* freccia *f*

indifferent (in-di-*di*-fö-rönt) *adj*
indifferente

indigestion (in-di-*dʒêss*-tʃön) *n*
indigestione *f*

indignation (in-digh-*nei*-ʃön) *n*
indignazione *f*

indirect (in-di-*rêkt*) *adj* indiretto

individual (in-di-*vi*-dʒu-öl) *adj*
singolo, individuale; *n* singolo *m*,
individuo *m*

Indonesia (in-dö-*nii*-si-ö) Indonesia *f*

Indonesian (in-dö-*nii*-si-ön) *adj*
indonesiano

indoor (*in*-doo) *adj* in casa

indoors (in-*doos*) *adv* in casa

indulge (in-*daldʒ*) *v* cedere

industrial (in-*da*-sstri-öl) *adj*
industriale; **~ area** zona industriale

industrious (in-*da*-sstri-öss) *adj*
laborioso

industry (*in*-dö-sstri) *n* industria *f*

inedible (i-*nê*-di-böl) *adj*
immangiabile

inefficient (i-ni-*fi*-ʃönt) *adj* inefficace

inevitable (i-*nê*-vi-tö-böl) *adj*
inevitabile

inexpensive (i-nik-*sspên*-ssiv) *adj*
economico

inexperienced (i-nik-*sspiᵒ*-ri-önsst)
adj inesperto

infant (*in*-fönt) *n* neonato *m*

infantry (*in*-fön-tri) *n* fanteria *f*

infect (in-*fêkt*) *v* infettare, contagiare

infection (in-*fêk*-ʃön) *n* infezione *f*

infectious (in-*fêk*-ʃöss) *adj* contagioso

infer (in-*föö*) *v* *dedurre

inferior (in-*fiᵒ*-ri-ö) *adj* inferiore

infinite (*in*-fi-nöt) *adj* infinito

infinitive (in-*fi*-ni-tiv) *n* infinito *m*

inflammable (in-*flæ*-mö-böl) *adj*
infiammabile

inflammation (in-flö-*mei*-ʃön) *n*
infiammazione *f*

inflatable (in-*flei*-tö-böl) *adj*
gonfiabile

inflate (in-*fleit*) *v* gonfiare

inflation (in-*flei*-ʃön) *n* inflazione *f*

inflict (in-*flikt*): **~ on** *v* infliggere a;

procurare a

influence (*in*-flu-önss) *n* influenza *f*; *v* influire

influential (in-flu-*ên*-ʃöl) *adj* influente

influenza (in-flu-*ên*-sö) *n* influenza *f*

inform (in-*foom*) *v* informare; *mettere al corrente, comunicare

informal (in-*foo*-möl) *adj* informale

information (in-fö-*mei*-ʃön) *n* informazione *f*; comunicazione *f*; ~ **centre** ufficio informazioni

infra-red (in-frö-*rêd*) *adj* infrarosso

infrequent (in-*frii*-kʷönt) *adj* infrequente

ingredient (ing-*ghrii*-di-önt) *n* ingrediente *m*

inhabit (in-*hæ*-bit) *v* abitare

inhabitable (in-*hæ*-bi-tö-böl) *adj* abitabile

inhabitant (in-*hæ*-bi-tönt) *n* abitante *m*

inhale (in-*heil*) *v* aspirare

inherit (in-*hê*-rit) *v* ereditare

inheritance (in-*hê*-ri-tönss) *n* eredità *f*

inhibit (in-*hi*-bit) *v* inibire

initial (i-*ni*-ʃöl) *adj* iniziale; *n* iniziale *f*; *v* *siglare

initiate (i-*ni*-ʃi-eit) *v* avviare

initiative (i-*ni*-ʃö-tiv) *n* iniziativa *f*

inject (in-d**ʒ**êkt) *v* iniettare

injection (in-d**ʒ**ê-ʃön) *n* iniezione *f*

injure (*in*-d**ʒ**ö) *v* ferire; *offendere

injury (*in*-d**ʒ**ö-ri) *n* ferita *f*; lesione *f*

injustice (in-d**ʒ***a*-sstiss) *n* ingiustizia *f*

ink (ingk) *n* inchiostro *m*

inlet (*in*-lêt) *n* insenatura *f*

inn (in) *n* locanda *f*

inner (*i*-nö) *adj* interno; ~ **tube** camera d'aria

innocence (*i*-nö-ssönss) *n* innocenza *f*

innocent (*i*-nö-ssönt) *adj* innocente

inoculate (i-*no*-kʲu-leit) *v* vaccinare

inoculation (i-no-kʲu-*lei*-ʃön) *n* vaccinazione *f*

inquire (ing-kʷ*aiᵒ*) *v* informarsi; indagare

inquiry (ing-kʷ*aiᵒ*-ri) *n* domanda *f*; indagine *f*; inchiesta *f*; ~ **office** ufficio informazioni

inquisitive (ing-kʷ*i*-sö-tiv) *adj* curioso

insane (in-*ssein*) *adj* pazzo

inscription (in-*sskrip*-ʃön) *n* iscrizione *f*

insect (*in*-ssêkt) *n* insetto *m*; ~ **repellent** insettifugo *m*

insecticide (in-*ssêk*-ti-ssaid) *n* insetticida *m*

insensitive (in-*ssên*-ssö-tiv) *adj* insensibile

insert (in-*ssööt*) *v* inserire

inside (in-*ssaid*) *n* interno *m*; *adj* interno; *adv* dentro; *prep* dentro, dentro a; ~ **out** alla rovescia; **insides** interiora *fpl*

insight (*in*-ssait) *n* comprensione *f*

insignificant (in-ssigh-*ni*-fi-könt) *adj* insignificante; irrilevante; futile

insist (in-*ssisst*) *v* insistere; persistere

insolence (*in*-ssö-lönss) *n* insolenza *f*

insolent (*in*-ssö-lönt) *adj* impertinente, insolente

insomnia (in-*ssom*-ni-ö) *n* insonnia *f*

inspect (in-*sspêkt*) *v* ispezionare

inspection (in-*sspêk*-ʃön) *n* ispezione *f*; controllo *m*

inspector (in-*sspêk*-tö) *n* ispettore *m*, -trice *f*; controllore *m*

inspire (in-*sspaiᵒ*) *v* ispirare

install (in-*sstool*) *v* installare

installation (in-sstö-*lei*-ʃön) *n* installazione *f*

instal(l)ment (in-*sstool*-mönt) *n* rata *f*

instance (*in*-sstönss) *n* esempio *m*; caso *m*; **for** ~ per esempio

instant (*in*-sstönt) *n* istante *m*

instantly (*in*-sstönt-li) *adv* all'istante, subito, immediatamente

instead: ~ **of** (in-*sstêd* ov) invece di

instinct (*in*-sstingkt) *n* istinto *m*

institute (*in*-ssti-t'uut) *n* istituto *m*; istituzione *f*; *v* istituire

institution (in-ssti-*t'uu*-ʃön) *n* istituto *m*, istituzione *f*

instruct (in-*sstrakt*) *v* istruire

instruction (in-*sstrak*-ʃön) *n* istruzione *f*

instructive (in-*sstrak*-tiv) *adj* istruttivo

instructor (in-*sstrak*-tö) *n* istruttore *m*, -trice *f*

instrument (*in*-sstru-mönt) *n* strumento *m*; **musical ~** strumento musicale

insufficient (in-ssö-*fi*-ʃönt) *adj* insufficiente

insulate (*in*-ss'u-leit) *v* isolare

insulation (in-ss'u-*lei*-ʃön) *n* isolamento *m*

insult[1] (in-*ssalt*) *v* insultare

insult[2] (*in*-ssalt) *n* insulto *m*

insurance (in-*fu*ᵒ-rönss) *n* assicurazione *f*; **~ policy** polizza di assicurazione

insure (in-*fu*ᵒ) *v* assicurare

intact (in-*tækt*) *adj* intatto

integrate (*in*-tö-ghreit) *v* integrare

intellect (*in*-tö-lêkt) *n* intelletto *m*

intellectual (in-tö-*lêk*-tʃu-öl) *adj* intellettuale

intelligence (in-*tê*-li-dʒönss) *n* intelligenza *f*

intelligent (in-*tê*-li-dʒönt) *adj* intelligente

intend (in-*tênd*) *v* *intendere

intense (in-*tênss*) *adj* intenso; veemente

intensify (in- *tênss*-ssi-fai) *v* intensificare; acuirsi; intensificarsi

intention (in-*tên*-ʃön) *n* intenzione *f*

intentional (in-*tên*-ʃö-nöl) *adj* intenzionale

intercourse (*in*-tö-kooss) *n* rapporto *m*

interest (*in*-trösst) *n* interesse *m*; interessamento *m*; *v* interessare

interested (*in*-tröss-sstiid) *adj* interessato; **be ~ in** interessarsi di; **thanks, but I'm not ~** grazie, non mi interessa

interesting (*in*-trö-ssting) *adj* interessante

interfere (in-tö-*fi*ᵒ) *v* interferire; **~ with** intromettersi in

interference (in-tö-*fi*ᵒ-rönss) *n* interferenza *f*

interim (*in*-tö-rim) *adv* temporaneamente

interior (in-*ti*ᵒ-ri-ö) *n* interiore *m*

interlude (*in*-tö-luud) *n* intermezzo *m*

intermediary (in-tö-*mii*-d'ö-ri) *n* intermediario *m*, -a *f*

intermission (in-tö-*mi*-ʃön) *n* intervallo *m*

internal (in-*töö*-nöl) *adj* interno

international (in-tö-*næ*-ʃö-nöl) *adj* internazionale

Internet (*in*-tö-net) *n* Internet *m*; **on the ~** su Internet; **~ service provider** provider di servizi Internet

interpret (in-*töö*-prit) *v* *fare da interprete; interpretare

interpreter (in-*töö*-pri-tö) *n* interprete *m/f*

interrogate (in-*tê*-rö-gheit) *v* interrogare

interrogation (in-tê-rö-*ghei*-ʃön) *n* interrogatorio *m*

interrogative (in-tö-*ro*-ghö-tiv) *adj* interrogativo

interrupt (in-tö-*rapt*) *v* *interrompere

interruption (in-tö-*rap*-ʃön) *n* interruzione *f*

intersection (in-tö-*ssêk*-ʃön) *n* intersezione *f*; incrocio *m*

interval (*in*-tö-völ) *n* intervallo *m*

intervene (in-tö-*viin*) *v* *intervenire

interview (*in*-tö-v'uu) *n* intervista *f*

intestine (in-tê-sstin) *n* intestino *m*

intimate (*in*-ti-möt) *adj* intimo *m*

into (*in*-tu) *prep* in

intolerable (in-to-lö-rö-böl) *adj* intollerabile

intoxicated (in-*tok*-ssi-kei-tid) *adj* ubriaco

intrigue (in-*triigh*) *n* intrigo *m*

introduce (in-trö-d'*uuss*) *v* presentare; *introdurre

introduction (in-trö-*dak*-ʃön) *n* presentazione *f*; introduzione *f*

invade (in-*veid*) *v* *invadere

invalid¹ (*in*-vö-liid) *n* invalido *m*, -a *f*; *adj* invalido

invalid² (in-*væ*-lid) *adj* nullo

invasion (in-*vei*-ʒön) *n* irruzione *f*, invasione *f*

invent (in-*vênt*) *v* inventare

invention (in-*vên*-ʃön) *n* invenzione *f*

inventive (in-*vên*-tiv) *adj* inventivo

inventor (in-*vên*-tö) *n* inventore *m*

inventory (*in*-vön-tri) *n* inventario *m*

invert (in-*vööt*) *v* invertire

invest (in-*vêsst*) *v* investire

investigate (in-vê-sti-gheit) *v* investigare

investigation (in-vê-ssti-*ghei*-ʃön) *n* investigazione *f*

investment (in-*vêsst*-mönt) *n* investimento *m*

investor (in-vê-sstö) *n* finanziatore *m*

invisible (in-*vi*-sö-böl) *adj* invisibile

invitation (in-vi-*tei*-ʃön) *n* invito *m*

invite (in-*vait*) *v* invitare

invoice (*in*-voiss) *n* fattura *f*

involve (in-*vöol*) *v* *coinvolgere

inwards (in-ᵘöds) *adv* verso l'interno

iodine (*ai*-ö-diin) *n* iodio *m*

Iran (i-*raan*) Iran *m*

Iranian (i-*rei*-ni-ön) *adj* iraniano

Iraq (i-*raak*) Iraq *m*

Iraqi (i-*raa*-ki) *adj* iracheno

Ireland (*aiᵒ*-lönd) Irlanda *f*

Irish (*aiᵒ*-riʃ) *adj* irlandese

iron (*ai*-ön) *n* ferro *m*; ferro da stiro; di ferro; *v* stirare

ironical (ai-*ro*-ni-köl) *adj* ironico

irony (*aiᵒ*-rö-ni) *n* ironia *f*

irregular (i-*rê*-ghᵘu-lö) *adj* irregolare

irreparable (i-*rê*-pö-rö-böl) *adj* irreparabile

irrevocable (i-*rê*-vö-kö-böl) *adj* irrevocabile

irritable (*i*-ri-tö-böl) *adj* irritabile

irritate (*i*-ri-teit) *v* irritare

is (is) *v* (pr be)

island (*ai*-lönd) *n* isola *f*

isolate (*ai*-ssö-leit) *v* isolare

isolation (ai-ssö-*lei*-ʃön) *n* isolamento *m*

Israel (*is*-reil) Israele *m*

Israeli (is-*rei*-li) *adj* israeliano

issue (i-ʃuu) *v* pubblicare; *n* emissione *f*, tiratura *f*, edizione *f*; questione *f*, punto *m*; conseguenza *f*, risultato *m*, conclusione *f*, esito *m*; uscita *f*

it (it) *pron* esso; lo, la, le; ci; ne

Italian (i-*tæl*-¹ön) *adj* italiano

Italy (*i*-tö-li) Italia *f*

itch (itʃ) *n* prurito *m*; *v* prudere

item (*ai*-töm) *n* articolo *m*; punto *m*

itinerary (ai-*ti*-nö-rö-ri) *n* itinerario *m*

its (its) *pron* il suo *m*, la sua *f*, i suoi *mpl*, le sue *fpl*

itself (it-*ssêlf*) *pron* si; di per sé; **by ~** da solo; da sé

ivory (*ai*-vö-ri) *n* avorio *m*

ivy (*ai*-vi) *n* edera *f*

J

jack (dʒæk) *n* cricco *m*

jacket (*dʒæ*-kit) *n* giacchetta *f*, giacca *f*; copertina *f*

jade (dʒeid) *n* giada *f*

jail (dʒeil) *n* prigione *m*

jam (dʒæm) *n* marmellata *f*; ingorgo *m*

janitor (*dʒæ*-ni-tö) *n* portinaio *m*

January (*dʒæ*-nⁱu-ö-ri) gennaio

Japan (dʒö-*pæn*) Giappone *m*

Japanese (dʒæ-pö-*niis*) *adj* giapponese

jar (dʒaa) *n* barattolo *m*; vasetto *m*

jaundice (*dʒoon*-diss) *n* itterizia *f*

jaw (dʒoo) *n* mascella *f*

jealous (*dʒê*-löss) *adj* geloso

jealousy (*dʒê*-lö-ssi) *n* gelosia *f*

jeans (dʒiins) *pl* jeans *mpl*

jelly (*dʒê*-li) *n* gelatina *f*

jellyfish (*dʒê*-li-fiʃ) *n* medusa *f*

jersey (*dʒöö*-si) *n* jersey *m*; maglione *m*

jet (dʒêt) *n* getto *m*; jet *m*

jetty (*dʒê*-ti) *n* molo *m*

Jew (dʒuu) *n* ebreo *m*, -a *f*

jewel (*dʒuu*-öl) *n* gioiello *m*

jeweller (*dʒuu*-ö-lö) *n* gioielliere *m*, -a *f*

jewellery, jewelry *Am* (*dʒuu*-öl-ri) *n* gioielli *mpl*

Jewish (*dʒuu*-iʃ) *adj* ebraico

job (dʒob) *n* lavoro *m*; impiego *m*

jobless (*dʒob*-les) *adj* disoccupato

jockey (*dʒo*-ki) *n* fantino *m*

join (dʒoin) *v* unire; unirsi a, associarsi a; riunire

joint (dʒoint) *n* articolazione *f*; saldatura *f*; *adj* unito, congiunto

jointly (*dʒoint*-li) *adv* insieme

joke (dʒouk) *n* scherzo *m*; barzelletta *f*

jolly (*dʒo*-li) *adj* allegro

Jordan (*dʒoo*-dön) Giordania *f*

Jordanian (dʒoo-*dei*-ni-ön) *adj* giordano

journal (*dʒöö*-nöl) *n* giornale *m*

journalism (*dʒöö*-nö-li-söm) *n* giornalismo *m*

journalist (*dʒöö*-nö-lisst) *n* giornalista *m*/*f*

journey (*dʒöö*-ni) *n* viaggio *m*

joy (dʒoi) *n* gioia *f*

joyful (*dʒoi*-föl) *adj* allegro, gioioso

jubilee (*dʒuu*-bi-lii) *n* anniversario *m*

judge (dʒadʒ) *n* giudice *m*; *v* giudicare

judgment (*dʒadʒ*-mönt) *n* giudizio *m*

jug (dʒagh) *n* caraffa *f*

juggler (*dʒa*-glö) *n* giocoliere *m*, -a *f*

juice (dʒuuss) *n* succo *m*

juicy (*dʒuu*-ssi) *adj* succoso

July (dʒu-*lai*) luglio

jump (dʒamp) *v* saltare; *n* salto *m*

jumper (*dʒam*-pö) *n* golf *m*, maglia *f*

junction (*dʒangk*-ʃön) *n* incrocio *m*; crocevia *m*

June (dʒuun) giugno

jungle (*dʒang*-ghöl) *n* giungla *f*

junior (*dʒuu*-nⁱö) *adj* minore

junk (dʒangk) *n* spazzatura *f*

jury (*dʒuᵒ*-ri) *n* giuria *f*

just (dʒasst) *adj* giusto; esatto; *adv* appena; esattamente

justice (*dʒa*-sstiss) *n* giustizia *f*

justify (*dʒa*-ssti-fai) *v* giustificare

juvenile (*dʒuu*-vö-nail) *adj* giovanile

K

angaroo (kæng-ghö-*ruu*) *n* canguro *m*

eel (kiil) *n* chiglia *f*

een (kiin) *adj* appassionato; aguzzo

keep (kiip) *v* *tenere; *mantenere; continuare; ~ **away from** *tenersi lontano da; ~ **off** lasciar *stare; ~ **on** continuare; ~ **quiet** *tacere; ~ **up** perseverare; ~ **up with** *stare al passo con

ennel (*kê*-nöl) *n* canile *m*; cuccia *f*

enya (*kê*-n'ö) Kenia *m*

erosene (*kê*-rö-ssiin) *n* cherosene *m*

etchup (*kê*-tʃap) *n* ketchup *m*

ettle (*kê*-töl) *n* bollitore *m*

ey (kii) *n* chiave *f*

eyboard (*kii*-böd) *n* tastiera *f*

eyboarder (kii-*boo*-dö) *n* tastierista *m/f*

eycard (kii-kaad) *n* tessera magnetica

eyhole (*kii*-houl) *n* buco della serratura

haki (*kaa*-ki) *n* kaki *m*

ick (kik) *v* tirare calci, *prendere a calci; *n* calcio *m*, pedata *f*

ickoff (ki-*kof*) *n* calcio d'inizio

id (kid) *n* bambino *m*; capretto *m*; *v* stuzzicare

idney (*kid*-ni) *n* rene *m*

ill (kil) *v* ammazzare, *uccidere

ilogram (*ki*-lö-ghræm) *n* chilo *m*

kilometer *Am*, **kilometre** (*ki*-lö-mii-tö) *n* chilometro *m*

kind (kaind) *adj* gentile; buono; *n* genere *m*

kindergarten (*kin*-dö-ghaa-tön) *n* asilo infantile; scuola materna

king (king) *n* re *m*

kingdom (*king*-döm) *n* regno *m*

kiosk (*kii*-ossk) *n* chiosco *m*

kiss (kiss) *n* bacio *m*; *v* baciare

kit (kit) *n* corredo *m*

kitchen (*ki*-tʃin) *n* cucina *f*; ~ **garden** orto *m*; ~ **towel** canovaccio *m*

kleenex® (*klii*-nêkss) *n* fazzoletto di carta

knapsack (*næp*-ssæk) *n* zaino *m*

knave (neiv) *n* fante *m*

knee (nii) *n* ginocchio *m*

kneecap (*nii*-kæp) *n* rotula *f*

*kneel (niil) *v* inginocchiarsi

knew (n'uu) *v* (p know)

knife (naif) *n* (pl knives) coltello *m*

knight (nait) *n* cavaliere *m*

*knit (nit) *v* lavorare a maglia

knob (nob) *n* manopola *f*

knock (nok) *v* bussare; *n* colpo *m*; ~ **against** urtare contro; ~ **down** atterrare

knot (not) *n* nodo *m*; *v* annodare

*know (nou) *v* *sapere, *conoscere

knowledge (*no*-lidʒ) *n* conoscenza *f*

knuckle (*na*-köl) *n* nocca *f*

L

abel (*lei*-böl) *n* etichetta *f*; *v* etichettare

aboratory (lö-*bo*-rö-tö-ri) *n* laboratorio *m*

labo(u)r (*lei*-bö) *n* lavoro *m*; doglie *fpl*; *v* lavorare sodo, faticare; **labor permit** *Am* permesso di lavoro

labo(u)rer (*lei*-bö-rö) *n* operaio *m*, -a *f*

labo(u)r-saving (*lei*-bö-ssei-ving) *adj* che risparmia lavoro

labyrinth (*læ*-bö-rinθ) *n* labirinto *m*

lace (leiss) *n* merletto *m*; laccio *m*

lack (læk) *n* mancanza *f*; *v* mancare

lacquer (*læ*-kö) *n* lacca *f*

lad (læd) *n* giovane *m*, ragazzo *m*

ladder (*læ*-dö) *n* scala *f*

lady (*lei*-di) *n* signora *f*; **ladies' room** gabinetto per signore

lagoon (lö-*ghuun*) *n* laguna *f*

lake (leik) *n* lago *m*

lamb (læm) *n* agnello *m*

lame (leim) *adj* paralitico; zoppicante, zoppo

lamentable (*læ*-mön-tö-böl) *adj* lamentevole

lamp (læmp) *n* lampada *f*

lamppost (*læmp*-pousst) *n* lampione *m*

lampshade (*læmp*-ʃeid) *n* paralume *m*

land (lænd) *n* paese *m*, terra *f*; *v* atterrare; sbarcare

landlady (*lænd*-lei-di) *n* padrona di casa, proprietaria *f*; affittacamere *f*

landlord (*lænd*-lood) *n* padrone di casa, proprietario *m*; affittacamere *m*

landmark (*lænd*-maak) *n* punto di riferimento; pietra miliare

landscape (*lænd*-sskeip) *n* paesaggio *m*

lane (lein) *n* vicolo *m*, sentiero *m*; corsia *f*

language (*læng*-gh^uidʒ) *n* lingua *f*; ~ **laboratory** laboratorio linguistico

lantern (*læn*-tön) *n* lanterna *f*

lap (læp) *n* giro (di pista)

larder (*laa*-dö) *n* dispensa *f*

large (laadʒ) *adj* grande; spazioso

largely (*laa*dʒ-li) *adv* in gran parte

lark (laak) *n* allodola *f*

laryngitis (læ-rin-*dʒai*-tiss) *n* laringite *f*

last (laasst) *adj* ultimo; scorso; *v* durare; **at** ~ finalmente

lasting (*laa*-ssting) *adj* duraturo, durevole

late (leit) *adj* tardo; *adv* in ritardo

lately (*leit*-li) *adv* ultimamente, recentemente

lather (*laa*-ðö) *n* schiuma *f*

Latin America (*læ*-tin ö-*mê*-ri-kö) America Latina

Latin-American (læ-tin-ö-*mê*-ri-kön *adj* latino americano

latitude (*læ*-ti-t^uud) *n* latitudine *f*

laugh (laaf) *v* *ridere; *n* riso *m*

laughter (*laaf*-tö) *n* risata *f*

launch (loontʃ) *v* lanciare; *n* motonave *f*

launching (*loon*-tʃing) *n* varo *m*

launderette (loon-dö-*rêt*) *n* lavanderi automatica

laundry (*loon*-dri) *n* lavanderia *f*; bucato *m*

lavatory (*læ*-vö-tö-ri) *n* gabinetto *m*

lavish (*læ*-viʃ) *adj* prodigo

law (loo) *n* legge *f*; ~ **court** tribunale

lawful (*loo*-föl) *adj* legale

lawn (loon) *n* prato *m*

lawsuit (*loo*-ssuut) *n* processo *m*, causa *f*

lawyer (*loo*-^iö) *n* avvocato *m*; giurist *m/f*

laxative (*læk*-ssö-tiv) *n* lassativo *m*

*lay (lei) *v* collocare, *mettere, posar ~ **bricks** murare

layer (*lei*^ö) *n* strato *m*

layman (*lei*-mön) *n* profano *m*

lazy (*lei*-si) *adj* pigro

lead¹ (liid) *n* vantaggio *m*; guida *f*; guinzaglio *m*

lead² (lêd) *n* piombo *m*

*lead (liid) *v* *dirigere

leader (*lii*-dö) *n* leader *m*, dirigente

leadership (*lii*-dö-ʃip) *n* comando

leading (*lii*-ding) *adj* dominante,

principale

eaf (liif) n (pl leaves) foglia f

eague (liigh) n lega f

eak (liik) n perdita f

eaky (*lii*-ki) adj che perde

ean (liin) adj magro

***lean** (liin) v appoggiarsi

eap (liip) n salto m; ~ **year** anno bisestile

***leap** (liip) v balzare

***learn** (löön) v imparare

earner (*löö*-nö) n principiante m/f; studente m, -essa f

ease (liiss) n contratto di affitto; v *dare in affitto; *prendere in affitto

eash (liiʃ) n guinzaglio m

east (liisst) adj minimo; **at ~** almeno

eather (*lê*-ðö) n pelle f; di pelle

eave (liiv) n congedo m

***leave** (liiv) v partire, lasciare; ~ **out** *omettere

Lebanese (lê-bö-*niis*) adj libanese

Lebanon (*lê*-bö-nön) Libano m

ecture (*lêk*-tʃö) n lezione f; conferenza f

eft[1] (lêft) adj sinistro; a sinistra

eft[2] (lêft) v (p, pp leave)

eft-hand (*lêft*-hænd) adj a sinistra

eft-handed (lêft-*hæn*-did) adj mancino

eg (lêgh) n gamba f

egacy (*lê*-ghö-ssi) n eredità f

egal (*lii*-ghöl) adj legittimo, legale; giuridico

egalization (lii-ghö-lai-*sei*-ʃön) n legalizzazione f

egible (*lê*-dʒi-böl) adj leggibile

egitimate (li-*dʒi*-ti-möt) adj legittimo

eisure (*lê*-ʒö) n comodo m

emon (*lê*-mön) n limone m

emonade (lê-mö-*neid*) n limonata f

end (lênd) v prestare

***ength** (lêngθ) n lunghezza f

engthen (*lêng*-θön) v allungare

lengthways (*lêngθ*-ueis) adv per lungo

lens (lêns) n lente f; obbiettivo m

leprosy (*lê*-prö-ssi) n lebbra f

less (lêss) adv meno

lessen (*lê*-ssön) v diminuire

lesson (*lê*-ssön) n lezione f

***let** (lêt) v lasciare; affittare; ~ **down** *deludere

letter (*lê*-tö) n lettera f; ~ **of credit** lettera di credito; ~ **of recommendation** lettera di raccomandazione; ~ **opener** tagliacarte m

letterbox (*lê*-tö-bokss) n cassetta per le lettere

lettuce (*lê*-tiss) n lattuga f

level (*lê*-völ) adj piano; piatto, spianato; n livello m; livella f; v pareggiare, livellare; ~ **crossing** passaggio a livello

lever (*lii*-vö) n leva f

liability (lai-ö-*bi*-lö-ti) n responsabilità f

liable (*lai*-ö-böl) adj responsabile; ~ **to** soggetto a

liar (*lai*-ö) n bugiardo m, -a f

liberal (*li*-bö-röl) adj liberale; generoso, prodigo

liberation (li-bö-*rei*-ʃön) n liberazione f

Liberia (lai-*bi*[o]-ri-ö) Liberia f

Liberian (lai-*bi*[o]-ri-ön) adj liberiano

liberty (*li*-bö-ti) n libertà f

library (*lai*-brö-ri) n biblioteca f

licence, license Am (*lai*-ssönss) n licenza f; **driving ~** patente di guida; ~ **number** Am numero di targa; ~ **plate** Am targa automobilistica

license (*lai*-ssönss) v autorizzare

lick (lik) v leccare

lid (lid) n coperchio m

lie (lai) v mentire; n menzogna f

***lie** (lai) v *star disteso; ~ **down** sdraiarsi

life (laif) *n* (pl lives) vita *f*; ~ **insurance** assicurazione sulla vita
lifebuoy (*laif*-boi) *n* salvagente *m*
lifetime (*laif*-taim) *n* vita *f*
lift (lift) *v* alzare, sollevare; *n* ascensore *m*
light (lait) *n* luce *f*; *adj* leggero; chiaro; ~ **bulb** lampadina *f*
*light (lait) *v* *accendere
lighter (*lai*-tö) *n* accendino *m*
lighthouse (*lait*-hauss) *n* faro *m*
lighting (*lai*-ting) *n* illuminazione *f*
lightning (*lait*-ning) *n* lampo *m*
like (laik) *v* *voler bene; gradire; *adj* simile; *conj* come
likely (*lai*-kli) *adj* probabile
like-minded (laik-*main*-did) *adj* di idee affini
likewise (*laik*-ᵘais) *adv* nello stesso modo
lily (*li*-li) *n* giglio *m*
limb (lim) *n* arto *m*
lime (laim) *n* calce *f*; tiglio *m*; cedro *m*
limetree (*laim*-trii) *n* tiglio *m*
limit (*li*-mit) *n* limite *m*; *v* limitare
limp (limp) *v* zoppicare; *adj* floscio
line (lain) *n* riga *f*; tratto *m*; cordicella *f*, linea *f*; fila *f*; **stand in** ~ *Am* *fare la coda
linen (*li*-nin) *n* lino *m*; biancheria *f*
liner (*lai*-nö) *n* nave di linea
lingerie (*long*-ʒö-rii) *n* biancheria *f*
lining (*lai*-ning) *n* fodera *f*
link (lingk) *v* collegare; *n* legame *m*; anello *m*
lion (*lai*-ön) *n* leone *m*
lip (lip) *n* labbro *m*
lipstick (*lip*-sstik) *n* rossetto *m*
liqueur (li-*kᶦuᵒ*) *n* liquore *m*
liquid (*li*-kᵘid) *adj* liquido; *n* liquido *m*
liquor (*li*-kö) *n* bevande alcooliche; ~ **store** spaccio di liquori
liquorice (*li*-kö-riss) *n* liquirizia *f*
list (lisst) *n* elenco *m*; *v* elencare

listen (*li*-ssön) *v* sentire, ascoltare
listener (*liss*-nö) *n* ascoltatore *m*
liter (*lii*-tö) *nAm* litro *m*
literary (*li*-trö-ri) *adj* letterario
literature (*li*-trö-tʃö) *n* letteratura *f*
litre (*lii*-tö) *n* litro *m*
litter (*li*-tö) *n* rifiuti; figliata *f*
little (*li*-töl) *adj* piccolo; poco
live¹ (liv) *v* *vivere; abitare
live² (laiv) *adj* vivo
lively (*laiv*-li) *adj* vivace
liver (*li*-vö) *n* fegato *m*
living (*li*-ving) *adj* vivo; *n* sostentamento *m*; *n* ~ **room** soggiorno *m*, salotto *m*; **earn one's** ~ guadagnarsi da vivere; **what do you do for a** ~? che lavoro fai?; **standard of** ~ tenore di vita
lizard (*li*-zöd) *n* lucertola *f*
load (loud) *n* carico *m*; peso *m*; *v* caricare
loaf (louf) *n* (pl loaves) pagnotta *f*
loan (loun) *n* prestito *m*
lobby (*lo*-bi) *n* atrio *m*; ridotto *m*
lobster (*lob*-sstö) *n* aragosta *f*
local (*lou*-köl) *adj* locale; ~ **call** chiamata urbana; ~ **train** treno locale
locality (lou-*kæ*-lö-ti) *n* località *f*
locate (lou-*keit*) *v* localizzare
location (lou-*kei*-ʃön) *n* posizione *f*
lock (lok) *v* *chiudere a chiave; *n* serratura *f*; chiusa *f*; ~ **up** *chiudere a chiave
locker (*lo*-kö) *n* armadietto *m*
locomotive (lou-kö-*mou*-tiv) *n* locomotiva *f*
lodge (lodʒ) *v* alloggiare; *n* rifugio *m*
lodger (*lo*-dʒö) *n* inquilino *m*
lodgings (*lo*-dʒings) *pl* alloggio *m*
log (logh) *n* ceppo *m*
logic (*lo*-dʒik) *n* logica *f*
logical (*lo*-dʒi-köl) *adj* logico
lonely (*loun*-li) *adj* solitario
long (long) *adj* lungo; ~ **for** bramare

no longer non … più

longing (*long*-ing) *n* bramosia *f*

longitude (*lon*-dʒi-tʰuud) *n* longitudine *f*

look (luk) *v* guardare; sembrare, *aver l'aria; *n* occhiata *f*, sguardo *m*; aspetto *m*; ~ **after** occuparsi di, badare a; ~ **at** guardare; ~ **for** cercare; ~ **out** *stare attento, *fare attenzione; ~ **up** cercare

looking-glass (*lu*-king-ghlaass) *n* specchio *m*

loop (luup) *n* nodo scorsoio

loose (luuss) *adj* slegato

loosen (*luu*-ssön) *v* slegare

lord (lood) *n* lord *m*

lorry (*lo*-ri) *n* autocarro *m*, camion *m*

*lose (luus) *v* *perdere, smarrire

loser (*luu*-sö) *n* perdente *m/f*; sfigato *m*, -a *f*

loss (loss) *n* perdita *f*

lost (losst) *adj* smarrito; ~ **and found** oggetti smarriti; ~ **property office** ufficio oggetti smarriti

lot (lot) *n* sorte *f*; massa *f*, quantità *f*; **a** ~ **of** molto; molti

lotion (*lou*-ʃön) *n* lozione *f*; **aftershave** ~ lozione dopo barba

lottery (*lo*-tö-ri) *n* lotteria *f*

loud (laud) *adj* forte, alto

loudspeaker (laud-*sspii*-kö) *n* altoparlante *m*; cassa *f*

lounge (laundʒ) *n* salone *m*

louse (lauss) *n* (pl lice) pidocchio *m*

love (lav) *v* amare; *n* amore *m*; **in** ~ innamorato; ~ **story** storia d'amore

lovely (*lav*-li) *adj* delizioso, splendido, bello

lover (*la*-vö) *n* amante *m*

low (lou) *adj* basso; abbattuto; ~ **tide** bassa marea

lower (*lou*-ö) *v* abbassare; ribassare; calare; *adj* inferiore

lowlands (*lou*-lönds) *pl* bassopiano *m*

loyal (*loi*-öl) *adj* leale

lubricate (*luu*-bri-keit) *v* lubrificare

lubrication (luu-bri-*kei*-ʃön) *n* lubrificazione *f*; ~ **oil** lubrificante *m*; ~ **system** sistema lubrificante

luck (lak) *n* fortuna *f*; caso *m*; **bad** ~ sfortuna *f*

lucky (*la*-ki) *adj* fortunato; ~ **charm** portafortuna *m*

ludicrous (*luu*-di-kröss) *adj* ridicolo

luggage (*la*-ghidʒ) *n* bagaglio *m*; **hand** ~ bagaglio a mano; **left** ~ **office** deposito bagagli; ~ **rack** portabagagli *m*; ~ **van** bagagliaio *m*

lukewarm (*luuk*-ᵘoom) *adj* tiepido

lumbago (lam-*bei*-ghou) *n* lombaggine *f*

luminous (*luu*-mi-nöss) *adj* luminoso

lump (lamp) *n* nodo *m*, grumo *m*, pezzo *m*; gonfiore *m*; nodulo *m*; ~ **of sugar** zolletta di zucchero; ~ **sum** somma globale

lumpy (*lam*-pi) *adj* grumoso

lunacy (*luu*-nö-ssi) *n* pazzia *f*

lunatic (*luu*-nö-tik) *adj* pazzo; *n* pazzo *m*

lunch (lantʃ) *n* pranzo *m*

luncheon (*lan*-tʃön) *n* pranzo *m*

lung (lang) *n* polmone *m*

lust (lasst) *n* libidine *f*

luxurious (lagh-ʒuᵒ-ri-öss) *adj* lussuoso

luxury (*lak*-ʃö-ri) *n* lusso *m*

M

machine (mö-*fiin*) n apparecchio m, macchina f

machinery (mö-*fii*-nö-ri) n macchinario m; meccanismo m

mackerel (*mæ*-kröl) n (pl ~) sgombro m

mackintosh (*mæ*-kin-tof) n impermeabile m

mad (mæd) adj matto, pazzo, folle; rabbioso

madam (*mæ*-döm) n signora f

madness (*mæd*-nöss) n pazzia f

magazine (mæ-ghö-*siin*) n rivista f

magic (*mæ*-dʒik) n magia f; adj magico

magician (mö-*dʒi*-fön) n prestigiatore m

magistrate (*mæ*-dʒi-sstreit) n magistrato m

magnetic (mægh-*nê*-tik) adj magnetico

magneto (mægh-*nii*-tou) n (pl ~s) magnete m

magnificent (mægh-*ni*-fi-ssönt) adj magnifico; grandioso, splendido

magnify (*mægh*-ni-fai) v ingrandire; ingigantire

magpie (*mægh*-pai) n gazza f

maid (meid) n domestica f

maiden name (*mei*-dön neim) cognome da nubile

mail (meil) n posta f; v impostare; ~ order Am vendita per corrispondenza

mailbox (*meil*-bokss) nAm cassetta per le lettere

main (mein) adj principale; maggiore; ~ deck ponte di coperta; ~ line linea principale; ~ road strada principale; ~ street via principale

mainland (*mein*-lönd) n terraferma f

mainly (*mein*-li) adv principalmente

mains (meins) pl rete elettrica

maintain (mein-*tein*) v *mantenere

maintenance (*mein*-tö-nönss) n manutenzione f

maize (meis) n granoturco m

major (*mei*-dʒö) adj grande; maggiore; n maggiore m

majority (mö-*dʒo*-rö-ti) n maggioranza f

***make** (meik) v *fare; guadagnare; *riuscire; ~ do with arrangiarsi con; ~ good compensare; ~ up compilare

make-up (*mei*-kap) n trucco m

malaria (mö-*lê*º-ri-ö) n malaria f

Malaysia (mö-*lei*-si-ö) Malesia f

Malaysian (mö-*lei*-si-ön) adj malese

male (meil) adj maschile; n maschio m

malicious (mö-*li*-föss) adj malevolo

malignant (mö-*ligh*-nönt) adj maligno

mall (mool) n centro commerciale

malnutrition (mæl-n'u-*tri*-fön) n denutrizione f

mammal (*mæ*-möl) n mammifero m

mammoth (*mæ*-möθ) n mammut m

man (mæn) n (pl men) uomo m; **men's room** gabinetto per signori

manage (*mæ*-nidʒ) v *dirigere; *riuscire

manageable (*mæ*-ni-dʒö-böl) adj maneggiabile

management (*mæ*-nidʒ-mönt) n direzione f; gestione f

manager (*mæ*-ni-dʒö) n capo m, direttore m, -trice f; manager m

mandarin (*mæn*-dö-rin) n mandarino m

mandate (*mæn*-deit) n mandato m

manger (*mein*-dʒö) n mangiatoia f

manicure (*mæ*-ni-k'uº) n manicure f; v curare le unghie

manipulate (mæ-*ni*-piu-leit) v manipolare; maneggiare

mankind (mæn-*kaind*) *n* umanità *f*

mannequin (*mæ*-nö-kin) *n* indossatrice *f*

manner (*mæ*-nö) *n* modo *m*, maniera *f*; **manners** *pl* maniere

man-of-war (mæ-növ-*"oo*) *n* nave da guerra

mansion (mæn-*f*ön) *n* palazzo *m*; casa padronale

manual (*mæ*-n¹u-öl) *adj* manuale

manufacture (mæ-n¹u-*fæk*-tfö) *v* confezionare, fabbricare

manufacturer (mæ-n¹u-*fæk*-tfö-rö) *n* fabbricante *m*

manure (mö-n¹u⁰) *n* concime *m*

manuscript (*mæ*-n¹u-sskript) *n* manoscritto *m*

many (*mê*-ni) *adj* molti

map (mæp) *n* cartina *f*; mappa *f*; pianta *f*

maple (*mei*-pöl) *n* acero *m*

marble (*maa*-böl) *n* marmo *m*; pallina *f*

March (maatf) marzo

march (maatf) *v* marciare; *n* marcia *f*

mare (mê⁰) *n* cavalla *f*

margarine (maa-dʒö-*riin*) *n* margarina *f*

margin (*maa*-dʒin) *n* margine *m*

maritime (*mæ*-ri-taim) *adj* marittimo

mark (maak) *v* marcare; segnare; caratterizzare; *n* segno *m*; voto *m*; bersaglio *m*

market (*maa*-kit) *n* mercato *m*

marketplace (*maa*-kit-pleiss) *n* piazza del mercato

marmalade (*maa*-mö-leid) *n* marmellata *f*

marriage (*mæ*-ridʒ) *n* matrimonio *m*

marrow (*mæ*-rou) *n* midollo *m*

marry (*mæ*-ri) *v* sposare; **married** sposato; **married couple** coniugi *mpl*; **be married to ...** essere sposato con ...

marsh (maaf) *n* palude *f*

martyr (*maa*-tö) *n* martire *m*

marvel (*maa*-völ) *n* meraviglia *f*; *v* meravigliarsi

marvel(l)ous (*maa*-vö-löss) *adj* meraviglioso

mascara (mæ-*sskaa*-rö) *n* mascara *m*

masculine (*mæ*-ssk¹u-lin) *adj* maschile

mash (mæf) *v* schiacciare

mask (maassk) *n* maschera *f*

Mass (mæss) *n* messa *f*

mass (mæss) *n* massa *f*; ~ **production** produzione in serie

massage (*mæ*-ssaaʒ) *n* massaggio *m*; *v* massaggiare

masseur (mæ-*ssöö*) *n* massaggiatore *m*

massive (*mæ*-ssiv) *adj* massiccio

mast (maasst) *n* albero *m*

master (*maa*-sstö) *n* maestro *m*; padrone *m*; professore *m*, insegnante *m*; *v* dominare

masterpiece (*maa*-sstö-piiss) *n* capolavoro *m*

mat (mæt) *n* stuoia *f*; *adj* pallido, opaco

match (mætf) *n* fiammifero *m*; partita *f*; *v* intonarsi con

matchbox (*mætf*-bokss) *n* scatola di fiammiferi

material (mö-*ti⁰*-ri-öl) *n* materiale *m*; stoffa *f*; *adj* materiale

mathematical (mæ-θö-*mæ*-ti-köl) *adj* matematico

mathematics (mæ-θö-*mæ*-tikss) *n* matematica *f*

matrimony (*mæ*-tri-mö-ni) *n* matrimonio *m*

matter (*mæ*-tö) *n* materia *f*; affare *m*, questione *f*, faccenda *f*; *v* *avere importanza; **as a ~ of fact** effettivamente, infatti

matter-of-fact (mæ-tö-röv-*fækt*) *adj*

prosaico

mattress (*mæ*-tröss) *n* materasso *m*

mature (mö-*t'u*ᵒ) *adj* maturo

maturity (mö-*t'u*ᵒ-rö-ti) *n* maturità *f*

mausoleum (moo-ssö-*lii*-öm) *n* mausoleo *m*

mauve (mouv) *adj* lilla

May (mei) maggio

*may (mei) *v* *potere

maybe (*mei*-bii) *adv* forse

mayor (mêᵒ) *n* sindaco *m*

maze (meis) *n* labirinto *m*

me (mii) *pron* mi; me

meadow (*mê*-dou) *n* prato *m*

meal (miil) *n* pasto *m*

mean (miin) *adj* meschino; *n* media *f*

*mean (miin) *v* significare; *voler dire; *intendere

meaning (*mii*-ning) *n* significato *m*

meaningless (*mii*-ning-löss) *adj* insensato

means (miins) *n* mezzo *m*; **by no ~** in nessun modo

meantime (*miin*-taim): **in the ~** intanto, nel frattempo

meanwhile (*miin*-ᵘail) *adv* frattanto

measles (*mii*-söls) *n* morbillo *m*; **German ~** rosolia *f*

measure (*mê*-ʒö) *v* misurare; *n* misura *f*

meat (miit) *n* carne *f*

mechanic (mi-*kæ*-nik) *n* meccanico *m*

mechanical (mi-*kæ*-ni-köl) *adj* meccanico

mechanism (*mê*-kö-ni-söm) *n* meccanismo *m*

medal (*mê*-döl) *n* medaglia *f*

media (*mii*-diö): **the ~** *npl* i mass media

mediaeval (mê-di-*ii*-völ) *adj* medievale

mediate (*mii*-di-eit) *v* *fare da intermediario

mediator (*mii*-di-ei-tö) *n* mediatore *m*

medical (*mê*-di-köl) *adj* medico

medicine (*mêd*-ssin) *n* medicina *f*

meditate (*mê*-di-teit) *v* meditare

Mediterranean (mê-di-tö-*rei*-ni-ön) Mediterraneo *m*

medium (*mii*-di-öm) *adj* medio; *n* mezzo *m*

*meet (miit) *v* incontrare

meeting (*mii*-ting) *n* assemblea *f*, riunione *f*; incontro *m*; **~ place** punto d'incontro

melancholy (*mê*-löng-kö-li) *n* malinconia *f*

mellow (*mê*-lou) *adj* dolce; tenue; delicato

melodrama (*mê*-lö-draa-mö) *n* melodramma *m*

melody (*mê*-lö-di) *n* melodia *f*

melon (*mê*-lön) *n* melone *m*

melt (mêlt) *v* *fondere, sciogliere; sciogliersi

member (*mêm*-bö) *n* membro *m*; **Member of Parliament** deputato *m*

membership (*mêm*-bö-ʃip) *n* qualità di membro

memo (*mê*-mou) *n* (pl ~s) nota *f*

memorable (*mê*-mö-rö-böl) *adj* memorabile

memorial (mö-*moo*-ri-öl) *n* monumento commemorativo

memorize (*mê*-mö-rais) *v* imparare a memoria

memory (*mê*-mö-ri) *n* memoria *f*; ricordo *m*

mend (mênd) *v* rammendare, riparare

menstruation (mên-sstru-*ei*-ʃön) *n* mestruazione *f*

mental (*mên*-töl) *adj* mentale

mention (*mên*-ʃön) *v* nominare, menzionare; *n* citazione *f*

menu (*mê*-nᵘuu) *n* carta *f*, menu *m*

merchandise (*möö*-tʃön-dais) *n* merce *f*, mercanzia *f*

merchant (*möö*-tʃönt) *n*

commerciante *m*, mercante *m*

mercury (*möö*-kⁱu-ri) *n* mercurio *m*

mercy (*möö*-ssi) *n* misericordia *f*, clemenza *f*

mere (mi^ö) *adj* semplice

merely (*mi^ö*-li) *adv* soltanto

merge (mööd3) *v* unirsi; fondersi

merger (*möö*-d3ö) *n* fusione *f*

merit (*mê*-rit) *v* meritare; *n* merito *m*

merry (*mê*-ri) *adj* allegro

merry-go-round (*mê*-ri-ghou-raund) *n* giostra *f*

mesh (mêʃ) *n* maglia *f*

mess (mêss) *n* disordine *m*; **~ up** mettere in disordine

message (*mê*-ssid3) *n* messaggio *m*

messenger (*mê*-ssin-d3ö) *n* messaggero *m*

metal (*mê*-töl) *n* metallo *m*; metallico

meter (*mii*-tö) *n* metro *m*

method (*mê*-θöd) *n* metodo *m*; ordine *m*

methodical (mö-ϑ-di-köl) *adj* metodico

metre (*mii*-tö) *n* metro *m*

metric (*mê*-trik) *adj* metrico

Mexican (*mêk*-ssi-kön) *adj* messicano

Mexico (*mêk*-ssi-kou) Messico *m*

mice (mais) *n* (pl mouse)

microphone (*mai*-krö-foun) *n* microfono *m*

microwave oven (*mai*-krö-^ueiv a-vön) *n* forno a microonde

midday (*mid*-dei) *n* mezzogiorno *m*

middle (*mi*-döl) *n* mezzo *m*; *adj* mezzo; **Middle Ages** medioevo *m*; **~ class** ceto medio; **middle-class** *adj* borghese

midnight (*mid*-nait) *n* mezzanotte *f*

midst (midsst) *n* mezzo *m*

midsummer (*mid*-ssa-mö) *n* piena estate

midwife (*mid*-^uaif) *n* (pl -wives) ostetrica *f*

might (mait) *n* potenza *f*

*might (mait) *v* *potere

mighty (*mai*-ti) *adj* poderoso

migraine (*mi*-ghrein) *n* emicrania *f*

Milan (mi-læn) Milano *f*

mild (maild) *adj* mite

mildew (*mil*-dⁱu) *n* muffa *f*

mile (mail) *n* miglio *m*

mileage (*mai*-lid3) *n* distanza in miglia

milestone (*mail*-sstoun) *n* pietra miliare

milieu (*mii*-lⁱöö) *n* ambiente *m*

military (*mi*-li-tö-ri) *adj* militare; **~ force** forze militari

milk (milk) *n* latte *m*

milkman (*milk*-mön) *n* (pl -men) lattaio *m*

milkshake (*milk*-ʃeik) *n* frappé *m*

milky (*mil*-ki) *adj* con molto latte

mill (mil) *n* macinino *m*; fabbrica *f*

miller (*mi*-lö) *n* mugnaio *m*

million (*mil*-ⁱön) *n* milione *m*

millionaire (mil-ⁱö-*nê^ö*) *n* milionario *m*, -a *f*

mince (minss) *v* tritare

mind (maind) *n* mente *f*; *v* *fare obiezione a; badare a, *fare attenzione

mine¹ (main) *pron* il mio

mine² (main) *n* miniera *f*

miner (*mai*-nö) *n* minatore *m*

mineral (*mi*-nö-röl) *n* minerale *m*; **~ water** acqua minerale

mingle (minghl) *v* mischiarsi; mescolarsi

miniature (*min*-ⁱö-tʃö) *n* miniatura *f*

minimum (*mi*-ni-möm) *n* minimo *m*

mining (*mai*-ning) *n* industria mineraria

minister (*mi*-ni-sstö) *n* ministro *m*; pastore *m*; **Prime Minister** primo ministro

ministry (*mi*-ni-sstri) *n* ministero *m*

mink (mingk) *n* visone *m*

minor (*mai*-nö) *adj* piccolo, esiguo, minore; subordinato; *n* minorenne *m*

minority (mai-*no*-rö-ti) *n* minoranza *f*

mint (mint) *n* menta *f*

minus (*mai*-nöss) *prep* meno

minute¹ (*mi*-nit) *n* minuto *m*; **minutes** verbale *m*

minute² (mai-n*iuut*) *adj* minuscolo

miracle (*mi*-rö-köl) *n* miracolo *m*

miraculous (mi-*ræ*-k*i*u-löss) *adj* miracoloso

mirror (*mi*-rö) *n* specchio *m*

misbehave (miss-bi-*heiv*) *v* comportarsi male

miscarriage (miss-*kæ*-ridʒ) *n* aborto *m*

miscellaneous (mi-ssö-*lei*-ni-öss) *adj* misto

mischief (*miss*-tʃif) *n* birichinata *f*; male *m*, danno *m*

mischievous (*miss*-tʃi-vöss) *adj* birichino

miserable (*mi*-sö-rö-böl) *adj* misero, miserabile

misery (*mi*-sö-ri) *n* miseria *f*; bisogno *m*

misfortune (miss-*foo*-tʃên) *n* sfortuna *f*, avversità *f*

mishap (*miss*-hæp) *n* incidente *m*

*mislay (miss-*lei*) *v* smarrire

misplaced (miss-*pleisst*) *adj* inopportuno; sbagliato

mispronounce (miss-prö-*naunss*) *v* pronunciar male

miss¹ (miss) signorina *f*

miss² (miss) *v* *perdere

missing (*mi*-ssing) *adj* mancante; ~ **person** persona scomparsa

mist (misst) *n* foschia *f*, nebbia *f*

mistake (mi-*ssteik*) *n* sbaglio *m*, errore *m*

*mistake (mi-*ssteik*) *v* *confondere

mistaken (mi-*sstei*-kön) *adj* erroneo;

*be ~ sbagliarsi

mister (*mi*-sstö) signore *m*

mistress (*mi*-sströss) *n* signora *f*; padrona *f*; amante *f*

mistrust (miss-*trasst*) *v* diffidare di

misty (*mi*-ssti) *adj* nebbioso

*misunderstand (mi-ssan-dö-*sstænd*) *v* *fraintendere

misunderstanding (mi-ssan-dö-*sstæn*-ding) *n* malinteso *m*

misuse (miss-*iuuss*) *n* abuso *m*

mittens (*mi*-töns) *pl* muffole *fpl*

mix (mikss) *v* mescolare; ~ **with** frequentare

mixed (miksst) *adj* misto

mixer (*mik*-ssö) *n* frullatore *m*

mixture (*mikss*-tʃö) *n* miscuglio *m*

moan (moun) *v* gemere

moat (mout) *n* fossato *m*

mobile (*mou*-bail) *adj* mobile; ~ **phone** (telefono) cellulare *m*, telefonino *m*

mock (mok) *v* canzonare

mockery (*mo*-kö-ri) *n* derisione *f*

model (*mo*-döl) *n* modello *m*; indossatrice *f*, modella *f*; *v* modellare, plasmare

modem (*mou*-döm) *n* modem *m*

moderate (*mo*-dö-röt) *adj* moderato

modern (*mo*-dön) *adj* moderno

modest (*mo*-disst) *adj* modesto

modesty (*mo*-di-ssti) *n* modestia *f*

modify (*mo*-di-fai) *v* modificare

mohair (*mou*-hê°) *n* angora *f*

moist (moisst) *adj* bagnato, umido

moisten (*moi*-ssön) *v* inumidire

moisture (*moiss*-tʃö) *n* umidità *f*

moisturizing cream (*moiss*-tʃö-rai-sing kriim) *n* crema idratante

molar (*mou*-lö) *n* molare *m*

moment (*mou*-mönt) *n* attimo *m*, momento *m*

momentary (*mou*-mön-tö-ri) *adj*

momentaneo

monarch (*mo*-nök) *n* monarca *m*

monarchy (*mo*-nö-ki) *n* monarchia *f*

monastery (*mo*-nö-sstri) *n* monastero *m*

Monday (*man*-di) lunedì *m*

monetary (*ma*-ni-tö-ri) *adj* monetario; ~ **unit** unità monetaria

money (*ma*-ni) *n* denaro *m*; ~ **exchange** ufficio cambio; ~ **order** vaglia *m*

monk (mangk) *n* monaco *m*

monkey (*mang*-ki) *n* scimmia *f*

monologue (*mo*-no-logh) *n* monologo *m*

monopoly (mö-*no*-pö-li) *n* monopolio *m*

monotonous (mö-*no*-tö-nöss) *adj* monotono

month (manθ) *n* mese *m*

monthly (*man*θ-li) *adj* mensile; ~ **magazine** rivista mensile

monument (*mo*-n'u-mönt) *n* monumento *m*

mood (muud) *n* umore *m*

moon (muun) *n* luna *f*

moonlight (*muun*-lait) *n* chiaro di luna

moor (mu°) *n* brughiera *f*

moose (muuss) *n* (pl ~, ~s) alce *m*

moped (*mou*-pêd) *n* motorino *m*

moral (*mo*-röl) *n* morale *f*; *adj* morale; **morals** costumi *mpl*

morality (mö-*ræ*-lö-ti) *n* moralità *f*

more (moo) *adj* più; **once** ~ ancora una volta

moreover (moo-*rou*-vö) *adv* inoltre

morning (*moo*-ning) *n* mattino *m*, mattina *f*; ~ **paper** giornale del mattino; **this** ~ stamattina

Moroccan (mö-*ro*-kön) *adj* marocchino

Morocco (mö-*ro*-kou) Marocco *m*

morphia (*moo*-fi-ö) *n* morfina *f*

morphine (*moo*-fiin) *n* morfina *f*

morsel (*moo*-ssöl) *n* pezzetto *m*

mortal (*moo*-töl) *adj* letale, mortale

mortgage (*moo*-ghidʒ) *n* ipoteca *f*

mosaic (mö-*sei*-ik) *n* mosaico *m*

mosque (mossk) *n* moschea *f*

mosquito (mö-*sskii*-tou) *n* (pl ~es) zanzara *f*; ~ **net** (mö-*sskii*-tou-nêt) *n* zanzariera *f*

moss (moss) *n* muschio *m*

most (mousst) *adj* il più; **at** ~ al massimo, tutt'al più; ~ **of all** soprattutto

mostly (*mousst*-li) *adv* per lo più

motel (mou-*têl*) *n* motel *m*

moth (moθ) *n* tarma *f*

mother (*ma*-ðö) *n* madre *f*; ~ **of pearl** madreperla *f*; ~ **tongue** madrelingua, lingua madre

mother-in-law (*ma*-ðö-rin-loo) *n* (pl mothers-) suocera *f*

motion (*mou*-ʃön) *n* moto *m*; mozione *f*

motivate (*mou*-ti-veit) *v* motivare

motive (*mou*-tiv) *n* movente *m*

motor (*mou*-tö) *n* motore *m*; *v* viaggiare in automobile; ~ **body** Am carrozzeria *f*; **starter** ~ starter *m*

motorbike (*mou*-tö-baik) *nAm* motorino *m*

motorboat (*mou*-tö-bout) *n* motoscafo *m*

motorcar (*mou*-tö-kaa) *n* automobile *f*

motorcycle (*mou*-tö-ssai-köl) *n* motocicletta *f*

motoring (*mou*-tö-ring) *n* automobilismo *m*

motorist (*mou*-tö-risst) *n* automobilista *m*

motorway (*mou*-tö-ᵘei) *n* autostrada *f*

motto (*mo*-tou) *n* (pl ~es, ~s) motto *m*

mouldy (*moul*-di) *adj* ammuffito

mound (maund) *n* elevazione *f*

mount (maunt) v montare; n monte m

mountain (*maun*-tin) n montagna f; **~ pass** passo m; **~ range** catena di montagne

mountaineering (maun-ti-*ni*ö-ring) n alpinismo m

mountainous (*maun*-ti-nöss) adj montagnoso

mourning (*moo*-ning) n lutto m

mouse (mauss) n (pl mice) topo m

moustache (mö-*sstaa*ʃ) n baffi mpl

mouth (mauθ) n bocca f; fauci fpl; foce f

mouthwash (*mau*θ°oʃ) n acqua dentifricia

movable (*muu*-vö-böl) adj mobile

move (muuv) v *muovere; spostare; traslocare; *commuovere; n mossa f; trasloco m

movement (*muuv*-mönt) n movimento m

movie (*muu*-vi) n film m; **movies** Am cinema m; **~ theater** Am cinema m

much (matʃ) adj molto; **as ~** altrettanto; tanto

muck (mak) n melma f

mud (mad) n fango m

muddle (*ma*-döl) n pasticcio m; v incasinare

muddy (*ma*-di) adj fangoso

muffler (*maf*-lö) nAm silenziatore m

mug (magh) n boccale m, tazza f

mule (m'uul) n mulo m

multiplication (mal-ti-pli-*kei*-ʃön) n moltiplicazione f

multiply (*mal*-ti-plai) v moltiplicare

mumps (mampss) n orecchioni mpl

municipal (m'uu-*ni*-ssi-pöl) adj municipale

murder (*möö*-dö) n assassinio m; v assassinare

murderer (*möö*-dö-rö) n assassino m, -a f

muscle (*ma*-ssöl) n muscolo m

muscular (*ma*-ssk'u-lö) adj muscoloso

museum (m'uu-*sii*-öm) n museo m

mushroom (*ma*ʃ-ruum) n fungo mangereccio; fungo m

music (m'uu-sik) n musica f; **~ academy** conservatorio m; **~ hall** teatro di varietà

musical (m'uu-si-köl) adj musicale; n commedia musicale

musician (m'uu-*si*-ʃön) n musicista m/f

mussel (*ma*-ssöl) n cozza f

*must (masst) v *dovere

mustard (*ma*-sstöd) n senape f

mute (m'uut) adj muto

mutiny (*m'uu*-ti-ni) n ammutinamento m

mutton (*ma*-tön) n montone m

mutual (m'uu-tʃu-öl) adj mutuo, reciproco

my (mai) adj mio

myself (mai-*ssêlf*) pron mi; io stesso

mysterious (mi-*ssti*ö-ri-öss) adj misterioso

mystery (*mi*-sstö-ri) n enigma m, mistero m

myth (miθ) n mito m

N

nail (neil) n unghia f; chiodo m; **~ file** limetta per le unghie; **~ polish** smalto

per unghie; **~ scissors** forbicine pe le unghie

nailbrush (*neil*-braʃ) *n* spazzolino per le unghie

naïve (naa-*iiv*) *adj* ingenuo

naked (*nei*-kid) *adj* nudo; spoglio

name (neim) *n* nome *m*; *v* nominare; **in the ~ of** a nome di

namely (*neim*-li) *adv* cioè

nap (næp) *n* pisolino *m*

napkin (*næp*-kin) *n* tovagliolo *m*

Naples (*nei*-pöls) Napoli *f*

nappy (*næ*-pi) *n* pannolino *m*

narcosis (naa-*kou*-ssiss) *n* (pl -ses) narcosi *f*

narcotic (naa-*ko*-tik) *n* narcotico *m*

narrow (*næ*-rou) *adj* angusto, stretto

narrow-minded (næ-rou-*main*-did) *adj* meschino

nasty (*naa*-ssti) *adj* antipatico, sgradevole

nation (*nei*-ʃön) *n* nazione *f*; popolo *m*

national (*næ*-ʃö-nöl) *adj* nazionale; statale; **~ anthem** inno nazionale; **~ dress** costume nazionale; **~ park** parco nazionale

nationality (næ-ʃö-*næ*-lö-ti) *n* nazionalità *f*

nationalize (*næ*-ʃö-nö-lais) *v* nazionalizzare

native (*nei*-tiv) *n* indigeno *m*; *adj* nativo; **~ country** patria *f*, paese natio; **~ language** lingua materna, madrelingua

natural (*næ*-tʃö-röl) *adj* naturale; innato

naturally (*næ*-tʃö-rö-li) *adv* naturalmente

nature (*nei*-tʃö) *n* natura *f*; indole *f*

naughty (*noo*-ti) *adj* cattivo

nausea (*noo*-ssi-ö) *n* nausea *f*

naval (*nei*-völ) *adj* navale

navel (*nei*-völ) *n* ombelico *m*

navigable (*næ*-vi-ghö-böl) *adj* navigabile

navigate (*næ*-vi-gheit) *v* navigare; governare

navigation (næ-vi-*ghei*-ʃön) *n* navigazione *f*

navy (*nei*-vi) *n* marina *f*

near (niö) *prep* vicino a; *adj* vicino

nearby (*niö*-bai) *adj* vicino

nearly (*niö*-li) *adv* quasi

neat (niit) *adj* lindo, curato; puro

necessary (*nê*-ssö-ssö-ri) *adj* necessario

necessity (nö-*ssê*-ssö-ti) *n* necessità *f*

neck (nêk) *n* collo *m*; **nape of the ~** nuca *f*

necklace (*nêk*-löss) *n* collana *f*

necktie (*nêk*-tai) *n* cravatta *f*

need (niid) *v* *occorrere, *aver bisogno di; *n* bisogno *m*, necessità *f*; **~ to** *dovere

needle (*nii*-döl) *n* ago *m*

negative (*nê*-ghö-tiv) *adj* negativo; *n* negativa *f*

neglect (ni-*ghlêkt*) *v* trascurare; *n* negligenza *f*

neglectful (ni-*ghlêkt*-föl) *adj* negligente

negotiate (ni-*ghou*-ʃi-eit) *v* negoziare

negotiation (ni-ghou-ʃi-*ei*-ʃön) *n* trattativa *f*

neighbo(u)r (*nei*-bö) *n* vicino *m*

neighbo(u)rhood (*nei*-bö-hud) *n* vicinato *m*

neighbo(u)ring (*nei*-bö-ring) *adj* contiguo, adiacente

neither (*nai*-ðö) *pron* né l'uno né l'altro; **neither ... nor** né ... né

neon (*nii*-on) *n* neon *m*

nephew (*nê*-fʰuu) *n* nipote *m*

nerve (nööv) *n* nervo *m*; audacia *f*

nervous (*nöö*-vöss) *adj* nervoso

nest (nêsst) *n* nido *m*

net (nêt) *n* rete *f*; *adj* netto

Netherlands (*nê*-ðö-lönds): **the ~** Paesi Bassi

network (*nêt*-ʰöök) *n* rete *f*

neuralgia (n¹u⁰-*ræl*-dʒö) n nevralgia f
neurosis (n¹u⁰-*rou*-ssiss) n nevrosi f
neuter (n¹uu-tö) adj neutro
neutral (n¹uu-tröl) adj neutrale
never (nê-vö) adv non … mai
nevertheless (nê-vö-öö-*lêss*) adv tuttavia
new (n¹uu) adj nuovo; **New Year** anno nuovo
news (n¹uus) n notiziario m, novità f; notizie fpl
newsagent (n¹uu-sei-dʒönt) n giornalaio m
newspaper (n¹uus-pei-pö) n giornale m
newsstand (n¹uus-sstænd) n edicola f
New Zealand (n¹uu *sii*-lönd) Nuova Zelanda
next (nêksst) adj prossimo; ~ **to** vicino a
next-door (nêksst-*doo*) adv accanto
nice (naiss) adj carino, bellino, piacevole; buono; simpatico
nickel (ni-köl) n nichelio m
nickname (nik-neim) n soprannome m
nicotine (ni-kö-tiin) n nicotina f
niece (niiss) n nipote f
Nigeria (nai-dʒi⁰-ri-ö) Nigeria f
Nigerian (nai-dʒi⁰-ri-ön) adj nigeriano
night (nait) n notte f; sera f; **by** ~ di notte; ~ **cream** crema per la notte; ~ **flight** volo notturno; ~ **rate** tariffa notturna; ~ **train** treno notturno
nightclub (nait-klab) n locale notturno
nightdress (nait-drêss) n camicia da notte
nightingale (nai-ting-gheil) n usignolo m
nightly (nait-li) adj notturno
nightmare (nait-meö) n incubo m
nil (nil) zero
nine (nain) num nove

nineteen (nain-tiin) num diciannove
nineteenth (nain-tiinθ) num diciannovesimo
ninety (nain-ti) num novanta
ninth (nainθ) num nono
nitrogen (nai-trö-dʒön) n azoto m
no (nou) no; adj nessuno; ~ **one** nessuno
nobility (nou-bi-lö-ti) n nobiltà f
noble (nou-böl) adj nobile
nobody (nou-bo-di) pron nessuno
nod (nod) n cenno con la testa; v annuire
noise (nois) n rumore m; baccano m, chiasso m
noisy (noi-si) adj rumoroso; sonoro
nominal (no-mi-nöl) adj nominale
nominate (no-mi-neit) v nominare
nomination (no-mi-*nei*-ʃön) n nomina f
none (nan) pron nessuno
nonsense (non-ssönss) n sciocchezza f
noon (nuun) n mezzogiorno m
nor (noo) conj neanche; ~ **do I** neanch'io, neanche a me; adv né; **neither … nor** né … né
normal (noo-möl) adj normale
north (nooθ) n nord m; settentrione m; adj settentrionale; **North Pole** polo Nord
north-east (nooθ-iisst) n nord-est m
northerly (noo-öö-li) adj settentrionale
northern (noo-öön) adj nordico
north-west (nooθ-ᵘêsst) n nord-ovest m
Norway (noo-ᵘei) Norvegia f
Norwegian (noo-ᵘii-dʒön) adj norvegese
nose (nous) n naso m
nosebleed (nous-bliid) n sangue dal naso
nostril (no-sstril) n narice f

nosy (*no-*si) *adj* curioso
not (not) *adv* non
notary (*nou-*tö-ri) *n* notaio *m*
note (nout) *n* appunto *m*, biglietto *m*;
commento *m*; tono *m*, nota *f*; *v*
annotare; osservare, notare
notebook (*nout-*buk) *n* taccuino *m*;
computer portatile
noted (*nou-*tid) *adj* illustre
notepaper (*nout-*pei-pö) *n* carta da
lettere
nothing (*na-*θing) *n* nulla *m*, niente *m*
notice (*nou-*tiss) *v* rilevare,
*accorgersi di, notare; *vedere; *n*
avviso *m*, notizia *f*; attenzione *f*
noticeable (*nou-*ti-ssö-böl) *adj*
evidente; notevole
notify (*nou-*ti-fai) *v* notificare;
avvisare
notion (*nou-*ʃön) *n* nozione *f*
notorious (nou-*too-*ri-öss) *adj*
famigerato
nougat (*nuu-*ghaa) *n* torrone *m*
nought (noot) *n* zero *m*
noun (naun) *n* nome *m*
nourishing (*na-*ri-ʃing) *adj* nutriente
novel (*no-*völ) *n* romanzo *m*
novelist (*no-*vö-lisst) *n* romanziere *m*,
-a *f*
November (nou-*vêm-*bö) novembre
now (nau) *adv* ora; adesso; ~ **and then**

di tanto in tanto
nowadays (*nau-*ö-deis) *adv*
oggigiorno
nowhere (*nou-*ᵘê°) *adv* in nessun
luogo
nozzle (*no-*söl) *n* becco *m*
nuance (nⁱuu-*angss*) *n* sfumatura *f*
nuclear (*nⁱuu-*kli-ö) *adj* nucleare; ~
energy energia nucleare
nucleus (*nⁱuu-*kli-öss) *n* nucleo *m*
nude (nⁱuud) *adj* nudo; *n* nudo *m*
nuisance (*nⁱuu-*ssönss) *n* seccatura *f*
numb (nam) *adj* intorpidito; intirizzito
number (*nam-*bö) *n* numero *m*; cifra *f*;
quantità *f*
numeral (*nⁱuu-*mö-röl) *n* numerale *m*
numerous (*nⁱuu-*mö-röss) *adj*
numeroso
nun (nan) *n* monaca *f*
nunnery (*na-*nö-ri) *n* convento *m*
nurse (nöss) *n* infermiere *m*, -a *f*;
bambinaia *f*; *v* curare; allattare
nursery (*nöö-*ssö-ri) *n* camera dei
bambini; asilo *m*; vivaio *m*
nut (nat) *n* noce *f*; dado *m*
nutcrackers (*nat-*kræ-kös) *pl*
schiaccianoci *m*
nutmeg (*nat-*mêgh) *n* noce moscata
nutritious (nⁱuu-*tri-*ʃöss) *adj* nutriente
nutshell (*nat-*ʃêl) *n* guscio di noce
nylon (*nai-*lon) *n* nailon *m*

O

oak (ouk) *n* quercia *f*
oar (oo) *n* remo *m*
oasis (ou-*ei-*ssiss) *n* (pl oases) oasi *f*
oath (ouθ) *n* giuramento *m*
oats (outss) *pl* avena *f*
obedience (ö-*bii-*di-önss) *n*
ubbidienza *f*

obedient (ö-*bii-*di-önt) *adj* ubbidiente
obey (ö-*bei*) *v* ubbidire
object[1] (*ob-*dʒikt) *n* oggetto *m*;
obiettivo *m*
object[2] (öb-*dʒêkt*) *v* obiettare; ~ **to**
*opporsi a
objection (öb-*dʒêk-*ʃön) *n* obiezione *f*

objective (öb-*dʒêk*-tiv) *adj* oggettivo;
  n obiettivo *m*

obligatory (ö-*bli*-ghö-tö-ri) *adj*
  obbligatorio

oblige (ö-*blaidʒ*) *v* obbligare; ***be
  obliged to** *essere obbligato a;
  *dovere

obliging (ö-*blai*-dʒing) *adj*
  servizievole

oblong (*ob*-long) *adj* oblungo; *n*
  rettangolo *m*

obscene (öb-*ssiin*) *adj* osceno

obscure (öb-*ssk'uᵒ*) *adj* scuro, oscuro,
  buio

observation (ob-sö-*vei*-ʃön) *n*
  osservazione *f*

observatory (öb-*söö*-vö-tri) *n*
  osservatorio *m*

observe (öb-*sööv*) *v* osservare

obsession (öb-*ssê*-ʃön) *n* ossessione *f*

obstacle (*ob*-sstö-köl) *n* ostacolo *m*

obstinate (*ob*-ssti-nöt) *adj* ostinato;
  caparbio

obtain (öb-*tein*) *v* conseguire,
  *ottenere

obvious (*ob*-vi-öss) *adj* ovvio

occasion (ö-*kei*-ʒön) *n* occasione *f*;
  motivo *m*

occasionally (ö-*kei*-ʒö-nö-li) *adv*
  ogni tanto, occasionalmente

occupant (*o*-k'u-pönt) *n* occupante *m*

occupation (o-k'u-*pei*-ʃön) *n*
  occupazione *f*

occupy (*o*-k'u-pai) *v* occupare

occur (ö-*köö*) *v* *succedere, capitare,
  *accadere

occurrence (ö-*ka*-rönss) *n* evento *m*

ocean (*ou*-ʃön) *n* oceano *m*

October (ok-*tou*-bö) ottobre

octopus (*ok*-tö-pöss) *n* polipo *m*

oculist (*o*-k'u-lisst) *n* oculista *m/f*

odd (od) *adj* bizzarro, strano; dispari

odo(u)r (*ou*-dö) *n* odore *m*

of (ov, öv) *prep* di; ~ **course** certo,

naturalmente

off (of) *adv* via; *prep* giù da

offence (ö-*fênss*) *n* reato *m*; offesa *f*;
  infrazione *f*

offend (ö-*fênd*) *v* *offendere;
  trasgredire

offense (ö-*fênss*) *nAm* reato *m*; offesa
  f; infrazione *f*

offensive (ö-*fên*-ssiv) *adj* offensivo;
  insultante; *n* offensiva *f*

offer (*o*-fö) *v* *offrire; presentare; *n*
  offerta *f*

office (*o*-fiss) *n* ufficio *m*; funzione *f*; ~
  hours ore d'ufficio

officer (*o*-fi-ssö) *n* ufficiale *m*

official (ö-*fi*-ʃöl) *adj* ufficiale

off-licence (*of*-lai-ssönss) *n* spaccio di
  liquori

often (*o*-fön) *adv* spesso

oil (oil) *n* olio *m*; petrolio *m*; ~ **filter**
  filtro dell'olio; **fuel** ~ nafta *f*; ~
  painting pittura ad olio; ~ **pressure**
  pressione dell'olio; ~ **refinery**
  raffineria; ~ **well** pozzo petrolifero

oily (*oi*-li) *adj* oleoso

ointment (*oint*-mönt) *n* unguento *m*

okay! (ou-*kei*) d'accordo!

old (ould) *adj* vecchio; ~ **age** vecchiaia
  f

old-fashioned (ould-*fæ*-ʃönd) *adj*
  antiquato

olive (*o*-liv) *n* oliva *f*; ~ **oil** olio d'oliva

omelette (*om*-löt) *n* frittata *f*

ominous (*o*-mi-nöss) *adj* sinistro

omit (ö-*mit*) *v* *omettere

omnipotent (om-*ni*-pö-tönt) *adj*
  onnipotente

on (on) *prep* su; a

once (ᵘanss) *adv* una volta; **at** ~ subito,
  ~ **more** ancora una volta

oncoming (*on*-ka-ming) *adj*
  imminente

one (ᵘan) *num* uno; *pron* uno

oneself (ᵘan-*ssêlf*) *pron* se stesso

one-sided (ᵘan-*ssai*-död) *adj* unilaterale

one-way traffic (ᵘan-ᵘei-*træ*-fik) *n* senso unico

onion (a-nᵗön) *n* cipolla *f*

only (*oun*-li) *adj* solo; *adv* solo, soltanto, solamente; *conj* però

onwards (*on*-ᵘöds) *adv* avanti

onyx (*o*-nikss) *n* onice *f*

opal (*ou*-pöl) *n* opale *m*

open (*ou*-pön) *v* *aprire; *adj* aperto; franco

opener (*ou*-pö-nö) *n* apriscatole; apribottiglie

opening (*ou*-pö-ning) *n* apertura *f*

opera (*o*-pö-rö) *n* opera *f*; ~ **house** teatro dell'opera

operate (*o*-pö-reit) *v* agire, funzionare; operare

operation (o-pö-*rei*-ʃön) *n* funzionamento *m*; operazione *f*

operator (*o*-pö-rei-tö) *n* centralinista *m/f*

operetta (o-pö-*rê*-tö) *n* operetta *f*

opinion (ö-*pi*-nᵗön) *n* parere *m*, opinione *f*

opponent (ö-*pou*-nönt) *n* avversario *m*, -a *f*

opportunity (o-pö-*ᵗuu*-nö-ti) *n* opportunità *f*, occasione *f*

oppose (ö-*pous*) *v* *opporsi

opposite (*o*-pö-sit) *prep* di fronte a; *adj* contrario, opposto

opposition (o-pö-*si*-ʃön) *n* opposizione *f*

oppress (ö-*prêss*) *v* *opprimere

optician (op-*ti*-ʃön) *n* ottico *m*, -a *f*

optimism (*op*-ti-mi-söm) *n* ottimismo *m*

optimist (*op*-ti-misst) *n* ottimista *m/f*

optimistic (op-ti-*mi*-sstik) *adj* ottimistico

optional (*op*-ʃö-nöl) *adj* facoltativo

or (oo) *conj* o

oral (*oo*-röl) *adj* orale

orange (*o*-rindʒ) *n* arancia *f*; *adj* arancione

orbit (*oo*-bit) *n* orbita *f*; *v* orbitare intorno a

orchard (*oo*-tʃöd) *n* frutteto *m*

orchestra (*oo*-ki-sströ) *n* orchestra *f*

order (*oo*-dö) *v* comandare; ordinare; *n* ordine *m*; comando *m*; ordinazione *f*; **in** ~ in ordine; **in** ~ **to** allo scopo di; **made to** ~ fatto su misura; **out of** ~ fuori uso; ~ **form** modulo di ordinazione; **postal** ~ vaglia postale

ordinary (*oo*-dön-ri) *adj* solito, ordinario

ore (oo) *n* minerale *m*

organ (*oo*-ghön) *n* organo *m*

organic (oo-*ghæ*-nik) *adj* organico

organization (oo-ghö-nai-*sei*-ʃön) *n* organizzazione *f*

organize (*oo*-ghö-nais) *v* organizzare

Orient (*oo*-ri-önt) *n* oriente *m*

oriental (oo-ri-*ên*-töl) *adj* orientale

orientate (*oo*-ri-ön-teit) *v* orientarsi

origin (*o*-ri-dʒin) *n* origine *f*; discendenza *f*, provenienza *f*

original (ö-*ri*-dʒi-nöl) *adj* autentico, originale

originally (ö-*ri*-dʒi-nö-li) *adv* originariamente

ornament (*oo*-nö-mönt) *n* ornamento *m*

ornamental (oo-nö-*mên*-töl) *adj* ornamentale

orphan (*oo*-fön) *n* orfano *m*, -a *f*

orthodox (*oo*-θö-dokss) *adj* ortodosso

ostrich (*o*-sstritʃ) *n* struzzo *m*

other (a-ðö) *adj* altro

otherwise (a-ðö-ᵘais) *conj* altrimenti; *adv* altrimenti

*ought (oot) *dovere; **you** ~ **to know** dovresti saperlo; **you** ~ **to have done it** avresti dovuto farlo

ounce (auns) *n* oncia *f*

our (au⁰) *adj* nostro

ours (au⁰z) *pron* il nostro *m*, la nostra *f*, i nostri *mpl*, le nostre *fpl*

ourselves (au⁰-*ssêlvs*) *pron* ci; noi stessi

out (aut) *adv* fuori; ~ **of** fuori di; per

outbreak (*aut*-breik) *n* scoppio *m*

outburst (*aut*-böösst) *n* reazione *f* violenta; ~ **of anger** esplosione *f* di rabbia

outcome (*aut*-kam) *n* risultato *m*

***outdo** (aut-*duu*) *v* superare

outdoors (aut-*doos*) *adv* all'aperto

outer (*au*-tö) *adj* esterno

outfit (*aut*-fit) *n* equipaggiamento *m*

outing (*aut*-ing) *n* gita *f*

outline (*aut*-lain) *n* contorno *m*; *v* abbozzare

outlook (*aut*-luk) *n* prospettiva *f*; punto di vista

output (*aut*-put) *n* produzione *f*

outrage (*aut*-reidʒ) *n* oltraggio *m*

outside (aut-*ssaid*) *adv* fuori; *prep* fuori di; *n* esteriore *m*, esterno *m*

outsize (*aut*-ssais) *n* taglia forte

outskirts (*aut*-ssköötss) *pl* sobborgo *m*

outstanding (aut-*sstæn*-ding) *adj* eminente

outward (*aut*-ᵘöd) *adj* esterno

outwards (*aut*-ᵘöds) *adv* al di fuori

oval (*ou*-völ) *adj* ovale

oven (*a*-vön) *n* forno *m*

over (*ou*-vö) *prep* sopra; oltre; *adv* al di sopra; giù; *adj* finito; ~ **there** laggiù

overall (*ou*-vö-rool) *adj* globale

overalls (*ou*-vö-rools) *pl* tuta *f*

overcast (*ou*-vö-kaasst) *adj* coperto

overcoat (*ou*-vö-kout) *n* soprabito *m*

***overcome** (ou-vö-*kam*) *v* *vincere

overdo (ou-vö-*duu*) *v* esagerare; stracuocere; **you're overdoing things** ti stai strapazzando

overdraft (ou-vö-*draaft*) *n* scoperto *m* (di conto); **have an** ~ avere il conto scoperto

overdraw (ou-vö-*droo*) *v* emettere assegni per una somma eccedente; ~ **one's account** andare allo scoperto

overdue (ou-vö-*d'uu*) *adj* in ritardo; arretrato

overhaul (ou-vö-*hool*) *v* revisionare

overhead (ou-vö-*hêd*) *adv* lassù

overlook (ou-vö-*luk*) *v* trascurare

overnight (ou-vö-*nait*) *adv* di notte

overseas (ou-vö-*ssiis*) *adj* oltremare

oversight (*ou*-vö-ssait) *n* svista *f*

***oversleep** (ou-vö-*ssliip*) *v* dormire troppo

***overtake** (ou-vö-*teik*) *v* sorpassare; **no overtaking** divieto di sorpasso

over-tired (ou-vö-*tai⁰d*) *adj* esausto

overture (*ou*-vö-tʃö) *n* ouverture *f*

overweight (*ou*-vö-ᵘeit) *n* sovrappeso *m*

overwhelm (ou-vö-ᵘ*êlm*) *v* *sopraffare, schiacciare

overwork (ou-vö-ᵘ*öök*) *v* lavorare troppo

owe (ou) *v* *dovere; **owing to** a causa di

owl (aul) *n* gufo *m*

own (oun) *v* *possedere; *adj* proprio

owner (*ou*-nö) *n* proprietario *m*, -a *f*

ox (okss) *n* (pl oxen) bue *m*

oxygen (*ok*-ssi-dʒön) *n* ossigeno *m*

oyster (*oi*-sstö) *n* ostrica *f*

ozone (*ou*-zoun) *n* ozono *m*

P

pace (peiss) *n* andatura *f*; passo *m*; velocità *f*

Pacific Ocean (pö-*ssi*-fik ou-ʃön) Oceano Pacifico

pacifism (*pæ*-ssi-fi-söm) *n* pacifismo *m*

pacifist (*pæ*-ssi-fisst) *n* pacifista *m*

pack (pæk) *v* fare le valigie; riempire; ~ **up** imballare

package (*pæ*-kidʒ) *n* pacco *m*

packet (*pæ*-kit) *n* pacchetto *m*

packing (*pæ*-king) *n* imballaggio *m*

pact (pækt) *n* patto *m*

pad (pæd) *n* cuscinetto *m*; blocco per appunti

paddle (*pæ*-döl) *n* remo *m*

padlock (*pæd*-lok) *n* lucchetto *m*

pagan (*pei*-ghön) *adj* pagano; *n* pagano *m*

page (peidʒ) *n* pagina *f*

pail (peil) *n* secchio *m*

pain (pein) *n* dolore *m*; **pains** pena *f*

painful (*pein*-föl) *adj* penoso

painkiller (*pein*-ki-lö) *n* analgesico *m*

painless (*pein*-löss) *adj* indolore

paint (peint) *n* colore *m*; *v* pitturare; verniciare

paintbox (*peint*-bokss) *n* scatola di colori

paintbrush (*peint*-braʃ) *n* pennello *m*

painter (*pein*-tö) *n* pittore *m*, -trice *f*

painting (*pein*-ting) *n* pittura *f*; quadro *m*

pair (pëᵒ) *n* paio *m*

Pakistan (paa-ki-*sstaan*) Pakistan *m*

Pakistani (paa-ki-*sstaa*-ni) *adj* pachistano

pal (pæl) n amico *m*, -a *f*

palace (*pæ*-löss) *n* palazzo *m*

pale (peil) *adj* pallido; chiaro

palm (paam) *n* palma *f*

palpitation (pæl-pi-*tei*-ʃön) *n*

palpitazione *f*

pan (pæn) *n* tegame *m*

pancake (*pæn*-keik) *n* crêpe *f*, frittella dolce

pane (pein) *n* vetro *m*

panel (*pæ*-nöl) *n* pannello *m*

panelling (*pæ*-nö-ling) *n* rivestimento a pannelli

panic (*pæ*-nik) *n* panico *m*

pant (pænt) *v* ansimare

panties (*pæn*-tis) *pl* mutandine *fpl*, mutande *fpl*

pants (pæntss) *pl* mutande *fpl*; *Am* pantaloni *mpl*

pantsuit (*pænt*-ssuut) *n* giacca e pantaloni

panty hose (*pæn*-ti-hous) *n* calzamaglia *f*

paper (*pei*-pö) *n* carta *f*; giornale *m*; di carta; **carbon** ~ carta carbone; ~ **bag** sacchetto *m*; ~ **knife** tagliacarte *m*; ~ **napkin** tovagliolo di carta; **wrapping** ~ carta da imballaggio

paperback (*pei*-pö-bæk) *n* libro tascabile

parade (pö-*reid*) *n* parata *f*

paradise (*pæ*-rö-dais) *n* paradiso *m*

paraffin (*pæ*-rö-fin) *n* paraffina *f*; vaselina *f*

paragraph (*pæ*-rö-ghraaf) *n* capoverso *m*, paragrafo *m*

parakeet (*pæ*-rö-kiit) *n* cocorita *f*

paralyse (*pæ*-rö-lais) *v* paralizzare

parallel (*pæ*-rö-lêl) *adj* parallelo; *n* parallela *f*

parcel (*paa*-ssöl) *n* pacco *m*, pacchetto *m*

pardon (*paa*-dön) *n* perdono *m*

parent (*pëᵒ*-rönt) *n* genitore *m*; **parents** *pl* genitori *mpl*

parents-in-law (*pëᵒ*-röntss-in-loo) *pl* suoceri

parish (*pæ-riʃ*) *n* parrocchia *f*
park (paak) *n* parco *m*; *v* posteggiare
parking (*paa*-king) *n* parcheggio *m*;
 no ~ divieto di sosta; **~ disc** disco
 orario; **~ fee** tariffa del parcheggio; **~**
 light luci di posizione; **~ lot** *Am*
 parcheggio *m*; **~ meter** parchimetro
 m; **~ ticket** multa; **~ zone** zona di
 parcheggio
parliament (*paa*-lö-mönt) *n*
 parlamento *m*
parliamentary (paa-lö-*mên*-tö-ri) *adj*
 parlamentare
parrot (*pæ*-röt) *n* pappagallo *m*
parsley (*paa*-ssli) *n* prezzemolo *m*
parson (*paa*-ssön) *n* pastore *m*
parsonage (*paa*-ssö-nidʒ) *n*
 presbiterio *m*
part (paat) *n* parte *f*; pezzo *m*; *v*
 separare; **spare ~** pezzo di ricambio
partial (*paa*-ʃöl) *adj* parziale
participant (paa-*ti*-ssi-pönt) *n*
 partecipante *m/f*
participate (paa-*ti*-ssi-peit) *v*
 partecipare
particular (pö-*ti*-k¹u-lö) *adj* speciale,
 particolare; esigente; **in ~** in
 particolare
parting (*paa*-ting) *n* congedo *m*;
 scriminatura *f*, riga *f*
partition (paa-*ti*-ʃön) *n* divisorio *m*
partly (*paat*-li) *adv* in parte
partner (*paat*-nö) *n* compagno *m*, -a *f*;
 socio *m*, -a *f*
partridge (*paa*-tridʒ) *n* pernice *f*
party (*paa*-ti) *n* partito *m*; festa *f*;
 gruppo *m*
pass (paass) *v* *trascorrere, passare,
 sorpassare; **~ by** passare accanto; **~**
 through attraversare
passage (*pæ*-ssidʒ) *n* passaggio *m*;
 traversata *f*; brano *m*
passenger (*pæ*-ssön-dʒö) *n*
 passeggero *m*, -a *f*; **~ car** *Am* vagone

m; **~ train** treno passeggeri
passer-by (paa-ssö-*bai*) *n* passante
 m/f
passing (*pæ*-ssing) *adj* passeggero; *n*
 passaggio *m*; **no ~** *Am* divieto di
 sorpasso
passion (*pæ*-ʃön) *n* passione *f*; collera
 f
passionate (*pæ*-ʃö-nöt) *adj*
 appassionato
passive (*pæ*-ssiv) *adj* passivo
passport (*paass*-poot) *n* passaporto
 m; **~ control** controllo passaporti; **~**
 photograph foto per passaporto
password (*paass*-ᵘööd) *n* parola
 d'ordine; password *f*
past (paasst) *n* passato *m*; *adj* scorso,
 passato; *prep* lungo, al di là di
paste (peisst) *n* pasta *f*; *v* incollare
pastime (*paasst*-taim) *n* passatempo
 m
pastry (*pei*-sstri) *n* pasticcino *m*; **~**
 shop pasticceria *f*
pasture (*paass*-tʃö) *n* pascolo *m*
pasty (*pei*-ssti) *adj* smorto
patch (pætʃ) *v* rappezzare
patent (*pei*-tönt) *n* brevetto *m*
path (paaθ) *n* sentiero *m*
patience (*pei*-fönss) *n* pazienza *f*
patient (*pei*-fönt) *adj* paziente; *n*
 paziente *m/f*
patriot (*pei*-tri-öt) *n* patriota *m/f*
patrol (pö-*troul*) *n* pattuglia *f*; *v*
 pattugliare; sorvegliare
pattern (*pæ*-tön) *n* disegno *m*
pause (poos) *n* pausa *f*; *v*
 *interrompersi
pave (peiv) *v* lastricare, pavimentare
pavement (*peiv*-mönt) *n* marciapiede
 m; selciato *m*
pavilion (pö-*vil*-ᶦön) *n* padiglione *m*
paw (poo) *n* zampa *f*
pawn (poon) *v* impegnare; *n* pedina *f*
pay (pei) *n* salario *m*, paga *f*

*pay (pei) *v* pagare; ***valere la pena;** ~ **attention to** *stare attento a; ~ **desk** cassa *f*; ~ **off** saldare; ~ **on account** pagare a rate; ~ **phone** telefono pubblico

payee (pei-*ii*) *n* beneficiario *m*, -a *f*

paying (pei*ng*) *adj* rimunerativo

payment (pei-mönt) *n* pagamento *m*

pea (pii) *n* pisello *m*

peace (piiss) *n* pace *f*

peaceful (piiss-föl) *adj* pacifico

peach (piitʃ) *n* pesca *f*

peacock (pii-kok) *n* pavone *m*

peak (piik) *n* vetta *f*; cima *f*; ~ **hour** ora di punta; ~ **season** alta stagione

peanut (pii-nat) *n* arachide *f*

pear (pê^ö) *n* pera *f*

pearl (pööl) *n* perla *f*

peasant (pê-sönt) *n* contadino *m*

pebble (pê-böl) *n* ciottolo *m*

peculiar (pi-kʲuul-'ö) *adj* strano; speciale, particolare

peculiarity (pi-kʲuu-li-æ-rö-ti) *n* singolarità *f*

pedal (pê-döl) *n* pedale *m*

pedestrian (pi-dê-sstri-ön) *n* pedone *m*; **no pedestrians** vietato ai pedoni; ~ **crossing** passaggio pedonale

peel (piil) *v* sbucciare; *n* buccia *f*

peep (piip) *v* spiare

peg (pêgh) *n* gancio *m*

pelican (pê-li-kön) *n* pellicano *m*

pelvis (pêl-viss) *n* bacino *m*

pen (pên) *n* penna *f*

penalty (pê-nöl-ti) *n* punizione *f*; pena *f*; ~ **kick** calcio di rigore

pencil (pên-ssöl) *n* matita *f*; ~ **sharpener** temperamatite *m*

pendant (pên-dönt) *n* pendente *m*

penetrate (pê-ni-treit) *v* penetrare

penguin (pêng-ghʷin) *n* pinguino *m*

penicillin (pê-ni-ssi-lin) *n* penicillina *f*

peninsula (pö-nin-ssʲu-lö) *n* penisola *f*

penknife (pên-naif) *n* (pl -knives)
temperino *m*

penny (pên-ni) *n* penny *m*

pension[1] (pang-ssi-ong) *n* pensione *f*

pension[2] (pên-ʃön) *n* pensione *f*

Pentecost (Pen-ti-kast) Pentecoste *f*

people (pii-pöl) *pl* gente *f*; *n* popolo *m*

pepper (pê-pö) *n* pepe *m*

peppermint (pê-pö-mint) *n* menta piperita

per (pöö) *prep* a; **100 km ~ hour** 100 km all'ora; **50 ~ night** 50 a notte; ~ **annum** all'anno

perceive (pö-ssiiv) *v* percepire

percent (pö-ssênt) *n* percento *m*

percentage (pö-ssên-tidʒ) *n* percentuale *f*

perceptible (pö-ssêp-ti-böl) *adj* percettibile

perception (pö-ssêp-ʃön) *n* percezione *f*

perch (pöötʃ) (pl ~) pesce persico *m*

percolator (pöö-kö-lei-tö) *n* caffettiera a filtro

perfect (pöö-fikt) *adj* perfetto

perfection (pö-fêk-ʃön) *n* perfezione *f*

perform (pö-foom) *v* compiere, eseguire

performance (pö-foo-mönss) *n* rappresentazione *f*

perfume (pöö-fʲuum) *n* profumo *m*

perhaps (pö-hæpss) *adv* forse

peril (pê-ril) *n* pericolo *m*

perilous (pê-ri-löss) *adj* pericoloso

period (pi^ö-ri-öd) *n* epoca *f*, periodo *m*; punto *m*

periodical (pi^ö-ri-o-di-köl) *n* periodico *m*; *adj* periodico

perish (pê-riʃ) *v* perire

perishable (pê-ri-ʃö-böl) *adj* deperibile

perjury (pöö-dʒö-ri) *n* spergiuro *m*

perm (pööm) *n* permanente *f*; *v* fare la permanente a

permanent (pöö-mö-nönt) *adj*

duraturo, permanente; stabile, fisso;
~ **press** stiratura permanente; ~
wave permanente f

permission (pö-*mi*-ʃön) *n* permesso
m, autorizzazione *f*; licenza *f*

permit[1](pö-*mit*) *v* *permettere

permit[2](pöö-mit) *n* permesso *m*

peroxide (pö-*rok*-ssaid) *n* acqua
ossigenata

perpendicular (pöö-pön-*di*-k¹u-lö)
adj perpendicolare

Persia (*pöö*-ʃö) Persia *f*

Persian (*pöö*-ʃön) *adj* persiano

person (*pöö*-ssön) *n* persona *f*; **per** ~ a
persona

personal (*pöö*-ssö-nöl) *adj* personale

personality (pöö-ssö-*næ*-lö-ti) *n*
personalità *f*

personnel (pöö-ssö-*nêl*) *n* personale
m

perspective (pö-*sspêk*-tiv) *n*
prospettiva *f*

perspiration (pöö-sspö-*rei*-ʃön) *n*
traspirazione *f*, sudore *m*

perspire (pö-*sspai*ᵒ) *v* traspirare,
sudare

persuade (pö-*ssᵘeid*) *v* *persuadere;
*convincere

persuasion (pö-*ssᵘei*-ʒön) *n*
convinzione *f*

pessimism (*pê*-ssi-mi-söm) *n*
pessimismo *m*

pessimist (*pê*-ssi-misst) *n* pessimista
m/f

pessimistic (pê-ssi-*mi*-sstik) *adj*
pessimistico

pet (pêt) *n* animale domestico;
favorito *m*

petal (*pê*-töl) *n* petalo *m*

petition (pi-*ti*-ʃön) *n* petizione *f*

petrol (*pê*-tröl) *n* benzina *f*; ~ **pump**
pompa di benzina; ~ **station**
distributore di benzina; ~ **tank**
serbatoio di benzina

petroleum (pi-*trou*-li-öm) *n* petrolio
m

petty (*pê*-ti) *adj* piccolo, futile,
insignificante; ~ **cash** cassa per
piccole spese

pewter (*p¹uu*-tö) *n* peltro *m*

phantom (*fæn*-töm) *n* fantasma *m*

pharmacist (*faa*-mö-ssisst) *n*
farmacista *m/f*

pharmacology (faa-mö-*ko*-lö-dʒi) *n*
farmacologia *f*

pharmacy (*faa*-mö-ssi) *n* farmacia *f*

phase (feis) *n* fase *f*

pheasant (*fê*-sönt) *n* fagiano *m*

Philippine (*fi*-li-pain) *adj* filippino

Philippines (*fi*-li-piins) *pl* Isole
Filippine

philosopher (fi-*lo*-ssö-fö) *n* filosofo
m, -a *f*

philosophy (fi-*lo*-ssö-fi) *n* filosofia *f*

phone (foun) *n* telefono *m*; *v*
telefonare, chiamare

phonetic (fö-*nê*-tik) *adj* fonetico

photo (*fou*-tou) *n* (pl ~s) foto *f*

photocopy (*fou*-tö-ko-pi) *n* fotocopia
f; *v* fotocopiare

photograph (*fou*-tö-ghraaf) *n*
fotografia *f*; *v* fotografare

photographer (fö-*to*-ghrö-fö) *n*
fotografo *m*

photography (fö-*to*-ghrö-fi) *n*
fotografia *f*

phrase (freis) *n* frase *f*; ~ **book**
manuale di conversazione

physical (*fi*-si-köl) *adj* fisico

physician (fi-si-*ʃ*ön) *n* medico *m*

physicist (*fi*-si-ssisst) *n* fisico *m*

physics (*fi*-sikss) *n* fisica *f*

physiology (fi-si-*o*-lö-dʒi) *n* fisiologia
f

pianist (*pii*-ö-nisst) *n* pianista *m/f*

piano (pi-*æ*-nou) *n* pianoforte *m*;
grand ~ pianoforte a coda

pick (pik) *v* *cogliere; *scegliere; *n*

scelta f; ~ **up** *raccogliere; andare a prendere

pickles (*pi*-köls) pl sottaceti mpl

pick-up van (*pi*k-ap-vön) n camionetta f

picnic (*pik*-nik) n picnic m; v *fare un picnic

picture (*pik*-tʃö) n pittura f; illustrazione f, stampa f; figura f, quadro m; ~ **postcard** cartolina illustrata; **pictures** cinema m

picturesque (pik-tʃö-*rêssk*) adj pittoresco

piece (piiss) n pezzo m

pie (pai) n torta f; pasticcio m

pier (piö) n molo m

pierce (piöss) v perforare

pig (pigh) n maiale m; porco m

pigeon (*pi*-dʒön) n piccione m

pig-headed (pigh-*hê*-did) adj testardo

piglet (*pigh*-löt) n porcellino m

pigskin (*pigh*-sskin) n pelle di cinghiale

pike (paik) n (pl ~) luccio m

pile (pail) n mucchio m; v ammucchiare; **piles** pl emorroidi fpl

pilgrim (*pil*-ghrim) n pellegrino m, -a f

pilgrimage (*pil*-ghri-midʒ) n pellegrinaggio m

pill (pil) n pillola f

pillar (*pi*-lö) n pilastro m, colonna f; ~ **box** buca delle lettere

pillow (*pi*-lou) n cuscino m

pillowcase (*pi*-lou-keiss) n federa f

pilot (*pai*-löt) n pilota m

pimple (*pim*-pöl) n pustoletta f

pin (pin) n spillo m; v appuntare; **bobby ~** Am fermaglio per capelli

pincers (*pin*-ssös) pl tenaglie fpl

pinch (pintʃ) v pizzicare

pineapple (*pai*-næ-pöl) n ananas m

ping-pong (*ping*-pong) n ping-pong m

pink (pingk) adj rosa

pint (paint) n pinta f

pioneer (pai-ö-*ni*ö) n pioniere m

pious (*pai*-öss) adj pio

pip (pip) n seme m

pipe (paip) n pipa f; tubatura f; ~ **cleaner** curapipe m; ~ **tobacco** tabacco da pipa

pipeline (*paip*-lain) n conduttura f; **in the ~** in arrivo

pirate (*pai*ö-röt) n pirata m

pistol (*pi*-sstöl) n pistola f

piston (*pi*-sstön) n stantuffo m; ~ **ring** fascia elastica

pit (pit) n buca f; miniera f

pitcher (*pi*-tʃö) n brocca f

pity (*pi*-ti) n pietà f; v provare compassione per, compatire; **what a pity!** peccato!

placard (*plæ*-kaad) n cartellone m

place (pleiss) n posto m; v possare, *porre; ~ **of birth** luogo di nascita; *take ~ *aver luogo

plague (pleigh) n flagello m

plaice (pleiss) n (pl ~) platessa f

plain (plein) adj chiaro; semplice; n pianura f

plan (plæn) n progetto m; pianta f; v progettare

plane (plein) adj piano; n aereo m; ~ **crash** incidente aereo

planet (*plæ*-nit) n pianeta m

planetarium (plæ-ni-*tê*ö-ri-öm) n planetario m

plank (plængk) n asse f

plant (plaant) n pianta f; impianto m; v piantare

plantation (plæn-*tei*-ʃön) n piantagione f

plaster (*plaa*-sstö) n stucco m, gesso m; cerotto m

plastic (*plæ*-sstik) adj plastico; di plastica; n plastica f; ~ **bag** sacchetto di plastica; ~ **money** carte di credito; ~ **surgeon** chirurgo plastico; ~

plate 278

surgery chirurgia plastica

plate (pleit) *n* piatto *m*; lamiera *f*

plateau (*plæ*-tou) *n* (pl ~x, ~s) altopiano *m*

platform (*plæt*-foom) *n* binario *m*, banchina *f*

platinum (*plæ*-ti-nöm) *n* platino *m*

play (plei) *v* giocare; suonare; *n* gioco *m*; rappresentazione teatrale; **one-act** ~ commedia in un atto; ~ **truant** marinare la scuola

player (plei⁰) *n* giocatore *m*, -trice *f*

playground (*plei*-ghraund) *n* parco giochi

playing card (*plei*-ing-kaad) *n* carta da gioco

playwright (*plei*-rait) *n* drammaturgo *m*, -a *f*

plea (plii) *n* difesa *f*

plead (pliid) *v* perorare

pleasant (*plê*-sönt) *adj* gradevole, simpatico, piacevole

please (pliis) per favore; *v* *piacere; **pleased** lieto

pleasing (*plii*-sing) *adj* gradevole

pleasure (*plê*-ʒö) *n* diletto *m*, divertimento *m*, piacere *m*

plentiful (*plên*-ti-föl) *adj* abbondante

plenty (*plên*-ti) *n* abbondanza *f*

pliers (plai⁰s) *pl* pinze *fpl*

plimsolls (*plim*-ssöls) *pl* scarpe da ginnastica

plot (plot) *n* congiura *f*, complotto *m*; trama *f*; appezzamento *m*

plough (plau) *n* aratro *m*; *v* arare

plucky (*pla*-ki) *adj* coraggioso

plug (plagh) *n* spina *f*; ~ **in** *connettere

plum (plam) *n* susina *f*, prugna *f*

plumber (*pla*-mö) *n* idraulico *m*, -a *f*

plump (plamp) *adj* grassottello

plural (*plu*⁰-röl) *n* plurale *m*

plus (plass) *prep* più

pneumatic (n'uu-*mæ*-tik) *adj* pneumatico

pneumonia (n'uu-*mou*-ni-ö) *n* polmonite *f*

poach (poutʃ) *v* cacciare di frodo

pocket (*po*-kit) *n* tasca *f*

pocketknife (*po*-kit-naif) *n* (pl -knives) temperino *m*, coltellino *m*

poem (*pou*-im) *n* poema *m*

poet (*pou*-it) *n* poeta *m*, -essa *f*

poetry (*pou*-i-tri) *n* poesia *f*

point (point) *n* punto *m*; punta *f*; *v* additare; ~ **of view** punto di vista; ~ **out** indicare

pointed (*poin*-tid) *adj* appuntito

poison (*poi*-sön) *n* veleno *m*; *v* avvelenare

poisonous (*poi*-sö-nöss) *adj* velenoso

Poland (*pou*-lönd) Polonia *f*

Pole (poul) *n* polacco *m*

pole (poul) *n* palo *m*

police (pö-*liiss*) *pl* polizia *f*; ~ **station** posto di polizia

policeman (pö-*liiss*-mön) *n* (pl -men) agente *m*, poliziotto *m*

policewoman (pö-*liiss*-ᵘu-mön) *n* (pl -women) agente *f*, poliziotta *f*

policy (*po*-li-ssi) *n* procedimento *m*; polizza *f*

polio (*pou*-li-ou) *n* polio *f*, poliomielite *f*

Polish (*pou*-liʃ) *adj* polacco

polish (*po*-liʃ) *v* lucidare

polite (pö-*lait*) *adj* cortese

political (pö-*li*-ti-köl) *adj* politico

politician (po-li-*ti*-ʃön) *n* politico *m*, -a *f*

politics (*po*-li-tikss) *n* politica *f*

poll (pöl) *n* sondaggio *m*; *v* fare un sondaggio tra; guadagnare; **the polls** le elezioni; **go to the polls** andare alle urne

pollute (pö-*luut*) *v* inquinare

pollution (pö-*luu*-ʃön) *n* contaminazione *f*, inquinamento *m*

pond (pond) *n* stagno *m*

pony (*pou*-ni) *n* pony *m*

pool (pool) *n* piscina *f*; pozza *f*; pool *m*

poor (pu⁰) *adj* povero; misero; scadente

pope (poup) *n* Papa *m*

pop music (pop *m'uu*-sik) musica pop

poppy (*po*-pi) *n* papavero *m*

popular (*po*-p'u-lö) *adj* popolare

population (po-p'u-*lei*-ʃön) *n* popolazione *f*

porcelain (*poo*-ssö-lin) *n* porcellana *f*

porcupine (*poo*-k'u-pain) *n* porcospino *m*

pork (pook) *n* carne di maiale

port (poot) *n* porto *m*; babordo *m*

portable (*poo*-tö-böl) *adj* portatile

porter (*poo*-tö) *n* facchino *m*; portiere *m*

porthole (*poot*-houl) *n* oblò *m*

portion (*poo*-ʃön) *n* porzione *f*

portrait (*poo*-trit) *n* ritratto *m*

Portugal (*poo*-t'u-ghöl) Portogallo *m*

Portuguese (poo-t'u-*ghiis*) *adj* portoghese

posh (poʃ) *adj* elegante; snob

position (pö-*si*-ʃön) *n* posizione *f*; situazione *f*; atteggiamento *m*

positive (*po*-sö-tiv) *adj* positivo; *n* positiva *f*

possess (pö-*sêss*) *v* *possedere; **possessed** *adj* indemoniato

possession (pö-*sê*-ʃön) *n* possesso *m*; **possessions** possedimenti *mpl*

possibility (po-ssö-*bi*-lö-ti) *n* possibilità *f*

possible (*po*-ssö-böl) *adj* possibile; eventuale

post (pousst) *n* palo *m*; impiego *m*; posta *f*; *v* impostare; **~ office** ufficio postale, posta *f*

postage (*pou*-sstidʒ) *n* affrancatura *f*; **~ paid** franco di porto; **~ stamp** francobollo *m*

postcard (*pousst*-kaad) *n* cartolina *f*; cartolina illustrata

poster (*pou*-sstö) *n* cartellone *m*, poster *m*

poste restante (pousst rê-*sstaɴgt*) fermo posta

postman (*pousst*-mön) *n* (pl -men) postino *m*

post-paid (pousst-*peid*) *adj* porto franco

postpone (pö-*sspoun*) *v* rimandare

pot (pot) *n* pentola *f*

potato (pö-*tei*-tou) *n* (pl ~es) patata *f*

pottery (*po*-tö-ri) *n* ceramica *f*; stoviglie *fpl*

pouch (pautʃ) *n* sacchetto *m*

poulterer (*poul*-tö-rö) *n* pollivendolo *m*, -a *f*

poultry (*poul*-tri) *n* pollame *m*

pound (paund) *n* libbra *f*; sterlina *f*

pour (poo) *v* versare

poverty (*po*-vö-ti) *n* povertà *f*

powder (*pau*-dö) *n* polvere *f*; **~ compact** portacipria *m*; **talc ~** talco *m*; **~ room** toilette delle signore

power (pau⁰) *n* potenza *f*, energia *f*; potere *m*; **~ station** centrale elettrica

powerful (*pau⁰*-föl) *adj* potente, poderoso; forte

powerless (*pau⁰*-löss) *adj* impotente

practical (*præk*-ti-köl) *adj* pratico

practically (*præk*-ti-kli) *adv* praticamente

practice (*præk*-tiss) *n* pratica *f*

practise (*præk*-tiss) *v* praticare; esercitarsi

praise (preis) *v* lodare; *n* elogio *m*

pram (præm) *n* carrozzina *f*

prawn (proon) *n* gambero *m*

pray (prei) *v* pregare

prayer (prê⁰) *n* preghiera *f*

preach (priitʃ) *v* predicare

precarious (pri-*kê⁰*-ri-öss) *adj* precario

precaution (pri-*koo*-ʃön) *n*

precauzione *f*

precede (pri-*ssiid*) *v* precedere

preceding (pri-*ssii*-ding) *adj* precedente

precious (*prê*-ʃöss) *adj* prezioso

precipice (*prê*-ssi-piss) *n* precipizio *m*

precipitation (pri-ssi-pi-*tei*-ʃön) *n* precipitazione *f*

precise (pri-*ssaiss*) *adj* preciso, esatto; meticoloso

predecessor (*prii*-di-ssê-ssö) *n* predecessore *m*

predict (pri-*dikt*) *v* *predire

prefer (pri-*föö*) *v* preferire

preferable (*prê*-fö-rö-böl) *adj* preferibile

preference (*prê*-fö-rönss) *n* preferenza *f*

prefix (*prii*-fikss) *n* prefisso *m*

pregnant (*prêgh*-nönt) *adj* incinta

prejudice (*prê*-dʒö-diss) *n* pregiudizio *m*

preliminary (pri-*li*-mi-nö-ri) *adj* preliminare

premature (*prê*-mö-tʃuᵒ) *adj* prematuro

premier (*prêm*-iᵒ) *n* primo ministro

premises (*prê*-mi-ssiss) *pl* stabile *m*, sede *f*

premium (*prii*-mi-öm) *n* premio *m*

prepaid (prii-*peid*) *adj* pagato in anticipo

preparation (prê-pö-*rei*-ʃön) *n* preparazione *f*

prepare (pri-*pêᵒ*) *v* preparare

preposition (prê-pö-*si*-ʃön) *n* preposizione *f*

prescribe (pri-*sskraib*) *v* *prescrivere

prescription (pri-*sskrip*-ʃön) *n* ricetta *f*

presence (*prê*-sönss) *n* presenza *f*

present¹ (*prê*-sönt) *n* regalo *m*, dono *m*; presente *m*; *adj* attuale; presente

present² (pri-*sênt*) *v* presentare

presently (*prê*-sönt-li) *adv* fra poco; ora

preservation (prê-sö-*vei*-ʃön) *n* preservazione *f*

preserve (pri-*sööv*) *v* conservare; *mettere in conserva

president (*prê*-si-dönt) *n* presidente *m*, -essa *f*

press (prêss) *n* stampa *f*; *v* schiacciare, premere; stirare; ~ **conference** conferenza stampa

pressing (*prê*-ssing) *adj* pressante, urgente

pressure (*prê*-ʃö) *n* pressione *f*; tensione *f*; **atmospheric ~** pressione atmosferica; ~ **cooker** pentola a pressione

prestige (prê-*sstiiʒ*) *n* prestigio *m*

presumable (pri-sⁱ*uu*-mö-böl) *adj* presumibile

presume (pri-*sium*) *v* presumere; ~ **to do** permettersi di fare

presumptuous (pri-*samp*-ʃöss) *adj* presuntuoso

pretence (pri-*tênss*) *n* pretesa *f*

pretend (pri-*tênd*) *v* *fingere, *pretendere

pretext (*prii*-têksst) *n* pretesto *m*

pretty (*pri*-ti) *adj* bello, carino; *adv* alquanto, piuttosto, abbastanza

prevent (pri-*vênt*) *v* impedire; *prevenire

preventive (pri-*vên*-tiv) *adj* preventivo

preview (pri-*vⁱuu*) *n* anteprima *f*

previous (*prii*-vi-öss) *adj* precedente, anteriore, previo

pre-war (prii-*ᵘoo*) *adj* d'anteguerra

price (praiss) *v* prezzare; *n* prezzo *m*; ~ **list** listino prezzi

priceless (*praiss*-löss) *adj* inestimabile

prick (prik) *v* *pungere

pride (praid) *n* fierezza *f*

priest (priisst) n prete m

primary (prai-mö-ri) adj primario; primo, principale; elementare

prince (prinss) n principe m

princess (prin-ssêss) n principessa f

principal (prin-ssö-pöl) adj principale; n preside m/f, direttore m, -trice f

principle (prin-ssö-pöl) n principio m

print (print) v stampare; n positiva f; stampa f; **printed matter** stampe

printer (prin-tö) n stampante f; tipografo m, -a f

printout (print-aut) n stampato m

prior (prai°) adj anteriore

priority (prai-o-rö-ti) n precedenza f, priorità f

prison (pri-sön) n prigione f

prisoner (pri-sö-nö) n detenuto m, -a f, prigioniero m, -a f, ~ **of war** prigioniero di guerra

privacy (prai-vö-ssi) n intimità f

private (prai-vit) adj privato; personale

privilege (pri-vi-lidჳ) n privilegio m

prize (prais) n premio m; ricompensa f

probable (pro-bö-böl) adj probabile

probably (pro-bö-bli) adv probabilmente

problem (pro-blöm) n problema m

procedure (prö-ssii-dჳö) n procedimento m

proceed (prö-ssiid) v procedere

process (prou-ssêss) n procedimento m, processo m

procession (prö-ssê-ʃön) n processione f, corteo m

proclaim (prö-kleim) v proclamare

produce¹ (prö-d'uuss) v *produrre

produce² (prod-¹uuss) n prodotto m

producer (prö-d'uu-ssö) n produttore m

product (pro-dakt) n prodotto m

production (prö-dak-ʃön) n

produzione f

profession (prö-fê-ʃön) n professione f

professional (prö-fê-ʃö-nöl) adj professionale

professor (prö-fê-ssö) n professore m, -essa f

profit (pro-fit) n profitto m, guadagno m; vantaggio m; v approfittare

profitable (pro-fi-tö-böl) adj fruttuoso

profound (prö-faund) adj profondo

programme (prou-ghræm) n programma m

progress¹ (prou-ghrêss) n progresso m

progress² (prö-ghrêss) v progredire

progressive (prö-ghrê-ssiv) adj progressista; progressivo

prohibit (prö-hi-bit) v proibire

prohibition (prou-i-bi-ʃön) n divieto m

prohibitive (prö-hi-bi-tiv) adj proibitivo

project (pro-dჳêkt) n piano m, progetto m

promenade (pro-mö-naad) n passeggiata f

promise (pro-miss) n promessa f; v *promettere

promote (prö-mout) v *promuovere

promotion (prö-mou-ʃön) n promozione f

prompt (prompt) adj sollecito, pronto

pronoun (prou-naun) n pronome m

pronounce (prö-naunss) v pronunciare

pronunciation (prö-nan-ssi-ei-ʃön) n pronuncia f

proof (pruuf) n prova f

propaganda (pro-pö-ghæn-dö) n propaganda f

propel (prö-pêl) v spingere

propeller (prö-pê-lö) n elica f

proper (pro-pö) adj giusto; decente,

conveniente, adatto, appropriato
property (*pro*-pö-ti) *n* proprietà *f*
prophet (*pro*-fit) *n* profeta *m*
proportion (prö-*poo*-ʃön) *n*
proporzione *f*
proportional (prö-*poo*-ʃö-nöl) *adj*
proporzionale
proposal (prö-*pou*-söl) *n* proposta *f*
propose (prö-*pous*) *v* *proporre
proposition (pro-pö-*si*-ʃön) *n*
proposta *f*
proprietor (prö-*prai*-ö-tö) *n*
proprietario *m*, -a *f*
prospect (*pro*-sspêkt) *n* prospettiva *f*
prospectus (prö-*sspêk*-töss) *n*
prospetto *m*
prosperity (pro-*sspê*-rö-ti) *n*
prosperità *f*
prosperous (*pro*-sspö-röss) *adj*
fiorente
prostitute (*pro*-ssti-t'uut) *n* prostituta
f
protect (prö-*têkt*) *v* *proteggere
protection (prö-*têk*-ʃön) *n* protezione
f
protein (*prou*-tiin) *n* proteina *f*
protest[1] (*prou*-têsst) *n* protesta *f*
protest[2] (prö-*têsst*) *v* protestare
Protestant (*pro*-ti-sstönt) *adj*
protestante
proud (praud) *adj* fiero; orgoglioso
prove (pruuv) *v* dimostrare, provare;
mostrarsi
proverb (*pro*-vööb) *n* proverbio *m*
provide (prö-*vaid*) *v* fornire,
*provvedere; **provided that** purché
province (*pro*-vinss) *n* provincia *f*
provincial (prö-*vin*-ʃöl) *adj*
provinciale
provisional (prö-*vi*-ʒö-nöl) *adj*
provvisorio
provisions (prö-*vi*-ʒöns) *pl* provviste
fpl
prune (pruun) *n* prugna secca

psychiatrist (ssai-*kai*-ö-trisst) *n*
psichiatra *m/f*
psychic (*ssai*-kik) *adj* psichico
psychoanalyst (ssai-kou-æ-nö-lisst) *n*
psicoanalista *m/f*
psychological (ssai-ko-*lo*-dʒi-köl) *adj*
psicologico
psychologist (ssai-*ko*-lö-dʒisst) *n*
psicologo *m*, -a *f*
psychology (ssai-*ko*-lö-dʒi) *n*
psicologia *f*
pub (pab) *n* taverna *f*; bar *m*
public (*pa*-blik) *adj* pubblico;
generale; *n* pubblico *m*; ~ **garden**
giardino pubblico; ~ **house** taverna *f*
publication (pa-bli-*kei*-ʃön) *n*
pubblicazione *f*
publicity (pa-*bli*-ssö-ti) *n* pubblicità *f*
publish (*pa*-bliʃ) *v* pubblicare
publisher (*pa*-bli-ʃö) *n* editore *m*,
-trice *f*
puddle (*pa*-döl) *n* pozzanghera *f*
pull (pul) *v* tirare; ~ **out** partire; ~ **up**
fermarsi
pulley (*pu*-li) *n* (pl ~s) carrucola *f*
pullover (*pu*-lou-vö) *n* maglione *m*
pulpit (*pul*-pit) *n* cattedra *f*, pulpito *n*
pulse (palss) *n* polso *m*
pump (pamp) *n* pompa *f*; *v* pompare
pun (pan) *n* gioco di parole
punch (pantʃ) *v* sferrare pugni; *n*
pugno *m*
punctual (*pangk*-tʃu-öl) *adj* puntual
puncture (*pangk*-tʃö) *n* foratura *f*,
bucatura *f*
punctured (*pangk*-tʃöd) *adj* bucato
punish (*pa*-niʃ) *v* punire
punishment (*pa*-niʃ-mönt) *n*
punizione *f*
pupil (p'uu-pöl) *n* scolaro *m*, -a *f*
puppet show (*pa*-pit-ʃou) *n*
rappresentazione di marionette
purchase (pöö-tʃöss) *v* comprare; *n*
compera *f*, acquisto *m*; ~ **price** prezz

d'acquisto
purchaser (*pöö*-tʃö-ssö) *n*
compratore *m*, -trice *f*
pure (p¹u⁰) *adj* puro
purple (*pöö*-pöl) *adj* viola
purpose (*pöö*-pöss) *n* proposito *m*,
fine *m*, intenzione *f*; **on ~** apposta
purse (*pööss*) *n* borsellino *m*
pursue (pö-ss¹uu) *v* perseguire
pus (pass) *n* pus *m*
push (pu ʃ) *n* urto *m*, spinta *f*; *v*

*spingere; *farsi largo; **~ button**
pulsante *m*
***put** (put) *v* collocare, posare,
*mettere; *porre; **~ away** *mettere a
posto; **~ off** rinviare; **~ on** indossare; **~
out** *spegnere
puzzle (*pa*-söl) *n* rompicapo *m*;
enigma *m*; *v* sconcertare; **jigsaw ~**
puzzle
puzzling (*pas*-ling) *adj* imbarazzante
pyjamas (pö-dʒaa-mös) *pl* pigiama *m*

Q

quack (kᵘæk) *n* guaritore *m*,
ciarlatano *m*
quail (kᵘeil) *n* (pl ~, ~s) quaglia *f*
quaint (kᵘeint) *adj* bizzarro; antiquato
qualification (kᵘo-li-fi-*kei*-ʃön) *n*
qualifica *f*; riserva *f*, restrizione *f*
qualified (kᵘo-li-faid) *adj* qualificato;
competente
qualify (kᵘo-li-fai) *v* *addirsi
quality (kᵘo-lö-ti) *n* qualità *f*;
caratteristica *f*
quantity (kᵘon-tö-ti) *n* quantità *f*;
numero *m*
quarantine (kᵘo-rön-tiin) *n*
quarantena *f*
quarrel (kᵘo-röl) *v* litigare; *n* litigio *m*,
lite *f*
quarry (kᵘo-ri) *n* cava *f*
quarter (kᵘoo-tö) *n* quarto *m*;
trimestre *m*; quartiere *m*; **~ of an
hour** quarto d'ora
quarterly (kᵘoo-tö-li) *adj* trimestrale
quay (kii) *n* molo *m*
queen (kᵘiin) *n* regina *f*

queer (kᵘi⁰) *adj* singolare, strano;
bizzarro
query (k¹i⁰-ri) *n* domanda *f*; *v*
domandare; *mettere in dubbio
question (kᵘéss-tʃön) *n* questione *f*;
domanda *f*; problema *m*; *v*
interrogare; *mettere in dubbio; **~
mark** punto interrogativo
queue (k¹uu) *n* coda *f*; *v* *fare la coda
quick (kᵘik) *adj* svelto
quick-tempered (kᵘik-*têm*-pöd) *adj*
irascibile
quiet (kᵘai-öt) *adj* quieto, calmo,
tranquillo; *n* quiete *f*, tranquillità *f*
quilt (kᵘilt) *n* trapunta *f*
quit (kᵘit) *v* cessare, *smettere
quite (kᵘait) *adv* interamente,
completamente; alquanto,
abbastanza, piuttosto; assai, molto
quiz (kᵘis) *n* (pl ~zes) quiz *m*
quota (kᵘou-tö) *n* quota *f*
quotation (kᵘou-*tei*-ʃön) *n* citazione *f*;
~ marks virgolette *fpl*
quote (kᵘout) *v* citare

R

rabbit (*ræ*-bit) *n* coniglio *m*

rabies (*rei*-bis) *n* rabbia *f*

race (reiss) *n* gara *f*, corsa *f*; razza *f*

racecourse (*reiss*-kooss) *n* pista da corsa; ippodromo *m*

racehorse (*reiss*-hooss) *n* cavallo da corsa

racetrack (*reiss*-træk) *n* pista da corsa; ippodromo

racial (*rei*-ʃöl) *adj* razziale

racket (*ræ*-kit) *n* racchetta *f*; chiasso *m*

radiator (*rei*-di-ei-tö) *n* radiatore *m*

radical (*ræ*-di-köl) *adj* radicale

radio (*rei*-di-ou) *n* radio *f*

radish (*ræ*-diʃ) *n* ravanello *m*

radius (*rei*-di-öss) *n* (pl radii) raggio *m*

raft (raaft) *n* zattera *f*

rag (rægh) *n* straccio *m*

rage (reidʒ) *n* furore *m*, rabbia *f*; *v* infierire

raid (reid) *n* irruzione *f*

rail (reil) *n* ringhiera *f*, parapetto *m*

railing (*rei*-ling) *n* inferriata *f*

railroad (*reil*-roud) *nAm* ferrovia *f*

railway (*reil*-ᵘei) *n* ferrovia *f*

rain (rein) *n* pioggia *f*; *v* *piovere

rainbow (*rein*-bou) *n* arcobaleno *m*

raincoat (*rein*-kout) *n* impermeabile *m*

rainproof (*rein*-pruuf) *adj* impermeabile

rainy (*rei*-ni) *adj* piovoso

raise (reis) *v* sollevare; aumentare; allevare, coltivare; *Am* aumento *m*

raisin (*rei*-sön) *n* uvetta *f*

rake (reik) *n* rastrello *m*

rally (*ræ*-li) *n* raduno *m*

ramp (ræmp) *n* rampa *f*

ramshackle (*ræm*-ʃæ-köl) *adj* sgangerato

rancid (*ræn*-ssid) *adj* rancido

random (*ræn*-döm) *adj* casuale

rang (ræng) *v* (p ring)

range (reindʒ) *n* portata *f*; ~ **finder** telemetro *m*

rank (rængk) *n* rango *m*; fila *f*

ransom (*ræn*-ssöm) *n* riscatto *m*

rape (reip) *v* violentare

rapid (*ræ*-pid) *adj* veloce, rapido

rapids (*ræ*-pids) *pl* rapida *f*

rare (rêᵒ) *adj* raro

rarely (*rêᵒ*-li) *adv* raramente

rascal (*raa*-ssköl) *n* birbante *m*, monello *m*

rash (ræʃ) *n* eruzione cutanea, sfogo *m*; *adj* avventato, sconsiderato

raspberry (*raas*-bö-ri) *n* lampone *m*

rat (ræt) *n* ratto *m*

rate (reit) *n* prezzo *m*, tariffa *f*; velocità *f*; **at any** ~ ad ogni modo, comunque; ~ **of exchange** corso del cambio

rather (*raa*-ðö) *adv* abbastanza, alquanto; piuttosto

ration (*ræ*-ʃön) *n* razione *f*

raven (*rei*-vön) *n* corvo *m*

raw (roo) *adj* crudo; ~ **material** materia prima

ray (rei) *n* raggio *m*

rayon (*rei*-on) *n* raion *f*

razor (*rei*-sö) *n* rasoio *m*; ~ **blade** lametta *f*

reach (riitʃ) *v* *raggiungere; *n* portata *f*

react (ri-*ækt*) *v* *reagire

reaction (ri-*æk*-ʃön) *n* reazione *f*

*read (riid) *v* *leggere

reader (*rii*-dö) *n* lettore *m*, -trice *f*

reading (*rii*-ding) *n* lettura *f*; ~ **lamp** lampada da tavolo; ~ **room** sala di lettura

ready (*rê*-di) *adj* pronto

ready-made (rê-di-*meid*) *adj* confezionato

real (riᵒl) *adj* reale

reality (ri-æ-lö-ti) *n* realtà *f*

realizable (*ri*ᵒ-lai-sö-böl) *adj* realizzabile

realize (*ri*ᵒ-lais) *v* realizzare; attuare

really (*ri*ᵒ-li) *adv* davvero, veramente; in realtà

rear (riᵒ) *n* parte posteriore; *v* allevare; ~ **light** fanalino posteriore

reason (*rii*-sön) *n* causa *f*, ragione *f*; senso *m*; *v* ragionare

reasonable (*rii*-sö-nö-böl) *adj* ragionevole

reassure (rii-ö-ʃuᵒ) *v* tranquillizzare

rebate (*rii*-beit) *n* riduzione *f*, sconto *m*

rebellion (ri-*bêl*-¹ön) *n* rivolta *f*, ribellione *f*

recall (ri-*kool*) *v* ricordarsi di; richiamare; revocare

receipt (ri-*ssiit*) *n* ricevuta *f*; ricevimento *m*

receive (ri-*ssiiv*) *v* ricevere

receiver (ri-*ssii*-vö) *n* ricevitore *m*

recent (*rii*-ssönt) *adj* recente

recently (*rii*-ssönt-li) *adv* di recente, recentemente

reception (ri-*ssêp*-ʃön) *n* ricevimento *m*; accoglienza *f*; ~ **office** accettazione *f*

receptionist (ri-*ssêp*-ʃö-nisst) *n* receptionist *m/f*

recession (ri-*ssê*-ʃön) *n* recessione *f*

recipe (*rê*-ssi-pi) *n* ricetta *f*

recital (ri-*ssai*-töl) *n* recital *m*

reckon (*rê*-kön) *v* *fare i calcoli; considerare; credere

recognition (rê-kögh-*ni*-ʃön) *n* riconoscimento *m*

recognize (*rê*-kögh-nais) *v* *riconoscere

recollect (rê-kö-*lêkt*) *v* ricordarsi

recommence (rii-kö-*mênss*) *v* ricominciare

recommend (rê-kö-*mênd*) *v* raccomandare; consigliare

recommendation (rê-kö-mên-*dei*-ʃon) *n* raccomandazione *f*

reconciliation (rê-kön-ssi-li-*ei*-ʃön) *n* riconciliazione *f*

record¹ (*rê*-kood) *n* disco *m*; primato *m*; registrazione *f*

record² (ri-*kood*) *v* registrare; ~ **player** giradischi *m*

recorder (ri-*koo*-dö) *n* registratore *m*

recording (ri-*koo*-ding) *n* registrazione *f*

recover (ri-*ka*-vö) *v* recuperare; guarire

recovery (ri-*ka*-vö-ri) *n* guarigione *f*

recreation (rê-kri-*ei*-ʃön) *n* ricreazione *f*, svago *m*; ~ **ground** parco giochi

recruit (ri-*kruut*) *n* recluta *f*

rectangle (*rêk*-tæng-ghöl) *n* rettangolo *m*

rectangular (rêk-*tæng*-ghʲu-lö) *adj* rettangolare

rector (*rêk*-tö) *n* pastore *m*

rectory (*rêk*-tö-ri) *n* presbiterio *m*

rectum (*rêk*-töm) *n* retto *m*

recycle (ri-*ssai*-köl) *v* riciclare

red (rêd) *adj* rosso

reduce (ri-*d¹uuss*) *v* *ridurre, diminuire

reduction (ri-*dak*-ʃön) *n* ribasso *m*, riduzione *f*

redundant (ri-*dan*-dönt) *adj* ridondante

reed (riid) *n* giunco *m*

reef (riif) *n* banco *m*

refer (ri-*föö*) *v* riferire; ~ **a decision to someone** riferire una decisione a qualcuno; ~ **to ...** riferirsi a ...; consultare ...

referee (re-fö-*rii*) *n* arbitro *m*; referenza *f*

reference (*rêf*-rönss) *n* referenza *f*, riferimento *m*; relazione *f*; **with ~ to**

riguardo a

refill (rii-fil) n ricambio m

refinery (ri-fai-nö-ri) n raffineria f

reflect (ri-flêkt) v *riflettere

reflection (ri-flêk-∫ön) n riflesso m; immagine riflessa

reflector (ri-flêk-tö) n riflettore m

reformation (rê-fö-mei-∫ön) n riforma f

refresh (ri-frê∫) v rinfrescare

refreshment (ri-frê∫-mönt) n rinfresco m

refrigerator (ri-fri-dʒö-rei-tö) n frigorifero m

refugee (re-fiu-dʒii) n profugo m, -a f, rifugiato m, -a f

refund¹ (ri-fand) v rimborsare

refund² (rii-fand) n rimborso m

refusal (ri-fⁱuu-söl) n rifiuto m

refuse¹ (ri-fⁱuus) v rifiutare

refuse² (ri-fⁱuuss) n immondizia f

regard (ri-ghaad) v considerare; osservare; n riguardo m; **as regards** per quanto riguarda

regarding (ri-ghaa-ding) prep riguardo a; in relazione a

regatta (ri-ghæ-tö) n regata f

régime (rei-ʒiim) n regime m

region (rii-dʒön) n regione f

regional (rii-dʒö-nöl) adj regionale

register (rê-dʒi-sstö) v registrarsi; raccomandare; **registered letter** raccomandata f

registration (rê-dʒi-sstrei-∫ön) n registrazione f; ~ **number** numero di targa; ~ **plate** targa automobilistica

regret (ri-ghrêt) v *rimpiangere; n rimpianto m

regular (rê-ghⁱu-lö) adj regolato, regolare; normale

regulate (rê-ghⁱu-leit) v regolare

regulation (rê-ghⁱu-lei-∫ön) n regolamento m; regolamentazione f

rehabilitation (ri-hö-bi-li-tei-∫ön) n

rieducazione f

rehearsal (ri-höö-ssöl) n prova f

rehearse (ri-hööss) v *fare le prove

reign (rein) n regno m; v regnare

reimburse (rii-im-bööss) v *rendere, rimborsare

reindeer (rein-diö) n (pl ~) renna f

reject (ri-dʒêkt) v rifiutare, *respingere; vomitare

relate (ri-leit) v raccontare

related (ri-lei-tid) adj imparentato

relation (ri-lei-∫ön) n relazione f, attinenza f; parente m/f

relationship (ri-lei-∫ön-∫ip) n relazione f, rapporto m

relative (rê-lö-tiv) n parente m; adj relativo

relax (ri-lækss) v rilassarsi

relaxation (ri-læk-ssei-∫ön) n rilassamento m

reliable (ri-lai-ö-böl) adj fidato

relic (rê-lik) n reliquia f

relief (ri-liif) n sollievo m; aiuto m; rilievo m

relieve (ri-liiv) v mitigare; *dare il cambio

religion (ri-li-dʒön) n religione f

religious (ri-li-dʒöss) adj religioso

rely on (ri-lai) contare su

remain (ri-mein) v *rimanere, restare

remainder (ri-mein-dö) n avanzo m, resto m, residuo m

remaining (ri-mei-ning) adj rimanente

remark (ri-maak) n osservazione f; v osservare

remarkable (ri-maa-kö-böl) adj notevole

remedy (rê-mö-di) n rimedio m

remember (ri-mêm-bö) v ricordarsi

remembrance (ri-mêm-brönss) n ricordo m

remind (ri-maind) v (*far) ricordare

remit (ri-mit) v *rimettere

remittance (ri-*mi*-tönss) *n* rimessa *f*

remnant (*rêm*-nönt) *n* resto *m*, rimanenza *f*, residuo *m*

remote (ri-*mout*) *adj* distante, remoto

removal (ri-*muu*-völ) *n* allontanamento *m*

remove (ri-*muuv*) *v* rimuovere

remunerate (ri-*m*ᵗ*uu*-nö-reit) *v* rimunerare

remuneration (ri-m*ᵗ*uu-nö-*rei*-ʃön) *n* rimunerazione *f*

renew (ri-n*ᶦuu*) *v* rinnovare

rent (rênt) *v* affittare; *n* affitto *m*

repair (ri-*pê*ᵒ) *v* riparare; *n* restauro *m*

reparation (rê-pö-*rei*-ʃön) *n* riparazione *f*

***repay** (ri-*pei*) *v* rimborsare

repayment (ri-*pei*-mönt) *n* rimborso *m*

repeat (ri-*piit*) *v* ripetere

repellent (ri-*pê*-lönt) *adj* ripugnante, repellente

repentance (ri-*pên*-tönss) *n* pentimento *m*

repertory (*rê*-pö-tö-ri) *n* repertorio *m*

repetition (rê-pö-*ti*-ʃön) *n* ripetizione *f*

replace (ri-*pleiss*) *v* sostituire

reply (ri-*plai*) *v* *rispondere; *n* risposta *f*; **in ~** in risposta

report (ri-*poot*) *v* riferire; presentarsi; *n* relazione *f*, rapporto *m*

reporter (ri-*poo*-tö) *n* reporter *m/f*, cronista *m/f*

represent (rê-pri-*sênt*) *v* rappresentare; raffigurare

representation (rê-pri-sên-*tei*-ʃön) *n* rappresentanza *f*

representative (rê-pri-*sên*-tö-tiv) *adj* rappresentativo

reprimand (*rê*-pri-maand) *v* rimproverare

reproach (ri-*prout*ʃ) *n* rimprovero *m*; *v* rimproverare

reproduce (rii-prö-*d*ᵗ*uuss*) *v* *riprodurre

reproduction (rii-prö-*dak*-ʃön) *n* riproduzione *f*

reptile (*rêp*-tail) *n* rettile *m*

republic (ri-*pa*-blik) *n* repubblica *f*

republican (ri-*pa*-bli-kön) *adj* repubblicano

repulsive (ri-*pal*-ssiv) *adj* ributtante

reputation (rê-p*ᶦ*u-*tei*-ʃön) *n* reputazione *f*; fama *f*

request (ri-k*ᵘ*ê*sst*) *n* richiesta *f*; domanda *f*; *v* *richiedere

require (ri-k*ᵘ*ai*ᵒ*) *v* *esigere

requirement (ri-k*ᵘ*ai*ᵒ*-mönt) *n* esigenza *f*

requisite (*rê*-k*ᵘ*i-sit) *adj* richiesto

rescue (*rê*-ssk*ᶦ*uu) *v* salvare; *n* salvataggio *m*

research (ri-*ssööt*ʃ) *n* ricerca *f*

resemblance (ri-*sêm*-blönss) *n* somiglianza *f*

resemble (ri-*sêm*-böl) *v* assomigliare a

resent (ri-*sênt*) *v* risentirsi per

reservation (rê-sö-*vei*-ʃön) *n* prenotazione *f*

reserve (ri-*sööv*) *v* riservare; prenotare; *n* riserva *f*

reserved (ri-*söövd*) *adj* riservato

reservoir (*rê*-sö-v*ᵘ*aa) *n* serbatoio *m*

reside (ri-*said*) *v* abitare

residence (*rê*-si-dönss) *n* residenza *f*; **~ permit** permesso di soggiorno

resident (*rê*-si-dönt) *n* residente *m*; *adj* residente; interno

resign (ri-*sain*) *v* *dimettersi

resignation (rê-sigh-*nei*-ʃön) *n* dimissioni *fpl*

resin (*rê*-sin) *n* resina *f*

resist (ri-*sisst*) *v* resistere

resistance (ri-*si*-sstönss) *n* resistenza *f*

resolute (*rê*-sö-luut) *adj* risoluto, deciso

respect (ri-*sspêkt*) *n* rispetto *m*; stima *f*; *v* rispettare

respectable (ri-*sspêk*-tö-böl) *adj* rispettabile

respectful (ri-*sspêkt*-föl) *adj* rispettoso

respective (ri-*sspêk*-tiv) *adj* rispettivo

respiration (rê-sspö-*rei*-ʃön) *n* respirazione *f*

respite (*rê*-sspait) *n* dilazione *f*

responsibility (ri-sspon-ssö-*bi*-lö-ti) *n* responsabilità *f*

responsible (ri-*sspon*-ssö-böl) *adj* responsabile

rest (rêsst) *n* riposo *m*; resto *m*; *v* riposarsi; ~ **home** casa di riposo

restaurant (*rê*-sstö-roᴺg) *n* ristorante *m*

restful (*rêsst*-föl) *adj* riposante

restless (*rêsst*-löss) *adj* inquieto; irrequieto

restrain (ri-*sstrein*) *v* *contenere, *trattenere

restriction (ri-*sstrik*-ʃön) *n* restrizione *f*

result (ri-*salt*) *n* risultato *m*; conseguenza *f*; esito *m*; *v* risultare

resume (ri-*s*ʲ*uum*) *v* *riprendere

résumé (*rê*-sʲu-mei) *n* riassunto *m*

retail (*rii*-teil) *v* vendere al minuto; ~ **trade** commercio al minuto, vendita al minuto

retailer (*rii*-tei-lö) *n* rivenditore *m*, -trice *f*

retina (*rê*-ti-nö) *n* retina *f*

retire (ri-*taiö*) *v* andare in pensione

retired (ri-*taiᵒd*) *adj* pensionato

retirement (ri-*taiᵒ*-mönt) *n* pensione *f*; pensionamento *m*

return (ri-*töön*) *v* ritornare; *n* ritorno *m*; ~ **flight** volo di ritorno; ~ **journey** viaggio di ritorno

reunite (rii-ʲuu-*nait*) *v* riunire

reveal (ri-*viil*) *v* svelare, rivelare

revelation (rê-vö-*lei*-ʃön) *n* rivelazione *f*

revenge (ri-*vênd*ʒ) *n* vendetta *f*

revenue (*rê*-vö-nʲuu) *n* entrate *fpl*; reddito *m*

reverse (ri-*vööss*) *n* contrario *m*; rovescio *m*; marcia indietro; rivolgimento *m*; *adj* inverso; *v* *far marcia indietro

review (ri-*vʲuu*) *n* recensione *f*; rivista *f*

revise (ri-*vais*) *v* revisionare

revision (ri-*vi*-ʒön) *n* revisione *f*

revival (ri-*vai*-völ) *n* ripristino *m*

revolt (ri-*voult*) *v* rivoltarsi; *n* ribellione *f*, rivolta *f*

revolting (ri-*voul*-ting) *adj* stomachevole, rivoltante, disgustoso

revolution (rê-vö-*luu*-ʃön) *n* rivoluzione *f*

revolutionary (rê-vö-*luu*-ʃö-nö-ri) *adj* rivoluzionario

revolver (ri-*vol*-vö) *n* rivoltella *f*

revue (ri-*vʲuu*) *n* rivista *f*

reward (ri-ᵘ*ood*) *n* ricompensa *f*; *v* ricompensare

rheumatism (*ruu*-mö-ti-söm) *n* reumatismo *m*

rhinoceros (rai-*no*-ssö-röss) *n* (pl ~, ~es) rinoceronte *m*

rhubarb (*ruu*-baab) *n* rabarbaro *m*

rhyme (raim) *n* rima *f*

rhythm (*ri*-ðöm) *n* ritmo *m*

rib (rib) *n* costola *f*

ribbon (*ri*-bön) *n* nastro *m*

rice (raiss) *n* riso *m*

rich (ritʃ) *adj* ricco

riches (*ri*-tʃis) *pl* ricchezza *f*

rid (rid): **get** ~ **of** sbarazzarsi di

riddle (*ri*-döl) *n* indovinello *m*

ride (raid) *n* corsa *f*

***ride** (raid) *v* *andare in macchina; cavalcare

rider (*rai*-dö) *n* cavallerizzo *m*

ridge (ridʒ) *n* cresta *f*

ridicule (*ri*-di-k'uul) *v* ridicolizzare

ridiculous (ri-*di*-k'u-löss) *adj* ridicolo

riding (*rai*-ding) *n* equitazione *f*; ~ **school** scuola di equitazione

rifle (*rai*-föl) *v* fucile *m*

right (rait) *n* diritto *m*; *adj* corretto, giusto; retto; destro; equo; **all right!** va bene!; ***be** ~ *avere ragione; ~ **of way** precedenza *f*

righteous (*rai*-tjöss) *adj* giusto

right-hand (rait-hænd) *adj* destro

rightly (*rait*-li) *adv* giustamente

rim (rim) *n* cerchione *m*; orlo *m*

ring (ring) *n* anello *m*; cerchio *m*; pista *f*

***ring** (ring) *v* suonare; ~ **up** telefonare

rinse (rinss) *v* sciacquare; *n* sciacquata *f*

riot (*rai*-öt) *n* sommossa *f*

rip (rip) *v* strappare

ripe (raip) *adj* maturo

rise (rais) *n* aumento *m*; altura *f*; rialzo *m*; ascesa *f*

***rise** (rais) *v* alzarsi; *sorgere; *salire

rising (*rai*-sing) *n* insurrezione *f*

risk (rissk) *n* rischio *m*; pericolo *m*; *v* rischiare

risky (*ri*-sski) *adj* rischioso

rival (*rai*-völ) *n* rivale *m/f*; concorrente *m/f*; *v* rivaleggiare

rivalry (*rai*-völ-ri) *n* rivalità *f*; concorrenza *f*

river (*ri*-vö) *n* fiume *m*; ~ **bank** argine *m*

riverside (*ri*-vö-ssaid) *n* lungofiume *m*

roach (routʃ) *n* (pl ~) lasca *f*

road (roud) *n* strada *f*; ~ **fork** *n* bivio *m*; ~ **map** carta stradale; ~ **restaurant** locanda *f*; ~ **system** rete stradale; ~ **up** strada interrotta

roadhouse (*roud*-hauss) *n* locanda *f*

roadside (*roud*-ssaid) *n* margine della strada

roadway (*roud*-ᵘei) *nAm* carreggiata *f*

roam (roum) *v* vagabondare

roar (roo) *v* mugghiare, ruggire; *n* ruggito *m*, rombo *m*

roast (rousst) *v* arrostire

rob (rob) *v* rubare

robber (*ro*-bö) *n* ladro *m*, -a *f*

robbery (*ro*-bö-ri) *n* rapina *f*, furto *m*

robe (roub) *n* tunica *f*; vestito *m*

robin (*ro*-bin) *n* pettirosso *m*

robust (rou-*basst*) *adj* robusto

rock (rok) *n* roccia *f*; *v* dondolare

rocket (*ro*-kit) *n* razzo *m*

rocky (*ro*-ki) *adj* roccioso

rod (rod) *n* barra *f*, stecca *f*

roe (rou) *n* uova di pesce

role (röul) *n* ruolo *m*

roll (roul) *v* rotolare; *n* rotolo *m*; panino *m*

roller-skating (*rou*-lö-sskei-ting) *n* pattinaggio a rotelle

Roman Catholic (*rou*-mön kæ-θö-lik) cattolico

romance (rö-*mænss*) *n* idillio *m*

romantic (rö-*mæn*-tik) *adj* romantico

Rome (röum) Roma *f*

roof (ruuf) *n* tetto *m*; **thatched** ~ tetto di paglia

room (ruum) *n* camera *f*, stanza *f*; spazio *m*, vano *m*; ~ **and board** vitto e alloggio; ~ **service** servizio in camera; ~ **temperature** temperatura ambientale

roomy (*ruu*-mi) *adj* spazioso

root (ruut) *n* radice *f*

rope (roup) *n* corda *f*

rosary (*rou*-sö-ri) *n* rosario *m*

rose (rous) *n* rosa *f*; *adj* rosa

rotten (*ro*-tön) *adj* marcio

rouge (ruuʒ) *n* fard *m*

rough (raf) *adj* disagevole, accidentato

roulette (ruu-*lêt*) *n* roulette *f*

round (raund) *adj* rotondo; *prep*

attorno a, intorno a; *n* ripresa *f*; **~ trip**
Am andata e ritorno

roundabout (*raun*-dö-baut) *n* rotonda
f

rounded (*raun*-did) *adj* arrotondato

route (ruut) *n* rotta *f*

routine (ruu-*tiin*) *n* abitudine *f*

row[1](rou) *n* fila *f*; *v* remare

row[2](rau) *n* lite *f*

rowdy (*rau*-di) *adj* turbolento

rowing boat (*rou*-ing-bout) *n* barca a
remi

royal (*roi*-öl) *adj* reale

rub (rab) *v* strofinare

rubber (*ra*-bö) *n* caucciù *m*; gomma
per cancellare; **~ band** elastico *m*

rubbish (*ra*-biʃ) *n* immondizia *f*;
sciocchezza *f*, stupidaggini *fpl*; **~ bin**
pattumiera *f*; **talk ~** *dire
stupidaggini

ruby (*ruu*-bi) *n* rubino *m*

rucksack (*rak*-ssæk) *n* zaino *m*

rudder (*ra*-dö) *n* timone *m*

rude (ruud) *adj* grossolano

rug (ragh) *n* tappeto *m*

ruin (*ruu*-in) *v* rovinare; *n* rovina *f*

rule (ruul) *n* regola *f*; regime *m*,
governo *m*, dominio *m*; *v* dominare,
governare; **as a ~** generalmente, di
norma

ruler (*ruu*-lö) *n* monarca *m*, sovrano
m; riga *f*

Rumania (ruu-*mei*-ni-ö) Romania *f*

Rumanian (ruu-*mei*-ni-ön) *adj*
romeno

rumo(u)r (*ruu*-mö) *n* diceria *f*

*run (ran) *v* *correre; amministrare; **~
into** incontrare per caso

runaway (*ra*-nö-ᵘei) *n* fuggitivo *m*

rung (ran) *v* (pp ring)

runner (*ra*-nö) *n* velocista *m/f*

runway (*ran*-ᵘei) *n* pista di decollo

rural (*ru*ᵒ-röl) *adj* rurale

ruse (ruus) *n* astuzia *f*

rush (raʃ) *v* affrettarsi; *n* giunco *m*; **~
hour** ora di punta

Russia (*ra*-ʃö) Russia *f*

Russian (*ra*-ʃön) *adj* russo

rust (rasst) *n* ruggine *f*

rustic (*ra*-sstik) *adj* rustico

rusty (*ra*-ssti) *adj* arrugginito

S

sack (ssæk) *n* sacco *m*

sacred (*ssei*-krid) *adj* sacro

sacrifice (*ssæ*-kri-faiss) *n* sacrificio *m*;
v sacrificare

sacrilege (*ssæ*-kri-lidჳ) *n* sacrilegio *m*

sad (ssæd) *adj* triste; afflitto,
malinconico

saddle (*ssæ*-döl) *n* sella *f*

sadness (*ssæd*-nöss) *n* tristezza *f*

safe (sseif) *adj* sicuro; *n* cassaforte *f*

safety (*sseif*-ti) *n* sicurezza *f*; **~ belt**
cintura di sicurezza; **~ pin** spilla da
balia

sail (sseil) *v* navigare; *n* vela *f*

sailing boat (*ssei*-ling-bout) *n* barca a
vela

sailor (*ssei*-lö) *n* marinaio *m*

saint (sseint) *n* santo *m*

salad (*ssæ*-löd) *n* insalata *f*; **~
dressing** condimento per l'insalata
~ oil olio per l'insalata

salary (*ssæ*-lö-ri) *n* stipendio *m*,
salario *m*

sale (sseil) *n* vendita *f*; **clearance ~**

svendita *f*; **for ~** in vendita; **sales** saldi

saleable (*ssei*-lö-böl) *adj* vendibile

salesgirl (*sseils*-ghööl) *n* commessa *f*

salesman (*sseils*-mön) *n* (pl -men) commesso *m*

salmon (*ssæ*-mön) *n* (pl ~) salmone *m*

salon (*ssæ*-lon͞g) *n* salone *m*

saloon (ssö-*luun*) *n* bar *m*

salt (ssoolt) *n* sale *m*; **~ cellar, ~ shaker** *Am* saliera *f*

salty (*ssool*-ti) *adj* salato

salute (ssö-*luut*) *v* salutare

salve (ssaav) *n* unguento *m*

same (sseim) *adj* stesso

sample (*ssaam*-pöl) *n* campione *m*

sanatorium (ssæ-nö-*too*-ri-öm) *n* (pl ~s, -ria) sanatorio *m*

sand (ssænd) *n* sabbia *f*

sandal (*ssæn*-döl) *n* sandalo *m*

sandpaper (*ssænd*-pei-pö) *n* carta vetrata

sandwich (*ssæn*-ᵘid͡ʒ) *n* tramezzino *m*

sandy (*ssæn*-di) *adj* sabbioso

sanitary (*ssæ*-ni-tö-ri) *adj* sanitario; **~ towel, ~ napkin** *Am* pannolino igienico

sapphire (*ssæ*-fai⁶) *n* zaffiro *m*

sardine (ssaa-*diin*) *n* sardina *f*

satchel (*ssæ*-t͡ʃöl) *n* cartella *f*

satellite (*ssæ*-tö-lait) *n* satellite *m*

satin (*ssæ*-tin) *n* raso *m*

satisfaction (ssæ-tiss-*fæk*-ʃön) *n* appagamento *m*, soddisfazione *f*

satisfactory (ssæ-tiss-*fæk*-tö-ri) *adj* soddisfacente; sufficiente; **this is not ~** non è sufficiente

satisfy (*ssæ*-tiss-fai) *v* *soddisfare; **satisfied** soddisfatto

Saturday (*ssæ*-tö-di) sabato *m*

sauce (ssooss) *n* salsa *f*

saucepan (*ssooss*-pön) *n* casseruola *f*

saucer (*ssoo*-ssö) *n* piattino *m*

Saudi Arabia (ssau-di-ö-*rei*-bi-ö)

Arabia Saudita

Saudi Arabian (ssau-di-ö-*rei*-bi-ön) *adj* saudita

sauna (*ssoo*-nö) *n* sauna *f*

sausage (*sso*-ssid͡ʒ) *n* salsiccia *f*

savage (*ssæ*-vid͡ʒ) *adj* selvaggio

save (sseiv) *v* salvare; risparmiare

savings (*ssei*-vings) *pl* risparmi *mpl*; **~ bank** cassa di risparmio

savio(u)r (*ssei*-v'ö) *n* salvatore *m*, -trice *f*

savo(u)ry (*ssei*-vö-ri) *adj* saporito; piccante

saw¹ (ssoo) *v* (p see)

saw² (ssoo) *n* sega *f*

sawdust (*ssoo*-dasst) *n* segatura *f*

sawmill (*ssoo*-mil) *n* segheria *f*

*say (ssei) *v* *dire

scaffolding (*sskæ*-föl-ding) *n* impalcatura *f*

scale (sskeil) *n* scala *f*; scala musicale; squama *f*; **scales** *pl* bilancia *f*

scandal (*sskæn*-döl) *n* scandalo *m*

Scandinavia (sskæn-di-*nei*-vi-ö) Scandinavia *f*

Scandinavian (sskæn-di-*nei*-vi-ön) *adj* scandinavo

scapegoat (*sskeip*-ghout) *n* capro espiatorio

scar (sskaa) *n* cicatrice *f*

scarce (sskê⁶ss) *adj* scarso

scarcely (*sskê⁶*-ssli) *adv* scarsamente

scarcity (*sskê⁶*-ssö-ti) *n* penuria *f*

scare (sskê⁶) *v* spaventare; *n* spavento *m*

scarf (sskaaf) *n* (pl ~s, scarves) sciarpa *f*, scialle *m*

scarlet (*sskaa*-löt) *adj* scarlatto

scary (*sskê⁶*-ri) *adj* allarmante

scatter (*sskæ*-tö) *v* sparpagliare

scene (ssiin) *n* scena *f*

scenery (*ssii*-nö-ri) *n* paesaggio *m*; scenario *m*

scenic (*ssii*-nik) *adj* pittoresco

scent (ssênt) n profumo m

schedule (ʃê-dᵗuul) n orario m

scheme (sskiim) n schema m; progetto m

scholar (ssko-lö) n erudito m; scolaro m; borsista m

scholarship (ssko-lö-ʃip) n borsa di studio

school (sskuul) n scuola f

schoolboy (sskuul-boi) n scolaro m

schoolgirl (sskuul-ghööl) n scolara f

schoolmaster (sskuul-maa-sstö) n insegnante m/f, maestro m, -a f

schoolteacher (sskuul-tii-tʃö) n insegnante m/f

science (ssai-önss) n scienza f

scientific (ssai-ön-ti-fik) adj scientifico

scientist (ssai-ön-tisst) n scienziato m, -a f

scissors (ssi-sös) pl forbici fpl

scold (sskould) v inveire

scooter (sskuu-tö) n scooter m; monopattino m

score (sskoo) n punteggio m; v segnare

scorn (sskoon) n scherno m, disprezzo m; v disprezzare

Scot (sskot) n scozzese m

Scotch (sskotʃ) adj scozzese; ~ tape® nastro adesivo

Scotland (sskot-lönd) Scozia f

Scottish (ssko-tiʃ) adj scozzese

scout (sskaut) n boy-scout m

scrap (sskræp) n pezzetto m

scrapbook (sskræp-buk) n album per ritagli

scrape (sskreip) v raschiare

scratch (sskrætʃ) v scalfire, graffiare; n scalfittura f, graffio m

scream (sskriim) v urlare, strillare; n strillo m, grido m

screen (sskriin) n riparo m; video m, schermo m

screw (sskruu) n vite f; v avvitare

screwdriver (sskruu-drai-vö) n cacciavite m

scrub (sskrab) v strofinare; n cespuglio m

sculptor (sskalp-tö) n scultore m

sculpture (sskalp-tʃö) n scultura f

sea (ssii) n mare m; ~ urchin riccio di mare; ~ water acqua di mare

seabird (ssii-bööd) n uccello marino

seacoast (ssii-kousst) n litorale m

seafood (ssii-fuud) n frutti di mare mpl

seagull (ssii-ghal) n gabbiano m

seal (ssiil) n sigillo m; foca f

seam (ssiim) n cucitura f

seaman (ssii-mön) n (pl -men) marinaio m

seamless (ssiim-löss) adj senza cucitura

seaport (ssii-poot) n porto di mare

search (ssöötʃ) v cercare; perquisire, perlustrare; n ricerca f

searchlight (ssöötʃ-lait) n riflettore m

seascape (ssii-sskeip) n marina f

seashell (ssii-ʃêl) n conchiglia f

seashore (ssii-ʃoo) n riva del mare

seasick (ssii-ssik) adj che ha il mal di mare

seasickness (ssii-ssik-nöss) n mal di mare

seaside (ssii-ssaid) n riva del mare; ~ resort stazione balneare

season (ssii-sön) n stagione f; high ~ alta stagione; low ~ bassa stagione; off ~ fuori stagione; ~ ticket abbonamento m

seat (ssiit) n sedia f; posto m; sede f; ~ belt cintura di sicurezza

second (ssê-könd) num secondo; n secondo m; istante m

secondary (ssê-kön-dö-ri) adj secondario; ~ school scuola media

second-hand (ssê-könd-hænd) adj d

seconda mano

secret (*ssii*-krŏt) *n* segreto *m*; *adj* segreto

secretary (*ssê*-krŏ-tri) *n* segretaria *f*; segretario *m*

section (*ssêk*-ʃŏn) *n* sezione *f*; reparto *m*

secure (ssi-*kⁱuᵒ*) *adj* sicuro; *v* assicurarsi

security (ssi-*kⁱuᵒ*-rŏ-ti) *n* sicurezza *f*; cauzione *f*

sedative (*ssê*-dŏ-tiv) *n* sedativo *m*

seduce (ssi-*dⁱuuss*) *v* *sedurre

*see (ssii) *v* *vedere; capire, *rendersi conto; ~ **to** occuparsi di

seed (ssiid) *n* semenza *f*

*seek (ssiik) *v* cercare

seem (ssiim) *v* sembrare, *parere

seen (ssiin) *v* (pp see)

seesaw (*ssii*-ssoo) *n* altalena *f*

seize (ssiis) *v* afferrare

seldom (*ssêl*-dŏm) *adv* raramente

select (ssi-*lêkt*) *v* selezionare, *scegliere; *adj* selezionato, scelto

selection (ssi-*lêk*-ʃŏn) *n* scelta *f*, selezione *f*

self (ssêlf) (pl selves) io

self-centred (ssêlf-*ssên*-tŏd) *adj* egocentrico

self-employed (ssêl-fim-*ploid*) *adj* autonomo

self-evident (ssêl-*fê*-vi-dŏnt) *adj* lampante

self-government (ssêlf-*gha*-vŏ-mŏnt) *n* autonomia *f*

selfish (*ssêl*-fiʃ) *adj* egoista

selfishness (*ssêl*-fiʃ-nŏss) *n* egoismo *m*

self-service (ssêlf-*ssöö*-viss) *n* self-service *m*

*sell (ssêl) *v* vendere

semblance (*ssêm*-blŏnss) *n* apparenza *f*

semi- (*ssê*-mi) semi-

semicircle (*ssê*-mi-ssöö-köl) *n* semicerchio *m*

semicolon (ssê-mi-*kou*-lön) *n* punto e virgola

senate (*ssê*-nŏt) *n* senato *m*

senator (*ssê*-nŏ-tö) *n* senatore *m*

*send (ssênd) *v* mandare, spedire; ~ **back** rinviare, rispedire; ~ **for** *far venire; ~ **off** spedire

sender (ssên-dö) *n* mittente *m*

senile (*ssii*-nail) *adj* senile

senior (*ssii*-niö) *n* più anziano; di grado superiore *m*; *adj* senior; anziano; ~ **citizen** gli anziani

sensation (ssên-*ssei*-ʃön) *n* sensazione *f*

sensational (ssên-*ssei*-ʃö-nöl) *adj* sensazionale

sense (ssênss) *n* senso *m*; ragione *f*; significato *m*; *v* percepire

senseless (*ssênss*-löss) *adj* insensato

sensible (*ssên*-ssö-böl) *adj* ragionevole

sensitive (*ssên*-ssi-tiv) *adj* sensibile

sentence (*ssên*-tönss) *n* frase *f*; sentenza *f*; *v* condannare

sentimental (ssên-ti-*mên*-töl) *adj* sentimentale

separate[1] (*ssê*-pö-reit) *v* separare

separate[2] (*ssê*-pö-röt) *adj* distinto, separato

separately (*ssê*-pö-röt-li) *adv* a parte

September (ssêp-*têm*-bö) settembre

septic (*ssêp*-tik) *adj* settico; ***become** ~ infiammarsi

sequel (*ssii*-kᵘöl) *n* continuazione *f*

sequence (*ssii*-kᵘönss) *n* successione *f*; serie *f*

serene (ssö-*riin*) *adj* calmo; sereno

serial (*ssiᵒ*-ri-öl) *n* romanzo a puntate

series (*ssiᵒ*-riis) *n* (pl ~) serie *f*

serious (*ssiᵒ*-ri-öss) *adj* serio

seriousness (*ssiᵒ*-ri-öss-nöss) *n* serietà *f*

sermon (ssöö-mön) n sermone m

serum (ssi°-röm) n siero m

servant (ssöö-vönt) n servitore m, -trice f

serve (ssööv) v servire

service (ssöö-viss) n servizio m; ~ **charge** servizio m; ~ **station** distributore di benzina

serviette (ssöö-vi-êt) n tovagliolo m

session (ssê-ʃön) n sessione f

set (ssêt) n assieme m, gruppo m

***set** (ssêt) v *mettere; ~ **menu** pranzo a prezzo fisso; ~ **out** partire

setting (ssê-ting) n scenario m; ~ **lotion** fissatore per capelli

settle (ssê-töl) v sistemare, fissare; ~ **down** sistemarsi

settlement (ssê-töl-mönt) n accomodamento m, accordo m

seven (ssê-vön) num sette

seventeen (ssê-vön-tiin) num diciassette

seventeenth (ssê-vön-tiinθ) num diciassettesimo

seventh (ssê-vönθ) num settimo

seventy (ssê-vön-ti) num settanta

several (ssê-vö-röl) adj diversi, parecchi

severe (ssi-vi°) adj violento; rigoroso, severo

sew (ssou) v cucire; ~ **up** suturare

sewer (ssuu-ö) n fogna f

sewing machine (ssou-ing-mö-ʃiin) n macchina da cucire

sex (ssêkss) n sesso m

sexual (ssêk-ʃu-öl) adj sessuale

sexuality (ssêk-ʃu-æ-lö-ti) n sessualità f

shade (ʃeid) n ombra f; tinta f

shadow (ʃæ-dou) n ombra f

shady (ʃei-di) adj ombreggiato

***shake** (ʃeik) v agitare

shaky (ʃei-ki) adj vacillante

***shall** (ʃæl) v *dovere

shallow (ʃæ-lou) adj poco profondo

shame (ʃeim) n vergogna f; disonore m; **shame!** vergogna!

shampoo (ʃæm-puu) n shampoo m

shamrock (ʃæm-rok) n trifoglio m

shape (ʃeip) n forma f; v formare

share (ʃê°) v *condividere; n parte f; azione f

shark (ʃaak) n pescecane m, squalo m

sharp (ʃaap) adj affilato

sharpen (ʃaa-pön) v affilare

shave (ʃeiv) v *radere; radersi, farsi la barba

shaver (ʃei-vö) n rasoio elettrico

shaving (ʃei-ving) n da barba; ~ **brush** pennello da barba; ~ **cream** crema da barba; ~ **soap** sapone da barba

shawl (ʃool) n scialle m

she (ʃii) pron essa; lei

shed (ʃêd) n capanno m; baracca f

***shed** (ʃêd) v versare; *diffondere

sheep (ʃiip) n (pl ~) pecora f

sheer (ʃi°) adj assoluto, puro; fino, trasparente, sottile

sheet (ʃiit) n lenzuolo m; foglio m; lamina f

shelf (ʃêlf) n (pl shelves) scaffale m

shell (ʃêl) n conchiglia f; guscio m

shellfish (ʃêl-fiʃ) n crostaceo m

shelter (ʃêl-tö) n riparo m, rifugio m; v riparare

shepherd (ʃê-pöd) n pastore m

shift (ʃift) n turno m

***shine** (ʃain) v brillare; scintillare, risplendere

ship (ʃip) n nave f; v spedire

shipowner (ʃi-pou-nö) n armatore m

shipping line (ʃip-ping lain) n linea di navigazione

shipyard (ʃip-¹aad) n cantiere navale

shirt (ʃööt) n camicia f

shiver (ʃi-vö) v tremare, rabbrividire; n brivido m

shock (ʃok) n scossa f; v *scuotere; ~

absorber ammortizzatore *m*

shocking (*ʃo*-king) *adj* scioccante

shoe (ʃuu) *n* scarpa *f*; **gym shoes** scarpe da ginnastica; **~ polish** lucido per scarpe; **~ shop** negozio di scarpe

shoelace (*ʃuu*-leiss) *n* laccio da scarpe

shoemaker (*ʃuu*-mei-kö) *n* calzolaio *m*

shook (ʃuk) *v* (p shake)

*shoot (ʃuut) *v* sparare

shop (ʃop) *n* negozio *m*; *v* *fare la spesa; **~ assistant** commesso *m*, -a *f*

shopkeeper (*ʃop*-kii-pö) *n* negoziante *m/f*

shoplifter (*ʃop*-lif-tö) *n* taccheggiatore *m*, -trice *f*

shoplifting (*ʃop*-lif-ting) *n* taccheggio *m*

shopping (*ʃo*-ping) *n* spesa *f*; **go ~** andare a fare acquisti; **~ bag** borsa per la spesa; **~ centre** centro commerciale; **do one's ~** fare la spesa

shopwindow (ʃop-ᵘ*in*-dou) *n* vetrina *f*

shore (ʃoo) *n* riva *f*, sponda *f*

short (ʃoot) *adj* corto; basso; **~ circuit** corto circuito

shortage (*ʃoo*-tidʒ) *n* carenza *f*, mancanza *f*

shorten (*ʃoo*-tön) *v* accorciare

shorthand (*ʃoot*-hænd) *n* stenografia *f*

shortly (*ʃoot*-li) *adv* presto, tra breve, prossimamente

shorts (ʃootss) *pl* calzoncini *mpl*; *plAm* mutande *fpl*

short-sighted (ʃoot-*ssai*-tid) *adj* miope

shot (ʃot) *n* sparo *m*; iniezione *f*; sequenza *f*

*should (ʃud) *v* *dovere

shoulder (*ʃoul*-dö) *n* spalla *f*

shout (ʃaut) *v* urlare, gridare; *n* grido *m*

shovel (*ʃa*-völ) *n* pala *f*

show (ʃou) *n* rappresentazione *f*, spettacolo *m*; esposizione *f*

*show (ʃou) *v* mostrare; *far vedere, esibire; dimostrare

showcase (*ʃou*-keiss) *n* bacheca *f*

shower (ʃauᵒ) *n* doccia *f*; acquazzone *m*, precipitazione *f*

showroom (*ʃou*-ruum) *n* show-room *m*

shriek (ʃriik) *v* strillare; *n* strillo *m*

shrimp (ʃrimp) *n* gamberetto *m*

shrine (ʃrain) *n* santuario *m*

*shrink (ʃringk) *v* *restringersi

shrinkproof (*ʃringk*-pruuf) *adj* irrestringibile

shrub (ʃrab) *n* arbusto *m*

shudder (*ʃa*-dö) *n* brivido *m*

shuffle (*ʃa*-föl) *v* mescolare

*shut (ʃat) *v* *chiudere; **~ in** *rinchiudere

shutter (*ʃa*-tö) *n* imposta *f*, persiana *f*

shy (ʃai) *adj* schivo, timido

shyness (*ʃai*-nöss) *n* timidezza *f*

Siamese (ssai-ö-*miis*) *adj* siamese

sick (ssik) *adj* ammalato; nauseato

sickness (*ssik*-nöss) *n* male *m*; nausea *f*

side (ssaid) *n* lato *m*; parte *f*; **~ street** traversa *f*

sideburns (*ssaid*-bööns) *pl* basette *fpl*

sidelight (*ssaid*-lait) *n* luce laterale

sidewalk (*ssaid*-ᵘook) *nAm* marciapiede *m*

sideways (*ssaid*-ᵘeis) *adv* lateralmente

siege (ssiidʒ) *n* assedio *m*

sieve (ssiv) *n* setaccio *m*; *v* setacciare

sift (ssift) *v* vagliare

sight (ssait) *n* vista *f*; veduta *f*, spettacolo *m*; curiosità *f*

sightseeing (*ssait*-siing) *n* visita turistica; **go ~** fare un giro turistico

sign (ssain) *n* segno *m*; gesto *m*, cenno

m; v *sottoscrivere, firmare

signal (*ssigh*-nöl) *n* segnale *m*; segno *m; v* segnalare

signature (*ssigh*-nö-tʃö) *n* firma *f*

significant (ssigh-*ni*-fi-könt) *adj* significativo

signpost (*ssain*-pousst) *n* cartello indicatore

silence (*ssai*-lönss) *n* silenzio *m; v* *far tacere

silencer (*ssai*-lön-ssö) *n* silenziatore *m*

silent (*ssai*-lönt) *adj* silenzioso; ***be ~** *tacere

silk (ssilk) *n* seta *f*

silly (*ssi*-li) *adj* sciocco

silver (*ssil*-vö) *n* argento *m*; d'argento

silverware (*ssil*-vö-ᵘêᵒ) *n* argenteria *f*

similar (*ssi*-mi-lö) *adj* analogo, simile

similarity (ssi-mi-*læ*-rö-ti) *n* rassomiglianza *f*

simple (*ssim*-pöl) *adj* ingenuo; semplice

simply (*ssim*-pli) *adv* semplicemente

simulate (*ssi*-mⁱu-leit) *v* simulare

simultaneous (ssi-möl-*tei*-ni-öss) *adj* simultaneo

sin (ssin) *n* peccato *m*

since (ssinss) *prep* da; *adv* da allora; *conj* da quando; poiché

sincere (ssin-*ssiᵒ*) *adj* sincero

sinew (*ssi*-nⁱuu) *n* tendine *m*

***sing** (ssing) *v* cantare

singer (*ssing*-ö) *n* cantante *m/f*

single (*ssing*-ghöl) *adj* singolo; celibe; nubile

singular (*ssing*-ghⁱu-lö) *n* singolare *m; adj* strano

sinister (*ssi*-ni-sstö) *adj* sinistro

sink (ssingk) *n* lavello *m*

***sink** (ssingk) *v* affondare

sip (ssip) *n* sorsetto *m*

sir (ssöö) *n* signore *m*

siren (*ssaiᵒ*-rön) *n* sirena *f*

sister (*ssi*-sstö) *n* sorella *f*

sister-in-law (*ssi*-sstö-rin-loo) *n* (pl sisters-) cognata *f*

***sit** (ssit) *v* *sedere; **~ down** *sedersi

site (ssait) *n* sito *m*; posizione *f*

sitting room (*ssi*-ting-ruum) *n* soggiorno *m*

situated (*ssi*-tʃu-ei-tid) *adj* situato

situation (ssi-tʃu-*ei*-ʃön) *n* situazione *f*; ubicazione *f*

six (ssikss) *num* sei

sixteen (ssikss-*tiin*) *num* sedici

sixteenth (ssikss-*tiin*θ) *num* sedicesimo

sixth (ssikssθ) *num* sesto

sixty (*ssikss*-ti) *num* sessanta

size (ssais) *n* grandezza *f*, misura *f*; dimensione *f*; formato *m*

skate (sskeit) *v* pattinare; *n* pattino *n*

skating (*sskei*-ting) *n* pattinaggio *m*; **rink** pista di pattinaggio

skeleton (*sskê*-li-tön) *n* scheletro *m*

sketch (sskêtʃ) *n* disegno *m*, schizzo *m; v* disegnare, abbozzare

ski¹ (sskii) *v* sciare

ski² (sskii) *n* (pl ~, ~s) sci *m;* **~ boot** scarponi da sci; **~ jump** salto con g sci; **~ lift** ski-lift *m;* **~ pants** calzoni d sci; **~ poles** *Am* bastoni da sci; **~ sticks** bastoni da sci

skid (sskid) *v* scivolare

skier (*sskii*-ö) *n* sciatore *m*, -trice *f*

skiing (*sskii*-ing) *n* sci *m*

skil(l)ful (*sskil*-föl) *adj* esperto, destro abile

skill (sskil) *n* abilità *f*

skilled (sskild) *adj* abile; esperto

skin (sskin) *n* pelle *f*; buccia *f;* **~ crear** crema per la pelle

skip (sskip) *v* saltellare; *omettere

skirt (sskööt) *n* gonna *f*

skull (sskal) *n* cranio *m*

sky (sskai) *n* cielo *m*

skyscraper (*sskai*-sskrei-pö) *n*

grattacielo *m*

slack (sslæk) *adj* lento

slacks (sslækss) *pl* pantaloni *mpl*

slam (sslæm) *v* sbattere

slander (*sslaan*-dö) *n* calunnia *f*

slang (sslæng) *n* slang *m* ; gergo *m*

slant (sslaant) *v* inclinare

slanting (*sslaan*-ting) *adj* obliquo, pendente, inclinato

slap (sslæp) *v* schiaffeggiare; *n* schiaffo *m*

slate (ssleit) *n* ardesia *f*

slave (ssleiv) *n* schiavo *m*

sledge (sslêdʒ) *n* slitta *f*

sleep (ssliip) *n* sonno *m*

***sleep** (ssliip) *v* dormire

sleeping bag (*sslii*-ping-bægh) *n* sacco a pelo

sleeping car (*sslii*-ping-kaa) *n* vagone letto

sleeping partner (sslii-ping-*paat*-nö) *n* socio inattivo

sleeping pill (*sslii*-ping-pil) *n* sonnifero *m*

sleepless (*ssliip*-löss) *adj* insonne

sleepy (*sslii*-pi) *adj* assonnato

sleeve (ssliiv) *n* manica *f*; copertina *f*

sleigh (sslei) *n* slitta *f*

slender (*sslên*-dö) *adj* snello

slice (sslaiss) *n* fetta *f*

slide (sslaid) *n* scivolata *f*; scivolo *m*; diapositiva *f*

***slide** (sslaid) *v* slittare

slight (sslait) *adj* leggero

slim (sslim) *adj* snello

slip (sslip) *v* scivolare; scappare; *n* svista *f*; sottoveste *f*

slipper (*ssli*-pö) *n* ciabatta *f*, pantofola *f*

slippery (*ssli*-pö-ri) *adj* viscido, sdrucciolevole

slogan (*sslou*-ghön) *n* motto *m*, slogan *m*

slope (ssloup) *n* pendio *m*; *v* pendere

sloping (*sslou*-ping) *adj* inclinato

sloppy (*sslo*-pi) *adj* disordinato

slot (sslot) *n* fessura *f*; ~ **machine** distributore automatico

slovenly (*ssla*-vön-li) *adj* sciatto

slow (sslou) *adj* lento; ~ **down** rallentare

sluice (ssluuss) *n* chiusa *f*

slum (sslam) *n* bassifondi *mpl*

slump (sslamp) *n* calo di prezzo

slush (sslaʃ) *n* neve fangosa

sly (sslai) *adj* astuto

smack (ssmæk) *v* picchiare; *n* ceffone *m*

small (ssmool) *adj* piccolo; scarso

smallpox (*ssmool*-pokss) *n* vaiolo *m*

smart (ssmaat) *adj* elegante; sveglio, intelligente

smash (ssmæʃ) *n* fracasso *m*; scontro *m*; schiacciata *f*; *v* spaccare; sbattere; frantumarsi; ~ **into** ... schiantarsi contro ...

smell (ssmêl) *n* odore *m*

***smell** (ssmêl) *v* odorare; puzzare

smelly (*ssmê*-li) *adj* puzzolente

smile (ssmail) *v* *sorridere; *n* sorriso *m*

smith (ssmiθ) *n* fabbro *m*

smog (ssmog) *n* smog *m*

smoke (ssmouk) *v* fumare; *n* fumo *m*

smoker (*ssmou*-kö) *n* fumatore *m*; scompartimento per fumatori

smoking (*ssmou*-king) *n* fumo *m*; **no** ~ vietato fumare; ~ **compartment** compartimento per fumatori

smooth (ssmuuð) *adj* levigato, piano, liscio; morbido

smuggle (*ssma*-ghöl) *v* contrabbandare

snack (ssnæk) *n* spuntino *m*; ~ **bar** tavola calda

snail (ssneil) *n* lumaca *f*

snake (ssneik) *n* serpente *m*

snapshot (*ssnæp*-ʃot) *n* istantanea *f*

sneakers (*ssnii*-kös) *plAm* scarpe da ginnastica

sneeze (ssniis) *v* starnutire

sniper (*ssnai*-pö) *n* franco tiratore

snooty (*ssnuu*-ti) *adj* arrogante

snore (ssnoo) *v* russare

snorkel (*ssnoo*-köl) *n* respiratore *m*

snout (ssnaut) *n* muso *m*

snow (ssnou) *n* neve *f*; *v* nevicare

snowstorm (*ssnou*-sstoom) *n* tormenta di neve

snowy (*ssnou*-i) *adj* nevoso

so (ssou) *conj* dunque; *adv* così; talmente; **and ~ on** e così via; **~ far** finora; **~ that** così che, affinché

soak (ssouk) *v* inzuppare; mettere ammollo

soap (ssoup) *n* sapone *m*; **~ powder** sapone in polvere

sober (*ssou*-bö) *adj* sobrio; assennato

so-called (*ssou-koold*) *adj* cosiddetto

soccer (*sso*-kö) *n* calcio *m*; **~ team** squadra di calcio

social (*ssou*-ʃöl) *adj* sociale

socialism (*ssou*-ʃö-li-ssöm) *n* socialismo *m*

socialist (*ssou*-ʃö-lisst) *adj* socialista; *n* socialista *m/f*

society (ssö-*ssai*-ö-ti) *n* società *f*; associazione *f*; compagnia *f*

sock (ssok) *n* calzino *m*, calza *f*

socket (*sso*-kit) *n* portalampada *m*

soda water (*ssou*-dö-ᵘoo-tö) *n* soda *f*

sofa (*ssou*-fö) *n* sofà *m*, divano *m*

soft (ssoft) *adj* morbido; **~ drink** bibita analcoolica

soften (*sso*-fön) *v* ammorbidire

software (*ssoft*-ᵘêᵒ) *n* software *m*

soil (ssoil) *n* suolo *m*; terreno *m*, terra *f*

soiled (ssoild) *adj* sudicio

sold (ssould) *v* (p, pp sell); **~ out** esaurito

soldier (*ssoul*-dʒö) *n* militare *m*, soldato *m*

sole¹ (ssoul) *adj* unico

sole² (ssoul) *n* suola *f*; sogliola *f*

solely (*ssoul*-li) *adv* esclusivamente

solemn (*sso*-löm) *adj* solenne

solicitor (ssö-*li*-ssi-tö) *n* procuratore legale, avvocato *m*

solid (*sso*-lid) *adj* robusto, solido; massiccio; *n* solido *m*

soluble (*sso*-lᶦu-böl) *adj* solubile

solution (ssö-*luu*-ʃön) *n* soluzione *f*

solve (ssolv) *v* *risolvere

somber *Am*, **sombre** (*ssom*-bö) *adj* tetro

some (ssam) *adj* alcuni, qualche; *pron* alcuni, taluni; una parte; **~ day** un giorno o l'altro; **~ more** ancora; **~ time** un giorno

somebody (*ssam*-bö-di) *pron* qualcuno

somehow (*ssam*-hau) *adv* in un modo o nell'altro

someone (*ssam*-ᵘan) *pron* qualcuno

something (*ssam*-θing) *pron* qualcosa

sometimes (*ssam*-taims) *adv* qualche volta

somewhat (*ssam*-ᵘot) *adv* alquanto

somewhere (*ssam*-ᵘêᵒ) *adv* in qualche posto

son (ssan) *n* figlio *m*

song (ssong) *n* canzone *f*

son-in-law (*ssa*-nin-loo) *n* (pl sons-) genero *m*

soon (ssuun) *adv* presto, tra poco; **as ~ as** non appena

sooner (*ssuu*-nö) *adv* piuttosto

sore (ssoo) *adj* indolenzito; *n* piaga *f*; **~ throat** mal di gola

sorrow (*sso*-rou) *n* tristezza *f*, dolore *m*, dispiacere *m*

sorry (*sso*-ri) *adj* spiacente; **sorry!** scusa!, scusate!, scusi!

sort (ssoot) *v* classificare; *n* genere *m*, specie *f*; **all sorts of** ogni sorta di

soul (ssoul) *n* anima *f*; spirito *m*

sound (ssaund) *n* suono *m*; *v* suonare; *adj* solido

soundproof (ssaund-pruuf) *adj* insonorizzato

soup (ssuup) *n* minestra *f*

sour (ssau⁰) *adj* agro

source (ssooss) *n* sorgente *f*

south (ssauθ) *n* sud *m*; **South Pole** polo Sud

South Africa (ssauθ æ-fri-kö) Africa del Sud

southeast (ssauθ-*iisst*) *n* sud-est *m*

southerly (ssa-ðö-li) *adj* meridionale

southern (ssa-ðön) *adj* meridionale

southwest (ssauθ-ᵘêsst) *n* sud-ovest *m*

souvenir (ssuu-vö-ni⁰) *n* ricordo *m*

sovereign (ssov-rin) *n* sovrano *m*

*sow (ssou) *v* seminare

spa (sspaa) *n* stazione termale

space (sspeiss) *n* spazio *m*; distanza *f*; *v* spaziare

spacious (sspei-ʃöss) *adj* spazioso

spade (sspeid) *n* zappa *f*, vanga *f*

Spain (sspein) Spagna *f*

Spanish (sspæ-niʃ) *adj* spagnolo

spanking (sspæng-king) *n* sculacciata *f*

spanner (sspæ-nö) *n* chiave *f*

spare (sspê⁰) *adj* di riserva; disponibile; *v* *fare a meno di; **~ part** pezzo di ricambio; **~ room** camera degli ospiti; **~ time** tempo libero; **~ tyre** pneumatico di scorta; **~ wheel** ruota di scorta

spark (sspaak) *n* scintilla *f*

sparking plug (sspaa-king-plagh) *n* candela d'accensione

sparkling (sspaa-kling) *adj* scintillante; spumante

sparrow (sspæ-rou) *n* passero *m*

spasm (sspæ-söm) *n* spasmo *m*

speak (sspiik) *v* parlare

speaker (sspii-kö) *n* oratore *m*, -trice *f*; annunciatore *m*, -trice *f*; altoparlante *m*

spear (sspi⁰) *n* lancia *f*

special (sspê-ʃöl) *adj* particolare, speciale; **~ delivery** per espresso

specialist (sspê-ʃö-lisst) *n* specialista *m/f*

speciality (sspê-ʃi-æ-lö-ti) *n* specialità *f*

specialize (sspê-ʃö-lais) *v* specializzarsi

specially (sspê-ʃö-li) *adv* particolarmente

species (sspii-ʃiis) *n* (pl **~**) specie *f*

specific (sspö-ssi-fik) *adj* specifico

specimen (sspê-ssi-mön) *n* esemplare *m*

speck (sspêk) *n* macchiolina *f*

spectacle (sspêk-tö-köl) *n* spettacolo *m*; **spectacles** occhiali *mpl*

spectator (sspêk-*tei*-tö) *n* spettatore *m*, -trice *f*

speculate (sspê-kᵘu-leit) *v* speculare

speech (sspiitʃ) *n* parola *f*; discorso *m*; linguaggio *m*

speechless (sspiitʃ-löss) *adj* muto

speed (sspiid) *n* velocità *f*; rapidità *f*, fretta *f*; **cruising ~** velocità di crociera; **~ limit** limite di velocità; **~ up** *v* accelerare

*speed (sspiid) *v* *correre; *correre troppo

speeding (sspii-ding) *n* eccesso di velocità

speedometer (sspii-*do*-mi-tö) *n* tachimetro *m*

spell (sspêl) *n* incanto *m*

*spell (sspêl) *v* compitare, sillabare

spelling (sspê-ling) *n* ortografia *f*

*spend (sspênd) *v* *spendere; impiegare

sphere (ssfi⁰) *n* sfera *f*

spiced (sspaisst) *adj* condito

spicy (sspai-ssi) *adj* piccante**

spider (*sspai*-dö) *n* ragno *m*; **spider's web** ragnatela *f*

*spill (sspil) *v* *spandere

*spin (sspin) *v* filare; *far girare

spinach (*sspi*-nidʒ) *n* spinaci *mpl*

spine (sspain) *n* spina dorsale

spinster (*sspin*-sstö) *n* zitella *f*

spire (sspaiö) *n* guglia *f*

spirit (*sspi*-rit) *n* spirito *m*; fantasma *m*; umore *m*; **spirits** bevande alcooliche; morale *m*; ~ **stove** fornello a spirito

spiritual (*sspi*-ri-tʃu-öl) *adj* spirituale

spit (sspit) *n* sputo *m*, saliva *f*; spiedo *m*

*spit (sspit) *v* sputare

spite (sspait): **in ~ of** nonostante, malgrado

spiteful (*sspait*-föl) *adj* malevolo

splash (ssplæʃ) *v* schizzare

splendid (*ssplên*-did) *adj* magnifico, splendido

splendo(u)r (*ssplên*-dö) *n* splendore *m*

splint (ssplint) *n* stecca *f*

splinter (*ssplin*-tö) *n* scheggia *f*

*split (ssplit) *v* *fendere

*spoil (sspoil) *v* guastare; viziare

spoke¹ (sspouk) *v* (p speak)

spoke² (sspouk) *n* raggio *m*

sponge (sspandʒ) *n* spugna *f*

spook (sspuuk) *n* spettro *m*

spool (sspuul) *n* rocchetto *m*

spoon (sspuun) *n* cucchiaio *m*

spoonful (*sspuun*-ful) *n* cucchiaiata *f*

sport (sspoot) *n* sport *m*; **sports car** macchina sportiva; **sports jacket** giacchetta sportiva

sportsman (*sspootss*-mön) *n* (pl -men) sportivo *m*

sportswear (*sspootss*-uê*ö*) *n* abbigliamento sportivo

spot (sspot) *n* chiazza *f*, macchia *f*; località *f*, luogo *m*

spotless (*sspot*-löss) *adj* immacolato

spotlight (*sspot*-lait) *n* riflettore *m*

spotted (*sspo*-tid) *adj* chiazzato

spout (sspaut) *n* getto *m*

sprain (ssprein) *v* slogarsi; *n* distorsione *f*

spray (ssprei) *n* spruzzi *mpl*; lacca *f*; spray *m*; *v* spruzzare

*spread (ssprêd) *v* *stendere

spring (sspring) *n* primavera *f*; molla *f*; sorgente *f*

springtime (*sspring*-taim) *n* primavera *f*

sprouts (ssprautss) *pl* cavolini di Bruxelles

spy (sspai) *n* spia *f*

squadron (*ssk*u*o*-drön) *n* squadriglia *f*

square (ssk*u*ê*ö*) *adj* quadrato; *n* quadrato *m*; piazza *f*

squash (ssk*u*oʃ) *n* spremuta

squeeze (sskuiis) *n* stretta *f*; *v* stringere; spremere; strizzare; **a ~ of lemon** uno spruzzo di limone

squirrel (*ssk*u*i*-röl) *n* scoiattolo *m*

squirt (ssk*u*ööt) *n* zampillo *m*

stable (*sstei*-böl) *adj* stabile; *n* stalla *f*

stack (sstæk) *n* pila *f*

stadium (*sstei*-di-öm) *n* stadio *m*

staff (sstaaf) *n* personale *m*

stage (ssteidʒ) *n* scena *f*; palcoscenico *m*; stadio *m*, fase *f*; tappa *f*

stain (sstein) *v* macchiare; *n* macchia *f*; **stained glass** vetro colorato; ~ **remover** smacchiatore *m*

stainless (*sstein*-löss) *adj* immacolato; ~ **steel** acciaio inossidabile

staircase (*sstê*ö-keiss) *n* scala *f*

stairs (sstê*ö*s) *pl* scala *f*

stale (ssteil) *adj* raffermo

stall (sstool) *n* bancarella *f*; poltrona in platea

stamp (sstæmp) *n* francobollo *m*; timbro *m*; *v* affrancare; pestare

stand (sstænd) *n* banco *m*; tribuna *f*

stood

*stand (sstænd) *v* *stare in piedi
standard (sstæn-död) *n* norma *f*; normale; **~ of living** livello di vita
stanza (sstæn-sö) *n* strofa *f*
staple (sstei-pöl) *n* graffetta *f*
star (sstaa) *n* stella *f*
starboard (sstaa-böd) *n* tribordo *m*
stare (sstê⁶) *v* fissare
starling (sstaa-ling) *n* stornello *m*
start (sstaat) *v* cominciare; *n* inizio *m*
starting point (sstaa-ting-point) *n* punto di partenza
state (ssteit) *n* stato *m*; *v* affermare; **the States** Stati Uniti
statement (ssteit-mönt) *n* dichiarazione *f*
statesman (ssteitss-mön) *n* (pl -men) uomo di stato
station (sstei-ʃön) *n* stazione *f*; posto *m*
stationary (sstei-ʃö-nö-ri) *adj* stazionario
stationer's (sstei-ʃö-nös) *n* cartoleria *f*
stationery (sstei-ʃö-nö-ri) *n* cartoleria *f*
statistics (sstö-ti-sstikss) *pl* statistica *f*
statue (sstæ-tʃuu) *n* statua *f*
stay (sstei) *v* *rimanere, *stare; soggiornare, *trattenersi; *n* soggiorno *m*
steadfast (sstêd-faasst) *adj* fermo
steady (sstê-di) *adj* stabile
steak (ssteik) *n* bistecca *f*
*steal (sstiil) *v* rubare
steam (sstiim) *n* vapore *m*
steamer (sstii-mö) *n* piroscafo *m*
steel (sstiil) *n* acciaio *m*
steep (sstiip) *adj* ripido
steeple (sstii-pöl) *n* campanile *m*
steer¹ (sstiö) *n* manzo *m*
steer² (sstiö) *v* guidare
steering wheel (sstiö-ring-ᵘiil) *n* volante *m*
steersman (sstiö's-mön) *n* (pl -men)

timoniere *m*
stem (sstêm) *n* gambo *m*
step (sstêp) *n* passo *m*; scalino *m*; *v* camminare
stepchild (sstêp-tʃaild) *n* (pl -children) figliastro *m*
stepfather (sstêp-faa-ðö) *n* patrigno *m*
stepmother (sstêp-ma-ðö) *n* matrigna *f*
stereo (sstê-ri-ou) *n* impianto stereo
sterile (sstê-rail) *adj* sterile
sterilize (sstê-ri-lais) *v* sterilizzare
steward (sstʰuu-öd) *n* steward *m*
stewardess (sstʰuu-ö-dêss) *n* hostess *f*
stick (sstik) *n* bastone *m*
*stick (sstik) *v* appiccicare, incollare
sticky (ssti-ki) *adj* appiccicaticcio
stiff (sstif) *adj* rigido
still (sstil) *adv* ancora; comunque; *adj* tranquillo
stimulant (ssti-mⁱu-lönt) *n* stimolante *m*
stimulate (ssti-mⁱu-leit) *v* stimolare
sting (ssting) *n* puntura *f*
*sting (ssting) *v* *pungere
stingy (sstin-dʒi) *adj* taccagno
*stink (sstingk) *v* puzzare
stipulate (ssti-pⁱu-leit) *v* stipulare
stir (sstöö) *v* *muovere; mescolare
stitch (sstitʃ) *n* punto *m*; fitta *f*
stock (sstok) *n* scorta *f*; *v* *tenere in magazzino; **~ exchange** borsa valori, borsa *f*; **~ market** borsa *f*; **stocks and shares** titoli
stocking (ssto-king) *n* calza *f*
stole¹ (sstoul) *v* (p steal)
stole² (sstoul) *n* stola *f*
stomach (ssta-mök) *n* stomaco *m*
stomachache (ssta-mö-keik) *n* mal di pancia, mal di stomaco
stone (sstoun) *n* sasso *m*, pietra *f*; pietra preziosa; nocciolo *m*; *adj* di pietra; **pumice ~** pietra pomice
stood (sstud) *v* (p, pp stand)

stop (sstop) *v* *smettere; terminare, cessare; *n* fermata *f*; **stop!** alt!

stopper (ssto-pö) *n* tappo *m*

storage (sstoo-ridȝ) *n* magazzinaggio *m*

store (sstoo) *n* riserva *f*; bottega *f*; *v* immagazzinare; ~ **house** magazzino *m*

stor(e)y (sstoo-ri) *n* piano *m*

stork (sstook) *n* cicogna *f*

storm (sstoom) *n* tempesta *f*

stormy (sstoo-mi) *adj* tempestoso

story (sstoo-ri) *n* racconto *m*

stout (sstaut) *adj* grosso, obeso, corpulento

stove (sstouv) *n* stufa *f*, cucina *f*

straight (sstreit) *adj* dritto; onesto; *adv* dritto; ~ **ahead** sempre diritto; ~ **away** direttamente, subito; ~ **on** avanti dritto

strain (sstrein) *n* fatica *f*; sforzo *m*; *v* forzare; filtrare

strainer (sstrei-nö) *n* colapasta *m*

strange (sstreindȝ) *adj* strano; bizzarro

stranger (sstrein-dȝö) *n* straniero *m*, -a *f*; estraneo *m*, -a *f*

strangle (sstræŋ-ghöl) *v* strangolare

strap (sstræp) *n* cinghia *f*

straw (sstroo) *n* paglia *f*

strawberry (sstroo-bö-ri) *n* fragola *f*

stream (sstriim) *n* ruscello *m*; corrente *f*; *v* *scorrere

street (sstriit) *n* strada *f*

streetcar (sstriit-kaa) *nAm* tram *m*

strength (sstrêŋgθ) *n* resistenza *f*, forza *f*

stress (sstrêss) *n* tensione *f*; accento *m*; *v* sottolineare

stretch (sstrêtʃ) *v* *tendere; *n* lasso di tempo

strict (sstrikt) *adj* severo; rigido

strike (sstraik) *n* sciopero *m*

*strike (sstraik) *v* picchiare; colpire; scioperare; ammainare

striking (sstrai-king) *adj* impressionante, notevole, vistoso

string (sstring) *n* spago *m*; corda *f*

strip (sstrip) *n* striscia *f*

stripe (sstraip) *n* striscia *f*

striped (sstraipt) *adj* striato

stroke (sstrouk) *n* colpo *m*

stroll (sstroul) *v* passeggiare; *n* passeggiata *f*

strong (sstrong) *adj* forte; robusto

stronghold (sstrong-hould) *n* roccaforte *f*

structure (sstrak-tʃö) *n* struttura *f*

struggle (sstra-ghöl) *n* combattimento *m*, lotta *f*; *v* lottare

stub (sstab) *n* matrice *f*

stubborn (ssta-bön) *adj* cocciuto

student (ssťuu-dönt) *n* studente *m*, -essa *f*

study (ssta-di) *v* studiare; *n* studio *m*

stuff (sstaf) *n* sostanza *f*; roba *f*

stuffed (sstaft) *adj* ripieno

stuffing (ssta-fing) *n* ripieno *m*

stuffy (ssta-fi) *adj* stantio

stumble (sstam-böl) *v* inciampare

stung (sstang) *v* (p, pp sting)

stupid (ssťuu-pid) *adj* stupido

style (sstail) *n* stile *m*

stylish (sstai-liʃ) *adj* elegante

subject[1] (ssab-dȝikt) *n* soggetto *m*; materia *f*; suddito *m*; ~ **to** soggetto a

subject[2] (ssöb-dȝêkt) *v* *sottomettere

submarine (ssöb-ma-riin) *n* sottomarino *m*, sommergibile *m*

submit (ssöb-mit) *v* *sottomettersi

subordinate (ssö-boo-di-nöt) *adj* subalterno; secondario

subscriber (ssöb-sskrai-bö) *n* abbonato *m*, -a *f*

subscription (ssöb-sskrip-ʃön) *n* abbonamento *m*

subsequent (ssab-ssi-kᵘönt) *adj* successivo

subsidy (*ssab*-ssi-di) *n* sovvenzione *f*

substance (*ssab*-sstönss) *n* sostanza *f*

substantial (ssöb-*sstæn*-ʃöl) *adj* solido; sostanziale; sostanzioso

substitute (*ssab*-ssti-t'uut) *v* sostituire; *n* sostituto *m*, -a *f*

subtitle (*ssab*-tai-töl) *n* sottotitolo *m*

subtle (*ssa*-töl) *adj* sottile

subtract (ssöb-*trækt*) *v* *sottrarre

suburb (*ssa*-bööb) *n* sobborgo *m*

suburban (ssö-*böö*-bön) *adj* suburbano

subway (*ssab*-ᵘei) *nAm* metropolitana *f*

succeed (ssök-*ssiid*) *v* *riuscire; *succedere

success (ssök-*ssêss*) *n* successo *m*

successful (ssök-*ssêss*-föl) *adj* riuscito

succumb (ssö-*kam*) *v* soccombere

such (ssatʃ) *adj* simile, tale; *adv* così; ~ **as** come

suck (ssak) *v* succhiare

sudden (*ssa*-dön) *adj* improvviso

suddenly (*ssa*-dön-li) *adv* improvvisamente

suede (ssᵘeid) *n* pelle scamosciata

suffer (*ssa*-fö) *v* *soffrire; subire

suffering (*ssa*-fö-ring) *n* sofferenza *f*

suffice (ssö-*faiss*) *v* bastare

sufficient (ssö-*fi*-ʃönt) *adj* bastante, sufficiente

suffrage (*ssa*-fridʒ) *n* suffragio *m*

sugar (*ʃu*-ghö) *n* zucchero *m*

suggest (ssö-*dʒêsst*) *v* suggerire

suggestion (ssö-*dʒêss*-tʃön) *n* suggerimento *m*

suicide (*ssuu*-i-ssaid) *n* suicidio *m*

suit (ssuut) *v* *andare bene a; adattare; *addirsi; *n* vestito da uomo *m*

suitable (*ssuu*-tö-böl) *adj* adeguato, adatto

suitcase (*ssuut*-keiss) *n* valigia *f*

suite (ssᵘiit) *n* appartamento *m*

sum (ssam) *n* somma *f*

summary (*ssa*-mö-ri) *n* sommario *m*, sunto *m*

summer (*ssa*-mö) *n* estate *f*; ~ **time** orario estivo; estate

summit (*ssa*-mit) *n* vetta *f*

sun (ssan) *n* sole *m*

sunbathe (*ssan*-beið) *v* *prendere il sole

sunburn (*ssan*-böön) *n* scottatura *f*

Sunday (*ssan*-di) domenica *f*

sunglasses (*ssan*-ghlaa-ssis) *pl* occhiali da sole

sunlight (*ssan*-lait) *n* luce del sole

sunny (*ssa*-ni) *adj* soleggiato

sunrise (*ssan*-rais) *n* aurora *f*

sunset (*ssan*-ssêt) *n* tramonto *m*

sunshade (*ssan*-ʃeid) *n* ombrellino *m*

sunshine (*ssan*-ʃain) *n* luce del sole

sunstroke (*ssan*-sstrouk) *n* colpo di sole

suntan (*ssan*-tæn) *n* abbronzatura *f*; ~ **oil** olio abbronzante

super (*ssuu*-pö) *adj* fantastico

superb (ssu-*pööb*) *adj* grandioso, superbo

superficial (ssuu-pö-*fi*-ʃöl) *adj* superficiale

superfluous (ssu-*pöö*-flu-öss) *adj* superfluo

superior (ssu-*piᵒ*-ri-ö) *adj* migliore, maggiore, superiore

superlative (ssu-*pöö*-lö-tiv) *adj* superlativo; *n* superlativo *m*

supermarket (*ssuu*-pö-maa-kit) *n* supermercato *m*

superstition (ssuu-pö-*ssti*-ʃön) *n* superstizione *f*

supervise (*ssuu*-pö-vais) *v* *sovrintendere

supervision (ssuu-pö-*vi*-ʒön) *n* sovrintendenza *f*, sorveglianza *f*

supervisor (*ssuu*-pö-vai-sö) *n* ispettore *m*, -trice *f* supper (*ssa*-pö) *n* cena *f*

supple (*ssa*-pöl) *adj* pieghevole, flessibile;

supplement (*ssa*-pli-mönt) *n* supplemento *m*

supply (ssö-*plai*) *n* rifornimento *m*, fornitura *f*; provvista *f*; offerta *f*; *v* fornire

support (ssö-*poot*) *v* appoggiare, *sostenere; *n* sostegno *m*

supporter (ssö-*poo*-tö) *n* tifoso *m*, -a *f*

suppose (ssö-*pous*) *v* *supporre; supposing that supposto che

suppository (ssö-*po*-si-tö-ri) *n* supposta *f*

suppress (ssö-*prêss*) *v* *reprimere

surcharge (*ssöö*-tʃaadʒ) *n* supplemento *m*

sure (ʃuᵒ) *adj* sicuro

surely (ʃuᵒ-li) *adv* certamente

surface (*ssöö*-fiss) *n* superficie *f*

surfboard (*ssööf*-bood) *n* tavola da surf

surgeon (*ssöö*-dʒön) *n* chirurgo *m*; veterinary ~ veterinario *m*

surgery (*ssöö*-dʒö-ri) *n* operazione *f*; chirurgia *f*; consultorio *m*

surname (*ssöö*-neim) *n* cognome *m*

surplus (*ssöö*-plöss) *n* eccedenza *f*

surprise (ssö-*prais*) *n* sorpresa *f*; meraviglia *f*; *v* *sorprendere; stupire

surrender (ssö-*rên*-dö) *v* *arrendersi; *n* resa *f*

surround (ssö-*raund*) *v* circondare

surrounding (ssö-*raun*-ding) *adj* circostante

surroundings (ssö-*raun*-dings) *pl* dintorni *mpl*

survey (*ssöö*-vei) *n* inchiesta *f*; perizia *f*

survival (ssö-*vai*-völ) *n* sopravvivenza *f*

survive (ssö-*vaiv*) *v* *sopravvivere

suspect¹ (ssö-*sspêkt*) *v* sospettare;

*supporre

suspect² (*ssa*-sspêkt) *n* sospetto *m*, -a *f*; indiziato *m*, -a *f*

suspend (ssö-*sspênd*) *v* *sospendere

suspenders (ssö-*sspên*-dös) *plAm* bretelle *fpl*

suspension (ssö-*sspên*-ʃön) *n* molleggio *m*, sospensione *f*; ~ bridge ponte sospeso

suspicion (ssö-*sspi*-ʃön) *n* sospetto *m*

suspicious (ssö-*sspi*-ʃöss) *adj* sospetto; sospettoso

sustain (ssö-*sstein*) *v* sopportare

Swahili (ssuᵒö-*hii*-li) *n* swahili *m*

swallow (ssuᵒo-lou) *v* ingoiare, inghiottire; *n* rondine *f*

swam (ssuᵘæm) *v* (p swim)

swamp (ssuᵘomp) *n* palude *f*

swan (ssuᵘon) *n* cigno *m*

swap (ssuᵘop) *v* barattare

*swear (ssuᵘêᵒ) *v* giurare; bestemmiare

sweat (ssuᵘêt) *n* sudore *m*; *v* sudare

sweater (ssuᵘê-tö) *n* maglione *m*

Sweden (ssuᵘii-dön) Svezia *f*

Swedish (ssuᵘii-diʃ) *adj* svedese

*sweep (ssuᵘiip) *v* scopare

sweet (ssuᵘiit) *adj* dolce; *n* caramella *f*; dolce *m*; sweets dolciumi *mpl*

sweeten (ssuᵘii-tön) *v* zuccherare

sweetheart (ssuᵘiit-haat) *n* amore *m*

sweetshop (ssuᵘiit-ʃop) *n* pasticceria *f*

swell (ssuᵘêl) *adj* magnifico

*swell (ssuᵘêl) *v* gonfiare

swelling (ssuᵘê-ling) *n* gonfiore *m*

swift (ssuᵘift) *adj* rapido

*swim (ssuᵘim) *v* nuotare

swimmer (ssuᵘi-mö) *n* nuotatore *m*, -trice *f*

swimming (ssuᵘi-ming) *n* nuoto *m*; ~ pool piscina *f*; ~ trunks costume da bagno

swimsuit (ssuᵘim-ssuut) *n* costume da bagno

swindle (ssuᵘin-döl) *v* truffare; *n* truffa

f

swindler (*ss"in*-dlö) *n* truffatore *m*, -trice *f*

swing (ss"ing) *n* altalena *f*

*swing (ss"ing) *v* dondolare

Swiss (ss"iss) *adj* svizzero

switch (ss"itʃ) *n* interruttore *m*; *v* cambiare; **~ off** *spegnere; **~ on** *accendere

Switzerland (*ss"it*-ssö-lönd) Svizzera *f*

sword (ssood) *n* spada *f*

swum (ss"am) *v* (pp swim)

syllable (*ssi*-lö-böl) *n* sillaba *f*

symbol (*ssim*-böl) *n* simbolo *m*

sympathetic (ssim-pö-*θê*-tik) *adj* cordiale, comprensivo

sympathy (*ssim*-pö-θi) *n* simpatia *f*; compassione *f*

symphony (*ssim*-fö-ni) *n* sinfonia *f*

symptom (*ssim*-töm) *n* sintomo *m*

synagogue (*ssi*-nö-ghogh) *n* sinagoga *f*

synonym (*ssi*-nö-nim) *n* sinonimo *m*

synthetic (ssin-*θê*-tik) *adj* sintetico

Syria (*ssi*-ri-ö) Siria *f*

Syrian (*ssi*-ri-ön) *adj* siriano

syringe (ssi-*rindʒ*) *n* siringa *f*

syrup (*ssi*-röp) *n* sciroppo *m*

system (*ssi*-sstöm) *n* sistema *m*; **decimal ~** sistema decimale

systematic (ssi-sstö-*mæ*-tik) *adj* sistematico

T

table (*tei*-böl) *n* tavola *f*; tabella *f*; **~ lamp** lampada da tavolo; **~ of contents** indice *m*; **~ tennis** ping-pong *m*

tablecloth (*tei*-böl-kloθ) *n* tovaglia *f*

tablespoon (*tei*-böl-sspuun) *n* cucchiaio *m*

tablet (*tæ*-blit) *n* pasticca *f*

taboo (tö-*buu*) *n* tabù *m*

tactics (*tæk*-tikss) *pl* tattica *f*

tag (tægh) *n* etichetta *f*

tail (teil) *n* coda *f*

taillight (*teil*-lait) *n* luce posteriore

tailor (*tei*-lö) *n* sarto *m*

tailor-made (*tei*-lö-meid) *adj* fatto su misura

*take (teik) *v* *prendere; accompagnare; capire; afferrare; **~ away** portar via; *togliere, levare; **~ off** decollare; **~ out** *togliere; **~ over** rilevare; **~ place** *aver luogo; **~ up** occupare

take-off (*tei*-kof) *n* decollo *m*

tale (teil) *n* storia *f*, racconto *m*

talent (*tæ*-lönt) *n* attitudine *f*, talento *m*

talented (*tæ*-lön-tid) *adj* dotato

talk (took) *v* parlare; *n* conversazione *f*

talkative (*too*-kö-tiv) *adj* loquace

tall (tool) *adj* alto; lungo

tame (teim) *adj* mansueto, addomesticato; *v* addomesticare

tampon (*tæm*-pön) *n* tampone *m*

tangerine (tæn-dʒö-*riin*) *n* mandarino *m*

tangible (*tæn*-dʒi-böl) *adj* tangibile

tank (tængk) *n* serbatoio *m*

tanker (*tæng*-kö) *n* petroliera *f*

tanned (tænd) *adj* abbronzato

tap (tæp) *n* rubinetto *m*; colpetto *m*; *v* bussare

tape (teip) *n* nastro *m*; **adhesive ~** nastro adesivo; **~ recorder** registratore *m*

tar (taa) *n* catrame *m*

target (*taa*-ghit) *n* bersaglio *m*

tariff (*tæ*-rif) *n* tariffa *f*

task (taassk) *n* compito *m*

taste (teisst) *n* gusto *m*; *v* *sapere; assaggiare

tasteless (*teisst*-löss) *adj* insipido

tasty (*tei*-ssti) *adj* gustoso, saporito

taught (toot) *v* (p, pp teach)

tavern (*tæ*-vön) *n* taverna *f*

tax (tækss) *n* tassa *f*; *v* tassare

taxation (tæk-*ssei*-ʃön) *n* imposta *f*

tax-free (*tækss*-frii) *adj* esente da tassa

taxi (*tæk*-ssi) *n* tassì *m*; ~ **driver** *n* tassista *m/f*; ~ **rank,** ~ **stand** *Am* posteggio di tassì

taximeter (*tæk*-ssi-mii-tö) *n* tassametro *m*

tea (tii) *n* tè *m*; merenda *f*; ~ **cloth** canovaccio per stoviglie; ~ **set** servizio da tè

*teach (tiitʃ) *v* insegnare

teacher (*tii*-tʃö) *n* docente *m/f,* insegnante *m/f*; professore *m,* -essa *f*; maestro *m,* -a *f*

teachings (*tii*-tʃings) *pl* insegnamento *m*

teacup (*tii*-kap) *n* tazzina da tè

team (tiim) *n* squadra *f*

teapot (*tii*-pot) *n* teiera *f*

tear¹ (tiⁿ) *n* lacrima *f*

tear² (tèⁿ) *n* strappo *m*

*tear *v* strappare

tearjerker (*tiⁿ*-dʒöö-kö) *n* romanzo (film, canzone) strappalacrime

tease (tiis) *v* stuzzicare

tea-shop (*tii*-ʃop) *n* sala da tè

teaspoon (*tii*-sspuun) *n* cucchiaino *m*

teaspoonful (*tii*-sspuun-ful) *n* cucchiaino *m*

technical (*têk*-ni-köl) *adj* tecnico

technician (têk-*ni*-ʃön) *n* tecnico *m,* -a *f*

technique (têk-*niik*) *n* tecnica *f*

technological (têk-no-*lo*-dʒi-köl) *adj* tecnologico

technology (têk-*no*-lö-dʒi) *n* tecnologia *f*

teenager (*tii*-nei-dʒö) *n* adolescente *m/f*

teetotaller (tii-*tou*-tö-lö) *n* astemio *m*

telegram (*tê*-li-ghræm) *n* telegramma *m*

telegraph (*tê*-li-ghraaf) *v* telegrafare

telephone (*tê*-li-foun) *n* telefono *m*; ~ **book** *Am* elenco telefonico; ~ **booth** cabina telefonica; ~ **call** chiamata *f*; ~ **directory** elenco telefonico; ~ **exchange** centralino *m*; ~ **operator** telefonista *m/f*

telephonist (ti-*lê*-fö-nisst) *n* telefonista *m/f*

television (*tê*-li-vi-ʒön) *n* televisione *f*; ~ **set** televisore *m*; **cable** ~ TV via cavo *f*; **satellite** ~ TV via satellite

telex (*tê*-lêkss) *n* telex *m*

*tell (têl) *v* *dire; raccontare

telly (*tê*-li) *n* tele *f*

temper (*têm*-pö) *n* temperamento *m*; **be in a** ~ essere arrabbiato

temperature (*têm*-prö-tʃö) *n* temperatura *f*

tempest (*têm*-pisst) *n* tempesta *f*

temple (*têm*-pöl) *n* tempio *m*; tempia *f*

temporary (*têm*-pö-rö-ri) *adj* provvisorio, temporaneo

tempt (têmpt) *v* tentare

temptation (têmp-*tei*-ʃön) *n* tentazione *f*

ten (tên) *num* dieci

tenant (*tê*-nönt) *n* inquilino *m,* -a *f*

tend (tênd) *v* *tendere a; badare a; ~ **to** *tendere a

tendency (*tên*-dön-ssi) *n* inclinazione *f*, tendenza *f*

tender (*tên*-dö) *adj* delicato, dolce; tenero

tendon (*tên*-dön) *n* tendine *m*

tennis (*tê*-niss) *n* tennis *m*; **~ court** campo da tennis; **~ shoes** scarpe da tennis

tense (tênss) *adj* teso

tension (*tên*-ʃön) *n* tensione *f*

tent (tênt) *n* tenda *f*

tenth (tênθ) *num* decimo

tepid (*tê*-pid) *adj* tiepido

term (tööm) *n* termine *m*; periodo *m*; condizione *f*

terminal (*töö*-mi-nöl) *n* terminal *m*; capolinea *m*

terrace (*tê*-röss) *n* terrazza *f*

terrain (tê-*rein*) *n* terreno *m*

terrible (*tê*-ri-böl) *adj* tremendo, spaventoso, terribile

terrific (tö-*ri*-fik) *adj* formidabile

terrify (*tê*-ri-fai) *v* sgomentare

terrifying spaventevole

territory (*tê*-ri-tö-ri) *n* territorio *m*

terror (*tê*-rö) *n* terrore *m*

terrorism (*tê*-rö-ri-söm) *n* terrorismo *m*

terrorist (*tê*-rö-risst) *n* terrorista *m/f*

test (têsst) *n* prova *f*, esame *m*; *v* mettere alla prova; sottoporre a un test

testify (*tê*-ssti-fai) *v* testimoniare

text (têksst) *n* testo *m*

textbook (*têkss*-buk) *n* manuale *m*; libro di testo

textile (*têk*-sstail) *n* tessuto *m*

texture (*têkss*-tʃö) *n* struttura *f*

Thai (tai) *adj* tailandese

Thailand (*tai*-lænd) Tailandia *f*

than (ðæn) *conj* che, di

thank (θængk) *v* ringraziare; **~ you** grazie

thankful (*θængk*-föl) *adj* riconoscente

that (ðæt) *adj* quello; *pron* quello; che; *conj* che

thaw (θoo) *v* disgelarsi; *n* disgelo *m*

the (öö, öi) *art* il, la, lo, i, le, gli, l'; **the ... the** più ... più

theater *Am*, **theatre** (*θiᵒ*-tö) *n* teatro *m*

theft (θêft) *n* furto *m*

their (ðêᵒ) *adj* loro

them (ðêm) *pron* li; loro

theme (θiim) *n* tema *m*, argomento *m*

themselves (ðöm-*sselvs*) *pron* si; loro stessi

then (ðên) *adv* allora; in seguito, poi; dunque

theology (θi-*o*-lö-dʒi) *n* teologia *f*

theoretical (θiᵒ-*rê*-ti-köl) *adj* teorico

theory (*θiᵒ*-ri) *n* teoria *f*

therapy (*θê*-rö-pi) *n* terapia *f*

there (ðêᵒ) *adv* là; di là

therefore (*ðêᵒ*-foo) *conj* quindi

thermometer (θö-*mo*-mi-tö) *n* termometro *m*

thermostat (*θöö*-mö-sstæt) *n* termostato *m*

these (ðiis) *adj* questi

thesis (*θii*-ssiss) *n* (pl theses) tesi *f*

they (ðei) *pron* essi, loro

thick (θik) *adj* spesso; denso

thicken (*θi*-kön) *v* ispessire

thickness (*θik*-nöss) *n* spessore *m*

thief (θiif) *n* (pl thieves) ladro *m*, -a *f*

thigh (θai) *n* coscia *f*

thimble (*θim*-böl) *n* ditale *m*

thin (θin) *adj* sottile; magro

thing (θing) *n* cosa *f*

*__thimk__ (θingk) *v* pensare; *riflettere; **~ of** pensare a; ricordare; **~ over** ripensare

thinker (*θing*-kö) *n* pensatore *m*, -trice *f*

third (θööd) *num* terzo

thirst (θöösst) *n* sete *f*

thirsty (*θöö*-ssti) *adj* assetato

thirteen (θöö-*tiin*) *num* tredici

thirteenth (θöö-*tiin*θ) *num* tredicesimo

thirtieth (*θöö*-ti-öθ) *num* trentesimo

thirty (*θöö*-ti) *num* trenta*

this (ðiss) *adj* questo; *pron* questo

thistle (θi-ssöl) *n* cardo *m*

thorn (θoon) *n* spina *f*

thorough (θʌ-rŏ) *adj* minuzioso, accurato

thoroughfare (θʌ-rŏ-fê°) *n* strada maestra, arteria *f*

those (ðous) *adj* quei; *pron* quelli

though (ðou) *conj* sebbene, quantunque, benché; *adv* però

thought[1] (θoot) *v* (p, pp think)

thought[2] (θoot) *n* pensiero *m*

thoughtful (θoot-föl) *adj* pensieroso; premuroso

thousand (θʌu-sönd) *num* mille

thread (θrêd) *n* filo *m*; refe *m*; *v* infilare

threadbare (θrêd-bê°) *adj* liso

threat (θrêt) *n* minaccia *f*

threaten (θrê-tön) *v* minacciare

threatening (θrê-tö-ning) *adj* minaccioso

three (θrii) *num* tre

three-quarter (θrii-kʷoo-tö) *adj* tre quarti

threshold (θrê-∫ould) *n* soglia *f*

threw (θruu) *v* (p throw)

thrifty (θrif-ti) *adj* parsimonioso

throat (θrout) *n* gola *f*

throne (θroun) *n* trono *m*

through (θruu) *prep* attraverso

throughout (θruu-aut) *adv* dappertutto

throw (θrou) *n* tiro *m*

*throw (θrou) *v* lanciare, gettare, buttare

thrush (θra∫) *n* tordo *m*

thumb (θʌm) *n* pollice *m*

thumbtack (θʌm-tæk) *nAm* puntina da disegno

thump (θʌmp) *v* *percuotere

thunder (θʌn-dö) *n* tuono *m*; *v* tuonare

thunderstorm (θʌn-dö-sstoom) *n*

thundery (θʌn-dö-ri) *adj* temporalesco

Thursday (θöös-di) giovedì *m*

thus (ðass) *adv* così

thyme (taim) *n* timo *m*

tick (tik) *n* spuntatura *f*; ~ **off** spuntare

ticket (ti-kit) *n* biglietto *m*; multa *f*; ~ **collector** controllore *m*; ~ **machine** biglietteria automatica

tickle (ti-köl) *v* solleticare

tide (taid) *n* marea *f*; **high** ~ alta marea; **low** ~ bassa marea

tidy (tai-di) *adj* ordinato; ~ **up** riordinare

tie (tai) *v* annodare, legare; *n* cravatta *f*

tiger (tai-ghö) *n* tigre *f*

tight (tait) *adj* stretto; attillato; *adv* strettamente

tighten (tai-tön) *v* serrare; *stringere; *restringersi

tights (taitss) *pl* calzamaglia *f*; collant *mpl*

tile (tail) *n* mattonella *f*; tegola *f*

till (til) *prep* fino a; *conj* finché non, finché

timber (tim-bö) *n* legname *m*

time (taim) *n* tempo *m*; volta *f*; **all the** ~ continuamente; **in** ~ in tempo; ~ **of arrival** ora d'arrivo; ~ **of departure** ora di partenza

time-saving (taim-ssei-ving) *adj* che fa risparmiare tempo

timetable (taim-tei-böl) *n* orario *m*

timid (ti-mid) *adj* timido

timidity (ti-mi-dö-ti) *n* timidezza *f*

tin (tin) *n* stagno *m*; barattolo *m*, latta *f*; ~ **opener** apriscatole *m*

tinned (tind) *adj* in scatola; ~ **food** conserve *fpl*

tinfoil (tin-foil) *n* stagnola *f*

tiny (tai-ni) *adj* minuscolo

tip (tip) *n* punta *f*; mancia *f*

tire[1] (tai°) *n* pneumatico *m*

tire² (tai⁰) *v* stancare

tired (tai⁰d) *adj* affaticato, stanco; **~ of** stufo di

tiring (*tai⁰*-ring) *adj* faticoso

tissue (*ti*-ʃuu) *n* tessuto *m*; fazzoletto di carta

title (*tai*-töl) *n* titolo *m*

to (tuu) *prep* fino a; a, per, da, verso, in; allo scopo di

toad (toud) *n* rospo *m*

toadstool (*toud*-sstuul) *n* fungo velenoso

toast (tousst) *n* crostino *m*; brindisi *m*

tobacco (tö-*bæ*-kou) *n* (pl ~s) tabacco *m*; **~ pouch** astuccio per tabacco

tobacconist (tö-*bæ*-kö-nisst) *n* tabaccaio *m*; **tobacconist's** tabaccheria *f*

today (tö-*dei*) *adv* oggi

toddler (*tod*-lö) *n* bimbo *m*

toe (tou) *n* dito del piede

toffee (*to*-fi) *n* caramella mou

together (tö-*ghê*-ðö) *adv* insieme

toilet (*toi*-löt) *n* gabinetto *m*; **~ paper** carta igienica

toiletry (*toi*-lö-tri) *n* articoli da toeletta

token (*tou*-kön) *n* segno *m*; prova *f*; gettone *m*

told (tould) *v* (p, pp tell)

tolerable (*to*-lö-rö-böl) *adj* tollerabile

toll (toul) *n* pedaggio *m*

tomato (tö-*maa*-tou) *n* (pl ~es) pomodoro *m*

tomb (tuum) *n* tomba *f*

tombstone (*tuum*-sstoun) *n* lapide *f*

tomorrow (tö-*mo*-rou) *adv* domani

ton (tan) *n* tonnellata *f*

tone (toun) *n* tono *m*; nota *f*; timbro *m*

tongs (tongs) *pl* pinze *fpl*

tongue (tang) *n* lingua *f*

tonic (*to*-nik) *n* tonico *m*

tonight (tö-*nait*) *adv* stanotte, stasera

tonsilitis (ton-ssö-*lai*-tiss) *n* tonsillite *f*

tonsils (*ton*-ssöls) *pl* tonsille *fpl*

too (tuu) *adv* troppo; anche

took (tuk) *v* (p take)

tool (tuul) *n* attrezzo *m*, arnese *m*; **~ kit** cassetta degli attrezzi

toot (tuut) *vAm* suonare il clacson

tooth (tuuθ) *n* (pl teeth) dente *m*

toothache (*tuu*-θeik) *n* mal di denti

toothbrush (*tuu*θ-braʃ) *n* spazzolino da denti

toothpaste (*tuu*θ-peisst) *n* dentifricio *m*

toothpick (*tuu*θ-pik) *n* stuzzicadenti *m*

top (top) *n* cima *f*; parte superiore; coperchio *m*; *adj* sommo; **on ~ of** in cima a; **~ side** lato superiore

topic (*to*-pik) *n* soggetto *m*

topical (*to*-pi-köl) *adj* attuale

torch (tootʃ) *n* torcia *f*; lampadina tascabile, pila *f*

torment¹ (too-*mênt*) *v* tormentare

torment² (*too*-mênt) *n* tormento *m*

torture (*too*-tʃö) *n* tortura *f*; *v* torturare

toss (toss) *v* gettare

tot (tot) *n* bimbetto *m*

total (*tou*-töl) *adj* totale; completo, assoluto; *n* totale *m*

totalitarian (tou-tæ-li-*tê*⁰-ri-ön) *adj* totalitario

touch (tatʃ) *v* toccare; colpire; *n* contatto *m*, tocco *m*; tatto *m*

touching (*ta*-tʃing) *adj* commovente

tough (taf) *adj* duro

tour (tu⁰) *n* gita turistica

tourism (*tu*⁰-ri-söm) *n* turismo *m*

tourist (*tu*⁰-risst) *n* turista *m/f*; **~ class** classe turistica; **~ office** agenzia viaggi

tournament (*tu*⁰-nö-mönt) *n* torneo *m*

tow (tou) *v* trainare

towards (tö-*ᵘoods*) *prep* verso

towel (tau⁰l) *n* asciugamano *m*

towel(l)ing (*tau^ö*-ling) *n* spugna *f*
tower (tau^ö) *n* torre *f*
town (taun) *n* città *f*; **~ centre** centro della città; **~ hall** municipio *m*
townspeople (*tauns*-pii-pöl) *pl* cittadinanza *f*
toxic (*tok*-ssik) *adj* tossico
toy (toi) *n* giocattolo *m*
toyshop (*toi*-ſop) *n* negozio di giocattoli
trace (treiss) *n* traccia *f*; *v* rintracciare
track (træk) *n* binario *m*; pista *f*
tractor (*træk*-tö) *n* trattore *m*
trade (treid) *n* commercio *m*; mestiere *m*; *v* commerciare; **~ union** sindacato *m*
trademark (*treid*-maak) *n* marchio di fabbrica
trader (*trei*-dö) *n* commerciante *m/f*
tradesman (*treids*-mön) *n* (pl -men) commerciante *m*
tradition (trö-*di*-ſön) *n* tradizione *f*
traditional (trö-*di*-ſö-nöl) *adj* tradizionale
traffic (*træ*-fik) *n* traffico *m*; **~ jam** ingorgo *m*; **~ light** semaforo *m*
trafficator (*træ*-fi-kei-tö) *n* indicatore di direzione
tragedy (*træ*-dʒö-di) *n* tragedia *f*
tragic (*træ*-dʒik) *adj* tragico
trail (treil) *n* traccia *f*, sentiero *m*
trailer (*trei*-lö) *n* rimorchio *m*; *Am* roulotte *f*
train (trein) *n* treno *m*; *v* ammaestrare, addestrare; **stopping ~** accelerato *m*; **through ~** treno diretto
trainee (*trei*-nii) *n* apprendista *m/f*
trainer (*trei*-nö) *n* allenatore *m*, -trice *f*; addestratore *m*, -trice *f*
training (*trei*-ning) *n* addestramento *m*
trait (treit) *n* tratto *m*
traitor (*trei*-tö) *n* traditore *m*
tram (træm) *n* tram *m*

tramp (træmp) *n* vagabondo *m*, barbone *m*; *v* vagabondare
tranquil (*træng*-kʰil) *adj* tranquillo
tranquillizer (*træng*-kʰi-lai-sö) *n* tranquillante *m*
transaction (træn-*sæk*-ſön) *n* transazione *f*
transatlantic (træn-söt-*læn*-tik) *adj* transatlantico
transfer (trænss-*föö*) *v* trasferire
transform (trænss-*foom*) *v* trasformare
transformer (trænss-*foo*-mö) *n* trasformatore *m*
transition (træn-*ssi*-ſön) *n* transizione *f*
translate (trænss-*leit*) *v* *tradurre
translation (trænss-*lei*-ſön) *n* traduzione *f*
translator (trænss-*lei*-tö) *n* traduttore *m*, -trice *f*
transmission (træns-*mi*-ſön) *n* trasmissione *f*
transmit (træns-*mit*) *v* *trasmettere
transmitter (træns-*mi*-tö) *n* trasmettitore *m*
transparent (træn-*sspɛ^ö*-rönt) *adj* trasparente
transport¹ (*træn*-sspoot) *n* trasporto *m*
transport² (træn-*sspoot*) *v* trasportare
transportation (træn-sspoo-*tei*-ſön) *n* trasporto *m*
trap (træp) *n* trappola *f*
trash (træſ) *n* robaccia *f*; **~ can** *Am* pattumiera *f*
travel (*træ*-völ) *v* viaggiare; **~ agency** agenzia viaggi; **~ agent** agente di viaggio; **~ bag** borsa da viaggio; **~ expenses** *npl* spese di viaggio; **~ insurance** assicurazione viaggi
travel(l)er (*træ*-vö-lö) *n* viaggiatore *m*, -trice *f*; **travel(l)er's cheque** assegno turistico
travel(l)ing (*træ*-vö-ling) *adj* da

viaggio; **~ expenses** spese di viaggio

tray (trei) *n* vassoio *m*

treason (*trii*-sön) *n* tradimento *m*

treasure (*trê*-ʒö) *n* tesoro *m*

treasurer (*trê*-ʒö-rö) *n* tesoriere *m*

treasury (*trê*-ʒö-ri) *n* Ministero del Tesoro *m*

treat (triit) *v* trattare

treatment (*triit*-mönt) *n* trattamento *m*

treaty (*trii*-ti) *n* trattato *m*

tree (trii) *n* albero *m*

tremble (*trêm*-böl) *v* tremare; vibrare

tremendous (tri-*mên*-döss) *adj* enorme

trendy (*træn*-di) *adj* alla moda

trespass (*trêss*-pöss) *v* trasgredire

trespasser (*trêss*-pö-ssö) *n* trasgressore *m*

trial (traiᵒl) *n* processo *m*; prova *f*

triangle (*trai*-æng-ghöl) *n* triangolo *m*

triangular (trai-*æng*-ghⁱu-lö) *adj* triangolare

tribe (traib) *n* tribù *f*

tributary (*tri*-bⁱu-tö-ri) *n* braccio *m*

tribute (*tri*-bⁱuut) *n* omaggio *m*

trick (trik) *n* tiro *m*; trucco *m*

trigger (*tri*-ghö) *n* grilletto *m*

trim (trim) *v* accorciare

trip (trip) *n* gita *f*, viaggio *m*

triumph (*trai*-ömf) *n* trionfo *m*; *v* trionfare

triumphant (trai-*am*-fönt) *adj* trionfante

troops (truupss) *pl* truppe *fpl*

tropical (*tro*-pi-köl) *adj* tropicale

tropics (*tro*-pikss) *pl* tropici *mpl*

trouble (*tra*-böl) *n* preoccupazione *f*, pena *f*; guaio *m*; *v* disturbare

troublesome (*tra*-böl-ssöm) *adj* molesto

trousers (*trau*-sös) *pl* pantaloni *mpl*

trout (traut) *n* (pl ~) trota *f*

truck (trak) *nAm* autocarro *m*,

camion *m*

true (truu) *adj* vero; reale, autentico; leale, fedele

trumpet (*tram*-pit) *n* tromba *f*

trunk (trangk) *n* baule *m*; tronco *m*; *Am* bagagliaio *m*; **trunks** *pl* calzoncini *mpl*

trunk-call (*trangk*-kool) *n* interurbana *f*

trust (trasst) *v* fidarsi di; *n* fiducia *f*

trustworthy (*trasst*-ᵘöö-ði) *adj* fidato

truth (truuθ) *n* verità *f*

truthful (*truuθ*-föl) *adj* veritiero

try (trai) *v* tentare; sforzarsi; *n* tentativo *m*; **~ on** provare

tube (tⁱuub) *n* tubo *m*; tubetto *m*

tuberculosis (tⁱuu-böö-kⁱu-*lou*-ssiss) *n* tubercolosi *f*

Tuesday (*tⁱuus*-di) martedì *m*

tug (tagh) *v* rimorchiare; *n* rimorchiatore *m*; strattone *m*

tuition (tⁱuu-*i*-ʃön) *n* insegnamento *m*

tulip (*tⁱuu*-lip) *n* tulipano *m*

tumbler (*tam*-blö) *n* bicchiere *m*

tumo(u)r (*tⁱuu*-mö) *n* tumore *m*

tuna (*tⁱuu*-nö) *n* (pl ~, ~s) tonno *m*

tune (tⁱuun) *n* aria *f*, melodia *f*; **~ in** sintonizzare

tuneful (*tⁱuun*-föl) *adj* melodioso

tunic (*tⁱuu*-nik) *n* tunica *f*

Tunisia (tⁱuu-*ni*-si-ö) Tunisia *f*

Tunisian (tⁱuu-*ni*-si-ön) *adj* tunisino

tunnel (*ta*-nöl) *n* galleria *f*

turbine (*töö*-bain) *n* turbina *f*

turbojet (töö-bou-*dʒêt*) *n* aereo a reazione

Turin (tⁱu-*rin*) Torino *f*

Turkey (*töö*-ki) Turchia *f*

turkey (*töö*-ki) *n* tacchino *m*

Turkish (*töö*-kiʃ) *adj* turco; **~ bath** bagno turco

turn (töön) *v* voltare; *volgere, girare; *n* cambiamento *m*, giro *m*; curva *f*; turno *m*; **~ back** ritornare; **~ down**

*respingere; ~ **into** trasformarsi in; ~
off *chiudere; *spegnere; ~ **on**
*aprire; *accendere; ~ **over**
*capovolgere; ~ **round** voltare;
rigirarsi

turning (*töö*-ning) *n* svolta *f*; ~ **point**
punto decisivo

turnover (*töö*-nou-vö) *n* giro d'affari;
~ **tax** tassa sugli affari

turnpike (*töön*-paik) *nAm* strada a
pedaggio

turpentine (*töö*-pön-tain) *n*
trementina *f*

turtle (*töö*-töl) *n* tartaruga *f*

tutor (*tʲuu*-tö) *n* precettore *m*; tutore
m, -trice *f*

tuxedo (tak-*ssii*-dou) *nAm* (pl ~s, ~es)
smoking *m*

TV (*tee vee*) *n* tv *f*; **on ~** alla tv

tweed (tʷiid) *n* tweed *m*

tweezers (*tʷii*-sös) *pl* pinzette *fpl*

twelfth (tʷêlfθ) *num* dodicesimo

twelve (tʷêlv) *num* dodici

twentieth (*tʷên*-ti-öθ) *num* ventesimo

twenty (*tʷên*-ti) *num* venti

twice (tʷaiss) *adv* due volte

twig (tʷigh) *n* ramoscello *m*

twilight (*tʷai*-lait) *n* crepuscolo *m*

twine (tʷain) *n* spago *m*

twins (tʷins) *pl* gemelli *mpl*

twist (tʷisst) *v* *torcere; *n* torsione *f*

two (tuu) *num* due

two-piece (tuu-*piiss*) *adj* in due pezzi

type (taip) *v* dattilografare; *n* tipo *m*

typewriter (*taip*-rai-tö) *n* macchina da
scrivere

typhus (*tai*-fös) *n* tifo *m*

typical (*ti*-pi-köl) *adj* caratteristico,
tipico

tyrant (*tai*ʳ-rönt) *n* tiranno *m*, -a *f*

tyre (taiʳ) *n* copertone *m*; ~ **pressure**
pressione gomme

U

ugly (*a*-ghli) *adj* brutto

ulcer (*al*-ssö) *n* ulcera *f*

ultimate (*al*-ti-möt) *adj* ultimo

ultraviolet (al-trö-*vai*ʳ-löt) *adj*
ultravioletto

umbrella (am-*brê*-lö) *n* ombrello *m*

umpire (*am*-paiʳ) *n* arbitro *m*

unable (a-*nei*-böl) *adj* incapace

unacceptable (a-nök-*ssêp*-tö-böl) *adj*
inaccettabile

unaccountable (a-nö-*kaun*-tö-böl)
adj inesplicabile

unaccustomed (a-nö-*ka*-sstömd) *adj*
non abituato

unanimous (ʲuu-*næ*-ni-möss) *adj*
unanime

unanswered (a-*naan*-ssöd) *adj* senza

riposta

unauthorized (a-*noo*-θö-raisd) *adj*
illecito

unavoidable (a-nö-*voi*-dö-böl) *adj*
inevitabile

unaware (a-nö-ʷêʳ) *adj* inconsapevole

unbearable (an-*bê*ʳ-rö-böl) *adj*
insopportabile

unbreakable (an-*brei*-kö-böl) *adj*
infrangibile

unbroken (an-*brou*-kön) *adj* intatto

unbutton (an-*ba*-tön) *v* sbottonare

uncertain (an-*ssöö*-tön) *adj* incerto

uncle (*ang*-köl) *n* zio *m*

unclean (an-*kliin*) *adj* sudicio

uncomfortable (an-*kam*-fö-tö-böl)
adj scomodo

uncommon (an-*ko*-mön) *adj* insolito, raro

unconditional (an-kön-*di*-ʃö-nöl) *adj* incondizionato

unconscious (an-*kon*-ʃöss) *adj* inconscio

uncork (an-*kook*) *v* stappare

uncover (an-*ka*-vö) *v* *scoprire

uncultivated (an-*kal*-ti-vei-tid) *adj* incolto

under (an-dö) *prep* sotto

underestimate (an-dö-*rê*-ssti-meit) *v* sottovalutare

underground (*an*-dö-ghraund) *adj* sotterraneo; *n* metropolitana *f*

underline (an-dö-*lain*) *v* sottolineare

underneath (an-dö-*niiθ*) *adv* sotto

underpants (*an*-dö-pæntss) *plAm* mutandine *fpl*

undershirt (*an*-dö-ʃööt) *n* maglietta *f*

*understand (an-dö-*sstænd*) *v* *comprendere, capire

understanding (an-dö-*sstæn*-ding) *n* comprensione *f*

understatement (an-dö-*steit*-ment) *n* understatement *m*

*undertake (an-dö-*teik*) *v* *intraprendere

undertaking (an-dö-*tei*-king) *n* impresa *f*

underwater (an-dö-*uoo*-tö) *adj* subacqueo

underwear (*an*-dö-ᵘê°) *n* biancheria intima

undesirable (an-di-*sai°*-rö-böl) *adj* indesiderabile

*undo (an-*duu*) *v* *disfare

undoubtedly (an-*dau*-tid-li) *adv* indubbiamente

undress (an-*drêss*) *v* spogliarsi

unearned (a-*nöönd*) *adj* non meritato

uneasy (a-*nii*-si) *adj* inquieto

uneducated (a-*nê*-dᶦu-kei-tid) *adj* ignorante

unemployed (a-nim-*ploid*) *adj* disoccupato

unemployment (a-nim-*ploi*-mönt) *n* disoccupazione *f*

unequal (a-*nii*-kᵘöl) *adj* ineguale

uneven (a-*nii*-vön) *adj* ineguale, ruvido; irregolare

unexpected (a-nik-*sspêk*-tid) *adj* inatteso, inaspettato

unfair (an-*fê°*) *adj* disonesto; ingiusto

unfaithful (an-*feiθ*-föl) *adj* infedele

unfamiliar (an-fö-*mil*-ᶦö) *adj* sconosciuto

unfasten (an-*faa*-ssön) *v* slacciare

unfavo(u)rable (an-*fei*-vö-rö-böl) *adj* sfavorevole

unfit (an-*fit*) *adj* inadatto

unfold (an-*fould*) *v* spiegare

unfortunate (an-*foo*-tʃö-nöt) *adj* sfortunato

unfortunately (an-*foo*-tʃö-nöt-li) *adv* disgraziatamente, sfortunatamente

unfriendly (an-*frênd*-li) *adj* poco gentile

ungrateful (an-*ghreit*-föl) *adj* ingrato

unhappy (an-*hæ*-pi) *adj* infelice

unhealthy (an-*hêl*-θi) *adj* malsano

unhurt (an-*hööt*) *adj* incolume

uniform (*uu*-ni-foom) *n* uniforme *f*; *adj* uniforme

unimportant (a-nim-*poo*-tönt) *adj* insignificante

uninhabitable (a-nin-*hæ*-bi-tö-böl) *adj* inabitabile

uninhabited (a-nin-*hæ*-bi-tid) *adj* disabitato

unintentional (a-nin-*tên*-ʃö-nöl) *adj* involontario

union (*uu*-nᶦön) *n* unione *f*; lega *f*, confederazione *f*

unique (*uu*-*niik*) *adj* unico

unit (*uu*-nit) *n* unità *f*

unite (*uu*-*nait*) *v* unire

united (uu-*nai*-tid) *adj* unito

United States (ˈuu-*nai*-tid ssteitss)
Stati Uniti

unity (ˈ*uu*-nö-ti) *n* unità *f*

universal (ˈuu-ni-*vöö*-ssöl) *adj*
generale, universale

universe (ˈ*uu*-ni-vööss) *n* universo *m*

university (ˈuu-ni-*vöö*-ssö-ti) *n*
università *f*

unjust (an-*dʒasst*) *adj* ingiusto

unkind (an-*kaind*) *adj* sgarbato,
scortese

unknown (an-*noun*) *adj* ignoto

unlawful (an-*loo*-föl) *adj* illegale

unleaded (an-*lê*-did) *adj* senza
piombo

unlearn (an-*löön*) *v* disimparare

unless (ön-*lêss*) *conj* a meno che

unlike (an-*laik*) *adj* diverso

unlikely (an-*lai*-kli) *adj* improbabile

unlimited (an-*li*-mi-tid) *adj*
sconfinato, illimitato

unload (an-*loud*) *v* scaricare

unlock (an-*lok*) *v* *aprire

unlucky (an-*la*-ki) *adj* sfortunato

unnecessary (an-*nê*-ssö-ssö-ri) *adj*
superfluo

unoccupied (a-*no*-kⁱu-paid) *adj*
vacante; vuoto

unofficial (a-nö-*fi*-ʃöl) *adj* ufficioso

unpack (an-*pæk*) *v* *disfare le valigie

unpleasant (an-*plê*-sönt) *adj*
increscioso, spiacevole; sgradevole

unpopular (an-*po*-pⁱu-lö) *adj*
impopolare

unprotected (an-prö-*têk*-tid) *adj*
indifeso

unqualified (an-*kᵘo*-li-faid) *adj*
incompetente; non qualificato

unreal (an-*rⁱöl*) *adj* irreale

unreasonable (an-*rii*-sö-nö-böl) *adj*
irragionevole

unreliable (an-ri-*lai*-ö-böl) *adj*
inaffidabile

unrest (an-*rêsst*) *n* agitazione *f*;

inquietudine *f*

unsafe (an-*sseif*) *adj* malsicuro;
pericoloso

unsatisfactory (an-ssæ-tiss-*fæk*-tö-ri)
adj insoddisfacente

unscrew (an-*sskruu*) *v* svitare

unselfish (an-*ssêl*-fiʃ) *adj*
disinteressato

unskilled (an-*sskild*) *adj* non
qualificato

unstable (an-*sstei*-böl) *adj* instabile

unsteady (an-*sstê*-di) *adj* barcollante,
malfermo; vacillante

unsuccessful (an-ssök-*ssêss*-föl) *adj*
infruttuoso

unsuitable (an-*ssuu*-tö-böl) *adj*
inadatto

unsurpassed (an-ssö-*paasst*) *adj*
insuperato

untidy (an-*tai*-di) *adj* disordinato

untie (an-*tai*) *v* slacciare

until (ön-*til*) *prep* fino a, finché

untrue (an-*truu*) *adj* falso

untrustworthy (an-*trasst*-ᵘöö-ði) *adj*
sleale

unusual (an-ˈ*uu*-ʒu-öl) *adj*
inconsueto, insolito

unwell (an-ᵘ*êl*) *adj* indisposto

unwilling (an-ᵘ*i*-ling) *adj* restio

unwise (an-ᵘ*ais*) *adj* incauto

unwrap (an-*ræp*) *v* *disfare

up (ap) *adv* verso l'alto, in su, su

upholster (ap-*houl*-sstö) *v* tappezzare

upkeep (*ap*-kiip) *n* mantenimento *m*

uplands (*ap*-lönds) *pl* altopiano *m*

upon (ö-*pon*) *prep* su

upper (*a*-pö) *adj* superiore

upright (*ap*-rait) *adj* diritto; *adv* in
piedi

upset (ap-*ssêt*) *v* turbare; *adj*
costernato

upside down (ap-ssaid-*daun*) *adv*
sottosopra

upstairs (ap-*sstê*ᵒs) *adv* di sopra; su

upstream (ap-*sstriim*) *adv* contro corrente

upwards (*ap-*ᵘöds) *adv* in su

urban (*öö*-bön) *adj* urbano

urge (ööd3) *v* stimolare; *n* impulso *m*

urgency (*öö*-d3ön-ssi) *n* urgenza *f*

urgent (*öö*-d3önt) *adj* urgente

urine (ᵗuᵒ-rin) *n* urina *f*

Uruguay (ᵗuᵒ-rö-ghᵘai) Uruguay *m*

Uruguayan (ᵗuᵒ-rö-*gh*ᵘai-ön) *adj* uruguaiano

us (ass) *pron* ci

usable (ᵗuu-sö-böl) *adj* usabile

usage (ᵗuu-sid3) *n* usanza *f*

use¹ (ᵗuus) *v* usare; ***be used to** *essere abituato a; ~ **up** consumare

use² (ᵗuuss) *n* uso *m*; utilità *f*; ***be of ~** giovare

useful (ᵗuuss-föl) *adj* utile

useless (ᵗuuss-löss) *adj* inutile

user (ᵗuu-sö) *n* utente *m/f*

usher (a-ʃö) *n* usciere *m*; maschera *f*

usherette (a-ʃö-*rêt*) *n* maschera *f*

usual (ᵗuu-3u-öl) *adj* solito

usually (ᵗuu-3u-ö-li) *adv* abitualmente

utensil (ᵗuu-*tên*-ssöl) *n* arnese *m*, utensile *m*

utility (ᵗuu-*ti*-lö-ti) *n* utilità *f*

utilize (ᵗuu-ti-lais) *v* utilizzare

utmost (*at*-mousst) *adj* estremo

utter (a-tö) *adj* completo, totale; *v* *emettere

V

vacancy (*vei*-kön-ssi) *n* posto libero

vacant (*vei*-könt) *adj* vacante

vacate (vö-*keit*) *v* sgombrare

vacation (vö-*kei*-ʃön) *n* vacanza *f*

vaccinate (*væk*-ssi-neit) *v* vaccinare

vaccination (væk-ssi-*nei*-ʃön) *n* vaccinazione *f*

vacuum (*væ*-kᵗu-öm) *n* vuoto *m*; *vAm* passare l'aspirapolvere su; ~ **cleaner** aspirapolvere *m*; ~ **flask** termos *m*

vague (veigh) *adj* vago

vain (vein) *adj* vano; inutile; **in ~** inutilmente, invano

valet (*væ*-lit) *n* cameriere *m*, -a *f*

valid (*væ*-lid) *adj* valido

valley (*væ*-li) *n* valle *f*

valuable (*væ*-lᵗu-böl) *adj* prezioso; **valuables** *pl* valori

value (*væ*-lᵗuu) *n* valore *m*; *v* valutare

valve (vælv) *n* valvola *f*

van (væn) *n* furgone *m*

vanilla (vö-*ni*-lö) *n* vaniglia *f*

vanish (*væ*-niʃ) *v* sparire

vapo(u)r (*vei*-pö) *n* vapore *m*

variable (*vê*ᵒ-ri-ö-böl) *adj* variabile

variation (vê*ᵒ*-ri-*ei*-ʃön) *n* variazione *f*; mutamento *m*

varied (*vê*ᵒ-rid) *adj* assortito

variety (vö-*rai*-ö-ti) *n* varietà *f*; ~ **show** spettacolo di varietà; ~ **theatre** teatro di varietà

various (*vê*ᵒ-ri-öss) *adj* vari, parecchi

varnish (*vaa*-niʃ) *n* lacca *f*, vernice *f*; *v* verniciare

vary (*vê*ᵒ-ri) *v* differire, variare; cambiare

vase (vaas) *n* vaso *m*

vaseline (*væ*-ssö-liin) *n* vaselina *f*

vast (vaasst) *adj* immenso, vasto

Vatican (*væ*-ti-kön): **the ~ n** Vaticano *m*

vault (voolt) *n* volta *f*; camera blindata

veal (viil) *n* vitello *m*

vegetable (*vê*-d3ö-tö-böl) *n* verdura *f*;

~ merchant fruttivendolo *m*, -a *f*

vegetarian (vê-dʒi-*te*ᵒ-ri-ön) *n* vegetariano *m*, -a *f*

vegetation (vê-dʒi-*tei*-ʃön) *n* vegetazione *f*

vehicle (*vii*-ö-köl) *n* veicolo *m*

veil (veil) *n* velo *m*

vein (vein) *n* vena *f*; **varicose ~** vena varicosa

velvet (*vêl*-vit) *n* velluto *m*

venerable (*vê*-nö-rö-böl) *adj* venerabile

venereal disease (vi-*ni*ᵒ-ri-öl di-*siis*) malattia venerea

Venezuela (vê-ni-sᵘ*ei*-lö) Venezuela *m*

Venezuelan (vê-ni-sᵘ*ei*-lön) *adj* venezuelano

Venice (*vê*-nis) Venezia *f*

ventilate (*vên*-ti-leit) *v* ventilare; aerare

ventilation (vên-ti-*lei*-ʃön) *n* ventilazione *f*; aerazione *f*

ventilator (*vên*-ti-lei-tö) *n* ventilatore *m*

venture (*vên*-tʃö) *v* arrischiare

veranda (vö-*ræn*-dö) *n* veranda *f*

verb (vööb) *n* verbo *m*

verbal (*vöö*-böl) *adj* verbale

verdict (*vöö*-dikt) *n* sentenza *f*, verdetto *m*

verge (vöödʒ) *n* bordo *m*

verify (*vê*-ri-fai) *v* verificare

verse (vööss) *n* verso *m*

version (*vöö*-ʃön) *n* versione *f*; traduzione *f*

versus (*vöö*-ssöss) *prep* contro

vertical (*vöö*-ti-köl) *adj* verticale

very (*vê*-ri) *adv* assai, molto; *adj* vero, preciso; estremo

vessel (*vê*-ssöl) *n* nave *f*, vascello *m*; recipiente *m*

vest (vêsst) *n* maglia *f*; *Am* panciotto *m*

veterinary surgeon (*vê*-tri-nö-ri *ssöö*-dʒön) veterinario *m*, -a *f*

via (vaiᵒ) *prep* via

viaduct (*vai*ᵒ-dakt) *n* viadotto *m*

vibrate (vai-*breit*) *v* vibrare

vibration (vai-*brei*-ʃön) *n* vibrazione *f*

vicar (*vi*-kö) *n* vicario *m*; parroco *m*

vicarage (*vi*-kö-ridʒ) *n* vicariato *m*

vice president (vaiss-*prê*-si-dönt) *n* vicepresidente *m*

vicinity (vi-*ssi*-nö-ti) *n* prossimità *f*, vicinanza *f*

victim (*vik*-tim) *n* vittima *f*

victory (*vik*-tö-ri) *n* vittoria *f*

video (*vi*-di-ou) *n* videocassetta *f*; video *m*; videoregistratore *m*; ~ registrare; **~ camera** videocamera *f*; **~ cassette** videocassetta *f*; **~ recorder** videoregistratore *m*

view (vᵛuu) *n* vista *f*; parere *m*, opinione *f*; *v* guardare

viewfinder (*vᵛuu*-fain-dö) *n* mirino *m*

vigilant (*vi*-dʒi-lönt) *adj* vigile

villa (*vi*-lö) *n* villa *f*

village (*vi*-lidʒ) *n* villaggio *m*

villain (*vi*-lön) *n* furfante *m*

vine (vain) *n* vite *f*

vinegar (*vi*-ni-ghö) *n* aceto *m*

vineyard (*vin*-ᵗöd) *n* vigna *f*

vintage (*vin*-tidʒ) *n* vendemmia *f*

violation (vaiᵒ-*lei*-ʃön) *n* violazione *f*

violence (*vai*ᵒ-lönss) *n* violenza *f*

violent (*vai*ᵒ-lönt) *adj* violento; intenso, impetuoso

violet (*vai*ᵒ-löt) *n* violetta *f*; *adj* violetto

violin (vaiᵒ-*lin*) *n* violino *m*

VIP (vii-ai-*pii*) VIP *m/f*

virgin (*vöö*-dʒin) *n* vergine *f*

virtue (*vöö*-tʃuu) *n* virtù *f*

visa (*vii*-sö) *n* visto *m*

visibility (vi-sö-*bi*-lö-ti) *n* visibilità *f*

visible (*vi*-sö-böl) *adj* visibile

vision (*vi*-ʒön) *n* visione *f*

visit (*vi*-sit) *v* visitare; *n* visita *f*

visiting hours (vi-si-ting auᵘs) *pl* orario delle visite

visitor (*vi*-si-tö) *n* visitatore *m*, -trice *f*

vital (*vai*-töl) *adj* vitale

vitamin (*vi*-tö-min) *n* vitamina *f*

vivid (*vi*-vid) *adj* vivido

vocabulary (vö-*kæ*-bⁱu-lö-ri) *n* vocabolario *m*; glossario *m*

vocal (*vou*-köl) *adj* vocale

vocalist (*vou*-kö-lisst) *n* cantante *m/f*

voice (voiss) *n* voce *f*

void (void) *adj* nullo

volcano (vol-*kei*-nou) *n* (pl ~es, ~s) vulcano *m*

volt (voult) *n* volt *m*

voltage (*voul*-tidʒ) *n* voltaggio *m*

volume (*vo*-lⁱum) *n* volume *m*

voluntary (*vo*-lön-tö-ri) *adj* volontario

volunteer (vo-lön-*tⁱö*) *n* volontario *m*

vomit (*vo*-mit) *v* rigettare, vomitare

vote (vout) *v* votare; *n* voto *m*; votazione *f*

voter (*vou*-tö) *n* elettore *m*, -trice *f*

voucher (*vau*-tʃö) *n* buono *m*, ricevuta *f*

vow (vau) *n* promessa *f*, giuramento *m*; *v* giurare

vowel (vauᵘl) *n* vocale *f*

voyage (*voi*-idʒ) *n* viaggio *m*

vulgar (*val*-ghö) *adj* volgare; triviale

vulnerable (*val*-nö-rö-böl) *adj* vulnerabile

vulture (*val*-tʃö) *n* avvoltoio *m*

W

wade (ᵘeid) *v* guadare

wafer (*ⁱei*-fö) *n* ostia *f*; cialda *f*

waffle (*ⁱo*-föl) *n* cialda *f*

wages (*ⁱei*-dʒis) *pl* stipendio *m*

wag(g)on (*ⁱæ*-ghön) *n* vagone *m*

waist (ᵘeisst) *n* vita *f*

waistcoat (*ⁱeiss*-kout) *n* panciotto *m*

wait (ᵘeit) *v* aspettare; ~ **on** servire

waiter (*ⁱei*-tö) *n* cameriere *m*

waiting (*ⁱei*-ting) *n* attesa *f*; ~ **list** lista di attesa; ~ **room** sala d'aspetto

waitress (*ⁱei*-triss) *n* cameriera *f*

wake (ᵘeik) *v* svegliare; ~ **up** svegliarsi

walk (ᵘook) *v* camminare; passeggiare; *n* passeggiata *f*; andatura *f*

walker (*ⁱoo*-kö) *n* camminatore *m*, -trice *f*

walking (*ⁱoo*-king) *adv* a piedi; ~ **stick** bastone da passeggio

wall (ᵘool) *n* muro *m*; parete *f*

wallet (*ⁱo*-lit) *n* portafoglio *m*

wallpaper (*ⁱool*-pei-pö) *n* carta da parati

walnut (*ⁱool*-nat) *n* noce *f*

waltz (ᵘoolss) *n* valzer *m*

wander (*ⁱon*-dö) *v* errare, vagare

want (ᵘont) *v* *volere; desiderare; *n* bisogno *m*; scarsezza *f*, mancanza *f*

war (ᵘoo) *n* guerra *f*

warden (*ⁱoo*-dön) *n* custode *m*, guardiano *m*

wardrobe (*ⁱoo*-droub) *n* guardaroba *m*

warehouse (*ⁱêᵒ*-hauss) *n* magazzino *m*, deposito *m*

wares (ᵘêᵒs) *pl* merci *f*

warm (ᵘoom) *adj* caldo; *v* scaldare

warmth (ᵘoomθ) *n* calore *m*

warn (ᵘoon) *v* avvisare

warning (*ⁱoo*-ning) *n* avvertimento *m*

wary ("ê⁰-ri) *adj* prudente
was ("os) *v* (p be)
wash ("oʃ) *v* lavare; **~ and wear** non si stira; **~ up** lavare i piatti
washable ("o-ʃö-böl) *adj* lavabile
washbasin ("oʃ-bei-ssön) *n* lavandino *m*
washing ("o-ʃing) *n* lavaggio *m*; bucato *m*; **~ machine** lavatrice *f*; **~ powder** detersivo *m*
washroom ("oʃ-ruum) *nAm* toilette *f*
wasp ("ossp) *n* vespa *f*
waste ("eisst) *v* sprecare; *n* spreco *m*; *adj* incolto
wasteful ("eisst-föl) *adj* spendereccio
wastepaper basket ("eisst-*pei*-pö-baa-sskit) *n* cestino *m*
watch ("otʃ) *v* guardare, osservare; *tenere d'occhio; *n* orologio *m*; **~ out** *stare in guardia
watchmaker ("otʃ-mei-kö) *n* orologiaio *m*, -a *f*
watchstrap ("otʃ-sstræp) *n* cinturino da orologio
water ("oo-tö) *n* acqua *f*; **iced ~** acqua ghiacciata; **running ~** acqua corrente; **~ pump** pompa dell'acqua; **~ ski** sci d'acqua
watercolo(u)r ("oo-tö-ka-lö) *n* acquerello *m*
watercress ("oo-tö-krêss) *n* crescione *m*
waterfall ("oo-tö-fool) *n* cascata *f*
watermelon ("oo-tö-mê-lön) *n* anguria *f*
waterproof ("oo-tö-pruuf) *adj* impermeabile
watt ("ot) *n* watt *m*
wave ("eiv) *n* ricciolo *m*; onda *f*; *v* sventolare
wavelength ("eiv-lêngθ) *n* lunghezza d'onda
wavy ("ei-vi) *adj* ondulato
wax ("ækss) *n* cera *f*

waxworks ("ækss-⁰öökss) *pl* museo delle cere
way ("ei) *n* maniera *f*, modo *m*; via *f*; lato *m*, direzione *f*; distanza *f*; **any ~** comunque; **by the ~** a proposito; **out of the ~** remoto; **the other ~ round** alla rovescia; **~ back** ritorno *m*; **~ in** entrata *f*; **~ out** uscita *f*
wayside ("ei-ssaid) *n* margine della strada
we ("ii) *pron* noi
weak ("iik) *adj* debole; diluito
weakness ("iik-nöss) *n* debolezza *f*
wealth ("êlθ) *n* ricchezza *f*
wealthy ("êl-θi) *adj* ricco
weapon ("ê-pön) *n* arma *f*
***wear** ("ê⁰) *v* indossare, vestire; **~ out** logorare
weary ("i⁰-ri) *adj* affaticato, stanco
weather ("ê-ðö) *n* tempo *m*; **~ forecast** previsioni del tempo
***weave** ("iiv) *v* tessere
weaver ("ii-vö) *n* tessitore *m*, -trice *f*
wedding ("ê-ding) *n* sposalizio *m*, matrimonio *m*; **~ ring** fede *f*
wedge ("êdʒ) *n* cuneo *m*
Wednesday ("êns-di) mercoledì *m*
weed ("iid) *n* erbaccia *f*
week ("iik) *n* settimana *f*
weekday ("iik-dei) *n* giorno feriale
weekend ("ii-kênd) *n* fine settimana
weekly ("ii-kli) *adj* settimanale
***weep** ("iip) *v* *piangere
weigh ("ei) *v* pesare
weighing machine ("ei-ing-mö-ʃiin) *n* bilancia *f*
weight ("eit) *n* peso *m*
welcome ("êl-köm) *adj* benvenuto; *n* accoglienza *f*; *v* *accogliere
weld ("êld) *v* saldare
welfare ("êl-fê⁰) *n* benessere *m*
well¹ ("êl) *adv* bene; *adj* sano; **as ~** pure, come pure; **as ~ as** come pure; **well!** allora!

well² (ᵘêl) *n* pozzo *m*
well-founded (ᵘêl-*faun*-did) *adj* fondato
well-known (ᵘêl-noun) *adj* noto
well-to-do (ᵘêl-tö-*duu*) *adj* agiato
went (ᵘênt) *v* (p go)
were (ᵘööö) *v* (p be)
west (ᵘêsst) *n* occidente *m*; ovest *m*
westerly (ᵘê-sstö-li) *adj* occidentale
western (ᵘê-sstön) *adj* occidentale
wet (ᵘêt) *adj* bagnato; umido
whale (ᵘeil) *n* balena *f*
wharf (ᵘoof) *n* (pl ~s, wharves) molo *m*
what (ᵘot) *pron* che cosa; quello che; ~ **for** perché
whatever (ᵘo-*tê*-vö) *pron* qualsiasi
wheat (ᵘiit) *n* frumento *m*
wheel (ᵘiil) *n* ruota *f*
wheelbarrow (ᵘiil-bæ-rou) *n* carriola *f*
wheelchair (ᵘiil-tʃêᵒ) *n* sedia a rotelle
when (ᵘên) *adv* quando; *conj* qualora, quando
whenever (ᵘê-*nê*-vö) *conj* ogni volta che
where (ᵘêᵒ) *adv* dove; *conj* dove
wherever (ᵘêᵒ-*rê*-vö) *conj* dovunque
whether (ᵘê-ðö) *conj* se; **whether ... or** se ... o
which (ᵘitʃ) *pron* quale; che
whichever (ᵘi-*tʃê*-vö) *adj* qualsiasi
while (ᵘail) *conj* mentre; *n* istante *m*
whilst (ᵘailsst) *conj* mentre
whim (ᵘim) *n* ghiribizzo *m*, capriccio *m*
whip (ᵘip) *n* frusta *f*; *v* sbattere
whiskers (ᵘi-sskös) *pl* basette *fpl*
whisper (ᵘi-sspö) *v* mormorare; *n* sussurro *m*
whistle (ᵘi-ssöl) *v* fischiare; *n* fischio *m*
white (ᵘait) *adj* bianco
whiting (ᵘai-ting) *n* (pl ~) merlano *m*
Whitsun (ᵘit-ssön) Pentecoste *f*
who (huu) *pron* chi; che

whoever (huu-*ê*-vö) *pron* chiunque
whole (houl) *adj* completo, intero; intatto; *n* totale *m*
wholesale (houl-sseil) *n* ingrosso *m*; ~ **dealer** grossista *m/f*
wholesome (houl-ssöm) *adj* salubre
wholly (houl-li) *adv* completamente
whom (huum) *pron* a chi
whore (hoo) *n* puttana *f*
whose (huus) *pron* il cui; di chi
why (ᵘai) *adv* perché
wicked (ᵘi-kid) *adj* malvagio
wide (ᵘaid) *adj* vasto, largo
widen (ᵘai-dön) *v* allargare
widow (ᵘi-dou) *n* vedova *f*
widower (ᵘi-dou-ö) *n* vedovo *m*
width (ᵘidθ) *n* larghezza *f*
wife (ᵘaif) *n* (pl wives) consorte *f*, moglie *f*
wig (ᵘigh) *n* parrucca *f*
wild (ᵘaild) *adj* selvatico; feroce
will (ᵘil) *n* volontà *f*; testamento *m*
*will (ᵘil) *v* *volere
willing (ᵘi-ling) *adj* compiacente
willingly (ᵘi-ling-li) *adv* volentieri
willpower (ᵘil-pauᵒ) *n* forza di volontà
*win (ᵘin) *v* *vincere
wind (ᵘind) *n* vento *m*
*wind (ᵘaind) *v* zigzagare; caricare, *avvolgere
winding (ᵘain-ding) *adj* serpeggiante
windmill (ᵘind-mil) *n* mulino a vento
window (ᵘin-dou) *n* finestra *f*
windowsill (ᵘin-dou-ssil) *n* davanzale *m*
windscreen (ᵘind-sskriin) *n* parabrezza *m*; ~ **wiper** tergicristallo *m*
windshield (ᵘind-ʃiild) *nAm* parabrezza *m*; ~ **wiper** *Am* tergicristallo *m*
windy (ᵘin-di) *adj* ventoso
wine (ᵘain) *n* vino *m*; ~ **cellar** cantina *f*; ~ **list** lista dei vini; ~ **merchant**

mercante di vini

wing (ʰing) *n* ala *f*

winner (ʰi-nö) *n* vincitore *m*, -trice *f*

winning (ʰi-ning) *adj* vincente;
  winnings *pl* vincita *f*

winter (ʰin-tö) *n* inverno *m*; ~ **sports**
  sport invernali

wipe (ʷaip) *v* strofinare; asciugare

wire (ʷaiᵒ) *n* filo *m*; filo di ferro

wireless (ʷaiᵒ-löss) *adj* senza fili

wisdom (ʰis-döm) *n* saggezza *f*

wise (ʷais) *adj* saggio

wish (ʰiʃ) *v* desiderare; *n* desiderio *m*

wit (it) n spirito *m*; persona di spirito

witch (ʰitʃ) *n* strega *f*

with (ʰið) *prep* con; presso; per

***withdraw** (ʰið-*droo*) *v* ritirare

within (ʰi-ðin) *prep* dentro; *adv*
  all'interno

without (ʰi-ðaut) *prep* senza

witness (ʰit-nöss) *n* testimone *m/f*

wits (ʰitss) *pl* ragione *f*

witty (ʰi-ti) *adj* spiritoso

wolf (ʷulf) *n* (pl wolves) lupo *m*

woman (ʷu-mön) *n* (pl women) donna *f*

womb (ʷuum) *n* utero *m*

won (ʷan) *v* (p, pp win)

wonder (ʷan-dö) *n* miracolo *m*;
  stupore *m*; *v* *chiedersi

wonderful (ʷan-dö-föl) *adj* stupendo,
  meraviglioso; delizioso

wood (ʷud) *n* legno *m*; bosco *m*

wooded (ʷu-did) *adj* boscoso

wooden (ʷu-dön) *adj* di legno; ~ **shoe**
  zoccolo *m*

woodland (ʷud-lönd) *n* terreno
  boscoso

wool (ʷul) *n* lana *f*; **darning** ~ lana da
  rammendo

wool(l)en (ʷu-lön) *adj* di lana

word (ʷööd) *n* parola *f*

wore (ʷoo) *v* (p wear)

work (ʷöök) *n* lavoro *m*; attività *f*; *v*

lavorare; funzionare; ~ **of art** opera
  d'arte; ~ **permit** permesso di lavoro

worker (ʷöö-kö) *n* lavoratore *m*, -trice *f*

working (ʷöö-king) *n* funzionamento
  m; ~ **day** giorno lavorativo, giorno
  feriale

workman (ʷöök-mön) *n* (pl -men)
  operaio *m*

works (ʷöökss) *pl* fabbrica *f*

workshop (ʷöök-ʃop) *n* officina *f*;
  gruppo di lavoro

world (ʷööld) *n* mondo *m*; ~ **war**
  guerra mondiale

world-famous (ʷööld-*fei*-möss) *adj* di
  fama mondiale

world-wide (ʷööld-ʷaid) *adj* mondiale

worm (ʷööm) *n* verme *m*

worn (ʷoon) *adj* (pp wear) consumato

worn-out (ʷoon-*aut*) *adj* usato

worried (ʷa-rid) *adj* preoccupato

worry (ʷa-ri) *v* preoccuparsi; *n* ansia *f*,
  preoccupazione *f*

worse (ʷööss) *adj* peggiore; *adv*
  peggio

worship (ʷöö-ʃip) *v* venerare; *n* culto
  m

worst (ʷöösst) *adj* pessimo; *adv* peggio

worth (ʷööθ) *n* valore *m*; *be ~ *valere

worthless (ʷööθ-löss) *adj* senza valore

worthwhile (ʷööθ-ail) *adj*
  conveniente; *be ~ valer la pena

worthy of (ʷöö-ði öv) degno di

would (ʷud) *v* (p will) *essere solito

wound¹ (ʷuund) *n* ferita *f*; *v*
  *offendere, ferire

wound² (ʷaund) *v* (p, pp wind)

wrap (ræp) *v* *avvolgere

wreck (rêk) *n* relitto *m*; *v* *distruggere

wrench (rêntʃ) *nAm* chiave *f*; storta *f*;
  v *storcere

wrinkle (*ring*-köl) *n* ruga *f*

wrist (risst) *n* polso *m*

wristwatch (risst-ʷotʃ) *n* orologio da

polso
*write (rait) *v* *scrivere; **~ down** annotare
writer (*rai*-tö) *n* scrittore *m*
writing (*rai*-ting) *n* scrittura *f*; **in ~** per iscritto; **~ pad** blocco per appunti, blocco di carta da lettere; **~ paper**

carta da lettere
written (*ri*-tön) *adj* (pp write) per iscritto
wrong (rong) *adj* erroneo, sbagliato; *n* torto *m*; *v* *fare un torto; ***be ~** *avere torto
wrote (rout) *v* (p write)

X

Xmas (*kriss*-möss) Natale
X-ray (*êkss*-rei) *n* radiografia *f*; *v*

radiografare

Y

yacht (¹ot) *n* panfilo *m*, yacht *m*; **~ club** circolo nautico
yachting (¹*o*-ting) *n* sport velico, velismo
yard (¹aad) *n* cortile *m*
yarn (¹aan) *n* filo *m*
yawn (¹oon) *v* sbadigliare
year (¹i⁰) *n* anno *m*
yearly (¹i⁰-li) *adj* annuale
yeast (¹iisst) *n* lievito *m*
yell (¹êl) *v* strillare; *n* strillo *m*
yellow (¹*ê*-lou) *adj* giallo
yes (¹êss) sì
yesterday (¹*ê*-sstö-di) *adv* ieri
yet (¹êt) *adv* ancora; *conj* eppure, però, ma
yield (¹iild) *v* *rendere; cedere
yoke (¹ouk) *n* giogo *m*

yolk (¹ouk) *n* tuorlo *m*
you (¹uu) *pron* tu; ti; Lei; Le; voi; vi
young (¹ang) *adj* giovane
your (¹oo) *adj* Suo; tuo; vostro, vostri
yours (¹oos) *pron* il tuo *m*, la tua *f*, i tuoi *mpl*, le tue *fpl*; il suo *m*, la sua *f*, i suoi *mpl*, le sue *fpl*; il vostro *m*, la vostra *f*, i vostri *mpl*, le vostre *fpl*; **a friend of ~** un tuo/suo/vostro amico; **yours ...** saluti ...; **~ sincerely** distinti saluti
yourself (¹oo-*ssêlf*) *pron* ti; tu stesso; Lei stesso
yourselves (¹oo-*ssêlvs*) *pron* vi; voi stessi
youth (¹uuθ) *n* gioventù *f*; **~ hostel** ostello della gioventù

Z

zap (zæp) *v* cancellare; annientare; colpire; mandare

zeal (siil) *n* zelo *m*

zealous (*sê*-löss) *adj* zelante

zebra (*sii*-brö) *n* zebra *f*; ~ **crossing** strisce pedonali

zenith (*sê*-niθ) *n* zenit *m*; apice *m*

zero (*si⁰*-rou) *n* (pl ~s) zero *m*

zest (sêsst) *n* gusto *m*

zinc (singk) *n* zinco *m*

zip (sip) *n* chiusura lampo; ~ **code** *Am* codice postale

zipper (*si*-pö) *nAm* chiusura lampo

zodiac (*sou*-di-æk) *n* zodiaco *m*

zone (soun) *n* zona *f*

zoo (suu) *n* (pl ~s) giardino zoologico

zoology (sou-*o*-lö-dʒi) *n* zoologia *f*

Lessico gastronomico
Cibi

à la carte secondo la lista delle vivande
almond mandorla
anchovy acciuga
angel food cake dolce a base di albumi
angels on horseback ostriche avvolte in fettine di pancetta, cotte alla griglia e servite su pane tostato
appetizer stuzzichino
apple mela
~ **charlotte** torta di mele coperta con fette di pane
~ **dumpling** mela ricoperta di pasta e cotta nel forno
~ **sauce** salsa di mele
apricot albicocca
Arbroath smoky varietà di merluzzo affumicato
artichoke carciofo
asparagus asparago
~ **tip** punta d'asparago
aspic gelatina
assorted assortito
aubergine melanzana
bacon pancetta
~ **and eggs** uova con pancetta
bagel panino a forma di ciambella
baked al forno
~ **Alaska** omelette alla norvegese; dessert con gelato alla vaniglia e meringhe
~ **beans** fagioli bianchi con salsa di pomodoro
~ **potato** patate cotte al forno con la buccia
Bakewell tart crostata con mandorle e marmellata di lamponi
baloney varietà di mortadella
banana banana

~ **split** banana tagliata a metà e servita con gelato, noci, sciroppo o cioccolata
barbecue 1) carne di manzo tritata, servita in un panino con salsa di pomodoro piccante 2) pasto all'aperto a base di carne ai ferri fatta al momento
~ **sauce** salsa di pomodoro molto piccante
barbecued ai ferri
basil basilico
bass branzino
bean fagiolo
beef manzo
~ **olive** involtino di manzo
beefburger medaglione di carne di manzo ai ferri, servito in un panino
beet, beetroot barbabietola
bilberry mirtillo
bill conto
~ **of fare** menù, lista delle vivande
biscuit 1) biscotto, pasticcino (GB) 2) panino (US)
black pudding sanguinaccio
blackberry mora
blackcurrant ribes nero
bloater aringa salata e affumicata
blood sausage sanguinaccio
blueberry mirtillo
boiled bollito
Bologna (sausage) mortadella
bone osso
boned disossato
Boston baked beans piatto di fagioli bianchi, cotti con pancetta e zucchero grezzo
Boston cream pie torta a strati, ripiena di crema e con glassa al cioccolato

brains cervella
braised brasato
bramble pudding budino di more a cui possono essere aggiunte mele tagliate a pezzetti
braunschweiger specie di paté di fegato
bread pane
breaded impanato
breakfast prima colazione
bream pagello
breast petto
brisket punta di petto
broad bean grossa fava
broth brodo
brown Betty torta di mele con spezie, coperta di uno strato di pasta frolla
brunch pasto abbondante, preso in tarda mattinata, che riunisce la colazione e il pranzo
brussels sprout cavolino di Bruxelles
bubble and squeak frittelle di purea di patate e di cavolo, a volte con pezzetti di manzo
bun 1) panino al latte con frutta secca (GB) 2) varietà di panino (US)
butter burro
buttered imburrato
cabbage cavolo
Caesar salad insalata con crostini all'aroma d'aglio, acciughe e formaggio grattugiato
cake torta, dolce
cakes pasticcini, biscotti
calf vitello
Canadian bacon filetto di maiale affumicato, tagliato a fette sottili
canapé panino imbottito
cantaloupe melone
caper cappero
capercaillie, capercailzie gallo cedrone
caramel caramello
carp carpa

carrot carota
cashew noce di acagiù
casserole casseruola; stufato
catfish pesce gatto
catsup ketchup, salsa di pomodoro con aceto e spezie
cauliflower cavolfiore
celery sedano
cereal fiocchi di mais, avena o altri cereali, serviti con latte freddo e zucchero
  hot ~ pappa di cereali calda
chateaubriand filetto di manzo di prima scelta cotto ai ferri
check il conto
Cheddar (cheese) formaggio di pasta dura, grasso e di gusto leggermente acido
cheese formaggio
  ~ board piatto di formaggio
  ~ cake dolce al formaggio doppia panna
cheeseburger amburghese con una fetta di formaggio fuso, servito in un panino
chef's salad insalata di prosciutto, pollo, uova sode, pomodoro, lattuga e formaggio
cherry ciliegia
chestnut castagna
chicken pollo
chicory 1) indivia (GB) 2) cicoria (US)
chili con carne piatto a base di manzo tritato, fagioli borlotti e pepe di Caienna
chili pepper pepe di Caienna
chips 1) patate fritte (GB) 2) patatine (US)
chitt(er)lings trippa di maiale
chive erba cipollina
chocolate cioccolato
  ~ pudding 1) budino al cioccolato (GB) 2) spuma al cioccolato (US)

choice scelta

chop cotoletta, braciola

~ **suey** piatto a base di carne o di pollo, verdure e riso

chopped sminuzzato, tritato

chowder zuppa densa di pesce, di frutti di mare o di carne

Christmas pudding budino a base di frutta candita, scorza di limone, cedro; a volte alla fiamma

cinnamon cannella

chutney salsa indiana molto piccante

clam vongola, tellina

club sandwich panino imbottito con pancetta, pollo, pomodoro, lattuga e maionese; a diversi strati

cobbler crostata di frutta, ricoperta di pasta frolla

cock-a-leekie soup minestra di pollo e di porri

coconut noce di cocco

cod merluzzo

Colchester oyster la più pregiata ostrica inglese

cold cuts/meat affettati

coleslaw insalata di cavolo

compote composta, conserva

condiment condimento

consommé brodo ristretto

cooked cotto

cookie biscotto

corn 1) grano (GB) 2) granturco (US)

~ **on the cob** pannocchia di granturco

cornflakes fiocchi di granturco

corned beef carne di manzo in scatola

cottage cheese formaggio bianco, fresco

cottage pie carne tritata ricoperta di cipolle e purea di patate, il tutto passato al forno

course portata

cover charge coperto

crab granchio

cranberry varietà di mirtillo

~ **sauce** marmellata di mirtilli rossi, servita con carne e selvaggina

crawfish, crayfish 1) gambero di fiume 2) aragosta (GB) 3) scampo (US)

cream 1) crema, panna 2) dessert 3) zuppa densa

~ **cheese** formaggio doppia panna

~**puff** bignè

creamed potatoes patate tagliate a dadi, in besciamella

creole alla creola; piatto preparato con salsa di pomodoro molto piccante, peperoni, cipolle e servito con riso

cress crescione

crisps patatine

croquette crocchetta

crumpet panino leggero di forma rotonda, tostato e imburrato

cucumber cetriolo

Cumberland ham prosciutto inglese molto rinomato

Cumberland sauce gelatina di ribes, con vino, succo d'arancia e spezie

cupcake varietà di pasticcino

cured salato, affumicato, marinato (pesce o carne)

currant 1) uva sultanina 2) ribes

curried con curry

custard crema, sformato

cutlet cotoletta, scaloppina

dab genere di pesce, simile alla sogliola

Danish pastry pasticceria danese

date dattero

Derby cheese tipo di formaggio piccante

devilled alla diavola; condimento molto piccante

devil's food cake torta al cioccolato, molto sostanziosa

devils on horseback prugne secche cotte nel vino rosso e ripiene di mandorle e di acciughe, avvolte nella pancetta, passate alla griglia e servite su pane tostato

Devonshire cream crema cagliata

diced tagliato a dadi

diet food cibo dietetico

dill aneto

dinner cena

dish piatto

donut, doughnut frittella a forma di ciambella

double cream doppia panna, panna intera

Dover sole sogliola di Dover, molto rinomata

dressing 1) condimento per insalata 2) ripieno per tacchino (US)

Dublin Bay prawn scampo

duck anatra

duckling anatroccolo

dumpling gnocchetto di pasta, bollito

Dutch apple pie torta di mele, ricoperta di un impasto di burro e zucchero grezzo

éclair pasticcino glassato ripieno di crema

eel anguilla

egg uovo

  boiled ~ alla coque

  fried ~ al tegame

  hard-boiled ~ sodo

  poached ~ in camicia

  scrambled ~ strapazzato

  soft-boiled ~ molle

eggplant melanzana

endive 1) cicoria, insalata riccia (GB) 2) indivia (US)

entrecôte costata

entrée 1) antipasto (GB) 2) piatto principale (US)

escalope scaloppina

fennel finocchio

fig fico

fillet filetto di carne o di pesce

finnan haddock varietà di merluzzo affumicato

fish pesce

  ~ **and chips** pesce fritto con contorno di patatine fritte

  ~ **cake** polpette di pesce

flan crostata alla frutta

flapjack frittella dolce e spessa

flounder passera di mare

forcemeat ripieno

fowl pollame

frankfurter wurstel

French bean fagiolino verde

French bread sfilatino (pane)

French dressing 1) condimento per insalata a base di olio e aceto (GB) 2) condimento per insalata un po' denso, con ketchup (US)

french fries patatine fritte

French toast fette di pane imbevute di uova battute e fritte in padella, servite con marmellata o zucchero

fresh fresco

fricassée fricassea

fried fritto

fritter frittella

frogs' legs cosce di rana

frosting glassa

fruit frutto

fry frittura

galantine galantina

game cacciagione

gammon prosciutto affumicato

garfish luccio

garlic aglio

garnish contorno

gherkin cetriolino

giblets rigaglie

ginger zenzero

goose oca

gooseberry uva spina

grape uva

grapefruit pompelmo
grated grattugiato
gravy sugo a base di carne
grayling temolo
green bean fagiolino verde
green pepper peperone verde
green salad insalata verde
greens verdura
grilled alla griglia, ai ferri
grilse salmone giovane **grouse** gallo cedrone
gumbo 1) legume di origine africana 2) piatto creolo a base di *okra* con pomodori e carne o pesce
haddock varietà di merluzzo
haggis frattaglie di pecora (o di vitello) tagliate a pezzetti e mescolate con fiocchi d'avena
hake nasello
half mezzo, metà
halibut passera di mare
ham prosciutto
  ~ **and eggs** uova con prosciutto
hamburger svizzera di carne di manzo tritata e cipolla, servita in un panino
hare lepre
haricot bean fagiolo
hash carne tritata o sminuzzata; piatto di carne sminuzzata, con patate e verdure
hazelnut nocciola
heart cuore
herb erbe, odori
herring aringa
home-made fatto in casa
hominy grits specie di polenta
honey miele
  ~**dew melon** melone molto dolce dalla polpa verde-gialla
hors-d'œuvre antipasto
horse-radish rafano
hot 1) caldo 2) piccante
  ~ **cross bun** brioche a forma di

croce, con uvetta e ricoperta di glassa (per la Quaresima)
  ~ **dog** wurstel caldo in un panino
huckleberry mirtillo
hush puppy frittella di farina di mais e di cipolle
ice-cream gelato
iced glassato, gelato
icing glassa
Idaho baked potato qualità di patata specialmente adatta per essere cotta al forno
Irish stew stufato di montone con cipolle e patate
Italian dressing condimento per insalata a base di olio e aceto
jam marmellata
jellied in gelatina
Jell-O dolce di gelatina
jelly gelatina
Jerusalem artichoke topinamburo
John Dory orata
jugged hare lepre in salmì
juice succo
juniper berry bacca di ginepro
junket latte cagliato zuccherato
kale cavolo ricciuto
kedgeree pesce sminuzzato, accompagnato da riso, uova e burro
kidney rognone
kipper aringa affumicata
lamb agnello
Lancashire hot pot stufato di cotolette e rognoni d'agnello, con patate e cipolle
larded lardellato
lean magro
leek porro
leg cosciotto, coscia
lemon limone
  ~ **sole** sogliola
lentil lenticchia
lettuce lattuga, lattuga cappuccina
lima bean specie di grossa fava

lime limoncino verde
liver fegato
loaf pagnotta
lobster astice
loin lombata
Long Island duck anitra di Long Island, molto rinomata
low-calorie povero in calorie
lox salmone affumicato
lunch pranzo
macaroon amaretto
macaroni maccheroni
mackerel sgombro
maize granturco, mais
mandarin mandarino
maple syrup sciroppo d'acero
marinade salsa di aceto e spezie
marinated marinato
marjoram maggiorana
marmalade marmellata d'arance
marrow midollo
~ **bone** osso con midollo
marshmallow caramella gelatinosa e gommosa
marzipan marzapane
mashed potatoes purea di patate
mayonnaise maionese
meal pasto
meat carne
~**ball** polpetta di carne
~ **loaf** polpettone cotto al forno e servito a fette
~ **pâté** pasticcio di carne
medium (done) cotto a puntino
melon melone
melted fuso
Melton Mowbray pie pasticcio a base di carne
meringue meringa
milk latte
mince carne tritata
~ **pie** dolce ripieno di frutta
minced tritato
~ **meat** carne tritata

mint menta
minute steak bistecca cotta velocemente a fuoco vivo da ambo le parti
mixed misto
~ **grill** spiedini con salsicce, fegatini, rognoni, cotolette e pancetta, alla griglia
molasses melassa
morel spugnolo (fungo)
mousse 1) dolce o dessert a base di panna o albumi battuti 2) spuma leggera di carne o di pesce
mulberry mora
mullet triglia
mulligatawny soup minestra di pollo, molto piccante, di origine indiana
mushroom fungo
muskmelon varietà di melone
mussel mitilo, cozza
mustard senape
mutton montone
noodle taglierini
nut noce
oatmeal (porridge) pappa d'avena
oil olio
okra baccelli di *gumbo* *utilizzati per rendere dense zuppe, minestre e stufati
olive oliva
omelet frittata
onion cipolla
orange arancia
ox tongue lingua di bue
oxtail coda di bue
oyster ostrica
pancake frittella
paprika paprica
Parmesan (cheese) parmigiano
parsley prezzemolo
parsnip pastinaca
partridge pernice
pastry pasta, pasticcino
pasty pasticcio

pea pisello
peach pesca
peanut arachide
 ~ butter burro di arachidi
pear pera
pearl barley orzo perlato
pepper pepe
 ~ mint menta piperita
perch pesce persico
persimmon cachi
pheasant fagiano
pickerel piccolo luccio
pickle 1) sottaceto 2) negli US si riferisce solo al cetriolino
pickled sott'aceto
pie pasticcio o torta, spesso ricoperta da uno strato di pasta, ripiena di carne, verdura, frutta o crema alla vaniglia
pig maiale
pigeon piccione
pike luccio
pineapple ananas
plaice passerino, pianuzza
plain liscio, al naturale
plate piatto
plum susina, prugna
 ~ pudding budino a base di frutta candita, scorza di limone, cedro; a volte alla fiamma
poached in camicia, affogato
popover piccolo dolce di pasta farcito alla frutta
pork maiale
porridge pappa di fiocchi d'avena o preparata con farina di altri cereali
porterhouse steak equivalente di bistecca alla fiorentina
pot roast arrosto brasato
potato patata
 ~ chips 1) patatine fritte (GB) 2) patatine (US)
 ~ in its jacket patata cotta con la buccia

potted shrimps gamberetti serviti in piccoli stampi con burro fuso aromatizzato
poultry pollame
prawn gambero
prune prugna secca
ptarmigan pernice delle nevi
pudding budino, sformato
pumpernickel pane di segale integrale
pumpkin zucca
quail quaglia
quince mela cotogna
rabbit coniglio
radish ravanello
rainbow trout trota fario
raisin uva passa
rare poco cotto, al sangue
raspberry lampone
raw crudo
red mullet triglia
red (sweet) pepper peperone rosso
redcurrant ribes rosso
relish condimento a base di verdura sott'aceto sminuzzata
rhubarb rabarbaro
rib (of beef) costola di manzo
rib-eye-steak grossa bistecca
rice riso
rissole polpetta di carne o di pesce avvolta in pasta frolla
river trout trota di torrente
roast(ed) arrosto
Rock Cornish hen galletto specialmente adatto per essere preparato arrosto
roe uova di pesce
roll panino
rollmop herring filetto di aringa, arrotolato attorno a un cetriolo, marinato nel vino bianco
round steak girello di manzo
Rubens sandwich carne tritata su toast, con crauti, emmental,

condimento per insalata; servita
calda

rump steak bistecca di girello

rusk pane biscottato

rye bread pane di segale

saddle la parte del dorso di un
animale macellato

saffron zafferano

sage salvia

salad insalata

~ **bar** vasta scelta di insalate

~ **cream** condimento per insalata a
base di panna, leggermente dolce

~ **dressing** condimento per insalata

salami salame

salmon salmone

~ **trout** trota salmonata

salt sale

salted salato

sardine sardina

sauce salsa, sugo

sauerkraut crauti

sausage salsiccia

sauté(ed) rosolato, fritto in padella

scallop 1) conchiglia S. Giacomo 2)
scaloppina di vitello

scone focaccia di pasta leggera a base
di farina d'avena o d'orzo

Scotch broth brodo di manzo o di
agnello con verdure sminuzzate

Scotch woodcock crostino coperto di
uova strapazzate e acciughe

sea bass spigola

sea kale cavolo di mare

seafood frutti di mare, pesce

(in) season (di) stagione

seasoning condimento

service servizio

~ **charge** prezzo del servizio

~ **(not) included** servizio (non)
compreso

set menu menù a prezzo fisso

shad alosa, salacca (genere di sardina)

shallot scalogno

shellfish crostaceo

sherbet sorbetto

shoulder spalla

shredded wheat fiocchi d'avena
serviti a colazione

shrimp gamberetto

silverside (of beef) controgirello

sirloin steak bistecca di lombo di
manzo

skewer spiedino

slice fetta

sliced a fette

sloppy Joe carne di manzo tritata con
salsa di pomodoro piccante, servita
in un panino

smelt eperlano

smoked affumicato

snack spuntino

sole sogliola

soup minestra, zuppa

sour agro, acido

soused herring aringa marinata in
aceto e spezie

spare rib costola di maiale o manzo

spice spezia

spinach spinaci

spiny lobster aragosta

(on a) spit (allo) spiedo

sponge cake pan di Spagna

sprat spratto (piccola aringa)

squash zucca

starter antipasto

steak and kidney pie stufato di
manzo e rognoni, coperto di pasta

steamed cotto a vapore

stew stufato, in umido

Stilton (cheese) uno dei più rinomati
formaggi inglesi a venatura blu

strawberry fragola

string bean fagiolino

stuffed ripieno, farcito

stuffing ripieno

suck(l)ing pig maialino da latte

sugar zucchero

sugarless senza zucchero
sundae varietà di cassata con noci, crema e talora sciroppo
supper cena
swede specie di rapa
sweet dolce, torta
  ~ **corn** granturco bianco
  ~ **potato** patata dolce
sweetbread animella
Swiss cheese emmental
Swiss roll brioche alla crema o marmellata
Swiss steak fetta di manzo brasata con legumi e spezie
T-bone steak bistecca di manzo formata dal filetto e dal controfiletto separati da un osso a forma di T
table d'hôte menù a prezzo fisso
tangerine specie di mandarino
tarragon dragoncello, estragone
tart torta di frutta
tenderloin filetto di carne
Thousand Island dressing condimento per insalata a base di maionese, peperoni, olive e uova sode
thyme timo
toad-in-the-hole carne di manzo o salsiccia avvolta in pasta e cotta al forno
toasted tostato
  ~ **cheese** crostino spalmato di formaggio fuso
tomato pomodoro
tongue lingua
tournedos medaglione di filetto
treacle melassa
trifle genere di zuppa inglese; charlotte allo sherry o al brandy con mandorle, marmellata e panna montata
tripe trippa
trout trota
truffle tartufo

tuna, tunny tonno
turbot rombo
turkey tacchino
turnip rapa
turnover calzone ripieno
turtle tartaruga
underdone poco cotto, al sangue
vanilla vaniglia
veal vitello
  ~ **bird** involtino di vitello
  ~ **escalope** scaloppina di vitello
vegetable verdura
  ~ **marrow** zucchino
venison cacciagione, capriolo
vichyssoise zuppa fredda a base di panna, patate e porri
vinegar aceto
Virginia baked ham prosciutto americano, steccato con chiodi di garofano, cotto al forno e decorato con fette di ananas, ciliege e glassato con lo sciroppo di questi frutti
vol-au-vent saccottino di pasta sfoglia ripieno di carne o altro intingolo
wafer cialda
waffle sorta di cialda calda
walnut noce
water ice sorbetto
watercress crescione
watermelon cocomero, anguria
well-done ben cotto
Welsh rabbit/rarebit formaggio fuso su un toast
whelk buccina (mollusco)
whipped cream panna montata
whitebait bianchetti
Wiener schnitzel scaloppina alla Milanese
wine list lista dei vini
woodcock beccaccia
Worcestershire sauce salsa piccante a base di aceto e soia
York ham uno dei più rinomati prosciutti inglesi, servito a fette sottili

Yorkshire pudding sformato a base di farina, latte e uova cotto con sugo di manzo; si mangia col rosbif

zwieback fette biscottate

Bevande

ale birra scura, leggermente dolce, fermentata ad alta temperatura

  bitter ~ scura, amara e forte

  brown ~ scura in bottiglia, leggermente dolce

  light ~ chiara in bottiglia

  mild ~ scura alla spina, dal gusto spiccato

  pale ~ chiara in bottiglia

applejack acquavite di mele

Athol Brose bevanda scozzese composta da whisky, mele e talora fiocchi di avena

Bacardi cocktail cocktail al rum e al gin, con sciroppo di melagrana e succo di limone verde

barley water bibita rinfrescante a base di orzo e aromatizzata con limone

barley wine birra scura a forte gradazione alcoolica

beer birra

  bottled ~ in bottiglia

  draft, draught ~ alla spina

black velvet champagne con *stout* (servito spesso con le ostriche)

bloody Mary vodka con succo di pomodoro e spezie

bourbon whisky americano, distillato soprattutto dal granturco

brandy 1) appellazione generica dell'acquavite distillata dall'uva o da altra frutta 2) cognac

  ~ **Alexander** acquavite, crema di cacao e panna

British wines vini fatti con uva (o succo d'uva) importata in Gran Bretagna

cherry brandy liquore di ciliege

chocolate latte al cacao

cider sidro

  ~ **cup** miscuglio di sidro, spezie, zucchero e ghiaccio

claret vino rosso di Bordeaux

cobbler *long drink* ghiacciato, a base di frutta, al quale si aggiunge vino o altra bevanda alcoolica

coffee caffè

  ~ **with cream** con panna

  black ~ nero

  caffeine-free ~ decaffeinato

  white ~ con latte

cordial cordiale

cream panna

cup bevanda rinfrescante composta da vino molto freddo, seltz, liquore, e guarnita con una fetta di limone, di arancia o di cetriolo

daiquiri bevanda composta da rum, succo di limone verde e di ananas

double doppia quantità

Drambuie liquore fatto da whisky e miele

dry martini 1) vermuth secco (GB) 2) cocktail al gin con un po' di vermuth secco (US)

egg-nog bevanda preparata con rum e altro liquore forte, tuorli battuti e zucchero

gin and it gin e vermut italiano

gin-fizz bevanda composta da gin, zucchero, succo di limone e soda

ginger ale bevanda non alcoolica allo

zenzero

ginger beer bevanda leggermente
alcoolica a base di zenzero e
zucchero

grasshopper bevanda composta da
crema di menta, crema di cacao e
panna

Guinness (stout) birra molto scura e
dal gusto dolciastro, ad alta
gradazione di malto e luppolo

half pint misura di capacità: circa 0,3
litri

highball whisky o altri superalcoolici
con acqua gasata o con *ginger ale*

iced ghiacciato

Irish coffee caffè con zucchero, un po'
di whisky irlandese e ricoperto di
panna montata

Irish Mist liquore irlandese a base di
whisky e miele

Irish whiskey whisky irlandese, più
secco dello *scotch*, fatto non solo da
orzo ma anche da segale, avena e
grano

juice succo

lager birra chiara e leggera, servita
molto fredda

lemon squash succo di limone

lemonade limonata

lime juice succo di limoncini verdi

liqueur liquore

liquor bevanda molto alcoolica

long drink bevanda alcoolica
allungata con acqua o acqua tonica e
ghiaccio

madeira madera

Manhattan bevanda a base di whisky
americano, vermut secco e angostura

milk latte

~ **shake** frappè

mineral water acqua minerale

mulled wine vin brûlé; vino caldo con
spezie

neat liscio

old-fashioned bevanda a base di
whisky, zucchero, angostura e ciliege
al maraschino

on the rocks con cubetti di ghiaccio

Ovaltine Ovomaltina

Pimm's cup(s) bevanda alcoolica con
aggiunta di succo di frutta e talvolta
seltz

~ **No. 1** a base di gin

~ **No. 2** a base di whisky

~ **No. 3** a base di rum

~ **No. 4** a base di acquavite

pink champagne champagne rosé

pink lady cocktail composto da
albumi, calvados, succo di limone,
succo di melagrana e gin

pint misura di capacità: circa 0,6 litri

port (wine) porto

porter birra scura e amara

quart misura di capacità: 1,14 litri (US
0,95 litri)

root beer bevanda gasata e
analcoolica dolce, ricavata da erbe e
radici varie

rye (whiskey) whisky di segale, più
forte e più aspro del *bourbon*

scotch (whisky) miscuglio di whisky
di grano e d'orzo

screwdriver vodka e succo d'arancia

shandy *bitter ale* con l'aggiunta di
limonata o di *ginger beer*

sherry sherry

short drink bevanda alcoolica liscia

shot piccola dose di whisky o di altro
liquore

sloe gin-fizz liquore di prugnola con
soda e succo di limone

soda water acqua gasata, seltz

soft drink bevanda analcoolica

spirits bevande molto alcooliche

stinger cognac e crema di menta

stout birra scura, aromatizzata
fortemente con il luppolo

straight liscio

tea tè
toddy grog, ponce
Tom Collins bevanda a base di gin, succo di limone, acqua di seltz e zucchero
tonic (water) acqua brillante, acqua tonica
water acqua
whisky sour bevanda a base di whisky, succo di limone, zucchero e soda
wine vino
  dry ~ secco
  red ~ rosso
  rosé ~ rosato, rosatello
  sparkling ~ spumante
  sweet ~ dolce
  white ~ bianco

Mini-grammatica

L'articolo

L'articolo determinativo (il, lo, la, i, gli, le) ha una sola forma: *the*.

the room, the rooms	la camera, le camere

L'articolo indeterminativo (un, una, uno) ha due forme: *a*, che si usa davanti a consonante, *an*, che si usa davanti a vocale e *h* muta.

a coat	un cappotto
an umbrella	un ombrello
an hour	un'ora

Some (del, dello, della, dei, degli, delle) indica una quantità o un numero indefiniti.

I'd like some water, please.	Vorrei dell'acqua, per favore.
Please bring me some biscuits.	Per favore, portami dei biscotti.

Any si usa nelle frasi negative e nelle interrogative.

There isn't any soap.	Non c'è sapone.
Do you have any stamps?	Avete francobolli?
Is there any message for me?	C'è un messaggio per me?

Il sostantivo

Il plurale della maggior parte dei sostantivi si forma aggiungendo *-(e)s* alla forma del singolare.

cup — cups (tazza — tazze)	**dress — dresses** (abito — abiti)

Nota: se un sostantivo termina con *-y* preceduta da una consonante, la desinenza del plurale sarà *-ies*, se la *-y* è preceduta da una vocale, il sostantivo segue la regola generale.

lady — ladies (signora — signore)	**key — keys** (chiave — chiavi)

Alcuni plurali irregolari:

man — men (uomo/uomini)	**foot — feet** (piede/-i)
woman — women (donna/-e)	**tooth — teeth** (dente/-i)
child — children (bambino/-i)	**mouse — mice** (topo/-i)

Il complemento del nome (genitivo)

1. Il possessore è una persona: se il sostantivo non termina in *-s*, si aggiunge *'s*.

the boy's room	la camera del ragazzo
the children's clothes	gli abiti dei bambini

Se il sostantivo termina in *s*, si aggiunge l'apostrofo (').

the boys' room	la camera dei ragazzi

2. Il possessore non è una persona: si usa la preposizione *of*:

the key of the door	la chiave della porta

L'aggettivo

Gli aggettivi di solito precedono il sostantivo.

a large brown suitcase	una grande valigia marrone

Vi sono due modi per formare il comparativo e il superlativo degli aggettivi:
1. Gli aggettivi di una sillaba e molti aggettivi di due sillabe aggiungono -(e)r ed -(e)st.

small (piccolo) — **smaller** — **smallest**
pretty (carino) — **prettier** — **prettiest***

2. Gli aggettivi di tre o più sillabe e alcuni aggettivi di due sillabe (in particolare quelli che terminano in -*ful* e -*less*) formano il comparativo e il superlativo con *more* e *most*.

expensive (caro) — **more expensive** — **most expensive**
careful (attento) — **more careful** — **most careful**

Alcune forme irregolari:

good (buono)	**better**	**best**
bad (cattivo)	**worse**	**worst**
little (poco)	**less**	**least**
much/many (molto)	**more**	**most**

L'avverbio

Numerosi avverbi si formano aggiungendo -*ly* all'aggettivo.

quick — **quickly**	veloce — velocemente
slow — **slowly**	lento — lentamente

Il pronome

	Soggetto	Complemento (dir./indir.)	Possessivo 1	1
Singolare				
1ª persona	**I**	**me**	**my**	**mine**
2ª persona	**you**	**you**	**your**	**yours**
3ª persona (m.)	**he**	**him**	**his**	**his**
(f.)	**she**	**her**	**her**	**hers**

---

* La *y* diventa *i* quando è preceduta da una consonante.

	Soggetto	Complemento (dir./indir.)	Possessivo 1	1
(n.)	it	it	its	—

Plurale				
1ª persona	we	us	our	ours
2ª persona	you	you	your	yours
3ª persona	they	them	their	theirs

Nota: in inglese non c'è distinzione come in italiano fra il "tu" e il "Lei". Si usa una sola forma: *you*.

Il pronome personale complemento si usa anche dopo le preposizioni.

Give it to me.	Dammelo.
He came with us.	È venuto con noi.

La forma 1 del possessivo corrisponde a "mio", "tuo", ecc., la forma 2 a "il mio", "il tuo", ecc.

Where's my key?	Dov'è la mia chiave?
That's not mine.	Non è la mia.

L'aggettivo dimostrativo

This (questo; plurale *these*) si riferisce a una cosa vicina nello spazio o nel tempo. *That* (quello; plurale *those*) si riferisce a una cosa più lontana.

Is this seat taken?	È occupato questo posto?

Verbi ausiliari

a) **to be** (essere)

	Forma contratta	Negativo — forme contratte		
I am	I'm	I'm not	o	
you are	you're	you're not		you aren't
he is	he's	he's not		he isn't
she is	she's	she's not		she isn't
it is	it's	it's not		it isn't
we are	we're	we're not		we aren't
you are	you're	you're not		you aren't
they are	they're	they're not		they aren't

Interrogativo: **Am I? Are you? Is he?** ecc.

Nota: nella lingua corrente si usano quasi sempre le forme contratte.

Le forme "c'è" e "ci sono" si traducono: *there is* (*there's*) e *there are*.

b) **to have** (avere)

	Contrazione		Contrazione
I have	I've	we have	we've
you have	you've	you have	you've
he/she/it has	he's/she's/it's	they have	they've

Negazione:	**I have not (I haven't)**
Interrogazione:	**Have you? — Has he?**

c) **to do** (fare)

	Negativo contratto		Negativo contratto
I do	I don't	we do	we don't
you do	you don't	you do	you don't
he/she/it does	he/she/it doesn't	they do	they don't

Interrogazione:	**Do you? Does he/she/it?**

Altri verbi

L'infinito si usa per tutte le persone del tempo presente; si aggiunge solo -(*e*)*s* alla terza persona singolare.

	to love (amare)	to come (venire)	to go (andare)
I	love	come	go
you	love	come	go
he/she/it	loves	comes	goes
we	love	come	go
you	love	come	go
they	love	come	go

La negazione si forma per mezzo dell'ausiliare *do/does* + *not* + verbo all'infinito.

We do not (don't) like this hotel.	Non ci piace questo albergo.
She does not (doesn't) smoke.	Lei non fuma.

L'interrogazione si forma con l'ausiliare *do* + soggetto + infinito.

Do you like it?	Ti piace?
Does he live here?	Lui vive qui?

Presente continuo

Si forma con il verbo *to be* (essere) + il participio presente del verbo coniugato. Il participio presente si forma aggiungendo -ing all'infinito (eliminando la -e finale quando c'è). Il presente continuo si impiega solo con certi verbi, in quanto indica un'azione o uno stato che sta avvenendo nel momento in cui si parla.

What are you doing?	Cosa stai facendo?
I'm writing a letter.	Sto scrivendo una lettera.

Imperativo

L'imperativo (singolare e plurale) ha la stessa forma dell'infinito (senza to). La negazione si forma con don't.

Please bring me some water.	Per favore, portami dell'acqua.
Don't be late.	Non far tardi.

Verbi irregolari inglesi

Vi elenchiamo qui di seguito i verbi irregolari inglesi. I verbi composti o quelli con prefisso si coniugano come i verbi semplici, es. *mistake* e *overdrive* si coniugano come *take* e *drive*.

Infinito	*Passato remoto*	*Participio passato*	
arise	arose	arisen	*alzare*
awake	awoke	awoken	*svegliare*
be	was	been	*essere*
bear	bore	borne	*portare*
beat	beat	beaten	*battere*
become	became	become	*diventare*
begin	began	begun	*cominciare*
bend	bent	bent	*curvare*
bet	bet	bet	*scommettere*
bid	bade/bid	bidden/bid	*comandare*
bind	bound	bound	*legare*
bite	bit	bitten	*mordere*
bleed	bled	bled	*sanguinare*
blow	blew	blown	*soffiare*
break	broke	broken	*rompere*
breed	bred	bred	*allevare*
bring	brought	brought	*portare*
build	built	built	*costruire*
burn	burnt/burned	burnt/burned	*bruciare*
burst	burst	burst	*scoppiare*
buy	bought	bought	*comprare*
can*	could	—	*potere*
cast	cast	cast	*gettare*

---

* indicativo presente

catch	caught	caught	*afferrare*
choose	chose	chosen	*scegliere*
cling	clung	clung	*aderire*
clothe	clothed/clad	clothed/clad	*vestire*
come	came	come	*venire*
cost	cost	cost	*costare*
creep	crept	crept	*strisciare*
cut	cut	cut	*tagliare*
deal	dealt	dealt	*trattare*
dig	dug	dug	*scavare*
do (he does)	did	done	*fare*
draw	drew	drawn	*tirare*
dream	dreamt/dreamed	dreamt/dreamed	*sognare*
drink	drank	drunk	*bere*
drive	drove	driven	*guidare*
dwell	dwelt	dwelt	*abitare*
eat	ate	eaten	*mangiare*
fall	fell	fallen	*cadere*
feed	fed	fed	*nutrire*
feel	felt	felt	*sentire*
fight	fought	fought	*combattere*
find	found	found	*trovare*
flee	fled	fled	*fuggire*
fling	flung	flung	*gettare*
fly	flew	flown	*volare*
forsake	forsook	forsaken	*abbandonare*
freeze	froze	frozen	*gelare*
get	got	got	*ottenere*
give	gave	given	*dare*
go	went	gone	*andare*
grind	ground	ground	*macinare*
grow	grew	grown	*crescere*
hang	hung	hung	*appendere*
have	had	had	*avere*
hear	heard	heard	*udire*
hew	hewed	hewed/hewn	*spaccare*
hide	hid	hidden	*nascondere*
hit	hit	hit	*colpire*
hold	held	held	*tenere*
hurt	hurt	hurt	*dolere*
keep	kept	kept	*tenere*
kneel	knelt	knelt	*inginocchiarsi*
knit	knitted/knit	knitted/knit	*congiungere*
know	knew	known	*conoscere*

lay	laid	laid	*posare*
lead	led	led	*dirigere*
lean	leant/leaned	leant/leaned	*inclinare*
leap	leapt/leaped	leapt/leaped	*balzare*
learn	learnt/learned	learnt/learned	*imparare*
leave	left	left	*lasciare*
lend	lent	lent	*prestare*
let	let	let	*permettere*
lie	lay	lain	*giacere*
light	lit/lighted	lit/lighted	*accendere*
lose	lost	lost	*perdere*
make	made	made	*fare*
may*	might	—	*potere*
mean	meant	meant	*significare*
meet	met	met	*incontrare*
mow	mowed	mowed/mown	*falciare*
must*	—	—	*dovere*
ought (to)*	—	—	*dovere*
pay	paid	paid	*pagare*
put	put	put	*mettere*
read	read	read	*leggere*
rid	rid	rid	*sbarazzare*
ride	rode	ridden	*cavalcare*
ring	rang	rung	*suonare*
rise	rose	risen	*sorgere*
run	ran	run	*correre*
saw	sawed	sawn	*segare*
say	said	said	*dire*
see	saw	seen	*vedere*
seek	sought	sought	*cercare*
sell	sold	sold	*vendere*
send	sent	sent	*mandare*
set	set	set	*mettere*
sew	sewed	sewed/sewn	*cucire*
shake	shook	shaken	*scuotere*
shall*	should	—	*dovere*
shed	shed	shed	*spandere*
shine	shone	shone	*splendere*
shoot	shot	shot	*sparare*
show	showed	shown	*mostrare*
shrink	shrank	shrunk	*restringere*
shut	shut	shut	*chiudere*

---

* indicativo presente

sing	sang	sung	*cantare*
sink	sank	sunk	*affondare*
sit	sat	sat	*sedere*
sleep	slept	slept	*dormire*
slide	slid	slid	*scivolare*
sling	slung	slung	*scagliare*
slink	slunk	slunk	*sgattaiolare*
slit	slit	slit	*fendere*
smell	smelled/smelt	smelled/smelt	*fiutare*
sow	sowed	sown/sowed	*seminare*
speak	spoke	spoken	*parlare*
speed	sped/speeded	sped/speeded	*affrettarsi*
spell	spelt/spelled	spelt/spelled	*compitare*
spend	spent	spent	*spendere*
spill	spilt/spilled	spilt/spilled	*versare*
spin	spun	spun	*(far) girare*
spit	spat	spat	*sputare*
split	split	split	*spaccare*
spoil	spoilt/spoiled	spoilt/spoiled	*viziare*
spread	spread	spread	*spargere*
spring	sprang	sprung	*scattare*
stand	stood	stood	*stare in piedi*
steal	stole	stolen	*rubare*
stick	stuck	stuck	*ficcare*
sting	stung	stung	*pungere*
stink	stank/stunk	stunk	*puzzare*
strew	strewed	strewed/strewn	*spargere*
stride	strode	stridden	*camminare a grandi passi*
strike	struck	struck/stricken	*percuotere*
string	strung	strung	*legare*
strive	strove	striven	*sforzarsi*
swear	swore	sworn	*giurare*
sweep	swept	swept	*scopare*
swell	swelled	swollen	*gonfiare*
swim	swam	swum	*nuotare*
swing	swung	swung	*dondolare*
take	took	taken	*prendere*
teach	taught	taught	*insegnare*
tear	tore	torn	*stracciare*
tell	told	told	*dire*
think	thought	thought	*pensare*
throw	threw	thrown	*gettare*
thrust	thrust	thrust	*spingere*

tread	trod	trodden	*calpestare*
wake	woke/waked	woken/waked	*svegliare*
wear	wore	worn	*indossare*
weave	wove	woven	*tessere*
weep	wept	wept	*piangere*
will*	would	—	*volere*
win	won	won	*vincere*
wind	wound	wound	*avvolgere*
wring	wrung	wrung	*torcere*
write	wrote	written	*scrivere*

---

* indicativo presente

Abbreviazioni inglesi

AA	*Automobile Association*	Automobile Club Britannico
AAA	*American Automobile Association*	Automobile Club Americano
ABC	*American Broadcasting Company*	società privata radio-televisiva americana
A.D.	*anno Domini*	A.D.
Am.	*America; American*	America; americano
a.m.	*ante meridiem (before noon)*	di mattina (00.00—12.00)
Amtrak	*American railroad corporation*	società di ferrovie americana
AT & T	*American Telephone and Telegraph Company*	società americana dei telefoni e telegrafi
Ave.	*avenue*	viale
BBC	*British Broadcasting Corporation*	Radio-Televisione Britannica
B.C.	*before Christ*	a. C.
bldg.	*building*	edificio
Blvd.	*boulevard*	viale
B.R.	*British Rail*	ferrovie britanniche
Brit.	*Britain; British*	Gran Bretagna; britannico
Bros.	*brothers*	fratelli
¢	*cent*	1/100 di dollaro
Can.	*Canada; Canadian*	Canada; canadese
CBS	*Columbia Broadcasting System*	società privata radio-televisiva americana
CID	*Criminal Investigation Department*	polizia giudiziaria britannica
CNR	*Canadian National Railway*	ferrovie nazionali canadesi
c/o	*(in) care of*	presso (negli indirizzi)
Co.	*company*	compagnia
Corp.	*corporation*	tipo di società
CPR	*Canadian Pacific Railways*	società di ferrovie canadesi
D.C.	*District of Columbia*	Distretto Federale della Columbia (Washington, D.C.)
DDS	*Doctor of Dental Science*	dentista
dept.	*department*	reparto, sezione
e.g.	*for instance*	per esempio
Eng.	*England; English*	Inghilterra; inglese
EU	*European Union*	Unione europea
xcl.	*excluding; exclusive*	esclusivo, non compreso
t.	*foot/feet*	piede/piedi
GB	*Great Britain*	Gran Bretagna
H.E.	*His/Her Excellency; His Eminence*	Sua Eccellenza; Sua Eminenza
H.H.	*His Holiness*	Sua Santità
H.M.	*His/Her Majesty*	Sua Maestà
H.M.S.	*Her Majesty's ship*	nave della marina reale inglese

hp	*horsepower*	cavallo (vapore)
Hwy	*highway*	autostrada, superstrada
i.e.	*that is to say*	cioè
in.	*inch*	pollice (2,54 cm)
Inc.	*incorporated*	tipo di società anonima americana
incl.	*including, inclusive*	inclusivo, compreso
£	*pound sterling*	lira sterlina
L.A.	*Los Angeles*	Los Angeles
Ltd.	*limited*	società anonima
M.D.	*Doctor of Medicine*	Dottore in Medicina
M.P.	*Member of Parliament*	deputato
mph	*miles per hour*	miglia all'ora
Mr.	*Mister*	Signor
Mrs.	*Missis*	Signora
Ms.	*Missis/Miss*	Signora/Signorina
nat.	*national*	nazionale
NBC	*National Broadcasting Company*	società privata radio-televisiva americana
No.	*number*	numero
N.Y.C.	*New York City*	città di New York
O.B.E.	*Officer (of the Order) of the British Empire*	Ufficiale (dell'Ordine) dell'Impero Britannico
p.	*page; penny/pence*	pagina; 1/100 di lira sterlina
p.a.	*per annum*	per anno
Ph.D.	*Doctor of Philosophy*	Dottore in Filosofia
PLC	*public limited company*	Società per azioni
p.m.	*post meridiem (after noon)*	del pomeriggio o della sera (12.00—24.00)
PO	*Post Office*	ufficio postale
POO	*post office order*	vaglia postale
pop.	*population*	abitanti
P.T.O.	*please turn over*	vedi retro
RAC	*Royal Automobile Club*	Real Automobile Club Inglese
RCMP	*Royal Canadian Mounted Police*	polizia reale canadese a cavallo
Rd.	*road*	strada
ref.	*reference*	riferimento
Rev.	*reverend*	reverendo della chiesa anglicana
RFD	*rural free delivery*	distribuzione della posta in campagna
RR	*railroad*	ferrovia
RSVP	*please reply*	si prega rispondere
$	*dollar*	dollaro
Soc.	*society*	società
St.	*saint; street*	santo; strada

STD	*Subscriber Trunk Dialling*	telefono automatico
UN	*United Nations*	N.U., Nazioni Unite
UPS	*United Parcel Service*	servizio spedizione pacchi americano
US	*United States*	Stati Uniti
USS	*United States Ship*	nave della marina americana
VAT	*value added tax*	I.V.A.
VIP	*very important person*	V.I.P., persona molto importante
Xmas	*Christmas*	Natale
yd.	*yard*	iarda (91,44 cm)
YMCA	*Young Men's Christian Association*	A.C.D.G., associazione cristiana dei giovani
YWCA	*Young Women's Christian Association*	U.C.D.G., unione cristiana delle giovani
ZIP	*ZIP code*	codice di avviamento postale

Numeri

Numeri cardinali		Numeri ordinali	
0	zero	1st	first
1	one	2nd	second
2	two	3rd	third
3	three	4th	fourth
4	four	5th	fifth
5	five	6th	sixth
6	six	7th	seventh
7	seven	8th	eighth
8	eight	9th	ninth
9	nine	10th	tenth
10	ten	11th	eleventh
11	eleven	12th	twelfth
12	twelve	13th	thirteenth
13	thirteen	14th	fourteenth
14	fourteen	15th	fifteenth
15	fifteen	16th	sixteenth
16	sixteen	17th	seventeenth
17	seventeen	18th	eighteenth
18	eighteen	19th	nineteenth
19	nineteen	20th	twentieth
20	twenty	21st	twenty-first
21	twenty-one	22nd	twenty-second
22	twenty-two	23rd	twenty-third
23	twenty-three	24th	twenty-fourth
24	twenty-four	25th	twenty-fifth
25	twenty-five	26th	twenty-sixth
30	thirty	27th	twenty-seventh
40	forty	28th	twenty-eighth
50	fifty	29th	twenty-ninth
60	sixty	30th	thirtieth
70	seventy	40th	fortieth
80	eighty	50th	fiftieth
90	ninety	60th	sixtieth
100	a/one hundred	70th	seventieth
230	two hundred and thirty	80th	eightieth
500	five hundred	90th	ninetieth
1,000	a/one thousand	100th	hundredth
10,000	ten thousand	230th	two hundred and thirtieth
100,000	a/one hundred thousand	500th	five hundredth
1,000,000	a/one million	1,000th	thousandth

L'ora

I Britannici e gli Americani usano il sistema di dodici ore. L'espressione *a.m.* (*ante meridiem*) indica le ore che precedono mezzogiorno e *p.m.* (*post meridiem*) quelle fino a mezzanotte. Tuttavia in Inghilterra gli orari vengono anche indicati alla maniera continentale.

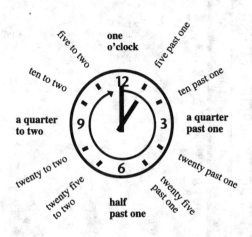

I'll come at seven a.m.	Verrò alle 7 (del mattino).
I'll come at two p.m.	Verrò alle 2 (del pomeriggio).
I'll come at eight p.m.	Verrò alle 8 (di sera).

I giorni della settimana

Sunday	domenica	*Thursday*	giovedì
Monday	lunedì	*Friday*	venerdì
Tuesday	martedì	*Saturday*	sabato
Wednesday	mercoledì		

Conversion tables/
Tavole di trasformazione

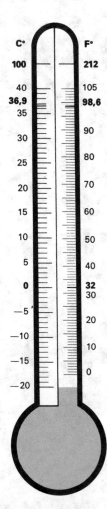

Metres and feet
The figure in the middle stands for both metres and feet, e.g. 1 metre = 3.281 ft. and 1 foot = 0.30 m.

Metri e piedi
I numeri al centro del seguente specchietto valgono sia per i metri sia per i piedi. Es.: 1 metro = 3,281 piedi e 1 piede = 0,30 m.

Metres/Metri		Feet/Piedi
0.30	**1**	3.281
0.61	**2**	6.563
0.91	**3**	9.843
1.22	**4**	13.124
1.52	**5**	16.403
1.83	**6**	19.686
2.13	**7**	22.967
2.44	**8**	26.248
2.74	**9**	29.529
3.05	**10**	32.810
3.66	**12**	39.372
4.27	**14**	45.934
6.10	**20**	65.620
7.62	**25**	82.023
15.24	**50**	164.046
22.86	**75**	246.069
30.48	**100**	328.092

Temperature
To convert Centigrade to Fahrenheit, multiply by 1. and add 32.
To convert Fahrenheit to Centigrade, subtract 3 from Fahrenheit and divide by 1.8.

Temperatura
Per trasformare i gradi centigradi in Fahrenhe moltiplicare i centigradi per 1,8 e aggiungere 32.
Per convertire i Fahrenheit in centigradi sottrarre 3 dai Fahrenheit e dividere per 1,8.

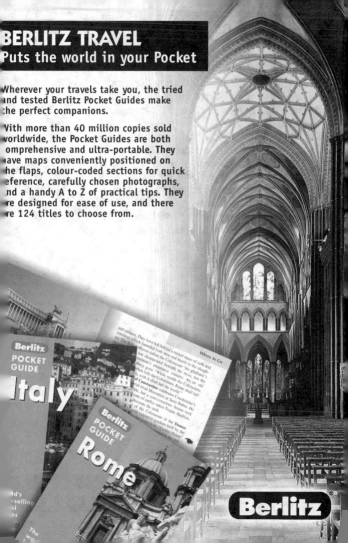

OCEAN CRUISING
& CRUISE SHIPS

This cruise guide, updated annually, contains more ships, more charts, more analytical data and more advice than any other guide.

Running to more than half a million words, it has established itself over 20 years as the definitive reference work for both novice and veteran passengers and for travel agents. Its author, Douglas Ward, has spent 4,500 days at sea, aboard more than 800 cruises and has been described by the London *Times* as the industry's most feared critic.